CLASSIC READINGS IN
CANADIAN PUBLIC
ADMINISTRATION

MW00714714

CLASSIC READINGS IN
CANADIAN PUBLIC
ADMINISTRATION

Edited by

BARBARA WAKE CARROLL

DAVID SIEGEL

MARK SPROULE-JONES

OXFORD
UNIVERSITY PRESS

OXFORD
UNIVERSITY PRESS

70 Wynford Drive, Don Mills, Ontario M3C 1J9
www.oup.com/ca

Oxford University Press is a department of the University of Oxford.
It furthers the University's objective of excellence in research, scholarship,
and education by publishing worldwide in

Oxford   New York

Auckland   Cape Town   Dar es Salaam   Hong Kong   Karachi
Kuala Lumpur   Madrid   Melbourne   Mexico City   Nairobi
New Delhi   Shanghai   Taipei   Toronto

With offices in

Argentina   Austria   Brazil   Chile   Czech Republic   France   Greece
Guatemala   Hungary   Italy   Japan   Poland   Portugal   Singapore
South Korea   Switzerland   Thailand   Turkey   Ukraine   Vietnam

Oxford is a trade mark of Oxford University Press
in the UK and in certain other countries

Published in Canada
by Oxford University Press

Copyright © Oxford University Press Canada 2005

The moral rights of the author have been asserted

Database right Oxford University Press (maker)

First published 2005

All rights reserved. No part of this publication may be reproduced,
stored in a retrieval system, or transmitted, in any form or by any means,
without the prior permission in writing of Oxford University Press,
or as expressly permitted by law, or under terms agreed with the appropriate
reprographics rights organization. Enquiries concerning reproduction
outside the scope of the above should be sent to the Rights Department,
Oxford University Press, at the address above.

You must not circulate this book in any other binding or cover
and you must impose this same condition on any acquirer.

Library and Archives Canada Cataloguing in Publication Data

Classic readings in Canadian public administration / edited by Barbara Wake Carroll,
David Siegel and Mark Sproule-Jones.

ISBN-13: 978-0-19-542167-5   ISBN-10: 0-19-542167-1

1. Public administration -- Canada. I. Carroll, Barbara Wake, 1947-
II. Siegel, David III. Sproule-Jones, Mark, 1941-

JL108.C605 2005   351.71   C2005-901826-7

Cover and text design: Brett J. Miller

1 2 3 4 – 08 07 06 05
This book is printed on permanent (acid-free) paper ∞.
Printed in Canada

Contents

Introduction

The idea for this collection of classic readings has been percolating for a long time. It started with our desire for a collection of the articles that we have used in our courses for years—a collection that would spare us arranging for our students to retrieve 'archival' materials and seeing our own copies of books and journals dog-eared by repeated photocopying. But in the end we realized that the book also serves a very important purpose on its own, reminding us of some of the enduring issues in Canadian public administration.

The more we read, re-read, and discussed the various candidates for inclusion, the more we realized that they represented, if not a 'golden age' of Canadian public administration, at least a very distinctive era. Our reactions varied. 'Is this article only twenty years old? It reads as if it was written before the flood.' Those articles tended to pre-date Canada's embrace of multiculturalism and inclusion. In other cases we had exactly the opposite reaction: 'Can this paper really be twenty years old? The issues it addresses are still so relevant now.' Our final selection was heavily biased towards material of the latter type.

As we went on we kept finding more works that we had forgotten but now recognized for the gems they are. Many of these were recommended by other members of the academic public administration community when we canvassed them for suggestions. We realized that the earlier generation of public administration scholars in Canada had produced an immense body of engaging theoretical material that is often overlooked today.

One by-product of our search for classics was a fresh appreciation of the central role that the Institute of Public Administration of Canada (IPAC) has played in the development of the academic discipline and the profession of public administration. Our selection was 'blind' in the sense that we tried to assess each article without regard to its provenance. However, we were not particularly surprised when we discovered that exactly half of the articles chosen originated with IPAC (most came from its flag-ship journal, *Canadian Public Administration*). Obviously the field of public administration would look very different today without IPAC's tremendous contribution.

There is a strong tendency among academics and practitioners to focus their attention on recent publications. As a result, insights from older sources are often forgotten. Are there parallels between the 'horizontal management' of the 1990s and the interdepartmental and intergovernmental 'coordination' of the 1970s? Does the bureaucracy today function differently as a result of the shift in representational focus from language groups to 'designated groups'? Questions of this kind can be extremely useful, but we cannot even ask them unless we know something about the work of our predecessors. We hope this book will help to revive some valuable memories.

As we continued our research, we became aware of several changes in the literature over the past two decades. First, we noticed that twenty years ago a single article could address several new theoretical questions. Today, by contrast, the theoretical field has become so fragmented that no single article can adequately explore even one theme. This could be a reflection of how complex public administration has become, but we suspect it also has something to do with the academic pressure to publish. Why write just one article when you could get more credit for writing two?

Second, we realized that the disconnect between the world of the theoretical academic and the world of the practitioner has become even greater than it was in the past. Twenty years ago, the academic journals published articles by practitioners as well as academics, addressing both normative and empirical aspects of public administration. Government documents offered well-reasoned philosophical justifications for government action. At the same time, academic articles were not necessarily written by Ph.Ds for Ph.Ds: they were accessible.

Third, we realized how many of the core issues for the public service—values, accountability, responsiveness, effectiveness of service delivery—have not changed. On these issues, many articles written in the 1960s and 1970s (and even earlier) still have resonance today. Not all could be accommodated in this volume, but we tried to find what we thought were the best, the classics. At the same time we noticed that some of the issues that are dominant today were not discussed at all two decades ago. For example, questions of ethics apparently did not arise before 1985, perhaps because traditional values were assumed to be the norm. Finally, we became aware that the day of academic/practitioner scholars such as A.W. Johnson, H.L. Laframboise, and R.H. MacFarlane has probably passed. Today the time demands on practitioners are such that they have no opportunity to write, while the requirement of specialization discourages academics from standing back and looking at the bigger picture. We are simply noting these trends, not deploring them. But we do feel that the 28 articles reproduced here represent the best of Canadian, and perhaps comparative, theoretical work on the subject of public administration.

Most of the authors will be familiar to readers. The articles are arranged loosely by subject under four broad headings: 'Structures', 'Human Resources', 'Financial Management', and 'Policy and Administration'. Each part begins with a general discussion of the articles to follow and the reasons we regard them as classics. We had originally planned on a more specific thematic approach, but decided that many of the articles were too wide-ranging to be pigeon-holed. Teachers who want to focus on more specific themes will find some suggestions in the introductions.

The most recent article in this collection dates from 1985. We chose that year as our cut-off point because the articles from before that date were the most difficult for students to find, and because two decades seemed to represent a reasonable 'test of time'. As a result we have left out some likely classics-to-be, but perhaps they can be included in a future edition.

In the winter of 2004 a draft of this book was used as a primary text in both an introductory public administration course and a graduate course. It was well received by the students, who often forgot the articles were 'old' until they came across references to 'Canadian Pacific' and 'Trans-Canada' airlines! But the collection may be equally useful for reference purposes. Some of the articles are very long, and we had considered abridging them until we recognized the risk that we might inadvertently edit out some crucial material. The abridging of the early classic *Papers on the Science of Public Administration* (1937) has over the years led to major misunderstandings about the classical structural theory, and we did not want to make the same error.

It should be noted that the primary focus of this collection is the federal level of government. This is an accurate reflection of the Canadian public service before the era of 'province-building'. We still feel the need for a substantive body of administrative theory looking at other levels of government in Canada, but much of the material in this book will be relevant at the provincial or municipal level. That this collection is entirely Canadian is a major strength. Much of the literature of public administration today is American and therefore reflects the unique political system of the United States. By contrast, the issues addressed in this book are firmly rooted in the Westminster model of government and Canada's own unique federal culture.

We would like to thank all the academics and practitioners we consulted both formally and informally over the last several years, along with the students who were guinea pigs for early versions of this work. Their advice has been invaluable. We would also like to thank Laura Macleod and Mark Piel of Oxford University Press for their assistance from the inception of this project to its completion.

Barbara Wake Carroll
David Siegel
Mark Sproule-Jones

PART I

Structures

Institutional analysis and design are the areas of public administration concerned with the organizational structures of government, including the laws and regulations that govern their operations. Structural analysis is a fertile field in Canada, where governments have frequently organized commissions and special committees to study the academic literature on structural issues with a view to solving practical problems. Between the early 1960s and the early 1980s five inquiries—the royal commissions on Government Organization (Glassco, 1965), Bilingualism and Biculturalism (Laurendeau-Dunton, 1967), Financial Management and Accountability (Lambert, 1979), and Equality in Employment (Abella, 1984), and the Special Committee on the Review of Personnel Management and the Merit Principle (D'Avignon, 1979)—all commissioned academic papers on various structures and recommended changes, many of which were implemented in subsequent years. Most provinces have held similar inquiries from time to time.

Governments in Canada have experimented with a variety of structures in an effort to address the practical problems of the day. For example, Canada invented the Crown corporation when it created the Board of Works in 1841. Crown corporations deliver marketable goods and services on behalf of the government, but are insulated against day-to-day political control: their structure balances accountability to government with entrepreneurial freedom. Horizontal management or policy networks—in effect, intergovernmental partnerships—may also have been invented in Canada, to enable governments to work around a difficult constitutional division of powers and deliver services to two unilingual communities.

Canada has also borrowed structural forms from other countries. These include the office of ombudsman, borrowed from Scandinavia and now adopted by nine provinces; the organization of the Prime Minister's Office, from Britain; and the 'value for money' auditing system from the US, UK, and other 'new public management' countries. The more standard form of bureaucracy—the departmental hierarchy that reports to a cabinet and parliament through a responsible minister of the Crown—remains the central agency for the implementation of public policy in

Canada. It is a structure that has attracted both positive and negative comment, as our selections will suggest.

In the early twenty-first century, the international literature on public administration comes from a variety of global sources and a variety of political administrative regimes. For most of twentieth century, however, that literature was dominated by American scholarship. Of the relatively few Canadian contributions in the area of organizational structure, we have selected ten of the most important. Our first selection offers a broad overview of the sociological, economic, and technological factors influencing structural designs in Canada. Then four pieces focus on the standard line departments of government. The remaining five deal with different organizational forms or 'structural heretics' like Crown corporations, ombudsmen, regulatory agencies, and the structures of executive federalism.

The first of two contributions by J.E. Hodgetts is a synopsis of the major 'environmental' factors—geography, culture, and economics—that influence organizational structures and in turn are influenced by them. This piece can also be used as an introduction to 'contingency theory'. Hodgetts' work has enriched the field of public administration for two or three generations of scholarship.

The second selection, from the Glassco Commission, is a fine example of structural analysis in the classic tradition of the 'scientific theory of organizations', much of which was developed before the Second World War. Similarly, the critique of structural change in the federal public service offered by H.L. Laframboise is a useful Canadian introduction both to 'transaction costs theory' and to the history of structural developments between the Second World War and the early 1970s.

The long selection from Colin Campbell and George J. Szablowski's book of the late 1970s is perhaps the first and certainly the most comprehensive overview of the evolution and functions of the three central agencies of the federal government: the Privy Council Office, the Treasury Board Secretariat, and the Prime Minister's Office. These agencies continue to play key roles in the federal policy process, and a solid understanding of their operations is essential for anyone interested in exploring newer theories such as the 'new public management' or 'rational policy analysis'.

The next two selections are part of the ongoing debate about the structure of the senior bureaucracy, its permanency, power, and accountability. Their respective authors, Mitchell Sharp and Hugh Segal, were both senior public servants who became political staffers. Both eventually ran for political office themselves, and Sharp served in several senior Cabinet positions. Thus both men were familiar with both sides of the political–administrative interface.

Hodgetts's second piece is a review of several non-standard forms of public organization that operate at every level of government in Canada. These 'structural heretics' merit close study, as their mandates, funding arrangements, composition, and formal lines of accountability vary widely. Next, Bruce Doern provides an overview of regulatory agencies, the rationales for their creation, and their effects on society (particularly the economic effects). His classic article is still a useful overview for scholars new to the field. C.A. Ashley and R.G.H. Smails's article on Crown corporations is similarly useful, even though it dates from 1965.

Donald Rowat's overview of 'ombudsman' operations provides a good starting point for understanding a parliamentary/legislative structure designed to remedy complaints of maladministration. Rowat was a pioneer in the study of this particular structure of government. It is significant that ombudsman's offices, like the office of the Auditor General, or the Freedom of Information Office, report directly to parliaments and legislatures rather than to ministers and the executive branch.

Our final selection is by Donald Smiley, who wrote extensively on executive federalism during the 1960s and 1970s. This article, in which he reflects on the dysfunctions of executive federalism, is a precursor of modern theory on horizontal management in the context of Canadian federalism.

1

Challenge and Response: A Retrospective View of the Public Service of Canada

J.E. Hodgetts

John Donne's comment that 'no man is an island' applies with equal relevance to organizations created by man to serve his needs. Thus, the central proposition I hope to demonstrate by this excursion into the past is that our public service has been shaped to the environment in which it has had to operate and that changes in the environment bring about alterations in the public service.

When the Founding Fathers met one hundred years ago they were seeking to grapple with the forces of change then confronting them. The result was a constitutional document that has proven surprisingly durable over the ensuing years. But constitutions are notably rigid, and it has been largely within the public services— local, provincial, and federal—that we find the main evidences of adaptation to changing conditions and emergent social needs which have provided the necessary flexibility. I see no evidence for claiming that this administrative adaptation has followed any iron laws of administrative growth. We are here concerned with a most complex set of interacting forces in which the organization acted upon, i.e., the public service, is far from passive. While the public service bears the marks of environmental factors that press upon it, society also bears the imprint of the activities and enhanced authority of public servants.

In considering the environmental pressures that have set the goals and moulded the shape of the public service over our first century, we find that some have remained relatively unchanged. These we may describe as the constant or 'the givens' with which the public service must live. They include the pervasive impact of our geographical setting, the constitutional framework, the legal base of administration, and the political system. The elements of the environment subject to the greatest change and requiring the greatest flexibility of response from the public service have been economic, technological, cultural, and philosophical factors. I should like to show briefly how each of these has contributed to the public service we know today.

The powerful persuasion of geography has been noted by Sir Ernest Barker in his examination of the growth of European public services. The large Egyptian bureaucracy, for example, he attributed to the Nile and the costly irrigation works

J.E. Hodgetts, 'Challenge and Response: A Retrospective View of the Public Service of Canada', *Canadian Public Administration* 7 (1964): 409–21. Courtesy of The Institute of Public Administration Canada.

required to harness it. England's insular position, on the other hand, delayed the emergence of the large centralized bureaucracies which grew up on the Continent largely to service the needs of standing armies. In Canada, for the better part of its first half century, geography dictated the major goals which the public service was to pursue. The Department of the Interior, the giant amongst early federal departments, was described as late as 1926 as 'the barometer of Western conditions'. The so called barometric departments were those concerned with opening up the west, encouraging its population and settlement, and providing the water or rail transportation to serve as the linkage for these activities.

Not only did geography dictate the goals, it also imposed the conditions which governed the way in which the tasks of public servants had to be performed. If administrative apoplexy was to be avoided at the centre, public servants had to be widely dispersed: police and protective services, agents for immigration, for colonization and Indian affairs, fisheries overseers, customs collectors, surveyors, and construction teams on railways and canals, spread often in isolated places across a continental domain.

New means of communication have alleviated the problems of communication and administration in remote outposts. But the harsh facts of our geography still exact a high price for preserving a union based on an artificial East–West axis against the counterpull of the geographically more natural North–South axis.

Thus, from the outset, geography forced Canada to adapt its services to dispersed operations. The subsequent expansion of welfare and regulatory activities necessitated the continuation of dispersed or area administration, governed now less by the limitations on our means of communication but more by the need to preserve a face-to-face relationship with individual citizens seeking benefits and services. Consequently a physical decentralization of the work force, which took root as a logical response to the challenge of administering across a continent, continues in being as a vital necessity to provide the flexible response to the contemporary state's positive welfare and regulatory functions. Decentralization is now as much dictated by the need to preserve democratic responsiveness of the administrative machine as it is a natural outcome of the original geographic challenge.

It is passing strange that this, perhaps the most obvious feature of our public service, has received so little formal analysis. It is one of a number of areas that warrant fuller discussion and study.

The second constant feature of the environment is the constitutional framework which was evolved one hundred years ago. It is no reflection on the Founding Fathers to claim that a division of labour between provinces and dominion made one hundred years ago is bound to become outmoded. Formal constitutional amendment has been infrequent and judicial interpretation has not always been in conformity with rapid changes in social philosophy, new needs, or revolutionary transformation in technology. Flexibility has been provided by the development of what the Rowell–Sirois Commission called 'administrative expedients'. These have ranged from the sporadic assembling of a diplomatic conference between dominion and provincial leaders, ministerial or official conferences for more limited purposes—often in conjunction with national interest groups (as happened, for example, in the case of labour and agriculture), formal agreements rather like treaties, joint advisory committees, the use of federal officers to perform provincial tasks (and vice versa), and the employment of federal funds to finance provincial programs.

At the outset, most of these expedients were not developed because potential conflict was restrained by the limited undertakings of public organizations at all levels. Beginning with fisheries and then moving into labour and industrial relations, on to health and welfare and the regulation of interprovincial trade, the respective jurisdictions began to touch, then overlap: inevitably friction was generated. The limitations on and unevenness of provincial revenues required action on a broader front. Thus, throughout the years, one can see the administrative response of the federal public service gathering momentum in distinct stages. First, it began to act as a centralized data collecting source; from statistics it went on to research; research results required dissemination and so we move to extensive publication (and some would say public relations); next came conditional grants that required 'policing' by federal officials; ultimately certain programs came to be operated by the federal government.

Two factors contribute to the perpetuation and even the continued expansion of the federal public service in such areas. First, there is the natural reluctance to dismantle an organization by giving up these programs. The historic rationale has been that the provincial services were less than adequate for the task involved—an estimate that today bears hard critical examination. The other factor has been the inability of the tax-poor provinces to carry the burden of these new services. Once again, I would offer this entire area as a rewarding subject for fresh examination: we need full-scale studies of provincial public services to begin with and of the administrative interrelations that have developed between provincial and federal public departments. Here, we must content ourselves with noting that the cumulative results of these developments have induced the federal government to assume fact-gathering, research, promotional, and grant-dispensing responsibilities that are quite different in kind from the more directly program-oriented, operational jobs undertaken by the provinces. At the same time, these activities have introduced in unprecedented numbers new types of professional, scientific, and technical personnel into the public service whose problems of adaptation to the traditional hierarchical organization have received far less study than they deserve.

The third fixed element of the environment is the legal foundation for public administration. At Confederation, the tension between executive and legislature built up during the previous period of colonial rule inclined the Canadian Parliament to adopt a more assertive attitude than the British Parliament towards the public service. The British North America Act bears signs of this attitude in the oft-invoked phrase tied to the few sections concerning the disposition of the public service 'until the Parliament of Canada [or the provincial legislature] otherwise provides.' The fact is that the Parliament of Canada has 'otherwise provided' in much more detail than has ever been the case in the United Kingdom, the most outstanding testimonial being the Civil Service Act of 1868, which had its precursors in pre-Confederation times and continues to this day with its counterpart in every province. No such act, significantly, has ever been passed in Britain.

This is not the place to thread my way through a most complex maze. That it is a maze, I know, for in a personal effort to explore the legal foundations of public administration I found to my surprise that there were few available guides in this lonely enterprise. I do not propose to inflict the details of my explorations on you but I can at least state the problem and its implications for the public service.

The essential difficulty derives from the union of executive and legislative functions which we have inherited from Britain. That union creates what I might call a legal ambivalence from which it is hard to say whether the public service is directed by sovereign parliament or by the executive. Put in another way, the question is: are public servants employees of parliament or employees of the executive, standing in the place of the Crown?

That this is not an academic question can be readily demonstrated by indicating the problem of identifying the centres of authority for handling the organization and management of the public service. Parliament clearly must authorize the creation of a department, but the executive determines when the department shall begin to function. Moreover, since a new department involves a money bill and only the executive can initiate such a bill, one must assume that even the major organizational units are dictated by the executive, with rather automatic ratification by parliament. For more detailed re-organization, parliament has in effect devolved authority on the executive through the Public Services Rearrangement and Transfer of Duties Act. A glance at the organic acts for each department shows that parliament has made no effort to bind the executive's hands by stipulating a detailed organizational breakdown. Equally, the day-to-day organization-and-methods work has been left by parliament entirely to the discretion of departments or to other management bodies.

In the field of management, the dichotomy is much more evident and perplexing. First, there is the question, previously noted, of the apparently dual allegiance of the public servant. For all practical purposes, including appointment, classification, promotion, pay scales, and tenure, the civil servant appears to be a servant of the executive (which in practical terms might be logically extended to read a servant of the party in power). In the performance of his functions, he is responsible through the hierarchy to his minister. Yet many members of parliament, stressing the term 'public' in public servant, claim to occupy the role of employer. When at the same time they claim the Civil Service Commission as their specially selected agency to perform this function on their behalf, further problems arise. Indeed the Civil Service Commission is perhaps the chief victim of this legal dualism, on the one hand being regarded as the peculiar instrument of parliament in its role of employer but on the other often sharing management functions with executive agencies, such as Treasury Board, which parliament in its indecision has divided between them. It is enough, perhaps, to add that the Pay Research Bureau of the Commission has at times been caught in the crossfire of this legal uncertainty and the current investigation of arbitration for federal public servants must also find some resolution of the problem.

This commentary on the legal basis of administration could be prolonged, but I have perhaps said enough to support the conclusion that because the legal ambivalence of our system has not been confronted head on we have grown into a confused system of divided management responsibilities that is cumbersome to work and difficult to live with.

The fourth and final fixed feature of the environment is our political system or, more accurately, the conventions that have grown up around that system. The three elements of this system that have left the deepest imprints on the public service are the conventions surrounding cabinet-making, the doctrine of ministerial responsibility and, that handmaiden of the party system, patronage.

The well-known convention that cabinets must be so constructed as to represent significant regional, provincial, religious, and ethnic groupings in a pluralistic community needs no elaboration. Its implications for the public service, though obvious, have scarcely ever been noted. Even in 1867, a cabinet of fourteen members was needed to meet all the claims for weighted representation. Critics at the time asked how it was that in the United States as compared to Canada 'forty million instead of four were ably governed by an administration of seven members instead of fourteen'. But the necessity of securing a representative cabinet over-rode any objections. On the other hand, if the American model did not commend itself, neither did the British system of making a distinction between the cabinet and the much larger Ministry. The Canadian convention in short was and continues to be that all Ministers should be in the cabinet.

The rejection of both the American and British models had these consequences: (1) for nearly half a century we were overstocked with departments and the slow accretion of government duties could readily be absorbed within a relatively static group of portfolios; (2) but, when the duties of the state began to mount at an accelerated pace, we were left little room to manoeuvre. If more departments were created to embrace the new tasks and if all ministerial heads by convention had to be in the cabinet, that body would soon reach an unmanageable size. The alternative was to create a variety of non-departmental entities to undertake the newer tasks. The generous provision of departmental portfolios and their extremely elastic walls enabled us to absorb a great deal of this expansion and necessitated surprisingly few additions to the original departmental roster. But it has meant that some departments have come to embrace a variety of ill-assorted functions simply as a means of housing what otherwise might become administrative orphans. The consequent problems of co-ordination through the cabinet and other centralized agencies have been acute.

The practical restrictions on the number of departmental portfolios also account in part for the profusion and variety of non-departmental entities. The effort to seat them comfortably within the traditional framework of ministerial responsibility has led to an incoherent 'second' public service that represents a piecemeal, haphazard response to the growing burden of state activities, even as it confuses the legislator and general citizen.

Indeed, the doctrine of ministerial responsibility is the second feature of the political setting whose implications for the public service need brief elaboration. The principle not only establishes a bridge across which most of the traffic between parliament and the public service is routed but, applied collectively to the cabinet, it ensures a unity of purpose and a coordination of direction at the top. Parliament benefits by being able to home in on one identifiable target; the public servant benefits because he does not have to debate publicly any challenge of his political overlords. His anonymity preserves the constitutional fiction of his political non-commitment and thus ensures his permanency in office whenever there is a change in the governing political party.

The benefits of the doctrine are obvious and desirable but a literal application in today's enlarged public service poses an impossible burden on the Minister. This was recognized on the administrative side at the very beginning by giving the Minister a permanent Deputy and on the legislative side, but much more recently, by giving him a Parliamentary Secretary. But the fact remains that there have been constant pressures that force the Minister into a 'managing' rather than a 'directing' role, thereby compelling Ministers in both their individual and collective capacities, to concern themselves with too much detail, at the expense of general coordinating and policy-making functions. The convention that the cabinet provides regional representation makes sense only if most matters are brought before cabinet. Thus, in contrast to England where statutes generally confer authority on individual Ministers, in Canada they more commonly confer powers on the Governor-in-Council, i.e., Ministers in their collective capacity. If to this we add the historic reliance on patronage, we can see why Ministers have been unable to extricate themselves from direct involvement in the details of management. Sir George Murray's succinct epitaph (written in 1912) accurately described a predicament that certainly existed until 1939. 'Ministers,' he concluded, 'both have too much to do and try to do too much.'

The significance of patronage, the third element of the political system to be examined here, is that the measures taken to eradicate it have left an enduring mark on the public service. A formal self-denying ordinance is necessary, at some time or another, if patronage is to be eliminated. In Britain, this was done by executive decree but in Canada, as has been noted, by statute, authorizing a Civil Service Commission to institute a rigorous regimen of controls. Over time the desired result was achieved of preventing the unfit from gaining admission to the public service; but for many years this negative approach dominated to the exclusion of more positive measures required to attract the best candidates available. The Civil Service Commission was given additional and comprehensive authority over most of the personnel management field. Thus the orientation toward control, generated by its primary function as patronage eliminator, tended (so to speak) to rub off on to the other management responsibilities that demanded a more positive, service-minded approach.

A somewhat parallel development occurred in the field of expenditure control in an effort to prevent peculation and patronage. When the Glassco Commission came to examine this situation, it found that departmental managers had been caught in the pincers of centralized agencies and have had to operate in that atmosphere of distrust which had been responsible in the first place for the imposition of such controls. It was the thesis of the Glassco Commission that, while the system had been a legitimate and logical response to the evils of patronage and dishonesty, the departments were, in the vernacular, 'big boys now' and should be put more on their own mettle. The readjustments required to meet this thesis will make heavier calls on the initiative and ability of departmental managers and will require centralized agencies to think less in terms of negative control and more in positive terms of guidance, service, and setting standards for the departments.

I may remind you at this stage that I distinguished at the beginning between the constant and variable elements of the environment that have helped mould our public service. Having touched on the constants, let me now turn to the variables, beginning with the economic setting.

Economic historians have familiarized us with the importance of staple products to Canada's economic growth and well being. The characteristic feature of staples such as fish, fur, timber, minerals, wheat, and pulpwood is that they are all extractive enterprises, based on the exploitation of a great wealth in natural resources requiring bulk transportation and access to markets abroad. Neither the exploitation, transportation or marketing of these staples has taken place within an Adam Smith type of economy. Government has been heavily committed from the outset to mapping out and making inventory of these resources; it has been deeply engaged as regulator, constructor, and operator of transport systems by water, rail, and air; it moved early into promotional activities—the first trade commissioner dates back to the 1880s as does the agricultural research station, and only slightly later do we find such services as forecasting facilities. Governments have even engineered the formation of economic interest groups such as the livestock producers and the pulpwood producers—presumably the better to deal with them. Today the major concern of at least one third of our federal departments is still with problems associated with the production, conservation, and transportation of and the trade in our main staple products.

This clear-cut identification of the departments with staple products is only one example—though a most persistent one—of how the unique features of the Canadian economy have shaped the public service. As government has more and more been drawn into an operating and regulatory role, we find that the new responsibilities have largely devolved on non-departmental agencies. A point has now been reached where the number of people employed in these sectors of the public service is nearly as large as the number employed in the departmental system proper. It is not surprising that, in devising non-departmental forms, governments have looked to the private industrial or commercial concerns for their models. We are still struggling to find a solution to the problems of grafting the consequent collection of heterogeneous administrative entities on to the conventional departmental system with its tradition of ministerial responsibility. We are also still seeking for ways to bridge the gap between the personnel in the civil service proper and in the other portion excluded from it, to the end that there may be truly *one* public service. In short, the mixed economy, with its avoidance of outright governmental monopoly and its favouring of a system of economic parallelism in transport, communication, and finance, has produced a corresponding organizational 'mix' in the public service itself.

Nor does the impact of the world of private economic organization end here.

It finds expression in a pervasive assumption that only a 'businessman's approach' to the public service can produce efficiency. We find early expression of this philosophy in the attempt to levy appropriate charges for the services that governments provide specific groups of beneficiaries. And, in the report of the Glassco Commission, dozens of such services have been identified, accompanied by evidence that some pay their way, others are given free, some make a profit, others lose money. The Royal Commission's reminder that we need to set this part of our administrative house in order is merely a reiteration of the old plea to inject sound business principles into public administration. The Commission's recommendation that many of these services might well be contracted out to private concerns is not so much a free enterpriser's special pleading but a legitimate concern to help public organizations keep their attention focused on their main job, subject to as few peripheral distractions as possible.

The major impact of the businessman's approach is to be found in the contemporary reliance on private management consultant firms that are refinements on the early school of efficiency experts nourished at the beginning of this century by Taylor and his followers. We owe to this school the detailed classification plans which were inaugurated after World War I in the civil service. The modern consultant is in the main an offshoot of the accountant, though his advice now ranges from financial and accounting practices through paperwork and systems analyses to feasibility studies on computers. His main customer is government and one of his most lasting marks will be found in the reports of the Glassco Commission. We find here the accountant's concern for identifying 'real' costs; the businessman's concern for relating revenues from services to the costs of providing them, the need to import the new techniques of systems analyses that have proven effective in private business. In brief, there is the assumption that the differences between private and public organization are not so substantial that practices proven successful in the private realm cannot be applied with equal effectiveness to the public organization. This is an assumption that in my view must constantly be tempered by the other environmental factors I have been discussing and to which private organizations need pay much less attention.

Turning from the economic setting to the impact of changing technology on the public service, we find a two-edged situation. In the broadest sense, changing techniques affect the substance of administrative activity—they alter the things that have to be done by administrators, by inducing the state either itself to sponsor the development of the techniques or else to grapple with the social and other problems posed by their widespread adoption. In the narrower sense, new techniques influence administrative procedures. We live in an age of gadgetry and public servants are no more immune to the charm of applying gadgets to their daily labours than are others in private organizations.

The Canadian public service has grown up during a century in which there have been more technological innovations than in all of man's past history. It was born in the steamboat and railway age, witnessed the emergence of telegraph and telephone, saw the origin and full onslaught of the internal combustion engine and, while still adjusting to these developments, has had to make its peace with the air age, the electronics revolution, the atom, and now outer space.

The incredible fertility of man, the innovating engineer and scientist, has left man, the social scientist, staggering for breath. The steamboat and railway brought the state into the centre of activity as owner, maintenance man, and operator or regulator. The automobile age has left its most indelible imprint on provincial and local public services, as they have had to grapple with highway construction, traffic regulations, and all the social and economic problems of urban concentration that have sprung up in the wake of the automobile.

Jurisdiction over the air for transportation and communication purposes was settled in favour of the federal government in 1932 and the stage was set for a fresh crop of agencies and further adaptation of the public service to meet the challenges. From virtual monopolies of national services, designed to pioneer in these new fields, the state has gradually permitted the private sector to emerge as a full partner. Similarly, in responding to the nuclear revolution, the state has harnessed the conventional component by regulatory action but has assumed, itself, nearly the full burden of research and development. With the largest research resources and establishments in the country, the federal government's relationship with universities and the increasing importance of science in government now raise problems that we are only beginning to assess, let alone solve.

One should also observe that many technological changes have affected the means of communication and transportation. These have required such substantial capital investment that the state has had to become an active participant as developer and owner. The consequent fostering of an interdependent economy brought new regulatory problems, most of which had to be met on a national front. Worldwide application of these techniques has shrunk the world and produced further problems of international trade and communication that also fall naturally on the shoulders of the federal government.

Apart from these broad repercussions of technological change, there are also the products which derive from the new technology and affect the procedures of the public service. One of the most important consequences of the age of gadgets is the ease with which paper can now be created and the resulting problems of record keeping, storage, filing, and so on. Historically, the mechanics of paper management were characterized unflatteringly but accurately as the 'donkey work' in the civil service. (There is more than a shadow of home truth in the classification of the first females in the British public service as 'female typewriters'.) Yet, as the Glassco Commission has emphasized, the new gadgets and procedures necessitate an upgrading of those concerned with the management of paper if the government is not, like the sorcerer's apprentice, to be drowned in a flood of its own creation. At this point we can confidently coin a neo-Parkinsonian Law: the quantity of paper will rise to meet the capacity of the machines available for processing it. It is still difficult to know how the electronics revolution will affect an organization where there is so much routine repetitive work that lends itself to automation. At the least, its widescale application will necessitate major retraining programs.

The high costs of the more versatile automatic data processing equipment imply that the new technology may force a reversal of the traditional pattern of dispersed and decentralized operations as work gets concentrated in a few large electronic machine shops. On the other hand, it may well be that centralized processing is quite compatible with—indeed, a genuine encouragement to—more effective decentralization, because the new machines can improve reporting and control techniques. It would be pure speculation to carry this line of inquiry further but, now we are in the throes of numbering the nation, it may not be too unrealistic to visualize our master cards going into the computer and slipping us anything from a birth certificate to an old age pension, a request for payment of back taxes to a passport. At the best we should see improved, though depersonalized, service to the public and the collation of new masses of data from which our social planners in the future should be able to make more confident and accurate predictions.

From this Orwellian world that is less fantastic than it seemed less than a decade ago, let us turn to the cultural setting. Canada is a middle power both in the figurative and literal sense, geographically positioned next door to the United States and still bound by tradition and sentiment to England. At good neighbour rallies, we extol the virtues of our undefended frontier, which on closer inspection is seen to bristle with defences, most of them of the Canadian government's own making. Tariffs and the all-Canadian railway were but the precursors of a host of other expressions of the do-it-yourself philosophy inspired by national pride and a reluctance to be beholden to our more powerful neighbour. The airplane and radio brought government monopolies as chosen instruments of national policy. The Canada Council was a far-too-modest answer to the American foundations, the proposal to redirect the Canadian advertisers' dollars to Canadian publications and the BBG's prescription of a fifty-five per cent quota of 'Canadian content' for broadcasting are all recent evidences of the same spirit.

If a number of the federal government's most important cultural activities have evolved in response to our defensive posture toward United States cultural penetration, it is equally true that the organization of the public service itself bears marks of our constant borrowing. Here, however, we have tended to gyrate between American practices and British tradition. Our Civil Service Act and the Civil Service Commission are more American than British in conception, intent and in the powers conferred; so, too, is our classification system. Our attempts to create a cadre of senior administrative officers and the abortive reports of such Royal Commissions as the Murray and Gordon Commissions show much clearer traces of the British pattern. The most recent reports from the Glassco Commission are an interesting amalgam of American management practices and British institutional devices, both adapted to the Canadian setting.

Apart from the significant and continuing pressure from these external cultural influences the Canadian public service has to face a unique indigenous cultural factor—the principle of bilingualism enshrined in the BNA Act. The hyphenated premierships, the double-barrelled ministries and, more particularly, the rotating capitals that characterized the pre-Confederation public service reveal that the bicultural nature of the earlier union gave much blunter expression than we have since given to the concept. For nearly a century the federal public service has shown at times even a deliberate disregard of this cultural fact of life and is now an obvious target for the moderate nationalist as well as the extremist in French-speaking Canada. The problem goes deeper than a mere recognition of two official languages, for it extends to the whole cultural context and will not be easily ameliorated by well-intended gestures on the part of English-speaking groups. The situation is probably most acute at headquarters, particularly at the senior officer level. Working within an essentially unilingual communication system, bilingualism becomes a one-way street where the only person who needs to be bilingual is the French-speaking officer. That he is called upon to make his home in an alien cultural environment only adds to the difficulties. With the rapid industrialization and bureaucratization of the Province of Quebec, the opportunities for advancement in executive ranks are so enhanced that it will probably be increasingly difficult to make the Ottawa service attractive to French-speaking recruits. On the other hand, Canada, as an officially bilingual country, has a potentially important contribution to make in fulfilling obligations to the international community. This fact by itself should be additional incentive to mount a more effective campaign to bring the federal public service into line with the realities of its long and much neglected bicultural tradition.

I close with a brief reference to what might be called the philosophical pressures that have shaped the public service. I am referring here to the familiar transition from a laissez-faire to a collectivist philosophy which is a worldwide phenomenon. The repercussions on the public service have been obvious. The new expectations and demands for broader and better services have led to an enormous growth in the number of public servants and an increasing complexity and variety of administrative organizations. It is an expansion shared by all levels of government and by no means confined to the federal public service. The vast expansion in the scale of operations means that more and more attention must be devoted to the auxiliary or housekeeping services that exist simply to look after the 'care and feeding' of the public bureaucracy. Problems of internal management, as the Glassco Commission reveals, assume much more significant proportions and older techniques of centralized control prove incapable of coping with the new situations or else, in trying to cope, bring irritation and frustration in their wake. Public services geared to a slower, steadier breathing rhythm find that each day now brings what appears to be a new crisis, until the realization dawns that these are not crises, but part of the speeded-up rhythm of our lives. No organization, let alone any public official, can cope for long with crisis administration unless interested in abnormal psychology and ready to become a patient of the psychiatrist. Current preoccupation with planning evidences an effort to meet the new problems of administrative change not on a crisis basis but as part of normal administrative life.

The collectivist philosophy has changed the scale, the pace, the very tone of administration. These are problems of which the working civil servant is aware. The general public probably goes on believing in its old stereotype of the public servant who, like the fountains in Trafalgar Square, 'plays from ten until four'. And it is the response of the general public that brings me to my final point. The shift from laissez-faire to collectivism has been accompanied by an unprecedented shift in the balance of real power, discretion, and initiative—away from courts, legislatures, and even cabinets to public servants. The shift is inescapable and necessary but the public cannot be blamed for suspecting that the 'faceless' men, the establishment, the mandarins, or what you will are up to no good, that their rights are being invaded even as they are ostensibly being served by public employees. It is from this sense of unease that the proposals for an ombudsman, a public defender, emanate.

I have, perforce, had to use the technique of the quick-sketch artist to present this hasty, episodic perspective on our developing public services. I trust that if you stand far enough back the likeness is reasonably accurate in its general outlines and focus, even if many of the details need much more amplification, qualification, or clarification.

2

The Tasks of Management: A New Approach

Royal Commission on Government Organization

The frustrating effects of the preoccupation with controls have, in recent years, become increasingly evident both within the public service and among the public. The urgent need now is to identify the tasks of management facing the Government of Canada under present and foreseeable conditions, and to devise patterns of organization and guides to action which will best accomplish these tasks.

The needs of effective management fall into two general categories: first, those associated with the administration of departmental operations; and second, those involved in the central direction and coordination of government activities as a whole.

THE NEEDS OF DEPARTMENTAL ADMINISTRATION

The departments, as the active operating organizations of government, must be taken as the starting point in any search for greater efficiency and economy or improved service to the public.

The typical modern department is a large-scale organization, charged with a wide variety of services to or on behalf of the public or with the enhanced housekeeping tasks of accommodating, equipping, and servicing the new operations. Its activities may encompass a large commercial undertaking like the postal service, the operation of harbours, airports, research laboratories and experimental farms, hospitals and schools, or marketing, lending, and insurance services. It may need specialists in purchasing, design and construction, transportation, communications, economic and social research, statistical analysis, records management, data processing, or public relations. The lists could be extended almost indefinitely.

Each extension of government operations has increased the need for ministerial attention to policy. Simultaneously, it has increased the complexity of the administrative apparatus and the demands on administrative leadership. As a consequence, it is virtually impossible for ministers to be, in any real sense, the managers of their departments.

Royal Commission on Government Organization, 'Report 1: A Plan for Management', (Ottawa: Queen's Printer, c. 1962): 48–63. Reproduced with the permission of the Minister of Public Works and Government Services, 2004, and courtesy of the Privy Council Office.

The size and complexity of departments also create a growing need to distinguish between the actual conduct of operations and the task of departmental administration. The former requires skill in the special operating techniques, the latter in the more generalized functions of management. To confuse the two functions within a department may be as damaging as to confuse the respective functions of departmental management and central directing agencies.

This distinction between administration and operations is of particular importance to organization. Administration is concerned with functions which must be performed at the directing centre of each department, regardless of its size, its program responsibilities, or the geographic dispersion of its activities. The organization of operations, on the other hand, must be devised with precisely these considerations in mind. Unless operations are dispersed and operating responsibility delegated, administrators may be diverted from their essential task by the intrusion of operational questions. Where operations involve dealings with the general public, dispersion and delegation will make departments most responsive to public needs.

It is the task of departmental administration which needs to be clearly defined— the task common to all departments. Its principal elements can be set out as follows:

- To advise the minister, with the assistance of the chief operating personnel on matters of departmental policy, and to serve as the channel through which ministerial direction flows to all parts of the department.
- To prepare plans of future programs for consideration by ministers, and to forecast future needs for money, staff, and other resources.
- To adapt the departmental organization to its program responsibilities.
- To ensure the availability of qualified staff and other resources needed for departmental programs, within the general limits authorized by ministers and to allocate such resources.
- To develop and apply the tools of management appropriate to its operations.
- To appraise the performance of the operating units and of the administrative staff itself.

The fact that these functions are common to departmental administration throughout the public service means, in effect, that senior administrative staff can be used interchangeably among departments. Rotation of such senior personnel can be highly advantageous in promoting consistency, strengthening areas of weakness and, more generally, sustaining vigour within departments and among the administrators themselves. Administrators and the more specialized professional staffs should not, however, be treated as castes separate one from the other. Senior administrative posts should be accessible to all who have the essential qualifications of an interest in and an aptitude for the practice of management. But administrators should not be chosen because of professional qualifications unrelated to the functions of management. There must be other roads of advancement open to the specialist whose interest lies in the practice of his professional skills.

There is some evidence of a partial recognition of the proper role of departmental management in the public service. A number of departments have in recent years made substantial progress in the use of appropriate accounting techniques and other tools of management. The control agencies themselves have shown a growing awareness of departmental needs, and one of the major innovations in the Civil Service Act of 1961 is the provision that the Commissioners may delegate certain of their powers to the permanent heads of departments. But such changes have been marginal and the general system of control remains substantially undiminished.

The costly, frustrating, and unproductive character of the existing system has been most strikingly acknowledged in the frequent resort to the use of semi-autonomous boards, commissions, and corporations. By such devices, the established patterns of control have been abandoned in favour of forms of organization borrowed from the private sector. Ministers to whom such agencies formally report have tended to disclaim responsibility for their day-to-day operations on the grounds that these were the concern of the corporations' management. Thus, the agencies enjoy an administrative independence denied to departments, despite the fact that many of the activities of the two differ little, either in character or in their public impact.

In a few cases accountability is to Parliament directly; more frequently, a minister is answerable. While not intervening in day-to-day actions of these agencies, ministers are deemed to be accountable for their broad policies and the general efficiency of operations. And against this ultimate accountability are set ultimate powers: to choose and remove the top managers; to define their objectives and policies in varying degrees of detail; to control their capital programs and, in many cases, their operating budgets; and to require management audits at will. These are, in fact, the only powers which, realistically, a minister can normally exercise over his department. Tradition and the need for a reserve of power will require that all formal authority and the corresponding formal responsibility continue to reside in ministers, but they should be held personally accountable only for the policies and general effectiveness of their departments.

A further conclusion to be drawn from the experience with the agencies is that the meticulous controls to which the departments are subject are not essential to ensure the honesty and efficiency of operations or their conformity to public policy. What has been demonstrated is the utility in large-scale government operations of many of the management concepts and techniques of internal control developed in the private sector of the economy.

Almost certainly, the emergence of these non-departmental forms of organization must be regarded as a response to the changing role of government. This change has been of equal relevance to the departments, and the new agencies are therefore evidence of the failure to adapt the traditional forms and their underlying concepts to the new circumstances.

Above all, departments should, within clearly defined terms of reference, be fully accountable for the organization and execution of their programs, and enjoy powers commensurate with their accountability. They must be subject to controls designed to protect those general interests of government which transcend departmental interests. But every department should be free of external controls which have no such broad purpose.

THE NEEDS OF CENTRAL DIRECTION

Although the departments are the primary operating units, each, as has just been noted, is only a segment of a single entity—the Government of Canada. The policies and programs of each must be balanced against and harmonized with those of other departments and agencies; they must justify themselves, in the last analysis, in terms of their contribution, not to the department itself or its particular interests, but to the general interests of the Canadian people. The money it spends is not departmental money available as of right, but public money, and the ultimate test of its spending is not of its legality but of its effectiveness in the view of the public. The members of its staff are not departmental employees but members of a single public service, whose abilities must be so developed and so employed as to secure the best use for Canada. Thus, the authority of each department, however much it should be strengthened, must be subject to the overriding needs of the government for unity, coherence, and a proper regard for the general interests of the Canadian public.

The functions of overriding concern to the government collectively include the following:

- To weigh public desires for federal government action against the willingness and ability of the public to bear the financial burdens involved, and to establish the limits of action and the apportionment of burdens in an overall financial plan—the annual budget.
- To assess the financial, administrative, and organizational implications, both immediate and long-term, of existing and proposed programs, including the costs and benefits of each and its relationship to other programs, and to define priorities and allocate the resources available within the limits of the total financial plan.
- To establish policies and standards governing the use, throughout the government, of money, staff, and other resources, defining the objectives to be sought and guidelines to be observed by departments, but without trying to prescribe the application of administrative policies and standards in detail.
- To ensure that all departments and agencies have strong administrative leadership and that the human resources available are consistently used for the greatest benefit of the public service as a whole.
- To foster the development and application of effective management practices for the control and improvement of operations throughout the government.
- To assess the general effectiveness of departmental activities and, in particular, the performance of departmental administrators in discharging their functions, as defined above.
- To maintain accounts in a form meeting the needs of Parliament and the Executive, which disclose the sources of public funds and the purposes for which they have been spent.
- To adapt the machinery of government to its changing tasks and objectives.

These functions of administrative direction are, of course, subordinate to the overriding task of political leadership: to define the goals of national interest to which government action is to be directed. The machinery for accomplishing this task embraces, in fact, the entire political process.

The tasks of central direction listed above are, of necessity, the collective responsibility of the government as a whole. But a collective responsibility for management can only be met effectively if there is one person whose job it is to furnish initiatives and ensure that the collective decisions are executed. In effect, this is essentially the same job individual ministers have in relation to their portfolios since, in the last analysis, all government policies and actions are the collective responsibility of all ministers.

Among the functions of central direction, only one, the preparation of the budget, has been assigned on this basis to an individual minister—the Minister of Finance. And it is significant that this is, at present, the only highly developed function among the eight listed. All others remain wholly collective concerns in varying states of underdevelopment.

In a private organization, it is the task of the chief executive officer or general manager to ensure that these needs are met. But the Government of Canada has not, and probably cannot have, a single chief executive in this sense. Other than the Prime Minister, no member of the Cabinet could occupy such a position in view of the powers of control over all other ministers which it would entail. For the same reason, it is clear that no official could do the job.

A Prime Minister has, of course, a recognized pre-eminence among his colleagues, but other matters even more important than the general management of the machinery of government demand almost all the time and energy of any man in this office. He will, of necessity, feel a special responsibility for the general efficiency and effectiveness of government operations, but cannot be expected to involve himself on any but very major or contentious questions.

Since Confederation, matters of central management have been progressively delegated by the Cabinet to its statutory committee, the Treasury Board, and the functions contemplated for that body under the Financial Administration Act of 1951 bear a close resemblance to the tasks of central direction identified here. A board of management on these lines can relieve the Cabinet of most of this work, but the Treasury Board has laboured under two handicaps.

First of all, it is composed of ministers who, as a general rule, have heavy departmental responsibilities and can give little time or attention to its work.

Historically, the primary responsibility for the direction of the Treasury Board has rested with the Minister of Finance, who by law has been its chairman since its inception, and whose department has provided its staff. But as the need has grown for energetic central direction of administration, so too have the departmental responsibilities of the Minister of Finance and his special concern with the financial plan of the government. Fiscal and monetary policy, public borrowings, cash management, international economic policy, the status of the domestic economy, and the economic impact of government policies and programs—responsibilities such as these leave the Minister of Finance little time to devote to the day-to-day task of central administrative direction. Except during the annual review of departmental estimates, which has relevance to the budget, Ministers of Finance have had progressively less time to devote to the work of the Board.

The result has been to place most of the burden of central direction on the permanent staff of the Board and especially its Secretary. Even if this unintentional devolution of such functions to appointed officials were acceptable—which is seriously questioned—it cannot be effective on any major issues of program control or administrative policy. Such issues, which arise constantly can be settled only at the ministerial level, and there is, therefore, a need for continuous leadership by a minister with no departmental responsibilities to divert his attention or prejudice his viewpoint.

It is our conclusion that the Treasury Board needs to be strengthened by the appointment of a presiding minister with no departmental responsibilities, who would give day-to-day guidance to its staff, provide the initiative needed within the Board itself, and ensure that general considerations of good management find adequate expression within Cabinet on all matters to which they are relevant.

The Minister of Finance will obviously continue to have an interest in those functions of the Treasury Board which bear directly on his budgetary responsibilities and must be a member *ex officio*, of the Board. There is, in fact, a close reciprocal relationship between his responsibilities and those of the Board. In its evaluation of departmental programs and plans, the Board must consider among other things, their probable impact on the economy and will normally look to the Department of Finance for guidance on this score. And the probable effects on future expenditure levels of program changes considered by the Board are of obvious interest to the Minister. Moreover, the Board's year-round evaluation of programs and of departmental performance provides the basis for its annual review of departmental estimates of expenditures for the subsequent fiscal year, and the approved body of estimates, in turn, is one of the elements to be reconciled by the Minister in his budget. But the preparation and review of estimates must take account of the Minister's advice as to the desirable limits within which expenditure plans would be settled. There must, therefore, be close working relations at all times between the Minister of Finance and the President of the Treasury Board. Recognizing this convergence of interest in financial affairs, the position of President might well be associated with the Department of Finance, comparable in status to the Minister but different in function.

The second major handicap under which the Treasury Board now works is the tradition of detailed control of departmental administration, as a result of which it has to consider about 16,000 submissions annually. Under these conditions, the proposed new President of the Treasury Board would find his time so occupied with individual cases concerning day-to-day administration that the essential tasks of the Board would receive scarcely more attention than they now do. The necessary abandonment of this tradition of control, to permit the proper functioning of departmental management, is therefore scarcely less essential as a means of freeing the Treasury Board to meet the needs of central direction.

There will remain certain categories of departmental action which will require specific approval by the Board. Ministers will wish to review proposals that entail very large expenditures or represent the launching of major programs with heavy future commitments, actual or implied. But the limits of departmental authority to act independently must be raised substantially, and include all routine and recurring needs almost regardless of the sums involved. The greatest prospect of eliminating detailed review lies in the area of day-to-day administration: the adjustment of establishments within approved program limits; the application of policies and standards governing accommodation, equipment and supplies, travel and entertainment, and the various allowances granted to staff to meet special conditions. The test of what is properly subject to specific approval by the Treasury Board must be its relevance to the essential functions of central direction.

With the strengthening of the functions and provision for day-to-day ministerial direction of the Treasury Board, there must be a redefinition of the role and character of its staff.

It must be recognized that the essential task of the staff is to assist ministers in discharging their collective responsibility for program priorities and administrative standards. Their present location in the Department of Finance tends to encourage among the staff a preoccupation with the detailed scrutiny of expenditures. Among departmental administrators, this has engendered an undue emphasis on justifying the minutiae of operations at the expense of a proper concern with functions of management. It is desirable that this concept be dispelled and that there be a common awareness of both the central and departmental tasks of management.

The ultimate authority lies with the Cabinet and is exercised by the Treasury Board only by delegation; this delegation may, on any matter, be withdrawn or overridden by the Cabinet. When Cabinet chooses to concern itself directly with these functions of central direction it must have at its disposal the staff support normally possessed by the Treasury Board. For this reason, the Treasury Board staff should be transferred from the Department of Finance to the Privy Council Office, where it would be more properly identified with the Cabinet and with the Treasury Board itself as a committee of Cabinet.

At the same time, the status of the Secretary of the Treasury Board needs reassessment. As the chief official adviser to the government on the coordination of programs and the organizational and administrative needs of the public service, his importance is clearly at least equal to that of the permanent heads of departments. He must, therefore, have the status of a deputy minister.

This would mean the existence, within the Privy Council Office, of two deputy ministers—the Clerk of the Privy Council and the Secretary of the Treasury Board. In fact, however, the roles and interests of the two are complementary. The Clerk is concerned in the main with policy, and the Secretary with the functions of administrative direction.

The staff of the Treasury Board, while having no direct administrative responsibilities, clearly occupies a crucial position—as the group making the examination of programs and estimates, drafting administrative policies and standards, evaluating departmental performance, and generally stimulating effective management practices throughout the public service. Invested with such functions, and having access to the central authority of government, such a staff could conceivably destroy the proper balance between central and departmental responsibilities and powers. To prevent such an occurrence, there must be safeguards.

The development and maintenance of strong administrative organizations within the departments will provide a counterweight to any attempts at encroachment on their authority by the Treasury Board staff. But the existence of a state of conflict between the departmental and Treasury Board staffs would be scarcely less damaging than the aggrandizement of the latter.

The most effective safeguard lies in strict adherence to the rule that the Treasury Board staff be formed by the rotation of experienced administrators from departments. No officer should serve the Board until he has acquired a working knowledge of administration and demonstrated his ability and judgment, preferably within a department. Nor should appointments to the Treasury Board staff be of long duration. The benefits of such a rotational policy would accrue to Treasury Board and the departments alike, and such a policy would forestall the growth of pretensions to superior virtue in the central group.

In addition, the size of the Treasury Board staff must be held to a minimum, the emphasis being on experience and outstanding ability rather than numbers. With the abandonment of detailed and often routine controls, and with the concentration of Treasury Board on the essential functions of central direction, the need for numbers—especially of junior staff—disappears. Moreover, the staff should be composed of officers of general administrative experience. Various individuals or groups among them may have to concentrate on particular aspects of the Board's responsibilities, to which more specialized experience in their past service will be relevant. But their responsibilities are essentially non-technical, and whatever technical assistance may be needed by the staff in the course of its work should be sought from the departments and agencies, whose operating needs require the use of highly qualified specialists of every conceivable kind.

An agency of central direction can rarely expect to be popular among departments. Although it should be concerned with encouraging energetic and imaginative administration within departments, there will be times when the Board must exert a restraining influence on departmental ambitions. But as long as it confines itself to its proper functions, it will be respected as an essential element of government. As a body serving broader interests and staffed with officers familiar with the needs of departmental administration, it will be welcomed by the departments as a source of guidance when new and unfamiliar problems arise.

THE PROVISION OF COMMON SUPPORTING SERVICES

The unity of the public service, which creates the need for central direction, is also relevant to the provision of administrative services for which departments have common needs.

As has already been noted, considerations of public policy may influence the administrative practices of the government in meeting its operating needs for staff, accommodation and engineering works, and supplies and equipment. Such considerations may necessitate not only the formulation of standards to govern such practices, but also the creation of common service departments and agencies charged with specific responsibility for ensuring that the public interest is recognized and served.

The pooling of common services may also be warranted by considerations of economy or administrative advantage. From the viewpoint of the departments, while the definition of needs for supplies and services is inescapably a part of departmental responsibility, the actual satisfaction of those needs may be only a chore which intrudes on the essential functions of devising and applying solutions to public problems.

Smaller operating units encounter a special problem in meeting their needs for a wide variety of administrative services, because of the prohibitive cost of maintaining staffs to cater to such needs and the impossibility of keeping such staffs fully employed. Common service organizations, where they exist, can meet some of these needs, but for others the small unit may have to become the client of a larger operating unit. Although this problem exists for some departments and agencies in Ottawa, it is most prevalent and acute in the field, where little has been done to develop remedies.

No uniform pattern is proposed for the organization of common services. Instead, specific solutions are suggested in reports dealing with such matters as accounting, the improvement of office management and systems, accommodation, and purchasing. It is possible, however, to postulate certain general principles which should govern the provision of administrative services by one organization to another.

The first principle is that such arrangements must not impair the essential authority and responsibility of operating departments. This means that, within any general standards enunciated by the Treasury Board (which should be neither minutely detailed nor inflexible), the user of the services shall define his needs. Moreover, in order to emphasize to both the user and the supplier where responsibility lies, and to ensure that relevant costs are allocated to programs, the cost of services should be chargeable to the user.

Second, service and control must be sharply differentiated. The suppliers of services should exercise no control over the users except within the strict limits of any responsibility for applying special considerations of public policy. The only general element of control will be exercised centrally in the form of an assessment of the level of service demanded by users and the degree of satisfaction given by supplying agencies, as part of the general evaluation of administrative performance throughout the machinery of government.

Third, means must also be adopted for ensuring that common service organizations do not become inbred and complacent. Their direction must be in the hands of senior administrators who come within the general rotational program for the top levels of the public service and who will, therefore, be conscious of and sympathetic to the needs of the user departments. Moreover, to the extent that operations similar to those of a service organization are carried on in other parts of the public service, there should be rotation of the technical staffs involved. In addition, where similar operations exist outside the government, the staffs of service organizations should be encouraged to keep in touch with external developments in techniques, and the services of the government should be strengthened by the employment from time to time of experts from such outside services, either by contract or by the exchange of personnel for periods of several years.

Fourth, the organization of each common service must be designed to serve the needs of its clientele. Certain professional staff services—legal, statistical, and economic, for example—are needed primarily for the support of administrative activity in the head offices of departments, and might properly be concentrated in Ottawa. Other services, however, such as those concerned with accommodation, construction, supply, and communications, must support the operating elements of the public service, which lie predominantly outside Ottawa; consequently, the organization of such services may require strong regional and even local components.

Finally, common service organizations can serve the Treasury Board and its staff as sources of technical guidance in the framing of policies and standards to govern administrative practices throughout the government. In addition, the government itself has need of a central service organization to maintain the financial records required for the central direction and evaluation of administration and for Parliament. This accounting agency can also provide related services to the departments but without the existing connotation of control.

The Importance of Administrative Leadership

A good plan of organization and an appropriate concept of management—essential as they are—provide no automatic guarantee of good administration. The essential ingredient is good people, especially at the top. The goals pursued by departments are matters of public policy but the effectiveness of their activity will depend primarily on the quality of administrative leadership. There must be, throughout the public service, senior administrators of outstanding ability with a strong sense of purpose and a clear grasp of their responsibilities.

The development of senior administrators is of concern to central and departmental authorities alike. But the Treasury Board staff must bear a special responsibility for ensuring that the available resources of leadership are used to the greatest advantage of the government as a whole. It is not too much to say that this is the most important task of constant concern to the central staff. The essentials of this task will be:

- To assess the strengths and weaknesses of individual senior officers throughout the public service and the relative urgency of bolstering departmental management in one respect or another.
- To secure such appointments and transfers of officials as seem most likely to match individual abilities with departmental needs at any given time.
- To be actively concerned, in association with departments, with the development of future generations of leaders.

As in the past, the appointment and transfer of deputy ministers should be made by Order in Council, on the recommendation of the Prime Minister. This traditional practice serves admirably to underscore the role of the deputy minister in providing the bridge between the political world of ministers and the administrative world of the department, and provides a reminder to them of their need for a perspective encompassing the whole range of government. At the same time it emphasizes the collective interest of the ministers, and the special interest of the Prime Minister, in the effectiveness of management in the public service.

In framing his recommendations, the Prime Minister will naturally consult whom he chooses—including, as a matter of course, the ministers of the departments concerned. But the two permanent heads of the central staff—the Clerk of the Privy Council and the Secretary of the Treasury Board—should have a special role to play. Each is concerned—in complementary ways—with the whole range of government operations and is therefore able to measure departmental needs for leadership against the men available. And in their respective positions they represent, in a sense, the two aspects which are fused in varying proportions in the office of a deputy minister: the development of policy and the management of operations. Thus they bear a joint responsibility for advising the Prime Minister on the appointment or transfer of deputy ministers whenever circumstances or their own assessment of need dictate.

The concern of the centre of government, however, must reach below the deputy ministers and take account of the development and use of other senior administrative staff throughout the public service. To ensure the satisfactory development and distribution of such staff on a government-wide basis, the central machinery must be actively concerned with appointments and transfers relating to certain positions in each department.

This central concern should extend, first, to those positions immediately below the deputy minister. Movement among departments at this level provides the last opportunity for achieving the broadening of experience and outlook which is so essential to the development of administrative leadership.

Special considerations apply to two other senior officials in each department: the chief financial officer and the chief personnel officer. These two are most directly concerned with the use of staff and public money, and with the application of the general policies and standards of the government relating to administration. Rotation of such officers among departments and the staff of Treasury Board itself will do more than anything else to ensure that the general policies and standards are applied with consistency throughout the government.

Moreover, it is important that these two officers should have the sense that their future careers rest primarily—though not exclusively—on the assessment of their performance by the staff of the Treasury Board, rather than on their ability to please the heads of their departments. They must be in all respects members of their respective departments and so regard themselves, and could not be empowered to veto the wishes of their departmental heads and thereby impair the necessary authority and responsibility of the minister and his deputy. But they would, in effect, provide a 'presence' of the central authority within the department, and their reluctance to concur in courses of action proposed by their departmental heads would not be lightly ignored.

For these positions—immediate subordinates of deputy ministers and the chief financial and personnel officers—it is proposed that the Treasury Board staff should, whenever the prospect of vacancies or their own assessment of needs dictate, initiate discussions with the department or departments concerned, with a view to securing the most effective use and development of senior administrators throughout the public service. Appointments to such positions should be subject to approval by the Treasury Board.

In addition to their specific responsibilities relative to these senior positions, the Treasury Board staff would have a general responsibility, in common with the departments, for identifying and developing promising officials in the middle ranks of administration. They must also, in evaluating performance, ensure that the departments themselves attach proper importance to the development and effective use of all their personnel. Moreover, in an organization as large as the public service, there is a constant danger of blind alleys, and particular care must be taken by departmental and Treasury Board staffs to guard against such pockets of frustration and to find new opportunities for able people caught in isolated or uncongenial positions.

As has been noted, the federal administration is fortunate today, and has been in recent decades, in the quality of its senior administrators. The distribution of ability is uneven and could be improved by greater flexibility in the use of senior officers. But this need is overshadowed by the more urgent need for a concept and plan of management which will provide greater opportunities for administrative leadership to become effective.

CHECKS AND BALANCES

There remains only the question of safeguards against those weaknesses in the public service which gave rise to the existing regime of control. The dangers of political patronage in the staffing of the public service, and of irresponsibility in the handling of public money must be recognized, and safeguards must be provided. But the remedies must be sought within a framework which fosters rather than frustrates good management.

The first guarantee of administrative integrity lies in the proposed new concept of management, with its emphasis on the sharper definition of responsibility, authority, and accountability, and on the systematic encouragement of strong administrative leadership. But, in fact, the proposed new concept offers more specific guarantees in the form of checks and balances. The balancing of functions between departments and the Treasury Board, and between the Clerk of the Privy Council and the Secretary of the Treasury Board; the rotation of senior administrative personnel; the creation within departments of a 'presence' of the Treasury Board—all serve as checks not only on the misuse, but equally on the ineffectual use of staff and public money. Yet none of these, unlike the existing controls, can act in any way to inhibit or impede energetic and imaginative administration.

In addition, the essential safeguards, independent of the framework of management under the authority of ministers, will remain: the Civil Service Commissioners and the Auditor General.

For the Civil Service Commissioners there will be a continuing task of certifying appointments to the public service, after satisfying themselves that selection has been made in a manner which establishes merit. Moreover, the new concept of management should end the confusion which has existed in the Civil Service Act and its administration, between the ideal of a unified service and the quite separate and unrealistic goal of uniformity in the treatment of public servants. Such matters as the basis and method of remuneration, and the special procedures which may be appropriate in the recruitment and management of different classes of people, would become more properly identified as functions of management. Thus, many sections of the public service which have had to be excluded from the Act because the uniform standards and procedures were inappropriate could now be brought within the protection of the Commissioners, and the ideal of a unified service could be more nearly realized.

The other external safeguard rests with the Auditor General, in his responsibility for judging the efficacy of government accounting systems, internal control and audit procedures, and other techniques of financial management, and ensuring that public funds are adequately protected against misuse and are legally spent. This function and his duty of disclosing to Parliament and the public any evidence of illegality, irresponsibility, and dishonesty in the handling of money, serve as powerful deterrents.

In the last analysis, the ultimate safeguard lies in the political process itself—in the accountability of ministers, both individually and collectively, to Parliament and through it to the public. The methods by which Parliament exacts this accounting from ministers and the public service are, of course, beyond your Commissioners' terms of reference. It is only noted, therefore that the growth and increasing complexity of government, which have generated new problems for the management of the public service, may well create new problems of accountability to the public and their elected representatives. Such, indeed, has been the experience of other parliamentary systems, resulting in a growing resort, in recent years, to new methods for the scrutiny of administrative action.

The importance to the public of efficiency and integrity in the machinery of government by which it is served is unquestionably great and grows with each new increase in the size and scope of government. But even greater is the importance of a service responsive to public wants and expectations. No plan of management and no system of checks and balances can, by themselves, offer guarantees of this responsiveness. This is the test, not merely of the machinery of government, but also—and principally—of the political process by which its goals are set.

3

Administrative Reform in the Federal Public Service: Signs of a Saturation Psychosis

H.L. Laframboise

Abstract. The thesis of this article is that managers in the federal public service have been required, in the past five years, to introduce and administer internal reforms which, in total, are far beyond the capacity of the system to absorb. As a result, managers have had to neglect their primary task of serving the public and are becoming increasingly impatient with the imposition of administrative reforms and the proportion of time required for their introduction and operation.

In support of his thesis, the author spells out the consequences, in terms of the diversion of managerial effort, in implementing recommendations of the Glassco Report, collective bargaining, bilingualism, and the decision to establish the Treasury Board Secretariat as 'general manager and employer' of the public service.

The purpose of the article is to generate a debate which would lead to a more careful approach to introducing reforms and might even reverse some of the changes whose results do not warrant the effort required.

Sommaire. La thèse de cet article, c'est que les cadres de la fonction publique fédérale ont dû, dans les cinq dernières années, initier et administrer des réformes internes qui, dans leur totalité, dépassent de beaucoup la capacité d'absorption du système. En conséquence, les cadres ont dû négliger leur tâche principale qui est de servir le public et ils tolèrent de moins en moins bien l'imposition de réformes administratives et la perte du temps consacré à leur mise en vigueur.

A l'appui de cette thèse, l'auteur expose les conséquences, du point de vue de la dispersion de l'effort des cadres, de l'application des recommandations du Rapport Glassco, des négociations collectives, du bilinguisme, et de la décision de faire du Secrétariat du Conseil du trésor « le directeur général et l'employeur » de la fonction publique.

Le but de cet article est de susciter un débat qui aurait pour conséquence de faire aborder les réformes de façon plus prudente et qui pourrait même faire marche arrière lorsque les résultats des changements ne justifient pas l'effort requis.

H.L. Laframboise, 'Administrative Reform in the Federal Public Service: Signs of a Saturation Psychosis', *Canadian Public Administration* 14, 3 (1971): 303–25. Courtesy of The Institute of Public Administration Canada.

INTRODUCTION

Up the Organization[1] and *The Peter Principle*[2] are two recent management books written in the same half-serious, half-humorous but highly critical vein as *Parkinson's Law*.[3] Of the three, *Up the Organization* is perhaps the one which takes deadliest aim at prevalent management practices and at the flocks of specialists whose job it is to improve these practices and provide management services.

What makes these and other similar books and articles more than just amusing is that the examples and arguments so often square with phenomena as observed daily in business life. Even a dedicated management improvement specialist cannot avoid feeling, in reading them, a twinge akin to a rap on the funny-bone—a quick sharp pain followed by a lingering numbness—as he recalls frequent episodes in his own experience that reinforce the criticisms put forth by the writers.

From my point of view, i.e., that of a federal official who is deeply involved in both managing subordinates and offering management advice to colleagues and superiors, these books raise two critical questions: (a) are federal programs over-managed, and, even more important, (b) are managers, through waves of massive administrative innovation, being overwhelmed? These are the questions which will be dealt with in this article.

Admittedly this paper expresses a personal view. On the other hand, that view is based on participation in management studies in some thirty federal departments and agencies, two large Canadian companies, and two international organizations over the past twenty years. It is also a view from the centre of one of the largest and most complex of federal departments. Finally, it is the view of someone who has been deeply involved in both the giving and receiving ends of management training over many years. Even all this falls short of assuring competence to deal with the questions asked and the subject treated in this paper.

But the increasing signs of anguish indicate that federal managers are crying for solace. Figuratively speaking, federal managers are exhibiting twitches and tics at such an accelerating rate that the question of whether they are approaching the critical point where they will cut off their channels of communication with the innovators must be asked.

The symptoms of conflict are strong. They must be heeded if we are to avoid either of two unacceptable consequences: (a) the psychological immobilization of our managers in the face of insistent and conflicting demands, (withdrawal and apathy); (b) a revolt by the managers against innovators leading to an outright hostility to change, whatever its real or apparent merit (aggression).

We may now be reaching a point where we must try to regulate the rate of administrative innovation at a level which can be digested without alienating public service managers, or reducing services to Canadians to a trickle, and absorbed without adding staff in such numbers as to put federal tax rates out of sight.

I would like to define some terms. First, the innovation critically described in this paper is limited to reform internal to the public service and does not include new programs and activities for the direct benefit of Canadians. I am writing of administrative reform and not of changes in substantive programs.

Second, my concern is *not* with reform arising in a specific activity as a result of a study initiated or requested by the manager, with recommendations which that manager is entirely free to accept or reject. In these cases the manager can control implementation according to the availability of staff and his own priorities. What I am concerned with are internal reforms imposed upon the manager by the government of the day or through the exercise of functional authority, either by a central agency or by one of the administrative specialist professions.

Third, I would like it to be noted that I am fully aware that we live in a complex and changing environment, and that novelty and experimentation are necessary to progress. As an official who has made a career of management innovation, I would be negating my own raison d'être of these past twenty years if I were to deny the progress that has been made. The breadth of my subject, however, forces me to limit my comments to the problem of excessive administrative innovation.

Fourth, I will define a manager, for the purpose of this article, as someone who directs two or more subordinates toward the accomplishment of given tasks which contribute to a better life for Canadians. A manager's job may be to operate a post office, to direct a team of tax assessors, to carry out a research program on the effects of air pollution, to manage a national park, to run a statistical division, or to direct the provision of an engineering service. It is jobs like these which I will refer to as 'substantive' or as those with which a manager has been charged, and it is the time needed for these duties which must be given a measure of protection against excessive demands by administrative specialists, such as accountants and personnel officers.

Finally, I will attempt to define what I mean by 'excessive' administrative reform. I will assume, first, that there is an upper limit to the amount of time and effort a manager can devote to administrative work which is peripheral to his principal mission. Second, I will propose that there are several components to be assessed in arriving at an 'acceptable' rate of innovation. Third, I will admit at the outset that an 'acceptable' rate, however arrived at, will at best be a matter of judgment. It would be useful, in any case, to have some base, even for the sake of argument.

The elements to be considered are: the amount of work-time needed to plan and implement a change; the amount of time needed for the ongoing administration of a new procedure; the amount of psychic energy consumed in any change process including uncertainty, friction, overcoming inertia, and so on; the limits of a manager's span of attention; the time needed for operational changes which the manager himself wants to make, over and above the administrative reforms imposed by others.

Taking these together, it is my opinion that a manager should be involved in only two major changes at one time; that these should not require more than 20 per cent of his work-time; and that unless the manager is convinced that a worthwhile purpose is being served, after a year, the change should be reversed or at least re-evaluated.

INNOVATION IN AN HISTORICAL CONTEXT

The years 1945–60 were not a golden age of administrative reform. In retrospect it is plain that we neglected to move quickly, if at all, in such matters as employee relations, bilingualization, program budgeting, and large-scale systems analysis. In particular, management consultants in government, as a rule, failed to raise their sights to major problems requiring solution. Attached to, and ensnared by, the concept that their duty lay in responding to requests and not in initiating reform, they spent much of their time helping managers to swat flies while failing to communicate to them that the foundations of their overall administrative system were being eaten away by termites.

Nevertheless, in the 1940s and 1950s the civil service administrators of the Canadian federal government basked in the light of an unrivalled international reputation for competence. The federal Civil Service had established substantial control over the patronage problem which continued to dog so many other jurisdictions. The best minds of the country were at the helm, and a list of some 'deputy heads' is, in retrospect, impressive: Stewart Bates (Fisheries, CMHC); Charles H. Bland (Public Service Commission); R.B. Bryce (Finance, Treasury Board, Privy Council); W.C. Clark (Finance); Edmond Cloutier (Queen's Printer); George F. Davidson (National Welfare); C.M. Drury (National Defence); A. Davidson Dunton (Canadian Broadcasting Corporation); J.J. Deutsch (Finance, Treasury Board); Arnold Heeney (Privy Council Office, External Affairs, Civil Service Commission); Hugh Keenleyside (Mines and Technical Surveys); C.J. MacKenzie (National Research Council); Gen. A.G.L. McNaughton (International Joint Commission); M.W. Sharpe (Trade and Commerce); O.M. Solandt (Defence Research Board); W.J. Turnbull (Post Office); W.E. Van Steenburgh (Energy, Mines and Resources), are some of the names which come readily to mind.

In the period 1945–60, most of the innovation took place in the implementation of new programs for Canadians. Keynesian principles dominated economic thinking, an awakening conscience dominated social thinking, and Canada was the voice of the middle powers on the international stage.

The rate of management innovation was exceedingly low and eminently digestible. Even an assessment of administrative needs by such an eminent authority as Walter Gordon (*Gordon Report*, c.1946) was viewed as a document for quiet contemplation and moderate action.

Modest resources were allocated in 1948 to a central management consulting function, and even by 1960 there were only some twenty-five consultants in the unit to serve the whole government. Departmental consulting units were small and few in number. Computers, which started to merit serious consideration in 1956, were dealt with by the Interdepartmental Committee on Electronic Data Processing. There was no bargaining with employee associations and the process of consultation was carried out by a handful of officials in the Civil Service Commission and the Treasury Board. Appeals under the Civil Service Act were heard by officers with other principal duties. Management Audit did not exist as a specialist function. Planning units were relatively unknown. Departmental personnel management was limited to filling vacancies, keeping leave and attendance records, looking after pay, and promoting modest training endeavours. The first separate personnel unit was only established in Taxation about 1947. Bilingualization did not exist as an issue; it was not even a topic of casual conversation. Judged by the resources allocated, the most important management innovations were in the fields of forms design, office mechanization, office and filing systems, and stores accounting.

The Civil Service Commission exercised almost all of the powers that affected management innovation. It controlled recruitment and promotion; it classified all positions; its approval was required for changes in organization structure; it made the recommendations, at least *de jure*, for pay increases to the Treasury Board; it controlled numbers of employees through the control of establishments, i.e., the number of authorized positions. By and large its principal duties had not altered in twenty years, the main change being in the volume of work rather than in its nature. The Civil Service Commission's principal analytical and control tool was the unit survey, and it is worth recording just what a unit survey was.

When the upward pressure on position classification and staff numbers in a particular unit became too great to be dealt with on the usual case-by-case basis, the Commission sent in one of its organization and classification officers to conduct a unit survey.

This survey reported on: (a) the appropriateness of the classifications of all positions in the unit; (b) the appropriateness of the staff numbers in relation to the workload; (c) the necessity for doing the work actually being done; (d) the structure of the unit's organization; (e) the working relationships of the Unit with other Units with which it was involved, including evidence of duplication; (f) the relevance of the unit's goals to the law and to departmental objectives.

This combination study resulted in a report which became the basis for negotiation between the department concerned and the Civil Service Commission. Evidence of good faith in implementing survey recommendations was rewarded by a tolerance of some anomalies, but by and large the Commission was very tough-minded.

It was from its experience with unit surveys that the Commission recognized the need for specialists in the analysis of administrative problems; the first operations and methods unit was created about 1948 as an adjunct to the Organization and Classification Branch in the Commission.

The Treasury Board Secretariat, charged with keeping over-all expenditures within ceilings established by the government of the day, concentrated on controlling the allocation of resources through percentage expenditure increments. Individual departments were permitted percentage increases in over-all expenditures or in certain cases were required to make percentage cuts. It was largely up to the department to determine where money would be allocated internally, although the Secretariat did pass judgment on programs. Specific Treasury Board authority had to be obtained for certain spending decisions and thousands of 'routine' Treasury Board submissions had to be processed, most of a minor nature.

Accounting was under an independent Comptroller of the Treasury whose role was created as a result of the chaos in government accounting brought to light by the Bennett administration. No spending commitment could be entered into by a department unless the Comptroller's staff was satisfied that it was for the purpose intended by Parliament when the funds were voted, that funds were in fact available during the fiscal year, and that the commitment was entered into by an authorized official. On the paying end the Comptroller paid all bills, ensuring the goods and services had been received and that the account had been submitted against an authorized commitment.

Departmental financial units were small and served mainly as a liaison unit between the Comptroller of the Treasury staff and departmental officials.

Whatever the shortcomings of the foregoing personnel, resources control, and accounting systems in limiting the powers of line managers, they had the advantage of simplicity; the line managers could concentrate on substantive programs for Canadians without undue distraction by the uncertainties of widespread administrative innovation.

FOUR CRITICAL DECISIONS

Four decisions by the government in the 1960s spelled the doom of this tidy little world. In a short span of years it was decided (a) to establish a Royal Commission on Government Organization (the Glassco Commission) and to implement its recommendations; (b) to introduce collective bargaining for federal employees; (c) to bilingualize the federal service; (d) to establish the Treasury Board Secretariat as the 'general manager' of the public service, and 'the employer' as required for collective bargaining.

Taken one at a time the merits of these decisions are defensible or at least arguable. Taken in their totality, and considering the changes consequent upon them, they have resulted in such an increase in the internal administrative workload that only huge increases in staff numbers and unprecedented demands on available managerial work-time have made their imperfect implementation possible.

The consequences of implementing Glassco recommendations, in terms of managerial energy and resources consumed, have not yet been compiled. It is fair to state, however, that it is from Glassco recommendations that the federal service has introduced: (a) 'modern' financial management; (b) 'modern' personnel management; (c) increased centralization of common services; and (d) increased decentralization, to managers, of what were formerly specialist tasks.

The introduction of collective bargaining, in addition to requiring added resources in the Treasury Board and in departmental personnel branches, has placed additional burdens on managers. Not only are there multitudinous contracts to administer but certain rigidities have been built in to the use of staff. The revised job classification system, which was introduced concurrently with collective bargaining, is often extremely time-consuming for managers. In order that full weight will be given to subordinates' duties, managers must spend countless hours in writing up detailed job descriptions. One manager, with a staff of less than 10, told me recently he had spent ten full working days in the past four weeks on writing job descriptions. The grievance system takes more time, and so on.

Increased bilingualism (i.e., the ability to use both English and French effectively) in the federal service is a national policy that is widely accepted by federal managers as necessary for Canada's survival. Yet it creates a dilemma for the manager since he and his subordinates are required to take time from their regular duties in order to learn another language. This time must be dedicated to language training without any compensating reduction in workload and without the addition of compensating manpower. The goal of national unity therefore conflicts with a manager's drive for operational productivity. In the absence of clear and consistent guidance as to where day-to-day priorities lie, managers juggle their manpower around to try to fit in language training. 'Being pulled off French' to help meet a pressing deadline is a common phenomenon that results from this ambiguity and conflict of priorities.

Many managers justifiably fear that concern with productivity will be interpreted as a prejudice against the increased use of the French language and there is not yet an open dialogue on the subject.

Finally, the enhancement of the Treasury Board's roles as 'general manager' and 'employer' has caused added demands for information. This may take the form of demands on departments, and subsequently on managers, for more detailed data on personnel, say actual and planned use of manpower by category and occupational group. It may require more quantitative justification for requests for funds. It may demand more accurate output measures. It may promote the implementation of more elaborate personnel management systems, resource allocation systems, vehicle control systems, expenditure forecast systems, and so on. In each case the Treasury Board Secretariat can initiate by edict any system which, in its opinion, will improve management in the public service or supply it with data it believes it needs to carry out its role as 'general manager'. None of these initiatives, to my knowledge, diminish the manager's workload, and, because the Treasury Board Secretariat is a major force in the annual allocation of funds, and the control of personnel policy, no department can risk incurring its displeasure by resisting its demands.

A SURFEIT OF ALPHABET SOUP

New management concepts are often, but not always, reduced to their first initials so that they can be spoken more quickly, freeing time to concentrate the conversation on the glorious results that could be achieved by their implementation. For those who may not know all the recent and current acronyms here is a glossary: 1. *O and M*: organization and methods—the design of systems and organization structures, principally at the micro or working level. 2. *PPBS*: planning-programming-budgeting system—an integrated system of resource allocation and control by program and activity. 3. *MBO*: management by objective—a system by which units of organization and individuals are reviewed according to their quantitative and qualitative contribution to agreed objectives. 4. *EDP*: electronic data processing—the application of computers to the processing of data and the maintenance of records. 5. *OR*: operations research—the application of the scientific method to the solution of business problems. 6. *C/B analysis:* cost-benefit (sometimes benefit-cost, sometimes cost-effectiveness) analysis—the calculation of the ratio between expenditures and returns for a defined course of action. 7. *MIS:* management information system—this term is capitalized because it refers to The System, i.e., the all-inclusive integrated system by which management gets its information.

In addition to the management concepts which have been 'acronymized' there are a number which have been retained in whole phrases. 8. *Participative decision-making*: a system by which all those affected by a decision are given opportunities to make an effective input to the decision. 9. *Responsibility accounting:* a technique whereby each manager is required to manage his own budget and to report on the results achieved. 10. *Value analysis:* in the field of procurement, the analysis of relative values for alternative material purchase options. 11. *Manpower planning:* a planning system which strives to ensure the availability of manpower resources in the right kinds and quantities as they are needed. It includes training and development, manpower forecasting, job rotation, etc. 12. *Datastream:* the name of the computerized data system operated by the Public Service Commission to assist in filling managerial and professional positions. 13. *Program forecast:* the systematic projections of spending plans for a five-year period, prepared by departments and submitted annually to the Treasury Board Secretariat. 14. *Sensitivity training:* training designed at inducing desired personality changes in individuals. 15. *Managerial grid training:* a variation of sensitivity training aimed at assisting individuals in recognizing the degrees of concern they have for production and for people. The 'grid' is a matrix of the two values on a scale of 1 to 9 in each dimension. 16. *Synergetics:* the techniques of working together to achieve common goals. 17. *Kepner-Tregoe system:* a copyright system by which managers are trained to make non-quantitative decisions with a minimum of unproductive effort. 18. *Decision theory:* the application of mathematical and statistical techniques to the making of business or government decisions (very similar to OR see above). 19. *Matrix organization:* a plan of organization which 'matrixes' functions with projects or products so that each activity is subject to dual subordination by the manager of the function concerned and the manager of a project or product line. 20. *Integrated dual supervision:* the result of matrix organization. 21. *Work study:* a technique for training and motivating workers to improve the procedures they are carrying out.

All of the foregoing, it will be noticed, are designed to assist 'the Manager', at whatever level, to do a better job. By improving the means it is hoped that the ends will be achieved more quickly, and/or, at lower cost, and/or, with greater effect.

This goal is entirely laudable, and there can be little argument that the various techniques appeal to logic. However, and this is the big 'however', they can demand so much of the manager's attention that unless they are taken by the spoonful they can literally rob him of the time he should be spending on rendering service to the public. He can, in brief, suffer from a surfeit of alphabet soup.

WHAT BELONGS TO WHOM?

In general each management concept is promoted by a particular category of administrative specialist. It is important, then, to know what belongs to whom at a given time or when a concept has taken on enough canvas to sail away on its own, with its own specialists.

In the federal government today, the big push of the finance community is for PPBS (planning-programming-budgeting system) and the prize concept of the personnel community is MBO (management by objective). The fact that PPBS is management by objective through the budget system and MBO, as interpreted by the personnel community, is management by objective through the performance of individuals, has not yet been sufficiently admitted to require that they be implemented under immediate common direction.

C/B (cost/benefit) analysis is a technique that is being fought over by finance and operations research. EDP (electronic data processing) sometimes stands alone, is sometimes amalgamated with MIS (management information systems) and sometimes with O and M (organization and methods). Work study belongs to O and M. Responsibility accounting and program forecast are protegés of finance, while manpower planning, participative decision-making, Kepner-Tregoe training, and sensitivity training emanate from personnel. Decision theory is, like OR (operations research), the domain of the management scientists, i.e., those who apply scientific methods to management decisions.

The lack of coordination between the specialties is most evident at the level of the manager who is at the receiving end of their respective exhortations. The manager's attention is a prize for which all compete.

LANGUAGE TRAINING AND ITS EFFECT ON EFFICIENCY

Language is the vehicle of persuasion, and success in persuasion is the key to managerial success. Persuasion takes many forms. It may consist of getting one's ideas accepted, or of having one's job performance viewed as superior, or of being chosen by interview for promotion over another. Whatever form it takes, persuasion through language, spoken or written, is a critical element in the climb up the managerial ladder.

Because of this, French-speaking Canadians with a faulty command of English have been under an insuperable disadvantage in the public service of Canada. Good ideas imperfectly expressed, or worse, not expressed at all because of difficulties of language, cannot receive consideration. Their originators are erroneously judged as confused, if they express themselves poorly, and as dunces, if they express themselves not at all.

Working under this handicap few French-Canadians rose to the upper echelons of the public service during the period 1945–60 unless their command of English was excellent. In the partial list of 'mandarins', given earlier in this paper for the period 1945–60, French-Canadian names are remarkable for their scarcity.

Not only were French-Canadians at a disadvantage in the public service, but French-speaking citizens were under a continuing handicap in obtaining services and information in their own official language.

In belated recognition of the need drastically to augment the use of the French language in the public service, a program of bilingualization was launched, a principal element of which has been language training, particularly the teaching of French to English-speaking public servants.

This long preamble is necessary in order to make it crystal clear that in exposing problems of efficiency and productivity I am not attacking the goal of bilingualism. My aim instead is to generate a debate as to how this goal can better be achieved, taking into account the nature and scale of the burden created by language training and the effects of this burden on the expedition of public business. To further limit the subject I will only analyse the effect of taking officials away from their substan-

TABLE 1—*Target Percentages by Category of Bilingual Officials, 1975*

Category	Percentage
Executive	60
Admin. and foreign service	50
Admin. Support	35
Scientific and professional	15
Technical	15
Operations	15

tive work for lengthy periods of language training. With a given amount of manpower to perform a specific mission the manager needs more guidance than he now receives as to what proportion of that manpower he is expected to dedicate to language training.

The calculation of the amount of language training required to bring language skills up to the goals of the government is an exercise in simple arithmetic.

The first element in the calculation is the average amount of classroom training required to advance a unilingual official to bilingual status. One department estimates this as twelve months. If a more accurate figure is available it can be used in the calculation.

The second element consists of determining how many bilingual officials will be required according to the target percentages by category of bilingual officials. Those for 1975 are shown in Table 1.

The third element is the determination of the number of officials in each category who are now bilingual and the assumption that this number will remain constant as an exclusion from the number who will require training.

The fourth element is an estimate of the number of bilingual officials who will be obtained by recruitment rather than by language training.

The fifth and final element is, of course, the time-span within which targets must be reached. For a 1975 target this can be calculated as four years.

Where: A = the number of months of classroom training required to bring one unilingual official up to bilingual status, and B = the number of officials required to be bilingual according to target percentages, and C = the number of officials who are now bilingual, and D = the number of bilinguals who will be recruited rather than trained, and E = the number of years in which targets are to be reached, then the following formula will determine the man-years to be devoted to language training in each year:

$$[A (B - C - D)]/[E \times 12 \text{ (to reduce to man-years)}].$$

As an illustration, let us substitute hypothetical figures in the formula as follows: A = 11 months classroom training per official; B = 1000 bilingual officers required by 1975 to meet targets; C = 105 bilingual already on strength; D = 125 to be recruited already bilingual; E = 4 years to target. Then:

$$[11 \times (1000 - 105 - 125)]/(4 \times 12)$$
$$= [11 \times (1000 - 230)]/48$$
$$= (11 = 770)/48 = 8470/48 = 176 \text{ man-years.}$$

This means that in the illustrative department 176 man-years would have to be dedicated to language training each year for the next four years in order to hit the targets. For the purpose of this paper, the most disquieting conclusion from the foregoing calculation is the great amount of manpower that will have to be dedicated to language training to meet present goals.

The effect of the language training program on the output of managers has many other facets. First, the training tends to be concentrated at upper-middle levels of management (see target percentages by category) where most decisions are taken.

Second, the man-years are not made up by wholly absenting a number of officials for a year but rather by annually absenting thousands of officials for three-week periods. If, as is the case for the few officials who take a year's language training and cultural development in Quebec City and Toronto, all officials were removed from their regular duties for a continuous one-year period, then replacements could take over the reins in their absence and disruption would be minimized. With the training provided in three three-week sessions, however, disruption is grave, and here are the reasons why.

Under present management practices, decisions of substance are normally taken only after consultation with superiors, colleagues, and subordinates. Unilateral decision-making, today, tends to be limited to technical and professional matters. In this era of participative decision-making, each manager is at the centre of a 'communications star' with lines out to those whose advice is needed or whose cooperation is required. It is bad form and poor management for a decision-maker to decide on an innovative course of action without advice from and consultation with affected parties. Three weeks is a relatively short period to wait for the return of a key official from language training and the tendency is very strong to delay a decision until that key official returns and can contribute to it. If on his return the key official raises questions or suggests alternatives that require discussion with another key official, and if, by now, the second official has left for a session of language training, then the decision is remitted for three more weeks, and so on. By this 'domino' series of postponements target dates are missed, and if the decision is one which is tied in to the budget cycle, a whole year can be lost.

Since the kind of decision which most requires consultation is one involving innovation or change, the continual absence of key officials is a major element in limiting the rate of innovation. This would be less serious if the amount of innovation being demanded by central agencies was small. It is not, as we shall now see, and therein lies another story.

INNOVATION ACTION AND REACTION

Demands for massive management innovation rarely, in my experience, arise in any organized way from the managers themselves. Contrary to opinions expressed at times by administrative specialists, they are not being besieged by managers asking them how to implement all of the concepts summarized in the section of this paper called 'A Surfeit of Alphabet Soup'. This is not intended to mean that officials are not progressive and innovative but merely that they normally give priority to more direct means of serving Canadians than to revising, for instance, the internal budget or position classification systems. Among management specialists this characteristic of managers of giving priority to direct program work is sometimes regarded as 'resistance to change'.

If the managers do not press for massive innovation then who does? There are two institutional sources: one source is the collection of central agencies with government-wide functional authority over administrative practices. Today this is principally the Treasury Board Secretariat but lesser contributors are such agencies as the Public Service Commission, the Department of Supply and Services, the Privy Council Office, and the Department of Public Works. The second institutional source is the collection of professions who consider management innovation more important, and more interesting I might add, than the provision of administrative services according to established procedures. In this collection are accountants, personnel specialists, management scientists (operations researchers), computer specialists, operations and methods analysts, and organization analysts. Of these, the accountants, personnel specialists, and data processing specialists are the most evangelistic by far. The other professions tend more often to react to requests for specific projects by the managers themselves rather than to initiate across-the-board administrative reforms. A corollary of the thesis that the institutional sources of innovation are central agencies and 'change agent' specialists, is that the greater the number of officials in these agencies and functions, and the greater their ability, the more time and skill they have for designing and promoting reforms and persuading managers to assist in their implementation.

The elevation in the middle 1960s of finance and accounting to its present high level of authority and strength was a direct consequence of the Glassco Report. After that Report was submitted pilot studies by outside consultants were carried out in several departments with the purpose of introducing 'modern' financial management. Since the consulting firms chosen to do the studies were outgrowths of established public accounting firms, it was predictable that they would recommend a pre-eminent role for accountants. In general, they recommended that each department should have a senior financial adviser reporting directly to the deputy minister, and that modern systems of responsibility accounting and financial reporting be established. Steps were also taken to repatriate, to the line departments, the pre-audit and commitment control work being done by the Comptroller of Treasury. Since this last change alone involved the absorption of some 1000 officials, these innovations have been of some magnitude.

If the innovations in accounting and finance had involved only the systems and techniques of the accountants themselves they would have added nothing to the workloads of managers generally, and might in fact have relieved them by providing faster service and better information. This is not, however, the way the game of managerial innovation is played. It is the manager whose needs circumscribe the financial system and he must take the time to identify and define those needs. It is also the manager who must act on the data provided, and he must therefore take the time to understand the significance of the financial reports he receives. The manager should develop a spending forecast, and an expenditure plan related to his objectives. He should learn to express his objectives in terms that are relevant to the costs of meeting them. He should learn why variances have occurred between planned spending and actual spending, track down the reasons for the variances, and take whatever actions those variances indicate. He should foresee impending discrepancies between the activities he controls and the funds made available for carrying them out. He should act to reconcile the discrepancies by contracting or expanding operations, or by developing alternatives for achieving his goals. In short, sophisticated financial systems designed to assist the manager, demand, in return for the help they provide, a substantial piece of the manager's available work-time. There is, in effect, a trade-off between the introduction of a better decision base on the one hand and the time available for matters of a more purely operational nature, on the other.

In theory, the investment of time by the manager in the design and operation of a sophisticated financial reporting system will pay off in the long run by facilitating his work. In my observation, there is no evidence that this promise has been fulfilled, partly because the system is constantly undergoing revision, partly because of the frequent mechanical errors in the processing of data and partly because of breakdowns in the operation of certain data sources such as the Central Pay Office. All too often the financial reports are too unreliable to provide a basis for decision and the manager feels cheated of the time he has contributed, and is contributing, to their production and use. It is now some six years since the wave of 'modern' financial management swept in in the wake of the Glassco Report. It has been a costly wave and its net benefits are doubtful.

In the field of personnel management, changes of an even greater order of magnitude have been introduced. The Public Service Commission has been relieved of its: (i) pay research function; (ii) job classification function; (iii) control over staff numbers (establishment control); (iv) management consulting function; (v) authority over organization structure; and (vi) role in consulting staff associations on pay and conditions of work.

All but (i) and (iv) above were transferred to the Treasury Board Secretariat concurrently with the introduction of collective bargaining; (i) has gone to the Public Service Staff Relations Board and (iv) to the Department of Supply and Services. Of its former powers the Commission retains only the staffing, training and appeals functions. To these has been added responsibility for language training. While retaining ultimate authority over staffing, the Public Service Commission has delegated much of the power to act to client departments and to the Department of Manpower and Immigration. Some 55,000 positions in the operational and administrative support categories were recently designated to be staffed through Manpower and Immigration, for instance. More and more the Public Service Commission has limited its direct involvement in staffing to executive, professional, and scientific recruitment and selection. The computerized Datastream system has been principally installed to this end.

In departments the growth in the numbers and salary costs of personnel administrators has been phenomenal. In 1960, one large department with which I am familiar had fewer than ten personnel administrators in the officer category. Where one officer used to do all the necessary liaison work with the former Civil Service Commission on classification and establishment control, and one CSC officer did the classifying as only part of his duties, there are now seven officials, an increase by a factor of five.

The growth in actual figures could not be determined without extensive research and even then comparisons would be invalid because of the changes in the content of personnel work. The growth has been due to many factors: (a) the introduction of collective bargaining; (b) the introduction of delegated classification authority and a new system of classification; (c) the assignment to personnel of the management of language training; and (d) the delegation of staffing authority.

'Modern' personnel management has also resulted in the establishment of certain personnel specialties such as manpower planning and organization planning. It is doubtful if, in the whole government, there is any other administrative function which has undergone such a revolution or one in which such a large and rapid increase in numbers has taken place.

To the manager, the net results of the personnel revolution and the vast increase in the number of personnel administrators appear to be two: (a) he perceives little improvement in the service, and (b) he must dedicate a much larger proportion of his time to doing work which was formerly done for him and to implementing innovations designed and enforced by the personnel branch.

Harsh as this judgment may seem, it is supported by evidence on every side. Instead of responding to periodic invitations to send his staff on training courses the manager must now submit an annual training plan six months in advance of the year in which it is to go into effect. Where he once supplied job descriptions in general terms, he now has to complete seven-page questionnaires couched in terminology which he does not clearly understand and which is crucial in protecting his subordinates from downgrading. Where appointments, promotions and transfers used to be made according to a single multi-stage system with which he was thoroughly familiar, there are now a multitude of different systems depending on the category of official, the state of delegation at a given time, and so on.

Positions are often filled by selecting possible candidates by computer and then interviewing those short-listed, rather than by responding to their much less frequent applications for specific vacancies. This all too often decreases their morale because: (a) they may be perfectly happy in their present employment; (b) they did not ask to be considered for the vacant position; (c) they are flattered by their selection for interview and their hopes are aroused; and (d) their hopes are dashed and they feel rejected when they are advised that they have not been chosen as the successful candidate.

This can happen several times a year to an individual official and can be shattering to his self-image. It is also disruptive of the work he is doing at the time.

Appeals against employment decisions used to be handled by officials in the former Civil Service Commission, as part of their duties, and in entering an appeal an aggrieved official had to provide sufficient evidence that his grounds for appeal were valid. Restrictions respecting appeals have been lifted. There are now eight appeals officers and the volume of appeals hearings has risen accordingly. This is good to the extent that it protects the merit system. To the manager, who is required to give evidence at a hearing, or to explain the basis of an employment decision in which he has participated, however, the prospect of having to attend a hearing is a threatening one, and he naturally will take whatever time he needs from his normal duties to prepare his evidence and to discuss with his personnel advisers the ramifications of the case. All too often, an appeal hearing is viewed by a manager as an exercise in harassment. Again by way of illustration, I recently spent a total of ten working days preparing for an appeal hearing which was ultimately cancelled due to the withdrawal of the appeal. The multiplication that has taken place in the number of appeals has proportionately increased the demands made on the time of managers. It has also resulted in a disproportionate attention to 'appeal-proof' procedures at the expense of attention to improving the evaluation of candidates. The manager sometimes feels that no one in personnel worries too much about whether he has chosen the best person just so long as he has made a decision according to a procedure that will stand up against an appeal.

With collective bargaining, and the establishment of specific conditions in employer–employee contracts, a grievance system has been instituted. The grievance system's sphere of adjudication is the administration of collective agreements and its process, culminating ultimately with the Public Service Staff Relations Board, is entirely separate from the appeals process. Once more, managers at various levels are required to consider grievances at various steps in the adjudication process. A grievance system is certainly a defensible innovation; with collective bargaining it is a necessity. But to a manager it is just one more increment in the demands which rob him of time to do substantive program work.

Of all the demands being made on managers by new personnel policy, there is probably none as irritating as the classification system introduced concurrently with collective bargaining. There is not only the time consumed to describe jobs in the detail required by the system but there is the disquieting knowledge that if the position is described in moderate terms it is likely to be classified at a lower level than if it is described in inflated terms. The game of words can be ignored only at the peril of an incorrect classification decision so the manager has to learn to avoid such indecisive verbs as 'consult', 'advise', and 'analyse', and to use such forceful ones as 'direct', 'decide', and 'recommend'. The manager's resentment is therefore double-barrelled: he begrudges the time it takes and his scruples are debased by the difference between the job as he knows it and the description he has had to write in order to give the true relative worth of the position to a classification specialist. There can be an element of fantasy between a job as it is and a job as it is described.

In the interests of flexibility the former system of authorizing for one year a given number of positions to carry out a particular function has been replaced by one which gives a manager a number of man-years and imposes on him a strength ceiling. He can use a man-year by employing two people for six months, or three people for four months, or one person for one year. He must not however, surpass a given ceiling of employee strength at a given time; nor must the annual cost of salaries exceed his dollar budget. The additional freedom in the use of manpower resources is commendable but a price is exacted in terms of the manager's time. Where he once had to give his attention only to keeping his authorized establishment filled, he must now manipulate a number of variables, staying within strength and dollar ceilings and making sure he is not caught out at year-end with more people than are permitted under his year-end strength ceiling. Under these circumstances there is an irresistible temptation to exploit flexibility by employing people as 'casuals' rather than as 'permanents', and since the employment rights of the former are much inferior to those of the latter, there are undoubtedly a number of cases where the employee suffers as a result of the system. Whether the advantages of the added flexibility outweigh the disadvantages in the increased time consumed by the manager and the increase in the number of 'second-class' employees is a moot point.

An interesting sidelight on flexibility in the use of man-years was pointed out to me recently by the Accommodations Officer for a federal department. He told me that the fluctuations in the number of officials employed at a given time resulted directly in fluctuations in the amount of office space needed. A manager who decides to use a man-year by employing three people for four months needs added accommodation for that period. At the end of the period, the space becomes available for re-layout and alternative use. The mind boggles at the potential time and cost of incessant space re-arrangements. Trying to stay on top of space needs under these circumstances could be as frustrating as catching canaries and putting them into a cage with an open door on its other side.

Turning now to some of the reports required by central agencies, I would like to write a few words about program forecast. Every year, about January, the call goes out from the Treasury Board Secretariat to all departments and agencies to prepare and submit their respective program forecasts by a given date in April or May. On receipt in the department a schedule of necessary events is prepared by the finance branch which will culminate in the provision of the program forecast report on the due date. The departmental program forecast, in its ultimate form, is a thick volume in a ring-binder, containing detailed data on anticipated fund and man-year requirements for the next fiscal year and for four ensuing years. It is intended, in effect, to be a five-year financial plan, but in practice attention is focused almost solely on next year.

Unfortunately, departments have no firm idea of what resources are going to be available for each year and the planning request is therefore analogous to asking a wife to list what she would like to spend without regard to her husband's income. Figures are provided at three levels of expenditure for the forthcoming year, i.e., funds required to finance presently authorized activities, funds required to finance proposed new activities and a list of activities that would be discontinued should a hypothetical 10 per cent cut be imposed. These levels are known, respectively as level A, level B and, ominously, level X.

Spending proposals are shown by program and activity, and by object of expenditure. Text is included to outline objectives and to justify resource requests.

In the department, the process of preparation is necessarily a cumbersome one. Fund requests are built up from the lower levels, and by consolidation and review are aggregated into program requests. Understandably, the managers at the various levels tend to include resource requests for all of the activities they have under way *plus* those that would further improve their services to Canadians. The result is an aggregation of requests for money which is far out of line with the amount of money that will be made available. The difference between the sum of funds requested by departments and agencies for the ensuing year, and the sum eventually authorized, is of the order of $500,000,000; that is, for emphasis, five hundred million dollars.

There are therefore a large number of managers whose requests for added funds, supported by quantitative and textual argument, will eventually be turned down, often after much time-consuming negotiation. Their resultant disillusion with the process to which they have contributed so much of their time is considerable. However, since no one is sure at the outset who will win the garlands in the annual race for resources, everyone has to put out his best effort. Next year, when the call goes out for program forecasts, this year's disappointments must be put aside and proposals again made with vigour and optimism.

The state of the art of evaluating the true worth of competing proposals is imperfect. The technique of ranking cost-benefit ratios is of such limited application so far as to be of little assistance in allocating resources. In the absence of quantitative criteria, decisions are made on other grounds and the manager who can most vividly depict the disaster that will befall the country if he is not given more money to spend has an excellent chance of getting it. The preparation of such arguments is time-consuming, and since the procurement of resources is a paramount function, it gets first priority. From my observations I would guess that 50 per cent of the time spent in developing proposals and in negotiation is wasted insofar as resulting in additional funds is concerned. This time, requiring as it does much minute detail and an extension of proposals over a five-year period, is necessarily consumed at the expense of managerial work with a more direct program benefit.

This section would be incomplete without further mention of the twin concepts of PPBS (planning-programming-budgeting system) and MBO (management by objectives). As explained earlier these concepts, respectively, are the progeny of the finance and accounting, and the personnel professions.

PPBS is, in theory, the answer to a manager's prayer. It is a system designed to rationalize the whole resource management spectrum from setting objectives and the logical selection from alternative courses of action to the measurement of returns for expenditures made. Objectives are formulated in a hierarchy, descending from national, to federal, to departmental, to program, to sub-program, to activity, and to sub-activity objectives.

Under the system, alternative courses of action are examined by which objectives can be achieved and a selection made according to criteria of efficiency and effectiveness. As funds are spent, data are fed back to measure both the productivity for the expenditures and ultimately the utility to the Canadian people. With these data, and with a continuing review of the needs of Canadians as expressed through the political process, plans are reformulated, objectives redefined, resources reallocated, manpower shifted, and so on. The process is tied in with the budget system which requires that funds be voted annually.

The problem with PPBS is that while its logic appears unassailable, its realization has been disappointing. There are uncontrollables, such as the determination of objectives through the political process rather than through bureaucratic analysis. The Canadian people do not express their needs according to the principles of cost-benefit analysis but rather according to a workable consensus among individuals and groups with substantially different and strongly held values. Second, there are rigidities which prevent a free-handed shifting of resources according to changed needs. Programs cannot be started and stopped according to new sets of annual priorities. Third, the quantification and assessment of alternative returns for expenditures (i.e., educate the young or provide income security to the aged) is difficult and, in some cases, value judgments only can be made. Finally, the data base and information required to support the system requires a huge input of time and money to maintain. Managers could be swamped with expensive data.

For these reasons the implementation of PPBS has been frustrating, in spite of the periodic glints of sunshine which come through the clouds. So far the managers for whose benefit the whole exercise is being undertaken are understandably in considerable doubt as to whether the results will be justified by the efforts expended. There remains, however, a substantial reservoir of managerial goodwill towards PPBS and there is still hope that results will be forthcoming that are commensurate with the time spent on analysis and implementation.

MBO (management by objectives) is a concept attributed to Peter Drucker, an eminent American management consultant. Its purpose is to clarify and focus management efforts by concentrating them on pre-determined goals. Many elements of PPBS are consistent with MBO. The interest of the personnel community is in the use of the MBO concept in the management of individual performance. It is contended that much better performance is likely when a superior and a subordinate have formulated mutually agreed goals, and when periodic but frequent consultation takes place to review achievements, remove barriers to further achievement, and reformulate specific objectives. These 'work-plan and review' sessions should also permit an official's performance to be appraised against his actual achievements rather than against a number of personality traits (intelligence, energy, punctuality, creativity, etc.). Implementing MBO for the management of individual performance is a very time-consuming process and requires infinite patience and skill. If review sessions are treated as a routine chore they are unproductive. If they deteriorate into periodic confrontations, they can damage morale. (Richard J. Needham, of *The Globe and Mail*, quotes Mignon McLaughlin as follows 'Nobody wants constructive criticism; it's all we can do to put up with constructive praise.') The form and frequency of the review must vary according to the nature of the work, and this requires that elements be tailor-made rather than standardized. Managers must not only be convinced of the utility of the concept but also must find the time and exert the effort necessary to make it work. And this time they must find at the expense of other demands.

So far in this section I have tried to describe the sources of managerial innovation and to delineate a representative number of the new concepts and techniques that are being fostered. There are many others, but I think I have covered enough ground to make it abundantly evident that we may be asking managers to invest too much of their time on implementing new techniques, leaving them insufficient time to operate the activities with which they have been charged.

There remains one important question to be answered before getting on to other things: are not the new concepts and techniques the very essence of management, and am I not guilty of sophistry in contending that there is other, more substantive work to be done? I contend not. I will agree that management decision-making and the motivation of employees are of critical importance but not that all of the techniques involved can be changed without consideration for the managerial time consumed in their implementation and operation.

The reaction of managers to excessive demands made upon their time by innovation has been to conceal their apprehension lest they be considered unprogressive or even reactionary. But now 'motherhood' concepts in management are being resisted. Outright refusals to cooperate with time-consuming innovators are no longer a novelty. Managers are expressing their concern openly, at management meetings, and are finding that their views are widely held among their colleagues. Even among the innovators considerable caution is becoming evident. If, as I strongly suspect, we are witnessing the start of a polite but firm revolt by the managers, we had better start now to defuse the situation.

REMEDIES

There are two principal courses of action, not mutually exclusive, open: (a) to reduce the rate of innovation to one that is more within the capacity of managers to absorb, and (b) to reverse some of the changes already implemented where it is clearly evident that the results produced do not warrant the effort required.

To implement (a), controls are required at two levels. The first control must be at the service-wide level. There could be a continuing body made up of deputy heads, with a secretariat, whose role would be to act as devil's advocates to any proposal for service-wide reform. Not only would an opinion be given to the government on proposed service-wide innovations (which was actually done for the new classification system), but it would audit the results achieved by those reforms which had been given the green light. The second control would be at the departmental or ministry level, and would consist of a small group of senior officials to whom proposals would have to be justified. Again, feedback would be obtained, particularly through the management audit or review unit which most departments have now established.

To implement (b), what is needed is a device by which managers can be heard by disinterested officials in respect of present administrative practices which they deem to be unproductive, a court of administrative ombudsmen. If this can be done without engendering an adversary atmosphere so much the better. It has obviously been of little use to complain to personnel managers about personnel procedures, or to material managers about procurement procedures, or to finance people about accounting procedures. In theory, representations can be made to the deputy head, but the limitations, in turn, on his time are such that it would be more practical if he were given the results of an evaluation rather than asked to listen to arguments in the first instance. Once more, at the departmental level, the evaluation could be carried out by the management audit or review unit.

These measures would constitute a start. Their very presence would cause management innovators to introduce more care into the development of proposals. More attention would be given to all of the likely consequences of a particular managerial reform, including the amount of time that would be demanded of managers, the target dates for completion of various stages, the cost of the time of the innovators themselves, the results anticipated, and so on. Proposals could, in many cases, be required to identify the criteria by which the success of the internal reform could eventually be audited. This hard-nosed and healthily skeptical attitude is commonplace in the private sector, where reforms are judged according to their contribution to long-term profits. Subject to especially close scrutiny in the private sector are staff propositions which can be implemented only through line managers, and at the expense of their principal production and marketing tasks. Since our program managers are stewards of funds entrusted to them by all Canadians to be spent for their benefit, can we do less than afford them a measure of the same kind of protection?

NOTES

1. Robert Townsend, *Up The Organization* (New York: Alfred A. Knopf, 1970).
2. Laurence J. Peter and Raymond Hull, *The Peter Principle* (New York: Morrow, 1969).
3. C. Northcote Parkinson, *Parkinson's Law* (Boston: Houghton Mifflin, 1957).

4

What Central Agencies May and Ought to Do: Structure of Authority

Colin Campbell and George J. Szablowski

Some eminent social scientists argue that governmental organizations emerge and develop like physical organisms.[1] A felicitous arrangement of inducing factors and conditions can produce a new department, agency, board, or commission. Decision makers, the argument goes, recognize that the gestation period is complete and give a formal 'birth certificate' to the new organizational offspring, either by passing a statute, by issuing an order-in-council, or by invoking some other instrument of authority. However, we might claim that this process of creation and growth is the product not of an inevitable bureaucratic evolution, but of conscious human design. Indeed, 'machinery of government' specialists who design and assemble new organizational structures would clearly reject the view that political man is at the mercy of his own institutions. Our aim in this chapter is not to defend either view, but to describe the sources of central agencies' authority, the birth of each, the content and limits of their mandates, and, finally, their organizational structures. At the conclusion of this chapter, the reader can reconsider the two views of how central agencies come into being and decide for him- or herself which is closer to the truth.

F.G. Bailey wrote:

> Only after we understand the rules can we start evaluating the behaviour and so in the end come to a judgment on the men, if we wish to do so.[2]

Our superbureaucrats operate strictly in organizational settings which are bound, first and foremost, by rules. The most fundamental set of rules defines the central agency's authority—it provides what the agency *may* and *ought to* do; that is, the realm of authority is both permissive and normative. We agree with Bailey that the study of rules must not be separated from the study of behaviour and we propose to follow this approach [. . .]

SOURCES OF EXECUTIVE AND BUREAUCRATIC AUTHORITY: CONVENTION AND STATUTORY LAW

There are two sources of authority which prescribe what central agencies may and ought to do: statutory (written) rules and conventional (unwritten) rules; both define

From Colin Campbell and George J. Szablowski, *The Superbureaucrats: Structure and Behaviour in Central Agencies* (Toronto: Macmillan of Canada, 1979): 16–53 plus notes. Reprinted by permission of Colin Campbell and George Szablowski.

the boundaries within which political institutions operate. Conventional rules hold particular sway over Canadian executive behaviour. Central agents operate at the boundary which separates the top political executive—the Prime Minister and his Cabinet—from the programmatic, line bureaucracies. Central agencies also provide the link and create the integrative forces which render this traditional boundary line much less distinct and sometimes downright illusory. Strict statutory rules often make little sense for central agents as they face modern political and institutional realities.

According to British constitutional and administrative theory, which Canada continues to follow, full executive authority belongs to the Crown or, as the British North America (BNA) Act states, 'is vested in the Queen'. In 1947, the monarch formally delegated this authority to the Governor General,[3] and under the recently unveiled Constitutional Amendment Bill, 1978 (if passed), the Governor General would actually replace the Queen as the ultimate source of executive authority. However, it is politically most significant that, whatever the source may be, executive authority is firmly under the control of the Prime Minister and his Cabinet. We propose to adopt a convenient description of executive authority: *it is the constitutional capacity to make policy decisions intended to be followed by all those to whom they are directed or whom they may affect.*

Policy is a difficult term and few political scientists are in agreement about its meaning. We borrow a definition from the Treasury Board Secretariat which emphasizes the distinction between executive acts (policy) and bureaucratic acts (programs), and permits us to demonstrate potential shortcomings of traditional constitutional theory and to question the authority enjoyed by some central agencies.

Policy

A policy is the Government's statement of a principle or set of principles it wishes to see followed, in pursuit of particular objectives, which may be stated in such a way as to suggest possible courses of action (programs) and as to indicate how success of the policy may be measured (criteria).

Program

A program is a course of action or instrument to implement a Government policy (or policies), sometimes involving legislative mandates and, usually, public expenditures. (A program also has objectives, which will in general be more operational than those of a policy, and be suggestive of possible criteria against which accomplishments of the objectives may be measured.)[4]

In general, policy decisions are not based on statutory authority; rather the Cabinet has a full constitutional mandate to act as it deems fit, on its own. Jennings's observation that 'Cabinet has a life and authority of its own' applies equally to Canada as it does to the United Kingdom. Its acts (decisions) cannot change the existing law, nor produce direct legal consequences, but they may initiate the legislative process and thereby eventually modify statutory authority. In principle, program decisions should always be based on statutory authority. Invariably, programs involve the expenditure of public funds and the accountability for it to Parliament. In constitutional theory, all is well as long as Cabinet makes policy, Parliament passes laws, and the bureaucracy faithfully implements programs. How and where do the central agencies and their authority fit into this tidy picture?

According to constitutional and administrative theory, bureaucratic authority should be express, specific, and delegated by Parliament to a department or agency created by it. The department's accountability to Parliament—through the intermediacy of a responsible cabinet minister—should cover all administrative acts and budgetary expenditures. On the other hand, executive authority exercised collectively by the Prime Minister and the Cabinet should be implied, general, and arising from the very obligation and commitment to govern. Policy decisions are the real political results of the use of executive authority; and there is no accountability to Parliament for policy making, except in the broadest sense—the Ministry must always have the confidence of the House in order to govern. If this confidence is lost, dissolution follows and the people are permitted to decide the fortunes of the party in power, unless another party can form a government and capture the confidence of the House.

Do central agencies exercise executive or bureaucratic authority? They administer virtually no programs, and their activities are most intimately related to the formulation, analysis, and implementation of policy decisions. If they are institutional extensions of the Cabinet and the Prime Minister, how much may they be permitted to grow without violating the principle of bureaucratic accountability? Should this new breed of executive-bureaucratic institutions, placed in a privileged and protected milieu, and operating largely under Cabinet's authority, continue to escape public scrutiny except for budgetary appropriations? Later chapters will deal with these issues in some detail. We do not question the political and practical necessity of meeting the continually increasing policy- and decision-making demands, nor the obvious benefits which accrue to the Ministry and to the government in general from the work performed in the central agencies. We simply claim that these developments, no matter how useful and necessary, should raise some doubt about the soundness of traditional constitutional theory.

Statutory law, as we have already stated, is the usual source of bureaucratic authority. It spells out, often with some precision, the exact content of what a depart-

TABLE 1 *Central Agencies' Sources of Authority*

	Statutory Authority	Conventional Authority
PCO	**Statutory law**	**Directives from Cabinet and PM**
	British North America Act	Strategic Planning
	Inquiries Act	Emergency Planning
	Governor General's Act	Machinery of Government, Senior
	Ministries and Ministers of	Personnel (Plans Division)
	State Act	Substantive Policy in
	Statutory Instruments Act	Discrete Sectors
	(Operations Division)	

continued

TABLE 1 *Central Agencies' Sources of Authority (cont'd)*

	Statutory Authority	Conventional Authority
FINANCE	**Statutory law** Financial Administration Act (Direction of financial affairs of Canada)	**Directives from Cabinet** Macro-economic Policy National Budget
PMO	**None**	**Directives from PM** Domestic Policy Advice Communications and Media Relations Legislative Advice Nominations and Appointments Correspondence
TBS	**Statutory law** Financial Administration Act (Administrative policy; Organization of the public service; Financial management; Expenditure plans and programs; Personnel management) Official Languages Act Public Service Staff Relations Act	**Directives from Cabinet** Priorities for Annual Expenditures Evaluation of Programs Management of the Public Service
FRPO	**None**	**Directives from Cabinet and PM** Political and Constitutional Strategies for Unity–Quebec (Coordination Secretariat) Conduct of Intergovernmental Relations and Coordination of Federal and Provincial Policies and Actions (Federal Provincial- Relations Secretariat)

ment or agency may and ought to do. It nearly always contains an enabling provision for a more detailed description by regulations which must fall strictly within the scope and the letter of the existing statute. Our statement that, pursuant to constitutional convention, Cabinet itself is the source of executive authority, requires some explanation. Originally, the monarch derived very extensive prerogative (meaning: natural and subject to no restriction) authority from English common law. In the course of history, statutory provisions either replaced or modified many of these prerogatives; in addition, political practice and constitutional convention harnessed and modernized them. Today the Prime Minister and his Cabinet have all authority necessary and sufficient for effective governing, whether of prerogative origin or not. Nevertheless, they still use it officially under a variety of labels, such as the Crown, the Governor General, or the Governor-in-Council. Because all remaining royal prerogative is now exercised only in accordance with constitutional convention and practice, it seems superfluous and merely legalistic to make more than token reference to it.[5] We will thus use exclusively the term 'conventional authority' and include under it everything that the Prime Minister and the Cabinet may and ought to do in the course of policy making as well as those directives and duties which they delegate to central agencies.

THE 'BIRTH' OF EACH CENTRAL AGENCY

The Privy Council Office

One might expect this to be a straightforward task of simple description. This may be true for some central agencies, but certainly not for others. Let us consider first the Privy Council Office (PCO). The standard, most frequently quoted statement about its origin refers to sections 11 and 130 of the BNA Act, 1867, and to the swearing in of the Clerk of the Executive Council of the United Province of Canada as Clerk of the Privy Council of the Dominion of Canada on the date of Confederation, July 1, 1867.[6] However, even a close reading of these two sections of the BNA Act does not yield a full understanding of how the PCO came to be and what the sources of its present authority are. For instance, section 11, which established the 'Queen's Privy Council for Canada', does not even mention the Prime Minister or the Cabinet. In fact, the authority of Prime Minister and Cabinet has no statutory basis, and their functions rest on convention and customs created in the evolution of the British parliamentary system. Paradoxically, however, it is the Prime Minister and Cabinet, not the Privy Council, that exercise effective authority as the political executive of Canada. We can, therefore, apply what Sir Ivor Jennings said of the UK Cabinet to our own:

> Cabinet has a life and an authority of its own. It is not concerned with prerogative powers alone; it acts whether there are already legal powers or not.[7]

We will return to this important principle of cabinet government later in this chapter. Its political implications are significant.

We see then that the question 'When was PCO established, and what are the present sources of its authority?' is more complex than it appears. Sections 11 and 130 of the BNA Act allow for only that part of the activities of PCO which deal with the preparation and registration of orders-in-council, that is, regulations and appointments made by the Cabinet acting under the name of Governor-in-Council. The great bulk of PCO's activities, however, including cabinet-committee secretariats and the Machinery of Government and Security and Intelligence secretariats, are carried on pursuant to the unwritten, conventional authority of the Prime Minister and the Cabinet. It was not until March 1940, indeed, that the cabinet secretariat obtained an organizational identity of its own. This occurred when the Clerk of the Privy Council took on as well the title 'Secretary to the Cabinet'. It was not until December 1974, moreover that the Secretary's title received legal sanction from Parliament.[8]

Finance

Unlike PCO, the Department of Finance operates under authority granted by statute. The department originally functioned under United Province of Canada statutes concerning financial administration, which were enacted before Confederation and administered by the Inspector General of Public Provincial Accounts. Two years after Confederation, the first federal Department of Finance Act, assented to in June 1869, gave the department 'supervision, control and direction of all matters relating to financial affairs and public accounts, revenue and expenditure of the Dominion, insofar as they are not by law or order of the Governor-in-Council assigned to any other Department.'[9] This provision directly relates to the authority under which the department operates today; that is, section 9 of the Financial Administration Act. Thus, the authority structure of the Privy Council Office stems mainly from convention, and that of the Department of Finance derives mainly from statute. Nevertheless, each may trace its roots directly to the period of Confederation. Either PCO or Finance spawned all three of the remaining central agencies in our study: the Treasury Board Secretariat, the Prime Minister's Office, and the Federal-Provincial Relations Office. TBS is the first of these itself to give birth to yet another central agency, that is, the Office of the Comptroller General.

Treasury Board Secretariat

Treasury Board Secretariat (TBS) was created by the Government Organization Act, 1966. The Act represented a modification of the celebrated Glassco Commission's recommendation (1962) that the secretariat of the Treasury Board—the cabinet committee responsible for expenditure control and management of the public service—be separated from the Department of Finance and housed in the PCO. The officials who sought a way to implement separation recommended that TBS be made an agency unto itself, reporting only to the president of the Treasury Board. This reform proposal sought essentially to institutionalize the division of financial affairs into two distinct categories: 1) intragovernmental control over the allocation of expenditure budgets and management of all in-house resources (TBS), and 2) national, intergovernmental, and international strategy to regulate and influence the economy (Finance). Also in 1966, Parliament delegated authority to the Treasury Board and to the Department of Finance, by means of the Financial Administration Act. Section 5 of the Act authorizes the Treasury Board to act on the Cabinet's behalf in relation to a number of specific matters falling under the umbrella of expenditure control and management policy. Today, the TBS is the organizational and operational arm of the Board. Its history, however, begins much earlier. An order-in-council originally established the Treasury Board in July 1867. Parliament subsequently gave it legislative sanction in 1869, again in 1878, and then again in 1951 when the first Financial Administration Act was placed on the statute books. During these years, however, the

Board's secretariat, as part of the Department of Finance, operated under the authority of the Minister of Finance.

On 1 February 1965, the first Secretary of the Treasury Board, George Davidson, announced the separate agency in an internal memo:

> We have discussed and agreed upon a plan of organization for the Treasury Board in conformity with the recommendations of the Glassco Commission, and with the duties and responsibilities which, now and in the foreseeable future, are likely to be assigned to it.[10]

In October 1966, the Treasury Board Secretariat officially became a legitimate issue of Finance. Along with the authority derived from the Financial Administration Act, it now also exercises additional statutory authority under the Public Service Staff Relations Act and the Official Languages Act. With respect to size, the Treasury Board Secretariat has caught up with, and surpassed, the Finance department itself in just eleven years of organizational independence.

The Prime Minister's Office

From the formal, legal point of view, the Prime Minister's Office (PMO) is an institutional enigma. Unlike the other four central agencies, it has not even been proclaimed by Governor-in-Council a distinct department under the Financial Administration Act. Thus, PMO's budget is hidden in PCO's estimates. No statutory or any other legal provisions, furthermore, indicate its origin or a mandate. Its chief executive officer, the principal secretary, lacks a legal title and his authority remains unspecified. Its history is further obscured because no one can say just when the shared orientations and responsibilities of the Prime Minister's staff turned the office into a full-fledged central agency. Thomas d'Aquino claims that 'PMO did not assume a clear identity of its own until Trudeau became Prime Minister in 1968.'[11] He is probably right; and yet ever since W.L. Mackenzie King regained office in 1935, every Prime Minister has had his own staff. No one doubts the institutionally distinct status of Finance or TBS, even though they share adjoining floors in one office building and a number of housekeeping services, as well as a common institutional history. PMO also shares quarters with PCO and the Federal-Provincial Relations Office, but FPRO's institutional beginning was blessed with a statutory enactment, while PMO seems doomed to continue its enigmatic existence.

There are, of course, very good reasons for this state of affairs. If no authority is formally specified, discretion and flexibility are increased. The conventional authority of the Prime Minister—which he is free to delegate to his principal secretary and PMO—is potentially enormous. He may change at will how much authority he delegates, to whom, and with respect to which issues or problems. All such delegation is informal and much of it is also implied, so that authority may be simply assumed by an officer in the PMO on his own and exercised in the name of the Prime Minister. As long as the Prime Minister is pleased with the results, he is not likely to interfere. With the complexity and size of government today, he does not have time to become personally involved with every issue. Although the authority of PMO defies one permanently valid definition, we shall attempt to describe its present-day content, though our findings will necessarily be subject to change and re-examination.

The Federal–Provincial Relations Office

The youngest central agency is the Federal–Provincial Relations Office (FPRO), established in December 1974 by the Act Respecting the Office of the Secretary of the Cabinet for Federal–Provincial Relations and Respecting the Clerk of the Privy Council. FPRO was designated, by order-in-council, a separate department under the Prime Minister in February 1975.[12] In spite of its apparent statutory origin, the authority exercised by the office is essentially conventional and unwritten. This means that the Prime Minister and the Cabinet may delegate to it any functions they deem expedient provided such functions fall within their responsibility for the federal government's relations with the provinces. Prior to 1975, the Cabinet's secretariat for federal–provincial relations was housed in the Privy Council Office. FPRO exhibits still an affinity to PCO similar to that of TBS to Finance back in the late 1960s. Newly created central agencies tend to solidify their independence over time and consolidate organizational objectives separate and distinct from those which they have once shared with their ascendants. There is reason to believe that FPRO will develop in a similar fashion to TBS.

CONTENT OF AUTHORITY AND ORGANIZATIONAL STRUCTURE

We have seen already that central agencies possess authority which in some cases is tantamount to a monopoly; in other cases, this authority overlaps and transgresses organizational boundaries; in still other cases, it appears to be diffuse and blurred. Unwritten, conventional authority increases officials' discretionary power and permits the central agency (PMO, PCO, and FPRO) to attend to the affairs of the PM and the Cabinet without feeling bound by specific functions defined by statute. Such a degree of flexibility makes public accountability very difficult, if not impossible. Indeed, under the present constitutional practice, agencies not created by Parliament and not possessing statutory authority are not publicly accountable for substantive acts, with the exception of budgetary expenditures. In this sense, accountability relates to the administration of existing policies and the management of allocated resources. It does not extend to policy in the making or allocations to be determined in the course of governmental decision making. To the extent that central agencies participate most intimately in the on-going decision-making process, the great bulk of their activities are beyond Parliament's and the public's reach. Two central agencies, TBS and Finance, operate largely under explicit written statutory authority. Yet, the broad and general language of the law often protects them from effective accountability.

Officials in central agencies are closer to the core of the policy process than public servants in other bureaucratic organizations in government. Indeed, they jealously guard access to their inner world, and are largely successful in this endeavour. Several years ago, a young, able, and ambitious MP was appointed by the Prime Minister as the parliamentary secretary to the president of the Treasury Board. He took this appointment seriously and felt that first he must learn and understand how TBS works. Being a methodical and serious man, he decided to arrange a series of introductory and informational meetings with the secretary of the Board, with all the deputy secretaries, with the assistant secretaries and, eventually, with the directors. His aim was simple and reasonable: to get to know officials in the TBS in order to understand how they work and what they do. He felt it would be particularly useful to attend the regular Monday morning senior-staff meeting chaired by the secretary of the Board. The secretary and the four deputy secretaries received him in their spacious and elegantly furnished offices; they listened to him and noted his serious intentions and willingness to participate. All agreed that this Member of Parliament was an excellent choice for parliamentary secretary and that his intellect and curiosity were most refreshing. They also felt, however, that he misinterpreted his role. The secretariat needed neither additional links with the House nor words of wisdom from an MP. His place was on the floor of the House or in committee, and to be at the disposal of his minister, the president of the Treasury Board, whenever he might want to use him. They informed him politely that further meetings with TBS officials would not be useful and that his proposed attendance at the Monday senior-staff meetings was out of the question. Of course, the secretary of the Board wanted to have lunch with him from time to time 'just to keep in touch'. The young MP was, to say the least, disappointed. He decided to see his minister and seek his support. The minister listened to his story and did not appear unsympathetic; after all the man's intentions were pure and motivated by willingness to serve. However, he decided not to intervene, concluding that this entire episode was a useful learning process for the MP and for all those concerned, and that it should be left at that.

The inner world of central agencies which this eager and promising MP failed to penetrate is largely confined to five broad functions:

1. Development of strategic planning and formulation of substantive policy;
2. Development of integrated economic and fiscal policy;
3. Allocation of budgets and management of resources;
4. Management of senior personnel;
5. Conduct of federal-provincial relations from the perspective of federal and national interests.

In order to carry out these functions, central agencies require appropriate organizational structures. We have already described the origins of central agencies' authority. It remains now to spell out the content of authority reflected in the web of formal organizations. We would, however, like to remind our readers again that the discussion in this chapter is confined to what central agencies may and ought to do and it only incidentally touches upon what they in fact do, or how effective or successful they are in doing it.

Strategic Planning and Formation of Substantive Policy (Lead Agency: PCO)

Strategic planning refers to choices open to governmental decision makers about issues to be resolved over a longer term. It is 'planning' in that it deals with possible future actions of the government. It is 'strategic' because the decisions concern the

TABLE 2 *Structure of Authority: Key Officials and Units (August 1978)*

	Strategic Planning and Substantive Policy	Integrated Economic and Fiscal Policy	Allocation of Budgets and Management	Management of Senior Personnel of Resources	Federal–Provincial Relations
PCO	**Lead Agency** Secretary: Pitfield Deputy Secretary: Teschke Deputy Secretary: Marchand Machinery of Government Secretariat Security, Intelligence, and Emergency Planning Secretariat Plans Secretariat Operations Secretariat	**Key inputs** Economic Policy Secretariat Economic Advisor: Stewart	**Key inputs** Priorities and Planning Secretariat	**Co-lead agency** Secretary: Pitfield COSO (Committee on Senior Officials) Senior Personnel Secretariat	**Key inputs** Secretary: Pitfield Security, Intelligence, and Emergency Planning Secretariat Priorities and Planning Secretariat
FINANCE	**Key inputs** Deputy Minister: Shoyama Associate Deputy Minister:Hood	**Lead agency** Deputy Minister: Shoyama Associate Deputy Minister:Hood	**Key inputs** Fiscal Policy and Economic Analysis Branch	**Key inputs** None	**Key inputs** Deputy Minster: Shoyama Tax Policy and Federal-Provincial Relations

					Branch Fiscal Policy and Economic Analysis
	Fiscal Policy and Economic Analysis Branch Tax Policy and Federal- Provincial Relations Branch	Tax Policy and Federal- Provincial Relations Branch Economic Programs and Government Finance Branch Fiscal Policy and Economic Analysis Branch International Trade and Finance Branch			
PMO	**Key inputs** Principal Secretary: Coutts Designated Policy Advisors and Consultants in Domestic Policy Sector	**Key inputs** Senior Consultant: Breton Designated Policy Advisors	**Key inputs** Designated Policy Advisors	**Key inputs** Principal Secretary: Coutts Nominations Secretary	**Key inputs** Principal Secretary: Coutts Designated Policy Advisors and Consultants
TBS	**Key inputs** Secretary: LeClair Program Branch Planning Branch	**Key inputs** Secretary: LeClair Program Branch Planning Branch	**Lead agency** Secretary: LeClair Program Branch Planning Branch	**Co-lead agency** Secretary: LeClair Personnel Policy Branch	**Key inputs** None

continued

TABLE 2 *(continued)*

	Strategic Planning and Substantive Policy	Integrated Economic and Fiscal Policy	Allocation of Budgets and Management	Management of Senior Personnel of Resources	Federal–Provincial Relations
TBS	Key inputs	Key inputs	**Lead agency** Administrative Policy Branch Personnel Policy Branch Efficiency Evaluation Branch Financial Administration Branch	**Co-lead agency** Official Languages Branch	Key inputs
FPRO	**Key inputs** Secretary: Robertson Deputy Secretary: Masse Constitutional Advisor: Carter	**Key inputs** Policy and Program Review Secretariat	**Key inputs** Policy and Program Review Secretariat	**Key inputs** Secretary: Robertson	**Lead agency** Secretary: Robertson Deputy Secretary: Masse Coordination Secretariat; Federal–Provincial Relations Secretariat

Note: This table does not take into account the changes made to the TBS in 1978 or the establishment of the Office of the Comptroller General under the stewardship of Harry Rogers.

future and attempt to place a given issue in circumstances which will lead to its most effective resolution. This can only be accomplished if all the critical factors in governmental decision making are considered together. These factors include: the annual expenditure budget; the forecast of revenues; the design of the legislative program; the timing of other policy innovations; the evaluation of the performance of senior governmental personnel; and the adequacy of the machinery of government.[13] In other words, strategic planners look at all vital conditions which will affect the outcome of a policy issue or problem. These conditions include the future availability of money, competent personnel and administrative machinery, and the political feasibility of future legislative action in relation to the other proposals which compete for the time and attention of decision makers. Policy proposals which are thus granted high priority must, however, constantly give way to the day-to-day and week-to-week concerns of the government, and to sudden, unanticipated issues and problems. When it does work, though, strategic planning represents an approach to decision making which challenges the short-term, fire-fighting type of decision making characteristic of pluralistic, liberal–democratic political systems.

The broad function of strategic planning in central agencies may be broken down into at least five components. These are:

1. priority determination for the longer term and for the annual allocation of expenditure budgets;
2. major reviews of specific policy areas, such as the review of foreign and defence policies in 1969–70 and immigration in 1976–7.
3. security and emergency planning which has been prominent since the 1970 October crisis;
4. changes and innovations in the machinery of government; that is, in the organizational structure of government and in the jurisdictions of key officials and decision makers; and
5. legislative strategy for effective passing of bills and control of the House of Commons.

The PCO has become the lead agency for strategic planning. Its Plans Division houses the key analytic and advisory personnel grouped into small secretariats which focus on all of the components of strategic planning. Thus, the Priorities and Planning Secretariat supports the Cabinet Committee on Priorities and Planning chaired by the Prime Minister, and helps determine and circulate to other departments priorities and broad policy objectives. The Legislation and House Planning Secretariat reviews draft government bills before they are introduced in Parliament and attempts to control the legislative process. The Machinery of Government Secretariat designs new organizational models and controls changes in departmental mandates and jurisdictions. It directly serves the Prime Minister and supports the ad hoc Committee on the Public Service chaired by him.

Substantive policy has been divided into five discrete sectors, each being the responsibility of 'subject matter' standing cabinet committees, each supported by its own secretariat of analysts and advisors housed in the Operations Division of PCO.

Currently, the standing committees include Economic Policy, Social Policy (health, welfare, social insurance, manpower, and housing), External Policy and Defence, Culture and Native Affairs, and Government Operations. Government Operations embraces policy issues involving both renewable and non-renewable natural resources, as well as items which do not clearly fall within the mandate of any other sector.

An interesting jurisdictional question may arise when a particular minister, supported by his departmental officials, wishes to submit a policy proposal before one sectoral cabinet committee while other ministers want it to come before another committee. For instance, a recent conflict between the domestically oriented policy assigned to the Foreign Investment Review Agency and Canada's traditional international commitments to the Paris-based Organization for Economic Co-operation and Development (OECD) had to be resolved at the cabinet-committee level. OECD exerted pressure, through the Department of External Affairs, in favour of a lenient and liberal foreign-investment policy consistent with Canada's international position. External Affairs would have liked to have had the matter discussed and resolved by the Cabinet Committee on External Policy and Defence. However, Donald MacDonald, the Minister of Finance at that time, chose a very strong line *vis-á-vis* OECD. He forced the referral of the issue to the economic-policy cabinet committee, largely controlled by Finance. There a compromise was finally worked out between the two factions' policy objectives. PCO indeed plays a highly significant role in all difficult jurisdictional disputes, but in the normal course of business a great majority of policy items are placed on the agenda without squabbles.

PCO's authority to serve as the lead agency for strategic planning and the formulation of substantive policy is not based in statute; rather it derives from the constitutional convention which obligates the government to govern. The precise content and scope of this authority is unclear. It has been correctly observed by S.A. de Smith that

> Some of the conventions about . . . the working of the Cabinet system are either blurred or experimental. Codification would purchase certainty at the expense of flexibility; informal modifications to keep the constitution in touch with contemporary political thinking or needs would be inhibited . . . in some contexts the rules ought not to be crystal clear. Clarification would tend to stultify one purpose of conventions—keeping the constitution up to date. . . . Nevertheless [he adds], it is unsatisfactory that the content, and indeed the very existence, of some of the most important conventions should be indeterminate.[14]

PCO's authority with respect to this broad function of strategic planning and substantive policy formulation is unquestionably predominant, but it is not absolutely exclusive. The remaining central agencies, within their respective areas of competence, also play a role in it. In particular, PMO's expected yet much-misunderstood contribution must be acknowledged. Its involvement focuses on those consequences and implications of policy decisions which have to do with:

1. how the public and the mass media perceive the Prime Minister's image and leadership;

2. the overall chances for re-election;
3. the government party's specific national and regional interests;
4. the Prime Minister's individual preferences, objectives, and ideology.

Especially during the past three to four years, this mandate has not been well served, primarily because the PMO lacks highly qualified, seasoned, and influential officials. The many changes in the organizational structure of PMO—which continues to be in a state of flux—reflect the fact that no principal secretary since Marc Lalonde (1968–72) has been able to sustain and staff the office fully in accordance with its mandate. Subsequent chapters will deal with this important matter.

The statute which grants the Department of Finance its authority imparts to it responsibility to forecast government revenues as well as general economic and fiscal conditions. To the extent that these responsibilities become critical factors in strategic planning and substantive policy formulation, Finance possesses a strong potential leverage in this area. The Federal–Provincial Relations Office must evaluate the impact of strategic planning and substantive policy on provincial governments and attempt to predict and deal with their responses. In addition, FPRO now has a special mandate assigned by the Prime Minister and the Cabinet to monitor events and to prepare scenarios for action *vis-á-vis* the government of Quebec and the issue of independence. Like Finance, the Treasury Board Secretariat has a specific statutory authority which, when exercised, may have a critical effect on strategic planning. TBS may determine priorities limited to programs (as distinct from policies), with respect to annual and longer-term expenditures, including the allocation of public-service personnel. Policies are the ken of the Priorities and Planning cabinet committee and the secretariats supporting it in PCO. Similarly, TBS authority over 'personnel management' in the public service excludes order-in-council appointments and other senior-level promotions; these are the domain of PCO's Senior Personnel Secretariat reporting to Gordon Robertson and the Prime Minister's nominations secretary. Thus, PCO maintains unchallenged supremacy in strategic planning and substantive policy formulation, although all central agencies exercise considerable authority which, in some instances, appears to overlap and to conflict.

The Development of Integrated Economic and Fiscal Policies (Lead Agency: Finance)

The development of integrated economic, fiscal, and tax policies is the second broad function of central agencies. The primary authority for this function is statutory and derives from the Financial Administration Act, section 9, which reads as follows:

> The Minister [of Finance] has the management and direction of the Department of Finance, . . . and the supervision, control and direction of all matters relating to the financial affairs of Canada not by law assigned to the Treasury Board or to any other Minister.[15]

In 1976 Michael Pitfield, the Clerk of the Privy Council, called Finance a 'lead department . . . responsible for stabilization policy and a court of last review for economic policy'. He pointed out further that in order to encourage countervaillance (that is, several competing approaches) in financial affairs, the government has created 'a number of new economic departments, such as Regional Economic Expansion, Manpower and Immigration, Consumer and Corporate Affairs, Energy, Mines, and Resources, and Environment—each with its own expert skills.'[16] How does this development affect the authority of Finance to supervise, control, and direct 'all matters relating to the financial affairs of Canada'? Each of the five new departments mentioned by Pitfield enjoys statutory authority, which, at least to some degree, reduces Finance's hegemony in the economic-policy field. At the same time, however, the existence of several economic units, each with its own specialty and orientation, increases the need for an overseeing eye. Regional Economic Expansion, for example, works to stimulate growth in the economically underdeveloped parts of Canada. Its clients are industries situated in those areas which seek federal support, along with labour organizations and other local groups. Manpower and Immigration promotes the development and placement of Canada's manpower. Consumer and Corporate Affairs furthers the ideas associated with controlled competition, stable price structure, and a gentle regulation of business and industry. Energy, Mines, and Resources, on the other hand, works along with business and industry to increase development of natural resources and to further technological expansion in this sector. Environment represents interests which promote ecological protection, conservation, and limits to growth. There are, of course, other economically oriented departments of an older vintage, such as Labour, or Industry, Trade, and Commerce, which promote their own points of view at the decision-making table. The authority of Finance as a central agency is supposed to transcend all these special approaches and interests; for the sake of economic stability it coordinates and controls their efforts.

In consequence, during recent years Finance has divested itself of nearly all operational programs and has assumed a clear central-agency posture. Once some 6,000 strong, the staff of the department today numbers approximately 700. These highly skilled public servants develop and analyse policy in four main areas. Together, the four sectors make up the current content of Finance's authority. They are:

Tax Policy
Here, one division of departmental specialists analyses existing tax measures and new proposals from the perspective of the business community. Within the division a personal-income-tax section examines proposals relating to personal taxation, deferred-income plans, trusts, and partnerships, while a commodity-tax division develops policy concerned with all excise taxes and duties. A legislation division develops tax bills and participates directly in the drafting of sections of the budget concerning taxation. Finally, a social development and manpower policy division represents Finance's interest, especially as related to taxation, in the field of social policy.

Economic Development and Government Finance
Here, policy analysts monitor government's attempts to encourage the development of Canada's natural resources; these include energy, oil, gas, and minerals. Another unit oversees other departments' promotion of industrial development in general; this

includes secondary industry, transportation, communications, nuclear energy, science policy, and research. A third unit allots government loans and other financial guarantees (primarily to Crown corporations) and plans investments.

Fiscal Policy and Economic Analysis

One unit within this sector provides central economic intelligence on the overall economic conditions of the country and prepares forecasts used in the development of national budgets. Another unit, responsible for the fiscal policy, draws up the annual fiscal framework, which forms the basis for the expenditure budget, and forecasts the financial requirements of the government. This unit maintains a very close link with the Program Branch in TBS. A long-range analysis unit employs various mathematical models to project national economic performance. Finally, a capital-markets unit develops policy with respect to private financial institutions and management of the public debt.

International Trade and Finance

The tariffs unit investigates and reports on proposals regarding the Canadian customs tariff pursuant to the General Agreement on Tariffs and Trade (GATT) and bilateral trade agreements. Another unit makes recommendations on international trade policy, particularly with regard to imports. Still another group of experts maintains liaison with international financial organizations and promotes export development. Finally, the international-finance division is concerned with the balance of payments and foreign exchange.

It is evident that the statute which delegates general authority to Finance is so vague that the department can interpret its content more or less as it pleases. Only the Prime Minister and his Cabinet can check this important bureaucratic discretion. For example, Finance once served as the lead agency for federal-provincial relations because of the overriding fiscal and economic implications. Since FPRO was established in 1974–5, however, Finance's authority in this area has diminished; we would not be surprised if FPRO took over most of it in the near future. To be sure, Finance will continue to advise the Prime Minister and the Cabinet in federal-provincial financial arrangements, but FPRO will make the strategic decisions, as it does now. This illustrates our point that the conventional authority vested in the Prime Minister and his Cabinet, rather than statutory authority, dominates the role of central agencies. Constitutional conflict is avoided because, conveniently, statutory authority is so general and vague that the agencies can add or take away particular functions at will.

The controlling and coordinating role of Finance in financial and economic matters is, of course, crucial to the effective discharge of the four other broad functions (listed in Chapter 1) performed by central agencies. In strategic planning, Finance provides the fiscal limits, at the national level, within which any major policy issue must be resolved. In the allocation and management of physical resources and expenditure budgets, Finance plays a similar role at the intragovernmental level. In the conduct of federal-provincial relations, Finance's advisory role at the intragovernmental level is self-evident. Typically, then, the predominant authority of Finance in economic and financial affairs is complemented by its increased involvement in other broad functions which characterize the role of central agencies. In other words, because of its presence in several fields, its influence is felt much more profoundly by other departments than if it simply handed down financial and economic edicts.

The Allocation and Management of Physical Resources and Expenditure Budgets (Lead Agency: TBS)

The allocation and management of human and physical resources and expenditure budgets throughout government is the work of the Treasury Board, a cabinet committee. TBS, the committee's secretariat, bases its activities on the Treasury Board's statutory authority derived from section 5 of the Financial Administration Act.

Specifically, this authority includes:

1. general administrative policy in the public service of Canada;
2. the organization of the public service or any portion thereof, and the determination and control of establishments therein;
3. financial management, including estimates, expenditures, financial commitments, accounts, fees or charges for the provision of services or the use of facilities, rentals, licences, leases, revenues from the disposition of property, and procedures by which departments manage, record, and account for revenues received or receivable from any source whatever;
4. the review of annual and longer-term expenditure plans and programs of the various departments of government, and the determination of priorities with respect thereto;
5. personnel management in the public service, including the determination of terms and conditions of employment of persons employed therein;
6. such other matters as may be referred to it by the Governor-in-Council.[17]

Money and physical resources are in great demand throughout the government apparatus. To make the best use of them consistently is the work of a successful bureaucratic executive. Operational departments and agencies in Ottawa are, in many respects, like business establishments competing for markets, sales, and profits. The bureaucratic 'marketplace', however, permits only competition for person-years, budgets, and physical assets, all of which the Treasury Board is supposed to control and manage centrally. This, perhaps, is only one side of the story. If incremental allocations are the order of the day (or rather, the year), and if operational departments and agencies get at least enough to continue essentially as they are, what is the real meaning of central allocation and TBS control?

Let us examine in some detail four aspects of authority delegated to TBS by statute.[18] We will discuss the fifth, personnel management, in a separate section.

General Administrative Policy

A statutory definition of this function does not exist. In consequence, we must rely on a long accepted bureaucratic definition which refers to rules based on 'equity, probity, and prudence'. Their purpose is to govern the acquisition, use, and consumption of various kinds of property by departments and agencies for greater 'efficiency and effectiveness'. TBS develops and enforces these rules, but the degree of enforcement varies. The rules apply to such highly expensive commodities as computers, telecommunication systems, and office buildings, as well as to desks, rugs, and stationery. An entire branch of TBS is engaged in the development and direction of this policy area.

Organization of the Public Service

This authority seems wide enough to encompass nearly everything in government. A formal organization will contain a complex group of offices or bureaus having explicit objectives, clearly stated rules, and a system of specifically defined roles, each with clearly designated rights and duties; but obviously, TBS cannot prescribe all of these for the entire federal public service. But, does TBS have exclusive statutory authority to do so? Once again we find that the general language of the law permits a competing central-agency secretariat, the machinery-of-government unit in PCO, to assume considerable responsibility in this area in accordance with conventional authority derived from the Cabinet and Prime Minister. The PCO unit organizes the governmental apparatus, establishes jurisdictional boundaries between departments and agencies, and designs new organizational units in the public service. In 1971, PCO's machinery-of-government unit was instrumental in creating ministries of state, notwithstanding the strong opposition of some otherwise influential senior TBS officials. More recently, the TBS's organization division conducted special studies on the effectiveness of particular types of organizational structure, on the relationship between policy-making departments (e.g., ministries of state) and policy-implementing units, and on the advantages and disadvantages of bureaucratic decentralization. *Prima facie,* all these subjects fall within the statutory authority of TBS *as well as* within the conventional authority of PCO. Who wins, and who loses? TBS retains strong authority over the classification changes at the lower senior-management levels (SX-1 to SX-3 positions) and the increases to management complements of departments. It chairs the Coordinating Committee on Organization (CCO) in which PCO and Public Service Commission officials regularly participate. In all likelihood, PCO and TBS will continue to share authority in this area. Such sharing creates serious problems of public accountability, particularly when one central agency (PCO) claims exemption from Parliament's scrutiny.

Financial Administration

Until recently, financial administration had been combined with administrative policy in the Administrative Policy Branch. With the re-organization of TBS, the new Financial Administration Branch has found itself in the newly created Office of the Comptroller General (OCG). The term 'financial administration' is misleading; it appears to mean the same thing as Finance's authority to direct and control the financial affairs of Canada. However, 'administration' here refers to internal or in-house control of expenditures to ensure that departments and agencies actually follow the intentions and aims for which money has been allocated. In this context, moreover, 'financial' refers to those rules which promote good accounting practices recognized by professional accountants. Under this authority TBS established methods for control of accounts and internal audits which are now under the stewardship of the OCG.

Review of Expenditures and Determination of Program Priorities
This authority is, in our view, the most crucial in the discharge of TBS activities. Two branches, the Program Branch and the Planning Branch, drew on it until 1978, one directly, the other indirectly. The Program Branch is organized according to five functional groupings of government programs: a) Industry and Natural Resources; b) Transportation, Communications, and Science; c) Defence, External Affairs, and Cultural Affairs; d) Social and Manpower Policy; and e) General Government Services. It controls the annual budgetary cycle; this is when the departmental program forecasts are reviewed, an overall expenditure plan for the coming fiscal year is approved, and the Main Estimates and Supplementary Estimates are prepared, scrutinized, and presented to Parliament. Apart from the cyclical activity, the branch analyses and evaluates new policy proposals from operational departments and agencies. It comments on the implications for the existing resources that such proposals may have, and on the extent to which governmental objectives and priorities are promoted. In this respect, the branch maintains a close relationship with the secretariat in PCO which drafts the policy guidelines for the Priorities and Planning cabinet committee. The committee's guidelines set out expenditure priorities for the forthcoming budgetary exercise. No wonder, then, that the Program Branch has become the springboard from which senior-rank executives rise to higher-level appointments offered by programmatic departments and agencies. For example, of the ten directors in the branch in 1970, seven became assistant deputy ministers by 1976; in addition, its deputy secretary and assistant secretary became deputy ministers. No governmental unit of similar size and expertise can match this extent and rapidity of upward mobility.

The activities of the Planning Branch rested on the proposition that the evaluation of program effectiveness and program efficiency is an essential prerequisite for control of public resources. In the words of Gordon Osbaldeston, a former Secretary of TBS, evaluation of bureaucratic performance completes the Planning-Programming-Budgeting 'cycle'.[19] Planning Branch came into its own in 1970 under the direction of Douglas Hartle, a University of Toronto economist; three years later he left public service doubting the practical value of the very analytical techniques and methodologies which he helped to introduce.[20] His contribution, however, has significantly influenced the development of policy and program analysis in government. A quantitative-analysis school operated by the branch trained numerous new specialists who subsequently returned to their respective departments and agencies to man policy- and program-evaluation units. Although, as we said earlier, the Financial Administration Act provided the authority under which this branch was established, its main activities concerned strategic planning and the role played in it by the Priorities and Planning cabinet committee. In addition to the statutory authority, consequently, the branch also acted under conventional authority which the Cabinet delegated to it. By late 1978, Planning Branch had undergone metamorphosis. The in-house quantitative-analysis school disbanded in 1976; the efficiency-evaluation division had been transferred and elevated to a branch in the newly created Office of the Comptroller General; and the organization division had moved to the Program Branch. What was left, the effectiveness-evaluation unit designed for in-depth analysis of programs for the secretary of the Treasury Board, finally dissolved.

Clearly, TBS's statutory authority is more specific and better defined than that of Finance. This does not, however, afford TBS any better protection against encroachment by competing central agencies which rely to a greater extent on conventional authority. PCO in particular has built units and expertise in areas of policy development which, to say the least, coincide with those bestowed by statute on TBS. How does one distinguish the TBS's 'organization of the public service' from the PCO's 'machinery of government'? It is evident that the ultimate control in this area resides in PCO.

Barely six years ago, A. W. Johnson, then secretary of the Treasury Board, put forward an interesting theory about TBS's authority.[21] He described the Treasury Board itself as a dual purpose cabinet committee responsible for: 1) the management of the public service; and 2) the expenditure budget. In the discharge of these two functions, the Board forms an integral part of the cabinet–committee system and acts on the decisions made in Cabinet or in one of its regular committees. As we have already noted, early in each year the Priorities and Planning cabinet committee formulates a set of decisions, subsequently confirmed by full Cabinet, called 'policy guidelines', which contain specific authority for the allocation of expenditure budgets. It is the task of TBS (Program Branch) to carry out these policy guidelines in the course of the budgetary cycle. Thus, in addition to authority derived from statute (Financial Administration Act), TBS relies and acts upon conventional authority granted to it from time to time by Cabinet. The former is public and subject to parliamentary scrutiny, while the latter remains secret and exempt from it. Johnson's theory permits TBS to claim the status of a cabinet secretariat with exclusive authority over the two areas of policy which, accordingly, are outside the competence of PCO. Moreover, the theory places TBS closer to the apex of power, ahead of Finance, and parallel to PMO, PCO, and FPRO.

Does this study accept Johnson's theory? The answer is both yes and no. The Prime Minister and his colleagues are free to create any committees and secretariats they wish, and to endow them with conventional authority, provided it is not contrary to existing statutory authority. The authority contained in the policy guidelines is merely an example of broader statutory authority to 'review . . . annual expenditure plans and programs'. In this sense, the Board may act as a dual-purpose cabinet committee, and TBS may be a cabinet secretariat like PCO. But one further qualification must be added. Strictly speaking, from the standpoint of law, the Treasury Board is not a cabinet committee but a Parliament-created committee of the Privy Council, and is ultimately responsible to Parliament. Neither the Board nor its secretariat may exercise greater or different authority from that provided in the statute. If TBS acts as well under the authority passed to it secretly by Cabinet or a cabinet committee, who is to tell whether that authority conforms with or exceeds the provisions of the Financial Administration Act?

In our view, Johnson's theory allows TBS too much discretion and reduces the possibility of parliamentary supervision. TBS's officials are given an opportunity to claim exemption from accountability whenever they act according to cabinet authority as distinct from the authority contained in statute. The distinction between authority obtained from Cabinet and that contained in the statute is, in too many instances, either exceedingly difficult to make or plainly illusory. If TBS forms an integral part of the cabinet-committee system which still operates according to the traditional rules of secrecy and solidarity, enjoying a privileged and protected milieu, it should not at the same time be, nor pretend to be, a publicly created department with full accountability to the House of Commons.

Management of Senior Personnel (Joint Lead Agencies: PCO and TBS)

Highly skilled, loyal, and capable men and women constitute the most-precious asset of any governmental bureaucracy. Authority to recruit, train, promote, and compensate these individuals is equally precious and crucial. Until 1967, much of this authority was exercised by the Civil Service Commission, a quasi-independent government agency. During the reforms of 1967, the newly created Public Service Commission did not retain the authority of its predecessor, the Civil Service Commission. Its role is now confined to three tasks: staffing, which it shares with programmatic departments and agencies; training and development; and handling appeals on all staffing decisions. The most important aspect of personnel management in general—the classification of positions and employees and the determination of compensation rates and scales—is now in the hands of TBS. J.E. Hodgetts states unequivocally that the present distribution 'leaves little room for querying the location of [the] ultimate repository of managerial authority over the public service.'[22] He is right, up to a point. The highly trained staff of TBS's Personnel Policy Branch oversees collective bargaining, pensions, and other non-negotiable benefits; the classification and compensation of all ranks of public servants; and other related duties. However, its authority over the highest level of officials, i.e., the SX or senior-executive category and the DM or deputy-minister category, has been diluted by four developments. These are:

1. the creation of an advisory committee of private-sector executives, at the time of our interviews under the chairmanship of Allen Lambert (Toronto Dominion Bank), who became chairman of the Royal Commission on Financial Management and Accountability;
2. the powerful impact of the Committee on Senior Officials (COSO), chaired by Michael Pitfield and composed of Gordon Robertson (Secretary to the Cabinet for Federal-Provincial Relations), Maurice LeClair (Secretary of the Treasury Board), Edgar Gallant (Chairman of the Public Service Commission), and four other deputy ministers;
3. the work of the Senior Personnel Secretariat in PCO under the direction of Ian Dewar; and
4. extensive and effective use by the government of the GC category, or governor-in-council appointments, where, in Michael Pitfield's words, 'lies the key to better administration and better policy development'.[23]

The SX and DM classifications are the highest a career public servant can earn. Normally, directors and directors-general merit SX-1 to SX-3; assistant deputy ministers and associate deputy ministers range from SX-3 to SX-4; and deputy ministers range from DM-1 to DM-3—the top of the ladder. Each class is related to a specific salary scale. Promotion to a new managerial position may not always coincide with a higher classification. An individual may become a director and work as such for some time, while his/her SX classification may be held up pending a pay-related performance assessment, or the lifting of a general freeze on the SX category. Statutory authority to develop policy about the SX classification, to approve individual promotions, to assess performance, and to approve compensation scales is held by TBS. However, it must be recognized that the Prime Minister attaches great importance to the selection of top officials. The Priorities and Planning committee which the Prime Minister chairs evaluates annually the performance of senior personnel; the senior-personnel secretariat of PCO which reports to the PM through Gordon Robertson screens candidates for senior SX and DM vacancies and recommends appointments. In addition, this PCO unit, reporting through Michael Pitfield, advises the PM and the Cabinet on senior-personnel policy.

The Prime Minister approves all governor-in-council appointments, which include DM-1, 2, and 3, and SX-4, in addition to members of federal boards, commissions, and task forces, and directors and senior executives of Crown corporations. Although the Prime Minister has ultimate authority to make appointments to these positions, most of which are provided for by statute, the process of selection is governed by rules developed in PCO under the conventional authority of the Prime Minister and Cabinet.

The Committee on Senior Officials (COSO) advises the Prime Minister and the Cabinet on key aspects of personnel policy for senior public servants (i.e., those in SX, DM, and GC categories), and reports through Michael Pitfield. Its broad mandate embraces also such issues as bilingualism policy, conflict of interest in the public service, the relationship between ministers and officials, post-employment regulations (i.e., restrictions on former public servants to engage in competitive or conflicting business activities or employment), and the work of the Royal Commission on Financial Management and Accountability. The advisory committee of private-sector executives, on the other hand, regularly reviews the salaries of senior officials, making its recommendations to PCO and TBS.

All the activities of the PCO and the advisory committees vitally affect the lives and careers of senior officials and determine the quality and composition of the top bureaucratic elite. They are carried out under conventional authority from the Prime Minister and the Cabinet over and above the statutory authority which Parliament delegates to TBS and to the Public Service Commission.

Policy on bilingualism in the public service must be viewed as an aspect of personnel management. The Official Languages Branch of TBS serves as the coordinating secretariat in this sector of activity. The branch monitors throughout government the implementation of the Official Languages Act, and a resolution adopted by Parliament in 1973. The branch also implements modifications to the policy developed by a special committee of officials and sanctioned by Cabinet. Thus, the branch's authority is both statutory and conventional.

Conduct of Federal–Provincial Relations (Lead Agency: FPRO)

This is the last of the five broad functions which we have ascribed to central agencies; in its breadth and scope it is the most pervasive, for in Canada no policy issue or problem is exempt from intergovernmental concern. Sections 91 and 92 of the BNA Act, which provide a legal framework for the distribution of legislative authority between Ottawa and the provinces, have been truly put aside by political practice. Although the courts once declared the two governmental jurisdictions 'water-tight compartments' in a sailing ship,[24] today the constitution in no way inhibits the intricate interdependency developed in the federal/provincial political system. Ontario, for example, uses policy-making authority to influence the design of the federal budget; Quebec (even before November 1976) insists on consultations in cultural and educational aspects of foreign policy; Alberta effectively forces reassessments of national energy policy to suit its own interests; and a number of provinces lead the way to major revisions in federal tax policy and federal–provincial fiscal arrangements.

Authority to conduct intergovernmental affairs is simply one aspect of the executive authority to govern. No federal government has paid as much attention to this activity as that of Pierre Trudeau. Indeed until 1977, Trudeau chaired the cabinet committee on Federal–Provincial Relations. This committee, which fashioned Ottawa's overall strategy *vis-à-vis* the provinces, now has merged with the Priorities and Planning committee and consists of the same ministers. Since 1975, FPRO has acted as a full-fledged *second* cabinet secretariat developing policy-review capabilities in all substantive issue areas and in all geographic regions of the country. The organization of FPRO remains flexible and responsive to changing political needs. Until just shortly before the time of writing (summer 1978), its staff comprised two deputy secretaries to the Cabinet, one for operations and one for coordination *vis-à-vis* national-unity questions. The operations unit directs a section on regional analysis, a studies and research group, and a policy- and program-review section. The review section is divided according to four issue areas: finance and economic matters; resources; social policy; and urban affairs and transportation. The coordination secretariat under Paul Tellier confines its activities to thorny political problems brought to the fore by the recent election of the separatist Parti Québécois government in Quebec. D.S. Thorson, a former deputy minister in the Department of Justice, served (until his elevation to the Ontario Court of Appeal in the summer of 1978, when Frank Carter took over from him) in a special capacity as the constitutional advisor to the Prime Minister during the entire period in which Trudeau developed his package of constitutional reforms in response to the constitutional crisis brought on by the separatist threat in Quebec. There can be little doubt that Ottawa has locked a full complement of its bureaucratic horns with the government in Quebec. At stake is not only the unity of the country, but also the future of the federal bureaucratic machinery, of the federal Liberal party, and of the elites associated and identified with it. In a struggle of such importance, the government will muster and employ all the authority it can. FPRO has been the principal organizational beneficiary of the government's resolve to save federalism.

We thus see that, as with the other broad functions of central agencies, federal–provincial relations fall within the domain of one institution designed primarily to control it. Yet, other central institutions are involved as well. For example, without the expertise and the knowledge generated by Finance in the area of economic, fiscal, and tax policy, conduct of federal-provincial relations is impossible. At the decision-making table, whether in cabinet committee, in an intergovernmental commit-tee, or in an interdepartmental committee, Finance presents its case and its particular point of view which is maintenance of the country's economic stability. Such a view may not always mesh with the more delicate and illusory requirements of political stability, nor with the short-term tactics and scenarios which FPRO may want to employ to gain a political advantage over one or more provinces. Similarly, the TBS, conscious of its own mandate to manage physical and manpower resources of the government, may and will advocate a position at odds with that of FPRO. Because PMO, PCO, and FPRO are literally each other's neighbours and consult together fre-quently and intimately, the attitudes of the three agencies often dovetail nicely; nev-ertheless, the individual mandates of PMO, PCO, and FPRO may also produce conflicting views of key federal-provincial issues. These positions clash at many deci-sion-making meetings at various levels and stages of policy formulation, until they reach the cabinet committee on Priorities and Planning, the ultimate forum for fed-eral-provincial relations. Thus, the content of authority in the conduct of federal-provincial affairs is truly multifarious; each central agency makes a significant contribution to the process from the perspective of its own policy responsibility, while FPRO maintains the primary authority in the field. We stress that this unique multifariousness and flexibility in the content and exercise of authority is made pos-sible by the absence of statutory authority in this field, and by a total reliance on con-stitutional convention and usage emanating from Cabinet.

SUMMARY AND CONCLUSIONS

This chapter first described the sources of executive and bureaucratic authority and identified its two types: *conventional*—originating from the Cabinet and the Prime Minister and their overall responsibility to govern, including the royal prerogative inherited from English common law and the Crown; and *statutory*—delegated by Parliament. It has shown that conventional authority is by far the most significant for central agencies. PMO, PCO, and FPRO rate highest in conventional authority and rely almost exclusively on it; TBS enjoys a mixture of conventional and statutory author-ity, while Finance is wedded to the highest amount of statutory authority, albeit of a very mild form due to its very broad and general mandate.

Next, the chapter dissected the content of authority into five broad functions:

1. strategic planning and substantive policy formulation which; belongs pri-marily to PCO, but concerns the remaining agencies as well;
2. development of integrated economic, fiscal, and tax policies and mainte-nance of economic stability, which is the domain of Finance but subject to the countervailing forces of others;
3. allocation of expenditure budgets, management of physical resources, and financial management, which form the mandates of TBS and OCG but which cannot be separated from the interests and influences of other agencies;
4. management of senior personnel, which is a shared concern of PCO and TBS, although PCO dominates; and

5. conduct of federal–provincial relations—a field clearly assigned to FPRO, yet so wide and pervasive that it cannot be managed without significant assistance from other agencies.

In summary, the authority structure of Canadian central agencies reveals the following characteristics:

—It is extremely broad and general, even when statutory, permitting engagement in all policy areas under a variety of labels, such as 'allocation', 'management', 'coordination', and 'control'.

—Conventional authority clearly transcends statutory authority. Central agencies strive for the former and shy away from too much of the latter. Moreover, it is often difficult to determine in each particular case whether an agency acts according to one or the other.

—Each central agency (with the notable exception of PMO) enjoys supremacy in one broad policy function; yet upon examination, it becomes evident that, in reality, jurisdictional and authority boundaries between the agencies are blurred; there is much overlapping and sharing. There is also some tendency for competition and conflict, which, however, is carefully managed and contained.

—The constitutional principle that Cabinet (subject only to the wishes of the Prime Minister) is the exclusive master of its own structure and the source of its own executive authority gives central agencies great freedom in the design of their organization and in the functions and responsibilities they assume.

Finally the chapter described central agencies as extensions of Cabinet and of the Prime Minister, speaking for and supporting them as well as guiding their decisions and actions. This is why the men and women who operate the agencies deserve to be called super bureaucrats.

NOTES

1. For example, see Victor A. Thompson, *Organizations as Systems* (Morristown, NJ: General Learning Press, 1973).
2. F.G. Bailey, *Stratagems and Spoils* (Oxford: Basil Blackwell, 1970), p. xii.
3. Letters Patent constituting the office of the Governor General, 1947. The Prime Minister, Mr St Laurent, described the effect of this delegation as follows: '. . . when the letters patent come into force, it will be legally possible for the Governor General, on the advice of the Canadian ministers, to exercise any of these powers and authorities of the Crown in respect of Canada without the necessity of a submission being made to Her Majesty . . .', *House of Commons Debates*, 1948, p. 1126.
4. *Treasury Board*, mimeo. (Ottawa: Treasury Board Secretariat, November 1975), p. 5.
5. For a good discussion of the royal prerogative, see S.A. de Smith, *Constitutional and Administrative Law* (Harmondsworth, Middlesex: Penguin Books, 1971), pp. 114–29.
6. *Organization of the Government in Canada* (Ottawa: Ministry of Supply and Services, 1976), p. 6001.

7. Sir W.I. Jennings, *The Law and the Constitution*, 3rd edn (London: Cambridge University Press, 1943), p. 88.

8. An Act respecting the office of the Secretary to the Cabinet for Federal-Provincial Relations and respecting the Clerk of the Privy Council, 23 Elizabeth II, chapter 16. See also J.R. Mallory, 'The Two Clerks: Parliamentary Discussion of the Role of the Privy Council Office', *Canadian Journal of Political Science* 10 (March, 1977), pp. 3–19.

9. Dr A.A. Sterns, *History of the Department of Finance*, unpublished monograph (Ottawa: Department of Finance, May 1965), p. 4.

10. *Treasury Board Organization Manual*, mimeo. (Ottawa: Treasury Board, January 1967), p. 1.

11. Thomas d'Aquino, 'The Prime Minister's Office: Catalyst or Cabal?', *Canadian Public Administration* 17 (Spring 1974), p. 57.

12. Order-in-Council P.C. 1975–250.

13. Donald Gow, *The Progress of the Budgetary Process in the Government of Canada*, Special Study No. 17 (Ottawa: Economic Council of Canada, 1973).

14. S.A. de Smith, *Constitutional and Administrative Law* (Harmondsworth, Middlesex: Penguin Books, 1971), pp. 54–5.

15. Revised Statutes of Canada (R.S.C.), 1970, chapter F–10.

16. Michael Pitfield, 'The Shape of the Government in the 1980s: Techniques and Instruments for Policy Formulation at the Federal Level', *Canadian Public Administration* 19 (Spring 1976), p. 14.

17. R.S.C., 1970, chapter F–10.

18. This examination is partially based on information contained in a loose-leaf internal manual entitled *Functions and Responsibilities of the Treasury Board Secretariat* (Ottawa: Treasury Board, 1974, as amended).

19. Gordon F. Osbaldeston, 'Implementation of Performance Measurement in the Federal Public Service: A Progress Report', *Optimum* 7, iv (1976), p. 6.

20. Douglas G. Hartle, 'Techniques and Processes of Administration', *Canadian Public Administration* 19 (Spring 1976), p. 21.

21. A.W. Johnson, 'The Treasury Board and the Machinery of Government', p. 346.

22. J.E. Hodgetts, *Canadian Public Service: A Physiology of Government, 1867–1970* (Toronto: University of Toronto Press, 1973), pp. 284–5.

23. Pitfield, 'The Shape of Government', p. 15.

24. Lord Atkin in *Attorney General of Canada v. Attorney General of Ontario* (1937), Appeal Cases 327.

5

The Role of the Mandarins:
The Case for a Non-Partisan Senior Public Service

Mitchell Sharp

In a recent article in *Policy Options* Flora MacDonald says 'Regrettably too few Canadian Ministers have provided a first hand account of the relationship between the Minister and the bureaucracy'. I am among the few who have done so and I do so again because my account differs substantially from that given by Miss MacDonald.

I have been on both sides of the relationship. For 16 years—between 1942 and 1958—I was a senior civil servant. Towards the end of that period the media called me a mandarin. For 13 years—between 1963 and 1976—I was a Minister. In between I was, for 5 years, a businessman.

My previous experience as a civil servant helped me enormously when I became a Minister. I understood the functions of my departmental advisers. I consulted them daily, every morning that I was in town, following the pattern of strong independent Ministers under whom I had served like Ilsley, Abbott, and Howe. I asked questions and listened to their answers. Sometimes I agreed; sometimes I didn't. In the end I made my decisions and they carried them out. Once they knew my views they prepared drafts of policy speeches and announcements for my consideration.

Top public servants are powerful persons in the machinery of government at the federal level in Canada. They wield great influence. They do so because they are, in the main, professionals who have been selected for proven administrative ability and who devote their full time to government. In many cases, they have a greater influence upon the course of events than have Ministers, particularly the weaker and less competent Ministers.

This may seem somehow to be anti-democratic but it needn't be and in my experience it isn't. Government is, in fact, a specialized affair which cannot be run successfully by amateurs without professional advice and professional execution. With rare exceptions, in a parliamentary system politicians are amateurs in any field of government administration, at least at the beginning of their political careers.

Few of them will be experts in fiscal and monetary policy, or in nuclear policy, or in foreign affairs, for example, when they offer themselves as candidates in a local

Mitchell Sharp, 'The Role of the Mandarins: The Case for a Non-Partisan Public Service', *Policy Options* 2, 2 (1981): 43–4. Reproduced with permission of the Institute for Research on Public Policy (IRPP) at www.irpp.com.

constituency. Yet they may find themselves having to make decisions in any or all those complex fields once in office. Prime Ministers are limited in their selection of Ministers to those of their party who have been elected. Sometimes, given the necessity in a federal state for geographical distribution in Cabinet, the choice may be extremely limited.

At a political meeting during the 1968 election campaign, I was asked by a young man in the audience what qualifications I had to be foreign Minister of Canada. I replied that my essential qualification was that I had been elected to Parliament.

Politicians, particularly Ministers, require the best impartial advice that they can get if they are to make wise decisions. Sycophants who echo their boss's views are of little value; indeed they can be positively dangerous as advisers if they are not prepared from time to time to tell their bosses the painful truth that a pet idea is unworkable. That is one of the reasons why I am not in favour of the principle, which is sometimes advanced, that the top positions—the heads of departments—should be filled by those who are in sympathy with the views of the party in power, who should depart with their Ministers when the Government is replaced.

After some 35 years observing the process of government at close range, I am also more convinced than I was at the beginning that there is virtue in continuity in the senior administrative jobs, and in promoting career public servants to them. Competent people are not going to be prepared to enter the public service and make a career of it if they are to be denied access to the top jobs where they can bring their talents fully to bear.

The contrary argument that senior civil servants would resist change in the event that a government with radically different views from its predecessor took office has never been very convincing to me. In the first place, knowing my own country and its political parties, I doubt that any change would be in fact very radical. In the second place, it is precisely under those circumstances, were they to come about, that an experienced senior civil service would be most valuable, one that could guide a new government in the implementation of its innovative policies and enable it to avoid the administrative pitfalls of which it might otherwise not be aware.

I can testify from my own experience and my own observation that changes of government such as occurred in 1957 and 1979 were considered in the civil service as providing a challenge, an opportunity to prove that the service is non-partisan, notwithstanding the long years of Liberal administration. It is useful in this connection to observe that nearly all the deputy Ministers at the time of both changes were drawn from the ranks of public servants who had originally qualified for entry to the public service by the independent Public Service Commission. As nearly as I can determine, something like 80 percent of the present heads of departments are drawn from the ranks of non-political civil servants.

That there were some transitional difficulties in 1957 and 1979 is not surprising. Even when there is no change of government—only change of Minister—there are bound to be some awkward adjustments in relations between the incoming Minister and the incumbent deputy minister, which sometimes necessitate a switch in responsibilities. However, I neither saw nor heard evidence that the transition was difficult because the senior public service was committed to the policies of the previous government and was determined to resist change.

What a new Minister finds—I had the experience four times in my political career—when he or she takes over a department is that the problems are more complicated than they looked to be from the outside and that he or she needs plenty of advice to avoid making mistakes.

There is need, of course, for Ministers to have in their offices men and women to help them perform as Members of Parliament and political leaders. Such temporary appointees, however valuable they may be, are no substitute for permanent non-partisan senior civil servants.

From time to time, too, Governments may wish to be able to call on the services of qualified Canadians from the business or professional world who have special expertise of one kind or another. This they should be able to do and are able to do. I myself inherited a Deputy Minister appointed by the Diefenbaker administration who had not been drawn from the ranks of the permanent public service. I advised Mr. Pearson to retain him, which he did. The test of such appointments should be the competence of the appointee and not his or her personal politics.

Admittedly the system does give rise to serious questions. Do senior civil servants exert too much influence upon the Government? Are Ministers puppets being manipulated by the mandarins, as is sometimes asserted or implied? These are difficult questions to answer satisfactorily because so much depends upon the way individual Ministers react to advice. I don't think anyone who knew him thought that C.D. Howe was manipulated by his civil service advisers, yet he had excellent working relationships with them. The key to that good working relationship was that Mr Howe gave them his confidence and they responded with loyalty and respect.

When I was a civil servant, I think it is fair to say that individual Ministers and the Cabinet as a whole depended more upon the advice of senior civil servants than they do today and they did so deliberately. When a difficult problem arose, the customary response was to refer it for study and report to a committee of senior public servants. There was also a period during the war and in the immediate post-war years when influential public servants like Clifford Clark, Norman Robertson, Graham Towers, and Donald Gordon were active promoters of new ideas and approaches that they persuaded their Ministers and the Cabinet to adopt.

The federal mandarins then, however, were a tightly knit group of personal friends drawn from various walks of life who had been invited to Ottawa to join the public service during both Conservative and Liberal regimes. They were not lifetime civil servants recruited at time of graduation who had risen through the ranks, as is now the pattern.

Today when difficult problems arise, they are more often referred to Ministerial Committees than to Committees of civil servants. Innovative ideas still emerge from the civil service, but the process of decision-making at the Cabinet level is so complex nowadays that individual contributions are quickly submerged in a deluge of documentation. The present Ministers, I suspect, long for a return of the general rule, under which as a civil servant I operated, which was that memoranda for Ministers should not exceed two pages, otherwise they might not be read.

I sympathize with those Ministers who like myself had to wade through pages and pages of memoranda, some of which became available barely in time to be read before decisions had to be taken. However, it was our own fault for letting the system get out of hand.

I sometimes thought that as Ministers we were much too zealous and that, particularly under Mr Trudeau, we worked far too hard and spent far too much time in Cabinet and Cabinet Committees reading and discussing each other's proposals. Decisions might have taken less time, we might have had a better perspective on events and more time for politics, had we delegated more to our civil service advisers and left more time for reflection.

A first-class non-partisan public service dedicated to the public interest is one of the bulwarks of parliamentary government. It enables the elected amateurs, gifted or otherwise, to make the political decisions and govern the country.

6

The Accountability of Public Servants: Our Governments Would be Better if Senior Mandarins Were Less Secure

Hugh D. Segal

There is much interest in the recent dialogue and implicit dialectic between the Hon. Flora MacDonald and the Hon. Mitchell Sharp, over the role of the public service and its relationship to the successful discharge of ministerial responsibility. Their discussion is thought-provoking because of the issue that is not addressed.

It is implied that the public service enjoys greater public confidence and trust if it operates in a fashion which is responsive to its own needs for continuity, rather than to the politics of the government of the day. This view is highly suspect.

The British norm is a permanent public service at all levels, so that senior personnel and their tenure are largely impervious to choices made at the ballot box. The assumption that this model is fully acceptable in Canada should not be taken for granted by too many public servants.

In fact, while very few election campaigns feature the public service and its neutrality as an issue, many election campaigns focus on 'cleaning the rascals out', 'a new beginning', and 'fresh ideas for a better tomorrow', and so implicitly deal with the broad directions of government, as they are marshalled by both the elected and appointed public servant.

The illusion maintained by many senior public servants that they can sustain a position of personal importance and centrality to the overall governmental process, however the people may choose to pass judgment upon their political masters, is both childish and naive. The notion of ministerial responsibility does not imply senior public service irresponsibility.

In my opinion, the Canadian public service generally, together with the organization and fundamental direction of many of our federal and provincial governments, would benefit greatly from a more blunt and frank view of the responsibility—for policies, programs, initiatives, and decisions—which senior public servants share with the government of the day.

This is not to say that all senior public servants fall into the same category. Governments in this country are blessed with many senior public servants who have obtained their seniority as a result of long and distinguished careers in the public

Hugh D. Segal, 'The Accountability of Public Servants: Our Governments Would be Better if Senior Mandarins Were Less Secure', *Policy Options* 2, 5 (1981): 11–12. Reprinted with permission of the Institute for Research on Public Policy (IRPP) at www.irpp.com.

service, in business, and in the academic world. They provide a level of continuity, technical expertise, and solid experience which is unrelated to the politics of any of the governments under which they have served, and very much related to a sense of professionalism and commitment to a non-political public service.

These public servants are very rarely the ones singled out as being too close in their views to one government to be able to serve the government that replaces it.

But to suggest rather blithely that while governments may come and go, there is at the apex of both power and influence an elite public service that should always stay, is, in my view, to sanction a fundamental subversion of both the democratic and parliamentary processes of government.

As is the case with many of our governmental institutions, Canadians find themselves perched between the British tradition of a static and professional public service and the American tradition of significant and wide-ranging changes at senior policy-making levels within the bureaucracy in response to the change of an administration. In some respects, the present system in Canada may be the worst of both worlds.

On the one hand, we find senior public servants who have, for their lifetime, largely served governments of one political affiliation and who have absolutely no experience in serving those of another affiliation. That is not the case in the United Kingdom.

> A newly elected government . . . should not be constrained by civil service tenure in shaping its direction.

On the other hand, we find newly elected administrations in Canada sometimes reluctant to make the kind of large-scale and fundamental change necessary to ensure that those who voted for them not only get politicians chosen at the ballot box, but also policy-making and policy-development at the bureaucratic level which responds to the decision made by the electorate.

What we have now is a growing level of frustration, not only among those who traditionally express suspicion about all things governmental and political but by both opposition and government parties who feel unable, during their tenure in office, to get the kind of responsiveness they feel appropriate in order that they might effectively discharge their mandate.

Our system rests on effective translation of parliamentary decision-making through a responsive and efficient bureaucracy, together with an overall sense of political accountability. That system would be immeasurably advanced by a more frank and realistic appraisal of the role of senior public servants and the degree to which their tenure should not, as a matter of both principle and practice, outstrip that of those whom they advise.

It surely seems a matter of both personal honour and self-respect that those who advise a Cabinet, and whose advice may be taken, should not themselves be insulated from the effect of that advice if it is wrong, particularly when those who took the advice may find themselves out of work as a result.

It is true that no single piece of advice, no explicit issue, no particular interchange between bureaucrat and politician can ever be seen as the unique cause of electoral defeat or change of government. One may expect that there is advice given from time to time by all senior bureaucrats in this country, to all the governments they serve, which the bureaucrats may believe to be absolutely right, and which the politicians know to be politically unacceptable.

The ensuing Solomon-like decision is made by politicians. Decision-making is what they are elected to do. They must live with their conscience as senior bureaucrats must live with their own.

At the present time, there is a fundamental inequality in the degree and nature of the consequences faced by the two partners to the process.

A newly elected government, even a government newly constituted after the election of a new leader within the mandate of the same party, should not be constrained by civil service tenure in shaping its direction. We would be well served if all government positions in this country at or above the assistant deputy minister rank, at the agency head or deputy agency head rank, and in some cases at the executive director's rank, were contract positions with terms no longer than three years.

We would also be well served if the convention were clearly established that upon the election of a new government, and upon the election by the governing party of a new leader, all those at the deputy's rank or equivalent submitted their resignations so as to give those who have gained the responsibility to govern complete and absolute freedom to make the selections which they believe to be essential to the discharge of their mandate.

This convention might be very hard to enforce; it should, however, be a matter of honour, not enforcement. In my view, it would be a fundamental improvement to our style of government and to the accountability which those in senior levels should be expected to have.

Those who find accountability and the concomitant risks too high would simply have to face up to the fact, as others do in all sectors of society, that one cannot attain the significant opportunities to contribute to and affect public policy, which do exist at the highest level of various public services in this country, without facing a much higher risk factor than would be the case at lower levels.

Acceptance of that fundamental reality would improve the quality of government in Canada, enhance the freedom of operation of those we elect to public office, and diminish the sense of frustration, cynicism, and stagnation which is so often rampant when one discusses the bureaucracies of our various Canadian governments with one's fellow citizen.

7

Structural Heretics:
The Non-Departmental Forms

J.E. Hodgetts

Flanking the departmental structure that makes up the 'civil service' proper there exists another, numerically much larger, group of administrative entities whose functions and structures are so varied that they virtually defy classification. Taken in conjunction with the departments they make up what might properly be called, in a global sense, the 'public service of Canada'.[1] This chapter attempts to describe the way in which the programs allocated to departments have spilled over into this motley collection of non-departmental agencies. In the course of the analysis it will be possible to show why the departmental containers have been unable to absorb the accumulating workload assigned to the state, for in the reasons given for resorting to other types of administrative entities we discover the defects from which departments are claimed to suffer. Some attempt is also made to 'type' and categorize this miscellany, but it should be admitted at the outset that each entity is to some extent *sui generis* and any catalogue is essentially an oversimplification of the infinite variables found among these different containers.

The resort to non-departmental forms of administrative units is rooted in two basic considerations. First, there is the straightforward and, simple proposition that as the workload of a conventional department expands a point is reached where the tasks become unmanageable and ways must be sought to lighten the load. The obvious response when this situation arises is to create another department; but, as we have seen, the political conventions surrounding the Canadian cabinet system impose a limit on the number of departments. Thus, a solution had to be found by adopting some administrative variant of the departmental form. The second governing consideration which has grown in importance is that not only do the functions of government expand but, to an increasing extent, they tend to differ so much in kind from the traditional functions that the conventional department is no longer deemed appropriate.

These two considerations provide a convenient frame of reference within which our exploration of these non-departmental entities can be conducted. Since the first consideration dominated in the early stages of growth of the Canadian public service and the second factor has become more influential in recent times, the analysis can follow a reasonably chronological path.

J.E. Hodgetts, 'Structural Heretics: The Non-Departmental Forms' from *The Canadian Public Service*. © 1973 University of Toronto Press: 138–56. Reprinted by permission of the publisher.

THE 'SPILL-OVER' PROBLEM

Despite the modest dimensions of the early post–Confederation civil service it was not long before the government had to face up to the question of overburdened ministries. The exact nature of the remedy adopted is described in a memorandum prepared for Sir John A. Macdonald in 1883 for presentation to council; it deals with the proper disposition of the Mounted Police and Geological Survey:[2]

> Though a quasi–military organization, the Mounted Police Force being, as its name implies, one with the maintenance of law and order in the Territories in which it is placed, it might from a certain point of view be supposed to come properly under the supervision of the Department of Justice, but as, for other reasons, Government has decided that the force should be under the control of the Minister of the Interior, there exists the apparent anomaly of the management of such force through a Department that is, otherwise, to a great extent, if not exclusively, a land department.
>
> It is therefore suggested that the Comptroller of the Mounted Police Branch should be given the rank of a Deputy Head, and the branch be constituted another Department of the service under the Minister of the Interior.
>
> The operations of the Geological and Natural History Survey are so largely professional in their nature, and so entirely dependent on their effective prosecution upon the skill and judgment of its director that he should be immediately responsible to the Head of the Department.
>
> It is therefore suggested that he also should have the rank of a deputy head and that the business of his branch should become that of a separate department under the Minister of the Interior.

In essence, the solution, as advocated in this memorandum and adopted by the cabinet, was to relieve an overloaded department by singling out a large, distinctive function that had no organic connection with the other activities for which the department was responsible and then to give its permanent managerial head the same status as a deputy minister. The normal constitutional chain of command and control was retained by having the statutory head report directly to the minister. The fact that such segregated, self-contained functions were sometimes statutorily defined as 'departments' confuses the nomenclature, as we have already seen, and for our purposes they are best viewed as 'junior' departments which, even though answerable to a minister, lack direct ministerial representation in the cabinet. In Britain, typically, these might well have been given a junior minister of their own but without a place on the cabinet; however, in Canada the idea of junior ministers never really gained acceptance.

These two organizational expedients established a precedent for similar reassignment of workloads in situations where a function was large enough, sufficiently complete within itself, and, on the whole, somewhat remote from the normal operation of a regular line department. In addition to the Royal Canadian Mounted Police and the Geological Survey other specimens of this genre include the following: the Public

Archives, the Department of Public Printing and Stationery, the commissioner of penitentiaries, the Department of Insurance, the inspector general of banks, the master of the Mint (in 1969, transformed into a corporation), the chief electoral officer, the custodian of enemy property, the dominion statistician, the national librarian, the commissioner of the Yukon, the director of the Prairie Farm Rehabilitation Administration, the government film commissioner, and the director of the Veterans Land Act. All of these were set up in the same general form in pursuit of the same objective of devolving the workload. The only feature shared by this wide range of dependent departmental entities is that they are each concerned with a function that can be severed sharply from the normal department with a minimum of 'bleeding'. They also share the same direct relationship to a minister, rather than reporting as part of the regular departmental hierarchy through the deputy head to the minister. In the main, these junior appendages are required to report to a minister whose main portfolio is not totally unrelated to the special, separate function they perform.

One must assume, if the purpose of this junior departmental organization is to drain off some of the workload of a department and lighten the minister's supervisory responsibilities, that they will receive less active attention from the minister (or his deputy) than is given to the function of the department proper. Indeed, a feature common to most of these entities is that they function in areas where policy issues do not arise (for example, the Mint or the Archives) or where policy can be laid down so clearly that no important discretionary powers are involved (for example, chief electoral officer, custodian of enemy property, etc.). Thus, it is possible to visualize a single minister capable of answering for several of these junior appendages as an almost routine operation, with no great addition to his regular departmental duties and no undue stretching of his effective span of control.

In short, the creation by statute of these quasi-departmental appendages does the least violence to the constituted system of ministerial responsibility, even as it provides a means of removing selected, self-contained functions from overburdened major departments.

In recent times a variation on the 'junior' department approach to overloading has been introduced; this is the so-called 'departmental corporation'. Once again, as with the junior departments, a particular, self-contained function has been singled out from the normal work of a department and a special legal status of a 'corporation' has been conferred on the agencies set up to perform the function. We shall have occasion in the next section of this chapter to consider the use of the corporate form of administrative entity for activities that are similar to those performed by private industrial and commercial concerns. This is not the type of function, however, for which the departmental corporations have been brought into existence: they are, to quote the definition provided by the Financial Administration Act, section 76(3)(a), 'responsible for administrative, supervisory, or regulatory services of a governmental nature'. In short, they are performing functions which a branch of any department might well be expected to perform, but their relationship both to the regular department and to the central financial and personnel agencies of the government is by no means uniform. The only common feature to be found among these agencies is that each is managed by a board rather than by a single head, and one must assume that collegial management (and hence the corporate status) is deemed more appropriate for the particular functions than is the conventional one-man direction provided through the departmental hierarchy.

If the board form of organization is, indeed, at the base of this type of structure, one may well ask why for one set of functions such as those carried out by the National Research Council it is essential to give independent corporate status, while for other and apparently similar functions (for example, in Agriculture or Energy Mines and Resources) no such corporate board form has been instituted. Moreover, why should some of the agencies in this group be quite free from the central personnel control imposed on the normal department (for example, the NRC) while in other cases they are treated by the Public Service Commission and the Treasury Board like the staff of a department (for example, the Unemployment Insurance Commission)? In some cases, such as the Agriculture Stabilization Board, the Fisheries Prices Support Board, the Canadian Maritime Commission, and the Dominion Coal Board, the board members are all drawn from the permanent staff of the parent department. In other cases, such as the National Research Council, the National Gallery, and the Unemployment Insurance Commission, the boards are separate and distinct from any departments. The Atomic Energy Control Board, on the other hand, is a composite agency—essentially a device for bringing together the heads of the bodies that have operating and research responsibilities in the field of atomic energy. Nor is there any consistency in the method by which these agencies are associated with the formal structure of ministerial command and responsibility that is a feature of the regular departmental system. Several of the agencies appear to be precisely in the same position *vis-à-vis* the minister as are any of the conventional branches of the same department; others are subject only to such directives as the minister cares to issue.

No useful purpose is served by expanding on these contradictions and inconsistencies found among this particular group of agencies. Our primary concern is with discovering a rationale for the particular mode of work division selected and, in this instance, the clue is the board form of organization. Obviously, the ordinary hierarchical pattern within a department is not adapted to vesting responsibilities in a collegial body, hence we must see what justifications there are for adopting a board form of organization that forces the entity out of the conventional departmental structure.

Broadly speaking, there appear to be two justifications for a board in this particular context. First, the nature of the work assigned is such that it is desirable to provide a means of representing various expert or interested opinions—an objective which only a collegial arrangement could meet. Thus, the National Gallery, the National Research Council, and the Unemployment Insurance Commission all specifically provide in their statutes for the representation of outside interests whose opinions are regarded as essential for policy making, regulating, or operations. If this be so, then we have every reason to add to this group—even though they may not share the same corporate legal status—such bodies as the Fisheries Research Board, the National Film Board, the Canada Council, and the Economic Council and the Science Council.

A board may also be essential—on the premise that several heads are better than one—in the handling of special funds. This would appear to explain the Agriculture Stabilization Board, the Fisheries Prices Support Board, the Maritime Commission, and the Coal Board, as well as the long-lingering Halifax Relief Commission. In all these cases, however, the board is much more a part of the regular departmental structure than is the case with the other boards mentioned immediately above. The necessity for such formal arrangements to provide what is, in essence, an intradepartmental committee for conducting a particular operation is not nearly so apparent and one may well query the solution adopted in these cases since many special funds are administered elsewhere in the public service by conventional branches of a particular department.

In summary, the organizational response to what we have termed the problem of 'spillover' in the workload assigned to departments has been the creation of a veritable jungle of quasi-departmental agencies. Many of these are virtually junior departments—in some instances even bearing the statutory label of 'department'; an equally large number are under collegial management, in some instances carrying the legal status of a 'corporation' but with few, if any, similarities so far as their relation to a minister, department, and central financial or personnel control agencies is concerned. The mutual inconsistencies and contradictions reflect the pragmatic nature of the response to the growing burdens of government. In consequence, the conventional channels of ministerial responsibility and control are clogged up or obscured, while parliamentary supervision and public comprehension are correspondingly diminished.

THE CHANGING CHARACTER OF STATE FUNCTIONS

It is when we come to the second consideration, the change in the character of government functions, that a whole new complex of non-departmental administrative forms is brought into view. The first important demonstration of the potency of this factor is to be found in the creation of the original Board of Railway Commissioners. Such a board was envisaged in the report of a royal commission on transportation in 1886–7.[3] Its recommendations were clearly influenced by the evolution of regulatory machinery in the United States that culminated in 1887 with the setting up of the Inter-State Commerce Commission. A new term and a new organizational concept entered the administrator's vocabulary at this time: the word was 'independent' and the concept was an autonomous board or commission. Since both the legislature and the judiciary, as a result of the many years' experience with railway regulation, were deemed to be incapable of handling, on a day-to-day basis, the complex tasks to be faced in this area, the executive branch had to assume the burden. But, in the process, the executive was being asked to undertake functions which called for both adjudicative and law-making operations that were substantially different from those traditionally associated with conventional departmental operations. It followed, therefore, that a new type of administrative entity was required that could take on the impartial and independent stamp of the judiciary and could be entrusted with subordinate law-making functions that would have to be delegated to it.

In some such terms as these the case for allocating work to a non-departmental agency was framed. The primary consideration, as distinct from the purely practical question of how to relieve an overburdened department, was, in this instance, the allegedly unique character of the function which in turn necessitated a departure from the administrative entity through which conventional governmental activities had traditionally been performed.

The first significant organizational response to this line of reasoning was, as noted, the Board of Railway Commissioners, which came into being in 1903, was enlarged and strengthened as the Board of Transport Commissioners in 1938, and in 1967, with the merging of two other regulatory bodies, became a part of the Canadian Transport Commission. The precedent established by this first organization was shortly followed up, this time as a device for collaborating on a governmental basis with the United States, by the creation of the International Joint Commission in 1909, followed by an International Boundary Commission in 1925.[4] After a wartime interregnum a renewed spate of similar bodies appeared, each vested with the broad power to legislate through the issuance of rules and orders and to adjudicate all controversial questions arising from the application of the legislation. The Board of Grain Commissioners, the Tariff Board,[5] the Air Transport Board, the Restrictive Trades Practices Commission, the Board of Broadcast Governors (as of 1968 the Canadian Radio-Television Commission), the Atomic Energy Control Board, the Copyright Appeal Board, and the National Energy Board were the major representatives in this new category of semi-independent, 'quasi-judicial', administrative agencies.

It is interesting to observe that practically all of these non-departmental agencies function in sectors of the economy which, as a reference to the previous chapter will show, had not been included as part of the jurisdiction of the conventional departments. But the impact of the changing character of governmental activities extended beyond those areas of the economy that increasingly required regulation. In addition, the mounting momentum of the welfare state began to reveal itself in an increasing number of benefits and services directed to selected categories of citizens. At once the question arose: who should be entitled to qualify for the benefits which parliament had declared should be made available? Traditionally, the law courts have been assigned the tasks of adjudicating questions involving individual rights. But as we have pointed out elsewhere the typical *modus operandi* of the courts was 'compensatory and punitive'.[6] They have been geared to a leisurely pace dictated by the historical interest in showing that justice manifestly be done—an interest safeguarded by cumbersome and expensive procedures along with a hierarchy of appeals. With these new benefits to be allocated, the number of individual cases would have swamped the regular judicial machinery which, in any event, was unsatisfactory because of its cost and deliberateness. Again, the judicial character of the work suggested the value of assigning it to a non-departmental entity. These considerations were operative, for example, when numerous benefits were conferred on the returning soldiers: the Canadian Pension Commission and the War Veterans Allowance Board were, therefore, created to adjudicate the individual claims of the veterans. The Merchant Seamen's Compensation Board plays a similar role with respect to a much more limited group of claimants. The largest and most important of the agencies in this category is the Unemployment Insurance Commission.

Two other important agencies in this category are concerned with appeals against decisions made by government departments rather than with specific claims to benefits. These are the Tax Appeal Board (1958), first created in 1946 as the Income Tax Appeal Board, and the Immigration Appeal Board (1967). Before these bodies were brought into being appeal on decisions was strictly internal, ending with the minister or the cabinet. Finally, we might place in this group the Canada Labour Relations Board (1949) and its counterpart for government employees, the Civil Service Staff Relations Board (1967). It should be noted that the number of bodies empowered to adjudicate individual or group claims is much larger in the provinces than at the federal level because so many benefits and rights are conferred under provincial programs.[7]

There has been an inconsistent organizational response to the judicial qualities of the type of work embraced by the foregoing agencies. In the cases just noted the argument for a special extradepartmental agency has been acknowledged; but in many other instances functions of an adjudicative nature have been left within the department. This was true until quite recently for immigration appeals and tax assessments and still holds true for such matters as claims for patents, courts martial, and regulation under the food and drug acts.

The interests and rights of individuals and firms are intimately affected by the action and decision taken by regulatory boards or agencies adjudicating claims, as well as by a number of departmental divisions that have somewhat similar authority. The possibility that injustices may be perpetrated by these administrative courts of the first instance—whether outside a department or as part of it—has been recognized in the creation of yet another tier of non-departmental agencies—this time primarily appellate bodies, though still part of the administrative organization rather than the judiciary. Thus, the Copyright Appeal Board exists, in part, to hear appeals from the commissioner of patents. Or again, decisions rendered by such non-departmental agencies as the Pension Commission and the Board of Grain Commissioners can be reviewed, respectively, by pension appeal boards or grain appeal tribunals; while the decision of administrators within the Prairie Farm Rehabilitation Administration and the Veterans Land Administration are equally subject to review by special boards.

It is important to observe that in most instances these appellate bodies are creations of (if not the creatures of) the agency whose decisions are being contested. Thus, grain inquiries tribunals—*ad hoc* creations of the Board of Grain Commissioners—usually have at least one member of the board's inspection staff represented on them. In a few important cases there is an opportunity for transferring the appeal process from this administrative setting to the conventional judicial setting of the law courts (as, for example, in income tax or labour relations cases) but the limitations on this transaction and the disposition to give the administrative tribunals the last word raise fundamental questions about the accountability of the public service that cannot be further explored here.[8]

Yet another distinctive type of non-departmental administrative entity has emerged in response to the factors which have contributed to the rise of regulatory and adjudicative organs. This extremely large group may be characterized as advisory bodies, and it is no accident that their appearance coincides with the multiplication of the other types of agencies already described. In the performance of their regulatory functions, departments and agencies are required to impose standards, inspect, license, and make orders of both a specific or general nature. It is therefore desirable that the vital interests affected by the regulations can be induced to co-operate by being given an opportunity to influence the administrator's decision. Perhaps the increasing resort to advisory bodies implies a failure of our conventional party and legislative machinery to provide the necessary liaison and 'inputs' into the political system. In this sense, public administrators are seeking ways of devising their own 'constituencies' with which they can maintain a direct relationship. Possibly a restructuring of the committee system of the legislature, paralleling the structure in the United States Congress, would reduce the need for such extraparliamentary institutions and improve the capacity of parliament to channel the interested public's views to the bureaucracy.

The chief value of advisory bodies lies in their ability to give the affected interests the opportunity to forestall complaints and criticisms that would ultimately plague the adjudicative and appellate bodies described above. They are also an obvious alternative to placing such interests directly on the regulatory bodies. Some of the typical advisory bodies falling in this category are: the Feeding Stuffs Advisory Board, Fertilizer Act Advisory Board, Livestock Products Advisory Committee, Pest Control Products Advisory Board, Proprietary or Patent Medicine Act Advisory Board, Salt Fish Marketing Advisory Committee. At a much more general and sophisticated level the Science Council of Canada, the Economic Council, and, most recently, the Prices and Incomes Commission play the role of advisers to the cabinet, as in part does the Tariff Board. In a special advisory relation to parliament itself is the Office of Representation Commission,[9] while, since 1969, the Commissioner of Official Languages has been accorded a status akin to that of the Auditor General in performing his 'ombudsman' functions.

Among the advisory bodies associated with agencies responsible for distributing welfare and social benefits the following may be listed: Blind Pensions Advisory Board, Canadian Fishermen's Local Loan Advisory Board, Maritime Marshland Rehabilitation Advisory Committee, Old Age Assistance Advisory Board, Unemployment Insurance Advisory Committee, Veterans Land Act Advisory Committee, Vocational Training Advisory Committee, Prairie Farm Rehabilitation Administration Advisory Committee, National Employment Committee, the Labour Management Co-operation Service Advisory Committee.

This list does not even begin to touch the much larger number of advisory bodies that exist primarily for dealing with problems of coordinating administrative services in which both the federal and the provincial governments have an interest. A recent compilation reveals that in a period of about a decade the number of these bodies has doubled from 65 to 125; this list does not include *ad hoc* advisory agencies set up for specific purposes.[10]

Advisory bodies must be considered an indispensable part of the Canadian public service organization—although they stand at the margin of the public service proper. They are an obvious response to changing functions of government that bring the public service into close contact with the public, either through its regulatory powers or its relatively new role as a dispenser of benefits. They may also be identified with the increasing technical complexity of the matters now coming within the purview of the state and the corresponding need of the state to avail itself of every possible source of skilled advice, not only in policy-formation but in the execution of programs. As noted above, for such agencies as the National Research Council or the Film Board, one way by which the government can avail itself of such assistance is by representing various groups on the directing board itself; advisory committees offer an alternative or, at times, supplementary means of bringing such views to bear on policy and administration.[11]

The changing character of state functions is attributable not only to growing responsibilities for regulating the economy and dispensing a variety of benefits, it is also related to the appearance of the state as an entrepreneur—the owner and operator of concerns destined to provide goods and services to the Canadian public. This is not altogether a novel role for the Canadian public service despite notions concerning the essentially laissez-faire nature of Canadian economic growth that erroneously depend on a rather romantic view of a 'pioneer' world in which the sturdy 'Canuck' is observed to shoulder his axe and independently carve out his own destiny from the bush. The fact is that the sturdy pioneer has always leaned heavily on the government, whether for land grants, roads, canals, or railways. The price of cementing and expanding the Canadian union has constantly necessitated a state involvement in settlement, transportation, and communication. Nevertheless, all these activities in early days were contained within the regular departmental system until their growing size and expanding responsibilities, fostered by the philosophical trend that supported positive state intervention in the economy, burst the walls of the old departments.[12] The First World War, rapid changes in technology affecting transportation, communication, and the exploitation of resources, and then the Second World War, all hastened the trend towards state operation and ownership—and the pace, if anything, is accelerating.

The organizational response to these trends has been the allocation of entrepreneurial functions to government corporate entities obviously modelled on the structures that have proven successful in private industry and commerce.[13] The corporate form has not been used solely for such new functions because, as noted above, it has also been employed as a means of injecting the board form of organization into the departmental structure. At this point, however, we shall concentrate on its use for activities of a commercial or industrial nature that have close parallels in private sectors. It should also be added that the corporate form has not been employed for certain traditional functions which would appear to fit all the reasons given by its protagonists; for example, the Post Office, Public Printing and Stationery, and the Mint are essentially business operations that might easily be regarded as suitable candidates for the corporate form of organization.[14] On the contrary, there are any number of agencies that have been accorded corporate status even though their functions afford no ready clue as to the necessity of distinguishing them in this fashion from ordinary departments.

The procession of corporate entities engaged in the provision of goods and services is headed by the Canadian National Railways which was set up in 1919 and is still, by far, the largest governmental enterprise. With its subsidiary, Canadian National (West Indies) Steamship Limited, set up in 1927, this corporate entity occupied for over a decade the position of sole representative of the strictly business-type government enterprise. The second experiment with this particular form of administrative entity came in 1927 with the creation of the Federal Farm Loan Board—subsequently renamed the Canadian Farm Loan Board in 1935 and reconstituted again in 1959 as the Farm Credit Corporation. In the 1930s the corporate device came into full bloom: in 1932 the Canadian Radio Broadcasting Commission—the forernnner of the Canadian Broadcasting Corporation of 1936; in 1932, again, the first experiment with a central bank designated by Prime Minister R. B. Bennett as 'a privately owned public trust' was fully converted through successive stages into the present Bank of Canada by 1938; the Canadian Wheat Board appeared in 1935; in 1936 the National Harbours Board was added to the list; and two years later Trans-Canada Airlines (Air Canada) made its appearance as a subsidiary to the CNR. But it was in the decade of the forties that the heaviest additions were made to the roster. Several important corporations were set up to engage in lending and guaranteeing transactions, including the Industrial Development Bank, 1944 (a subsidiary of the Bank of Canada); Export Credits Insurance Corporation, 1944; and Central Mortgage and Housing Corporation, 1945. Another category of corporation emerged to carry on commodity trading and procurement functions, some of which were absorbed or abandoned after the war: Commodity Prices Stabilization Corporation Limited, 1941 (now defunct); War Assets Corporation (which became Crown Assets Disposal Corporation in 1950); two price support boards for agriculture and fisheries products in 1944; Canadian Commercial Corporation, 1946; Canadian Sugar Stabilization Corporation the following year; and Defence Construction, 1944 (which in 1951 assumed the charter of Wartime Housing Limited). Corporate agencies concerned with industrial and commercial enterprises included Polymer Corporation Limited, 1942; Eldorado Mining and Refining Limited, 1944; Northern Transportation Company Limited, 1947 (a subsidiary of Eldorado); Canadian Arsenals Limited, 1945; Northwest Territories Power Commission, 1948 (as of 1956 Northern Canada Power Commission); and Canadian Overseas Telecommunication Corporation, 1949. In the 1950s the crop was smaller but included such important newcomers as Atomic Energy of Canada Limited, 1952; the St Lawrence Seaway Authority, 1952; and Northern Ontario Pipe Line Crown Corporation, 1956. The 1960s witnessed an acceleration of the trend, beginning with the Atlantic Development Board in 1962 (but transformed from corporation to advisory body in 1969 and renamed Atlantic Development Council); the National Arts Centre Corporation, 1966; the Cape Breton Development Corporation, 1967; and the National Museums of Canada, 1968, that swept into a species of cultural holding corporation the National Gallery and the three museums of Human History, Natural History, and Science and Technology. Closing out the decade with a flourish, the Government Reorganization Act of 1969 conferred corporate status on the Mint, the Science Council, and the Medical Research Council, even as a separate act created the Canadian Film

Development Corporation. The decade of the seventies opened auspiciously with the launching of the Canada Development Corporation (1971), even as long-deferred proposals for converting the Post Office and the Department of Public Works into Crown corporations were still waiting in the wings.

The Financial Administration Act categorizes the various agencies listed above as either 'proprietary' or 'agency' corporations. The former category includes the corporations that most closely resemble their counterparts in the private businessworld: they provide goods and/or services for a fee or set price; they enjoy substantial freedom in the realm of policy, finance, and personnel; their organization is modelled closely on the board-management structure of the private corporation. The agency corporations include those that are engaged in governmental trading, lending, and procurement functions, as distinct from the sale of commodities or services at a price designed to make their operations self-sufficient. These agencies are all closely tied in with the system of central control to which regular departments must submit, but at the same time enjoy a measure of financial autonomy usually provided by means of revolving funds which relieve them of the annual necessity of seeking parliamentary appropriations to undertake their transactions.

Included in the list of agencies presented above is a group of variants known as 'Crown companies', immediately distinguishable from the others by virtue of the word 'Ltd' which is appended to their title. Many of these administrative entities were born in the war—some three dozen Crown companies having been on the list at the peak period of their use. Some of them have been continued as permanent additions to the non-departmental roster. They differ from the public corporations proper in a number of ways. While the latter obtain their authority from specific acts of parliament, Crown companies receive their powers in a more complicated, indirect fashion. The right to recommend, for cabinet approval, creation of a Crown company is vested by separate statutes in four agencies: the Minister of Defence Production, the Atomic Energy Control Board, the National Research Council, and the St Lawrence Seaway Authority.[15] Issuance of an order in council provides authority for the next step in the creation of the Crown company, namely an application to the Secretary of State under the terms of the Companies Act[16] for a charter of incorporation as a 'private' company. In 1965, the Companies Act became the Canada Corporation Act[17] (c. 52, 1964–5) and in 1970 the Minister of Consumer and Corporate Affairs took over the Secretary of State's functions. In addition to complying with the obligations outlined in the Canada Corporation Act an additional document, an 'Agreement' between the Crown company and the sponsoring minister or agency, sets out in more explicit terms the structure, financing, and powers of the company.

When the wartime boom in incorporation was over, the government sought to rationalize and standardize the arrangements for the Crown companies that still remained. In 1946 the Government Companies Operation Act[18] was passed with a view to unifying the legal and fiscal position of these companies. This measure was largely supplanted in 1951–2 by the Financial Administration Act in which the Crown company was thoroughly mixed in with the regular statutory corporations by including it in either Schedule C (agency corporations) or Schedule D (proprietary corporations). A classification legitimately concerned with grouping agencies in relation to their degrees of fiscal independence and specific function tends, however, to conceal the very real differences between the legal bases of the Crown companies and of the public corporations.

Even this sketchy survey of the use of the corporate form of administrative organization is enough to reveal that the resort to this practice has been extremely unsystematic and haphazard. Included in the schedule to the Financial Administration Act are many agencies that are there simply because they are in law 'bodies politic and corporate', in no way concerned with functions akin to the industrial or commercial activities which gave rise to the corporate form in the private sector. Moreover, even if we separate out the corporate entities whose functions are not of a commercial or industrial nature, we are still left with a collection of public agencies characterized by almost infinite organizational variations, paradoxical relations with the conventional chain of ministerial command, viewed by the law courts in contradictory decisions, and possessing little in common so far as their alleged autonomy is concerned. While the indirect means of bringing Crown companies into being was appropriate to a wartime situation where secrecy and speed were essential, the permission accorded the executive by several statutes to continue this procedure in peacetime seems to reduce unnecessarily the already meagre opportunities afforded to parliament to discuss the creation and subsequent operations of such agencies. Agreeing that part of the charm of the public corporation is its flexibility and adaptability to the peculiar circumstances surrounding the performance of a special function, this variability and inconsistency can only add to the confusion of parliament and the public as they contemplate the public service organization.[19]

The allocation of the government's workload, over the years, has resulted in the creation of a bewildering variety of organizational containers. The pragmatic and haphazard approach to the problem of work allocation makes the effort to order this universe a rather forced and artificial exercise. Nevertheless, some design must be superimposed on this disorderly structure if we are to gain even an impressionistic conspectus of the public service organization. The primary division has been made between the major operating departments and the myriad of non-departmental administrative entities. The first group is relatively small—only twenty-six active departments with ministerial heads in the cabinet having been identified.[20] There has, in fact, been astonishingly little increase in the number of departments with which we began one hundred years ago. Within the four walls of each of the major departments, however, there has been an expansion of staff and activities that makes today's departments quite unrecognizable in terms of the original. It is this internal growth that generates the problems of subdivision of labour [. . .]

The non-departmental organizations are so varied and have arisen in response to so many special problems of work allocation that they present a forbidding problem for the classifier. The closest equivalent to the departments proper are those agencies which we have characterized as junior or quasi-departments. All of these are statutory creations, each has a permanent head, reports to a relevant minister, but none can be said, for this reason, to have the status of a major department. These are the agencies which, by and large, have absorbed what we have called the 'spillover' of functions from the conventional departments. They will invariably be found administering a specific program which can be severed from the regular departmental hierarchy because it is not organically related to the main purposes of a department and because it is a complete unit in itself. Something of the order of sixteen such agencies can be fitted into this group.

A variant on the quasi-department is the agency that is set up under collegial supervision. Many of these have been vested with corporate status by their sponsoring statutes—a practice that has led to their confusion with another array of corporate governmental agencies that are engaged in commercial or business transactions. The board form has been adopted primarily as a method of giving representation to 'outside' interests (or the interests of several departments) in the management and execution of a particular program—the program itself, as in the case of the quasi-departments, comprising a self-contained activity that may have little organic connection with what goes on in a regular department. Roughly a dozen such entities fit into this category.

The remaining non-departmental units have, in the main, emerged in response to two basic changes in the conventional functions assigned to departments, quasi-departments, and operating boards. The first change is associated with the state's increasing responsibilities for regulating various sectors of the economy and dispensing a number of individual benefits. In the course of these transactions functions of a judicial and legislative nature had to be assumed by the public service. While it is true that some of these were, in fact, absorbed within the regular departmental apparatus, to an increasing extent they have been assigned to special deciding tribunals, separated off from the departments so as to emphasize their independence—an independence which was deemed essential if they were to arbitrate among conflicting interests that had to be regulated or to settle the claims of individuals for various benefits. This line of reasoning has led to the creation of more than a dozen regulatory or deciding tribunals whose functions are akin either to the law courts or to the legislature itself but who are part of the executive machinery of government.

Supplementing these bodies, yet another group of non-departmental agencies have evolved to act as appellate tribunals sitting in judgment on the decisions rendered by administrative courts of first resort. Some five or six of these can be identified.

The need to bring the outside point of view to bear on the programs administered by the public service has encouraged the growth of boards on which such interests could be directly represented; it also encouraged the resort to advisory committees which, so to speak, stand at the margin of the public service organization acting as two-way channels of communication between outside interests and the civil servants responsible for implementing programs. The profusion of these advisory committees makes difficult even a crude count of their number, but the reasons for their appearance are clear. The regulatory and dispensing functions of government necessitate the creation of close links with various sections of the public; moreover, the increasing complexity of decision-making and execution in highly technical fields forces heavy reliance on such devices to bring the best available expert knowledge to bear on such problems.

The second major change in the character of government functions has been

occasioned by the advances of the government into various commercial and industrial undertakings, infrequently as a monopolist and more often to supplement facilities and services provided by private enterprise. It has been argued that whenever
such entrepreneurial activities are undertaken they ought to be assigned to organizations that are moulded to the pattern of private enterprise. Thus, the public or Crown
corporation has come into existence, endowed with special autonomy in financial
and staffing matters, and removed from the direct play of politics so that policies can
be evolved independently of the normal 'line' operations of departments, and day-to-
day administration can be conducted on 'sound business' lines. A mode of reasoning
that is strictly relevant to the direct business undertakings of government has, as we
have seen, been extended to embrace a significant number of other non-departmental agencies whose functions do not really fit this pattern. The result has been an
undue extension of corporate status to agencies that have nothing to gain by it and
yet whose inclusion with the Crown corporations has simply added confusion to an
already complex organizational structure. One can single out some two dozen Crown
corporations and Crown companies that genuinely represent these new entrepreneurial functions of government for which the claims of autonomy may legitimately
be made.

NOTES

1. The Public Service Staff Relations Act (Stats Can. 1967, c.72) in its definitions, sec-
    tion 2(x), reads: '"Public Service" means the several positions in or under any depart-
    ment or other portion of the public service of Canada specified from time to time
    in Schedule A.' Part I of Schedule A lists those portions of the public service for
    which the Treasury Board is the employer; part II has a much smaller list of 'portions
    of the public service of Canada that are separate employers'. A number of the agen-
    cies to which this chapter will refer are not in either part of the schedule, and there-
    fore not in the strictly legal sense part of the 'public service of Canada'. On the other
    hand, in the context of a comprehensive conspectus of all the non-departmental
    public organizations, I shall continue to use the term 'public service' in a more global
    and inclusive sense than the legal definition would admit.
2. P.C. 2122, 17 Oct. 1883.
3. A concise résumé of the rise and development of the Board of Railway
    Commissioners is to be found in Arthur R. Wright, 'An Examination of the Role of
    the Board of Transport Commissioners for Canada as a Regulatory Tribunal',
    Canadian Public Administration 6 (Dec. 1963), pp. 349–85, and extensive references
    contained in footnotes.
4. The International Boundary Commission, in 1960 (Stats Can. 1960, c.31) had its
    original functions of inspection, repair maintenance, and arbitration of disputes
    extended to include the regulation of all works or construction within ten feet of
    the international boundary. The International Joint Commission is concerned with
    the use, obstruction, and diversion of boundary waters and rivers crossing between
    Canada and the United States.
5. The Tariff Board operates in a judicial fashion in making inquiries and tendering

reports to the government; it also acts in an appellate fashion in rulings from the Customs and Excise division of the Department of National Revenue. The board therefore occupies both an advisory and adjudicative position.

6. J.A. Corry and J.E. Hodgetts, *Democratic Government and Politics* (3rd edn, Toronto, 1959), pp. 415, 528.

7. For the province of Ontario, see (Gordon) Committee on the Organization of Government in Ontario, *Report* (Toronto, 1959); for a critical analysis of this development, see Peter Silcox, 'The Proliferation of Boards and Commissions', in *Agenda 1970: Proposals for a Creative Politics*, ed. Trevor Lloyd and Jack McLeod (Toronto, 1968), pp. 115–34.

8. There is an extensive literature on this topic, but for a useful, concise treatment of the problems as they affect labour relations, see Canada, Department of Labour, *Judicial Review of Decisions of Labour Relations Boards in Canada* (Ottawa, 1969).

9. Public organizations such as the Science Council and the Economic Council represent an 'institutionalization' of the advisory functions performed by temporary, *ad hoc*, advisory teams such as are found in task forces and royal commissions. The Economic Council, for example, may be said to have been fostered as a device for continuing on a permanent, on-going basis, the kind of analyses developed by the Royal (Gordon) Commission on Canada's Economic Prospects. However, the Government Reorganization Act of 1969 transformed the Science Council into a public corporation, signifying a change in its purely advisory role.

10. See *The Canadian Public Service* (University of Toronto Press, 1973), c. 3, n. 2.

11. An interesting strategic problem for organized interest groups seeking 'access' to government is whether it is preferable to secure a place by direct representation on a deciding tribunal or to maintain a more independent arm's length relationship by seeking representation on an advisory body. Given this choice by the government when the Agricultural Prices Support Board was being created in 1944, organized agriculture opted for representation on the powerful Agricultural Advisory Committee. See *Can. H. of C. Debates*, 1944, p. 5377 ff.

12. The Board of Works for the Province of Canada in pre-Confederation times would be viewed today as a forerunner of the Crown corporation. See my *Pioneer Public Service* (Toronto, 1955), pp. 176, 180, 190.

13. For more detailed discussion, see my 'The Public Corporation in Canada', in *Government Enterprise: A Comparative Study*, ed. W. Friedmann and J.F. Garner (London, 1970), c. 12.

14. In 1972 the government had still to produce its long-promised white paper, recommending the reconstitution of the Post Office as a public corporation; under the Government Organization Act of 1969 the Royal Canadian Mint, for thirty-eight years reporting to the Department of Finance, was scheduled for conversion to a public corporation. In March 1964 the technical side of the Department of Public Printing and Stationery was transferred to the Department of Supply and Services, leaving the former as a centralized servicing agency. The Canadian Government Printing Bureau reports through its general manager to the deputy minister of its new foster parent, and to this extent remains in the traditional line of command rather than occupying the more autonomous role conferred on statutory executives

that report directly to the minister (for example, Statistics Canada, formerly the Dominion Bureau of Statistics).

15. Stats Can. 1951, c. 4, s. 7; Stats Can. 1946, c. 37, s. 10; Stats Can. 1946, c. 31, s. 9; Stats Can. 1956, c. 11, s. 24A, respectively.

16. R.S.C. 1952, c.53.

17. 1964–5, c.52.

18. Stats Can. 1946, c. 24.

19. For analysis and critique by the Royal Commission on Government Organization, see *Report, v, The Organization of the Government of Canada* (Ottawa, 1963), report no 24: 'The Organization of the Government of Canada', p. 58ff.

20. In the current (March 1972) roster of the 'Ministry' the prime minister, the leader of the government in the Senate, two ministers of state for designated purposes—urban affairs and science and technology, and one minister of state, along with twenty-seven parliamentary secretaries, are listed, for a total of fifty-seven. Although there are twenty-six separate departments of the conventional type, two of these—Fisheries and Forestry and Environment—are held by one minister. Assuming that all ministers of state are in the cabinet, it numbers thirty persons as of 1972.

8

Regulatory Processes and Regulatory Agencies

G. Bruce Doern

The regulatory process is clearly a central process of government. But, alas, it is a central process without any obvious central agency and hence does not parallel the more direct and visible connection between the expenditure and budgetary process and the Treasury Board. Regulation profoundly affects private budgets and public expenditure but regulatory values are not as normally or regularly converted into the common denominator of money. Regulation is the hidden half of government, so to speak, and the regulatory process and the behaviour of regulatory agencies, boards, and commissions must be examined as an integral part of public policy and of the organizational modes available to policy-makers. Three views about regulation will help illustrate the problem of understanding the nature of regulation.

The *process of regulation*, says Sir Geoffrey Vickers, is a continuing transaction between the governors and the governed. It is a 'mutual transaction: persuasion, authority, bargain and threat move from the governed to the governors, no less than from governors to governed.'[1] In the opinion of a 1969 special committee of Parliament on Statutory Instruments, a *regulation*:

> is a rule of conduct, enacted by a regulation making authority pursuant to an Act of Parliament, which has the force of law for an undetermined number of persons; it does not matter if this rule of conduct is called an order, a decree, an ordinance, a rule, or a regulation.[2]

Others have asserted that *regulatory agencies* tend to become captured by the industries they were intended to regulate.[3]

The above statements about regulation are diverse. They illustrate why an understanding of the regulatory process in Canada must be based on at least an analytical distinction between the theory and practice of the governmental performance of the *regulatory function* and the theory and behaviour of *regulatory agencies*, boards, and commissions. Vickers gives to the concept of regulation the widest definitional scope by equating it with the total political process and by subsuming under it a number of

G. Bruce Doern, 'Regulatory Processes and Regulatory Agencies' in *Public Policy in Canada*, G. Bruce Doern and Peter Aucoin, eds (Toronto: Gage, 1979): 158–89. Reprinted by permission of G. Bruce Doern.

mechanisms of 'transaction' such as persuasion, authority, bargain (inducements), and threat. He sees it as a transaction with private non-governmental centres of power also capable of wielding the same array of transactional tools. The second statement about regulation treats it more narrowly by viewing it as a rule of conduct backed by the sanctions of the state. It is similar in nature to Theodore Lowi's classification of policy outputs in that it suggests that regulation is only one of several governmental functions or instruments.[4] The second concept avoids, however, the evolving minutiae of administrative distinctions (rules, guidelines, orders) which are properly viewed to be generally meaningless for any *general* understanding of the regulatory process.[5] The third statement deals with a frequently hypothesized pattern of behaviour by 'regulatory' *agencies*, organizations which in fact usually perform both regulatory and non-regulatory functions (that is, adjudicative, expenditure, and advisory functions).[6]

The organization of this chapter reflects the need to make some theoretical and practical distinctions between the issues inherent in the first two concepts on the one hand, and the third concept on the other hand. Thus, we will first examine a number of the central dimensions of the political economy of regulation in Canada, concentrating on regulation as *one governmental* function but cognizant of Vickers' more catholic concept of the two-way transactions between governed and governors. We will then examine the processes and, in some cases, the performance or effect of selected regulatory *agencies*. While it is important to separate agency behaviour from the broader dimensions of the *regulatory process*, it is obvious that the two significantly affect each other. This will be more apparent in later parts of the chapter as well as in my concluding comments on the relationships between 'process' and 'performance' and on the possibilities and limits of regulatory reform [. . .]

The chapter will stress that no theory of regulation or regulatory processes and no answer to the question of why and when governments regulate can make complete sense except in relation to some understanding of the role which the choice of governing instruments plays in the political behaviour of governing politicians. We have referred to this concept of governing instruments in the introduction to this book and hence will only note it again here. While ideologies, and the specific economic rationales outlined later in this chapter, undoubtedly exert their causal influence, they are inadequate for a full explanation of regulatory phenomena. To regulate is merely to choose one instrument of governing from a range of other instruments.[7] A regulation can be viewed *politically* as a rule of behaviour backed up more directly by the legitimate sanctions of the state. It is a more directly coercive way of achieving objectives and can be distinguished in part from somewhat more pleasant ways of governing such as spending (offering an incentive) or exhortation (soliciting voluntary compliance). The types of instrument to be used and/or the sequence in which they are used (for indeed all may be tried or may be necessary) does matter *politically*. It matters because the way one secures legitimate compliance in a democratic state is not merely a matter of technique. The selection of instruments is, in part, an *end* in itself. Subtle and not so subtle *degrees* of legitimate coercion *are* important.[8]

In addition to asking questions about why and when governments choose to regulate as opposed to other instruments of governing it is also important to ask why certain organizational modes of regulation are chosen.[9] Why are the legal and medical professions and some agricultural commodity producers accorded virtually self-regulatory status with little or no 'third-party' membership in the organization charged with carrying out the regulation?[10] Why are other sectors regulated by multi-membered commissions and representative boards, and still others by regular departments headed by ministers and deputy ministers? These questions are not merely to be asked by those fascinated by abstract organizational form. Rather, they go to the root of *positional* policy in that they address those who will control the positions of authority in defined sectors of day-to-day decision-making.[11] These are questions which, to the main protagonists, are as important as the supposedly more substantive regulatory values and objectives themselves.

Because these positional questions are important, we will be concerned with the notion of the 'independent' regulatory agency. We do so however, with a healthy skepticism about the American pluralist notion of independent tribunals. While some degrees of independence are not unimportant in Canada, the degree is always relative to the dependence created by the Cabinet system of government, a system in which the executive is inherently more integrated, by the persistent use of state enterprise and by the presence of state corporations (federal and provincial). The physical, political, and economic realities of communication, transportation, and energy in Canada have brought the presence of state enterprise and regulation. The presence of the CBC, Air Canada, the CNR, the Atomic Energy of Canada Ltd, and provincial electric power utilities as part of the clientele of federal regulatory boards means that government is in part regulating itself as well as centres of private- and foreign-owned economic power. The role of the state as regulator cannot help but be somewhat different in the context of these configurations of the Canadian political economy.[12]

The organization of the chapter will reflect these two levels of concern. At the aggregate level we will first review the aggregate economic rationales for regulation or, more accurately, the rationales advanced by economists. That these rationales are ultimately founded on political economy rather than abstract economics will be stressed. Further, aggregate 'political' factors will be examined briefly, including in particular the influence of cabinet-parliamentary government and federalism. The chapter will then survey the more particular organizational forms for regulation. the legal and procedural determinants of agency behaviour, the characteristics of regulators, and the theory and practice of agency behaviour. [. . .]

THE ECONOMICS OF REGULATION: RATIONALE AND CONSEQUENCES

There are a number of points of intervention in which the state has regulated the operations and production cycle of business enterprises, both publicly and privately owned. These points include regulation of access to the industry, prices, rates of return on investment, market share, technology, ownership, and health and safety.[13] This is in addition to other general regulations effecting the acquisition of capital, labour relations, and competition. In general, however, experience has shown how infrequently governments in general, and specific agencies in particular, systematically assess the expenditure and economic consequences of regulation. High levels of inflation and massive regulatory interventions such as the incomes policy administered by the Anti-Inflation Board have sensitized powerful economic groups to the need to assess the marginal and comparative costs of regulation in relation to other devices for achieving policy results.[14]

Virtually all regulations directly affect and alter private spending. The difficulty in assessing the costs of regulation is that the private expenditure *consequences* (on individuals and corporations) do not normally appear in government budgets.[15] The budgetary process in government is a highly visible and central rhythm of activity in which values are at least partly converted into the common denominator of money. There is a central budgetary process and there is a treasury board. There is no such equivalent central rhythm to the regulatory process. Money is needed and is calculated to operate the regulatory machinery, but the expenditure *consequences* of regulation are rarely calculated in any direct financial sense, although they certainly are calculated in more general political terms.[16]

For example, in response to increases in urban crime, governments could respond by hiring more policemen and police patrol cars, an act which would appear directly in public budgets. On the other hand, governments could regulate a requirement that all homes be equipped with burglar alarms, an act which would affect private budgets but not appear in public budgets at all. While governments would typically not directly calculate the financial costs, they would certainly be aware in general political terms of who was paying the price.

Even the above example, however, does not adequately reveal the nature of who wins and who loses in the regulatory process. It fails to reveal the *redistributive effects* of regulation. For less wealthy home owners the cost of the burglar alarm would effectively be a regressive tax in comparison with a wealthy owner. The redistributive effects are a central issue in such areas as the regulation of occupational health and environmental hazards, since the costs of regulation fall disproportionately on different economic classes (e.g., workers and lower-income families who live near industrial plants because they cannot afford to live in the suburbs).[17]

The basic traditional economic justification for the regulation of economic activity is to control and prevent the improper allocation of resources that may be caused by either excessive 'destructive' competition or natural monopoly.

> The fundamental argument for having the government regulate a particular industry is that it, e.g., a telephone company, will develop a natural monopoly because the economies of scale, production, or distribution are so pronounced that a single producer or single seller will dominate the industry. In achieving such a dominant position, the firm could extract monopoly rents or in other words charge whatever the market could bear. In more specific terms, by regulating the price or limiting the profits of the firm, the idea is to increase the output of the particular product or service beyond that which would be evident in the case of a monopoly position.[18]

Regulatory intervention to control the problems of excessive competition arises when there are very low barriers to entry in the industry which cause instability and perhaps disruption of basic services (e.g., bus routes and taxi service). Generally speaking, the economic literature is less sympathetic to excessive competition as a rationale for government regulation than it is to natural monopoly.

Regulation is often used as a proxy for fiscal policy. This occurs when regulators permit the charging of prices well above the incremental costs of some services to offset losses of other services caused by prices below cost. In this way one service cross-subsidizes another service (e.g., railway freight service subsidizing passenger service, or urban telephone service subsidizing rural service).

All these economic aspects of regulation involve the closely related activities of price regulation and licensing. Economists have generally been very critical of the typical approaches taken in both pricing and licensing. Their criticism of pricing arises out of the different ways in which the economist, on the one hand, and the regulator, on the other, view the role of prices. As Roger Noll points out, 'economists see prices as guides to efficient productive agents—labour, machines, natural resources—with incentive to produce a combination of goods and services that maximizes consumer welfare. The price system can serve this function only if each price is a measure of all of the costs—private and social—of producing one more unit of output—the incremental or marginal cost.'[19]

The regulator, on the other hand, does not tend to relate price with cost in the same sense or to the same extent. Prices of particular services tend to be viewed as merely one component of a general corporate or industry price structure which must be assessed in the aggregate to ensure that sufficient revenue is generated to permit the regulated firms to cover costs plus some allowable profits. This total revenue perception of the regulator prompts a consideration of cross-subsidization. By this process uneconomic services are sustained by economic ones. The economist would argue that if the economically unviable services are highly valued by society, then costs of an inefficient price structure are worth bearing. This may be done by direct social subsidization or by indirect subsidization; the difference will depend on who bears the cost of subsidization, the users alone or the general taxpayer.

The control of market entry of regulated firms is obviously related to price regulation in that the price structure can be used to promote cross-subsidization only if there is some control over the number of firms who can enter the high price parts of the market. The firms required to continue providing an uneconomical service would be unwilling to do so if their highly priced economical services were subject to easy entry and competition from firms with no uneconomical service obligation.

If, as sometimes occurs, the licensing function and the pricing function are not handled together, the economist's concern is that the licensing authority will give too much attention to the interests of the licensee. The effect will be to limit competition needlessly at the cost of wider questions of general welfare. Some licensing is clearly justified in the public interest to prevent individuals or firms from 'trying to broadcast on the same frequency', and so on. Where this is necessary, some economists suggest the licences ought to be auctioned so that the government can capture the monopoly profits from the highest bidder able to provide the service.

While the traditional economic concerns have dealt with monopoly and excessive competition and related licensing and pricing practices, more recent analysis has
been directed as assessing the cost of regulation itself. As McManus has pointed out,
'the fallacy in the traditional case is that regulation is treated as if it were "free". . . .'
One of the costs of regulation is the inefficiency in production that will result from
the attenuation of profit incentives on managerial behaviour.'[20] Because of regulations, corporate management has incentives to incur costs above the minimum in
pursuit of non-pecuniary objectives. As a result,

> there is no practical way for a regulatory board to detect such cost increasing
> behaviour. Imagine the problem we would have in determining whether
> investment was excessive or whether it was efficiently allocated among alterna-
> tive applications. How could a regulatory board detect inefficient employee
> performance or excessive managerial prerequisites or wasteful advertising cam-
> paigns? The difficulty boards have in estimating and assigning actual, experi-
> enced costs strongly suggests that potential cost savings will remain
> undiscovered.[21]

The above analysis suggests that there are no *a priori* grounds for regulating on
the basis of either monopoly or excessive competition. Economists are not necessarily arguing that regulation should not take place (although some deregulation may in
fact be beneficial) but rather that the costs and benefits of regulation as a policy
instrument ought to be more critically assessed in relation to other instruments.

A related concern has been expressed in the economic literature about the
extent to which regulation of prices and of market entry inhibits the adoption of new
technology.[22] Concern in price regulation for overall revenue and for the rate of
return on investment militates against adopting cost-saving new technologies.
Control of entry likely prevents the entry of new firms possessing new technology
which, if they were permitted entry, would alter the distribution of wealth among
existing firms. It is felt that these inherent tendencies are exacerbated by regulatory
agencies' attitudes to two issues: the tendency to be obsessed with sunk costs and to
abhor abandoning an existing capital investment (e.g., a rail line), and the tendency
not only to stress continuity of service but to protect regulated firms from as much
uncertainty as possible.

The raw economics of the adoption of technology also fundamentally affect the
corporate response to workers and environmental health and safety.[21] Part of a corporation's response to the suggestion of building better and safer production processes
is influenced by the question of sunk capital costs. A corporation is reluctant to invest
new capital when it will only yield new costs rather than new efficiencies. The standard response in matters concerning new safety technology is either to say it cannot
be done (usually accompanied by suggested scientific evidence to show that the new
technology does not exist to meet suggested new standards), or that it cannot be done
for several years or months. In some instances a time lag is clearly necessary. In others, time is merely another way of expressing the higher priority to be accorded to

capital as opposed to labour (or other bearers of the costs of less superior safety-production technologies).

The foregoing economic concern about, and pressure to insure the 'timeliness' of, major investments, profoundly affects regulators in that it reinforces their preference for continuity and reliability and the need for their regulatory organization to have sound everyday relationships with its clientele.

The above reference to the regulation of workplace and occupational health and safety cannot pass by without pointing to one of the remaining ironies (and weaknesses) of the economics of regulation. While the regulation of access to the market, prices, rate of return, and the like will, in the usual nomenclature of economics be called 'economic' regulation or regulated industries, the regulation of the health of the workplace is more likely than not to be characterized as social 'qualitative' regulation[24] or merely as health and safety. Nothing could be further from the truth. That health and safety is the other half of the same economic and regulatory coin should be patently obvious.

Not all analysis by economists subjects regulation to the often artificial microeconomic tests of the marketplace. Paquet's analysis also assesses regulation in the context of the historic evolution of economic institutions and, building on the insights of Vickers and others, relates recent regulatory experiments to the broader context of governing relations and values.[25] Paquet suggests that much recent regulation must be seen to be in the realm of 'mezzo' economics, thus suggesting a middle range of analysis located uncomfortably between the traditional, usually quite arbitrary categories of 'micro and macro economics'.

CABINET–PARLIAMENTARY GOVERNMENT AND FEDERALISM

The constraints and the political values inherent in the central pillars of Canada's 'constitution', cabinet-parliamentary government and federalism, make the concept of the 'independent regulatory agency', as used in American literature, largely, though not totally, inapplicable in Canada.[26]

The Governor-in-Council or Cabinet is the officially designated regulatory authority in the great majority of federal statutes.[27] The Cabinet or individual ministers frequently are given statutory power to order agencies to do their bidding. The scope of Court review is also constrained by Cabinet government. These formal attributes are often reinforced by more informal pressures such as those which arise when the regulatory agency, and a Crown corporation regulated by that agency, report to or through the same minister (for example, the CNR and CTC to the Minister of Transport, and the AECL and AECB to the Minister of Energy, Mines and Resources).[28] The fact that regulatory agencies need the administrative and political support of other ministers and departments, and that the career patterns of board members and staff are linked to other parts of the bureaucracy also reinforces these formal dependencies.

Federalism also imposes its curses and its blessings on the regulatory process. Federalism divides constitutional jurisdiction. Politically it legitimizes the right of provinces and of the federal government to pursue independent and different priorities, albeit taking into account the 'national' pressures imposed on them by their interdependence. The division of political authority enables corporations, unions, and interest groups to lobby on a multilateral basis, having 'their' preferred political party in power in some provinces but not in others. Differences in policies, in regulatory standards, and in compliance strategies and practices are partly explained by the political opportunities which federalism encourages. Federalism also requires the striking of bargains between regulation-making and compliance. Because many areas of jurisdiction are blurred, or are thought to be blurred, the political trade-offs between levels of government are frequently made not just in the area of regulations themselves, but also in the enforcement of regulations.

Recent analysis by Richard Schultz traces the growing interdependencies which federalism imposes on the Canadian regulatory process.[29] In a very important sense recent regulatory developments are reinforced by what Smiley has called 'executive federalism'.[30] The sources of regulatory conflict arise not only out of traditional constitutional concern over which level of government can regulate in particular areas (e.g., cable television, wages and prices, competition) but also out of overlapping regulatory responsibilities (e.g., in energy and transportation), the actual decisions of appointed regulatory authorities, and the procedures of regulatory bodies before which provincial governments must increasingly appear.

Federalism has always affected regulation but the movement of federal-provincial relations in the 1970s relatively more into the regulatory arena may make the forms of intergovernmental collaboration and compromise, called for by Richard Schultz, more difficult to achieve than in the past. The federal-provincial policies of the 1950s and 1960s were dominated primarily by *expenditure politics* centred on elaborate *joint conditional grant programs* (e.g., medicare, vocational training, social security). This was followed in the late 1960s by another form of expenditure politics, reflected in programs such as the Opportunities for Youth (OFY), Local Initiatives Program (LIP), and regional incentive grants in which the federal government used its spending power, but effectively 'bilateralized' certain aspects of federal–provincial relations. That is, expenditure politics came to include more bilateral negotiations between the federal government and particular provinces. The regulatory politics of the 1980s are likely to be much more difficult not only because the federal government has succeeded in placing ceilings on earlier open-ended spending programs, but also because it is probably more difficult to influence and bargain about regulatory issues, since they are issues which are more of a zero-sum game,[31] and they cannot as readily be converted into the common denominator of money. For example, Harris's analysis shows the conflicting consequences of regulating regional air carriers and hence on the regional development plans of provincial governments.[32] As Schultz points out, the levels of conflict are important because 'bad blood' between the federal government and one or a few provincial governments in one area of regulatory activity not only can affect that area, but also related or other areas of regulation.[33]

While the inapplicability of the 'independent agency' model has been stressed above (especially in the context of American comparisons), one can only carry the argument so far. Analysis by Windsor and Aucoin shows how the regulation of telephone service in Nova Scotia has been characterized by the considerable effort, through long tenure of appointment, independent powers to 'tax', and other operating norms, to make the regulatory authority more independent than the Canadian experience would otherwise suggest.[34] One should, therefore, not underestimate the importance, at certain strategic points in the evolution of many policy fields, of the general view that partisan elected politicians should not be trusted and that the 'politics', defined in these terms, should therefore be taken out of regulation, whether the regulatory area involves adjudication or quasi-judicial functions or not.

That politics (in the sense of making value-laden choices) is *not* in fact, removed by such steps, or that the appointed bureaucrats who take the elected politicians' places are not inherently more trustworthy or are not as subject to their own forms of professional and occupational 'partisanship', will not, at such times, likely dissuade or impress those who advocate the need for independence. Nor should one underestimate the desire, and the need, at different times by politicians to escape obligation to make 'regulatory' choices (especially those which impose penalties as opposed to inducements) and hence their willingness to give such choices to others.

POLICY, DISCRETION, ORGANIZATIONAL FORMS, AND ADMINISTRATION

The *day-to-day* regulatory process, however, could not be understood merely by reciting the above general features of political and economic life. The choices available, and hence the regulatory dynamics, can take on numerous forms and can occur in numerous permutations and combinations. To understand these wider varieties one must explore in more detail the varying scope of regulatory policy mandates, the discretionary power they confer, the *finer ranges* of instruments available, and the *kinds of organizations* in which these instruments might be grouped and located.

While, in broad political terms, it is appropriate to present a broad range of instruments such as regulation, spending, and exhortation, the choices available in day-to-day legal and administrative terms are much finer. At the regulatory end of the continuum, for example, one can include sanctions which would encompass imprisonment, fines, revocation of licences, stop-orders, and reporting requirements. Within the spectrum of spending instruments one can envisage grants, subsidies, transfer payments, and conditional or shared grants. At the other end of the continuum one might group under exhortation, such devices as information programs, research, and direct consultative and advisory committees and processes.

While it can be argued that this chapter is about the 'regulatory' process and therefore we ought to focus on the *regulatory* end of the spectrum only, it is important to stress that such a narrow focus would indeed be a distortion of reality. It would distort reality in two major respects. First, the realization of policy objectives may be frustrated by the fact that regulatory functions may be housed in one government organization and expenditure functions in another and the two may be working at cross-purposes. Second, even so-called 'regulatory' agencies frequently, indeed usually, do not just regulate. They are more normally multi-functional and perform functions such as adjudication of disputes, research, the distribution of subsidies, and policy advice. This in turn affects how they behave, how aggressively the 'regulatory' agency regulates and enforces, and how 'court-like' are their procedures. It also affects the normative standards against which we might measure the processes followed by the particular agency concerned, and how much discretion, and ultimately, power it possesses.[35]

Hence, it is important to stress that the *regulatory processes* are *not* confined to *regulatory activity* precisely because the specific organizations which regulate are not usually just performing regulatory functions, nor can the resolution of the policy problems or the implementation of policy objectives usually be achieved only by regulatory means.

Three subsidiary but important issues arise from the above points, each of which takes us further into the day-to-day realm of the political economy of regulation. The first issue is the range of discretionary power of regulatory agencies both over the interpretation of the policy mandate and over procedure. The second are the differences between regular departments, independent 'third-party' commissions, and self-regulatory bodies as organizational forms of regulation. The third issue is the relationship between regulation-making and compliance within regulatory organizations.

The regulation-making mandates and compliance processes, as they are now legally enshrined, confer enormous discretionary powers on regulatory authorities. Discretion exists, in many instances, in the determination of which values will be maximized, how open the regulatory process will be, who will be consulted, how early in the process particular groups will be consulted, whether reports and the results of monitoring will be released (and, if so, to which parties), whether sanctions will be applied, the type of sanction and the sequence in which multiple sanctions are to be applied, and a host of other related questions.

Discretion itself is clearly not an evil.[36] A great deal obviously depends upon how it is exercised and how openly it is exercised. The more uncertainty that exists in the process, however, and the more closed the process, the more affected groups will likely (and accurately) perceive themselves to be the objects of arbitrary power.

Regulatory and compliance processes also, as we have seen, are not without costs, both in financial and human terms. Paquet's analysis shows that some regulatory agencies, such as the Foreign Investment Review Agency, have such wide mandates and imprecise standards of performance that they have become virtually 'negotiating' tribunals designed to wring out of industry somewhat better terms for Canadian society than would be possible without them. In this sense it is somewhat academic to view such bodies in the context of a narrow view of micro-economics.[37] Ralph Harris's discussion of regional air transportation regulation shows the inherent conflict in which regulators are put when their mandate contains both positive promotional or managerial policy goals as well as negative sanctions to prevent certain forms of behaviour.[38]

At first glance one usually thinks of regulation in the context of the major quasi-independent regulatory 'boards' or 'commissions' such as the National Energy Board or the Canadian Transport Commission. These boards are created with decision-making responsibilities lodged in a collective group of commission members. Their formal relationship to a Cabinet minister or to the Cabinet as a whole is intended to be more arm's length or quasi-independent. Under a cabinet system of government, as we have seen, they are never fully independent, even when the justification for the board often is to remove, and/or to *appear* to remove, certain kinds of decisions from elected politicians. The multi-member commission may also facilitate 'representation' of key interests on the board itself, and this *seems* to imply greater obligations to consult the affected interests.

This form of regulatory agency can be contrasted in theory and partly in practice with regulation performed by regular departments headed directly by ministers and deputy ministers (for example, mines and labour departments). These single-headed, more traditionally hierarchical organizations tend to operate more guardedly as a traditional bureaucracy. There seems at times to be less of a clamour for these regular agencies to encourage participation and to create formal channels of consultation. Regular departments seem to be bound more directly by the norms of Cabinet and ministerial accountability and responsibility.

The major 'self-regulating' professions such as medicine and law and self-regulating agricultural producer groups have been accorded apparently even more independence, the former through their self-governing agencies and the latter through marketing boards or arrangements. Explanations are noticeably lacking for the existence of these specific modes of regulation.[39] One might speculate that the association of these producers of services and commodities with questions of life and death, and with the basic necessities of life and the climatic vicissitudes of nature might help explain their regulatory good fortune. But these speculations break down when other groups (professions and producers) are examined who have perhaps similar characteristics but have not succeeded in reaching the self-regulatory millennium. Neo-Marxist theories of the state similarly flounder as explanations for the existence of such modes because such producers do not readily conform to the elegant simplicity of class divisions and conflict.[40] Micro 'market' economists invariably have little good to say about any marketing boards but cannot explain their existence. Similarly, public-choice economic theory, which stresses self-interest behaviour, has difficulty explaining why some groups get self-regulatory privileges while others do not.[41]

While the analysis in this chapter makes no claims to unravelling these mysteries of organizational form, it does imply that existing macro theories are unlikely to be unsatisfactory as bases for explaining the organizational variety in the Canadian regulatory terrain. Whether independent regulatory agencies and regulatory departments behave any differently in fact, as opposed to in theory, is difficult to say. Whether one form is more responsible and responsive depends upon a host of factors in each case. Whether the independent form promotes more legitimacy than the departmental form depends in part on how one ranks the concept of ministerial accountability held by *elected* politicians, as opposed to more indirect forms of representation by collective boards *appointed* by elected politicians. Both forms are equally susceptible in theory to be captured over time by the interests they were intended to regulate. Both forms must develop good relationships with interests they are regulating or regulation becomes virtually impossible.

Differences in organizational form may or may not be illusory. It is, however, instructive to point out that the task of regulating occupational health is carried out primarily by regular departments. With the exception of the Atomic Energy Control Board (AECB) in the radiation field, and the several Workers' Compensation boards, most of the regulations are carried out by regular departments of labour, health, mines and resources, and environment.[42] It is not unimportant to note that in areas of long recognized 'economic' regulation there has been much more of a tendency to assign regulation to quasi-independent bodies while in the 'softer' areas of economic regulation (which is, of course, what occupational health is too often perceived to be) the regulation seems to be kept more closely to the bosom of ministers and of the collective Cabinet.

Regulation is also influenced by the compelling demands of day-to-day administration. Analyses of the CTC, NEB, and AECB give some flavour of the inherent administrative complexity of regulatory activity.[43] Growing 'case' loads and licensing applications, the demands of hearings, the agency's role as adviser to ministers, and inadequacies in staff and information all contribute to what at times is an impossible administrative task. The actual effective implementation of regulations obviously requires a considerable amount of 'voluntary' compliance by the parties being directly regulated, a considerable and visible inspection and compliance capability in the regulatory organization's own staff, the co-operation of compliance personnel located in other public organizations, and the technical capability to develop and/or utilize existing or required compliance and monitoring technology. The compliance function everywhere encounters a need to resolve the natural human desire for effective and fair enforcement without the annoying presence of too many 'enforcers'. A number of other factors influence the overall compliance capability.

Most regulatory agencies in Canada tend to be rather sparsely staffed. Their compliance capability does not usually measure up to their regulatory intent. There is a considerable tendency to avoid unnecessary duplication of personnel, to 'piggyback' one agency's compliance needs on the backs of agencies already in the field. Up to some undefined point, *more* effective regulatory compliance does require more staff (although more staff is clearly not itself a sufficient condition for more effective compliance). This fact implies bureaucratic growth at a time when many arguments are being mounted against the growth of government and of public bureaucracies.

While some growth is necessary, the concern about excessive bureaucratic growth should counsel a more intelligent search for other compliance mechanisms. In the workplace, for example, this may suggest some very practical advantages to the use of joint worker-management committees as a complementary compliance device as well as to serve other purposes.[44] It may also suggest the value of wider legal remedies by outside parties (e.g., class actions). Obviously these alternative compliance mechanisms will not be assessed only on the grounds of avoiding the formal growth of bureaucracy, but they do suggest the need to consider the compliance capability in somewhat broader and more catholic terms.

Considerations of compliance capability should also take into greater account the conditions under which field-level inspectors operate in contemporary public bureaucracies. In recent years especially, greater status has been accorded the high policy and policy-advisory roles in government. The 'nuts and bolts' line operators and field-inspection personnel tend to have been downgraded both relatively and absolutely. The formal educational qualifications of inspectors also tends to be regarded as inferior. From the point of view of the regulated parties, the inspectors often are viewed as second-class policemen.[45] These factors complicate a situation in which it is already difficult, in many fields, to get and retain qualified and experienced technical manpower at the inspectorate and monitoring levels.

None of the above is intended to suggest that no co-operative relationships are developed in particular regulatory areas between inspectors and colleagues in government and in the regulated organizations. What is suggested, however, is that the inspection and compliance functions are grossly under-supported or devalued in the current Canadian climate of public administration.

This situation is made worse by the 'piggy-backing' phenomenon referred to above. Its recent practice has reached a stage where inspectors from *other* departments are utilized by a regulatory agency not so much as *part-time* inspectors but rather as *over-time* inspectors. The same phenomenon occurs between the federal and provincial governments as well as among departments within each level of government. The likelihood of 'piggy-backing' is greater in the current Canadian climate since budgetary constraints cause requests for new staff to be viewed with skepticism by central treasury officials.

LEGAL AND PROCEDURAL DETERMINANTS

What is a 'regulatory lag' for one party to the regulatory process may be regulatory justice for another. That the costs and benefits of more openness and procedural fairness in the Canadian regulatory process are being persistantly raised is clear. While Trebilcock's analysis of the economic disincentives that preclude or discourage individual and interest group participation accurately reflects a major overriding cause of the current regulatory imbalance, this general cause is reinforced by the fewer procedural opportunities inherent in the Canadian legal system.[46] The general absence of an enshrined bill of rights or of an administrative procedures act, as present in the American system for example, means that current reform proposals have somewhat less of a base on which to work.

In a review of the Ontario McRuer Commission recommendations on regulatory reform, Professor John Willis characterized the commission's preference for narrow statutory discretions as the triumph of 'lawyers' values' over 'civil servants' values':

> Consider the normal lawyers' biases. Because he acts for individuals he necessarily empathizes with the individual. Because he is steeped in the common law he views with alarm any departures from the eighteenth century constitution which he finds in the law reports. Because he lacks experience in the facts of governmental life he has little interest in what actually happens there. Because he is familiar with law as a shield to be used in the defence of his clients he over-estimates the importance of legal safeguards and underestimates the

importance of the, to him, less familiar but more efficacious ones of fairminded civil servants, a vigilant press, and a 'watch that government' atmosphere in the general public.[47]

While recent analysis by legal and non-legal academics does not display any excessive trust of 'civil servants' values' it also does not reflect an uncritical embrace of legal procedural reforms such as those suggested by an administrative procedures act.[48] There is clearly a recognition, however, that procedures matter a great deal and that reforms are needed to achieve the proper balance between public and private interests, and between legal formalism and informal modes of participation. These twin balances are best reflected in Trebilcock's view that direct representation on boards for consumer interests is largely ineffective and that a *combination* of a consumer advocacy institution and reimbursement for the costs of participation (on the model of the Alberta Public Utilities Board practice) is the most direct and effective way of enhancing consumer participation and, at the same time, acknowledging the realities of political division among consumer groups. Based upon his own experience as a practising legal counsel to consumer groups, however, Andrew Roman cautions, against the reliance too much informalism and amateurism.[49] The procedural realities are such that expertise, procedural and substantive, must consistently be challenged, through quasi court-like mechanisms, by competing expertise.

THE REGULATORS

If the evolution of regulatory mandates has been such as to confer wider and wider areas of policy and procedural discretion on regulators, then who the regulators are matters a great deal. The background characteristics of regulators and the *behaviour* of regulators are not the same thing,[50] but the former can influence the latter. Knowledge of regulators also assists in evaluating how formally representative a particular board, or boards collectively, might be. Data on career patterns might also alert us to the probabilities that boards are, or are likely to become, captives of the interests they are intended to regulate. The analysis by Caroline Andrew and Réjean Pelletier examines the regulators on several federal regulatory agencies in terms of experience, education, Francophone representation, age, and sex.

The most interesting finding, particularly in comparison with the US, is the significant extent to which Canadian regulators are drawn from bureaucratic careers as opposed to industry. Given our earlier discussion, this characteristic should not perhaps have been surprising. In addition to the qualifications which Andrew and Pelletier outline, the analysis has to be qualified by the fact that it generally treats all regulators in the sample as being equal.[51] The background of chairmen or of full-time members only might give more precise indicators of the characteristics of regulators from which future statements about behaviour could be derived. For example, analysis of the AECB shows a very closed bureaucratic career system between the AECB and the publicly owned nuclear enterprises. It also shows how the appointment in 1975 of the first President without a strong AECB background has helped alter the perceptions and behaviour of the AECB.[52]

THE THEORY AND PRACTICE OF REGULATION AGENCY BEHAVIOUR

In the analysis above a number of points have already been noted about the day-to-day factors influencing regulatory agency behaviour.[53] These can be summarized briefly as follows:

a) The scope of the legislative mandates and the degree of conflict among the goals the agency is expected to pursue.

b) The degree of multi-functionality of the agency—that is, its range and mix of regulatory, adjudicative, expenditure, consultative, advisory, and research functions.

c) The opportunities for and modes of cabinet or ministerial intervention, e.g., review, appeal, power to order and instruct.

d) The degree of agency dependence on its clientele for research and information.

e) The role of agency leaders and career patterns of agency members (and staff).

f) The nature and evolution of clientele pressure, including pressure from industry, state enterprise, provincial governments, and public-interest groups.

The above list does not exhaust the variables. For instance, the degree of media attention and criticism is an increasingly important factor as is the degree to which the agency's mandate is characterized by technological complexity (a variable of considerable importance in the case of the AECB).

Recent analyses enable us to make some statements about agency behaviour, particularly in relation to the most well-known hypothesis about agency behaviour, namely Bernstein's view that regulatory agencies go through a *natural* cycle of decay ending in the agency's capture by the industry it is regulating.[54] We will leave other observations about the relationships between agency processes and performance to our concluding observations at the end of the chapter.

The 'clientele capture' thesis developed in the American context by Marver Bernstein utilized both political and organizational variables to suggest that regulatory agencies go through a predictable life cycle characterized initially by a responsible, highly aggressive attitude towards the industry being regulated but which gradually deteriorates until the board is captured. The agency is initially created after a struggle between a loose, transient majority wanting regulation, whose political vigilance wanes after the creation of the legislation, and a smaller, more cohesive minority who opposes the creation of the agency but who lives on to develop the daily *modus operandi* with the board. The processes of capture begin when the supporting clientele weakens. Gradually the agency begins to think and act as if it was the protector of the industry.

Bernstein's theory has been criticized in a number of ways, even in the context of American regulatory processes.[55] First, as a 'theory' it suffers from the fact of non-falsifiability. Second, the thesis has been questioned on the grounds that many regulatory mandates envisaged the agencies as managers and quasi-promoters rather than as mere policemen. Hence, captivity is built in from the beginning. Third, it is argued that the lack of statutory precision made it both inevitable and necessary that the agency would seek out day-to-day, case-by-case, ways of carrying out its functions. Finally, even Bernstein's vaguely expressed hope for greater executive supervision was criticized as being an unlikely remedy given the numerous demands on presidential time.

Some useful advance on Bernstein's theory has been offered by Paul Sabatier who offers a more 'optimistic' view of agency behaviour.[56] His focus is on ways in which the agency can maintain constituency support, the support which Bernstein felt subsided almost immediately after the initial legislative victory. He examines two case studies in which a regulatory agency successfully organized a supportive constituency, and in which a supportive constituency effectively participated in monitoring the implementation of the regulatory program. Sabatier thus goes on to invoke interest group pluralism (despite what he acknowledges to be its shortcomings) as a sufficient condition for preventing the cycle of decay.[57]

While other typologies[58] have been suggested for the analysis of regulatory agencies, the captives thesis remains the most enduring hypothesis. The presentation of the factors listed above and the evidence provided by other published analyses permit us to make some tentative comments about its relevance to Canada.

With respect to the second and third of the above-mentioned criticisms levelled against the thesis in the United States, it can be argued that they apply with even greater force in the Canadian context. In analyses of the AECB, CTC, and NEB it is clear that the wide and vague scope of their mandates, their wide degree of multi-functionality, the significant opportunities for Cabinet and ministerial intervention (even though they are not always exercised), the presence of large state corporations as part of their clientele, and their administrative dependence on other federal and provincial departments, all suggest that Canada's major regulatory agencies are more accurately viewed as being intended to perform more of a managerial function over their policy field (along with other important departments of government) rather than being strictly regulatory policemen. Thus, the CTC manages a large program of subsidies and has responsibilities for research and policy advice, in addition to its rate-setting, safety, and other regulatory roles. The AECB has important, indeed critical, policy-advisory roles as well as research and regulative tasks. Hence, if captivity exists, it is more of a governmental or state captivity, rather than a clientele captivity as such. Moreover, if countervailing quasi-pluralist constituencies are evolving, or are to be created, they are more likely in the Canadian context to be found in the *combined* form of increasing provincial government interventions and emerging and increasingly permanent public-interest groups, many of which are funded by the state, through other government departments whose mandates themselves partly countervail those of the regulatory agency.[59]

Different agencies fit the above configuration in different degrees. For example, the AECB and NEB seem to have been more cohesively managerial in nature partly because their industrial clientele is itself more cohesive, the former consisting primarily of a few large state enterprises and the latter of a handful of giant oil companies. Also the policy assumptions under which the two boards operated were not seriously challenged until relatively recently. The NEB's mandate was basically unchallenged from 1960 to 1970 and the AECB's from 1946 to about 1974.[60] The CTC (and to a lesser extent provincial public utility boards such as the Nova Scotia board) has a much more cumbersome mandate and a clientele that is much more diffuse and whose interests are thus potentially more divided.[61]

Career background data reinforce and reflect the above dependencies. Studies of the AECB provide background data showing the exceedingly close career links between the AECB and the largely state-owned industry. Bureaucratic career links are also especially strong among NEB members.[62] They tend not to come from the private energy industry as such but rather from the governmental energy management and career system. Paradoxically, the CTC has a higher proportion of members with transportation industry careers than the NEB.[63]

In arguing that the major Canadian regulatory boards are more a part of a government managerial system, one is not necessarily arguing that the boards are blatant promoters of the industry. Nor is one suggesting that for each board different *degrees of independence* from the Cabinet do not apply. For example, the analysis of telephone regulation in Nova Scotia suggests that the Nova Scotia Public Utilities Board has been given considerable independence. Thus, agencies do have regulatory functions to perform but they also do a great deal more and hence they warrant a characterization that goes well beyond the elegant and misleading simplicity of either the 'independent' board or the captive thesis.

REGULATORY PROCESS AND PERFORMANCE

This chapter has dealt more with regulatory processes than performance. The attempt to differentiate process from performance is, in part, a product of the intellectual division of labour among academic disciplines, with law and political science presumably specializing in 'process' and economics in 'performance'. However, even the most superficial reading of recent analyses would strongly suggest that regulatory process and performance are relatively more a seamless web rather than two totally distinct categories of analysis.

Process and performance are linked in several important respects. First, in a democratic state, the openness and legitimacy of processes are *ends* in themselves, rather than matters of mere technique. Second, the more complex the processes, the more likely the regulatory agency will have to be judged on multiple performance criteria, some of which will be in partial or direct conflict with others. Thirdly, complex processes may be such that failure to achieve performance criteria may not be attributable to any single agency. That a number of these linkages affect current proposals for regulatory reform is obvious.

NOTES

The analysis in this chapter is adapted from my earlier edited book The Regulatory Process in Canada (*Toronto, 1978*).

1. Sir Geoffrey Vickers, *Freedom in a Rocking Boat* (London, 1970), p. 145. See also Sir Geoffrey Vickers, *The Act of Judgement* (New York. 1965).

2. Quoted in G.B. Doern and V.S. Wilson, eds, *Issues in Canadian Public Policy* (Toronto, 1974), p. 15.

3. Especially Marver Bernstein, *Regulating Business by Independent Commission* (Princeton, 1955).

4. See T. Lowi, 'Four Systems of Policy, Politics and Choice', *Public Administration Review* XXXII (May-June 1970), pp. 314–25.

5. The minutiae are, of course, not unimportant in *day-to-day* administrative terms. These finer ranges of inducements and sanctions are discussed below. See also *Policy Implementation: Guidelines,* special issue of *Policy Sciences* VII, 4 (December 1976), pp. 399–518.

6. See G. Bruce Doern, Ian Hunter, Don Swartz, and V.S. Wilson, 'The Structure and Behaviour of Canadian Regulatory Boards and Commissions. Multi-Disciplinary Perspectives', *Canadian Public Administration* XVII, 2 (Summer 1975), pp. 189–215.

7. Because of this we part company with Sir Geoffrey Vickers' conception of regulation, quoted at the beginning of the chapter, which treated regulation as encompassing all modes of governing. To treat it so generally is to make it impossible to fully develop an understanding of the important features of other modes of governing. We do, however, share Vickers' view of the need to view the regulatory *process* as a series of transactions between governors and governed. See Vickers, *Freedom in a Rocking Boat.*

8. In this sense the theories of governmental expenditure growth and theories of the use of devices such as royal commissions and task forces as outputs and instruments of governing are related to theories of regulation. See Richard Bird, *The Growth of Government Spending in Canada* (Toronto, 1970) and V.S. Wilson, 'The Role of Royal Commissions and Task Forces', in Doern and Aucoin, *The Structures of Policy-Making in Canada*, Chapter 6.

9. Albert Breton has stressed the need to develop theory about particular forms or modes of regulation. See his *The Regulation of Private Economic Activity* (Montreal, 1976). See also Ontario Economic Council, *Government Regulation* (Toronto, 1978).

10. For an analysis of marketing boards see Grant Vinning, 'Regulation and Regulatory Modes in Canadian Agriculture', unpublished MA thesis, School of Public Administration, Carleton University, Ottawa, 1978. On professional self-regulation see C. Tuohy and A. Wolfson, 'The Political Economy of Professionalization: A Perspective', *Four Aspects of Professionalism* (Ottawa, 1977), pp. 41–90; and Peter Aucoin, *Public Accountability in the Governing Professions* (Toronto, 1978).

11. On the concept of positional policy, see P. Aucoin 'Public Policy Theory and Research', in Doern and Aucoin, *The Structures of Policy-Making in Canada*, Chapter 1.

12. See G. Bruce Doern, ed., *The Regulatory Process in Canada* (Toronto, 1978).

13. See Alfred E. Kahn, *The Economics of Regulation*, vols. I and II (New York, 1970). See also G.B. Reschenthaler, 'Regulatory Failure and Competition', *Canadian Public Administration* XIX, 3 (Fall 1976), pp. 466–86.

14. See Breton, *The Regulation of Private Economic Activity.*

15. See Albert Breton, *The Economic Theory of Representative Government* (Chicago, 1974) and George J. Stigler, *The Citizen and the State: Essays on Regulation* (Chicago, 1975).

16. Perhaps the main exception to this tendency is in the area of regulating tax changes where the private expenditure consequences are quite extensively assessed. These are now increasingly called 'tax expenditures'. See Allan Maslove, 'Tax Expenditures: The Other Side of Public Spending', paper presented to a conference on Forums and Methods for the Evaluation of Public Spending, School of Public Administration, Carleton University, Ottawa, 18–20 October 1978.

17. See G. Bruce Doern, 'The Political Economy of Regulating Occupational Health: The Ham and Beaudry Reports', *Canadian Public Administration* XX, 1 (Spring 1977), pp. 1–30.

18. David Bond, 'The Consumer and the Independent Regulatory Commission', paper presented to School of Public Administration, Carleton University, Ottawa, February 1973, pp. 2–3.

19. Roger Noll, *Reforming Regulation*. (Washington, DC, 1971), pp. 2–3.

20. John C. McManus, 'Federal Regulation of Transport in Canada ', paper prepared for Consumer Council of Canada, Ottawa, 1972, p. 10. See also R.A. Posner. 'Natural Monopoly and Its Regulation', *Stanford Law Review* XXI (1968–9), pp. 548–63.

21. McManus, 'Federal Regulation of Transport in Canada'.

22. See William M. Capron, ed., *Technological Change in Regulated Industries* (Washington, DC, 1971); Robert E. Babe, 'Public and Private Regulation of Cable Television: A Case Study of Technological Change and Relative Power', *Canadian Public Administration* XVII, 2 (Summer 1974), pp. 187–225; and Carl Beigie, 'An Economic Framework for Policy Action in Canadian Telecommunications', in H. Edward English, ed., *Telecommunications in Canada* (Toronto. 1973), pp. 37–212.

23. See Doern, 'The Political Economy of Regulating Occupational Health'.

24. See *Report of the Royal Commission on Corporate Concentration* (Ottawa, 1978), p. 395.

25. See Gilles Paquet, 'Regulation and Economic Performance', in Doern, *The Regulatory Process in Canada*, Chapter 2.

26. See Bernstein, *Regulating Business by Independent Commission*, and President's Advisory Council on Executive Organization, *A New Regulatory Framework*, Report on Selected Independent Regulatory Agencies (Washington, DC, 1971).

27. *Report of the Special Committee on Statutory Instruments,* House of Commons, *Votes and Proceedings*, 22 October 1969, pp. 1448–9.

28. Among other things the 'ministry system' has to be used to exert control over the regulatory agencies which are a part of a minister's portfolio. For further analysis, see John Langford, *Transportation in Transition* (Montreal, 1976).

29. R. Schultz, 'Regulation and Federal-Provincial Relations', in Doern, *The Regulatory Process in Canada*, Chapter 5.

30. Donald Smiley, *Canada in Question*, 2nd edn (Toronto, 1975).

31. See Lowi, 'Four Systems of Policy'. See also Paul Sabatier, 'Social Movements and Regulatory Agencies: Toward a More Adequate—and Less Pessimistic—Theory of "Clientele Capture"' *Policy Sciences* VI (1975), pp. 301–42.

32. See Doern, *The Regulatory Process in Canada*, Chapter 9.

33. Schultz, 'Regulation and Federal-Provincial Relations'.

34. H. Windsor and P. Aucoin, 'The Nova Scotia Public Utilities Board', in Doern, *The Regulatory Process in Canada*, Chapter 10.

35. For example, the Immigration Appeal Board is expected to be more passive and court-like because it is more exclusively adjudicatory than the CTC and the NEB. See Ian A. Hunter, *The Immigration Appeal Board* (Ottawa, 1976).

36. See K.C. Davis, *Discretionary Justice* (Baton Rouge, 1969).

37. See Paquet, 'Regulation and Economic Performance'.

38. See Harris, in Doern, *The Regulatory Process in Canada*. The contemporary Canadian example, *par excellence* on this point is the Anti-Inflation Board. Again, other numerous examples are given in Doern, ibid. (the managerial nature of Canadian regulatory boards like the CTC, NEB, and AECB are stressed in Part II). See also T. Abdel-Malek, and A.K. Sarker, 'An Analysis of the Effects of Phase II Guidelines of the Foreign Investment Review Act', *Canadian Public Policy* III, 1 (Winter 1977), pp. 36–49, and L. A. Skeoch, et al., *Dynamic Change and Accountability in the Canadian Market* (Ottawa, 1976).

39. See Vinning, 'Regulation and Regulatory Modes in Canadian Agriculture'.

40. For example, it is not at all clear where regulation fits into the analysis of the role of the state in work by Panitch and others. See Leo Panitch, *The Canadian State* (Toronto, 1977).

41. See Vinning, 'Regulation and Regulatory Modes in Canadian Agriculture'.

42. See Doern, 'The Political Economy of Regulating Occupational Health'.

43. See Doern, *The Regulatory Process in Canada,* chapters 7–11.

44. G. Bruce Doern, *Regulatory Processes and Jurisdictional Issues in the Regulation of Hazardous Substances in Canada*, Report prepared for the Science Council of Canada, Ottawa, August 1976, Chapter VII.

45. This is a more subjective view on my part but it is based on extensive discussions with officials of numerous departments and agencies over the past few years. The most conspicuous growth in numbers and salary has been in the policy and planning branches rather than in operating personnel. Recent concern about decentralization has also reflected, in part, concern about the weaknesses and neglect of field-level operating capability as opposed to so-called 'high' policy matters.

46. See Trebilcock, 'Must the Consumer Always Lose'.

47. John Willis, 'The McRuer Report: Lawyers' Values and Civil Servants' Values', *University of Toronto Law Journal* XVIII (1968), p. 353.

48. See Albert Abel, 'Appeals Against Administrative Decisions: In Search of a Basic Policy', *Canadian Public Administration* V, 1, p. 67.

49. See A. Roman, 'Regulation and Legal Processes', in Doern, *The Regulatory Process in Canada*, Chapter 3.

50. On the methodological limitations of the analysis of 'elites' see Lewis J. Edinger and Donald D. Searing, 'Social Background in Elite Analysis', *American Political Science Review* LVI (1967), pp. 428–45, and Robert D. Putnam, *The Beliefs of Politicians* (New Haven, 1973).

51. Andrew and Pelletier, in Doern, *The Regulatory Process in Canada*, Chapter 6.

52. Doern ed., *The Regulatory Process in Canada*, Chapter 11.

53. For an initial effort at developing an inventory of Canadian agencies, see L. Brown-John, 'Regulatory Policy Making', paper presented to Annual Meeting, Canadian Political Science Association, Edmonton, June 1975.

54. Bernstein, *Regulating Business by Independent Commission*.

55. See Louis Jaffe, 'The Independent Agency—A New Scapegoat', *Yale Law Journal* LXV (1956), pp. 1068–76; T. Lowi, *The End of Liberalism* (New York, 1969), Chapter 5; and Sabatier, 'Social Movements and Regulatory Agencies', pp. 301–42.

56. Sabatier, 'Social Movements and Regulatory Agencies', p. 305.

57. Ibid.

58. We have earlier referred to 'public interest' theory and to models of organizational sub-systems by Katz and Kahn and by Perrow as potentially useful ways to examine agency behaviour. See Doern, et al., 'The Structure and Behaviour of Canadian Regulatory Boards and Commissions' pp. 189–215.

59. Thus the Department of Consumer and Corporate Affairs, the Secretary of State Department, and the Department of Indian Affairs and Northern Development have developed funding programs to aid public participation in their respective policy domains.

60. See Doern, *The Regulatory Process in Canada,* chapters 10 and 11. Other analyses have suggested how the NEB is part of what we have called the managerial form of regulatory apparatus. See Ian McDougall, 'The Canadian National Energy Board: Economic "Jurisprudence" in the National Interest or Symbolic Reassurance', *Alberta Law Review* XI, 2 (1973), pp. 327–82; and John N. McDougall, 'Oil and Gas in Canadian Energy Policy', in Doern and Wilson, *Issues in Canadian Public Policy,* pp. 115–36.

61. See Doern, *The Regulatory Process in Canada,* Chapter 7. For further analysis of the CTC's role in the transportation-policy process see Langford, *Transportation in Transition*. Given the CTC's modal committees, it may be more meaningful to assess the clientele-capture thesis in relation to each committee separately.

62. See Doern, *The Regulatory Process in Canada,* Chapter 6. See also Ian Roger, 'Are There Too Many Career Bureaucrats Among Members of the National Energy Board?' *The Globe and Mail,* 23 January 1975, p. 134.

63. See H. Janisch, Agency Study, *The Canadian Transport Commission* (Ottawa, September 1974), pp. 86–92.

9

From *Canadian Crown Corporations*

C.A. Ashley and R.G.H. Smails

Survey of the Field

In Canada, a Crown corporation is an institution with corporate form brought into existence by action of the Government of Canada[1] to serve a public function. This definition is, perhaps, as satisfactory as any likely to be put forward. Part VIII of the Financial Administration Act, which is reproduced as an appendix to this study, states: 'In this Part . . . "Crown corporation" means a corporation that is ultimately accountable, through a Minister, to Parliament for the conduct of its affairs. . . .' This definition has been rejected on the grounds that its meaning is uncertain: 'through a Minister' may be taken as meaning either that the minister has a responsibility for the conduct of the corporation or that he acts merely as a messenger. As will be seen later, one corporation may be subject to complete control by a minister, while another may be entirely independent of ministerial control; other corporations are found between these two extremes.

The reasons for setting up Crown corporations were well stated by Lord Morrison of Lambeth.

> If we establish the public corporation, it must be for certain reasons. What are they? They are that we seek to combine the principle of public accountability, of a consciousness on the part of the undertaking that it is working for the nation and not for sectional interests, with the liveliness, initiative, and a considerable degree of the freedom of a quick-moving and progressive business enterprise. Either that is the case for the public corporation, or there is no case at all.[2]

The reasons for setting up a particular Crown corporation are, of course, another thing.

The only political party in Canada that has favoured public ownership as a main instrument of economic policy is the New Democratic Party (and its predecessors), and it has never formed the government of Canada, whereas in Britain such a party has formed the government. Labour unions here have not seriously sought direct political power, nor a share in the day-to-day management of industry, whereas in

C.A. Ashley and R.G.H. Smails, *Canadian Crown Corporations* (Toronto: The Macmillan Company of Canada Limited, 1965).

Britain they have been an important factor in the Socialist party, and at one time aimed at sharing in the management of publicly owned industries. However, the acts passed under Socialist governments in Britain for the nationalization of industries have not provided for trade union representation on the boards of management, and trade union officials who have been appointed to such boards have severed their union affiliation. In both countries, Conservative and Liberal parties have resorted to public ownership, not for doctrinaire reasons, but to carry out particular functions. During the Second World War a large number of Crown corporations were established in Canada because C.D. Howe, as Minister of Munitions and Supply, was of the opinion —probably quite rightly—that this was the most effective way of getting certain goods produced quickly. After the war, a flood of legislation was passed in Britain to nationalize key industries and services. Probably no such extensive nationalization has taken place in so short a time elsewhere without a revolutionary change in the system of government.

J.E. Hodgetts suggests[3] that the first Crown corporation in Canada was the Board of Works, formed in 1841; it became a department of government in 1846. The first annual report of the Nova Scotia Railway Company appeared in 1859,[4] and a number of harbour boards were set up as Crown corporations before Confederation; so we are not dealing with a new phenomenon. The traditional method of creating a Crown corporation is by special act, but the amendment of the Department of Munitions and Supply Act in 1940 provided that the minister might procure the incorporation of companies under the Companies Act and delegate powers and duties to them. Twenty-eight such Crown corporations were incorporated for war purposes;[5] of these Eldorado Mining and Refining Limited and Polymer Corporation Limited are still operating. Some corporations created by special act were given power to procure the incorporation of subsidiaries under the Companies Act and, as will be seen later, still have this power, although they have not exercised it for many years. Under the Defence Production Act, the minister still has power to procure incorporation under the Companies Act, subject to approval of the Governor in Council. This is a very undesirable state of affairs, for Crown corporations could be incorporated without Parliament's being made aware of it, or having control over the purposes for which they were created and the form of organization and management under which they were to be operated: matters determined by their letters patent and bylaws, which are not readily obtainable. Unless some member became aware of the incorporation of such a corporation and asked a question in the House, it is possible that no discussion would take place until some item in respect of the corporation appeared in the estimates.[6] In 1946 a member of the House drew attention to the fact that incorporation under the Companies Act gives wide and undesirable ancillary powers. [7]

The Financial Administration Act provides for the classification of Crown corporations as departmental, agency, or proprietary; in addition there are some unclassified corporations. Each of these types of corporations is dealt with later. Writing of experience in Britain, where some of the problems are similar to those in Canada, Lord Citrine says: 'The broad structure of the nationalized industries has been laid down by Parliament in the separate Acts. The first thing that strikes the observer is their diversity.'[8] The diversity is even greater in Canada, for there is no equivalent in Britain of the departmental corporations or the agency corporations of Canada. The diversity of structure is the natural result of the diversity of functions, and any attempt to impose a set pattern, even on corporations of the same class, would serve no useful purpose and would create endless difficulties. There are, however, occasions when people, even ministers, refer to Crown corporations in general when they are thinking only of *some* Crown corporations, usually the large proprietary together with the large unclassified corporations. These include the corporations enjoying the greatest degree of independence.

The New Democratic Party has consistently favoured the use of Crown corporations for the conduct of the business of key industries and services. Liberal governments have created most of the Crown corporations. (If those created for war purposes but no longer in existence are included, this party has created a large majority of them.) Conservative governments passed the original legislation in respect of four of the most important Crown corporations (Canadian National Railways, Bank of Canada, Canadian Broadcasting Corporation, and Canadian Wheat Board), but the party has been critical of this form of organization and equivocal in its attitude. A Conservative member said in the House in 1949: 'The official opposition does not believe in Crown corporations. We think that is one method of getting away from control by Parliament.'[9] This member was, a few years later, a member of the Diefenbaker cabinet which was responsible for the creation of an entirely new Crown corporation (Canadian World Exhibition Corporation), and for a large increase in the operations of a number of Crown corporations, including the one that provoked the speech just quoted, and was accused by the new 'official opposition' of frustrating the efforts of Parliament to exercise control. The same administration was accused of '. . . doing its best to tear down the Crown corporations of the country'. The leader of the New Democratic Party said: 'I have good reason to be suspicious. When I see what the government has done to the Canadian Broadcasting Corporation, which they have undermined in the interests of the private broadcasting network; when I see what they have done to the TCA, which they have sabotaged in the interests of Canadian Pacific Airlines; when I see what they have been doing to the Canadian National Railway . . .' (He was interrupted and did not continue this line of thought.)[10] The conclusion one arrives at is that no government has formulated any consistent over-all policy, acceptable to all its party, in respect of Crown corporations.

'It has been pointed out by nearly all the writers that government enterprise is found where for some reason private enterprise is found wanting. The usual condition where this occurs is the existence of some public need having commercial characteristics which private enterprise is unwilling to fill, should not be expected to fill or is unsuitable to fill . . .'[11] The alternative to the Crown corporation for operating government enterprise is the government department.[12] The reasons for preferring the Crown corporation are, J.H. Perry writes, manifold and confusing.

> Starting with the proposition that government departments are neither by structure nor tradition designed for carrying on commercial activities it is not

unexpected that governments would turn to some other form of organization for this purpose. The commercial world is said to require greater initiative, flexibility, independence and freedom from redtape than can be assured in a government department, and the separate board or corporation achieves this end, both in day-to-day operations and in the hiring of staff. The desire to remove a function from politics and to attract business men who are familiar with the corporate entity . . . and incidentally to pay them salaries higher than the civil service level—are also given as reasons.[13]

The case against the use of a department of government to operate government enterprise has been stated by J.A Corry.

The weaknesses of direct government or municipal operation of public utilities became clear early in the century. They fall into two distinct types. There are those arising from the traditional inflexibility of government administration and there is a smaller but, if anything, more serious group, due to the baneful intrusion of political partisanship in the affairs of government. Any human organization operating on such a scale that policy must be executed by subordinates is necessarily cursed with the rigidity of rules. Red tape was the essential discovery of the first despot who extended his sway beyond the village. Constitutional government is the perfection of that discovery—how to manipulate rolls of it that are longer and redder. Wherever men have learned to govern their rulers, this incubus has weighed heavily on state administration. Tradition grows immensely strong here, feeding on the ceremonial of state, and new tasks have to be performed in old ways. So when governments begin to operate public utilities, they turn the dynamics of trade into the statics of routine administration. The illogical situation forced into the logical category, the impersonal touch in personal contacts, the curious operation of prestige incentives, the sad procession of files to the last pigeon hole, and the budgetary system of accounting, audit and finance all tend to make government operation of commercial undertakings cumbrous and expensive. In large part, these difficulties are structural. As such they are not a reproach to the efficiency of a civil service nor are they to be allowed to obscure the steady improvement in the art of public administration.[14]

The report of the Liberal Industrial Inquiry of 1928 in the United Kingdom stated:

. . . we are inclined to think that it would have been better if in the first instance the post office, telephones and telegraphs had been in the hands of an *ad hoc* administrative body detached from the central administration. There are weighty arguments for requiring government undertakings to be conducted in a form analogous to that of joint-stock companies, the capital of which is owned and the directors appointed by the state. This is the present method of administering, for example, the Belgian and German railways and the German post office. Amongst its advantages are a greater detachment from politics and from political infiuence.[15]

Detachment from politics is difficult to define. When speaking of it in this context, people usually mean detachment from constant haggling for partisan purposes. But Crown corporations (unless they enjoy the exceptional freedom of the Canada Council) cannot be entirely detached from politics in a wider and more respectable sense. They are brought into being by a government which determines the purpose to be served, the form of administration, and the composition of the management; they perform a public function. 'Politics involves policy, and if the cabinet is to remain responsible for policy an important sector of the economy run by a government corporation cannot be taken out of politics.'[16] Lord Citrine writes: 'With the ordinary private company, the Annual Accounts are usually regarded as providing an efficiency test, but where monopolies are concerned, whether they be private or public, they would not be accepted in any responsible quarters as the sole test of efficiency.'[17] But some means are necessary by which Parliament can judge whether a Crown corporation is performing the task assigned to it with reasonable efficiency.

The degree of independence enjoyed by the boards of Crown corporations depends to some extent on the financial control exercised over them, particularly if they need appropriations by Parliament to carry out their policies. It also depends to some extent on the tenure of office of the chief executive and other members of the board and, of course, on the personal relations between the board and the minister and his deputy minister.

The Companies Act does not give shareholders power to remove a director during his term of office. However, the letters patent of some Crown corporations incorporated under that act (e.g., Polymer Corporation Limited) do confer this power. The only formality involved would be the calling of a special meeting of shareholders. The Defence Production Act, which gives the minister power, with the approval of the Governor in Council, to procure the incorporation of Crown corporations under the Companies Act, also provides that he shall have the power to remove any directors or officers of such corporations and appoint others in their place.

The tenure of members of the boards of other corporations is stated later, but a considerable number of the members hold office at pleasure, and it can be argued that under these circumstances it is difficult for the government to escape responsibility for their actions. Some Crown corporations have boards consisting wholly or partly of officials of government departments. If the former, the government must necessarily be held directly responsible in the same way as it is responsible for the departments; if the latter, then the degree of responsibility is more difficult to determine. An official of the Department of Finance is a non-voting member of the board of the Bank of Canada. The function he was intended to perform when the act was passed could probably be better carried out by a requirement that the minutes of meetings of the board and of its executive committee should be submitted to the minister. There are, as shown later, cogent reasons why departmental officials should not serve on the boards of Crown corporations.

To whatever extent the minister or the government exercises control over

Crown corporations, their actions, except as specifically provided for by statute, should be known by Parliament and subject to question and examination. This form of control would be additional to the general right of question and examination which can, however, be limited by the statutes passed by Parliament to create individual corporations. To provide corporations with a certain degree of independence by act of Parliament, and then to complain—endlessly—of their acting within that degree of independence is senseless.[18]

As for the power of the minister or the government to exercise control, J.W. Dafoe wrote: '. . . where the power of intervention is exercised it should be in the open and a matter of public record for the information of the people. The necessity of intervention in the interests of the community must be established.'[19] In the United Kingdom, ministerial directives to the nationalized industries are all made public. After the general election in Canada in 1963, the following appeared in the Toronto *Globe and Mail:* 'It has been customary in the past for [advertising] agencies handling the accounts of government departments or Crown corporations to change with the fortunes of the political parties. There are no indications that things will be different this time.'[20] Do the Crown corporations receive directives on advertising contracts?

The operations of some Crown corporations have an appreciable effect on the economy of the country, and directives by the minister, made public, may be desirable, for the boards of corporations are not in a position to judge the effect of their policy on the economy as a whole. The difficulties, however, may be very great, as has been seen in the United Kingdom, where British Overseas Airways Corporation has twice received instructions from the minister as to the type of aircraft to purchase, with heavy loss resulting to the corporation.[21] Faced with the making of a decision in 1963 on the type of plane to order for future use, and the fact that attempts were being made to influence public opinion on a regional basis on the question, Trans-Canada Air Lines reported its decision to the minister. The cabinet decided not to interfere with the decision made by the corporation.[22] The president of Eldorado Mining and Refining Limited stated in 1961 that any major change in the operations of its subsidiary, Northern Transportation Company Limited, would be referred to the government.[23] There was a long discussion in 1935 about the purchase of supplies by Canadian National Railways, to be paid for out of the Unemployment Relief Fund. It appeared that the transaction was at least suggested by the government, and the opposition was annoyed that particulars of the contracts had been refused as being a matter of internal management of the corporation.[24] From time to time members of the House have urged that Crown corporations should 'buy Canadian', and the question arises whether, in the absence of a directive, the corporations should do this or buy in the cheapest market. 'Crown corporations have multiplied in the past few years and have increased in importance to the point where their purchasing impact has become of major importance. These Crown companies need pay no attention to the policy of the government, but can set their own policy, and in many cases this policy does not conform to either the policy of this government or of previous governments in regard to a Canadian preference.'[25]

The Canada Council Act states that the council is not an agent of the Crown.

The National Productivity Council was not an agent of the Crown, but its successor, the Economic Council of Canada, is stated by its act to be an agent of the Crown. All other Crown corporations are agents of the Crown. The method by which legal proceedings are taken by or against the Crown is different from that in respect of other persons; the actions are brought in the Exchequer Court and certain time limits are imposed. This is true also of agents of the Crown unless they have been put into the position of ordinary persons by statute, as most Crown corporations have.[26] The statutes concerned are the individual acts setting up particular corporations, and the Government Companies Operation Act, which applies to all Crown corporations incorporated under the Companies Act. The relevant section of that act states: 'Actions, suits or other legal proceedings in respect of any right or obligation acquired or incurred by a Company on behalf of Her Majesty, whether in its name or the name of Her Majesty, may be brought or taken by or against the Company in the name of the Company in any court that would have jurisdiction if the Company were not an agent of Her Majesty.' Provisions to this effect are found in the acts governing the other Crown corporations except for five departmental and two agency corporations.[27]

> Under the Financial Administration Act all agency and proprietary corporations prepare annual capital budgets which are submitted to the appropriate minister and the Minister of Finance for their recommendation to the Governor in Council and after approval by council are laid before parliament. These capital budgets are not normally submitted in great detail. Major projects or expenditures are set out, including estimates of proposed capital expenditures for land, buildings, plant and equipment, increases in working capital, and amounts required for redeeming maturing indebtedness, and, in the case of those companies that administer lending programmes, the amount required for loans. An estimate is usually made of the overall cost of the programme, of the estimated commitments for future years, and of the cash required for the year under review. Some indication is also given of the sources from which the funds required will be obtained. The approval of the budget does not constitute an authority for the corporation to borrow nor does it signify an undertaking on the part of the government to lend or to guarantee loans. These powers must be specifically granted by parliament, either annually or in a general continuing authority and the terms are usually subject to the approval of the Governor in Council.
>
> Agency corporations are also required to submit their operating budgets for the approval of the two ministers but there is no specific requirement to lay these before parliament. Proprietary corporations generally are not required to submit operating budgets for the approval of ministers or the Governor in Council or for tabling in parliament, presumably on the ground that they should be freer than agency bodies in the management of their own affairs. However, there are exceptions. The Canadian National Railways and the Canadian Broadcasting Corporation are required to submit both their operating and capital budgets to parliament. In addition, the Canadian Broadcasting

Corporation is required every five years to submit to the two ministers for transmission to the Governor in Council a five year capital programme together with a forecast of the effect of the programme on the Corporation's operating requirements.

However, the nature and magnitude of operations of both agency and proprietary corporations are matters of concern to the House of Commons when funds are sought to cover operating deficits and are appropriate subjects for criticism and debate when the estimate items are under consideration.[28]

The author of this quotation, who is Comptroller of the Treasury, has kindly amplified it in a letter:

The capital budgets of Crown corporations annually laid before Parliament concern proposals for the current year only. However, those corporations which receive direct assistance by means of grants, etc., are presently required to submit a three-year forecast of requirements to the Treasury Board for consideration when the Main Estimates of expenditure are being prepared. Such corporations would include Atomic Energy of Canada Limited, Canadian Arsenals Limited, National Harbours Board and the Canadian Broadcasting Corporation. In addition to the CNR and the Canadian Wheat Board, Polymer Corporation receives financial accommodation from public sources. Certain other corporations, such as the St Lawrence Seaway Authority, may borrow publicly, but such authority has never been used.

The funds used by Crown corporations are drawn from a variety of sources. The special act setting up a corporation may specify how funds may be obtained from the government; appropriations may be made by Parliament through the Estimates or, for Canadian National Railways, by annual enactment; or Parliament may authorize government advances. Some corporations which show a profit on operations are permitted to retain their surplus, and those corporations that own fixed assets may have funds available through the annual provision made for depreciation. Section 82 of the Financial Administration Act allows the Minister of Finance, at the request of the minister and with the approval of the Governor in Council, to make limited loans to corporations for working capital, repayable within a year. Such loans have to be reported to Parliament. The limit set in this act may be exceeded for those corporations whose special acts make provision for larger advances.

In the accounts given of individual Crown corporations, it will be seen that some of them are required by statute to hand over surplus cash to the Receiver General of Canada each year, and that others have been required to do so as provided in the Financial Administration Act. That act also provides for the voluntary deposit of funds, at interest, with the Receiver General. Some corporations are allowed to invest surplus cash in government securities, a practice criticized by the Royal Commission on Government Organization on the grounds that there is a risk of loss to the corporations through fluctuations in market values, and because the national debt is overstated as a result; deposit with the Receiver General was stated in the

Commission's report to be preferable.[29] A further criticism by the Commission was that some corporations had very large sums on deposit with chartered banks, and that a large proportion of these deposits were not interest bearing.[30] It is remarkable that, considering the time the House and its committees have spent on Crown corporations, this point does not appear to have been discussed.

An objection to the maintenance of large funds by corporations is that they may be able to expand operations without Parliament's being aware of it because no appropriation is called for. This point has been noticed.[31] Members would, of course, be aware of what was being done if they examined the capital budgets, which are tabled in Parliament.

The Crown is not subject to taxation, nor are its agents, unless the immunity is removed by statute; this is true of federal, provincial, and municipal taxes. Complaints having long been made that certain Crown corporations benefited from municipal services but made no contribution towards them, the government announced in 1949 that it had authorized Crown corporations to make agreements for the payment of allowances in lieu of taxes to municipalities;[32] this move was followed by an Order in Council instructing the corporations to make such agreements.[33] The Minister of Finance emphasized the point that these allowances were *ex gratia* payments;[34] they have continued to be paid.

Nothing was done in respect of provincial taxation of Crown corporations in general until 1962,[35] when the government put forward a motion to consider the introduction of a bill to deal with the matter, but did not persist;[36] the same thing happened in 1962–3.[37] The new government in 1963 got a first reading of the bill late in the session;[38] in the next session the bill was introduced again and was carried through.[39] The act provides for the payment of sales and gasoline taxes and motor vehicle licence fees by all Crown corporations in Schedules C and D of the Financial Administration Act, except Canadian Arsenals Limited, Crown Assets Disposal Corporation, and Defence Construction Limited (excluded because their function is almost entirely to provide service for government departments), and by the Bank of Canada, Canadian Wheat Board, Industrial Development Bank, Northern Ontario Pipe Line Crown Corporation, Seaway International Bridge Corporation Limited, and the Canada Council. The last but one of these took the place of Cornwall International Bridge Company Limited. As the Canada Council is not an agent of the Crown it may not have been necessary to include it in the schedule.

As for federal taxes, an amendment to the Income Tax Act was passed in 1952 to make all the Crown corporations in Schedule D of the Financial Administration Act liable for income tax. The government stated that the effect would be to make possible a better or more accurate comparison of the relative efficiency of these Crown corporations and privately owned companies operating in the same field,[40] but did not explain why a comparison before charging income tax was less effective. The official opposition welcomed the measure, but a private member suggested that there was something anomalous in taxation by a state of its own agencies. 'This will undoubtedly require more red tape, more bureaucratic control and more civil servants; it will increase the cost of administration. In a word, it will increase the taxpayer's burden and nothing more.'[41] There was something more: the effect on those Crown corporations liable to the tax and operated profitably would be for them to have less in liquid resources available for expansion without further appropriations by Parliament. On the disposition of surplus moneys of Crown corporations, the Comptroller of the Treasury writes:

> Agency corporations are usually required to surrender their profits to the Receiver General. The Canadian Commercial Corporation, which may retain for its own purposes all moneys received in the course of its business, is an exception, although the Minister of Defence Production may direct it to pay over to the Receiver General any of the moneys administered by it that he considers to be in excess of requirements.
>
> The proprietary corporations usually have a greater degree of freedom in using their own funds, and many are permitted to retain their profits. However, the practices followed differ from corporation to corporation. Canadian Overseas Telecommunication Corporation, Eldorado Mining and Refining Limited, Polymer Corporation Limited, and Trans-Canada Air Lines retain their profits but some, following commercial practice, declare dividends and pay these to the Receiver General. Central Mortgage and Housing Corporation, the Farm Credit Corporation and the Bank of Canada may retain their earnings to establish reserve funds, but when the statutory limits of these have been reached all additional earnings are payable to the Receiver General. The Northern Canada Power Commission may retain its surplus earnings to be used, subject to the approval of the Governor in Council, in the reduction of rates to consumers, but the Canadian National Railways pays any annual profits to the Receiver General. The Export Credits Insurance Corporation must pay excess moneys to the Receiver General on demand. The Financial Administration Act contains a variation of this provision, whereby the Minister of Finance and the appropriate minister, with the approval of the Governor in Council, may require a corporation to pay to the Receiver General any moneys considered to be in excess of requirements, to be used to discharge any debt owing by the corporation to the Crown, or to be applied as revenues of Canada. This provision, however, is operative only when it is not inconsistent with any legislation applicable to a corporation. Moreover, as the latter part is in effect an authority for the Governor in Council to require the declaration of a dividend, it is probably not intended to be used except under exceptional circumstances.[42]

All Crown corporations, with the exception of most of the departmental corporations, whose employees are covered by the Public Service Superannuation Act, have freedom in the appointment of employees and are not subject to the Civil Service Act. They have power to set up schemes for superannuation of employees, subject to approval by the Governor in Council. Those Crown corporations with employees doing work similar to that of unionized workers in private enterprise have had to negotiate with trade unions. Whether other employees could form unions was in doubt, and difficulties arose, particularly in the Canadian Broadcasting Corporation.[43] In 1948, the Industrial Relations and Disputes Investigation Act put the employees of Crown corporations in the same position as employees in private enterprise, unless excluded from the provisions of the act by the Governor in Council. The employees of Canadian Arsenals Limited and National Research Council have been so excluded.[44]

In 1936, an amendment to its act made the Bank of Canada a 'mixed' corporation; that is to say, its shares were held partly by the government and partly by the general public; some of its directors were appointed by the Governor in Council and the others by the outside shareholders. This arrangement persisted for only a short time before a further amendment resulted in all the shares being held by the government. Before the creation of Trans-Canada Air Lines, the government hoped that a mixed corporation would be formed, but this proved to be impracticable at that time; the act still provides for the general public to be allowed to acquire shares, but there seems little likelihood of its happening.

The difficulty with a mixed corporation is to decide what rights the government shall have to interfere with the management in the public interest, and what forms of control shall be exercised by Parliament. This form of corporation has been used, apparently with reasonable success, in Sweden.[45] Examples are also found in France, Germany, and Italy; in many parts of Europe, publicly owned enterprises seem to be freer from criticism and obstruction than in Canada and the United Kingdom.[46]

The corporate form of organization invites the drawing of parallels between Crown corporations and ordinary limited companies. The people of Canada, it has often been stated, are the shareholders of Crown corporations, and members of the House are shareholders' proxies. Members have put this point of view forward particularly to justify their demands for information on the internal management of such large corporations as Canadian National Railways and the Canadian Broadcasting Corporation.[47] A comparison between publicly owned and privately owned corporations shows, however, that the affairs of the former are submitted to far greater scrutiny than those of the latter. The annual general meeting of a privately owned company seldom lasts for more than an hour or so, and its chairman is part of the management. The affairs of a Crown corporation may be discussed in the House with no member of the management present, and in a committee of the House, with the chief executive officer appearing as a witness for days on end.[48]

NOTES

1. That is, the federal government. Corporations set up by the provinces are not dealt with in this study.
2. *Government and Parliament,* p. 292.
3. *Proceedings of Fifth Annual Conference of Institute of Public Administration of Canada,* p. 389.
4. G.R. Stevens, *Canadian National Railways,* vol. I, p. 163.
5. J. de N. Kennedy, *History of the Department of Munitions and Supply,* vol. I, p. 286 ff.

6. See views of D.M. Fleming, *House of Commons Debates,* 1946, p. 2158.

7. *Minutes of Public Accounts Committee,* 1951, p. 130.

8. *Public Administration,* vol. XXIX, p. 319.

9. *House of Commons Debates,* 1949 (Second Session), p. 1035.

10. See *House of Commons Debates,* 1960–1, pp. 7252–3; 1962, p. 2954; 1962–3, p. 1958.

11. J.H. Perry, *Proceedings of Eighth Annual Conference of Institute of Public Administration of Canada,* p. 146.

12. Or, particularly for public utilities in the United States of America, private enterprise regulated by the government or some public body set up for that purpose.

13. Op. cit., p. 147.

14. *Canadian Journal of Economics and Political Science* II, 3, p. 304.

15. *Britain's Industrial Future,* p. 76.

16. J.E. Hodgetts, *Proceedings of Fifth Annual Conference of Institute of Public Administration of Canada,* p. 395. See also G.P. de T. Glazebrook, *A History of Transportation in Canada,* vol. II, p. 216–9.

17. *Public Administration* XXIX, p. 323.

18. See, for example, *House of Commons Debates,* 1952–3, pp. 1365–6.

19. *Canadian Journal of Economics and Political Science* II, 3, p. 329; see also p. 320.

20. April 11, 1963.

21. Parliament and the press were giving daily attention to this in July 1964.

22. See postscript to section on Trans-Canada Air Lines.

23. *Minutes of Committee on Research,* 1960–1, p. 473.

24. *House of Commons Debates,* 1935, pp. 1200, 2679, 2728 ff.

25. *House of Commons Debates,* 1960–1, p. 1513.

26. See D.W. Mundell, *Remedies against the Crown.* Special Lectures of the Law Society of Upper Canada, 1961, pp. 149–82.

27. See later sections dealing with these classes of Crown corporations.

28. H.R. Balls, in *Indian Journal of Economics,* January 1960, pp. 228–9.

29. *Report,* vol. I, pp. 218–9.

30. Ibid., pp. 216–7.

31. e.g., *Minutes of Public Accounts Committee,* 1951, p. 131.

32. *House of Commons Debates,* 1949 (Second Session), p. 1706.

33. *House of Commons Debates.* 1950, p. 4217.

34. *House of Commons Debates,* 1951, p. 4224.

35. The Bank of Canada was reported to be paying provincial taxes earlier, *House of Commons Debates,* 1964, p. 3196.

36. *House of Commons Debates,* 1962, pp. 1556–8.

37. *House of Commons Debates,* 1962–3, p. 40.

38. *House of Commons Debates,* 1963, p. 5519.

39. Crown Corporations (Provincial Taxes and Fees) Act.

40. *House of Commons Debates,* 1952, pp. 2092–3. Possibly only four corporations were likely to be operated at a profit and also to be in competition with private enterprise.

41. Ibid., p. 1763.

42. H.R. Balls, op. cit., pp. 232–3.

43. *House of Commons Debates,* 1941, pp. 3990 and 3994–5; *Minutes of Radio Broadcasting*

Committee, 1943, pp. 15–16.

44. A.H. Hanson, ed., *Public Enterprise,* p. 95.

45. D.V.Verney, *Public Enterprise in Sweden* (Liverpool: Liverpool University Press, 1959), p. 42 ff.

46. P. Lowell, in *Lessons of Public Enterprise,* ed. M. Shanks, pp. 283 ff. See also W.A. Robson, *Nationalized Industry and Public Ownership,* p. 492.

47. *House of Commons Debates,* 1920, p. 4194; 1924, p. 2632. See also L.D. Musolf, *Public Ownership and Accountability,* pp. 28–9.

48. See views expressed by Lord Heyworth in *Public Administration* XXXI, p. 270; see also XXIX, p. 323 ff. and XXX, p. 27 ff.

Boards of Corporations

Parliament has not paid much attention to the composition of the boards of Crown corporations except to push local interests and to charge the government of the day with making political appointments. On one occasion, the Public Accounts Committee noted in its report that the composition of boards varied widely.

> A year ago when the committee had Crown Assets Disposal Corporation before it for examination it learned that the corporation's directors were members of the public service, while in the case of Export Credits Insurance Corporation and the other corporations examined there was a mixed board of directors, half from the public service and half from private industry. When the committee examined Polymer Corporation Limited this year, it learned that all the directors were from private industry. This variation raises the question as to what is the most desirable way of organizing Crown corporations' directorates in given sets of circumstances so as to facilitate their operation to the greatest possible extent along commercial lines, while at the same time retaining an appropriate measure of ministerial and parliamentary control.[1]

Many opinions have been expressed in Canada and elsewhere on the question of how members of the boards of Crown corporations, or of nationalized industries, should be appointed, and what kind of member should be sought. The functions of the boards are varied, and there is no reason why the policy in making appointments should be the same for different corporations. In the separate studies of Crown corporations to be found later, the procedure is stated, and in those and elsewhere in this book opinions that have been advanced are mentioned. The general question is now under discussion.

As in private enterprise,[2] it is important that a board should be harmonious in its deliberations. This makes it difficult to draw members from representative bodies or groups, such as producers, consumers, and employees. A Committee of Inquiry into the British Broadcasting Corporation 'rejected the suggestion that the governors should represent the various interests concerned with broadcasting because this might lead to a divided allegiance. The governors should, it recommended, be persons of judgment and independence, who would inspire public confidence.'[3] The Port of London Authority, however, has a long and successful history with representative members. Advisory councils have been used more extensively in the United Kingdom than in Canada to forward the interests of particular groups. In Canada, some of the acts incorporating Crown corporations have forbidden the appointment of members affiliated with certain interests; others have required it. The matter of public confidence is much more important when services are being provided for the general public than when services or goods are being supplied for a limited market.

In Canada there has not been, as there was for a time in England, any body of opinion strongly in favour of employee or labour representation on boards. The few representatives of labour on boards have been appointed by the Governor in Council, and no suggestion appears to have been made of disharmonies having arisen on the boards. A motion for the direct appointment by employees of two members of the board of Canadian National Railways on its formation was defeated.[4] The president of Viceroy Aircraft Limited, a wartime Crown corporation, resigned when the government initiated a policy of requiring at least one representative of organized labour on each board of that type of corporation. He stated that in accepting his position he had done so with the understanding that he would have freedom in choosing members of his board.[5] It was stated in the United Kingdom that representatives of labour on boards were placed in an intolerable position: '. . . no man can act as an employer one day and as his own employee the next day';[6] but this objection is not valid if a person is chosen by the government from organized labour to serve on a board of which he is not an employee.

Lord Simon of Wythenshawe proposed that appointments to a board should be made only after full consultation with the chairman (he had in mind boards whose chairman was not the chief executive officer) and with acceptance by the board,[7] and something analogous to this procedure is to be found in some Crown corporations in Canada. It was stated by the president of Polymer Corporation Limited that when vacancies on the board occurred, '. . . the board would consider the matter and make a recommendation to the Minister of Defence Production, usually in the form of recommendations one, two, three, and the Minister of Defence Production has then acted on that recommendation.'[8]

A private bill was introduced in the House to enable the government to appoint members of the House to boards of Crown corporations. 'The House of Commons and the parliamentary committees would then be better informed on the decisions taken by the management of the Crown corporations. At the same time, certain prejudices entertained by the public when some of these Crown corporations show deficits would be removed.'[9] A very optimistic statement! Such appointments would almost inevitably be political. Would the member on a board act mainly as a watchdog, or would he take a full share in the board's activities? If the former, he would hamper the management; if the latter, he would probably do little to satisfy the inquisitive propensities of the opposition. His relations with the minister, who would probably recommend his appointment, would not be very happy if he started to inform the House and its committees of matters which ministers have consistently refused to disclose.

The clashing interests of different geographic regions of Canada are a constant source of trouble and appear to have been introduced artificially and gratuitously into the affairs of some Crown corporations. Many instances are reported and recorded elsewhere in this study. If a member is appointed with the avowed purpose of giving representation to a particular area, he is presumably expected to place before the board any regional needs or points of view, but these have probably already been brought to the attention of the board by members of the House, who tend to exaggerate such things. In some corporations, local interests do not arise, but that does not always prevent clamour for representation. Presumably, the appointment of members from places far distant from headquarters adds to the cost, but that would be a small matter if any benefits resulted. The Bank of Canada Act provides for regional representation on the board of the bank, and one of the reasons for increasing the number of directors of Trans-Canada Air Lines in 1953 was to provide for representation from Winnipeg.[10] In the same year, the Minister of Transport said that the directors of Canadian National Railways gave a pretty good geographical representation.[11] This point was argued in relation to the original broadcasting commission:

> In the provision for appointing the board we are at once impressed by the fact that the delegation of an important sector of public policy to an independent agency does not automatically solve the problem of keeping politics out of administration. The board has supplanted the cabinet as policymaker in the field of radio broadcasting, hence it has been deliberately organized to give representation to the same sort of interests that have plagued prime ministers in forming their cabinets. The act provides for the appointment of nine governors to give representation to the 'principal geographic divisions of Canada'. In addition, the board, like the cabinet, has also been expected to give representation to important functional interests, such as labour and agriculture.[12]

When the Bank of Canada was formed, R.B. Bennett, the Prime Minister, said: 'Shall men be appointed to the bank because they reside in a particular locality? Shall men be appointed to the bank because of their religion? —politics? —race?'[13]

More serious than the problem of regional representation is that of making political appointments.

> I think it is important that, as members of Parliament, we should give much closer attention to appointments to boards of directors of Crown corporations. It seems that there is a lack of good sense or good business judgment exhibited in the picking of directors of these companies. It would appear that in the case of one member of the board . . . the appointment depended entirely on the size of the contribution made to a candidate during the last election campaign.[14]

In the United Kingdom, governments have appointed members of boards from opposing political parties,[15] and the same thing may have been done in Canada in respect of corporations created for war-time purposes, but there have been endless charges of appointments being made for political purposes. J. W. Dafoe recorded some strange suggestions for appointing the board of Canadian National Railways:[16] from Lapointe that the Conservatives should appoint three members and the Liberals two; from Thornton that the board should consist of the two chief officers of the railway, one member to represent the minister, two each from the Conservatives, the Liberals, and the Progressives, and one representing labour; and one from Dafoe himself that the board should be appointed by a body of some sixty trustees representing the government, the provincial governments, farmers, labour, manufacturing, shipping, and other interests. In the United Kingdom in 1952, 'A government White Paper [on the BBC] proposed that governors should be appointed by a statutory committee, apparently with the idea of avoiding arbitrary and one-sided action by any future government. The proposal met with widespread disapproval and was very sensibly dropped.'[17] This suggestion had greater merit, however, than those just described, for they would almost certainly lead to the appointment of boards lacking in common purpose, and might easily lead to the appointment of totally unsuitable people.

In those Crown corporations which most closely resemble private enterprise, the boards consist of a chief executive officer and other, part-time members drawn from a variety of sources. If the board does not meet frequently, there is likely to be provision for an executive committee. It was reported in 1956 that the board of the Bank of Canada met only four or five times a year[18] but, more recently, the Royal Commission on Banking and Finance referred to seven or eight times a year, and recommended more frequent meetings.[19] The chairman of the Canadian Broadcasting Corporation stated in 1961 that the directors served in rotation on the executive committee:[20] an arrangement that seems likely to result in greater power being concentrated in the management. This corporation has a president as its chief executive officer and also a chairman. The same arrangement is provided for in Canadian National Railways, but the two positions have always been filled by the same man.

Some Crown corporations have government officials as members of their boards. When the board consists entirely of government officials no particular difficulty arises, although it may be doubted whether such a body should have corporate form. When the board contains only one or two government officials, it is not clear what their function is. It may be to remind the board of departmental or expressed government policy; to report to the minister on the proceedings of the board; or to take a full part in the discussions of the board and, unless denied voting power, to accept some responsibility for decisions. It is extraordinary that this matter has received so little attention from Parliament in view of the fact that Canadian National Railways and Trans-Canada Air Lines both had a deputy minister on their boards for years, that the Bank of Canada has a deputy minister as a non-voting member of the board and of its executive committee, and that two deputy ministers are directors of the Industrial Development Bank. The mixture of government officials and others on the board of Central Mortgage and Housing Corporation is not so important because the board operates subject to direction by the minister.

The relationship between the executive head of a Crown corporation and the other members of the board has been discussed,[21] but not at any length, for it must vary greatly from one corporation to another. The president of Canadian National Railways objected in 1960 to the calling of other members of the board as witnesses by a committee of the House, but an earlier president raised no such objection,[22] and Polymer Corporation Limited arranged in 1961 for another director to appear before a committee.[23] It appears, however, to be a sound principle that the president should be the only witness called to give evidence on matters of policy.

Although the ideal may be to appoint the best people available as members of boards, no great harm is done provided those appointed are reasonably sensible people, without violent prejudices and fixed preconceptions. Unless they hold executive positions, it is probably best for them not to possess technical knowledge of the operations. The really important appointments are those of full-time members of boards and, sometimes, the part-time members of executive committees.

The chief executive officer should be chosen with the utmost care, and he should also have the power to choose his own officials. The 'top' management will then carry on the operations of the corporation, making reports at meetings of the board. The relations between the management and the board will depend on the personalities involved. The less frequently a board meets, and the more frequently its membership changes, the stronger will be the position of the management.[24]

During the war many Crown corporations were set up to carry out urgent work, and business men were appointed to their boards. Some of them were impatient of the forms of parliamentary control and raised suspicions of Crown corporations in members of the House, while themselves becoming suspicious of any form of government ownership.[25] C.D. Howe, who was responsible for many of these corporations, became exasperated when he thought that parliamentary routine was slowing down or reducing the efficiency of the men he had appointed to boards. 'To me one of the discouraging features of public life is the objection that certain members have to using the experience of men who have gained that experience in the hard way and have emerged successful men of business . . .', but not for the only time he mistook a legitimate argument for a personal attack on people in whom he had confidence.[26] The attitude of members of the House has sometimes, however, been misguided: an unflagging pursuit of trivialities and search for petty political advantage, known also in Britain. 'When, in addition, officials are subject to continual political sniping, to which they cannot by the conventions answer back, the position becomes intolerable. They leave for the higher paid anonymity of private enterprise.'[27]

Two of the boards which are commonly supposed to enjoy a marked degree of independence have in fact kept the minister well informed. In 1950 the president of Eldorado Mining and Refining Limited stated that the minutes of board meetings were submitted to the minister, and that a report was made to the minister on all matters of major policy.[28] The same sort of procedure was reported in 1961 by Polymer Corporation Limited.[29] As shown in the study of the Bank of Canada, the uncertainty about the relations of the president and board with the minister caused a good deal of trouble in 1959–61. Of all Crown corporations (other than the Canada Council, which is not an agent of the Crown) the one whose board appears to have been given the greatest degree of statutory independence is the Canadian Broadcasting Corporation.

The chairman of Canadian National Railways, after his appointment, is prevented by the act from becoming, otherwise than by reappointment, a director in a privately owned company. Asked in 1961 if any senior executive officers of the corporation held outside directorships, the minister replied that the board of directors saw no objection to this provided that there was no conflict of interest and that it did not interfere with the officer's performance of his duties. The board, however, considered that such a matter should be referred to the president for decision. He added that the Vice President, Atlantic Region, was a director of an insurance company, and the Traffic Manager, Foreign Freight, was a director of a steamship supplies company.[30]

Three other instances of outside directorships being held by members of the boards of Crown corporations had been discussed during the last years of the previous government, and one during the earlier days of the new government. The question was asked in 1956 whether the man appointed to be general manager of the Northern Ontario Pipe Line Crown corporation was a director of other companies. Howe replied that he was the chairman of one company and a director of three others, but that these companies had no connection with his new job; that he would cease to hold these outside appointments in nine months' time, and that until then he was to receive no pay from the Crown corporation. His questioner showed what he thought was a connection between the official and outside positions. Howe referred to his argument as devious, and said: 'A man that is not connected with any company is one of the army of unemployed, and as such, in this country at this time, I do not want him.'[31]

A question was asked in 1957 about the report that the president and managing director of Polymer Corporation Limited had been appointed to the board of McIntyre Porcupine Gold Mines Limited. Howe replied that he had seen the report, but had not inquired if it was true; he would do so if his questioner so wished. Asked if he thought it appropriate for a managing director of a Crown corporation to be on the board of a private company, he said that it was a question of ethics on which he would need to get expert opinion.[32] The matter became very complex before the end of the session and the dissolution of Parliament. Howe was asked whether he himself had suggested to anyone connected with McIntyre Porcupine that this man should be appointed to its board. Howe replied that the president had spoken to him about it; that he had expected to be consulted later, but was not. Another member asked the Prime Minister, L. St Laurent, for a statement of policy, and was told that there was no policy, for the matter had not arisen.[33]

Before the discussion of this case was finished, a further one was raised and the two were discussed together. The Prime Minister was asked whether he was aware that the president and head of Atomic Energy of Canada Limited, Eldorado Mining and Refining Limited, and Northern Transportation Company Limited was a director of Investors Mutual of Canada Limited, and whether he thought it appropriate that the top man in uranium in the country should be connected with an investment company. He replied that he would take inquiries and reply later, and in spite of pressure refused to express an opinion before he had the facts.[34] Later, St Laurent said that the facts were as stated, but that the man concerned had no part in the investment policy of the investment company, and that he had submitted his resignation from its board on account of pressure of work. The Prime Minister was then asked about the report that Avro interests and McIntyre Porcupine were going to buy the Algoma Steel empire, and was referred again to the consultations Howe had had about the appointment of the president of Polymer Corporation to the board of McIntyre Porcupine. St Laurent replied that the newspaper report had no bearing on the propriety of the matter. Asked if the three companies were making contributions to the party's election fund, he stated that he knew nothing about contributions to party funds.[35]

Reverting to the investment company, a member stated that whether the president of Eldorado had anything to do with investment policy or not, the investment company held share in uranium mining companies. He then referred to the fact that Algoma and Avro had contracts with the government, that McIntyre received subventions from the government, and that Howe was executor of an estate that held a controlling interest in Algoma.[36] This question arose again, and Howe explained that as executor of the estate of Sir James Dunn he had to dispose of the estate's holding in Algoma, but denied that there was any impropriety in his conduct.

After the change in government, a question was asked whether the heads of any Crown corporations were directors of private corporations. The Minister of Trade and Commerce replied that as far as the corporations that reported through him were concerned, there was one such instance. The president of the Atomic Energy Control Board, after he ceased to be president of the National Research Council and Atomic Energy of Canada Limited, had become a director of Canadian Chemical and Cellulose Company. He received no pay as president of the Crown corporation.[37] No reply was given in respect of Crown corporations reporting through other ministers.

Federal ministers and civil servants do not accept appointments to outside boards of directors, and there is good reason why full-time officers of the Crown corporations should be prevented from doing so. The question of whether or not they are paid appears to be irrelevant. As for part-time members of the boards of Crown corporations, it is obviously impossible to find people who have no outside interests, but it is desirable that there should be no clash of interests, and precautions have been taken by statute to prevent certain clashes of interests in respect of the Bank of Canada and Canadian Broadcasting Corporation.

The holding of outside directorships by some full-time and many part-time members of the boards of the nationalized industries in the United Kingdom was critically examined at length in 1956,[38] and clashes of interests in respect of full-time members of area boards of the Gas Council were shown. These apparently result, as do the clashes in respect of part-time members of other boards, from the appointment of members with some acquaintance with the problems of the particular industries concerned.

Notes

1. *Minutes of Public Accounts Committee,* 1960–1, p. 623 ff.
2. See C.A. Ashley and J.E. Smyth, *Corporation Finance in Canada,* ch. 2.
3. Lord Simon of Wythenshawe, *The B.B.C. from Within,* p. 30.
4. *House of Commons Debates,* 1919, p. 437.

5. Taylor Cole, *The Canadian Bureaucracy,* p. 167.
6. Quoted by C.N. Chester in A.H. Hanson, ed., *Nationalization,* p. 74.
7. *Public Administration* XXXVI, p. 89.
8. *Minutes of Committee on Estimates,* 1958, p. 504.
9. *House of Commons Debates,* 1962, p. 1338.
10. *House of Commons Debates,* 1952–3, p. 3758.
11. *Minutes of Committee on Railways and Shipping,* 1952–3, p. 199.
12. J.E. Hodgetts, in *Canadian Journal of Economics and Political Science* XII, 4, p. 456.
13. *House of Commons Debates,* 1934, p. 4152. See also 1952, pp. 2903 and 3389.
14. *House of Commons Debates,* 1960–1, p. 7899.
15. See J.A. Corry, in *Canadian Journal of Economics and Political Science* II, 3, p. 313.
16. In *Canadian Journal of Economics and Political Science* II, 3, pp. 321–7.
17. Lord Simon of Wythenshawe, *The B.B.C. from Within,* p. 332.
18. *Minutes of Committee on Banking and Commerce,* 1956, p. 425.
19. *Report,* p. 546.
20. *Minutes of Committee on Broadcasting,* 1960–1, p. 17.
21. *House of Commons Debates,* 1960–1, pp. 4846–7.
22. *Minutes of Committee on Railways and Shipping,* 1960, pp. 150–3; 1931, p. 217; 1932, pp. 8–29.
23. See study of this corporation in Part II.
24. In the United Kingdom, the chairman of the board is frequently not the chief executive officer, and although his may be a part-time appointment, he may have considerable power. Cf. Canadian Broadcasting Corporation.
25. See G.C. Power, in *Queen's Quarterly,* Winter 1957, p. 487.
26. *House of Commons Debates,* 1943, p. 3712.
27. R. Jenkins, in *Lessons of Private Enterprise,* ed. M. Shanks, p. 9.
28. *Minutes of Public Accounts Committee,* 1950, p. 628.
29. *Minutes of Public Accounts Committee,* 1960–1, pp. 335–6.
30. *House of Commons Debates,*1960–1, pp. 5964–5.
31. *House of Commons Debates,* 1956, pp. 6114–5.
32. *House of Commons Debates,* 1957, p. 3236.
33. Ibid., pp. 3297–8.
34. Ibid., pp. 3363–4.
35. Ibid., p. 3401.
36. Ibid., pp. 3472–6.
37. *House of Commons Debates,* 1957–8, pp. 134–5.
38. C. Jenkins, *Power at the Top, passim.*

10

From *The Ombudsman Plan:* The Case for the Plan in Canada

Donald C. Rowat

Canada shares the general characteristics of the parliamentary system that exists in the Commonwealth countries. Among its main features are: a union of executive and legislative powers in a politically dominant cabinet; a single-member, single-vote electoral system that often throws up a huge parliamentary majority which gives obedient support to that cabinet; a tradition of secrecy that permeates the whole administrative structure; and severely limited opportunities for the appeal or judicial review of administrative decisions. All of these lend support to the proposition that the citizens and parliament need the help of an ombudsman in any attempt to get at the facts regarding a complaint of maladministration or arbitrary administrative action.

In fact, there are good grounds for believing that the need for the ombudsman institution in Canada is more pressing than in many other Commonwealth countries. As in the United Kingdom, the liberties of the subject are not entrenched in a written constitution. But Canada has fewer administrative tribunals, where decisions can be made in a judicial manner, and no Council on Administrative Tribunals. Also, she has inadequate legislative prescription of administrative procedure; many regulatory boards and commissions with power to decide cases but no provision for appeal to the courts; antiquated laws on Crown privilege, expropriation and liability; weak arrangements for free legal aid to needy citizens; and no formal procedures in either the central Parliament or the provincial legislatures for settling the grievances of individuals. In addition to all this, the federal division of powers means that the provisions protecting the citizen's rights against administrative action are worse in some provinces than in others, and that the administration of justice varies because it is divided between the federal government, which appoints and pays the judges, and the provinces, which appoint all magistrates and control the organization and civil procedure of provincial and lower courts.

PRESENT INADEQUACIES

Let us review some of these points more fully. First, only in rare cases has an administrative procedure been laid down by law for departments, boards or administrative

Donald C. Rowat, 'The Case for the Plan in Canada' taken from *The Ombudsman Plan: Essays on the Worldwide Spread of an Idea* (Toronto: McClelland & Stewart Ltd., 1973): 86–96. Used by permission of McClelland & Stewart Ltd., *The Canadian Publishers*.

tribunals to follow in dealing with individual cases. On the other hand, the United States has had a general Administrative Procedure Act for the federal administration since 1946, and many American states have such an act. Similar acts for federal and provincial administration in Canada have been proposed for several years by the Canadian Bar Association, but so far only Ontario has adopted a general, comprehensive Procedures Act, proclaimed in 1972. The governments of both Britain and the US have had elaborate investigations of administrative procedure by official bodies, but in Canada little has been done about studying the problem, especially at the federal level. Moreover, in recent years Britain has created a Council on Administrative Tribunals to improve their procedures, while the federal government in the US has set up a similar body, the Administrative Conference of the United States.

In Canada the appeals available to a citizen in a case where he believes that an arbitrary decision has been made, or where he has some other grievance against official action or inaction, are very limited. True, both levels of government have set up some specialized appeal bodies, such as the federal Tax Appeal Board and the Immigration Appeal Board, and appeals from the federal bodies may be taken to the new Federal Court, set up in 1970. But there is no comprehensive system of administrative appeal courts as in several countries of western Europe, which have a complete network of courts covering all administrative actions. Besides the famous *Conseil d'État* in France, there is also an excellent system of administrative courts in West Germany. This had existed in Germany during the inter-war years, and its jurisdiction was greatly extended in West Germany under the 1949 constitution.

The opportunity for reviewing administrative decisions by the ordinary courts is also seriously limited in Canada. There are no general legislative provisions for court review, except in Ontario, where a Judicial Review Procedure Act was proclaimed in 1972. In fact, at both levels of government many pieces of legislation providing for the creation of an administrative board or commission include a privative clause stating that there shall be no appeal from its decisions to the courts. But even where there is an opportunity for appeal, the way in which the appeal may get before the courts is very complicated. This is done by ancient writs, and often it takes a very skilled lawyer to know which kind of writ should be used; if he makes a mistake, the case may fail. Hence, trying to get an appeal before the courts can be very complex.

Another serious limitation on court review is that the courts usually have taken the stand that they will make a decision on the law only, and an appeal on the merits of a case cannot be brought before them. Where legislation has granted a discretion to an official or a body, the courts have wisely taken the stand that they should not substitute their lay judgment for that of the expert administrator. But they have tended to interpret the scope of this discretion much too broadly.

Additional problems are that the courts operate very slowly and that their procedure is likely to be very costly in relation to the importance of the issue or the money involved. A citizen would therefore hesitate, especially in a minor case, to appeal an administrative grievance to the courts. Legal aid for the poor, though better in some provinces such as Ontario, is generally inadequate. Many other countries are far ahead of Canada in providing schemes of legal aid for people who cannot afford counsel to appear in the courts or to lodge appeals on their behalf. An example is the 'store-front' lawyers provided for the poor by the federal Office of Economic Opportunity in the United States. Another is the 8,500 mediation officers in Japan (described in Professor Gellhorn's book, *Ombudsmen and Others*), whose job is to provide help to citizens in appealing against official action. An ombudsman would be of considerable help in this respect. He would not only provide legal advice in minor cases; he would also recommend legal aid where it is necessary to fight administrative cases in the courts, as the ombudsman has done in Denmark.

Also, Canada is worse off than other Commonwealth countries in the opportunities available to citizens to air their grievances in parliament. Because of the breadth of the country, members cannot easily maintain contact with their constituents, as they can in Britain where many members on weekends hold 'surgery hours' for giving advice and receiving complaints. And, as Professor Kersell has pointed out in his thorough study of parliamentary control,

> Canadians and their representatives in Parliament have no procedure for ventilating grievances which compares with Australian 'Grievance Day', or for that matter, with British Question Time or New Zealand public petitions. There is no procedure in the Canadian House which in practice provides the back bench Member of Parliament with an adequate opportunity to air a constituent's bona fide grievance without first gaining the co-operation of his party in Parliament.[1]

But if a grievance were to demand the attention of his whole parliamentary party, it would have to be a very serious one indeed. Even so, there is no parliamentary procedure for sifting evidence or making recommendations. Thus under Canada's parliamentary system, involving the executive's dominance over the legislature and its tradition of secrecy, there is no easy way for cases of maladministration to come to light. Although we know that there is a serious problem, we cannot judge how large it is. To assess its extent in Britain the Whyatt Committee had to resort to inquiring of two *private* organizations that had been created to handle citizens' complaints.

In Canada, one of the most frequently voiced objections to the ombudsman proposal has been that it is not needed: citizens' rights seem to be adequately protected already, and one doesn't 'hear about' very many cases of persons who have been dealt with unfairly by officials. The objectors do not appreciate that only some of the most serious cases are revealed and that, since they concern isolated individuals, often they are not widely publicized by the press and are soon forgotten by the public.

CASES OF MALADMINISTRATION

To meet this objection, I have made a point of collecting cases of maladministration, arbitrariness, and outright injustice which have been publicly reported within the past few years. In all of them an ombudsman could have improved the situation for the complainant, usually by finding out the true facts at a much earlier date, by obtaining either redress or a change in the decision, and by doing so with far less injurious publicity than under existing procedures. In several cases he would no doubt have secured administrative and perhaps even legislative reforms.

These cases reveal a bewildering variety of bureaucratic bungling at all three levels of government—federal, provincial, and local. They range from simple (but none the less serious) cases of red tape such as failure to answer an inquiry or make a decision, to heart-rending stories which are shocking enough to show that something must be done. Examples from the 1950s are: the case in which a sane young man was incarcerated for three years, and others for shorter periods, in a Montreal prison madhouse amid unspeakable conditions of filth and squalor; the case of the Doukhobor children of British Columbia, who were hunted down by police and placed in 'educational concentration camps' because their parents' religious beliefs prevented their going to public schools.

The young man's case came to light only because an unofficial volunteer ombudsman, Jacques Hébert, wrote a book about it and persistently publicized his plight in a newspaper. The case of the Doukhobor children is one that graphically points up the need for ombudsmen in all provinces, because of the division of authority between the federal and provincial governments. The children's parents were admittedly breaking the province's school attendance law. The wrong lay in the harsh and inhuman manner in which the law was enforced by the province. Yet the federal government looked on from the sidelines, reluctant to act or even to comment because the case lay in the delicate area of provincial rights.

On the whole, Canadian public servants are noted for their integrity. Yet many instances of abuse of office have been revealed in recent years at all levels of government. Typical examples are: the notorious case in which personnel at the military base in Petawawa organized a system for pilfering army materials on a large scale, and are even alleged to have put the names of horses on the payroll; a case in which a provincial cabinet minister in British Columbia accepted a bribe; and numerous cases at the municipal level in which civic officials have used their offices for personal gain. Most of these cases came to light only through public agitation and special arrangements for investigation. Their detection would have come much sooner—and no doubt others would have been detected—had ombudsmen been on the scene.

All of the above examples were such serious cases that they gained the public's attention. But there are countless others of individual grievance that are never brought to light and in which the aggrieved person may suffer years of heart-breaking frustration. This was revealed after I wrote my first magazine article on the ombudsman idea and spoke on radio an television about it in 1961. I became a kind of unofficial ombudsman myself, and received complaints from aggrieved citizens all across Canada, some complete with frighteningly complicated documentation. These cases were of much the same type that an ombudsman would receive and investigate. The situation was much the same in Britain before the adoption of an ombudsman scheme there. The number of potential complainants was so great that, when the first Danish ombudsman had been interviewed about the idea on British television, after his return to Denmark he began to receive complaints from British citizens against maladministration in Britain!

On the basis of the Scandinavian experience, one can estimate that the total case-load for ombudsmen at all levels of government in Canada might be about

7,000 per year, with perhaps 3,000 at the federal level. Even using the low Danish figure of about 10 per cent that require some kind of corrective action, this would mean that the number of cases of uncompensated administrative injustice in Canada must be at least 700 per year. However, these figures are probably far too low because of the earlier-mentioned inadequacy of Canada's protections against arbitrary administration. Also, the federal division of the country into two levels of government causes administrative conflict and delay, and creates confusion for the citizens, who are likely to complain to the wrong level of government at first, thus increasing the total case load at both levels. Another significant difference from the Scandinavian countries is Canada's higher level of immigration and the accompanying administrative problems of eligibility for admission and citizenship.

THE ROLE OF MEMBERS OF PARLIAMENT

While opponents may admit that most of an ombudsman's cases could not be handled by the courts in Canada, they frequently object that in a single-member district it is the job of the member of parliament to handle such cases for his district. In effect, they say, Canada already has 264 ombudsmen at the federal level of government, to say nothing of those at the lower levels. To investigate this argument—to find out how many and what kinds of complaints MPs receive, how they handle them and whether they think an ombudsman would help—Mr Llambias sent a questionnaire to all members of the House of Commons in the spring of 1964, and received 80 replies.[2] Nine of these were refusals of information, of which two were from ministers who declined to express any opinion for fear that this might be interpreted as government policy. Although the remainder is probably a biased sample, in the sense that only the most interested and sympathetic MPs replied, it does reveal some interesting facts.

The MPs were asked to estimate 'how many complaints about some aspect of governmental administration in relation to individuals' they received per month from constituents, and there was a surprising scatter in the replies. Thirty-six MPs estimated they had fewer than 10 complaints per month while twelve said they received more than 30, and two indicated that they were burdened with as many as 65. The difference in the number of complaints seems to depend mainly on the rural or urban character of the constituencies and their total populations, which at present vary tremendously. The average number of complaints received by the forty-four MPs who replied to this question was–about 15. Extending this average to all MPs would mean that in total they receive an estimated 4,000 per month, or nearly 50,000 per year. Even if we assume that it was mainly the overburdened MPs that replied, and that an average for all MPs would be closer to 10 per month, this would still mean a total of 32,000 complaints per year. The replies indicated that a surprising number of complaints concern provincial or local government and even non-governmental bodies. Only about 70 per cent relate to federal departments or agencies, so that complaints of the latter type may total about 22,000 per year.

To a question on whether the complaints concern the personality of officials, the manner of proceeding or the substance of the action taken, there was considerable variation in the replies. However, most of the MPs thought that about 10 per cent concern personalities, 35 per cent the manner of proceeding, and that a majority are directed to the substance of the action. It is likely that many of the latter deal with the reasonableness of a decision or the effect of a law or policy. These matters an ombudsman would not ordinarily investigate. MPs would continue to handle such cases, as well as requests for help and information and demands for change in the laws or regulations.

When the MPs were asked to identify the areas of governmental activity into which complaints mainly fell, they named 41 different areas, departments, and agencies. However, there was a heavy concentration on certain areas. Decisions regarding pensions seemed to cause the most trouble, appearing in 20 questionnaires. The next most common areas of complaint were citizenship and immigration, income tax, health and welfare, unemployment insurance, and veterans' affairs.

Questions were also asked on the efficacy of the existing procedure for handling complaints. It is interesting that there was considerable disagreement about whether being on the government or opposition side of the House made a difference to the success of a complaint, although a majority of the MPs felt that it made no difference. Perhaps the reason for this disagreement, as one stated, is that being on either the government or opposition side has advantages and disadvantages. While access to information is easier for government MPs, they are reluctant to ask the minister a question in the House for fear of embarrassing the government. As one MP wrote, 'No questions to the minister, as I am on the government side!' An opposition MP, on the other hand, is free to publicize a case and to press an attack on the floor of the House.

A crucial question was: 'Do you ever handle complaints which are settled in a manner unsatisfactory to you and/or the complainant?' To this the great majority (55 out of 63) answered yes, and many said that half or more of their complaints were settled unsatisfactorily. Various reasons were given for the shortcomings of the existing system. One stated bluntly, 'Insufficient time and secretarial assistance to deal with each complaint.' Another felt that a basic inadequacy of the system was the 'weakness of individual MPs who are unwilling to intercede on behalf of constituents.' A third believed that not all MPs had the 'experience or training to deal with some of the issues which arise,' while two MPs pointed out that in most cases they could only obtain information at second-hand from the minister or civil servant, since they lacked access to the files.

The MPs were then requested to describe one or more typical cases, or cases in which they felt that the Minister's explanation and/or the department's action was unsatisfactory. Although many MPs felt that they could not take the time to do this, the others went to the trouble of presenting a great variety of interesting and sometimes shocking cases. While space does not permit an analysis of these cases here, it is clear that many of them would fall within the competence of an ombudsman.

To the final question, whether they thought that a Parliamentary Complaints Commissioner (Ombudsman) would be of help, 53 MPs answered yes, 13 said no, and 2 were doubtful. Of this sample of 68, then, the proportion in favour of an ombudsman exceeded three to one.

The results of this survey, then, clearly demonstrate that the number of griev-

ances against the federal and other levels of administration is great, and that legislators need the help of an ombudsman. They are too overloaded with work, too inad-
equately equipped, and not expert enough to handle the kind of case with which an
ombudsman should deal.

Applying the Plan to Canada

Let us now turn to the question of applying the ombudsman plan to Canada and
whether it will meet the need. New Zealand led the way in working out the problem of adapting the plan to a Commonwealth parliamentary system. But New
Zealand's scheme is of little help in telling us how the plan should be adjusted to fit
a large federal country. While it may have required considerable change to fit British
conditions, it does not seem to require major adjustment to suit Canada. In the first
place, Canada has a much smaller population than Britain. More important, because
Canada has a federal division of powers, there can be eleven separate offices—one to
look after complaints against federal administrative action, and the others to handle
complaints against the ten provincial administrations. Fortunately, this circumstance
has given us three advantages: we have had eleven chances of adopting the plan; we
have eleven opportunities of developing a scheme well fitted to our special needs; and
the work load of the ombudsman for each government will be small enough to be
manageable. Hence there is no danger of a single office that would become too big,
impersonal, and bureaucratic.

Yet the need for additional protections against arbitrary administrative action is
now so great in Canada that other reforms will be needed if the ombudsman system
is not to become overloaded. For instance, we need much simpler judicial remedies,
and wider opportunities for appeal to the courts, especially on points of fair legal procedure. The existing use of ancient writs is archaic, inadequate, and confusing. There
should be federal and provincial laws providing one simple method for appealing
administrative decisions to the courts on questions of law and procedure, and uniform provisions regarding which types of matters may and may not be appealed to
the courts.

There should also be federal and provincial laws on administrative procedure.
These laws would spell out in general terms, and protect, the elementary rights of an
individual affected by administrative action. For example, they would require that,
wherever possible, officials should give reasons for their decisions and should give a
fair hearing to persons likely to be adversely affected by a decision, as in the American
Administrative Procedure Act. Also, many more administrative appeal bodies are
needed. Court review is costly and mainly restricted to the question of whether an
agency exceeded its power, rather than whether its decision was fair and reasonable.
Hence, in the thousands of instances where officials make decisions on individual
cases, many more opportunities are needed for their review. Indeed, perhaps what we
need is a complete system of administrative courts, as in France and West Germany.

We also need a much better system of free legal aid in Canada. It is true that a
few provinces have recently improved their provisions for legal aid. But this is far
from meeting the need. As in Ontario, legal aid should be made available for actions

intended to redress administrative wrongdoing. And the federal government should stimulate the provinces to develop an acceptable minimum standard of legal aid across Canada.

In addition, the legal liability of federal and provincial officials needs to be clarified and codified. In many cases, citizens cannot successfully claim damages for injurious official action, either because the law does not regard the wrong done as actionable, or because only the official is considered liable and the prospect of recovering full damages from him is doubtful. The state should assume full liability for paying damages or making restitution to persons who are wrongfully injured by administrative action. At the same time, officials should be required to indemnify the state to the extent of their ability, for amounts paid by the state on account of their wrong-doing. This would increase their feeling of responsibility.

Furthermore, the rule of administrative secrecy should be reversed. Instead of our present rule that all administrative information should remain secret unless the government chooses to release it, the rule should be that all administrative documents are open to the public except in special cases where there is reason for them to remain secret, as in Sweden and Finland. This rule has worked successfully in these countries for many years. The witholding of official information not only denies the right of a citizen to have access to the reasons for a decision against him. It is inconsistent with the principle of free and open discussion of public policy in a democracy.

Though these other reforms are also necessary, ombudsman schemes in all provinces and at the federal level would help to bring them about. Many of the reforms are legally complicated and technical, and it is therefore difficult to create an informed public opinion about them. Yet a government does not easily submit to the limitations upon the free exercise of its own executive powers that such reforms imply. The ombudsman plan, on the other hand, is simple, easily understood and has great popular appeal. The public discussion generated by the creation of ombudsman schemes, and later by the ombudsmen's own proposals, will stimulate the kind of technical reforms of the law that require a fully informed public to promote them, and will help to form a strong public opinion that will insist upon their adoption.

In Canada we seem to have a general attitude of complacency about the protection of the citizen's rights, perhaps engendered by the strength of the inherited British tradition that the citizen is fully protected by the 'rule of law'. We do not realize that, due to the modern growth of administrative powers, the meaning of this tradition has lost much of its content, and that we are now living on our past reputation for the 'rule of law'. We are like the dog in the anonymous rhyme:

> There was a dachshund, one so long
> He hadn't any notion
> How long it took to notify
> His tail of his emotion;
> And so it was that, though his eyes
> Were filled with tears of sadness,
> His little tail went wagging on
> Because of previous gladness.

Faced with our failure to solve the problems of protecting the rights of the citizen in the modern administrative state, our eyes are 'filled with tears of sadness'. But our tails go wagging smugly on, because of previous gladness.

NOTES

Source: An expansion of the section on Canada in *The Ombudsman*, 186–93, by permission.

1. John E. Kersell, *Parliamentary Supervision of Delegated Legislation* (London, 1960), 149.
2. Mr. Llambias has given a full analysis of the results of this questionnaire, and has also recounted many cases of maladministration, in his MA thesis, *The Need for an Ombudsman System in Canada* (Ottawa: Carleton University, 1964).

11

An Outsider's Observations of Federal–Provincial Relations Among Consenting Adults

Donald V. Smiley

These are an outsider's observations of what I have come to call executive federalism. My credentials as an outsider if not an observer are outstanding. I have never attended a federal–provincial conference and my ignominous career as a minor functionary of the federal and then the Saskatchewan governments did not involve me in these relations. And I can assure Gordon Robertson and other guardians of official secrecy in the conduct of public business that since leaving government employment about 20 years ago I have never read a classified document—except of course those published by the media. I am a law-abiding man and I would not want to disobey the Official Secrets Act or provincial variants thereof or to connive that others should do so. Beyond that, I hold to another principle to the effect that I will sound off about governmental matters based on a reading of the public record alone and if my judgments are for that reason superficial and perverse the fault is with those who withhold the necessary information from me and other private citizens.

I am not totally an outsider of course because as a university teacher of Canadian government I 'live off' federalism. Perhaps I can be accused of gross ingratitude for being as critical of it as I am in this paper. In a sense I should regard myself as did a senior scholar of American law who responded in the 1950s to a query by saying that he would not have the slightest objection to taking an oath to support the Constitution of the United States because for over 40 years the Constitution had supported him. I have sometimes written as if the complex and mysterious system of executive federalism in Canada was one of the most distinguished achievements of the mind and heart of man and in this connection I have now and again quoted John Porter's contrary assessment with some derision '. . . it may be speculated that (Canadian) federalism as such has meaning only for politicians and senior civil servants who work the complex machinery they have set up, as well as for scholars who provide a continuing commentary on it, but that it has very little meaning for the bulk of the population.'[1] I am no longer as sure as I once was that Porter was totally wrong.

Donald V. Smiley, 'An Outsider's Observations of Federal–Provincial Relations Among Consenting Adults' in *Confrontation and Collaboration: Intergovernmental Relations in Canada Today*, Richard Simeon, ed. (Toronto: Institute of Public Administration of Canada): 105–13. Courtesy of the Institute of Public Administration Canada.

My charges against executive federalism are these:

First, it contributes to undue secrecy in the conduct of the public's business.

Second, it contributes to an unduly low level of citizen-participation in public affairs.

Third, it weakens and dilutes the accountability of governments to their respective legislatures and to the wider public.

Fourth, it frustrates a number of matters of crucial public concern from coming on the public agenda and being dealt with by the public authorities.

Fifth, it has been a contributing factor to the indiscriminate growth of government activities.

Sixth, it leads to continuous and often unresolved conflicts among governments, conflicts which serve no purpose broader than the political and bureaucratic interests of those involved in them.

First to secrecy. It is I believe undeniable that executive federalism contributes to the undue secrecy by which public affairs are conducted in Canada. This secrecy is not very profound—there is a great deal of information about federal–provincial affairs on the public record and journalists and even scholars can penetrate what confidentiality there is in many cases. However, we are likely to have a federal freedom of information act and corresponding legislation in most if not all of the provinces in the next five years or so and it is almost inevitable that these enactments will confer on governments the power to withhold from public scrutiny documents involving federal–provincial relations.

The second charge is that executive federalism contributes to an unduly low level of citizen-participation in public affairs. In part this is a result of the secrecy to which I have already referred. In larger part it is a result of the extra-ordinary complexity of the process. For example, how can one reasonably expect intelligent public or even parliamentary debate on the Federal–Provincial Fiscal Arrangements and Established Programs Financing Act of 1977—perhaps one of the most important enactments of the Canadian Parliament in recent decades? And I would also defy anyone without specialized training to make sense of the national dimension and emergency doctrines as these were argued in the Anti-Inflation reference of 1976. But apart from secrecy and complexity, executive federalism discourages citizen participation by contributing to a very minimal role for political parties in the formulation of public policy and in the articulation and aggregation of public demands. Political parties—and I am speaking here of the extra-parliamentary components of parties rather than caucuses and cabinets—are not very influential in matters related to policy, although they of course play a vital role in the nomination of candidates for public office and strive to elect such persons. So far as governments themselves are concerned, partisan complexions are not very important in federal–provincial relations and it would be a most extraordinary event if any intergovernmental conference divided on partisan lines. Executive federalism thus restricts the role of parties in public policy and the constructive participation of citizens in the formulation of policy by party activity.

Federalism in its Canadian variant weakens the accountability of governments to their respective legislatures and the wider public. As participation was the cause of a decade ago, so is the accountability of those who act in the name of governments today. In a formal sense the British-type parliamentary system meets the accountability criterion well—ministers are responsible for the acts carried out under the legal authority conferred upon them and the cabinet is collectively responsible for its policies to the legislature. It is almost trite to say that these traditional doctrines of ministerial and cabinet responsibility are now under question as being misleading or inoperative or impossible to attain. My own views on the matter are confused. The pristine doctrines of ministerial and cabinet responsibility cannot be applied without some significant modifications to governments with the scope of activity which prevails today. Yet to reject these doctrines completely is surely indefensible for without them we appear to have no guides to the most fundamental of political relations—between governments and legislatures, among members of the political executive, between elected politicians and bureaucrats, between governments and those whom they govern. At any rate, federalism contributes to the weakening of the responsibility of the executive to the legislature and Thomas Courchene has rightly judged this of the 1977 legislation concerning federal–provincial financial relations:

> . . . the entire negotiation process with respect to the new fiscal arrangements essentially by-passed the Parliament of Canada. It is true that the Fiscal Arrangements Act is an act of Parliament. But our federal representatives were effectively presented with a *fait accompli*, hammered out between representatives of Ottawa and the ten provincial governments. The bulk of the Commons debate on the bill was directed toward sorting out the details of the various provisions. There was no debate in the traditional sense of the term. . . . Public opinion was not brought to bear on the new arrangements. This is in marked contrast to the information that has been available in the print and electronic media relating to the upcoming revision of the new Bank Act, for example. Yet the Bank Act revision pales in comparison with renegotiating the financial bases of the federation in terms of the impact on the Canada of tomorrow.[2]

To the extent then that the actual locus of decision-making in respect to an increasing number of public matters has shifted from individual governments to intergovernmental groupings the effective accountability of executives both to their respective legislatures and to those whom they govern is weakened.

My argument then is that executive federalism contributes to secret, non-participatory, and non-accountable processes of government.

But in an even more crucial sense federalism puts some issues permanently or almost permanently on the public agenda and keeps others off. The American political scientist E.E. Schattschneider wrote: 'All forms of political organization have a bias in favor of the exploitation of some kinds of conflict and the suppression of others. . . . Some issues are organized into politics while others are organized out.'[3] There are important regional and provincial differences in Canada—Simeon and Elkins have demonstrated variations in basic orientations to government as one goes from province to province,[4] the provincial and regional economics differ in the levels of income they provide to their citizens and their kinds of development, most French-speaking Canadians live in Quebec and in areas contiguous to Quebec in Ontario and New Brunswick.

But as Simeon has cogently argued, these differences do not in themselves explain why Canadian politics is almost monopolized by territorially based conflicts to the neglect of other issues which divide Canadians along other cleavages[5]—for example, rich as against poor, authoritarians as against liberals, the upwardly-mobile as against those with stable or declining status and so on. Why is Ottawa so much more preoccupied with the reduction of regional economic disparities than with redistributive measures on an interpersonal basis? How was it that the crucial debate over public retirement pensions of the mid-1960s involved hardly at all the intergenerational distribution of burdens and benefits? I think I could argue that the continuing competition for tax points in respect to levies on individual incomes pales in significance with the circumstance that the existing system by any coherent standards of equity confers indefensible benefits on some citizens and imposes indefensible burdens on others but there is little or no debate on these latter lines. Let us be frank about it. Executive federalism 'organizes into politics' the interests of governments and of those private groupings which are territorially concentrated. The system almost by its inherent nature weakens the influence of other interests.

Federalism is thus an important influence in perpetuating inequalities among Canadians. This is so despite countervailing efforts of the central government to narrow regional economic disparities and to sustain national minimum standards of public expenditures and services by the provincial and local governments. One of the results of the continuing conflicts between Ottawa and the provinces is to displace other conflicts among Canadians, particularly those between the relatively advantaged and those who are less so. So long as the major cleavages are between governments, inequalities *within* the provinces are buttressed. I would also argue but in a tentative way that the processes of executive federalism have contributed to the somewhat indiscriminate growth of government activity in the past two decades. I am very much aware here of Richard Bird's caution in his distinguished study that '. . . the ratio of total government expenditure to GNP is not a meaningful subject for analysis. . . .'[6] and that in order to understand this general phenomenon we must look at the factors determining the levels of public expenditure on particular functions. Yet the expansion of the public sector seems not to have led and seems not to be leading in the direction of social and economic equality and in itself has created new forms of privilege. The relation between federalism and the increases in public expenditure is complex. I have the impression that the dynamics are somewhat different in the Atlantic region from those prevailing elsewhere in Canada. In a recent essay on Prince Edward Island where government and politics are the dominant industries Frank MacKinnon argues that 'individual and community effort decrease as large government takes over an increasing proportion of the activities of the society.'[7] The historian T.W. Acheson has said this of the recent involvement of the national authorities in the Maritime provinces:

> Another side effect of the federal intervention was the creation of a new, bourgeoisie elite composed of professional civil servants, medical doctors, and academics who joined the lawyer-politician-businessman leadership of the community and gave to it a distinctly professional flavour. Indeed, with its emphasis upon place and sinecures, and with the patron-client relationship which the monopolistic hierarchies of provincial governments and institutions of higher learning encouraged, Maritime society began more closely to resemble an eighteenth- than a nineteenth-century society. . . . It was a captive elite largely dependent for opportunity, position, and status on federal resources and ultimately subject to the will of the federal government. Most important, it was an elite with no resource base, one incapable of generating anything more than services, producers of primary or secondary goods played little role in its ranks.[8]

While governmental and political activity is less dominant in the larger provinces there has arisen a competitiveness between the federal and provincial authorities that has resulted in a costly duplication of effort.

My last charge against executive federalism which I shall discuss in somewhat more detail than the others is that it leads to continuing conflicts among governments and that, to borrow a horrible term from the sociologists, these conflicts are in large part dysfunctional. I should not for a moment deny that in public affairs and elsewhere there are useful conflicts among people—for example, students of the institution of marriage tell us that the most loving and long-lasting unions are of couples who fight a good deal. So far as our governmental system is concerned, both courts and legislatures proceed by adversarial methods, parties compete vigorously with one another for votes and there may be creative conflicts within individual governments such as those between functional departments and central agencies. And if we were to come to a situation where there were no differences between Ottawa and the provinces some of us would be uneasy because that would mean that one order of government was able to dominate the other completely.

One of the crucial elements in contemporary executive federalism is the increasing importance of intergovernmental affairs specialists, of officials and agencies not responsible for particular programs but rather the relations between jurisdictions. In the context of American federalism Samuel Beer of Harvard University has variously designated this complex of interests as the 'topocracy' and the 'intergovernmental lobby' and has analyzed its continuing conflicts with those responsible for specific functional activities of government.[9] Claude Morin and the able group of young people he gathered around him in the Quebec Department of Federal-Provincial Affairs in the 1960s were the harbingers of this new breed in Canada. The role of the inter-governmental affairs specialist is to protect and extend the powers of the jurisdiction for which he works, and an important element of this power adheres in its financial resources. Despite the high-flown justifications that such persons make for their occupations, this is in fact their only important role. The game is at least as intricate as international diplomacy, with which it shares many similarities, and the players have the satisfaction that no one has as yet been killed because of their activities. The context is clubby and when new members join they soon discover that they can't be very influential unless and until they accept the almost wholly implicit rules of the club. In his stance toward other governments the federal–provincial relations specialist has a single-minded devotion to the power of his jurisdiction. And because his counterparts in other governments have the same motivations, conflict is inevitable. In his relations with elements of his own government the objective of the federal–provincial specialist is to ensure that operating agencies will not by collaborative intergovernmental interactions weaken the power of federal or provincial jurisdiction as such.

I have come to the pessimistic conclusion that as governments become more sophisticated in their operations conflict among these governments will increase in scope and intensity.[10] Almost by definition, sophistication in this sense means that jurisdictions will rank and make more explicit their objectives and will be concerned with increasingly precise measures of evaluation of actual and projected policies. And as governments are disposed to conduct their operations in a less fragmented and haphazard way it is inevitable that they will strive to control their environments and to make these less uncertain. It is almost trite to say that an important part of these environments are composed of other governments. In general then, the related factors of the increasing influence of intergovernmental specialists and the increasing maturity of governments leads directly to continuous and unresolved conflicts between Ottawa and the provinces. My impression is that on both sides the power of one level or the other has become an important value independent of the objectives towards which the exercise of such powers are or could be directed.[11] Further, it seems that many of these actual and emergent conflicts are not susceptible to authoritative resolution. So far as such matters as the provision of costly health, welfare, and educational services are concerned the characteristic situation is that the provinces have the jurisdiction while Ottawa has superior fiscal resources. In A.D. Scott's terms the federal government will in such circumstances 'buy jurisdiction' at a mutually agreed 'price' between the two levels, although under the Canadian ground-rules the federal authorities will in perpetuity pay for jurisdiction they bought in the past and subsequently relinquished. The circumstances in respect to the regulatory activities of government—telecommunications, consumer protection, transportation, environmental control, and so on—are less susceptible to authoritative resolution. Here jurisdiction is often divided—and in many cases in dispute—and Ottawa's superior fiscal resources cannot be used to secure provincial compliance. And it is in respect to the regulatory activities of government, along with the new disputes about the administration of justice, where federal–provincial conflicts have become most intense.

I have perhaps been unduly severe on the intergovernmental specialists. Members of this burgeoning craft will no doubt argue that I have vastly exaggerated their influence both within their respective jurisdictions and in shaping the interactions among governments. It may well be true that the conventional wisdom about

Canadian government attributes more power to central agencies than these organizations in fact possess.[12] But a more persuasive defence might be that the intergovernmental relations specialists are merely the managers of the cultural, economic and other conflicts built into the elemental nature of Canadian society. I am less sure of this than I once was and I find compelling the argument presented by Alan Cairns in his 1977 Presidential Address to the Canadian Political Science Association. He was explaining the continuing and growing strength of the provinces and he raised this 'possibility';

> the support for powerful, independent provincial governments is a product of the political system itself, it is fostered and created by provincial government elites employing the policy-making apparatus of their jurisdiction, and that such support need not take the form of a distinct culture, society or nation as these are conventionally understood. . . . Passivity, indifference, or the absence of strong opposition from their environment may be all that provincial governments need in order to grow and thrive. The significant question, after all, is of the survival of provincial governments, not of provincial societies, and it is not self-evident that the existence and support of this latter is necessary to the functioning and aggrandisement of the former. Their sources of survival, renewal and vitality may well be within themselves, and in their capacity to mould their environments in accordance with their own governmental purposes.[13]

Although Cairns' analysis was devoted to explaining the vitality of the provinces, it can just as easily be applied to assert that federal powers arise from the national political system rather than the cultural, economic, or other underpinnings of the national community and the emotional allegiances of Canadians to that community.

I have been very critical of the workings of Canadian federalism. You may ask me what I would propose to remedy these deficiencies. I have no solution—one does not judge the ability of a medical diagnostician by his refusal to pronounce certain illnesses as terminal. Rather my approach is that of the economist attempting to evaluate the 'opportunity costs' of federalism, what we give up in these institutions and processes in terms of other things we value. I should thus like to turn to a brief consideration of how we might lower these costs in the light of the current proposals for constitutional reform.

It has now become the conventional wisdom that constitutional reform should strengthen the powers of the provinces in the institutions of the government of Canada. I share this conventional wisdom, partly perhaps because I think I was the first person to make such an argument—in an article published in 1971.[14] (The federal strategy for constitutional review as outlined by Prime Minister Pearson in the 1968 document *Federalism for the Future* proposed changes in the institutions of the central government but the focus here was almost exclusively on English–French duality). The most important of the new constitutional reforms would replace the Senate by a House of the Federation or House of the Provinces in which the provinces are directly represented.

The proposal of the government of Canada as made public in June 1978 provides for a House of the Federation of 118 members of whom half would be selected by the House of Commons and half by the provincial legislatures. The distribution of these members on a provincial/regional basis does not diverge markedly from the membership of the existing Senate, although the representation of the western provinces is increased. Members of the new House are chosen after each federal or provincial election and represent the balances of voter preferences in such elections. Complex provisions allow for a suspensive veto by the House of the Federation of bills passed by the House of Commons, with such vetoes not extending for more than 60 days and with the provisions that the House of Commons may enact laws without submission to the other House if two-thirds of the members of the Commons vote that such bills affect federal–provincial relations directly or are of urgent concern. There are special provisions for concurrent English–French majorities when legislation having 'special linguistic significance' is being enacted.

Because the federal proposals provide for the representation of legislatures rather than governments in the House of the Federation I would expect this to be a very marginal institution. Under normal circumstances at least half the members of HOF will be drawn from opposition rather than government parties and the scheme explicitly provides that no member of the House of Commons or of a provincial legislature shall be so appointed. Canadian federalism is after all *about* executives rather than legislatures, and it is my guess that if the new House of the Federation were established governments would continue to pursue these interests through the same kind of interactions as they now do without recourse to HOF.

I find somewhat more appealing the proposals for the direct representation of the provincial *governments* in a House of the Provinces as contained in the report of the Ontario Advisory Committee on Confederation [15] and of the Discussion Paper prepared for the Canada West Foundation by Professors Elton, Engelmann, and McCormick.[16] There is not the time to discuss these in detail but they both propose that provincial delegations in the new House be appointed by and be responsible to the provincial governments somewhat along the lines of the German Bundesrat. Thus there would be a more continuous and regularized provincial influence on federal policies and federal-provincial relations would be somewhat more open to public scrutiny than they now are. I would share in part at least Ian Macdonald's hope that this reform would reduce the adversarial nature of intergovernmental relations and enhance collaborative elements . . . (All three of the proposals for a new second chamber raise the difficult issue of the distinction to be made between legislation which can be enacted by the House of Commons alone and legislation subject to some kind of suspensive veto by the House of the Federation/House of the Provinces. On the basis of previous Canadian experience, a prudent person would be very hesitant to introduce a new division-of-powers issue into the Canadian constitutional system. But time does not permit discussion of this matter).

I end with the academic's characteristic plea for more investigation of the matter under discussion. For example, there are at least three provincial models for the conduct of federal–provincial and interprovincial relations—the Quebec/Alberta model where a Department under its own minister is responsible for these relations and for those with jurisdictions outside Canada, the Saskatchewan model where federal–provincial and interprovincial relations are conducted through the Premier's office and the Ontario procedure which combines in one department responsibility for federal–provincial, interprovincial and international relations with the treasury function and that of a department of municipal affairs.[17] How, if at all, do these different organizational forms influence the effectiveness of a province in pursuing its objectives and the general conduct of federal–provincial relations? How powerful *are* these evolving central agencies in relation to elements of government with program responsibilities? What has been the impact of the 1977 fiscal arrangements on relations between professionals in the field of health services? What is the impact of the struggle for Canadian survival—and more particularly of the agencies in the federal and Quebec governments whose work is explicitly devoted to waging this battle—on the ongoing processes of Canadian federalism? These are the kind of questions I should like to gain some enlightenment about in this seminar.

NOTES

1. *The Vertical Mosaic* (Toronto: University of Toronto Press, 1965), p. 384.
2. 'The New Fiscal Arrangements and the Economics of Federalism', *Options*, Proceedings of the Conference on the Future of the Canadian Federation, University of Toronto, 1977, p. 345.
3. *The Semi-Sovereign People*, (New York: Holt, Rinehart and Winston, 1966) p. 71.
4. Richard Simeon and David Elkins, 'Regional Political Cultures in Canada', *Canadian Journal of Political Science* 7 (September 1974) pp. 394–437.
5. 'Regionalism and Canadian Political Institutions', in J. Peter Meekison, ed., *Canadian Federalism: Myth or Reality*, 3rd edn (Toronto: Methuen of Canada, 1977), pp. 292–304.
6. *The Growth of Government Spending in Canada* (Toronto: Canadian Tax Foundation, 1970), p. 189.
7. 'Prince Edward Island: Big Engine, Little Body' in Martin Robin, ed., *Canadian Provincial Politics*, 2nd edn (Scarborough: Prentice-Hall of Canada, 1978), p. 242.
8. 'The Maritimes and "Empire Canada', in David Jay Bercuson, ed., *Canada and the Burden of Unity*, (Toronto: Macmillan of Canada, 1977), pp. 104–5.
9. See 'Federalism, Nationalism and Democracy in America', *American Political Science Review* 72 (March 1978) pp. 9–21 and 'The Adoption of General Revenue-Sharing: A Case Study in Public Sector Politics', *Public Policy* 24 (Spring 1976), pp. 127–95.
10. I have argued this in more detail in *Canada in Question: Federalism in the Seventies*, 2nd edn (Toronto: McGraw-Hill Ryerson of Canada, 1976), pp. 76–9.
11. A recent example of this is the way that the governments and various interest groups defended their constitutional preferences on the anti-inflation reference of 1976. The stakes as here perceived were not entirely or even mainly the 1975 legislation but rather the implications of the Supreme Court decision for future jurisdictional disputes. See Peter H. Russell 'The Anti-Inflation Case: The Anatomy of a Constitutional Decision' *Canadian Public Administration* 20 (Winter 1977), pp. 632–65.

12. For a questioning of this conventional wisdom, see Richard Schultz, 'Prime Ministerial Government, Central Agencies and Operating Departments: Towards a More Realistic Analysis', in Thomas A. Hockin, ed., *Apex of Power: The Prime Minister and Political Leadership in Canada,* 2nd edn (Scarborough: Prentice-Hall of Canada, 1977), pp. 229–36.

13. 'The Governments and Societies of Canadian Federalism', *Canadian Journal of Political Science* 10 (December 1977), p. 699.

14. 'The Structural Problem of Canadian Federalism', *Canadian Public Administration* 14 (Fall 1971), pp. 326–43.

15. Toronto, 1978.

16. *Alternatives: Towards the Development of an Effective Federal System for Canada* by David Elton, F.C. Engelmann, and Peter McCormick, Canada West Foundation, 1978 (mimeo).

17. Editorial note: shortly before the seminar, Ontario established a separate Ministry of Intergovernmental Affairs and Saskatchewan took similar action shortly after.

PART II

―――

Human Resources

The range of the institutions that make up the public sector is very broad, as Table 1 shows. In 2003 nearly 3 million people were employed, full- or part-time, by a government organization, and most of their jobs were in the health, social, and educational sectors. Thus human resources management in the public sector is mainly about nurses and teachers and gardeners and electricians. The classical literature, however, tends to focus on the top levels of the public service—notably the senior bureaucrats working in federal line departments and ministries.

This emphasis reflects the power of senior bureaucrats, in particular their power to influence the democratic process. In Part I Sharp and Segal addressed the accountability of top public servants. In this section we consider other rules of employment—specifically, appointment, promotion, remuneration, and dismissal practices—and codes of conduct prescribed by government for public administrators.

Canada was slow to develop formal rules regarding partisan appointments, promotions, and dismissals. The prescriptive impact of these rules, in the context first of partisan politics and then of francophone and female representation, was a frequent subject for the public administration literature of the 1970s and early 1980s. Another topic of interest was the first major effort to limit conflicts of interest by developing codes of ethical conduct.

The international public administration literature also stressed the importance of formal rules for appointment, promotions, remuneration, and dismissals. In part this reflected the Weberian tradition of emphasizing the importance of vocational careers for public servants within modern political systems. In part it also reflected the interest of scientific management theorists in controlling and channelling human behaviour in organizations. But sociological and psychological theory on social norms, human values, 'satisficing' behaviour, leadership traits, and so on found little resonance in the classical Canadian literature.

Perhaps the greatest Canadian contributions to the international literature prior to 1985 came in the areas of public-service unionization and job dismissal. Canada was also one of the first countries to introduce personal service contracts mandating

TABLE 1 *Public Sector Employment 2003*

	1999	2000	2001	2002	2003
	Employment (persons)				
Public sector	**2,769,996**	**2,786,491**	**2,812,251**	**2,842,928**	**2,910,419**
Government	2,508,169	2,520,387	2,545,911	2,579,027	2,638,743
Federal general government[1]	328,280	335,317	351,331	359,481	366,428
Provincial and territorial general government	336,158	339,285	340,320	336,509	349,820
Health and social service institut-ions, provincial and territorial	689,762	691,158	696,446	715,054	738,531
Universities, colleges, vocational and trade institutions, provincial and territorial	269,145	272,985	275,887	281,000	290,307
Local general government	341,485	340,827	341,339	344,609	362,362
Local school boards	543,340	540,815	540,587	542,374	531,293
Government business enterprises	261,827	266,104	266,340	263,901	271,676
Federal government business enterprises	89,990	89,743	89,131	88,429	89,471
Provincial and territorial government business enterprises	124,422	128,156	128,047	125,185	130,624
Local government business enterprises	47,414	48,206	49,162	50,287	51,582

Notes: Employment data are not in fulltime equivalent and do not distinguish between fulltime and partime employees. Includes employees both in and outside Canada.

[1] Federal general government data includes reservists and full-time military personnel.
Source: Statistics Canada, CANSIM, table 1830002. Last modified: 20040527.
Accessed at http://www.statcan.ca/english/Pgdb/govt54a.htm [7 June 2004].

policy goals for chief executives and deputy ministers; provincial ministries led the way in introducing this practice. Appointments and dismissals moved from a status to a contractual basis.

We have selected six items from the Canadian literature on human resources management that address these issues. First, the two articles by Kenneth Kernaghan outline the rules for bureaucratic behaviour in Westminster-style political systems—that is, systems based on the principle of ministerial responsibility. The 1978 article looks at administrative responsibilities and powers in government departments, while the 1980 piece discusses the growing need for ethical conduct codes to fill the gaps in the traditional rules governing bureaucracies. Next, Robert Vaison traces the history of the federal public service reforms that led to the introduction of the merit system and eventually collective bargaining. V. Seymour Wilson and Willard A. Mullins discuss the implications of rules requiring francophone representation in the federal public service—a particularly contentious issue in Canada but also one that reflects almost a century of international debate about the design and role of a 'representative bureaucracy' in a democratic polity. Kathleen Archibald's work on the representation and working conditions for women in the federal service was perhaps the earliest systematic study of that subject in Canada, but teachers may also find it useful as an introduction to study of the formal rules adopted by some provincial and local governments to designate particular groups for differential consideration in their recruitment and later public service careers. Finally, William Neilson provides an overview of the common law tradition of 'service at the pleasure of the Crown'—the tradition out of which the modern rules governing dismissal in the public service evolved.

12

Changing Concepts of Power and Responsibility in the Canadian Public Service

Kenneth Kernaghan

Public servants exercise power as key actors in the Canadian political system. However, they share a stage crowded with a variety of other political actors, including cabinet ministers, legislators, members of the general public, and pressure group representatives. These actors, by directing or influencing the decisions and recommendations of public servants, help to balance administrative power with administrative responsibility.

In this essay, the evolution and present status of these concepts of administrative power and administrative responsibility are examined in the context of the Canadian public service. The first part of the paper centres on the power of public servants; the second part deals with administrative responsibility. The focus of the paper is on the federal sphere of government but the paper should serve as a useful basis for discussing the extent to which similar patterns of change have occurred in other governmental jurisdictions.[1] In this discussion of the role of public servants in the political system, the word political is not used in the narrow sense of partisan activity; rather it is used in the broad sense of involvement in the authoritative allocation of social values. 'Political life concerns all those varieties of activity that influence significantly the kind of authoritative policy adopted for a society and the way it is put into practice.'[2]

ADMINISTRATIVE POWER

The precise nature and extent of administrative power in the contemporary political process are not well documented in Canadian social-science literature. It is generally acknowledged, however, that public servants exercise significant power both in policy formation and policy execution. In a recent lecture on the threat to parliamentary responsible government, the former leader of the Opposition, Robert Stanfield, stated that 'while the House of Commons has been losing control, so also has the Government. The ministers just do not have the time to run such a vast show and make such a vast range of decisions. Consequently, more and more is for all practical purposes being decided by and implemented by the bureaucracy.'[3] And in a reminis-

Kenneth Kernaghan, 'Changing Concepts of Power and Responsibility in the Canadian Public Service', *Canadian Public Administration* 21, 3 (1978): 389–406. Courtesy of The Institute of Public Administration Canada.

cence on thirty years as a senior public servant and a minister, Mitchell Sharp observed that 'top public servants are powerful persons in the machinery of government at the federal level. They wield great influence. They do because they are, in the main, professionals who have been selected for their proven administrative ability and who devote their full time to government. In many cases, they have a greater influence upon the course of events than have Ministers, particularly the weaker and less competent.'[4] The extent of this administrative power clearly varies in accordance with such factors as the government's view of the proper role of public servants in the political process, the policy or program under consideration, the department or agency involved, and the style and competence of ministers and their officials.

A framework for examining the power of public servants may be devised by utilizing the doctrine of political neutrality which explains the nature of the interaction between public servants and other actors in the political system. It also permits us to focus on the changing nature of administrative power and on the role of public servants in both policy development and implementation. The major elements of the traditional doctrine may be summarized as follows:

(a) politics and policy are separated from administration: thus politicians make policy decisions; public servants execute these decisions;

(b) public servants are appointed and promoted on the basis of merit rather than on the basis of party affiliation or contributions;

(c) public servants do not engage in partisan political activities;

(d) public servants do not express publicly their personal views on government policies or administration;

(e) public servants provide forthright and objective advice to their political masters in private and in confidence; in return, political executives protect the anonymity of public servants by publicly accepting responsibility for departmental decisions; and

(f) public servants execute policy decisions loyally and zealously irrespective of the philosophy and programs of the party in power and regardless of their personal opinions; as a result, public servants enjoy security of tenure during good behaviour and satisfactory performance.[5]

As a basis for explaining the nature of administrative power in the political process, each of these six statements will be examined briefly.

The Policy Role of Public Servants

For the purpose of this essay, the key element of the traditional doctrine of political neutrality is that politics and policy are separated from administration so that ministers formulate policy and public servants administer that policy. This strict dichotomy is a convenient means of differentiating between the responsibilities of politicians and public servants; it is not, however, an accurate portrayal of reality. Public servants are now actively involved in both the formation and the execution of public policy—and it is often difficult to distinguish between the two activities.

In the sphere of policy formation, the power of public servants was perceived to be so great by the late 1960s that Prime Minister Trudeau endeavoured to place more policy-making power in the hands of politically accountable authorities, especially cabinet ministers. To this end, the cabinet committee system and the parliamentary committee system were reformed, the coordinating capacity of the Privy Council Office was strengthened and the policy influence of the Prime Minister's Office was expanded. The use of such alternative sources of policy advice as task forces, white papers and advisory councils provided a competing influence to departmental advice. The impact of these changes has been discussed at length elsewhere. However, it is notable that these changes did increase the role of ministers in policy formation. Indeed, Mitchell Sharp has lamented that ministers expended too much effort discussing each other's proposals in cabinet and in committees. He notes that 'decisions might have taken less time, we might have had a better perspective on events and more time for politics had we delegated more to our civil service advisors and left more time for reflection.'[6] It appears also that the power of the so-called 'public service mandarins' has been diffused among a broader range of political actors and among a greater number of senior public servants.

Despite these reforms, certain public servants continue to exercise significant power by virtue of their central positions in the policy process (for example, the Deputy Minister of Finance, the Clerk of the Privy Council). Moreover, despite the greater variety of available sources of policy advice, the very technical, complex, and time-consuming nature of certain policy issues obliges ministers to continue to rely heavily on the advice of their expert and experienced officials.

In the sphere of policy execution, public servants also exercise substantial power. Many of the day-to-day decisions of public servants involve the straightforward, objective application of general rules to specific cases and require the exercise of little or no judgment. However, many other decisions permit or require public servants to exercise considerable judgment in the administration of policy. In the course of interpreting, clarifying, and applying policy, public servants may significantly influence the success of policy decisions taken by ministers and legislators. The accuracy and enthusiasm with which public servants administer policy determines to a large extent the success of that policy. A series of individual, relatively minor decisions in a particular policy area can have a significant cumulative impact on the extent to which the original intent of cabinet and Parliament is realized. Moreover, such decisions can help to determine the content of subsequent changes in existing policy. In wielding such discretionary powers, public servants are of course expected to ensure that their decisions are broadly attuned to the general policy of their minister and their department.

The discretionary powers of public servants in policy execution are especially evident in the making and enforcement of regulations under authority delegated to them by Parliament or sub-delegated to them by a minister or by cabinet. The statutory provisions authorizing the making of regulations are often phrased in general or imprecise language which permits public servants to exercise significant discretion both in the wording of the regulations and in the application of their provisions to particular cases. The delegation by Parliament of power to make regulations is now very common and a large number of regulations has been made. The Special

Committee on Statutory Instruments which reported in 1969 found that 420 of 601 statutes perused by the committee provided for delegated legislation and that an annual average of 530 regul' :ions had been passed between 1956 and 1968.[7] Then, in 1977, the Senate-Hc ,se Committee on Regulations and Other Statutory Instruments, on the basis of its inquiry into 'the subordinate law made by delegates of Parliament', provided examples not only of the substantial volume of subordinate law but also of cases where public servants had exceeded the regulation-making authority granted to them by Parliament.[8] The committee recognized the need for subordinate legislation but made a number of recommendations to ensure more effective parliamentary scrutiny of this legislation and more attention to the rights of individuals affected by it.

It is clear that administration has important implications for policy and that politics and policy cannot be easily separated from administration.

Contrary to the dichotomy enshrined in the traditional doctrine of political neutrality, public servants are engaged in both policy formation and policy execution. Moreover, this power of public servants in the political process is likely to continue to grow in pace with the scale and complexity of government operations.

Political Appointments

Preservation of the political neutrality of public servants requires that they be appointed and promoted on the basis of competence and performance rather than on the basis of service to a political party. Most political appointments to senior positions in government are made to agencies, boards, and commissions rather than to regular departments and central agencies. However, during the Trudeau administration, much publicity has been given to a small number of political appointments to senior departmental and central agency posts and to the staff of the Prime Minister's Office. Criticism of these appointments has been directed more to the commitment of the appointees to the governing party than to the appointees' lack of merit.

Political appointments to senior positions usually occupied by career public servants limit the influence of these public servants by blocking their access to some of the highest positions in government. Moreover, long-serving officials are obliged to share their influence in the policy process with newcomers who may have fresh ideas and unorthodox approaches and who may not share the administrative values to which most public servants have become socialized. It is generally acknowledged that the recent growth in the influence of officials in the Privy Council Office and the Prime Minister's Office has diminished to some extent the influence of departmental public servants. This shift in power is primarily the result of changes in policy-making structures, however, rather than of the fact that some positions in these offices are held by appointees aligned with the governing party. Moreover, officials dedicated to service of the state rather than service of a political party continue to hold the great majority of senior positions and to exercise the power associated with those positions.

Partisanship

Between 1918 and 1967 the convention that public servants do not engage in partisan political activities was buttressed by the Civil Service Act of 1918 which specifically prohibited such activities. In 1967 the Public Service Employment Act removed this prohibition. Most public servants who wish to seek political office are now permitted to take a leave of absence to stand for nomination and election. Also, despite continuing restrictions against working on behalf of a candidate, public servants may engage in such activities as making financial contributions to a political party or candidate and attending political meetings. Senior public servants and those holding 'sensitive posts' (such as those with personnel or regulatory responsibilities) are still excluded from partisan activities.

This change has not had significant influence on the exercise of administrative power, especially since those officials most actively involved in policy development are excluded from participation. Thus, the political sympathies of the most powerful public servants remain generally unknown. Indeed, open identification with the governing party would break with tradition and would not necessarily enhance a public servant's influence with his political superiors or his administrative colleagues. It would certainly jeopardize his administrative career in the event of a change in government.

Moreover, one of the attractions of government employment at the senior levels is the opportunity to exercise influence in relative privacy and anonymity. While there have been some notable examples of public servants being transformed into cabinet ministers, a cabinet post is by no means a sure reward for a public servant who is elected to political office. And a senior public servant may well exercise more influence on policy from his departmental office than from a backbench in Parliament.

Public Comment
It follows that unless public servants are involved in approved forms of political partisanship, they should not engage in public and political controversy. By convention, public servants are not permitted to influence public opinion by expressing in public their personal views on government policies or administration. However, this conventional rule does not reflect the complexity of the issue of public comment and the difficulty of defining its permissible limits. Public servants can engage in a variety of forms of public comment which permit, encourage, or require the expression of personal views but which do not usually involve criticism of government. It is important to distinguish public comment from public criticism.

In the performance of their duties public servants are often obliged to discuss (a) the meaning and administration of government policies, (b) available remedies to problems with existing policies, and (c) matters on which government policy is undecided. These three categories constitute a zone of discretion within which public servants may move from description and explanation of existing or proposed government policies to the expression of personal views on these policies. Public servants are increasingly involved in situations where opportunities arise for the expression of personal views on public matters. The large scale of government's service and regulatory activities has led to public demand for more information about government programs and intentions and for discussion of policy issues in public. This demand has increasingly been met by public servants, who are required to represent their ministers in public forums either because of severe demands on the time of ministers or because of the complicated and technical nature of certain policies and programs.

Public servants cannot, however, fulfill their ministers' partisan political role. They strive to retain their impartiality by resisting the temptation to advocate specific policy options or to support or reject the policy suggestions of others. They also try to avoid personal identification with views which may be rejected by their minister or by a subsequent government. The danger of straying over the line between administration and policy is especially great when public servants are discussing matters on which government policy is unclear or undetermined. However, experienced public servants tend to know when they are near the line and few of them have been caught on the wrong side of it.

Public servants are much less circumspect when meeting with various individuals and groups in private and in confidence. In this much less public milieu, public servants engage in such political activities as negotiation and accommodation on behalf of their ministers. It is on these occasions that members of the public may see most clearly the nature and extent of administrative power in the policy process.

Public servants will increasingly be required to appear at public meetings to provide information about the substance and implementation of government policies and programs. As a result, the public will become more aware of the influence which public servants bring to deliberations on public policy matters. It is often difficult for public servants to discuss government policy without indicating, inadvertently or otherwise, some measure of the influence they have—or could have—over the content of the policy.

Anonymity

By engaging more actively in public comment on government policies and programs, public servants have moved more directly into the public spotlight and have thereby lost some of their anonymity. Despite this development, public servants strive to retain as much anonymity as possible. They give frank and impartial advice to their ministers in a private and confidential manner. Ministers, for their part, are expected to shield their officials from public attack by bearing public responsibility for all the actions—good or bad—of their administrative subordinates. This is the essence of the doctrine of ministerial responsibility. Recent experience in Canada demonstrates, however, that ministers occasionally fail to protect their officials from public criticism in cases of real or alleged maladministration.

Although ministers are sometimes unwilling or unable to protect their public servants from being named or blamed by opposition members or by the media, the confidentiality of official advice, whether in oral or written form, is usually preserved. This private advisory function gives public servants enormous influence over the content of public policy. Their advice is persuasive because it is informed and supported by administrative and professional personnel within their departments. This advice is especially influential, however, because it is proffered in confidence where it cannot be openly challenged and debated by other political actors.

Thus the tradition and practice of administrative secrecy which are so ingrained in the Canadian parliamentary system help to maintain the influence of public servants in the policy process. To the extent that knowledge is power public servants are in a position to preserve and expand their power by keeping certain information secret. Public servants are becoming more visible to the public but the confidentiality and influence of their advice to ministers are retained.

The anonymity of public servants has been diminished by their more frequent appearances before parliamentary committees. Their diplomatic skills are often severely taxed as they strive to describe and explain their department's programs fully and frankly while preserving their loyalty to their minister and their reputation for impartiality. On occasion, however, legislators, pressure group members, media representatives, and others concerned with the committees' deliberations can discern the actual or potential power of public servants in the political process.

A further incursion on anonymity has resulted from the increasing interest of the news media in the activities of public servants, whether these activities take place in parliamentary committees, in public gatherings or in departmental offices. This media coverage makes public servants and their views better known to the public. Thus, it helps to limit the power of public servants by exposing their activities to public questioning and criticism.

Permanence

An important source of administrative power is the permanence in office which public servants enjoy as long as they serve their political masters loyally regardless of the party in power. This security of tenure enables a career public servant not only to establish and wield influence in the policy process but to continue to exercise such influence even if there is a change in the governing party. Long tenure in office enables public servants to acquire knowledge and experience both in specific policy fields and in the political–administrative system within which policy decisions are made.

The permanence in office of public servants increases their power *vis-à-vis* politicians. Ministers cannot hope to match the expertise of their senior officials, and the frequent rotation of ministers prevents them from accumulating much experience in particular policy areas. The effort of the Trudeau administration to rotate senior public servants more frequently has probably reduced somewhat the attachment of officials to certain policy fields and diminished the knowledge and experience they acquire in any single policy field.

There is some support in Canada for a system of political appointments similar to that in the United States. Under this system, the incumbents of the most senior public service positions would be replaced whenever a change in government occurred. Some senior appointments would thus be held on a temporary rather than a permanent basis. The power of career public servants would be reduced because they would not normally be appointed to the highest administrative posts in government. However, assuming regular changes in the governing party, the tenure in office of senior political appointees would be too brief to enable them to exercise as much power based on experience and expertise as career public servants do.

At present, there is little possibility of a shift to a system of political appointments. Such a shift would be more likely if the political neutrality of public servants declined much more than it has. Thus, to preserve their permanency in office, senior public servants must maintain their impartiality by avoiding partisan activity and inappropriate public comment and, so far as possible, preserving their anonymity. Despite the tenure in office which public servants in general enjoy, it is likely that a few political appointments to senior departmental and central agency posts will continue to be made.

On the basis of this examination of the major elements of the doctrine of political neutrality, two major conclusions may be drawn:

(a) public servants are more active participants in the political process than the traditional doctrine of political neutrality suggests;

(b) this participation accounts in large part for the nature and extent of the power which public servants exercise in contemporary Canadian government.

ADMINISTRATIVE RESPONSIBILITY

In democratic states, it is not the expansion of administrative power which arouses primary concern; rather it is the irresponsible exercise of that power. Thus, continuing attention centres on the means by which administrative power and administrative responsibility may be reconciled.

The concept of administrative responsibility, like that of administrative power, is difficult both to define and to measure. The evolution of the concept has been accompanied by conflicting views on its appropriate meaning. This evolution has culminated in a widespread acceptance today of two major interpretations of administrative responsibility, namely *objective* responsibility and *subjective* or *psychological* responsibility.[9] Objective responsibility is similar in meaning to accountability. It refers to the responsibility employees have to political and administrative superiors who may impose sanctions for failure to obey directions. Subjective responsibility is more similar in meaning to loyalty, identification, and conscience. It refers to the responsibility employees feel toward the various political actors with whom they interact.

These two meanings may conflict with one another. Objective responsibility requires employees to look upward to hierarchical superiors whereas subjective responsibility permits employees to look outward to a greater variety of political actors and to look inward to a sense of conscience. It is generally acknowledged, however, that the two interpretations are complementary and that administrative power can be most effectively controlled by requiring employees to adhere to objective responsibility in the event of a conflict between the two senses of responsibility.

While these broad classifications help to conceptualize administrative responsibility, they are not precise enough to provide a useful framework for assessing the present nature of administrative responsibility in the Canadian political system. Administrative responsibility may more fruitfully be discussed in terms of the administrative values associated with it. A number of values may be identified which are central both to the theoretical literature on administrative responsibility and to the evolution of the Canadian public service. The values linked to administrative responsibility vary in importance from one country to another and from one period to another. However, a review of Canadian administrative history suggests that the values most commonly associated with administrative responsibility in the Canadian context are accountability, neutrality, efficiency, effectiveness, integrity, responsiveness, and representiveness. With the exception of efficiency and effectiveness, which will be discussed together each of these values will be examined in turn.

Accountability

Accountability is a prime and enduring value associated with administrative responsibility: it is virtually synonymous with the notion of objective responsibility defined above. Accountability involves concern for the legal, institutional, and procedural devices by which public servants may be held accountable or answerable for their actions. In a democratic system of government it is deemed essential that appointed officials be held accountable to ministers, legislators, judges, and administrative superiors. This quest for accountability has become both more important and more challenging as administrative power over policy formation and execution has expanded.

Enforcing accountability for the exercise of such power is becoming increasingly difficult as contemporary public services continue to grow in size and as their responsibilities grow in complexity. The decision-making process in government is often so lengthy and complicated that it is difficult to single out those individuals who should be held accountable for specific recommendations and decisions. And we have already noted the inadequacy of the doctrine of ministerial responsibility in ensuring that the minister will be held responsible for maladministration in his department. Thus, the locus of responsibility is sometimes hard to find.

Several of the reforms in Canadian governmental institutions during the post-war period have had a significant impact on the accountability of public servants. There is not space in this essay to do more than note briefly the effect of these changes.

The reform of the PMO, the PCO, and the cabinet committee system, mentioned earlier, has helped to increase the accountability of public servants to the cabinet and to ministers in the sphere of policy development. Changes in the parliamentary committee system have enhanced the opportunities of legislators to supervise the executive. The recently established Committee on Regulations and Other Statutory Instruments has been constructively critical of the government's handling of subordinate legislation. It appears that the Auditor General's powers will be increased, particularly with respect to determining whether the government has received 'value for money' and that a Comptroller General will be appointed to help ensure effective government control of the public purse. And one of the major reasons for the creation of the Federal Court of Canada was to provide greater opportunities for appeals against administrative decisions.

Organizational reform in such departments as Transport, Public Works, and the Post Office was designed primarily to enhance efficiency and effectiveness rather than accountability. Similarly, the strengthening of Treasury Board and the introduction of such management techniques as PPBS, MBO, and performance measurement aim to make the administrative process more efficient and effective. However, these changes in organization and management, by bringing about clearer statements of objectives and of responsibility for meeting these objectives, can assist hierarchical superiors to hold public servants more accountable for their actions.

Neutrality

Responsible public servants are expected to be politically neutral. We have already seen that absolute political neutrality requires that public servants be neutral not only in regard to partisan conflicts but also in regard to the predominant values of the society they serve. However, the role of public servants in the contemporary political process is important in large part because they are *not* value neutral; rather they are actively involved in the authoritative allocation of values for society.

If value neutrality were possible, public servants would 'receive' their values from those political and administrative actors to whom they are accountable. Politically determined values would flow down the hierarchy as a framework for administrative action. Public servants are not, however, neutral instruments of political masters. They may feel responsible to a variety of political actors other than those to whom they are accountable in the legal or hierarchical sense. Moreover, their discretionary powers to give advice and make decisions enable them to take into account their personal values and their department's values as well as the values of those political actors with whom they interrelate. Public servants have never been value neutral and they tend to become less so as their discretionary powers increase.

In the exercise of their advisory and decision-making powers, however, public servants are expected to act within a policy framework determined by their political superiors. Where they have full discretion to make decisions, they are expected to anticipate the reactions of their ministers by making decisions which they believe the ministers would like them to make.

Efficiency and Effectiveness

Scholarly literature and government reports on the Canadian public service demonstrate that the dominant value in the evolution of responsible public administration in Canada is efficiency. Since 1962, implementation of the Glassco Commission recommendations has extended this historical emphasis on efficient public sector management. During this same period, 'effectiveness' has tended to supersede 'economy' as the companion value for efficiency.

The values of efficiency and effectiveness are interdependent but distinct in meaning. Efficiency is a measure of performance which may be expressed as a ratio between input and output. Effectiveness is a measure of the extent to which an activity achieves the organization's objectives.

During the Trudeau administration, relatively more attention has been paid to effectiveness than previously. Indeed, John Langford contends that effectiveness was one of the major organizational values driving the machinery of government between 1968 and 1972.[10] Treasury Board has been the prime mover since the late 1960s in promoting efficiency and effectiveness throughout the public service. The

Board has supported the introduction of more sophisticated techniques of achieving and evaluating efficiency and effectiveness, including planning, programming and budgeting, cost-benefit analysis, operational performance measurement, and management by objectives. Treasury Board is likely to continue to invest time, effort and money in developing evaluation techniques and its concern for improving efficiency and effectiveness will continue to pervade the public service.

The extensive organizational reform of several government departments in recent years has also been aimed at achieving the departments' objectives more efficiently and effectively. And under a new bill which broadens the powers of the Auditor General, he would report instances where money has been spent without 'due regard to economy or efficiency' or where 'satisfactory procedures have not been established to measure and report the effectiveness of programs, where such procedures could appropriately and reasonably be implemented.'

All these measures extend the importance which historically has been placed on the achievement of efficiency in the Canadian public service. It is notable that strong support—and in some cases the initiative—for these measures has come from senior public servants.

Integrity

Integrity refers here to ethics in public administration. The integrity of public servants is important to the preservation of public confidence in government. Some students of administrative responsibility take the integrity of public servants for granted. However, recent experience in Canada and elsewhere indicates that increased vigilance is required to ensure that public servants adhere to high ethical standards. The achievement of high standards is increasingly difficult because of the large number of employees in the public service and the discretionary decision-making powers which these employees enjoy.

Historically, public concern about the integrity of public servants has risen and declined as real or apparent cases of unethical conduct have been revealed, investigated, and then forgotten. In very recent years, however, the public's interest has been sustained by an unprecedented number of allegations of unethical conduct involving both public servants and politicians. The two major areas of concern have been conflicts of interest and unauthorized disclosures ('leaks') of government information.

For the first time in Canadian administrative history, these events have led to significant legislative action. In the conflict of interest sphere, the federal government has promulgated a code of conduct for public servants which includes conflict of interest guidelines and provision for disclosure of actual or potential conflicts. In the area of confidentiality, the government seems likely to yield to pressures by the opposition, the news media and other groups to provide more open access to government documents through a Freedom of Information Act.[11]

Some forms of administrative conduct are more readily seen to be unethical than others. The use of public office for personal gain is clearly unethical and may be prohibited by statute or regulation. However, the unauthorized disclosure of confidential information may on occasion involve an ethical dilemma in that public servants may believe that the public interest would be advanced through the leaking of confidential information. It may be argued that the public has the right to know, even if that knowledge is gained through the unauthorized release of information. On the other hand, it may be argued that 'leaks' constitute a violation of a public servant's oath of office and that integrity demands that public servants resign if they wish to oppose government policies outside government.

The encouragement of integrity as a defence against abuse of administrative power involves both objective and subjective responsibility in that it requires not only legislative constraints and penalties but also appeals to conscience and morality.

Responsiveness

The Glassco Commission concluded that 'the importance to the public of efficiency and integrity in the machinery of government . . . is unquestionably great. . . . But even greater is the importance of a service responsive to public wants and expectations.'[12] And Carl Friedrich, one of the foremost writers on administrative responsibility, claims that the responsible public servant exercises power with proper regard 'for existing preferences in the community, and more particularly the prevailing majority.'[13]

The responsiveness of public servants depends largely on their knowledge of public needs and desires. This knowledge may be gained directly through personal contacts with individual citizens and groups and indirectly through elected representatives, especially ministers. Interest in responsiveness through direct contact has been stimulated by the citizen participation movement which has pervaded North America during the last decade and which has been manifested at the federal level of government in Canada by the emphasis on participatory democracy. Citizen involvement requires that citizens be given access to the decision-making process by being actively consulted by public officials and having their views taken into account. Available evidence suggests that the federal government has been unsuccessful in bringing about a significant increase in citizen involvement in decision-making. The greatest success in opening up channels of access for citizen participation has been achieved in the municipal sphere of government.

The matter of confidentiality, discussed earlier in relation to integrity, is also closely related to the value of responsiveness. It is difficult for citizens to assess and contribute to decision-making if they do not have access to the information on which public servants base their decisions. Moreover, public access to such information obliges public servants to consider policy in terms of its impact on the citizenry and thereby tends to encourage public servants to be more responsive to public wants and expectations.

Responsiveness to the public, whether to citizens' groups or to organized special interest groups, often requires the exercise of subjective responsibility because it depends on the public servants' perception of what influences they should respond to in making decisions. Thus, responsiveness may on occasion conflict with accountability to political and administrative superiors. Responsiveness may also conflict with efficiency in that consultation with citizens tends to be time-consuming and disruptive to normal patterns of decision-making.

Representativeness

Advocates of a representative public service contend that it makes public servants more responsible by making them more responsive. A representative public service may be defined as one in which the employees are drawn proportionately from the major ethnic, religious, socio-economic, and other groups within society. Some of its proponents believe that a representative public service should be a 'mirror' of society; others are content with a public service in which the various groups are included in rough proportion to their numbers in the total population.

In the belief that the attitudes of representatives of the group will be similar to the attitudes of the whole group, a representative public service is deemed to be more responsive to the needs of the public and more effective in giving policy advice. Thus, a representative public service is seen as a partial remedy to the inadequacy of accountability as a means of controlling administrative power.

Although the propositions in the preceding paragraph have serious logical and empirical deficiencies, they have been influential in supporting efforts in various countries to bring about a more representative public service. In Canada, a representative public service has been presented as a means of bringing about a more responsive public service. For example, in regard to the representation of Francophones and Anglophones, a senior public servant wrote that

> if we wish our political and administrative institutions to reflect the norms and priorities of both groups, we must ensure that representatives from both communities are actively and jointly engaged in the process of policy making and policy implementation at the most senior levels of our public services. We must ensure not only that the representatives of these two communities can communicate with one another but, more important, that each can understand and appreciate the other's set of values. Only in this way can our governmental institutions acquire sensitivity and responsiveness to the predominant values and priorities within both communities.[14]

In addition to Francophones, the major groups for whom a more proportional representation has been sought during the postwar period are women, Indians, and Eskimos. For example, in an effort to increase participation, responsiveness and representativeness all at the same time, the President of the Treasury Board announced a new personnel management policy affecting Indians, Métis, Non-Status Indians, and Inuit. He said that 'greater participation of these people in the government's decision-making process will improve federal programs and services to their communities, while creating a public service that is more representative of all Canadians.'[15]

In the Canadian context, the symbolic value of representativeness is at least as important as improved responsiveness. A public service which is composed of representatives of the major groups in society symbolizes for members of these groups such benefits as equal opportunity and upward mobility. The group members tend to perceive that if they are represented at senior levels of the public services, the public policy process will be more responsive to their needs and desires. It is obvious also that the government attaches considerable political value to the symbolism of representativeness in the public service.

CONCLUSIONS

It is clear that the reconciliation of administrative power and administrative responsibility requires emphasis on values other that simply accountability. Accountability is a necessary but an insufficient means to achieve administrative responsibility. The contemporary challenge is not so much to check administrative power but to ensure that public servants use their power to meet public needs and wants. Reliance on formal controls over administrative action may stifle initiative and lead to inaction or to action which is inefficient, ineffective, or unresponsive. Thus, several values vie with accountability for precedence in the pursuit of administrative responsibility. Some of these values (for example, neutrality) tend to complement accountability; other values (for example, responsiveness) may conflict with accountability—or with one another (efficiency versus responsiveness). The strength of these administrative values depends on the priority attached to them by the political actors who control and influence public servants and by the public servants themselves. The way in which public servants use their power will be shaped by a mix of these values and the relative importance of the values will vary over time.

In keeping with the long-standing emphasis on accountability, scholars and practitioners concerned with the issue of administrative responsibility have centred their attention on the means by which political and administrative institutions and structures may be altered so as to achieve objective responsibility. As a result, comparatively little thought has been devoted to the means by which subjective responsibility may be encouraged. But the public service is now so large and complex that reliance on formal controls to achieve administrative responsibility is inadequate. It is important to create an environment in which responsibility may be elicited rather that enforced. Among the means by which subjective responsibility may be stimulated are the personal model of responsible conduct provided by administrative superiors, pre-service and in-service training and education regarding the problems and demands of administrative responsibility, and the increasingly professional composition of the public service.

Our ability to choose the best means to preserve and promote administrative responsibility depends on our knowledge of what we want to hold public servants responsible for. However, we have sparse empirical evidence on either the power of public servants in the political process in relation to specific policies and decisions, or the consequences for the allocation of public resources of the exercise of administrative power. Available evidence suggests that our concern should centre less on the fact of administrative power and more on the ends to which that power is directed.

Among the questions bearing on the power and responsibility of public servants to which this seminar might direct its attention are these:

(a) What means are available to elicit rather that to enforce responsible administrative conduct?

(b) What measure can be taken to fill the gap between ministerial responsibility and administrative responsibility?

(c) Is the public servant responsible solely to his minister or is he legitimately responsible to other actors in the public service?

(d) Will more openness in government promote or hinder the achievement of administrative responsibility?

(e) Will more citizen participation in government encourage or impede the attainment of administrative responsibility?

(f) Will the growing professionalization of the public service advance or retard the achievement of administrative responsibility?

(g) Is the importance of such values as efficiency, effectiveness, responsiveness, or representativeness increasing relative to the value of accountability?

(h) Can management functions be devolved from central agencies to departments with assurance that these functions will be performed responsibly?

NOTES

1. The organization and content of this paper have been determined in part by an effort to incorporate in a coherent fashion a lengthy list of concepts suggested by the conference organizers.

2. David Easton, *The Political System* (New York: Alfred A. Knopf, 1953), p. 128.

3. The George C. Nowlan Lecture, Acadia University, 7 February 1977. Reprinted in *The Globe and Mail,* 8 February 1977.

4. Mitchell Sharp. 'Reflections of a Former Minister of the Crown', address to the Toronto Regional Group of the Institute of Public Administration of Canada, 29 November 1976, pp. 6–7.

5. This framework is drawn from Kenneth Kernaghan, 'Politics, Policy and Public Servants: Political Neutrality Revisited', *Canadian Public Administration* 19, 3 (Fall 1976), pp. 432–56.

6. Sharp, 'Reflections', p. 15.

7. House of Commons, *Special Committee on Statutory Instruments,* 3rd Report (Ottawa: Queen's Printer, 1969), p. 4.

8. Senate and House of Commons, *Standing Joint Committee on Regulations and Other Statutory Instruments,* 2nd Report (Ottawa: Queen's Printer, 1977), esp. pp. 2–12.

9. See Frederick C. Mosher, *Democracy and The Public Service* (New York: Oxford University Press. 1968), pp. 7–10. See also Kenneth Kernaghan, 'Responsible Public Bureaucracy: A Rationale and a Framework for Analysis', *Canadian Public Administration* 16, 4 (Winter 1972), pp. 572–603.

10. John Langford, *Transport in Transition* (Montreal: McGill-Queen's University Press, 1976), pp. 7–15.

11. See Secretary of State, *Legislation on Public Access to Government Documents* (Ottawa: Supply and Services Canada, June 1977).

12. *Report of the Royal Commission on Government Organization* (Ottawa: Queen's Printer, 1962), 1, p. 63.
13. Carl J. Friedrich, 'Public Policy and the Nature of Administrative Responsibility', *Public Policy* 1 (1940), p. 12.
14. Sylvain Cloutier, 'Senior Public Servants in a Bicultural Society', *Canadian Public Administration* 11, 4 (Winter 1968), pp. 397–8.
15. Robert Andras, News Release, Treasury Board, 5 July 1977.

13

Codes of Ethics and Public Administration: Progress, Problems, and Prospects

Kenneth Kernaghan

From an international perspective, the 1970s may aptly be described as 'the ethics decade' in the historical development of the study and practice of public administration. This focus on the ethical conduct of public servants resulted not only from intense public and academic concern about ethics in government but also from the unprecedented response of governments to this concern. The continuing interest in this issue at the end of the 1970s suggests that the ethical behaviour of public servants will remain high on the agenda of public administration's concerns in the forseeable future.

The overarching theme of this paper is that the issue of ethical conduct among public servants is an integral part of the larger issue of reconciling administrative power and administrative responsibility. Ethics has traditionally been an important element of the broad concept of administrative responsibility and high ethical standards are widely viewed as one means of guarding against abuse of bureaucratic power.

Opportunities for public servants to become involved in unethical conduct arise from the power they exercise in both the development and administration of public policy. In particular, their discretionary decision-making powers and their access to confidential information provide considerable scope for unethical conduct. John A. Rohr argues that 'through administrative discretion, bureaucrats participate in the governing process of our society; but to govern in a democratic society without being responsible to the electorate raises a serious ethical question for bureaucrats.'[1] Ethical rules are designed to ensure the impartiality, objectivity and integrity of public servants in their conduct of the public's business. Public servants are enjoined to refrain from using their government position for personal, private, pecuniary, or partisan gain.

Historically, the public's interest in the ethical conduct of government officials, whether politicians or public servants, has waxed and waned as instances of wrongdoing have been exposed, publicized, debated, punished, and then forgotten. Moreover, there has been, in the past, little spillover of anxiety about ethics in government from one country to another. Instances or allegations of unethical conduct

Kenneth Kernaghan, 'Codes of Ethics and Public Administration: Progress, Problems, and Prospects', *Public Administration* vol. 58 (Summer 1980): 207–24. Reprinted by permission of Blackwell Publishing.

among government officials have tended to arise at different times in different countries. But in the early 1970s, the worldwide publicity given to ethical offences of high-ranking officials in the United States coincided with revelations of unethical activities by officials in other countries. These events stimulated a widespread mood of public concern, especially in western democratic states, about the ethical standards of government officials.[2]

During the 1970s, information and knowledge about ethical problems in government have been enormously expanded by the publications of academics and journalists and by government studies and reports. The statute books and administrative manuals of many governments contain new or revised sections on various aspects of ethical conduct.[3] Some governments are still engaged in the formulation of ethical rules while others are actively involved in the administration—and even the revision—of recently adopted measures.[4] Thus, at the end of the decade, it seems unlikely that public, governmental, and academic interest in the ethics of public officials will soon subside.

Yet there is little objective evidence of a substantial increase in the number or proportion of public servants engaged in unethical activities. What then has stimulated and sustained the high level of public and governmental concern about unethical conduct? The answer lies in several developments acting in combination and varying in importance from one country to another and from one government jurisdiction to another within a single country.

The *public's* concern about public service ethics has been prompted in large part by the knowledge of ethical offences actually or allegedly committed by public servants. In some countries, certain instances of official misconduct have been especially shocking or controversial (e.g., the Watergate affair, the Pentagon Papers); in other countries, the cumulative impact of offences of lesser moment has stimulated public agitation for higher standards of ethical performance. The news media have played a key role in exposing unethical conduct and in maintaining the public's interest in the extent of the offences and the fate of the offenders. In part as a result of this publicity, there is a widespread public perception that ethical standards are too low and a suspicion that many ethical infractions are never uncovered. These views are reinforced by sporadic but continuing revelations of ethical misconduct. Furthermore, the public's view as to what constitutes unethical behaviour has changed over time. For example, political activity by public servants has gradually become more acceptable while conflicts of interest, especially in the area of subsequent employment, have become less tolerable.

The concern of *governments* about public service ethics has been based on both administrative and partisan political considerations. It is difficult, however, to discover to what extent the adoption of ethical rules is a response to actual or anticipated ethical problems and to what extent it is intended to assure the public of the government's commitment to high ethical standards. The public's unhappiness about ethical transgressions together with confusion within and outside government as to what constitutes unethical conduct demonstrate the need to clarify and specify ethical standards. Elaboration of ethical rules is also required as a result of the efforts of public service unions to extend the rights of their members (e.g., in regard to political activity or outside employment). Finally, the political fortunes of the governing party tend to be enhanced by minimizing the number of ethical infractions committed by either elected or appointed officials.

This paper focuses on the conduct of appointed officials (hereinafter described as public servants). Attention is centred on Canadian governments but references are made to developments elsewhere and most of my observations are directly applicable to ethical issues in other countries. Also, emphasis is placed primarily, but not exclusively, on those ethical problem areas most troublesome in Canada, the United States, Britain, and Australia—namely conflicts of interest, confidentiality, political partisanship, and public comment.

This paper examines, in turn, recent Canadian developments affecting the ethical conduct of public servants; the form, content and administration of codes of ethics; the benefits and costs of these codes for public servants and for those whom they serve; and the implications of codes of ethics for administrative responsibility.

THE ETHICS OF CANADA'S PUBLIC SERVANTS

The Watergate revelations and their reverberations intensified government efforts in other countries to promote high ethical standards among public servants. But many countries had already adopted legal and administrative measures bearing on the ethics of public servants. In Canada, the federal and provincial governments had devised a variety of mechanisms to deal with ethical problems that had arisen before 1970. And disclosures of unethical conduct among government officials during the early 1970s had prompted several Canadian governments to assess the desirability of new measures.[5]

However, at that time, federal and provincial measures relating to the ethical conduct of public servants were rudimentary, fragmentary, and scattered. Such measures were virtually non-existent in municipal governments. Neither the federal government nor any provincial government had a code of ethics applicable to the public service as a whole. A few governments did have separate service-wide statutes or regulations on some aspects of conflict of interest situations, and on political partisanship and confidentiality. Within these governments, some departments had ethical rules in the form of written guidelines but most departments had none. Some of the departments with written rules provided relatively broad coverage of ethical problem areas but most were concerned primarily with conflicts of interest. The content of these rules differed from one department to another within the same government.

Then, in 1973, the federal government promulgated a code of ethics with major emphasis on the conflict of interest area.[6] During the same year, the Ontario and Newfoundland governments adopted measures regulating conflicts of interest.[7] These initiatives, together with continuing public criticism and cynicism regarding the ethical standards of government officials, had a snowballing effect. By the end of the decade, most provincial governments had adopted written rules to regulate the ethical behaviour of public servants. These rules differ greatly from one government to another in their form (i.e., statutes, regulations, guidelines, or a combination of these measures); in their content; in the types of government officials covered; in the provisions for administration; and in the penalties for violations. All governments focus primarily on the several variants of conflict of interest; some give attention, usually in separate statutes or regulations, to the areas of political activity, public comment, and confidentiality. Public servants in regular government departments are usually covered separately from politicians and often from other public employees, but the conflict of interest statute in one province applies to provincial and municipal elected and appointed officials, including employees in agencies, boards and commissions.[8] Some conflict of interest rules require disclosure of assets whereas others simply require a declaration that the public servant has no conflicts of interest. Sanctions for ethical offences range from the specific—'a fine of not more than $10,000' to the more general—'dismissal or other disciplinary action pursuant to . . . the Public Service Act.'[9] The diversity of these mechanisms for preventing and punishing ethical misconduct can be explained largely by the number, nature, and magnitude of ethical problems experienced by each government, by the legal and administrative measures already in existence, and by varying opinions as to the most effective means of administration and the most appropriate penalties for particular offences.

It is too early yet to assess adequately the utility of these written rules in enhancing the ethical conduct of Canada's public servants. Canadian governments have now had much experience in developing ethical rules, but to date they have had only brief experience in administering those rules formulated in recent years. In any event, it is difficult to measure accurately the impact of ethical rules because governments provide little or no data on the number and nature of ethical offences committed either before or after the development of the rules. During the early 1970s, it appeared that even if the public revelations of unethical conduct constituted only the tip of the iceberg of ethical offences, the iceberg was a very small one. Since that time, my discussions of ethical issues with many public servants at all levels of Canadian government have demonstrated that the iceberg is larger than it first appeared. Still, a very small percentage of public servants are actually involved in unethical conduct. It is important to note that ethical rules are not designed simply to catch offenders but to provide guidance to public servants who are uncertain as to what activities are permissible and what activities are prohibited.

THE STYLE AND SUBSTANCE OF ETHICAL RULES

In Canada, as in other countries, governments have taken varying approaches to the form, content, and administration of their written rules on the ethical conduct of public servants. It is generally acknowledged that the most appropriate form is a *code* of ethics which contains comprehensive coverage of the major ethical problems facing a particular government and effective means for the code's administration. It is useful to codify existing rules by bringing them together in a single document (e.g., Alberta's Code) or at least incorporating in that document reference to service-wide rules already existing in statutes and regulations (e.g., the federal Code). The codification of previously unwritten and scattered written rules provides a central reference source of rules on ethical conduct. The practice of most Canadian governments, however, has been to treat each problem area in a separate statute or regulation.

Safeguards against unethical conduct can take the form of statutes providing for prosecution and punishment by the regular courts (e.g., Criminal Code provisions on bribery and corruption) or of statutes or regulations administered and enforced within the government itself. Prosecution by the courts is too blunt an instrument to apply to most unethical practices. Many instances of unethical behaviour fall into a 'grey zone' in that they are unacceptable but cannot be effectively handled by the courts. In other cases, it is debatable as to whether an offence has actually been committed since many ethical issues are very complex and the offence may be more apparent than real. In such circumstances, governments are sometimes required to exercise a considerable measure of judgment as to what penalty, if any, is appropriate. This judgment may be based on such factors as the seriousness of the offence, the previous record of the official, and his experience and position in the public service. Moreover, if a penalty is imposed, it could range from reprimand through to dismissal. A persuasive argument can be made for ethical rules which take the form of regulations rather than statutes since regulations are subject to more flexibility in their interpretation and can be more easily amended to take account of experience and changing conditions. However, statutory provisions on ethical conduct can be and often are supplemented by administrative regulations or guidelines which elaborate on these provisions.

Codes of ethics may be depicted on a continuum from 'The Ten Commandments' approach to 'The Justinian Code' approach depending on the general and limited or the specific and comprehensive nature of their content. The Ten Commandments model is a comparatively brief statement of broad principles of ethical conduct which contains no provision for its administration and enforcement. The ten brief and general clauses of the United States *Code of Ethics for Government Service* adopted in 1958 constitute an excellent example of this model.[10]

The Justinian Code model, by way of contrast, is a lengthy document which provides comprehensive coverage of ethical problem areas in very specific language and makes detailed provision for the administration and enforcement of the code. A major advantage of a code based on this model is that it consolidates in a single reference document all rules relating to the ethical conduct of public servants. A significant disadvantage is that the code tends to be a lengthy and cumbersome document which may be difficult to understand and may appear unduly constraining both to existing and aspiring public servants. The code contained in the discussion paper drafted in 1978 by the Australian Public Service Board does not take this extreme form but lies close to the Justinian Code pole of the continuum.[11] This draft code contains five chapters covering relationships between officials, the government and Parliament; financial interests; use of official information; political and industrial participation; and personal behaviour. Codes based on the Justinian Code model could be abbreviated by excluding matters relating to personal rather than ethical conduct (e.g., dress and appearance, waste and extravagance).

The code of conduct of the Canadian federal government has some deficiencies but it has features which enable it to avoid the disadvantages at either end of the continuum. The eight clauses of the federal conflict of interest guidelines are broadly worded principles but the code of conduct explicitly recognizes this. It states that

Any attempt to identify the totality of potential areas of conflict . . . could never be totally comprehensive and would require constant review and interpretation. Instead a more workable approach has been taken to identify certain principles, the violation of which would clearly establish a situation of conflict of interest. With these published principles, the overall intent is established and actual situations can be scrutinized to determine whether the principles are respected.

The Code suggests also that individual departments and agencies 'supplement these guidelines with more specific provisions pertaining to their own operations'. These departmental provisions help compensate for the generality of the service-wide guidelines. Aspects of personal conduct are specifically excluded from the Code and 'the responsibility for developing such standards continues to rest with the management of individual departments'.

Regardless of the form of ethical rules developed by a government, the *content* of these rules reflects the ethical problems encountered by that government. In such countries as Canada, the United States, Britain, and Australia, ethical rules have focused primarily on conflicts of interest and to a lesser extent on confidentiality, political partisanship, and public comment. Thus, these four areas should constitute the principal elements of a code of ethics. Another area that merits coverage is the interaction of political leaders and public servants, with particular reference to conflicts of loyalty experienced by public servants. This subject has received little attention in Canadian discussions of codes of ethics but has been a major concern in other countries.

Senior public servants with discretionary authority and confidential information have the greatest opportunities to participate in and benefit from unethical conduct. But temptations to engage in unethical behaviour exist at all levels of the administrative hierarchy and at all levels of government (e.g., a senior official with contracting authority in a federal department or a secretary in a municipal government with access to confidential development plans). Thus, it is useful to describe briefly the nature of the ethical problem posed in each of the five areas mentioned above.

Conflicts of interest constitute the most pervasive and problematic area of unethical activities not only because of the prospect of financial gain from such activities but also because of the many varieties of the offence. A conflict of interest may be defined as 'a situation in which a public employee has a private or personal interest sufficient to influence or appear to influence the objective exercise of his official duties'. The varieties of conflict of interest include influence peddling, financial transactions, dealings with relatives, gifts and entertainment, corrupt practices, outside employment, and post-employment.

The development of ethical rules in some of these categories is more challenging than in others. For example, the drafting and enforcement of rules on post-employment activities are especially difficult. The public's confidence in the integrity and impartiality of the public service may be diminished if an official accepts employment from a firm with which he conducted official business before his resignation or retirement from government service. There would be grounds for suspicion that the official might have conferred benefits on the firm in the hope of future employment or that the firm might gain a competitive advantage by hiring an official who has had access to confidential information, including trade secrets.

Britain has had rules on post-employment activities since 1937 but Canada did not promulgate any rules in this area until 1978.[12] The problem is not a new one in Canada; nor is it confined to the most senior levels of the government. It was, however, given special prominence in 1976 by the well-publicized employment and commercial activities of retired deputy ministers. The major principle set out in the Canadian guidelines is that 'current and former holders of public office must ensure by their actions that the objectivity and impartiality of government service are not cast in doubt and that the people of Canada are given no cause to believe that preferential treatment is being or will be unduly accorded to any person or organization'. The guidelines apply to all existing and former ministers and public employees. Former holders of public office 'are requested not to engage' in certain specified activities for periods of time ranging from six months to two years depending on the nature and level of the position they held in the government.

The enforcement of rules on post-employment activities is no easier than their formulation. In Britain, no formal sanctions are provided. In Canada, the policy applies 'to all persons appointed to new positions within the government and its agencies, who will be expected to conform to it *as a matter of honour and personal choice*'. The policy also includes rules of practice designed to lessen the likelihood of conflicts of interest by regulating the granting of government appointments and personal service contracts to former public servants.

The ethical standards of public servants in respect to the *confidentiality* of government information is also of widespread public and governmental interest. During the 1970s, the unauthorized disclosure of government documents, of which the Pentagon Papers episode in the United States was the most celebrated example, troubled governments in several countries. In Canada, the leaking of confidential documents during this decade was unprecedented in the country's history.[13]

As with conflicts of interest, the formulation and the administration of rules on confidentiality are challenging tasks. It has been suggested that some documents have deliberately been leaked by political leaders for partisan political purposes but most leaks appear to be the work of public servants who wish to embarrass the government of the day or protect the public interest. The penalties provided by the *Official Secrets Act* are too severe for application to relatively minor incidents of unauthorized disclosure, and the public servant's oath of office and secrecy is widely viewed as an inadequate safeguard to confidentiality. There is a need for ethical rules on confidentiality which set out clearly the standards to which public servants are expected to adhere and the penalties for violations. Most conflict of interest rules prohibit the use of official information for financial benefit but this offence is only one aspect of the confidentiality issue.

Some proponents of freedom of information legislation contend that if members of the public had broader access to government information, the motivation for unauthorized disclosure would be significantly reduced. It is important to remember, however, that under a freedom of information act, many of the documents most eagerly sought by journalists, scholars, and others will be exempted from disclosure (e.g., Cabinet papers, information relating to security matters).

Rules on the *political activity* of public servants vary considerably from one country to another and indeed from one government to another within the same country. Constraints on political activity are justified primarily by the desire that public employees both serve and appear to serve the public and their political superiors in an objective, non-partisan manner. It is argued that under such circumstances, public servants are much more likely to be appointed and promoted on the basis of merit rather than party affiliation.

In Britain and the United States and in Canada at the federal level and in several provinces, the great majority of public servants are permitted to participate in a variety of political activities, including election to public office. But there is still disagreement and confusion in several jurisdictions, especially in Canada, as to precisely which public servants may participate in which activities. Regardless of the form adopted for rules on political activity, it is important to have a mechanism whereby public servants can learn quickly what is permissible and what is prohibited. Moreover, since debatable and marginal cases are bound to arise, this mechanism should allow for flexibility in the interpretation of the rules. Provision should also be made for amending the rules in the light of experience and changing opinions on this issue, especially in view of the widespread trend toward loosening the restraints on political activity.[14] Thus, a long list of dos and don'ts, enshrined in statutory form, may not be an appropriate means of regulating political activity.

In the Canadian federal government, the formal rules on political partisanship are contained in a section of the *Public Service Employment Act* and are elaborated to some extent by decisions in particular cases by the Public Service Commission which is responsible for administering that section of the Act.[15] Senior public servants and those in sensitive positions (e.g., personnel managers) are not permitted to stand for elected office but most public servants are permitted to participate in a broad range of political activities. Considerable uncertainty remains, however, as to whether some political activities are acceptable and there is therefore a need to amend the Act or to supplement it with administrative guidelines so as to provide greater clarity and specificity.

The reasons for limitations on the *public comment* of government employees are very similar to those noted above for restrictions on political activity. There is no service-wide coverage of this ethical problem in Canadian governments. Some governments have rules forbidding public statements which make use of confidential information. But for guidance on what types of public comment are permissible, public servants must rely on unwritten rules based on tradition. Stated broadly, the tradition is that public servants must not express publicly their personal views on government policy or administration.

The issue of public comment is too complex to be treated adequately by this unwritten rule. It is clear that public servants must not become involved in public or political controversy. But many public servants are obliged, by virtue of their government duties, to comment publicly on policy and administrative matters. At the same time, they are expected to restrict their comments to the explanation of policy and to refrain from speculating on future policy. The defence and formulation of policy is, at least in theory, the responsibility of their political superiors. But the information and conciliation roles now played by public servants sometimes cause them to step over the line between policy and administration and between the explanation of policy and its defence. In the absence of written guidelines on public comment, government employees tend to be unduly cautious and reticent in their public statements. The formulation of rules in the sphere of public comment is more difficult than in some of the other problem areas, but the draft Australian code contains a discussion of this subject together with some helpful guidelines.[16]

Much of the academic literature in Britain and the United States on the ethical conduct of public servants is concerned with conflict of loyalties, and the Australian draft code devotes several pages to relationships between public servants on the one hand and the government and Parliament on the other.[17] In continental European countries, much of the ethical code of public servants is prescribed by law in terms of their obligations to the state. In recent years, such countries as Canada, the United States, and Australia have moved in the direction of the formal codification of ethical rules. But the obligations of public servants are not discussed or expressed in terms of loyalty to the state. For example, F.F. Ridley notes that in Britain, 'where the state does not exist as a legal entity', the public servant 'holds office under the crown'. Moreover, 'for all practical purposes the crown is an abstraction embodied in the ministers who are themselves . . . ministers of the crown. No question of a higher loyalty to the state, a conflict of loyalties between state and government, need therefore arise.'[18]

The ethical rules of Canadian governments do not cover the subject of conflicts of loyalty. As a result, public servants must seek guidance in conventions and understandings. The paucity of written rules on this subject in Canada does not reflect a lack of public or governmental concern. Indeed, the broad issue of responsibility in government and the specific issue of where the loyalty of public servants lies have been of widespread interest in Canada during the 1970s. Yet there has been little inclination to provide written guidelines on this matter. Such rules could not solve a public servant's ethical dilemma involving, for example, responsibility to his political superior versus responsibility to his conscience. They could, however, inform public servants as to where their first loyalty usually lies and how to escape from certain conflict of loyalty situations. It is generally acknowledged that a public servant's first loyalty is to his political superior so long as his superior acts within the law. But occasions arise when public servants, on grounds of conscience, do not wish to obey certain lawful instructions. The Australian draft code notes that although public servants

> have their own sets of values and beliefs, the Service exists to provide advice and assistance to the Government and the public. Officials who feel unable to carry out particular duties or directions for reasons of conscience should discuss the matter with supervisors. This may result in the matter being resolved by relieving the officer of particular duties, or may necessitate the officer seeking transfer to another area of the Department or the Service.[19]

The effective *administration* of ethical rules is critical to their success in promoting high ethical standards. Regardless of the form and content of the rules, careful provision must be made for their administration, and authorities charged with the interpretation and application of the rules must take this responsibility seriously. Provisions for administration of the rules should include publicity, enforcement, and grievance procedures.[20] Ethical rules are likely to be administered most effectively when they are contained in a code of ethics that provides comprehensive coverage of ethical problem areas and involves as few authorities as possible in the administration of the code. In many governments, however, there is a diffusion of responsibility for preventing and punishing unethical conduct because the ethical rules are found in more than one document and are often administered by different authorities.

In governments with a large number of employees and administrative units, it is usually necessary to delegate to individual departments and agencies responsibility not only for elaborating on service-wide rules to suit their particular needs but also for administering the rules for their own employees.[21] Alberta's Code of Conduct includes explicit provision for such departmental responsibility and is accompanied by administrative instructions in support of the Code which are designed, among other things, to ensure the consistency of departmental instructions with the Code.

BENEFITS AND COSTS OF CODES OF ETHICS

Whether or not ethical rules take the form of a code, they confer benefits and impose costs on public servants and their political and administrative superiors. For the general public, the benefits of ethical rules far outweigh their costs.

Both the drafting and administration of codes of ethics require a balancing of political, administrative, and legal considerations. A central and pervasive concern should be to balance the desire for high ethical standards with the preservation of the individual rights of public servants. A major principle guiding the administration of a code in one Canadian government is that public servants 'should enjoy the same rights in their private dealings as any other citizen unless it can be demonstrated that a restriction is essential to the public interest'. Similarly, the Australian draft code states that 'where personal behaviour does not interfere with the proper performance of official duties, and where it does not reflect on the integrity or standing of the Service, it is of no interest or concern to the employing authority.'[22] Although some governments have paid little attention to the impact of codes of ethics on their employees' rights, most governments have been sensitive to this problem. But the fact remains that a well-drafted and well-administered code does tend to diminish the rights of public servants compared to the rights enjoyed by their fellow citizens outside government.

Perhaps the single greatest advantage of a code of ethics is the measure of certainty it provides for standards of ethical conduct expected from public servants. Unwritten rules in the form of understandings and practices leave much room for argument as to what the content of the rules actually is and what penalties must be paid for violating them. Written rules, especially in the form of a code of ethics, can reduce disagreement over permissible activities and provide a mechanism for resolving disputes where disagreement remains. The existence of a common set of ethical standards helps ensure that no public servants are exploiting their public office for private gain. It also ensures that all public servants have the same—or, at the very least, clearly differentiated—rights and restrictions in respect of activities outside government.

Some advantages accrue specifically to public servants, their superiors or the general public. It is often convenient for public servants to be able to cite chapter and verse of written rules that forbid their involvement in certain activities (e.g., the receipt of gifts and entertainment from members of the public). Also, the development of a code of ethics may prompt governments to reassess their existing written or unwritten rules so that the rights and participation of public servants in regard to certain activities (e.g., political partisanship, dual employment) may be enhanced. Both public servants and their political superiors benefit from the increased public trust in government that tends to result from the careful drafting and effective administration of a code of ethics. A code provides one means by which political leaders and senior managers can hold public servants accountable for their activities. Moreover, if ethical standards are raised by the existence of a code, the chances that the government of the day may suffer political embarrassment from the ethical misconduct of its employees are reduced. Members of the public receive both psychological and practical benefits from high ethical performance by public servants. Taxpayers are assured that employees on the public payroll are less likely to use their position for personal gain. And citizens can expect—indeed they can demand—that public employees serve them in an equitable and impartial manner.

The existence and administration of codes of ethics or of ethical rules in any form impose some costs, especially on public servants. Codes present obvious problems for public servants who are engaged or wish to engage in unethical activities. If their offences are revealed, they cannot claim in their defence ignorance of the rules or of the probable penalties. But since ethical rules are designed in large part to prevent and penalize ethical offences, it is important that these rules should not impose unduly heavy burdens on those public servants who are neither involved nor likely to become involved in unethical practices. The need to control offenders and to provide clear guidance for all public servants sometimes results in restrictions that public servants find repugnant or even unacceptable. For example, some governments deny to all public servants the right to participate in political activities so as to avoid problems arising from the participation of a few officials. As a result, a large number of public servants are relegated to second-class citizenship in respect of political rights. The approach adopted by most governments is a compromise between two extremes which permits broad participation by most public servants but still limits severely the activities of some. Restrictions in the conflict of interest sphere are particularly irritating to many public servants whose right to personal privacy may be infringed by requirements that they disclose their assets or whose participation in financial activities outside government may be curtailed. One of the hardest burdens for public servants to bear is restriction of their activities based not on actual or probable conflict of interest but on the appearance or possibility of conflict. In Canada, an adjudicator of the Public Service Staff Relations Board concluded in a conflict of interest case that 'even in the absence of evidence of wilful wrongdoing, a conflict of interest *or the appearance thereof* can be easily recognized by an intelligent citizen as contrary to public policy.'[23]

As a consequence of such strict measures to ensure that ethical standards are not only high but also appear to be high, governments may lose some of their employees and fail to attract new, well-qualified recruits who find the measures unduly constraining on their private lives and individual rights. This problem complicates the already difficult task of authorities responsible for administering ethical rules. For these authorities, the administration of the rules can often be a difficult, time-consuming, and frustrating task.

A central question for governments is whether the tasks of drafting and administering a code of ethics are worth the effort. In the absence of firm evidence over time on the nature and number of ethical offences and on the attitudes of public servants on ethical conduct, it is difficult to conduct a cost-benefit analysis. Nevertheless, a comparatively large cost in time and effort may be justified by even a marginal increase in public confidence in government and in the responsibility of public servants.

ETHICAL RULES AND ADMINISTRATIVE RESPONSIBILITY

Neither written nor unwritten rules alone are sufficient to ensure high ethical standards among public servants and thereby to promote administrative responsibility. There is room for debate among academics and practitioners as to the value of written codes of ethics in preventing and punishing ethical offences. But those who oppose all written rules in the belief that it is sufficient for public servants to internalize unwritten practices and understandings do not understand the complexity and magnitude of the issue of ethical conduct. In this regard, it is notable that the First Division Association in Britain observed in 1972 that 'the existence [in Britain] of a comprehensive but intangible and unwritten code would be hard to verify and runs counter to many people's experience. We believe reliance on it leads to dangerous complacency.'[24] Certainly, not all ethical problems can be handled by statutory or administrative prohibitions; nor can these prohibitions guarantee ethical behaviour by those who are determined to abuse their public office. But written rules can be very effective in promoting ethical conduct in certain problem areas and in informing actual or potential offenders of the standards to which they are expected to adhere and of the penalties for infractions of the rules.

The five areas of ethical conduct discussed earlier constitute only a small portion of the ethical issues that confront public servants in the exercise of their discretionary authority. For example, *Estacode,* the British code of conduct for public servants, covers each of these five areas but has been criticized for not providing adequate guidance with respect to the ethical aspects of the presentation and implementation of policy and of relations between officials and ministers, between departments, between senior and junior officials, between officials and outside interests, and between officials and the public.[25] It is significant, however, that the five ethical problem areas for which governments tend to have written rules are the areas that have received most publicity and that are most amenable to written treatment.

Aside from the extreme difficulty of formulating written rules to cover the whole field of ethical conduct for public servants, it is undesirable to depend on such rules to promote responsible administrative action. It is necessary to complement formal rules and sanctions by relying on the self-discipline of public servants. The focus of scholars and governments has been on the development of institutional and procedural mechanisms to achieve administrative responsibility. This emphasis has been to the detriment of a search for the means to stimulate and sustain a personal or individual sense of responsibility among public servants.

Self-discipline, in the sphere of ethical conduct as in other spheres of administrative activity, is developed during the socialization of the individual that precedes and follows entry into the public service. The challenge is to instil in public servants a code of behaviour which will reduce the likelihood of their involvement in unethical conduct. The critical components of the socialization process are education and training and the model of behaviour provided by one's fellow citizens and administrative colleagues.

The socialization of individuals before they join the public service provides them with a value system which includes beliefs about ethical standards considered generally acceptable in society. These beliefs are moulded by exposure to the standards of ethical conduct that prevail in society as a whole rather than by knowledge of standards that are unique to the public service. The majority of public servants have not taken formal courses in public administration before entering government service and many of those who have taken such courses have been taught little or nothing about the ethical problems that arise in the public service. The personal example provided by senior public servants whose ethical performance is faultless has traditionally been an important influence on the behaviour of their subordinates. In Canada, when the senior level of the public service was a smaller and more cohesive group often described as a 'bureaucratic elite', the superior ethical performance of this group tended to have a pervasive influence on the service. But as a result of the large scale and complexity of contemporary government, senior officials now have personal contact with a relatively small percentage of their employees and there is no assurance that their influence on ethical matters will flow down the administrative pyramid. This fact helps explain why many senior public servants support the codification of ethical standards.

A heavy burden for instilling high ethical standards in public servants rests on education for government service. A major emphasis on ethical issues during the pre-employment and in-service education and training of public servants would heighten their sensitivity to and understanding of ethical considerations. Both academic scholars and practitioners of public administration should devote more of their ingenuity and initiative to designing approaches and courses in public service education that will enhance ethical conduct in particular and responsible administrative behaviour in general.[26]

NOTES

1. *Ethics for Bureaucrats: An Essay on Law and Values* (New York: Marcel Dekker, 1978), p. 15.
2. As a result of worldwide concern about this issue, the International Association of Schools and Institutes of Administration established in 1975 a Study Group on Ethics

in the Public Service. See the Study Group's first report, *Public Service Ethics,* O.P. Dwivedi (Belgium: International Institute of Administrative Sciences, 1978). See also for Britain, *Report of the Committee on Local Government Rules of Conduct* (the Redcliffe-Maud Committee) (London: HMSO, Cmnd. 5636, May 1974) and *Report of the Royal Commission on Standards of Conduct in Public Life* (the Salmon Commission) (London: HMSO, Cmnd. 6524, July 1976). In 1978, the Government of Australia appointed a committee of inquiry into the conflict of interest area as it affects both politicians and government employees.

3. In the United States, for example, ethics laws have been adopted in more than forty states since 1973. See Richard G. Terapak, 'Administering Ethics Laws: the Ohio Experience', *National Civic Review* (February 1979), pp. 82–4, and Melvin G. Cooper, 'Administering Ethics Laws: the Alabama Experience', *National Civic Review* (February 1979), pp. 77–81, 110.

4. Throughout this paper, the term 'ethical rules' refers to statutes, regulations, or guidelines on ethical conduct and to any combination of these instruments.

5. See Kenneth Kernaghan, 'The Ethical Conduct of Canadian Public Servants', *Optimum* 4, 3 (1973), pp. 5–8.

6. The Privy Council, *Guidelines to be Observed by Public Servants Concerning Conflict of Interest Situations,* P.C. 1973–4065, 18 December 1973, and Treasury Board, *Standard of Conduct for Public Service Employees,* Circular no. 1973–183, 31 December 1973.

7. Ontario, *The Public Service Act,* Regulation 603/73, 1 October 1973. Newfoundland, *Statutes,* 1973, no. 113.

8. British Columbia, *Public Officials and Employees Disclosure Act, Statutes,* 1974, c. 73.

9. Ibid.; Alberta, *A Code of Conduct and Ethics for the Public Service of Alberta,* 1978.

10. House of Representatives Concurrent Resolution 175, 85th Congress, 2nd Session, 11 July 1958.

11. *Draft Guidelines on Official Conduct of Commonwealth Public Servants,* Canberra, March 1978.

12. For an examination of this matter in the British context, see *Report of the Royal Commission on Standards of Conduct in Public Life,* ch. 11. For Canadian rules, see *Post-Employment Activities Guidelines,* 1 January 1978, amended 24 April 1978.

13. See Gordon Robertson, 'Official Responsibility, Private Conscience and Public Information', *Optimum* 30, 3 (1972), pp. 5–18.

14. In this regard, note that a committee of the British Parliament recommended in 1978, among other things, that the percentage of public servants in the 'politically restricted' category be reduced from 26 per cent to 3 per cent. *Report of the Committee on Political Activities of Civil Servants* (London: HMSO, Cmnd. 7057, 1978).

15. Canada, *Statutes,* c. 71, s. 32. The Canadian Special Committee on Personnel Management and the Merit Principle concluded that 'the manner in which the British system regulates this matter [of political participation] provides an appropriate framework for the Canadian public service.' The Committee recommended that the public service of Canada be divided into three groups as in the British system. *Report* (Ottawa: Minister of Supply and Services, 1979), p. 172.

16. Public Service Board, *Draft Guidelines,* pp. 28–30.

17. On Britain, see First Division Association, 'Professional Standards in the Public

Service,' *Public Administration* 50 (Summer, 1972), pp. 167–82; Maurice Wright, 'The Professional Conduct of Civil Servants', *Public Administration* 51 (Spring 1973), pp. 1–16. On the United States, see George A. Graham, 'Ethical Guidelines for Public Administration: Observations on Rules of the Game', *Public Administration Review* 34 (January/February 1974), pp. 90–2.

18. 'Responsibility and the Official: Forms and Ambiguities', *Government and Opposition,* vol. 10, 1975, p. 453.
19. *Draft Guidelines,* p. 46.
20. For a discussion of each of these three areas and of the procedure for developing a code of ethics, see Kenneth Kernaghan, *Ethical Conduct: Guidelines for Government Employees* (Toronto: Institute of Public Administration of Canada, 1975), pp. 50–2.
21. See the impressive and comprehensive *Code of Conduct for Departmental Staff* issued by Canada's Department of Manpower and Immigration in March 1975.
22. *Draft Guidelines,* p. 2.
23. 'Public Service Staff Relations Act Decision, Between Maurice Dudley Atkins, Grievor, and Treasury Board (Ministry of Transport), Employer', 21 March 1974, File no. 166–2–889, p. 30 (emphasis added).
24. 'Professional Standards in the Public Service', p. 169.
25. Ibid., pp. 172–3. Note that *Estacode* has recently been replaced by two sets of information, namely *The Civil Service Pay and Conditions of Service Code,* which essentially contains rules and instructions for all employees, and *The Establishment Officer Guide,* which provides management with guidance parallel to, but fuller than, the Code.
26. For a novel and imaginative approach to the teaching of ethics in public administration in the United States, see Rohr, *Ethics for Bureaucrats,* especially ch. 2. See also Herman Mertins, Jr., ed., *Professional Standards and Ethics: A Workbook for Public Administrators* (Washington, DC: American Society for Public Administration, Professional Standards and Ethics Committee, 1979).

14

Collective Bargaining in the Federal Public Service: The Achievement of a Milestone in Personnel Relations

Robert A. Vaison

On 20 February 1967, the House of Commons assented to the so-called Public Service Staff Relations Act and two accompanying bills which taken together established a system of collective bargaining for the federal public service. This legislation in effect provided for a truly bilateral basis for negotiation and bargaining between management in the service and its employees collectively represented. The road to the realization of such a system of staff relations has been long, and one sometimes marked by unforeseen detours. Thus, to appreciate fully the significance of this recent development, one must retrace briefly the evolution of both personnel administration and management-staff interrelations in the public service.

EARLY EXPERIENCE

During the last quarter of the nineteenth century, the rights of workers to organize themselves into unions gradually crystallized within the industrial environment of the western world. The horrors of the working man's lot spurred more positive public attitudes and unions emerged as officially condoned in many nations. In 1872, the Dominion Parliament passed an act respecting trade unions which repealed 'both on the civil and criminal side the harsh measures [regarding union organizing activity] previously enforced. . . .'[1] Such legal toleration in the industrial sector coupled with unenviable working conditions, within the public service (including nepotism, the varied hazards of patronage, generally low pay, and inequality of remuneration in relation to work done) gave impetus to budding efforts to form employee associations among civil servants. In 1889 the Railway Mail Clerks' Association was created. Two years later, another organization attracting members from amongst letter carriers appeared. The post office was and still is the department most closely resembling a private business operation and its employees tended even at this early date to identify more closely with the labour movement than did other segments of the service.[2]

In the next couple of decades, during what Professor Dawson has deemed 'the most dismal period in civil service history,' other employee groupings timidly exper-

Robert A. Vaison, 'Collective Bargaining in the Federal Public Service: The Achievement of a Milestone in Personnel Relations', *Canadian Public Administration* 12, 1 (1969): 108–22. Courtesy of The Institute of Public Administration Canada.

imented with collective organization. Such bodies as did spring up were mainly confined to the outside service, i.e., the non–Ottawa based section, and were uncertain
regarding their rights, being effectively ignored by the senior officials of the service.
The prolonged depression of the 1890s no doubt put a damper on any vociferousness on the part of such groups; government service probably seemed a good place
to be, all in all. Nonetheless, conditions were far from ideal and the continued abuses
of the patronage tradition were perhaps at their zenith. Around the turn of the century, however, the emergent associations began to display a little more confidence.
Increased numbers of public servants banded together. The headquarters–based Civil
Service Union, soon to become the Civil Service Association, was formed in 1907
and was instrumental in the formation of the larger Civil Service Federation a couple of years later. Reform of the public service was accepted as their key goal and
lobbying was seen as the most effective and actually the only means to this end. In
1907, the Liberal regime of the day established a Royal Commission to delve into
various aspects of the public administration. Appearing before this body, the nascent
Union advocated among other things reform of the service along merit lines and
higher salaries for public employees. While satisfaction in regard to the second matter was not immediately forthcoming, the first long-sought objective of reform was
realized by the establishment of the Civil Service Commission in 1908. The
Canadian service was moving hesitantly toward the *rationalized* end of Max Weber's
spectrum of bureaucracies having at this one extreme the concept of a hierarchy in
which employment is based strictly on merit and which exhibits a lack of nonra-
tionalized factors such as patronage and nepotism.

While the staff associations strongly approved of this major step, it quickly
became evident that the desired state of affairs had not yet been realized. Patronage
remained less than a dead letter, in spite of overt opposition to it. The change of
administration in 1911 saw the practice very much in evidence, although for the most
part restricted to the outside service which had not been placed under the jurisdiction of the Commission. Further, the utilization of position classification schemes and
complementary pay scales remained an unresolved issue. The 1908 Act creating the
Commission had set out some relevent principles but, as the report of special inves-
tigator Sir George Murray noted a few years later, the machinery of implementation
was absent. During World War I expansion of the service occurred in response to
wartime conditions. Over this period the size of the civilian service roughly doubled.
To accomplish this, the Civil Service Act went into cold storage. Patronage was rampant in this era of bitter party politics. By the later years of the war, public administration was in a state little short of chaotic. Departmental organization had broken
down and considerable overstaffing existed. The promising merit reforms of 1908
seemed doomed. But the cause was picked up by the Union Government and
emphasized in its platform during the electoral campaign of 1917. With this coalition
victorious at the polls, the opportunity for further reform was availed of, initially by
Orders–in–Council which were the basis for a thoroughly revamped Civil Service
Act. This considerably strengthened the Civil Service Commission which was delegated extensive powers in the areas of appointment and promotion and was given the
responsibility of recommending all rates of remuneration. Provision was made for an

elaborate classification scheme, which was soon elaborated by an American firm of consultants. This fundamentally revised statute was accepted with very little controversy; it is remarkable that virtually all members of the House of Commons seemed suddenly cognizant of the evils inherent in the system they had condoned for years. This legislation stood, with only occasional amendment, until new concepts and conditions refocused attention on the subject four decades later. Within the reformed service, the associations had scope to operate as representatives of employees. They no longer had to fight for the basic framework deemed essential.

The significance of and the opportunities presented by these alterations in the public service milieu were not lost upon spokesmen for the employee side. The advantages to be realized via organization and collective voicing had been stressed at the founding convention of the Civil Service Federation. The twenty-three groups that united to form the Federation had been joined on the staff side by seventeen others by 1914.[3] Undoubtedly, contemporary developments in industrial relations— the marked growth of trade union membership and the passage of the Industrial Disputes Investigation Act in 1907—were not unnoticed by staff association leaders. There were parallels between public and private employment, for example, the appearance of large operating entities in which workers were more and more isolated from decision-making management. The philosophy enunciated by popular trade union figures such as Samuel Gompers had relevance to workers in all spheres. Some staff associations in the public service became outspoken during the first decades of the century. Their right of existence and of representation was tacitly recognized by the government. Their leaders were periodically granted audiences at which they persistently deplored at length the income plight of civil servants and demanded salary increases. Frustrated by the almost total lack of response to such petitions, the letter carriers did something without precedent in Canadian public service experience. They struck. While the strike did not last long, it found some support among postal clerks. Attention to staff relations matters was being forced upon management by employee action, a pattern that was to continue.

Measures of reform of public administration exerted their own influence on service staff associations. The extensive restructuring of classification created service-wide horizontal groupings of employees amenable to collective representation.[4] The location of virtually all personnel functions in one agency, the Civil Service Commission, might promise well for a simple negotiating arrangement. The Commission's responsibility for recommending salary levels enhanced that possibility. Suggesting reconsideration in the whole personnel policy area, the Report of Transmission which accompanied the proposal regarding the new classification scheme alluded to possible use of a Whitley-type of council in the Canadian public service as a sounding board for the presentation of various opinions. The point was rather cautiously advanced even though Whitley councils were functioning fairly satisfactorily in Great Britain at the time. The associations in Ottawa responded to the suggestion by pushing strongly for this or a similar medium of consultation. While nothing was done about it in the 1918–19 reorganization of federal personnel administration, the staff side found the 1923 House committee on the civil service more receptive to its point of view. While rejecting the Whitley scheme as such, the

Committee report did opt for 'creation of some type of board on which the civil servant shall be represented . . .'[5] Neither the government of the day nor the senior
administrative officials were yet ready to acquiesce in granting such a voice to
employees. There the matter lay until another House committee was established in
the late 1920s to study the concept of civil service councils, following approval in
principle of a private member's bill recommending the founding of such organs. This
committee agreed in favour of such councils and suggested that the objective could
be achieved most easily via Order-in-Council. This apparently satisfied the staff side.
In 1930, such an Order was issued authorizing the creation of a National Civil
Service Council.[6] However, the election of that year changed the party in power and
the Order was never promulgated. Positive action in the staff relations field had to
wait out the passing of the Depression. The decade of the 1930s hit the staff associations severely in morale, on the membership rolls, and in the treasury. Civil servants
had to absorb across-the-board pay cuts as part of Prime Minister Bennett's anti-
Depression austerity program. Though boasting an element of security, the public
service did not gain in prestige. The situation would change only as the role of the
public sector broadened and became more complex. Informal relationship doubtless
did exist between the staff and official sides of the table but it must have surprised
employee spokesmen to discover that, in the words of the chairman of the Civil
Service Commission, 'there is general negotiation between employees' organizations,
government departments, and the Civil Service Commission.'[7] Economic conditions
plus some abandonment of the reform measures (for example, circumvention of classification schemes, the appearance of many agencies exempt from the Civil Service
Act, and some echoes of patronage) made it seem inopportune for the staff side to
make strong demands backed by appropriate action. While certainly not declining
into nonexistence, the employee organizations muted their representations in
response to a Canadian environment characterized by hardship on many fronts.

THE POST-DEPRESSION ERA

By 1939, then, the staff side of the public service had not realized anything approaching a formalized negotiating set-up for the determination of salaries or related facets
of personnel policy. Associations could and did petition the Cabinet, various individual ministers, and some senior officials from time to time, as the situation seemed
opportune. The associations also made fairly regular representations to the Civil
Service Commission and presented usually well-documented briefs with supporting
personal appearances before House Committees and Royal Commissions set up to
study various aspects of the public service. But all of these were more or less *ad hoc*.
More importantly, the final policy decisions were still taken unilaterally. The associations functioned essentially as pressure groups and were only successful in achieving
their goals insofar as techniques of lobbying allowed. In short, there existed no staff
relations in the industrial sense of the term. The Civil Service Commission, after lis-
tening to and accepting or rejecting the staff side's views, as it saw fit, recommended
any salary changes to the Treasury Board who in turn acted upon such recommendations or not, as it saw fit.

The number of people employed in the central administration of the federal government increased substantially during World War II.[8] The staff associations for their part grew fairly rapidly in membership, both during and in the years following the war. To some extent this was due simply to the rise in potential membership brought about by the expansion of employment. But staff association growth was also related to the attitudes held by many of these new government employees. Thousands had joined the public service from industry, where well-organized trade unions bargained with employers. The Depression had for many put business in a bad light; some newly recruited employees probably sought and expected greater security in the public service and were thus amenable to collective organization. While undergoing this expansion, the staff associations continued to make salary representations to the government, generally with little immediate result. A war-time economy had forced up wage and salary levels in the industrial sector and the public service once again lagged perceptibly. Late in the war, a committee was established to advise the Treasury Board, the war-time locus of responsibility in the personnel area, on several personnel matters. The employee point of view was not represented on this Coon Committee, nor were its recommendations made public, thus adding fuel to a smouldering fire. The Civil Service Federation, largest of the staff organs, called for immediate implementation of the 1930 Order-in-Council providing for a joint management-staff body for the purposes of consultation on a variety of matters of mutual interest. The government could no longer ignore the demands. The result was an Order-in-Council of May 1944, establishing the National Joint Council of the Public Service of Canada. The ministerial statement accompanying the announcement stated a variety of purposes for this step. Briefly, a body modelled on the British Whitley Council scheme was envisaged.[9] The right of civil servants to organize had been tacitly recognized over years of *de facto* organization. The right to make representations, i.e., at least to be heard, albeit often only on an *ad hoc* basis, had been implicitly granted early in the twentieth century. The recognition of the associations as having a consultative role to play was now explicitly granted.

One of the first acts of this Council was to consider its constitution, a draft of which had been submitted to it by the government. The staff representatives (as selected by the various associations granted seats on the Council) and management whose representatives were seconded from various agencies and departments and one of whom was to act as chairman, agreed to three minor alterations to this draft. The National Joint Council was now ready for business. Early meetings focused upon transition to peacetime matters, such as the cessation of several wartime restrictions and the consolidation of various bonus schemes and related questions.[10] Very early a pattern began to emerge in the functioning of the Council. Meetings were held only irregularly. Items of business were dealt with in a purely tentative manner. The National Joint Council became an advisory body and no more. Disillusionment of the staff developed in the early period, primarily perhaps because the association leadership had expected too much out of this first real concession by the government. The Council as it evolved was clearly not all it might have been from their point of view. For one thing, no provision existed for carrying to arbitration or other form of binding settlement any inability to agree on items within the Council's purview. Further, the Council's existence was somewhat tenuously based on an Order-in-Council rather than on statute.

Its solely advisory nature was a strong conditioning factor. The consensus, if any, arising out of deliberations could be accepted, rejected, or totally ignored by the administration and all three eventualities occurred. There was apparently no compulsion, even of a moral nature, for the government or Treasury Board to accept even unanimous decisions of Council. The duality of responsibility, i.e., between the Civil Service Commission and Treasury Board, of management for personnel policy itself complicated the process and at times stymied action. To cap off the staff's chagrin, the view that salary matters were not within the Council's domain gradually came to dominate, even though the original enunciation of the Council's scope was broad. In the long run this latter element emerged as the key point of dissatisfaction. With another name, the regime was still unilateralism. As the *sole* machinery of negotiation in the public sphere, a consultative body such as the National Joint Council soon proved decidedly inadequate from the employees' standpoint.[11]

By the late 1940s, then, association leadership had become quite disillusioned with the Council and its limited role. While the system as it was then operating had its place and would continue to aid in the achievement of some desired changes, the limitations noted told heavily. The honeymoon following the founding of the Council was shortlived. In 1949, Professor Cole identified several factors, including larger membership, better organization, and a more favourable labour market, which would come to lend strength to the staff side's demands for a greater say in personnel management.[12] However, the role actually played by the associations remained minor. Any pressure brought to bear in relation to salary questions was only indirect, making use of briefs, appearances before official bodies, and outright lobbying. This approach obviously was fraught with possible frustrations. The initial presentations could be immediately rejected or laid aside and ignored. Delay seemed to be omnipresent. The formal presentations and the work involved in preparing them could and often did go for nought. Even if the Commission and Treasury Board officials were amenable to particular staff side demands, the government of the day could reject the recommendations forwarded it. Lobbying was not as a rule fruitful in overcoming this last stumbling block. A change in the political administration or the continued success of a party unsympathetic to association positions could jeopardize from the outset the achievement of pay increases. And, as already noted, the National Joint Council was of no value to the employees in matters of salary.

The shortcomings in civil servants' eyes of the extant system of staff relations were thrown into clearer perspective as the nature of the Council's management-worker relationship evolved—or, rather, failed to do so. The paternalism long characteristic of management in the service flavoured whatever negotiating did occur and the staff side representatives resented this more and more. Aside from the salary constraint, the National Joint Council's main shortcoming, as it was functioning, was the continued absence of machinery for enforcing the decisions it arrived at. The entire public service personnel environment was anchored in paternalism or benevolence. In a socioeconomic milieu in which trade unions were flexing an increasing amount of muscle, the public servants' spokesmen demanded not benevolence but a real voice in the determination of working conditions. The staff leadership sought to supplement the Council with arrangements that would allow for expansion of the scope of labour–management relations within the service. During the decade of the 1950s, association officials, often with the explicit support of annual convention resolutions, began to talk in terms of collective bargaining, usually without euphemism. The precise detail was not seen as being of crucial importance. What was essentially sought was bilateralism, viz., the joint final determination of pay scales and related matters. The staff groups had reached a sort of watershed in their existence. The informal recognition implicit in National Joint Council membership was insufficient; wholehearted acceptance was desired, coupled with and resting on a key place in the personnel picture.

While the staff representatives no doubt felt by the later 1950s that some form of collective bargaining was definitely required, and was perhaps even inevitable, an appreciation of the entire personnel scene must be obtained to evaluate such a point of view. Long-standing and often well-meaning paternalistic attitudes and practices obviously did not allow for the immediate institution of such measures. Basic change of this magnitude is only gradually brought about in a large bureaucratic organization such as the federal public administration. In defence of the status quo in the personnel field, much emphasis had traditionally been placed upon conventional legal concepts such as the sovereignty of the state which could be discredited only by degrees.[13] On the other hand, developments within the work environment tended to make for change and the re-evaluation of ancient policies. The growth in size of the service, unabated through the post-war decades, created an ever-widening distance between those who decided policy matters and those affected by such decisions, particularly as personnel questions were decided upon by two organs rather remote from most civil servants. Departmental management only slowly, and for the most part unofficially, came to acquire a real say in some facets of this administrative domain. The lack of official attention to a wide variety of minor grievances, attendant with the maintenance of numerous often rather petty rules and regulations, caused members of the service rank and file to turn to their staff associations for possible redress and rectification of such situations. In attempting to respond to such calls for action the associations often found themselves frustrated. The whole question of grievances became a continuing sore point. No recognized grievance procedure existed. Complaints were for the most part either handled summarily (and normally dismissed) or ignored. On this particular score, the rank and file membership was becoming restless. The association leadership was gradually able to count on support regarding some of its more radical demands. Civil servants, it appeared, were collectively losing some of their docility, a quality that long seemed to go hand in hand with public service. The difference between public and private employment was not as clearly perceived and accepted by civil servants as before. In the late 1950s an American academic surveying the Canadian public service concluded that the future of staff relations 'seems likely to revolve around the question of collective bargaining or compulsory arbitration.'[14] With hindsight we might well agree, recalling that collective bargaining was by then firmly established in the public services of most Canadian municipalities as well as at the provincial level in Saskatchewan. Efforts were being made contemporaneously to organize industrial white-collar workers.

THE ROAD TO MEANINGFUL NEGOTIATION

In 1956, a Public Service Pay Research Unit was set up in Britain to facilitate salary negotiations by providing yardsticks upon which pay comparisons and demands could be based. To Canadian staff associations, such a body in Ottawa would indicate a shift away from the repugnant unilateralism in salary determination. Thus when Prime Minister St Laurent hinted at the use of such a mechanism in 1957, the associations urged immediate implementation. The Diefenbaker Government proved receptive and early in its tenure of office the Pay Research Bureau was established. Although the staff side had desired a fully independent agency, the locating of the Bureau in the Civil Service Commission does not appear to have been seriously questioned.

Acceptance in practice of the organ would be the measure of its success. As time passed, its stature slowly grew. Along with the Bureau, an Advisory Committee on Pay Research was set up, presumably modelled on the representatively balanced Steering Committee to which the director of the British Pay Research Unit was responsible. The Canadian Committee, however, was chaired by an official of the Civil Service Commission, who could not be accepted as a neutral person by the employee representatives. The key aspect of independence was once again endangered by such an arrangement. Further, the persistent *advisory* nature of overall negotiating procedures remained a sore point. The Commission in drawing up its pay recommendations could still effectively do as it pleased with the Bureau's findings. Nonetheless the leaders of the associations began to see some light. Good faith utilization of the Bureau could well diminish the one-sided character of salary determination. Meanwhile, the newly elected minority Conservative Government was in a precarious position in the House of Commons; association spokesmen who approached the Prime Minister on the issue of collective bargaining were assured that the matter was not being neglected. But before a year was out, the administration was returned with a large majority. Sensitiveness to the civil service vote in a few ridings evaporated and the confident government concentrated its attention on other issues. But the movement toward collective bargaining kept gathering momentum.

One of the last acts of Prime Minister St Laurent had been to appoint a new chairman, Arnold Heeney, and two new commissioners to the Civil Service Commission. They were directed to survey in depth all aspects of personnel administration within the service with an eye to mapping out changes desirable in the Civil Service Act which had stood since 1918 without major overhaul. They were further to consider completely the potential role of the Commission itself as an impartial mediator in negotiations between management and staff in the public service. Prime Minister Diefenbaker tacitly confirmed the nature and scope of the review and the commissioners were thus presented with a bi-partisan mandate for their task. The report was foreshadowed by Chairman Heeney's address in 1958, suggesting that one might well find, in the Commission's alleged independence, the basis for an extension of that agency's responsibilities in the staff relations field.[15] Such preconceptions anticipated recommendation for the extension of the Commission's functions *vis-à-vis* negotiation and bargaining. While the authors saw no possibility of the industrial type of collective bargaining for the public sphere, they did suggest that, by enlarging the role of the Commission and by strengthening the National Joint Council, the essential objectives of the employees could be met.[16] As the associations' aim by this stage was some form of collective bargaining, clearly this did not nearly satisfy them, with its unaltered triangular personnel policy route and unilateral salary determination. The Report justifies the speculation that the commissioners having begun to perceive the writing on the wall, viz. the pressures making for a bilateral negotiating arrangement, had set about carving out a role for the Commission in such an environment. But with its long tradition of service to management, the Commission was not a body which possessed the neutrality required of a successful mediator.

An opportunity to test the system envisaged by the 1958 Report occurred the next year. After the Pay Research Bureau reported its findings on then existing wages and salary conditions in the economy, joint consultations under the guidance of the Chairman of the Commission took place. No definite agreements were reached. The Commission went ahead to make recommendations on possible salary increases to the Treasury Board, without forwarding a copy of the recommendations to the employee representatives. Furthermore, the government, after considerable delay, rejected the recommendations of the Commission—still without making them public. It appeared to the staff associations that, in spite of the façade, salary determination was not actually altered. Unilateralism remained. The whole episode succeeded only in arousing the ire of the staff leadership and many of the rank and file.

A bill aimed at re-writing the Civil Service Act, introduced in the House of Commons the next year, was allowed to lapse at the end of session. The administration of the day appeared to be using it as a feeler to gauge current attitudes and perhaps to assess how these had been altered by the recent developments sketched. This bill dealt with many aspects of public personnel management, but the sections pertaining to staff relations are our present concern. The bill rejected the 1958 Report's conclusions for a greater role for the Civil Service Commission and stated instead that the Commission and selected designees of the Minister of Finance should consult from time to time with staff representatives on matters of pay and other conditions of work. Initiation of consultation proceedings lay implicitly with the official side. Staff side reaction was quick and predictable. Their spokesmen demanded bilateral negotiation backed by arbitration (the strike weapon having been rejected as out of the question, a matter we shall return to). The government gave some ground. When the bill was introduced again during the next session, the clauses concerned had been altered to allow for consultation to be initiated by either side. This revised bill was sent to committee for a thorough examination. The staff associations expounded at length their demands for viable negotiation machinery. No group except the postal employees sought the right to strike. The latter body was a Canadian Labour Congress affiliate and the Congress itself officially advocated the right of public employees to strike.[17] The other associations had all taken unequivocal stands against pushing for the strike weapon as a possible recourse in case of inability to reach accord over salary matters. What was desired was compulsory arbitration machinery. This hope of the staff was disappointed by the arrangements envisaged by the version of the civil service act-to-be that emerged from committee hearings. Consultation and not negotiation was all that was provided for, and it was provided in the form of a rather complicated tripartite system of consultation which hinged upon the nature of the topic. While this act was doubtless an attempt to clarify responsibility for different aspects of personnel policy, the revised version looked to the employees like a move away from the coveted bilateralism. Formal granting of the right to consultation is not very significant if that right has informally existed in the past, as Professor Frankel observed.[18] The government deemed the new act an important milestone and perhaps silently hoped the vociferousness of the associations would be toned down as a result. From a later vantage point, one sees the 1961 legislation as yet another plateau in an evolutionary process that would see a new era of public service staff relations ushered in. The next year one of the larger associations commissioned Professor Frankel to study service employer-employee relations in depth; the resultant document[19] criticized the triangular Commission-Central Executive Staff relationship and proposed instead realistic negotiating machinery involving only the government, via its designated representatives and employee representatives. In many respects it summarized, not surprisingly, the staff side's reaction to the 1961 Act. Public servant spokesmen were in general not satisfied with the state of service employee relations even after the passage of this 'milestone' statute and further developments were to come. A transition period was at hand in the federal public administration.

During this time of flux, the Glassco Commission was appointed and directed to delve into the existing state of management in the public service. Much in the Commission's report was devoted to various aspects of personnel administration but the whole question of employer-employee relations was thought to have little direct bearing on its main concern, the efficiency and economy of management in the bureaucracy.[20] The commissioners apparently had studies prepared on the matter of collective bargaining; unfortunately these were never released. While the commissioners were undoubtedly aware of the importance and currency of the topic, they sought to maintain a neutral stance on it. But the whole Glassco Report was permeated with a business management orientation to administration in the service. Analogies to the industrial world, with its practices of collective bargaining, pervaded it. Perhaps as important to the ultimate realization of a new staff relations system within the public service was the clarification outlined by the commissioners regarding the locus of responsibility for personnel management in government. The Treasury Board was unequivocally vested with such responsibilities. To the Commissioners' thinking, the Civil Service Commission should accent its independence and retain responsibility for ensuring the preservation of the merit principle and related practices as well as for the provision of some common services to other areas of management.[21] The Treasury Board emerged as the central organ of personnel management as the recommendations of the Glassco Commission were gradually implemented, a central organ capable of fully representing the official side at any negotiating table. For their part, the staff associations had begun several years before to seek a basis agreeable to all of them upon which unification (or a reasonable facsimile thereof) of the staff voice could be achieved. While the final knot would not be tied until the formation of the Public Service Alliance in 1966, courtship was stepped up in the early 1960s in anticipation of a more nearly bilateral negotiation arrangement being created.

An astute observer of the public service scene might well have sensed that further change was possible and perhaps imminent. The staff association leadership was definitely so inclined and pressed the four national parties in the pre-election months of 1963 for clear-cut stands on the issue of collective bargaining for public servants, extracting statements varying in favourableness. The Liberals had taken a fairly unambiguous position on the question and, when returned to power, proceeded to honour their promise. The importance of this administration's minority status, and its consciousness of its strength in Ottawa area ridings, should not be underestimated. A Preparatory Committee on Collective Bargaining under the chairmanship of Heeney was established in August 1963 to prepare the way for instituting a system of bargaining culminating in compulsory arbitration.[22] This was a significant step, a group of top-level service management people being directed to iron out the practical features of a bona fide bargaining system.

At this stage the matter of a public service strike remained by and large academic: the terms of reference explicitly indicated a bargaining mechanism involving arbitration, and none of the nonpostal staff associations appearing before the Committee requested the right to strike. Moreover a strike had not occurred in the service for many years. Compulsory arbitration meant to most civil servants a means of circumventing the unilateral final determination of salaries and this was the gist of what was desired. The arrangement and supporting procedures worked out within this Committee were well received by all concerned. Its report became a virtual government white paper on personnel policy in this area.

The Report might well have been implemented shortly thereafter had not 17,000 letter carriers and mail sorters gone on strike some few weeks after the Report's release. This first public service strike since 1924 shocked the public, caught the government off guard, and generated extensive discussion of the strike question within governmental and press circles. Revenue Minister Benson was quick to announce that this development would not defer the administration plans, adding that the postal strike was not a 'part of collective bargaining or a result of collective bargaining' but a demonstration of what may happen when there exists no fruitful outlet for a group of men with a real sense of grievance.[23] The nonpostal associations' leaders probably accurately reflected the views of the majority of civil servants that, while a stronger voice was wanted, most would stop short of claiming the right to strike. But, with the postal strike a *fait accompli*, the position of the postal groups and their rank and file was clear.

Against this background after the 1965 election, the Cabinet examined collective bargaining and the strike question. The postal walkout had ended with the granting of a big pay increase. With the militant attitude exhibited by large segments of the postal work force, a repeat performance at some future date was far from unlikely. The position of the Canadian Labour Congress, representing at least formally hundreds of thousands of workers across the country, remained clear. It was opposed to using compulsory arbitration as the sole means of contract dispute settlement. The Cabinet appointment of a prominent labour figure, Jean Marchand, should not go unnoticed. Those actively opposed to the granting of a strike provision, i.e., that amorphous body the 'general public', were not organized to do so effectively. The upshot of the Cabinet deliberations was a compromise. The collective bargaining bill introduced in the House in early 1966 allowed an association seeking certification as a bargaining agent to indicate prior to being certified whether it would follow a compulsory arbitration route or a conciliation with a right to strike alternative. At the Special Joint Committee stage, this section of the bill was altered to give a bargaining agent the chance to select the desired path prior to the commencement of bargaining for each new contract, i.e., upon the expiration of a negotiated agreement the employee association representing the employees would be able to switch from, say, the arbitration option to the other route, the one that could culminate in a legal strike, if certain requisite procedures were followed during the bargaining process. During committee scrutiny, relatively minor alterations were made to the bill. This amended bill became the legislative basis for a new system for staff relations in the public service.

With the grant of Royal Assent in early 1967 to it and two companion minor bills, collective bargaining for the federal public service became a reality, on paper at least. An independent Public Service Staff Relations Board received responsibility for both determination and certification of bargaining agents for appropriate bargaining units of civil servants, for supervision of conciliation and arbitration processes, and for investigation of complaints alleging violation of the empowering statute. Overall, the powers and duties of the Board are like those of an industrial labour relations board.

In summary, a bilateral arrangement is provided for, with management, represented usually by the Treasury Board, and staff, represented by staff associations after certification, bargaining collectively under the supervision of the Board. The achievement of such a system has not been a simple task. Staff relations in the public and private sectors may still be different; but the difference will be one of detail and not of substance. It is much too soon to draw conclusions as to the functioning of the new machinery of staff relations. There has been yet another postal strike but there has also been the successful conclusion of several major bargaining agreements without resort to either strike or arbitration. Appraisal of this novel staff relations arrangement must await more experience under the legislation.

NOTES

1. R.H. Coats, 'The Labour Movement in Canada', in A. Shortt, ed., *Canada and its Provinces* (Toronto, 1914), p. 296.
2. In the United States and in several European nations, the pioneer public employee organizations tended also to be in the postal and railway areas of the service.
3. *The Civil Service of Canada* (a special issue of the civil servant journal *The Civilian*) (Ottawa, 1914), p. 205.
4. Similar developments had spurred the evolution of public service staff associations in Britain at an earlier date. See B.V. Humphreys, *Clerical Unions in the Civil Service* (London, 1958), p. 18.
5. *Proceedings of the Special Committee on the Civil Service Act* (1923), p. xi.

6. For more detail on personnel matters during this early era, see R.M. Dawson, *The Civil Service of Canada* (London, 1929).

7. C.H. Bland, 'The Present Status of the Civil Service,' in L.D. White et al., eds, *Civil Service Abroad* (New York, 1935), p. 79.

8. From approximately 46,000 at the outbreak of the conflict to over 115,000 by early 1946 in the service proper, i.e., excluding the armed forces, employees of proprietary bodies, etc.

9. The best treatment of the British system is found in J. Callaghan, *Whitleyism, A Study of Joint Consultation in the Civil Service* (London, 1953).

10. National Joint Council of the Public Service of Canada 1944–1964 (Ottawa, 1964), p. 17.

11. Consultation emerged as an accepted facet of industrial relations in the post-war years; but the significant aspect is that it emerged as a supplement to full-fledged collective bargaining.

12. In *The Canadian Bureaucracy, 1939–1947* (Durham, 1949), pp. 135–6.

13. On this issue see S.J. Frankel, 'Staff Relations in the Public Service: The Ghost of Sovereignty', *Canadian Public Administration* (June 1959).

14. H.A. Scarrow, 'Civil Service Commissions in the Canadian Provinces', *Journal of Politics* (May 1957), p. 398.

15. Address reprinted in *Canadian Journal of Economics and Political Science* (February 1959). See esp. p. 7.

16. *Personnel Administration in the Public Service* (Ottawa, 1958), p. 14.

17. See in this regard two collections of papers published by the Congress: *Collective Bargaining in the Public Service . . . A Look at the Inevitable* (Ottawa, 1960) and *Collective Bargaining in the Public Service . . . A Survey in Detail* (Ottawa, 1961).

18. *Staff Relations in the Civil Service: The Canadian Experience* (Montreal, 1962), p. 166.

19. *A Model for Negotiations and Arbitration between the Canadian Government and its Civil Servants* (Montreal, 1962).

20. *Report of the Royal Commission on Government Organization* I (Ottawa, 1965), p. 3.

21. Ibid., pp. 298–302.

22. For a description of this Committee's experience, see A.M. Willms, 'The Administration of Research on Administration in the Government of Canada', *Canadian Public Administration* (1967), pp. 413–15.

23. 'A Turning Point in Staff Relations,' an address reprinted in *Civil Service Review* (September 1965), pp. 38–9.

15

Representative Bureaucracy: Linguistic/Ethnic Aspects in Canadian Public Policy

V. Seymour Wilson and Willard A. Mullins

Abstract. This paper explores the historical background, logical contours, and policy implications of recent attempts by the Government of Canada to achieve the 'effectively balanced participation' of francophones in the federal public service. Historically, various crucial events concerning French Canadian participation in the federal bureaucracy are recounted with an eye to understanding both the roots of present policies and the distinctive inherited elements which shape them. Logically, the generic concept 'representative bureaucracy' is employed as a prism for shedding light on its Canadian variant, 'balanced participation': the logic of representative bureaucracy and the arguments for and against it are explicated, with concern for how these pertain to the Canadian case. Finally, the foregoing historical and logical elements are brought to bear on the question of sociological proportionality in the federal public service, especially as it might involve the use of quotas. It is maintained that sociological heterogeneity in the federal bureaucracy is a positive value, and that recruitment and promotion procedures should strive to attract people with manifold backgrounds, perspectives, and talents. The use of legislated quotas, however, is viewed as an inefficacious and potentially destructive means for addressing this task. With respect to the issue of francophone participation specifically, the adoption of legislated quotas would be superficial and anachronistic.

In the summer of 1976 Canadians experienced a bitter strike and factious debate which many, including the Prime Minister viewed as having the potential for dividing Canada as it had not been split since the conscription crisis of 1942. Indeed, the nine-day strike of the Canadian Air Traffic Controllers Association and the Canadian Airline Pilots Association in opposition to the use of French in Quebec airspace plunged the country into a passionate conflict that has ramifications far beyond the issues of airline safety. Private resentments and acrimonious exchanges only tangentially related to the immediate issues were exhibited by both of the immediate parties to the dispute, and even by members of the general public who did not allow an unfamiliarity with the essential facts of the situation to prevent them from expressing strong opinions.[1] What was involved, according to Prime

V. Seymour Wilson and Willard A. Mullins, 'Representative Bureaucracy: Linguistic/Ethnic Aspects in Canadian Public Policy', *Canadian Public Administration* 21 (1978): 513–38. Courtesy of The Institute of Public Administration Canada.

Minister Trudeau, was an 'underlying mistrust of the principle of bilingualism'—a policy which both the Pearson and Trudeau administrations have vigorously pursued for the last fifteen years.[2]

The principle of bilingualism goes to the very heart of Canadian democracy, and a failure to resolve the complex issues involved would surely threaten, perhaps even destroy, Canadian federalism. On this point all sides in the House of Commons apparently agree, for the principle of bilingualism has repeatedly received the full support of the majority of parliamentarians from all parties. What is in dispute, however, is the Trudeau government's policies for applying the principle.[3]

What has this policy been? At the outset, it seemed to encompass two basic themes: 'services to the public' and 'effectively balanced participation', the latter initially implying that Canadians who work for the federal public service should be able, generally, to work in the language of their choice. Permeating both of these themes was the more obvious concern with language proficiency, and, indeed, early government policy aimed to foster individual bilingualism by emphasizing the need for language training for individual public servants.

As the policy evolved, however, a quality of vagueness persisted. Many anglophones held that the problem was basically one of providing service to the public in both languages: presumably if enough anglophones were sufficiently bilingual they could provide the necessary service.[4] Others, including, of course, those francophones committed to federalism, demanded that the federal bureaucracy become a working environment in which francophones could advance as easily and feel as comfortable on the job as they would in the Quebec public service.[5]

Underlying these two interpretations was a fundamental divergence of outlook. English Canadian instrumentalism stressed how bilingualism as a means for services to the public can be operationalized: how French and English can be taught, language competency measured, and practical programs devised to correct deficiencies. French Canadians, however, were mainly concerned with a far less tractable but more basic problem politically: how styles of thought and other aspects of the French Canadian cultural outlook would be assured an influence in the boardrooms of the federal public service.

By the early 1970s, the government had moved to give further clarification to its bilingual policy. Addressing a committee of the House of Commons in 1971, the Honourable C.M. Drury, then President of the Treasury Board of Canada, called for vigorous recruitment methods to attract more French Canadians to the federal public service.[6] This new orientation in government policy led the minister to define a bilingual public service in terms of 'institutional bilingualism', namely, a bilingual policy to be grounded in the existence of a select collection of bilingual individuals buttressed by a support civil service divided into two groups of unilinguals.

Put into practice by the present government, institutional bilingualism or effectively balanced participation had important implications for the staffing needs of the public service. Various positions in the hierarchy were to be designated for bilingual persons, and a balance between the two unilingual groups was to be accomplished by recruitment, the aim being to achieve 'a more fully representative' public service which ensured 'adequate participation by francophones as well as anglophones, in terms of numbers and levels within the services'.[7] Reduced to its essentials, the thrust of government language policy has been to achieve a representative bureaucracy in Canada in ways which are deemed particularly suited to the Canadian experience.

Because the idea of 'effectively balanced participation' has achieved the status of public policy in Canada, and because it is likely to have a profound impact on both the Canadian public service and the Canadian political system, it is timely, and perhaps even imperative, that certain fundamental questions be raised about it. What is the historical background and distinctive character of balanced participation in Canada? What are its logical implications and possible empirical consequences? What might be its effects in Canadian politics—not only those effects which are desired and consciously anticipated, but also those which may be neither wanted nor recognized? Would it tend to promote political stability or undermine it? Would it tend to improve the public service or sabotage it? Is it compatible with merit or inherently antithetical to it? Finally, could it actually be used to promote merit in, and improve the overall performance of, the public service?

It is our belief that an informed and persuasive inquiry into these questions is best approached within the framework of the notion which underlies balanced participation—that of representative bureaucracy. Only by studying the pure type, together with the historical antecedents and special character of the Canadian variant, can the underlying issues be well understood. We will therefore focus, in turn, on the following: the historical background of balanced participation in Canada, the logic of representative bureaucracy, the arguments for and against representative bureaucracy, and, finally, the way in which the issue of representative bureaucracy or balanced participation should be approached within the Canadian political system.

SOME HISTORICAL ANTECEDENTS

It is important to remind Canadians in the 1970s that the sociologically proportional representation of francophones in governmental institutions existed in this country during the mid-nineteenth century, and that this greatly facilitated the federal union of 1867. In the 1840s, as the federal concept began to emerge as a feasible solution to the French–English dualism in Canada, institutional bilingualism was given full expression in the creation of dual administrative establishments in the United Provinces of Canada. The administration of education was perhaps the most distinctive of these establishments, but the departments of Law, the Provincial Secretary, and sections of the Crown Lands Department were other notable examples. J.E. Hodgetts has noted that, although some government departments maintained integrated bilingual establishments, others were linguistically 'split right down the middle, starting at the top with the political head and going down to the subdivisions of the various branches'.[8] Indeed, political equilibrium even dictated that the capital of the United Provinces be rotated between Toronto and Quebec City in the years following 1849.[9]

Thus, in the years immediately preceding Confederation, when the continued existence of French Canada as a separate cultural entity had become widely accepted as a political fact, the French Canadian political, religious and bureaucratic elite 'became the representatives of a separate unit of the population with its own rights and interests'.[10] After the Confederal settlement, however, the accession of new provinces meant that this pattern of dualism would be reformulated. Geographical representation grew rapidly in significance. Increasingly, questions in the House of Commons about representation (even fixed quotas) came not from French Canada but from the newly added Atlantic Provinces and subsequently from the West.[11] Early Canadian federal history therefore indicates that geographical rather than sociologically balanced representation was of much greater concern to federal politicians. The demands for French Canadian representation were assumed to be met by the careful institutional arrangements devised during the period of the United Canadas. But were they? What appeared as a French Canadian understanding of, and acquiescence in, this new political reality which Michel Brunet calls 'the Great Compromise',[12] contained from its inception the seeds of a disaffection which would mature at some later date.

Essentially the Confederation agreement was viewed by both the Church and the Quebec lawyer-politicians as a firm guarantee of Canadian dualism, a condition seen as being essential for the protection of French Canada's distinctive cultural values. Whether this interpretation of the agreement was accurate does not concern us here: the fact is that it was widely held in French Canada, and that many French Canadian nationalists were zealous in proposing formal blueprints for what Kenneth McRae has called 'the consociational accommodation of linguistic diversity'.[13] Moreover, these views of the agreement were never clearly disavowed by federal politicians or by the rest of Canada. Over time, discord concerning these fundamental understandings was therefore inevitable, for, as Alfred Dubuc observes:

> Confederation was much more than the enactment of a simple legal document: it established an institutional fabric deeply rooted in the economic, social and political structure of Canadian society in the middle of the nineteenth century. . . .The Confederation settlement endured a hundred years, but in the course of that century Canadian society has been profoundly transformed. Its economic structure is now that of an industrialized country, its social classes are more clearly defined and its aspirations for democracy are increasingly heard. . . .Today the most important conflicts are settled on the political level and become confrontations of power; these are the conditions of political chaos.[14]

'Political chaos' would surely be too strong a phrase for describing the normal state of Canadian politics; yet French Canada's several confrontations with the rest of the country, particularly in the last decade, have had profoundly unsettling effects.

French Canadians have correctly perceived that the idea of cultural dualism was being gradually eroded and increasingly ignored by English Canada. The elements underlying these changes are complex, and it would be impossible to summarize them in a few generalizations here.[15] Two aspects of this change which found expression in the recruitment patterns of the federal public service, however, demand comment. Data to substantiate these observations are difficult to garner, due in part to the fire in the Parliamentary Library in 1916, but one may nevertheless make some informed guesses. First, with the entry of Nova Scotia and New Brunswick into

Confederation there was an undoubted increase in the number of anglophones in the Dominion civil service, notably because only about 6 per cent of the people of Nova Scotia and about 15 per cent of those of New Brunswick were of French origin. Furthermore, within the Maritimes this minority counted for very little politically, economically, or culturally.[16]

Second, the French Canadians in the administration of education were bound to disappear from Ottawa to Quebec City with the transfer of education to the provinces. So were the French Canadians in the Department of Law, with the transfer of most civil law matters to the provinces, and those in the Crown Lands Department, with the transfer of Crown lands. Of course, for the same reasons a good many English Canadians went to Queen's Park in Toronto; but with a much larger total English-speaking population in the new confederation, it seems reasonable to assume that the total disappearance of French Canadians from education, civil law, and Crown Lands made a proportionately bigger hole in their numbers federally than the disappearance of large numbers of English Canadians from the same departments,[17] Unfortunately, the empirical evidence needed to substantiate these assumptions unequivocally is lacking.

There was a lack of institutional devices to avert this diminishing role of French Canada in the important federal institutions of the nation.[18] Yet, this change had far-reaching consequences. In the words of Hodgetts:

> After 1867, the larger Confederation with its subsequent accession of new provinces progressively reduced the French-speaking element from its former position of equality to one of a political minority. The situation was akin to that which had developed a generation or more earlier in the United States where the slave-owning southern states lost their position of political parity in the enlarging American Union. Lacking the political leverage provided by equal numbers, French Canada was unable to insist on the maintenance of the old administrative patterns of dualism—just as the southern states saw themselves deprived of the necessary leverage to maintain one of their cultural and economic mainstays, the institution of slavery. The response of the American South was the decision to secede from the Union—a decision that was countermanded by resort to arms and the ultimate victory of the North in the Civil War.
>
> French Canada's response was of a totally different order, for separatist agitation assumed significant proportions only a century later in the 1960s. In effect, as its minority position worsened in political terms, French Canada elected to use the federal framework to retreat into the enclave of provincial rights, there to concentrate on becoming *maîtres chez nous*. (The American South, after the trauma of post-Civil War reconstruction, in like fashion withdrew to lick its wounds and nurse its romantic visions of the past).[19]

Within the public service of Canada, these developments had a striking impact on staffing. In 1946, a brief by the Montreal Chamber of Commerce to the Royal Commission on Administrative Classifications provided statistics indicating that the overall representation of French Canadians in the federal bureaucracy fell from 21.58 per cent in 1918 to 19.90 per cent in 1936–7, and finally, to 12.25 per cent by 1944–5. In the senior positions of deputy minister rank, the Chamber's figures claimed that French Canadian representation in the senior hierarchy dropped from 14.28 per cent in 1918 to zero in 1946. The Chamber was blunt in affixing the blame for this state of affairs: a blatant neglect of bilingualism in the public service, coupled with a mechanistic classification system fashioned to correspond with English-language educational systems, were the principal reasons for this drastic decline.[20]

The introduction of scientific management in 1918 in the form of the classification system was hailed in English Canadian circles as a giant step forward in rationalizing the staffing practices of the federal bureaucracy.[21] The school of scientific management flourished in the United States at the beginning of the twentieth century, and this philosophy of organizational efficiency and economy with its strong Anglo-Saxon Protestant moral overtones was welcomed as a panacea to clean up 'the venal practices of patronage' existing in Canadian bureaucracies of the time. During this reform period, efficiency was associated with morality, lack of corruption and neutrality—all traditional values of the public service. Thus, as Nicholas Henry observed, a somewhat inconsistent but soothing amalgam of beliefs emerged that packaged together goodness, merit, morality, neutrality, efficiency, science, and the Protestant ethic into one conceptual lump.[22]

By creating a personnel system relatively free of bureaucratic patronage, these reforms also closed one of the principal avenues by which francophones had previously been recruited to the federal public service. At the same time, moreover, the reform legislation included a preferential system of recruitment for veterans which was diametrically at odds with the accompanying conception of merit. This, of course, also worked to the disadvantage of francophones, considering their general lack of enthusiasm for Canadian entry into the world wars, which entry many of them viewed as being mainly for the preservation of Crown and Empire. And no one in authority seemed to entertain serious thoughts of facilitating the principle of service to francophones in their language, or of ensuring that an adequate ethnic representation would be maintained in the federal bureaucracy.[23] The resulting imbalance became quite spectacular over time. In 1949, for example, a Civil Service Commission internal inquiry found that, of 865 applicants for positions of student assistant coming from Quebec and Ontario, only 6 per cent came from Laval University, 12.8 per cent from the Université de Montreal, and as much as 34.5 per cent from McGill and 46.7 per cent from the University of Toronto.[24]

These figures reveal more than they attempt to explain. Universities outside the Quebec–Ontario borders were not, in 1949, actively involved in supplying summer student manpower to the Canadian public service. Indeed, it was not until the 1950s that the Public Service Commission rectified this imbalance by consciously assuring a better geographical distribution of its recruits. In the late 1960s, this continuing policy was supplemented in public service recruitment procedures, as we have seen, by the additional notion of a more balanced ethnic representation.

Both of these changes, moreover, were accomplished without fixing quotas in legislation or devising bureaucratic structures to ensure that the letter of the law was carried out (despite significant pressures from within the Canadian public service to move in that direction). And the results are impressive: for example, between 1966 and 1976 the Public Service Commission, with quiet consistency, pushed French Canadian participation in the senior administrative category (SXS) from 14 to 21 per cent. Kenneth Kernaghan offers additional evidence for the effectiveness of PSC policies:

> The most tangible indicator of progress is the fact that francophones are now represented in the public service in almost exact proportion to their numbers in the total population—an increase from 12.25 per cent of the service in 1946 to 27.2 per cent in 1977. Perhaps of even greater significance in view of the important policy role of senior public servants is the fact that 21 per cent of the senior executive category is now composed of francophones. It is notable that these increases have been achieved without using the strategy of a quota system.[25]

It has been alleged, of course, that the educational system of Quebec was, in significant part, responsible for a lack of suitable and sufficient francophone recruits for the public service. Canadians, it is true, developed a curriculum emphasizing classical studies, medicine and law to the neglect of scientific and technical training. Why this happened is a matter for some dispute; but it was undoubtedly related, in large degree, to the Church's monopoly on education, combined with its opposition to secular values and modes of activity. And this was perhaps linked to certain wider political and economic variables too extensive to explore here.[26]

Whatever the reasons, however, the crucial issue is whether such classical training was, in actuality, as deficient for employment in the public service as anglophones often alleged it to be. In the words of Nathan Keyfitz:

> The argument is an attractive one to those who wish to devalue a rival educational system that has many humane aspects. There is no use, however, for this writer to become sentimental on the subject, since the Quebec colleges and universities are in a state of rapid change and will have attained within a very short time, that emphasis on science on which the modern world insists. As one offers the old system a regretful salute and farewell, however, one notes that it teaches a curriculum similar to that which formed many an empire builder at Oxford before he went out to India to be the absolute ruler of a district containing a million people, or to London to start climbing to the chairmanship of a large railway or bank.[27]

In competition with English Canadian applicants for public service jobs, therefore, French Canadian applicants did suffer from an educational disadvantage, which, viewed from one perspective, can be said to be of their own making; but this handicap was surely compounded, even caricatured, by the values of anglophones on merit and efficiency and a recruitment process that stemmed from those values. Over

time, the personnel recruitment standards and procedures were fashioned to correspond to the educational biases of anglophones concerning rationality and experience.[28] In 1965, the Royal Commission on Bilingualism and Biculturalism, as the
Montreal Chamber of Commerce brief of 1946 referred to earlier, summed up the
then existing situation:

> The rationalization of the federal Public Service along lines of efficiency and
> merit in the years after 1918 destroyed the old system of patronage under
> which there were always a number of Francophone civil servants appointed by
> Francophone cabinet ministers. No procedure or doctrine was evolved to
> replace the old system and, with few Francophones in the guiding councils of
> the Public Service, its explicit qualifications and implicit assumptions became
> more and more unfavourable to Francophones.[29]

To remedy this problem, the Royal Commission has advocated balanced participation, an idea which, as we have already indicated, implies representative bureaucracy. Accordingly, we will now turn to a more thorough examination of
representative bureaucracy, its relation to balanced participation, and its most important logical and empirical consequences.

THE LOGIC OF REPRESENTATIVE BUREAUCRACY

Stated simply, the idea of representative bureaucracy is that the public service should
be democratized, and that this can be accomplished by including, in the composition
of the bureaucracy, 'representatives' from the major social groups in proportion to
each group's numerical size within the total society.[30] In any society, at least in one
with a significant degree of social heterogeneity, the literal, arithmetical, application
of this idea is full of quandaries to the point of absurdity. Where do we cease dividing and subdividing the many social groups, cleavages, and stratification according to
which claims for proportional representation might be made? How do we weigh the
many cases of overlap which occur if non-exclusive categories such as sex, ethnic
background, and socio-economic status are conjointly used as a basis for asserting
claims to representation? Do we opt for the most capable of the population, or do
we logically seek a micro-reproduction of the society, giving proportional representation to, among others, the ignorant and the feebleminded? A good indication of the
extraordinary lengths to which the concept of representation can be taken is illustrated in a remark attributed to Senator Roman Hruska of Nebraska. In a speech to
the US Senate concerning whether the Senate should approve President Nixon's
nomination of G. Harrold Carswell to the US Supreme Court, Hruska conceded that
Carswell could be described as 'mediocre' in abilities, but added:

> Even if he is mediocre, there are a lot of mediocre judges and people and
> lawyers. They are entitled to a little representation, aren't they, and a little
> chance? We can't have all Brandeises and Frankfurters and Cardozos and stuff
> like that there.[31]

In political practice, however, such theoretical puzzles rarely concern us overmuch; exact proportionality remains an ideal which may be approached in greater or lesser degree, but never achieved. This is because the argument over representative bureaucracy necessarily centres on the most politically conscious and highly mobilized groups, who are also the most vocal and have the most salience. These may not always be the largest groups numerically, but they will be of major importance in the polity because there are tensions and cleavages among them, and because some who feel left out of the decision-making process organize, mobilize, and make claims to be let in. As we have seen in the Canadian case, we may therefore expect the argument for representative bureaucracy to take a variety of forms, depending on the sociological make-up, political structure, and major policy concerns of different countries. In every context, moreover, the notion of representative bureaucracy may not appear under that name. Whatever the label, however, there is a family of ideas which share certain features of representative bureaucracy, which entail some of its characteristic assumptions and implications and which may be illuminated by reference to the generic concept.

As conceived in the Commission's report, balanced participation is not a pure form of representative bureaucracy. This is because, first, the report views balanced participation as a supplement to, or modification of, the traditional merit system, not as its replacement. It is confined to the highest levels of the bureaucracy where the majority of positions are already filled by supplementing the formal merit system's 'standard appointment processes' with political considerations, and the system of merit at the lower levels, therefore, is not displaced. Second, the balancing effects solely the two founding linguistic groups, francophones and anglophones, but does not apply to any other linguistic groups in Canadian society.[32] And third, in achieving this balance, the report does not recommend strict proportionality:

> The balancing process is not a question of numbers or percentages. The appropriate ratio in one department is not necessarily the appropriate ratio in another. Our proposal does not impose a formal system of quotas or ratios, *but this approach might conceivably be used if the proposed adaptation fails.*[33]

Despite its moderate flavour, however, balanced participation is clearly a variant of representative bureaucracy; it is viewed as an antidote to the merit system's failure, or inability, to achieve an equitable sociological balance in bureaucratic recruitment and promotion, and it seeks to do this by deliberately altering the composition of the bureaucracy so that it more adequately represents the two most visible groups in Canadian politics.

The notion of representative bureaucracy plays upon certain ambiguities inherent in the notion of representation, and gains much of its persuasiveness from the assumption that if a bureaucracy is representative in a numerical-proportional sociological sense, (a representative sample) it will therefore be representative in the normal sense of political agency. There is a second, and also misleading, ambiguity which arises from confusing the notion of symbolic representation. We shall therefore discuss, in turn, three meanings of representation—as political agency, as representative sample and as symbol—and analyse their interconnections.

When the term 'representative' is used in politics, it usually refers to one who acts as an agent or spokesman for someone else. The styles of representation may vary: one might, for example, act as a delegate whose performance as representative is dictated by what the constituents desire or seem to desire; or one might act as a trustee who makes independent judgments concerning what policies are best for the constituents.

The types of constituencies and constituency interests for whom the representative acts also vary: they normally pertain to those who inhabit a particular geographical area, for example, a riding, a state, a province, or a nation; they may, however, concern groups and interests which are not necessarily conceived in geographical terms, for example, consumers, particular industrial or labour organizations, specified socio-economic strata such as classes, or racial and ethnic groupings. Although the possible combinations of representational styles and constituency types may be complex and even bewildering, the nature of representation as political agency is nevertheless clear: someone acts in lieu of someone else, and as their agent or spokesman.[34]

Second, there is a meaning of the term 'representative' which is primarily sociological, but which, in the context of representative bureaucracy and other theories of proportional representation, takes on political significance. This view conceives a representative as one who, in terms of the characteristics deemed to be important, is typical of a group, in other words is a representative sample. Viewed in organizational terms, what matters is that the institution includes individuals who are typical of their group, and in proportion to the group's numerical size in the wider population.

Here there is little concern with a representative's style—on what responsibilities and actions are appropriate for him. The key consideration is whether one is an accurate reflection or likeness of those who are represented; it is assumed that if this is the case, the representative will do what they would do if they were in the representative's place. Hence, when considering the representativeness of a bureaucracy, the key issue is composition. It is assumed that if the bureaucracy is a sociological miniature of the group or groups to be represented, it will also be representative in the first sense—it will be an effective agent or spokesman for the relevant group interests:

> The basic argument—stated in different ways in different contexts—is that bureaucrats carry their class attitudes and prejudices into their official life and only when all classes (or castes) are properly represented in the civil service will their different needs and interests find due consideration.[35]

Finally, the term 'representative' may be used in the primarily literary or philosophical sense of symbolic representation. Strictly speaking, a symbol calls to mind, stands for, or represents something else, but is not a likeness, even in miniature, of the thing stood for. In an obvious example, a flag may symbolize a nation but is not a likeness of it. Or a sacred symbol, such as the cross, may represent a religious community (partly visible, partly invisible), call to mind certain crucial and meaningful events in the community's history, and remind communicants of their shared convictions, values, and aspirations. But the cross is not a literal image of the things and events it represents.

In bureaucratic representation it is somewhat more difficult to isolate the purely symbolic element in cases where one or several members of a sociological group are brought into institutional positions, not in an effort to achieve proportional representation for the group, but as a signal that such positions are not henceforth closed to group members, or, in a familiar case of symbol manipulation, as a token gesture to group claims for admission to these positions. Nevertheless, we can recognize what occurs in these cases, and distinguish them from those where the symbolic element, while perhaps present, is secondary to the concrete achievement of proportionality along the lines advocated in representative bureaucracy.

There are other cases where representation as representative sample and representation as symbolization overlap and inter-penetrate—where the characteristics shared with a group or groups are connected with one's role as symbol. For example, Prime Minister Trudeau, because of his French–English origins, symbolizes the political duality of Canada; or the eloquent and commanding black leader, Martin Luther King Jr, came to symbolize the aspiration of black people for political equality and freedom. In these, as in the previous examples, the sociological and symbolic aspects of representation are subtly admixed, but nevertheless analytically distinguishable.

The discussion of representative bureaucracy normally centres, of course, on questions of representation. This, however, necessarily leads to the consideration of additional assumptions which are made concerning the nature of bureaucracy. The main assumption is that bureaucrats do not merely perform a 'phonograph' function which dutifully translates legislative policies into bureaucratic programs. It is assumed, in fact, that bureaucrats make policy and should be regarded as political actors. Without this assumption, the payoff to the individual who is part of the representative sample would be direct and material, with no implication that he is agent or spokesman for the group; put bluntly, the issue becomes one of who gets the desirable jobs. And the payoff to the group might be psychic and symbolic, but nothing more. Under such circumstances, there would be no significance to the argument for democratization—that political policy involves or effects group interests and that, in a democracy, all major group interests should be represented in the formulation and application of public policy.

It should therefore be noted that the argument for representative bureaucracy is not solely an argument for outsider groups who are entirely excluded from the bureaucratic structure and seek to be let in. It is also attractive to political groups that have arrived in one branch of the political system (the executive or Parliament) and are convinced that their aspirations have been frustrated by an unsympathetic bureaucracy which can, in fact, make policy. Thus, J. Donald Kingsley argues that, in England, Parliament became more broadly representative of the working class while the bureaucracy did not, and that the system would be improved by democratizing the bureaucracy too.[36] As has been demonstrated above, a similar situation exists in Canada with francophones who, while adequately represented in Parliament, feel frustrated from equal access to all levels of the public service.

THE CASE FOR REPRESENTATIVE BUREAUCRACY

In preceding pages, we have stated the argument for representative bureaucracy in a way that emphasizes its democratic core yet fails to articulate some of the less obvious justifications which may be given for it. The case for a more democratic bureaucracy, however, concerns not only the inherent value of democracy itself; it also includes values which are held to accompany the democratizing of human relationships both within bureaucracy and between bureaucracy and the public affected by it.

Hence, a heterogeneity of values, experiences and outlooks, with its built-in implications of dynamism, tension and 'provoking and unsettling encounters', may be considered healthy for bureaucracy.[37] It helps to assure that bureaucracy will be responsive to its members and to the wider public, both of whom must give their support if the organization is to continue in a viable way. Paradoxically, it is argued, the need for organizational security and authority is actually contradicted by excessive homogeneity of outlook at the higher levels and the insulation of leaders from views which challenge their uniformly narrow preconceptions.

This idea leads easily to another justification for representative bureaucracy—that it limits the abuse of bureaucratic power by allowing major groups to exercise checks over one another. The necessity for achieving consensus and for making compromises in order to carry out programs assures this. It may also be claimed, therefore, that representative bureaucracy is a way of keeping various groups in the system—of assuring them that they will have a voice in the bureaucracy which effects their interests. This, in turn, is a source of political stability.

Moreover, it may be argued that the effectiveness of bureaucracy *vis-à-vis* external challenges will also depend on a diversity of views, experiences and talents: otherwise, 'where is an organization to find the tools and flexibility to cope with changes in its environment?'[38] This argument is supported by certain aspects of systems theory such as the 'principle of variety' which states that those systems having the highest probability of successful adaptation to environmental charges are those with the greatest 'diversity in their composition'.[39] At the level of human social systems, where human intelligence plays an important role in system direction, the crucial element of variety is in the cultural and intellectual responses to external change.

This argument may be stated in a similar way, having obvious affinities with the sociological assumptions which underlie representative bureaucracy. In the 'sociology of knowledge' as developed by Karl Mannheim,[40] it is alleged that members of each group, because of their group's location in the system of social stratification and in the ongoing historical process, share unique experiences, develop distinctive concepts, and enjoy a novel perspective on society—a perspective which allows them but not members of other groups, to understand particular aspects of social reality. A complete picture of society and responsiveness to all group realities and aspirations, Mannheim argues, can only come from a group which, given the democratic nature of modern education, is recruited from all other social groups and is therefore a miniature of society as a whole.

This group, which Mannheim charged with representing a comprehensive, though composite, perspective in the bureaucracies of democratic states, is the so-called 'free-floating intelligentsia'. In principle, of course, representative bureaucracy is not confined to the intelligentsia, but as a practical matter it often is; for other social strata will be less likely to possess the skills and talents requisite for the proper functioning of a bureaucracy (at least as bureaucracy is conceived in the Weberian terms of efficiency and rationality). In the Canadian case, the notion of balanced participation at the higher levels of bureaucracy seems also to assume the recruitment of those with administrative skills and talents.

The advantage of the modern intelligentsia, Mannheim thought, is not in the one-sidedness or homogeneity of their views, but precisely in their diversity. This is useful, he maintained, because exposure to a variety of perspectives assures that one is no longer the captive of a single perspective. In dialectical fashion, being faced with the 'other' forces one to reflect on one's own values and presuppositions and to see their shortcomings. One becomes not only more appreciative of the views of others, but is therefore able to apprehend and promote a wider public interest or interests.

In this argument, the distinction between systems of proportional representation and systems of merit, which are usually thought to be in conflict, is ignored. For it is alleged that the excellence of bureaucratic performance rests upon the heterogeneity of outlook, breadth of understanding, and sharpened sensitivity to competing values, which bureaucratic recruitment from diverse backgrounds provides. Even if Mannheim's assumption that a representative sample automatically reflects the views of its parent group(s) is open to challenge—a point which will be developed in a moment—his argument alerts us to a contradiction that often afflicts the merit principle: measures of merit too narrowly conceived arbitrarily constrict the recruitment of those with talent. Moreover, the exposure to diverse values and perspectives can present a significant learning experience for public officials which also furthers the democratic ideal of a tolerant heterogeneity. In the Canadian case, this is at least implicitly recognized by the Commission on Bilingualism and Biculturalism: 'All Canadians are the poorer because the federal Public Service does not draw fully on the intellectual and organizational resources of French-speaking Canada.'[41]

THE CASE AGAINST REPRESENTATIVE BUREAUCRACY

Perhaps the most telling argument against representative bureaucracy (and, *pari passu,* Mannheim's sociology of knowledge) is that its basic assumption is incorrect. It is questionable whether persons continue, in their mature lives, to be dominated by early group experience. And it is therefore doubtful that a bureaucracy which is a miniature, or representative sample, of the larger society, will automatically or even probably represent the interests, values, and attitudes of society's groups.[42]

The inherently unique features of individual personality and the variability of individual psychological-intellectual development undermine the validity of generalizations which attempt to explain individual adult behaviour according to early group influences.[43] Add to this the observed tendency of upwardly mobile individuals to identify with the group to which they aspire rather than with the group from whence they came, or the tendency, described by Robert Michels, for able members of outsider groups to be coopted into establishment circles, thus neutralizing their opposition to the status quo. We are also aware that historically most lower-class social movements have been led by persons born into the middle or upper classes, thus casting doubt on the assumption that each group would find within itself effective spokesmen for its interests (as well as the assumption that these interests could not be represented by members of other strata).

We must also consider the Weberian claim that the norms of bureaucratic rationalization tend to neutralize the effects of previous sociological experience. At any rate, we may ask who members of the bureaucratic intelligentsia talk to on a day-to-day basis. The answer is, in most cases, with other bureaucrats having similar incomes, socio-economic status, and aspirations.

But we may also ask: If the assumptions of representative bureaucracy were true, would we want it then? For one thing, the notion of representative bureaucracy ignores an important expectation we normally have concerning the notion of representation. We usually assume that the task of a representative is to articulate the issues, take positions on them, offer programs and strategies for their solution, and stand or fall on the ability to gain continued constituency support at elections. In representative bureaucracy, however, there is no election to office, and there is no way of holding the representative responsible for his actions. It may therefore be argued that representative bureaucracy is not representative at all, 'that above all a representative is someone who will be held responsible to those for whom he acts, who must account to them for his actions.'[44]

Moreover, do we accept representative bureaucracy's uncompromising challenge to the norm of bureaucratic neutrality? We may admit that bureaucrats do, in both subtle and obvious ways, make policy, but should we encourage the practice, in its most negative ramifications, by building it into the very structure of bureaucratic institutions? And we may well ask: If it is his bias that makes a bureaucrat an effective representative of his own group, then isn't the corollary of this that he is also biased against members of other groups and dedicated to frustrating their aspirations? In an observation concerning the composition of committees in modern corporations, John Kenneth Galbraith makes this same point:

> Committees are not, as commonly supposed, alike. Some are constituted not to pool and test information and offer a decision but to accord representation to diverse bureaucratic, pecuniary, political, ideological, or other interests. . . . A committee with representational functions will proceed much less expeditiously, for its ability to reach a conclusion depends on the susceptibility of participants to compromise, attrition and cupidity. The representational committee, in its present form, is engaged in a zero sum game, which is to say what some win others lose. Pooling and testing information is nonzero sum— all participants end with a larger score.[45]

Viewed in this way, the conflicts built into a representative bureaucracy could immobilize the public service, making it impossible to respond either fairly or quickly and innovatively to emergencies. It could therefore frustrate the democratically elected legislature and undermine it. What effect this might have on a public who views the bureaucracy as being politicized, but in no way politically responsible, one can only guess. But the price, in terms of political instability, might be high indeed.

SUMMARY AND CONCLUSIONS

In summary, the basic assumption of representative bureaucracy is probably incorrect: it is doubtful that members of a bureaucracy chosen from various relevant groups will be likely to act as agents or spokesmen for their groups and group interests. If they did, the dangers of immobilization, negative bias toward other groups, politicization without political responsibility, loss of bureaucratic neutrality, diminished concern for a wider public interest, and bureaucratic instability would make representative bureaucracy unattractive. We therefore believe that the argument for representative bureaucracy on the assumption that it would be politically representative in any meaningful sense, is not only bogus, but also dangerous, and advocate that the debate in Canada be pursued on other grounds.

One possible alternative ground (which we do not advocate) abandons the intellectual justifications for representative bureaucracy altogether: it holds that the real issue is well paid and secure employment and whether it is to be distributed proportionally. This option might be welcomed by the relatively small percentage of persons who gain jobs and influence, but it would be of no advantage to their group or groups as a whole except perhaps for its symbolic and psychic benefits. At any rate, there is little doubt that this rationale would be rejected, for it is, in effect, no rationale at all.

The alternative grounds which we do find attractive draw from the arguments for representative bureaucracy, but without accepting certain theoretical and practical features of the notion which appear to us to be unsupportable or destructive. Indeed, we have maintained that the notion of representative bureaucracy actually illuminates and extends the principle of merit in its widest and most advantageous sense. Accordingly, the criteria of merit should be continuously re-examined and reformulated in light of the principle of heterogeneity and its advantages. With respect to Canada, in particular, there is evidence that the merit system has been too narrowly conceived and that it has therefore failed to recruit a broad range of talents that could help to revitalize and strengthen the public service.

This implies, of course, increased attention to the more effective recruitment of talented individuals from many groups, not only to francophones. For francophones in particular, a broader and more flexible interpretation of merit would not only symbolize the nation's commitment to bringing one of its major founding groups into the public service on the basis of equal opportunity for entry and advancement; it might also help to meet a special need in the public service itself. For it may be argued that the more classical and philosophical training to which francophones traditionally have been exposed is sorely needed in Western bureaucracies which, because they are increasingly run by experts and specialists, have tended to lose sight of broader human goals and values. The pertinence of this argument may well diminish when graduates of the more technically oriented CEGEPs, established in 1968–9, are of age to have reached the upper levels of the public service. But if the classical-philosophical training fades into insignificance we can only mourn its passing.

We should, at any rate, make concerted attempts to avoid an excessive preoccupation with narrowly technical competence or sameness of outlook in the public service. Bureaucracies need political vision, imagination, and the ability to interpret the imperatives and problems of bureaucracy into terms which are understandable for, and pertinent to, the politician and the citizen. Above all, in the face of the perplexing problems of contemporary civilization, where human wisdom appears so frail and limited, it seems foolish and arrogant to foster policies which encourage narrowly technical, homogeneous or standardized responses to unprecedented social problems.

How then is a more manifold public service to be achieved? One suggested approach has been the use of quotas. In the United States this policy has, in recent years, dominated many aspects of public, and even private, recruitment and hiring—mostly through the so-called affirmative action programs. And, as noted earlier, the Armed Forces of Canada have already instituted the legislated quota system as official military policy.[46] It is our contention, however, that the further extension of this policy in Canada would be unwise. One reason is that although the proponents of quotas rarely advocate the abandonment of merit, the logic of quotas is profoundly antithetical to the merit principle. Strictly speaking, quotas ignore individual qualifications: one applicant is as good as another inasmuch as he or she meets the relevant sociological criteria. What consequences the intensified use of quotas might have for public service morale and effectiveness—not only for those who are threatened or displaced, but for appointees in their relations with colleagues and the public, and in terms of their self-esteem—is still largely a matter for conjecture. The widespread and public use of quotas is a relatively recent phenomenon, and its concrete effects are just beginning to be studied.

In the understandable and admirable desire to achieve social justice, however, we should not become so intent on anticipated outcomes that we are mindless of the unrecognized and possible unwanted consequences of the means employed. If one seeks to assure the highest possible level of ability and performance in the public service, the use of quotas in hiring and promotion should be viewed as a last resort to eradicate deep existing social inequities, if it is to be used at all. We must be sure that in removing inequities we do not merely compound them, even for the group we are trying to help.

A recent article by economist Thomas Sowell demonstrates this point.[47] He has argued, with convincing statistical evidence, that affirmative action as practised in the United States under the Civil Rights Act of 1964 and its subsequent Executive orders and Labor Department regulations, has not been successful in advancing the cause of equal employment opportunity. Moreover, he argues, the program is potentially disastrous in its long-term social and political consequences. Writing in 1976, Sowell shows that, statistically, the pursuit of 'numerical proportions' in the hiring and remuneration of minorities and women for positions in higher educational institutions has had negligible results in the interval since 1971 when application of the policy became firmly established. His main concern, however, is not the mere failure of this policy to advance its ostensible objectives; it is the policy's observed and potential

side-effects. One of these is the enormous growth of both federal bureaucracies concerned with administering the program, and university bureaucracies devoted to
preparing the complex and weighty affirmative action reports. This exercise, he says,

> need not involve hiring a minority or female faculty member—and usually
> does not, as the statistics indicate—but does involve a legalistic and bureaucratic
> manner of recruiting, screening, and evaluating candidates in order to generate
> enough paperwork to show 'good faith efforts' to meet numerous 'goals and
> timetables' for minority and female employment. These charades take the place
> of meeting quotas which no one seriously expects to be met.[48]

Additional effects are probably even more serious in terms of their overall social
and political damage: increased resentment and frustration for both sides in the affirmative action debate; heightened public hostility to the legitimate aspiration of
women and minorities for equal employment opportunities; growing antagonisms
within the old Democratic Party 'ethnic coalition' once devoted to the cooperative
achievement of basic human rights; and the thorough obfuscation of underlying
social variables (not hiring practices) which explain the present distribution and levels of remuneration of women and minorities in various professions or occupations
(not always to the disvalue of women and minorities).

Perhaps most important of all, Sowell argues that affirmative action distorts the
public perception of those sizeable advances made by women and minorities independent of the program:

> What 'affirmative action' has done is to destroy the legitimacy of what had
> already been achieved, by making all black achievements look like questionable
> accomplishments, or even outright gifts. Here and there, this program has
> undoubtedly caused some individuals to be hired who would otherwise not
> have been hired—but even that is a doubtful gain in the larger context of
> attaining self-respect and the respect of others. The case of women is different
> in many factual respects, but the principle is the same.[49]

In our view, the policy of quiet consistency pursued by the Public Service
Commission of Canada in the last decade has therefore been a desirable one, and we
have tried to acknowledge its impressive gains made without legislated quotas or
fixed guidelines. With the sole exception of the Armed Forces, which does not come
under the Public Service Employment Act, specific legislation dealing with quotas—
or, to use the euphemism of the military, 'division in opportunities'—has not been
introduced in this country.

It is fortunate that it has not. For the further extension of quotas in Canadian
public life would tend to polarize an already splintered country, and would, as in the
United States, almost certainly obscure the more fundamental and abiding forces
involved. For example, with respect to francophone participation in the federal public service, the problem today is not how to assure more jobs for qualified francophones, but how to attract qualified francophones to the available jobs. Though it has

never been a secret that the Ottawa milieu is regarded by Quebec francophones as unattractive if not downright disagreeable, thus making their recruitment difficult, the problem seems to have become more acute in recent times. The 1977 annual report of the Public Service Commission openly frets about the increasing difficulty of attracting new graduates from French-speaking colleges, universities, and CEGEPs, and about the departure rate of francophones, even at senior executive levels, which, in the scientific and professional category, is almost twice that of their anglophone counterparts.[50] This situation would likely be exacerbated by the widely predicted decline of francophones outside Quebec as successive generations assimilate into the dominant anglophone society. Quotas are, we believe, irrelevant to the basic cultural, socio-economic, and political forces which underlie such developments, and they are utterly incapable of affecting them in some lasting and satisfactory manner.

We should therefore seek to eradicate or minimize, wherever possible, the attitudinal and structural impediments to equal opportunity in the public service. We should be willing to conceive imaginative programs for the recruitment—and, if necessary, even the training—of individuals from various groups, especially systematically disadvantaged ones such as the native people.[51] And we should entertain flexible and diverse conceptions of merit in our evaluation of talent and competence. If such ideas seem radical, we should be radical—for being radical means, in its profoundest sense, to get to the root of things. It means to scrupulously avoid superficial remedies, especially when their adoption obscures the understanding and retards the pursuit of meaningful solutions.

NOTES

This is a revised version of a paper presented to the Conference on Political Change in Canada, University of Saskatchewan, Saskatoon, 17–18 March 1977. For their helpful comments the authors are particularly indebted to J.J. Carson, John C. Courtney, G. Bruce Doern, Eugene Forsey, J.E. Hodgetts, Kenneth Kernaghan, A. Paul Pross, and D.V. Smiley. We are also grateful to participants in the Saskatoon conference, and to the senior federal public servants and faculty and graduate students visiting from Syracuse University with whom we first explored these ideas in seminars at Touraine, Quebec. However, the main conclusions and views expressed in this article are entirely those of the authors.

1. See, for example, 'Ignorance and Lack of Interest Plague the Issue of Bilingualism', *The Globe and Mail*, 5 July 1976.

2. Indeed, one well-known Quebec sociologist claimed that, to his knowledge, it was the first time in Canadian history that special interest groups [that is, the Canadian Air Traffic Controllers (CATCA), and the Canadian Airline Pilots Association (CALPA)] were: '. . . able to dictate to the Crown a "free vote" in Parliament on matters that are not related to issues of personal conscience. That this clause was not perceived as a direct threat to the very essence of British Parliamentary democracy is quite revealing. Even more so, when one realizes that this policy had been endorsed by all political parties.' Hubert Guindon, 'The Modernization of Quebec and the Legitimacy of the Federal State', in D. Glenday, H. Guindon, and A. Turowetz, eds, *Modernization and the Canadian State* (Toronto: Macmillan of Canada, 1978), pp. 217.

3. A good illustration of this comes from the former Commissioner of Official Languages to Parliament. Highly critical of the government's expensive language training program for public servants, Mr. Spicer argues that too many of the wrong people, chosen for the wrong reasons, have been getting the wrong training; their progress has been assessed by the wrong standards, and they have been sent back to jobs too often wrongly designated bilingual in the first place. Canada, Parliament, *Fifth Annual Report of the Commissioner of Official Languages, 1975* (Ottawa: Information Canada, 1976). For a good journalistic account see Sandra Gwyn, 'Speaking the Unspeakable, Bilingually', *Saturday Night*, July–August 1976, pp. 10–13.

4. The problem of perception is crucial. It has rarely been investigated whether the members of the ethnic minority feel that they are effectively represented by officials who, sociologically, belong to the majority group. A study of municipal governments in the National Capital Region (where, in various municipalities, either English or French is dominant) concluded that lack of direct representation of the linguistic minority tended to indicate satisfaction with the effective representation afforded by the majority, while direct representation by the minority tended to imply a lack of confidence by the minority that its interests would otherwise be effectively represented. See K.D. McRae, ed., *The National Capital: Government Institutions*, Royal Commission on Bilingualism and Biculturalism, Study No.1 (Ottawa: Queen's Printer, 1969).

5. Language policy at some provincial levels, notably Quebec and New Brunswick, and at the federal level, has been evolving continuously, and it is not our intention here to give an analysis of that evolution up to the present. For a discussion of that evolution up to 1974 see V. Seymour Wilson, 'Language Policy', in G. Bruce Doern and V. Seymour Wilson, eds., *Issues in Canadian Public Policy* (Toronto: Macmillan of Canada, 1974). We are aware of the distinctions made by the Royal Commission on Bilingualism and Biculturalism between 'anglophones' and 'francophones', and that its use of the terms has been criticized. We use both these terms in addition to the more traditional 'French Canadian' or 'Canadien' and 'English Canadian', however, in the conviction that a superficial attempt at redefinition here would only exacerbate the existing conceptual confusion.

6. Text of the statement by the Honourable C.M. Drury, President of the Treasury Board of Canada, before the Miscellaneous Estimates Committee on Management Objectives for Bilingualism in the Public Service, 9 March 1971.

7. Drury, ibid.

8. See J.E. Hodgetts, *Pioneer Public Service: An Administrative History of the United Canadas, 1841–1867* (Toronto: University of Toronto Press, 1955), p. 55.

9. Ibid., especially Chapter V, and Hodgetts, 'Our Early Peripatetic Government', *Queen's Quarterly*, 59 (Autumn 1952), pp. 316–22.

10. William Ormsby, *The Emergence of the Federal Concept in Canada, 1839–1845* (Toronto: University of Toronto Press, 1969).

11. This was drawn to our attention by Professor Hodgetts.

12. Michel Brunet, 'The French Canadians' Search for a Fatherland', in Peter Russell, ed., *Nationalism in Canada* (Toronto: McGraw-Hill, 1966), p. 51.

13. A good illustration is the proposal of Henri Bourassa which advocated a pan-Canadian nationalism built on dualistic cultural foundations. See Kenneth McRae, ed., *Consociational Democracy: Political Accommodation in Segmented Societies,* Carleton Library Series no. 79 (Toronto: McClelland and Stewart Ltd, 1974), pp. 257–8.

14. Alfred Dubuc, 'The Decline of Confederation and the New Nationalism', in Peter Russell, ed., *Nationalism in Canada,* p. 131.

15. Readings on this topic are extensive, but a few essential ones are: Pierre Elliott Trudeau, *Federalism and the French Canadians* (Toronto: Macmillan of Canada, 1968); Richard J. Joy, *Languages in Conflict: The Canadian Experience* (Toronto: McClelland and Stewart Ltd, 1972); Kenneth McRae, ed., *Consociational Democracy;* R.M. Burns, ed., *One Country or Two?* (Montreal: McGill-Queen's University Press, 1971); Michel Brunet, *Canadians and Canadiens* (Montreal: Fides, 1954); Conrad Winn and J. McMenemy, eds, *Political Parties in Canada* (Toronto: McGraw Hill Ryerson, 1976), chapters 4 and 11.

16. Hugh S. Thorburn, *Politics in New Brunswick* (Toronto: University of Toronto Press, 1961).

17. This assumption and the grounds for its credibility were suggested to us by Senator Eugene Forsey.

18. Two questions may be posed here: a) If the Church and the Quebec lawyer-politicians thought that Confederation gave them a firm guarantee of Canadian dualism, why were they content with three ministers in a cabinet of thirteen in 1867, with about the same proportion or less down to 1896, and, in Laurier's government with a smaller proportion still? Figures supplied by Senator Eugene Forsey indicate that Laurier's cabinet had 23.1 per cent francophone representation from 31 July to 16 November 1896, 25 per cent from 30 June 1897 to 18 July 1899, never rose above 21.4 per cent, and for two short periods sank to 18.8 per cent; b) Given this diminishing role of the French Canadians, why did we not adopt in Canada the American practice of modifying the merit system with quotas based on the population of each state (province)—a notion, incidentally, which was written into the US Civil Service Act but honoured perpetually in the breach?

19. J.E. Hodgetts, *The Canadian Public Service 1867–1970* (Toronto: University of Toronto Press, 1973), p. 35.

20. 'La classification des fonctionnaires est la source de difficultés et de mécontentements assez graves dont l'origine provient, selon nous, de trois causes principales: (a) la désuétude de la méthodologie appliquée, (b) la méconnaissance du bilinguisme, (c) le manque d'autorité en certains cas, des services d'organisation (organization branch). Voici nos remarques à ce sujet.
1 *La méthodologie de la classification*
La différence inacceptable des traitements entre le personnel administratif que nous signalions plus haut provient en grand partie de la classification préparée en 1919, par la maison Arthur Young de Chicago et incorporée dans le fameux Rapport de Transmission (Report of Transmission). . . . La plus grande faiblesse du Rapport de Transmission semble être l'importance exagérée accordée à l'expérience par rapport à l'instruction ou à l'éducation.' Public Archives of Canada. Files of the Royal Commission on Administrative Classifications. Chambre de Commerce du District

de Montréal. Mémoire soumis à la commission royale d'enquête sur le service civil fédéral, avril 1946.

21. For a more comprehensive treatment of this theme see: V. Seymour Wilson, 'The Relationship Between Scientific Management and Personnel Policy in North American Administrative Systems', *Public Administration* (London), Summer 1973, pp. 193–205; and J.E. Hodgetts, R.W. McCloskey, R. Whitaker, and V. Seymour Wilson, *The Biography of an Institution: The Civil Service Commission of Canada, 1908–1967* (Montreal: McGill-Queen's University Press, 1972).

22. Nicholas Henry, *Public Administration and Public Affairs* (New Jersey: Prentice Hall, 1975), p. 191. The Royal Commission on Bilingualism and Biculturalism rejected this packaging with the argument that 'The debate is no longer about efficiency, merit, patronage, and representation, but rather between thorough-going reform and schism. Change is imminent and no institution requires reform more urgently than does the federal administration.' Royal Commission on Bilingualism and Biculturalism, Book III, *The Work World*, p. 95.

23. No one considered that providing public services in English in a predominantly French-speaking environment is itself a highly inefficient practice. In 1938, after increasing demands for such services were made by French Canadians, Wilfred Lacroix, Liberal member for Quebec-Montmorency, succeeded in adding an amendment to the Civil Service Act to specify that a candidate must be qualified in the language of the majority of people with whom he would have to deal. By 1942–3 this amendment had become a virtual dead letter in the law. For a fuller treatment of this and related themes in administering the merit system, see Hodgetts et al., *The Biography of an Institution*, pp. 461–93.

24. Jean Boucher, *The Civil Service and the Universities*, an Internal Civil Service Commission Report, December 1949.

25. Kenneth Kernaghan, 'Representative Bureaucracy: the Canadian Perspective', *Canadian Public Administration* 21 (1978), p. 501.

26. See Hubert Guindon, 'The Modernization of Quebec and the Legitimacy of the Federal State', in Glenday, Guindon, and Turowetz, eds, *Modernization and the Canadian State*.

27. Nathan Keyfitz, 'Canadians and Canadiens', *Queen's Quarterly*, 70, no. 2,, Summer 1963, pp. 164–82. Keyfitz was of course referring to the then reform of college and university curricula, and the subsequent creation of the CEGEP in 1968–9. Thus, over the last decade and a half, the more classical and philosophical training of French Canadians has virtually disappeared from the Quebec educational curricula.

28. See V. Seymour Wilson, 'Language Policy', for a more comprehensive discussion of this. See also Beattie, Désy, and Longstaff, 'Bureaucratic Careers: Anglophones and Francophones in the Canadian Public Service', a study prepared for the Royal Commission on Bilingualism and Biculturalism, vol. 1, pp. 36–40.

29. Royal Commission on Bilingualism and Biculturalism, Book III, *The Work World*, p. 203. See also footnote 20 for comparison.

30. The origins of the concept have been traced to President Andrew Jackson's view that job rotation is the best possible means for insuring responsibility in a bureaucracy, but the first developed proposal for representative bureaucracy which would, as an

administrative arrangement, reflect the character of the social structure, was presented by J. Donald Kingsley, *Representative Bureaucracy: An Interpretation of the British Civil Service* (Yellow Springs, Ohio: Antioch Press, 1944). Some of the more recent literature is as follows: Samuel Krislov, *Representative Bureaucracy* (Englewood Cliffs, New Jersey: Prentice-Hall, 1974); Kenneth John Meier, 'Representative Bureaucracy: An Empirical Analysis', *American Political Science Review* 69 (June 1965), pp. 526–42; David H. Rosenbloom, 'Forms of Bureaucratic Representation in the Federal Service', *Midwest Review of Public Administration* 8 (July 1974), pp. 159–77; David H. Rosenbloom and David Nachmias, 'Bureaucratic Representation in Israel', *Public Personnel Management* (July–August 1974), pp. 302–13; Peta A. Sheriff, 'Unrepresentative Bureaucracy', *Sociology* 8 (September 1974), pp. 447–62; Gideon Sjoberg, Richard A. Brymer and Buford Farris, 'Bureaucracy and the Lower Class', *Sociology and Social Research* 50 (April 1966), pp. 325–37; and V. Subramaniam, 'Representative Bureaucracy: A Reassessment', *American Political Science Review* 61 (December 1967), pp. 1010–19. For an early, and very general, discussion of representative bureaucracy in Canada, see J. Porter, 'Higher Public Servants and the Bureaucratic Elite', *Canadian Journal of Economics and Political Science* 24, 4 (November 1958); and D.C. Rowat, 'On John Porter's Bureaucratic Elite' and Porter, 'A Reply to Professor Rowat', ibid., 25, 2 (May 1959).

31. Quoted in *The New Republic* 162, 13 (28 March 1970), p. 6.
32. Government policies seeking proportionality, however, now also apply to women and native peoples. For a summary and discussion of these policies, see Kernaghan, 'Representative Bureaucracy', pp. 502–7.
33. Royal Commission on Bilingualism and Biculturalism, Book III, *The Work World*, p. 272. Emphasis added.
34. In American literature on the subject, representative bureaucracy suggests a body of officials, broadly representative of the society in which it functions, and which, in social values, is as close as possible to the grass roots of the nation. See Norton Long, 'Bureaucracy and Constitutionalism', *American Political Science Review*, 46 (September 1952), p. 813; Paul Van Riper, *History of the United States Civil Service* (Evanston, Illinois: Row, Peterson and Co., 1958); Van Riper, et al., *The American Federal Executive* (New Haven: Yale University Press, 1963).

    In the British context, a case is usually made for class representation to ensure the responsiveness of bureaucracy. See, especially, R.K. Kelsall, *Higher Civil Servants in Britain* (London: Routledge and Kegan Paul, 1955), pp. 189–93. Some British writers, however, question this assumed connection between sociological representativeness and political responsiveness. See Kenneth Robinson, 'Selection and the Social Background of the Administrative Class', *Public Administration* (London) 33 (Winter 1955), pp. 383–8.
35. Subramaniam, 'Representative Bureaucracy', p. 1014.
36. Kingsley, *Representative Bureaucracy*.
37. See Alvin Gouldner, 'Metaphysical Pathos and the Theory of Bureaucracy', *American Political Science Review* 49 (June 1955), pp. 496–507, at p. 507
38. Ibid., p. 506.
39. See, for example, Edward Goldsmith, *Ecologist* 3 (September 1973), pp. 348–55, at p. 353.

40. See, especially, Mannheim's *Ideology and Utopia* (New York: Harvest Books, 1961), and Mannheim, *Freedom, Power, and Democratic Planning* (New York: 1950).

41. Royal Commission on Bilingualism and Biculturalism, Book III, *The Work World,* p. 263.

42. See the discussion by Kernaghan, 'Representative Bureaucracy', pp. 493–4, 496. Kernaghan cites Kenneth John Meier and Lloyd C. Nigro, 'Representative Bureaucracy and Policy Preferences: A Study in the Attitudes of Federal Executives', *Public Administration Review* 36 (July–August, 1976), pp. 458–69, and Porter, 'A Reply to Professor Rowat', p. 208.

43. For an important empirical study of this theme combining a rigorous and sophisticated use of social science theory with comparative data analysis, see John A. Armstrong, *The European Administrative Elite* (New Jersey: Princeton University Press, 1973), especially chapters 10 and 11.

44. Hanna Fenichel Pitkin, ed., *Representation* (New York: Atherton Press, 1969), p. 9.

45. John Kenneth Galbraith, *The New Industrial State* (New York: Signet, 1967), pp. 75–6.

46. See the White Paper on 'Defence in the 1970s' issued in August 1971, by the then Minister of Defence, Donald S. Macdonald.

47. Thomas Sowell, '"Affirmative Action" Reconsidered', *The Public Interest* 42 (Winter 1976), pp. 47–65.

48. Ibid., p. 58.

49. Ibid., p. 64.

50. See Geoffrey Stevens, 'Can it Survive?' *The Globe and Mail,* 10 May 1978, quoted from the Public Service Commission Annual Report for 1977. Stevens writes: 'The departure rate of Francophones from the senior executive category last year was 9.4 per cent (versus 6.7 per cent for Anglophones), from the scientific and professional category 14.2 per cent (versus 8.2 per cent). The main reason for this exodus of high-qualified francophones seems to be an increasing demand, and higher salaries, in the private sector for bilingual managers and specialists'.

51. The Department of Indian and Northern Affairs in concert with the Public Service Commission is making efforts in this direction. See Kernaghan, 'Representative Bureaucracy', pp. 505–7.

16

From *Sex and the Public Service*

Kathleen Archibald

Men and Women in the World of Work

> *No culture has failed to seize upon the conspicuous facts of age and sex in some way, whether it be the convention of one Philippine tribe that no man can keep a secret, the Manus' assumption that only men enjoy playing with babies, the Toda prescription of almost all domestic work as too sacred for women, or the Arapesh insistence that women's heads are stronger than men's.*
>
> —Margaret Mead

Many of our rules for social interaction derive from the fact that human beings come in two distinct packages as well as an assortment of ages. Just as older people are generally supposed to lead and younger people follow, so men are supposed to originate actions for women. Within the family there is a division of responsibilities based on sex. Men are the breadwinners, women the homemakers. Our definitions of masculinity and femininity reflect this[1] and children are socialized into these notions of sex roles from the day they graduate from stuffed animals to either toy cars or dolls.

The work roles of men and women are linked to their social roles and this is what makes the employment of women an issue. There is confusion about the current nature of this link and its consequences. More importantly, there is disagreement about the kind of link that should exist.

WHAT OF THE PAST?

Disagreements about the place of women have a long history; in every period of turmoil and social change, women's place has become an issue.[2] But since it was the move to an industrial economy that gave us our modem definition of 'work' as the performance of duties in exchange for a wage or salary, the historical period of particular interest starts just before the industrial revolution.

Women before the industrial revolution, 'were members of guilds, plied trades, harvested crops, managed commercial enterprises, and supervised the home workshops'.[3] In sixteenth-century England, women not only worked as thatcher helpers but also received the same pay as male thatcher helpers.[4] Both men and women

Kathleen Archibald, *Sex and the Public Service* (Ottawa: Information Canada, 1973): 1–32, 142–155.

worked primarily in and around the home, but the home then was a production unit as well as a consumption unit. Woman's place was in the home but as one feminine scholar remarked: 'Mankind . . . having once named a place "the home" thinks it makes no difference whether that home consists of a workshop or a boudoir.'[5]

When factories appeared on the landscape heralding the industrial revolution, it was women who first went to work in them, and children. Men stayed home to work the land since agriculture was then considered a more masculine and prestigious pursuit[6]—one of many switches in the definitions of male and female work since the tending of crops had been considered strictly women's work in all societies at an earlier time.[7]

Upper-class women did not go into the factories; they stayed home and managed their large domestic staffs. But most women were not upper class and even daughters of families which would today be considered middle class went to work in the textile mills. It was not until the second half of the nineteenth century that the distinction between 'working women' and 'middle class women' arose,[8] since this distinction required sufficient economic prosperity to permit a large class of men to support non-working wives and daughters.

Although many women were working throughout the nineteenth century, they were not working on equal terms with men. When doing the same work as men, their pay was lower; when doing different work, both their pay and the prestige of their occupation was lower. In no fields did their advancement opportunities equal those of men.[9] But to most people, men and women, this seemed right and proper since women were considered less competent in all fields whether requiring brains or brawn, whether involving repetitive or changing tasks. As long as everyone believed women were inferior, their differential treatment seemed only natural. But a few early observers, like John Stuart Mill, noted that the emperor was not fully clothed; why, if women were inferior by nature, was it necessary to place restrictive barriers in their occupational paths?

> One thing we may be certain of,—that what is contrary to women's nature to do, they never will be made to do by simply giving their nature free play. . . . What women by nature cannot do, it is quite superfluous to forbid them from doing. What they can do, but not so well as the men who are their competitors, competition suffices to exclude them from, since nobody asks for protective duties and bounties in favor of women; it is only asked that the present bounties and protective duties in favor of men should be recalled.[10]

One hundred years ago, when Mill wrote, protective legislation for women workers was not being sought; a few decades later it was. Working women in the sweat shops and factories wanted safeguards against exploitation. At the same time, middle and upper class suffragettes were demanding not differential treatment but equal treatment, not legal protection but full competitive participation. As Reeves has pointed out, these two strands within the feminist movement still exist: business and professional women tend to press for 'literal parity' via equal rights legislation, laboring women for 'practical parity via protective legislation'.[11]

MEN, WOMEN, AND EMPLOYEES

Equal treatment versus differential treatment remains one of the thorniest issues in the field of female employment today. Men and women are, without doubt, different. They are, just as indubitably, alike. When, in the world of work, is it appropriate to react to the differences, including differences in social roles, and when to the similarities?

Our occupational and employment structure as it has taken shape in the twentieth century was designed primarily as a masculine domain. The status of men came to be measured by success in the work world rather than family lineage; the status of women by their success in finding a husband who would be a good provider.

Equal Treatment vs Differential Treatment

The twentieth century saw the rise of a great middle class and it was generally expected that middle class women would work, at most, only until marriage. Thus women's work was seen as short-term and marginal. Few people thought of providing on-the-job training or advancement opportunities for women—they weren't going to be in the labour force long enough to worry about. The exclusion of women from all but the lowest occupational rungs was taken for granted at the beginning of the century and, until relatively recently, many employers refused even to hire married women.[12] Demands by women for equal opportunity and treatment arose from these aspects of the structure.

Arguments in favour of treating female employees differently than male ones are heard from employers as well as from women.

The argument of many employers runs, in brief, that since men are the primary work force, they should, under certain conditions, be given preference in employment. After all, men can be counted on to work throughout their adult years and women cannot. Men have to work to support their families; women do not. Men, they believe, are more competitive, more interested in their work, and have lower separation and absenteeism rates. It turns a man's world upside down to take orders from a woman, so generally supervisory and managerial positions should be reserved for men. So for responsible jobs, managerial jobs, jobs requiring on-the-job training, some employers think it is sensible to give preference to men over women.

They also think women should not be placed in onerous or unpleasant jobs, where the work is heavy or done outdoors in all weather, or in jobs in isolated areas or dangerous neighbourhoods. But they say, women should be given preference when manual dexterity is important, when a helpful, supportive attitude is needed rather than a competitive one.[13]

The argument made by some women in favour of differential treatment rests, as does part of the employers', on the differences between men and women arising out of differing family responsibilities. They say the employment structure has taken account of the family responsibilities of men and made adjustments and allowances for the man's roles as breadwinner, husband, and father. But it has scarcely made any adjustments, other than unpaid maternity leave, to the woman's family responsibilities as homemaker, wife, and mother. Yet, they point out, in the 1960s a majority of working women are married[14] and an increasing number of them are mothers.[15]

One of the responsibilities married women have had for some time is to be a secondary breadwinner, to go out to work while the husband finishes his education, when he is unemployed, or when the family needs supplementary income. So married women often work out of economic necessity,[16] just as do men and single women. Many well-educated married women have another kind of concern: they wish to be good wives and mothers but they feel they have a responsibility not to let their education go to waste.[17]

Thus married women—especially those who must work and those who wish to make use of their education—sometimes argue for differential treatment that takes account of women's family responsibilities. Current interest in paid maternity leave, child-care facilities, part-time employment, and refresher training for re-entrants into the labour force are based on the view that equal treatment is not necessarily equitable treatment.

The Risks of Differential Treatment

Differential treatment—of women and men, of Negroes and whites or of children and adults—always limits freedom of choice for one group, and often of both. It also entails a risk of inequity, since 'separate' easily becomes unequal. Therefore, if differential treatment is to be justifiable, it should produce at least enough progress toward economic or social goals to offset its obvious costs. Most differential treatment of children as compared to adults has this property, but is this true of differential treatment of men and women *in the work world?*

COSTS AND BENEFITS RELATED TO THE EMPLOYMENT OF WOMEN

Four basic values or objectives are involved in arguments about the advantages and disadvantages of equal opportunity for and equal treatment of male and female employees: economic efficiency or effectiveness, equity, freedom of choice, and the social health of the nation.

These four objectives are not always complementary, sometimes more of one means less of another. It is these trade-offs which make some decisions problematic for an employer. Therefore, some of the recommendations made in this study will reflect not only factual findings and interpretations, but also the relative importance of the four objectives. The objectives and the trade-offs between them are discussed in this chapter as a way of clarifying the major issues related to female employment and of making it easier for readers to evaluate the recommendations of this report in light of their own social and economic priorities.

Economic Efficiency and Effectiveness

Economic efficiency refers to maximizing output per unit cost; economic effectiveness is usually used more broadly to refer to optimal utilization of resources to attain desired objectives.

Labour or manpower is a resource, and to the extent that women (or men) have socially useful skills which are not put to the most productive use they are an underutilized economic resource. This may also be true of those persons in the labour force with underdeveloped skills, and, similarly, of a number of women outside the labour force, especially if workers with their particular qualifications, are in short supply.[18] For instance, manpower shortages in Switzerland in the mid-1960s led the Swiss government to state:

> The Government considers that, for women whose children no longer need constant attention, participation in economic activity is not only a personal right, but, in certain circumstances, also a social duty.[19]

Thus economic efficiency sometimes suggests using extraordinary methods to draw women with needed skills into the labour market. The argument is stronger if some public investment has been made in the education and training of women; not so firm for any individual employer unless he has invested in training himself.

For the individual employer, economic effectiveness must mean getting the best person available for a particular job. This implies selecting employees on the basis of individual merit rather than of gender.

But does it also imply equal pay for equal work? Wouldn't an employer save money if he paid women less than men? It is often assumed that salary discrimination is a cost-saving (less politely, exploitative) device and if one thinks in terms of paying women less than men, or Negroes less than whites, this seems to be so. But in giving the favoured group higher salaries, employers are actually paying a premium to the majority of workers (since the discriminated-against groups are usually minority groups, as women in the labour force are). This is more costly to employers than letting supply and demand alone determine wages.[20]

This argument applies in the long run and on a general level. In the short run, for the individual employer, moving to a policy of equal pay is costly, because women's wages have to be raised (it is impractical to think of lowering male wages). For this reason, England has implemented such a policy gradually.[21] The Canadian government has always subscribed to equal pay for equal work for men and women; the problem here has become one of defining what is equal work.

Equity

The notion of equity holds that everyone should have equal access, limited only by his or her ability, to the opportunities and rewards available in the society. In employment this means consideration of each individual on his or her merits, not in terms of that person's membership in a group. If an employer requires more evidence to decide a woman is capable than to decide a man is capable, the fundamental idea of equity is transgressed just as it is if a jury were to require less evidence for a verdict of guilty against a non-Caucasian than a Caucasian.

One common argument used to justify excluding women, or favouring men, for certain occupations is based on differences in turnover rates. Assume an employer knows that the turnover rate of women in a particular occupation is considerably higher than the rate for men. If he shows preference for men on this basis, he will be penalizing the majority of women for the minority who would quit, and levying no penalty on men, not even on those who quit. This is why judgments based on group tendencies—even when those tendencies are accurately measured—are considered discriminatory.

Note that economic efficiency, an employer's first concern, seems here to conflict with equity: if women have a higher turnover rate than men, it is more efficient to hire only men. Economic efficiency calls for lowering the incidence of false positives (giving jobs to those who would soon leave); equity calls for lowering the incidence of false negatives (denying a job to those who would, in fact, stay with it).

If this conflict is real, the employer must meet the requirements of one value at the expense of the other. But in the real world, such conflicts are often more apparent than real. The argument based on economic efficiency is of little value unless actual costs can be specified, and while differences in some job-relevant variables (turnover rates, absenteeism, etc.) can quite often be correlated with a particular group (sex, mother tongue, race), it is unlikely that membership in one of these groups is the best, or even a good predictor of these job-relevant variables. Sex and race are sometimes used to predict job performance because they are convenient, highly visible, and often support deeply held sentiments, not because they are good predictors. And if they are not good predictors, the chances for cost saving are minimal. If it is really important to lower the incidence of false positives, then it is worthwhile for the employer to do the research needed to discover good predictors of job performance. Using convenient but uncertain predictors sacrifices equity with little or no compensating gain in efficiency. Any judgment about an individual made on the basis of minority group membership runs this risk, and this is why such judgments are discriminatory.

Freedom of Choice

We have a fundamental notion that individuals should have freedom of choice where their activities do not infringe upon the rights of others. Yet social conventions in Canada—in every society—honour this ideal more in the breach than in the observance, most clearly in our conceptions of sex identities and roles.

One effect of this is to limit males more strongly than females: the woman with 'masculine' interests and behaviour is accepted with far less ambivalence than the man who demonstrates 'feminine' interests and behaviour (an indication of the superiority granted masculine pursuits).

In the work world, limitation on freedom of choice derives from the sex-typing of jobs. Some jobs are considered 'male', others 'female' and this produces a large degree of sex segregation. Here, in employment, alternatives are more limited for women than for men since more occupations, and especially more of the higher-status ones, are considered to be 'male' fields.[22] While this means women are more often a minority in formerly segregated occupations, it does not necessarily mean that male nurses have an easier time than female engineers.

Occupational segregation deserves as jaundiced an eye as the one directed to residential or educational segregation: separate is seldom equal. As *The Economist* has pointed out, 'tapping on the keyboard of a typewriter' uses skills similar to 'tapping on the keyboard of a composing machine', yet pay for the former—a female occupation—is considerably lower than for the latter, a male occupation.[23] So long as occupational segregation exists, equal pay for equal work can be subverted by gerry-mandering the definitional boundaries of equivalent work.

Social Health of the Nation

The health of the family is generally considered a matter of concern to the whole society, and there are strongly held and widely shared beliefs that a husband should support the family, a wife maintain the home and care for the children. Do these differing social responsibilities justify differential treatment for male and female employees?

Is it reasonable and fair for an employer to favour men, and women who are self-supporting, over married women? The Canadian public service has explicitly discriminated against married women during several lengthy periods. Employers often justify such treatment on economic grounds—for instance, married women have been restricted from working when a surplus of labour is expected, as during the transition from wartime to peace time. Is this reasonable?

Note first this is only secondarily an economic issue, it is primarily a social one. To simplify, assume a nation of 1,000 families with only 1,000 jobs available. The economically efficient employer will hire the best workers, whether male or female. But this will leave some families with two breadwinners, and some with none. On a national scale, the two-worker families will then have to support the no-worker families. Refusing to let married women work would help distribute income more equitably across family units.

This would not be unreasonable, assuming there were restrictions on moonlighting and on employment of the wealthy as well, but it would be more reasonable to prohibit a husband and wife both working, since this increases both equity and freedom of choice (and permits a more parsimonious set of restrictions[24]). Thus on the basis of social values, restricting employment opportunities for married women is not the best of available alternatives in periods of expected or actual unemployment.

But the economic arguments against such restrictions are even stronger. An employer will operate more efficiently if he hires the best employees regardless of sex and marital status. It is counter to any defensible view of the economy for the individual employer to attempt to ensure a more equitable distribution of family income. And, while for the nation as a whole the elasticity of the female labour supply is useful, natural economic and social forces appear sufficient to maintain this elasticity.[25]

The issue of greatest social concern is the potential conflict between married women's responsibilities to their families, particularly to their children, and their growing participation in the labour force. While the Swiss government in the mid-1960s thought mothers should be encouraged to work, the West German government thought they should be discouraged. The Minister of Labour and Social Affairs stated:

> I deem it necessary in connection with the promotion of the employment of
> women with family responsibilities to have regard not only to the needs of the

... economy but also to the social aspects of the problem. In the case of mothers who have children of school age or below, family duties should, as far as possible, take precedence over remunerative employment. We should hesitate, therefore, to promote measures which might serve the expansion of maternal employment. This does not, however, exclude attempts to create facilities for such mothers as cannot escape the double burden. . . .

If adverse social effects of the employment of mothers are to be avoided, more recourse will have to be taken to [other] possibilities of meeting manpower requirements instead of expanding the employment of mothers.[26]

Does the potential conflict between a woman's family responsibilities and her work responsibilities suggest that employers should respond differently to working mothers than to other employees?

Employers have, at various times and in various ways, taken maternal responsibilities into account. Some have done this by being reluctant to hire mothers of young children. Others have, although only when confronted with 'womanpower' shortages, provided child-care facilities to ease the burden for working mothers. The most common recent response to working mothers, however, on the part of public authorities as well as employers, has been to permit equal job access but provide no help on child-care arrangements. The absence of child-care facilities is 'usually defended with the argument that the employment of [mothers with pre-school children] should not be encouraged,'[27] in other words; a social-health-of-the-nation argument. But this response, as Klein points out in her 21 country survey of hours and services for women workers, is a 'kind of moral censorship' which rather than solving the problem actually intervenes between the 'Social need and its remedy'.[28]

Most Canadian women with children under six do not work and do not want to work: having pre-school children deters female labour force participation more powerfully than any other variable.[29] Nevertheless, about 20 per cent of married and once married women in the labour force do have children under six (and slightly over half have children under 16).[30] Since about half of all women in the labour force are married, this means that approximately 10 per cent of all women workers and of all women in the public service have children under six.[31]

Mothers of young children tend to be in the labour force either because their husbands' incomes are very low or because they are well-educated and, presumably, committed to a career. Thus increasing economic prosperity should decrease the proportion of mothers who work but, on the other hand, a greater interest in higher education and careers among women would increase it; so it is difficult to predict whether the number of working mothers in Canada will go up or down. The percentage of mothers in the Canadian labour force in the early 1960s was considerably higher than in the British labour force and about the same as in the United States labour force.[32] If Canada has continued to look more like the United States than like Britain, then working mothers have been on the upswing: in the United States, the number of working mothers with children under six rose 39 per cent between 1960 and 1967.[33]

It appears that the absence of child-care facilities has not served to keep mothers out of the work force. Their absence has, however, caused increasing concern among public authorities about the adequacy of child-care arrangements currently made by working mothers.[34]

Another way in which employers can respond to family and maternal responsibilities is by adjusting the working hours of married women, in particular, by permitting them to work part-time. Part-time employment can sometimes serve all four objectives: it increases freedom of choice and decreases the dual burden of working mothers; under certain conditions, it does not detract from and may even increase economic efficiency for the employer; and, as long as benefits and conditions are fair and the part-time alternative is equally available to all employees regardless of marital status and sex, it does not reduce equity in the work world.[35]

It is for these reasons that Klein has suggested that adjustments in the field of part-time employment 'would seem to promise the most fruitful results' in helping working wives and mothers bridge their two worlds.[36]

Summary

Should women in the work world be treated in just the same way as men? Should they be treated as women? Or should both men and women be treated as employees—a category of persons whose gender is irrelevant?

On almost all job-relevant variables there is considerable overlap in the distribution of men and the distribution of women. In other words, 'maleness' and 'femaleness' are seldom bona fide qualifications for particular jobs, so restricting access to employment or occupations on the basis of sex is almost always discriminatory.

Equal opportunity is not really problematic—women and men should be treated as individuals and judged on the basis of merit. But when it comes to equal treatment, things are a little more complicated. Benefits and conditions of employment, if originally intended to respond to the family responsibilities of male employees, may not when equally bestowed upon female employees meet their family responsibilities. The ILO Convention on discrimination in employment, while calling for 'equal treatment' without regard to sex, takes cognizance of this possibility by noting that certain

> special measures designed to meet the particular requirements of persons who, for reasons such as sex, age, disablement, family responsibilities or social or cultural status, are generally recognized to require special protection or assistance, shall not be deemed to be discrimination.[37]

THE GOVERNMENT OF CANADA AS AN EMPLOYER

In succeeding pages, attention is focused on the Government of Canada as an employer of women—in fact, the largest employer of women in Canada. As an employer, economic efficiency has to be the value of foremost concern to the government. It must get maximum output from tax dollars no less than a private firm with investment dollars. But the government is more than an employer; it is also responsible for the welfare and progress of the nation as a whole. Thus it can be expected to lead other employers with respect to social responsibilities as it often has in the past.

When no costs are involved in increasing equity, freedom of choice, or the social health of Canada, or when costs are relatively minor initial ones, there can be little question as to how the public service should act. When the costs are substantial or continuing, however, or when non-economic values conflict, reasonable men—and reasonable women—can be expected to disagree over the appropriate action.

Disagreements in themselves are not a problem, but battles fought with distorted facts over confused principles are. These have not been battles between the sexes; there are some who cherish tradition and others who welcome change on either side of the sex line. But if one can cherish the differences between men and women while welcoming the similarities, then one can also cherish tradition while welcoming change. The trick in both cases is to be selective—to decide when differences and traditions are important and when they are not. To be, in short, discriminating but not discriminatory.

NOTES

1. Lorraine Rand, 'Masculinity or Femininity? Differentiating Career-Oriented and Homemaking-Oriented College Freshman Women', *Journal of Counseling Psychology* 15 (1968), pp. 444–50.
2. Nancy Reeves, *Womankind: Beyond the Stereotypes* (New York: Aldine-Atherton, 1971), p. 16.
3. Ibid., p. 12.
4. Marjorie B. Turner, *Women & Work* (Los Angeles: Institute of Industrial Relations, University of California, 1964), p. 4.
5. Alice Clark, *Working Life of Women in the Seventeenth Century* (London, 1919), p. 8, as cited in Reeves, op. cit., p. 12.
6. Elizabeth Faulkner Baker, *Technology and Women's Work* (New York: Columbia University Press, 1964), p. 98.
7. Reeves, op. cit., p. 10.
8. Baker, op. cit., p. 99.
9. Ibid., pp. 99–334 and Eleanor Flexner, *Century of Struggle* (Cambridge: Belknap Press of the Harvard University Press, 1959).
10. Cited in Baker, op. cit., pp. 85–6.
11. Reeves, op. cit., p. 53.
12. See Chapter II of this report and Valerie K. Oppenheimer, 'The Interaction of Demand and Supply and its Effect on the Female Labour Force in the United States', *Population Studies* 21 (1967), pp. 239–59.
13. See subsequent chapters of this report and Edmund Dahlstrom, ed., *The Changing Roles of Men and Women* (London: G. Duckworth and Co., 1962).
14. *1961 Census of Canada*, Bulletin 7.2-1 (Ottawa: Dominion Bureau of Statistics).
15. Sylvia Ostry, *The Female Worker in Canada* (Ottawa: Dominion Bureau of Statistics, 1968), p. 4.
16. Ibid., pp. 24, 32, and Hortense M. Glenn, 'Attitudes of Women Regarding Gainful

Employment of Married Women', *Journal of Home Economics* 51 (1959), p. 250.

17. Ostry, op. cit. pp. 24, 32 and John D. Allingham and Byron G. Spencer, 'Women Who Work: Part 2, Married Women in the Labour Force . . .', *Special Labour Force Studies*, Series B, 2 (Ottawa: Dominion Bureau of Statistics, 1968).

18. As would be the case if they were highly educated in any of a number of fields. See Bruce Wilkinson, 'Studies in the Economics of Education' (Ottawa: Economics and Research Branch, Department of Labour, July, 1968).

19. Quoted in Viola Klein, *Women Workers: Working Hours and Services* (Paris: Organization for Economic Co-operation and Development, 1965), p. 63.

20. Becker has used such reasoning to show that discrimination against Negroes is costly to white capital as well as to Negro labour. It benefits white labour, however, and, by the same token, discrimination against female workers tends to benefit male workers. On economic grounds, unions with a predominantly male membership should be more interested in limiting equal access to occupations than employers. Gary S. Becker, *The Economics of Discrimination* (Chicago: The University of Chicago Press, 1957), pp. 11–16.

21. 'What Women Want', *The Economist*, 228, (6 July 1968).

22. Valerie K. Oppenheimer, 'The Sex-Labeling of Jobs', *Industrial Relations* 7 (1968), p. 230, and Edward Gross, 'Plus ça Change . . . ? The Sexual Structure of Occupations Over Time', *Social Problems* 16 (1968).

23. Op. cit. p. 13.

24. Restrictions against the employment of married women always have to exempt women who support their families.

25. Clarence D. Long, *The Labour Force Under Changing Income and Employment* (Princeton: Princeton University Press, 1958), p. 19.

26. Quoted in Klein, op. cit., pp. 62–3.

27. Ibid., p. 59.

28. Ibid.

29. Allingham, op. cit., p. 11.

30. Department of Labour, *Women's Bureau Bulletin* XI (January 1964; revised October 1964), Ottawa, p. 1.

31. In 1961, no more than 15 per cent of Canadian women with children under six were in the labour force, unless the husband's income was below $3,000 or unless the woman was a university graduate. If both, the rate was 36 per cent. Ostry, loc. cit.

32. Klein, op. cit., p. 61n.

33. US Department of Labor, Women's Bureau, *Working Mothers and the Need for Child Care Services* (Washington, DC, June, 1968), p. 7.

34. Ibid. and, for Canada, see Canadian Welfare Council, 'The Day Care of Children in Canada: Summary of Canadian Day Care Studies' (Ottawa, 1968).

35. For the complex set of empirical and value considerations involved, see Jean Hallaire, *Part-Time Employment* (Paris: Organisation for Economic Co-operation and Development, 1968), pp. 39–68.

36. Klein, op. cit., p. 85.

37. Discrimination (Employment and Occupation) Convention (1958) of the International Labour Organisation, Ratified by Canada in 1964.

Women in the Canadian Public Service

While the Commissioners readily acknowledge that many women are thoroughly enti-
tled to succeed in the public service, yet the influx of such a large number must, if con-
tinued, in the course of time, utterly swallow up the lower grades of the service and by
limiting the field for promotion to the higher classes prove detrimental to the development
of the higher and more responsible branches of the service; for it can hardly be admitted
yet that the work devolving on the departments can be carried on with a staff composed
entirely of women.

> First Annual Report, *Civil Service Commission,* 1909

At this point in time, at least, there are not enough women in the work world to prove
that they can do it.

> Male Interviewee No. 35, in 1968

This chapter examines both the history and, in broad terms, the current situation of
women in the Canadian federal service.

The pattern of female employment in Canada as a whole has changed considerably over the past 60 years. In the early 1900s, the proportion of women in the
Canadian labour force apparently remained static at just over 13 per cent (Table 1).
Since the First World War, however, this proportion has grown sometimes quite
slowly, as during the depression; sometimes very rapidly, as in the 1950s. Today almost
one-third of the labour force is female.[1]

TABLE 1 *Proportion of Women in the Canadian Labour Force,[a] 1901–67*

Year	Total	Women	Percentage of women in total	Percent increase in proportion of women
1901	1,783,000	238,000	13.3	.75
1911	2,724,000	365,000	13.4	
1921	3,164,000	489,000	15.5	15.6
1931	3,922,000	665,000	17.0	9.7
1941	4,516,000	834,000	18.5	8.8
1951[b]	5,286,000	1,147,000	22.1	19.5
1961[b]	6,458,000	1,764,000	27.3	23.5
1967[b]	7,730,000	2,395,000	31.0	13.6

[a] Excludes Yukon and Northwest Territories. Prior to 1921, includes those 10 years of age and older; 1921–1951, 14 years and over; after 1961, 15 years and over.
[b] Includes Newfoundland.
Sources: 1901–61 figures from Women's Bureau, *Women at Work in Canada.* Ottawa: Dept. of Labour, 1964, p. 10. 1967 figures from *Labour Gazette.* Ottawa: Dept. of Labour, Dec. 1967, p. 777.

TABLE 2 *Proportion of Women in the Canadian Civil Service, 1901–67*

Year	Total	Women	Percentage of Women in Total
1901[a]	5,000	113	2.3
1911[a]	10,000	807	8.1
1928[b]	30,655	5,775	18.8
1931[c]	45,581	7,617[c]	16.7
1937[d]	42,836	8,010	18.7
1943[e]	112,000	30,000	26.8
1961[f]	135,922	I38,480	28.3
1967[g]	150,245	40,999	27.3

[a] Inside and Outside Service.
[b] Civil Service except Post Office.
[c] Excludes postmistresses.
[d] Civil Service and salaried departmental employees
[e] Rough estimate, probably Civil Service and salaried departmental employees.
[f] Full-time employees under the Civil Service Act.
[g] Full-time employees under the Public Service Employment Act limited to types formerly under the Civil Service Act.

Sources: 1901, 1911: *Civil Service Lists*. 1928, 1931: House, *Proceedings of Select Special Committee on Civil Service*, 1932, Ottawa: King's Printer, 1932, pp. 243, 906. 1937: Glassco Commission, p. 315, and Judek, p. 8. 1943: statement tabled in the House, March 26, 1943, see *Civil Service Review*, 16 (March, 1943) p. 108. 1961, 1967: Pay Research Bureau.

While the number of women in the labour force, both married and single, has increased, the rate of increase has been much higher for married women. In 1931, 10 per cent of the female labour force was married.[2] In 1961, for the first time, there were more married women than single women in the labour force.[3]

HISTORY OF WOMEN IN THE FEDERAL SERVICE

Although the historical record is far from complete, the proportion of women working in the federal service appears to have followed the pattern in the labour force as a whole. Data grouped by sex were not available on a regular basis until 1960, but estimates—of varying quality—are available for some earlier years (Table 2). Women were evidently less well represented in the civil service in the early 1900s than in the labour force as a whole.

Early Status of Women

The first recorded female public servants were a matron and a deputy matron at the Kingston Penitentiary, both appointed in 1870. Another woman was appointed 'lock-labourer' on the Williamsburg Canal in 1871. By 1885, 23 of a total of 4,280 civil servants were women, more than one-third of them employed as third class clerks (the lowest clerical level at that time) by the Post Office Department.[4]

From the first, the Government of Canada adopted the principle of equal pay for equal work, which was not accepted in the United States Civil Service until 1923[5], nor in the British Civil Service until 1955 (with six years allowed to implement it[6]), and has yet to be accepted in the Australian Civil Service.[7]

In these early years, however, women were promoted more slowly than men. The Civil Service Lists of 1885, 1901, and 1911, make it possible to trace the employment and promotion of three female clerks in the Post Office Department and some male workers who started at the same time, class, level, and salary. From 1885 to 1911, the female clerks were promoted within their class only, with an average salary increase of $667. Their male counterparts were advanced to another class and level, with an average salary increase of $1,000 over the same 26 years.

The 'Problem' with Women

These three women are not isolated examples. Limitations on promotion for women were quite explicit in several early annual reports of the Civil Service Commission. Women were not considered suitable for, or capable of, work at more responsible levels. The Commission perceived its problem not as one of keeping women down—that was taken for granted—but as one of keeping down the number of women in the civil service.

The entry point for a civil service career, as in industry, had long been the lowest level clerical positions. But salaries in these positions were low, and few men applied, so the lower levels rapidly filled with women. A Royal Commission on the Civil Service reported in 1908 that women filled almost all the lower grades of the Post Office and the Department of the Interior.[8]

The Commission's annual report of 1918 included a brief history of the civil service. In discussing 'abuses still rampant' around the turn of the century, it said:

> The character and quality of the men entering the service declined. The lower-grade offices were filled with women, which limited the field from which promotions might be made to the higher divisions, and interfered with the development of competent male clerks.[9]

The first attempt to solve this 'problem', around 1909, was to permit deputy heads to specify a man or woman for a particular position (leading to occupational segregation with women becoming 'stenographers and typewriters' and men 'general clerks'[10]) and to limit appointments in all but the lowest levels 'almost entirely to men'.[11]

The Commission had estimated in 1908 that there were 3,000 government employees including labourers in Ottawa, and 700 of these were women[12]—an astounding 23.3 per cent, almost as high as the current proportion in the public service as a whole. Yet 1911 figures show that women accounted for only eight percent of the civil service as a whole.[13] How can this discrepancy be explained?

Surely the restrictions introduced in 1910 could not have had such a massive effect in only two years. Two other possible explanations both assume the surfeit of women plagued the service in Ottawa far more than elsewhere. Then as now, Ottawa required a greater proportion of office support positions than the rest of Canada, and these were the positions women were entering.

This is not a full explanation, however; the patronage system would also have affected women. Most employees in Ottawa were in the 'Inside Service' and thus appointed under the merit system of competitive examinations. Most employees outside Ottawa were in the 'Outside Service' where 'politics entered into every promotion and appointment'.[14] As women did not have the vote, selection based on merit would have given them a far better chance than procedures based on political influence.[15]

The important point, however, is that when opportunities were made available, as in the Ottawa civil service, women flooded in. This suggests the generally low labour force participation rates of women in the early part of this century were more a result of restricted opportunities than of female lack of interest in working.

Further Restrictions

The Civil Service Act of 1918 brought 'Outside Service' appointments under the Commission's jurisdiction, thus extending the merit system throughout the service. It also gave the Commission explicit authority to limit competitions on the basis of sex, as well as age, health, habits, residence, moral character, 'and other qualifications that are in the judgment of the Commission requisite to the performance of . . . duties'.[16]

In 1921, at about the time that the concept of permanent appointments was introduced in the civil service, stringent formal restrictions were placed upon the employment of married women. 'Married women could be appointed only when required to be self-supporting or on a temporary basis when a sufficient number of qualified candidates was not otherwise available.'[17] Women in the service who married were obliged to resign; if they wished to continue, and the service needed them, they were rehired as new appointees in a temporary position and paid the minimum rate in the class.[18]

During the depression, the government reduced salaries and introduced severe staff controls. Total appointments (particularly permanent appointments) under the Civil Service Act decreased abruptly. While the proportion of females appointed was only slightly less than in the 1920s, the proportional decrease in permanent appointments was greater for females than for males.[19]

The War Effort

During World War II, both the number and proportion of female appointments to the civil service increased sharply. Women were called into the labour force as a matter of patriotic duty and, throughout the economy, found themselves doing work women had seldom tackled before. More than 50 per cent of the civil service appointments made during the War were to women; female appointments had never before accounted for more than one-quarter of total appointments and usually far less.[20]

Post-War Restrictions

Restrictions on the employment of married women, relaxed during the War, were re-introduced in 1947. (This appears to have been completely unnecessary: married women were so eager to return home that the exodus of women from the labour force preceded the return of veterans.[21] The restrictions may have even harmed the civil service, since Ottawa faced a severe shortage of office help in the post-war years.) Married women could be retained or hired only under special circumstances, and even then their salaries and advancement opportunities were limited.[22]

Other restrictions also narrowed opportunities for women more than for men: veterans' preference; limiting permanent appointments to veterans with overseas service, and to persons who had qualified for such appointments before the war and served continuously during the war; and the maximum age limits (from which veterans were exempt) attached to a number of occupational classes.[23]

Before the end of 1946, the Commission made an exception and permitted permanent appointments for both stenographers and typists.[24] This move, and a part-time program for married women,[25] were attempts to cope with the shortage of office help in Ottawa.

Since women had first become a 'problem' before World War I, decisions on whether particular positions should be filled by a male, female, or either had been in the hands of deputy heads. At the end of World War II women's organizations began to complain about the number of competitions restricted to males. In response, the Commission sent a letter to deputy heads in 1946 which said in part:

> It is quite possible that heretofore sufficient consideration may not have been given in all cases to the question of restricting competition to one sex or another. . . .
>
> Accordingly it is strongly recommended that in future every consideration should be carefully weighed before the decision is shown by each department on its requisitions as to the desired sex of the appointees.
>
> In order that there might be no further doubt that this has been done, the following procedure is recommended: wherever on any requisition the sex is specified other than 'either' it should be emphasized by the addition of the word 'only', thereafter, e.g., 'male *only*' or 'female *only*'.
>
> The addition of the word 'only' will be assumed by the Civil Service Commission to signify that the department has made its final decision in each and every case. Consequently, delays due to further checking or inquiry will be obviated. This will apply to all requisitions whether for promotion or for a new appointment.[26]

The gentle reminder, with its explicit promise of 'no questions asked', seems, quite naturally, to have caused no more than a slight ripple in tradition and habit. Six months later, competitions for a Grade 5 Statistician and an Assistant Director of Information were restricted to males.[27]

The Dawn of the Modern Era
At the end of 1955, when one-third of all women working in Canada were married,[28] the Civil Service Regulations restricting employment of married women were finally revoked. Whether this caused an immediate influx of married women into

government cannot be determined since data on the marital status of appointees are not available. Also married women who were not self-supporting had been retained in both professional and office support categories for a number of years, since exceptions to the restrictions had been made wherever staff shortages existed. Lifting the restrictions did, however, have a major effect on the salaries and benefits of married women in the service.[29]

Immediately after the War, female appointments had dropped to about 30 per cent of all appointments. The proportion started to rise in the early 1950s, reaching 40 per cent by 1954. It jumped to 45.5 per cent in 1955 and 47 per cent in 1956—perhaps because more married women were appointed. Since then the proportion of women appointed each year has averaged about 45 per cent.[30]

The proportion of women in the service, as distinct from the proportion appointed each year, has remained rather steady in the 1960s at approximately 27 per cent.[31] This discrepancy can be accounted for both by the higher turnover rate of women and by the smaller proportion of women appointed in the years following World War II.

The Civil Service Act of 1961 ignored sex. The Act forbade discrimination on the basis of 'race, national origin, colour or religion', while permitting the Commission to 'prescribe qualifications as to age, residence or any other matters that in the opinion of the Commission are necessary or desirable having regard to the nature of the duties to be performed'.[32] Sex was not mentioned in the Civil Service Regulations of that period either.

The 1961 Act did represent progress of a sort over the 1918 Act. It reinstated the unrestricted competition which had, apparently without sufficient consideration of the female hordes waiting in the wings, been decreed in 1908.

Official Concern About Discrimination Begins

In the early 1960s, the Glassco Commission devoted one page out of several hundred on government personnel matters to the status of women, pointing out that—while there was no official discrimination against women in recruitment, selection, classification, or pay—in practice, a number of differences in the treatment of men and women could be considered discriminatory. It noted the government discriminated against women less than most employers, but was 'trailing behind the United States and the United Kingdom in terms of the number of women it allows to reach senior positions in the public service', and suggested, albeit hesitantly, that the government provide 'creative leadership' to the rest of the community in the matter of hiring and utilizing women.[33]

In 1964, Canada ratified the 1958 Discrimination (Employment and Occupational) Convention of the International Labour Organization (ILO). This instrument, which explicitly mentioned discrimination on the basis of sex, committed Canada to the pursuit of a 'national policy designed to promote . . . equality of opportunity and treatment in respect of employment and occupation, with a view to eliminating any discrimination in respect thereof'. The terms 'employment' and 'occupation' in this Convention include 'access to vocational training, access to employment and to particular occupations, and terms and conditions of employment'.[34]

Sex reappeared in the Public Service Employment Act of 1967—not, as in the 1918 Act, along with age and residence as one basis for restricting competition—but rather, in accordance with the ILO Convention, along with race and religion as a basis on which it was forbidden to discriminate.[35] Thus while equal pay for equal work had been official policy for nearly a century, the equal opportunity that would make equal pay meaningful was not endorsed in legislation until 1967.

Summary and Implications

The above does not comprise a complete history of women in the public service, but it does illustrate some general points.

Occupational segregation limits freedom of choice and tends to lead to inequality of opportunity. The historical record not only confirms this but reveals that occupational segregation was not inadvertent. It was instituted expressly to limit competition and to discourage females. Competitive examinations for higher level clerical positions and for positions with advancement opportunities were limited to men, not because women were uninterested, or incapable of passing the examinations, but precisely because they were interested and capable. The formal record shows this much. Informal practices and pressures undoubtedly also helped dampen the career ambitions of women in the civil service.

As soon as the merit system was introduced, women began to enter the civil service in great numbers. Just as soon, the Commission downgraded the importance of the qualifications measured by the merit system:

> It is freely admitted that there are women who have quite as good executive ability as men, and who might, on the *mere* ground of personal qualifications, fill the higher positions in the service.[36] [Italics added for emphasis.]

Moreover, the Commission introduced restrictions on the employment of women that were not completely lifted until 1955, and not formally and explicitly repudiated until 1967.

The greater success of women in professional than in executive classes, noticeable today,[37] has its roots in the early years of the civil service. Advancement to managerial positions was officially restricted for women, whereas discrimination in professional classes, while common,[38] was the product of more informal practices on the part of line managers. Alice E. Wilson was able to overcome these informal barriers and become a successful geologist in government service, although she did have to apply for leave to study for her doctorate each year for 10 years before she was granted it in 1926.[39] But the route to managerial positions remained blocked to women for years after that.

The history of women in the civil service is useful in revising the pervasive notion that women's interest in working is a new phenomenon. If anything is to be considered new, it should be the increasing opportunities for women to work.

It has been known for some time that the supply of female labour is quite responsive to shifts in demand for female labour. Recent studies elaborate on this, showing that today's large increases in the work rates of married and older women probably result from increased demand for female labour, coupled with a declining supply of the traditionally preferred young and single woman, rather than a growing interest in equity among employers. The growing interest in working among older married women is more a response to opportunities than itself a moving force. Changed attitudes, lower birth rates, shorter work weeks, and a reduction in household chores have all facilitated this response, but it is doubtful they initiated it.[40]

This record of discrimination is by no means peculiar to the Canadian public service. Other employers engaged in similar policies at the time. If this were merely a matter of past history, it would be of interest only to historians. But these early discriminatory policies were a resounding and still redounding success; they accomplished their purposes so well that their effects are still evident in today's employment structure.

CURRENT DISTRIBUTION OF WOMEN IN THE FEDERAL SERVICE

The terminology used to describe different kinds of federal employees has undergone many changes over the years. The terms 'federal service', 'public service', and 'civil service' were used rather loosely in the preceding historical section. To avoid confusing the general reader and for the sake of brevity, it will be necessary to take some liberties with current official terminology as well. The nature of these liberties is explained below.

Definitions
Major changes in official vocabulary were introduced in 1967 both by the Public Service Employment Act and the Public Service Staff Relations Act.

Before 1967, a 'public servant' was apparently any federal government employee; a 'civil servant' was one employed under the Civil Service Act. With the passage of the Public Service Employment Act in 1967, 'public servant' retained its broad meaning but 'civil servant' was banished from the federal vocabulary, so employees under the 1967 Act are generally referred to as 'employees under the Act'. For the sake of brevity, the term 'public servant' will be used in this report to refer to employees under the Act, while 'federal employee' will refer to anyone employed by the Government of Canada whether or not they are under the Act.

Further confusion results from the fact that some employees who were not under the 1961 Act are under the 1967 Act, but data on the composition of the public service in 1967, the most recent available for most tables in this report, included only those employees formerly under the Civil Service Act. So 'public servant' as used in this report actually means one who used to be a civil servant.

The Public Service Staff Relations Act, which established collective bargaining within the public service, necessitated a reclassification of occupations. With the reclassification came a new vocabulary. Reference used to be made to occupational 'classes' and 'grades' within a class; this has been changed to occupational 'groups' and 'levels' within a group. Families of related occupations were formerly called 'class groups'; they are now 'occupational categories'. The occupations included in a new 'class' are not the same as those under the old 'group'; the same holds for 'class groups' and 'occupational categories'.

Since occupational data from both the old and the new classification system are used in the report, the change in terminology causes some problems. The official terms are sometimes used in the report, but wherever possible they are avoided by, for instance, substituting 'occupation' for occupational 'class' or 'group'. Often 'occupational category' will be used in its generic sense to refer to both the old 'class groups' and the new 'categories'.

Composition of Federal Service

Federal employees numbered almost 400,000 in 1967, excluding the armed forces, but only 150,000 were under the Public Service Employment Act.[41] Others included 'salaried exempt' employees (Royal Canadian Mounted Police, sessional staff of Parliament, employees of various boards and commissions, etc.), employees in crown corporations, and certain other categories. More than one-half of all female civilian employees were under the Act, but only about one-third of male civilian employees.[42]

This report focuses on employees under the Public Service Employment Act. In particular, it focuses on those in the public service who usually wear dresses to work: 41,000 women.

Kind of Work

What do these women do when they go to work in the morning? Almost 83 per cent hold office support or administrative support jobs. A little over five per cent work in administrative jobs; an equal percentage in various hospital jobs. Another two per cent are in the 'technical and inspection' category and two per cent in the 'postal, customs, and immigration' category. One and a half per cent are professionals and scientists. Those remaining—one half per cent—work in service and maintenance.[43]

Table A–1 [at the end of this chapter] shows the proportion of women within these various occupational categories (formerly 'class groups') over the past few years. Conversion to the new classification system which began in 1966 and is not yet completed, seriously limits comparisons across the mid-1960s, especially within the administrative category. But Table A–1, since it spans the years 1960 to 1967, reveals trends which help distinguish real changes from effects of the 1966 reclassification.

For example, around 70 per cent of all office and administrative support employees were female from 1961 to 1966; in 1967 this dropped to 66 per cent, undoubtedly as an effect of reclassification. The actual number of women in the category increased, but the number of men increased far more—presumably an influx of those formerly under other categories.

The even sharper drop in the percentage of women in administration in 1966 and 1967 again appears to be a function of reclassification. Women in administration stayed at approximately 14 per cent until 1965, then dropped to 11 per cent in 1966 and to nine per cent in 1967. While the number of women in the category decreased slightly, the percentage change must again be attributed to a large influx of men, presumably from other categories.

Note that the reclassification did not change what women were doing, but it did downgrade their titles compared to men. Comparing 1967 with 1965, approximately

6,000 additional men show up in administrative support and office jobs, but almost 7,000 more show up in administrative and foreign service jobs. In the same period, almost 4,000 more women appear in the administrative support and office categories and 285 fewer in administrative and foreign service jobs. The complexity of classification shifts makes any hard and fast generalizations impossible, particularly regarding the major shifts in male employees. It is fairly clear, however, from Table A-1 and from additional information from the Public Service Commission Staffing Branch, that more women than men were reclassified from Administration C into Administrative Support because more women were in the lower grades of the occupational classes involved.

The increase in the proportion of women in professional fields—from seven per cent in 1960 to eight per cent in 1967—could be partly due to reclassification, but this is doubtful since a trend of incremental increases is obvious. The clearest increase is in the hospital category, from 46 per cent female in 1960 to 50 per cent in 1967. While percentage changes have occurred in some other groups, the representation of women is minimal and the number involved very small.

In summary, the proportion of women in broad occupational categories has remained quite stable over the past eight years. The few 'real' changes have been incremental. The two marked decreases in proportion in 1967 are both residual effects of reclassification—changes which merely register a change in what work is called and what people call themselves.

Table A–2 presents a breakdown into individual occupations rather than broad categories. The interest of this table is twofold. First, one can pick out individual classes which elicit comments of the did-you-know variety:

> Did you know that in 1967 only three of 349 Senior Officers were women?
> That while six per cent of Foreign Service Officers in External Affairs were women, there were no female Foreign Service Officers in Trade and Commerce? (External Affairs considered women postable in foreign countries; Trade and Commerce did not—this unwritten policy has, however, recently changed.)
> Did you know there were seven female Air Traffic Controllers, two Herdsmen, one Veterinarian, and one Lighthouse Keeper in the public service? [44]

The Lighthouse Keeper is of special interest, since several individuals within the personnel community, when interviewed for this study, specifically mentioned lighthouse keeper as one job where 'of course, you couldn't have a woman'. The Canadian government hired women as lighthouse keepers at least as early as 1911,[45] and the United States government as early as 1853.[46]

Occupational Segregation
Of far more significance, the percentages of women in each class, as shown in Table A–2, testify to the degree of *de facto* occupational segregation within the public service. If men and women were distributed equally in all occupations, about 27 per cent of each class would be female. Instead the pattern of percentages has many zeroes interspersed with a scattering of very large percentages of women in some classes.

This can be made more precise and more meaningful by computing an Index of Segregation. The Index used here, originally devised by Duncan and Duncan,[47] is expressed as a percentage. An Index of 40 per cent for a particular series of occupations means that 40 per cent of the women in that series would have to change occupations to produce a percentage distribution of females corresponding to that of males, or 40 per cent of the men would have to change occupations, or 20 per cent of the women and 20 per cent of the men, or any other combination adding up to 40 per cent (but not 40 per cent of the total employees unless there are an equal number of men and women).

The Index of Segregation for the Canadian public service, based on 1967 data, is 73.1 per cent. In other words, approximately three-quarters of the women, about 30,000, would have to change jobs for men and women to be distributed equally across occupational groups.

This same measure of occupational segregation by sex has been computed for the United States for each census year between 1900 and 1960. The Index of Segregation for the United States in 1900 was 66.9. Over the next 60 years, it fluctuated only slightly, ending up at 68.4 for 1960, an increase of 1.5. It may seem that women have been going into new and exciting fields once dominated by men, but, as the title of Gross's study of occupational segregation implies, *plus ça change, plus c'est la même chose.* Gross concludes that the Index has remained relatively stable because, while female occupations were becoming less segregated, male occupations were becoming more segregated.[48]

There is good reason to suspect that the Index of Segregation for the public service has changed little over time: distribution within occupational categories has not changed much over the past eight years. Furthermore, it is doubtful that the Canadian labour force, or the governmental portion of it, would show more change in this respect than the American labour force.

Today's occupational distribution undoubtedly reflects restricted opportunities for women in earlier years. Such purposeful segregation has not completely disappeared since employers have only recently begun to question the bases on which many jobs have been considered suitable for men only or women only.[49]

While the Index partially reflects employers' policies, it also reflects the occupational preferences and 'needs' of men and women. Preferences are both a cause of current *de facto* segregation and an effect of earlier *de jure* segregation. The occupational 'needs' of men and women are partially determined by their differing family responsibilities and these and other differences also contribute to segregation in the work world.

Location of Work

Male and female public servants are distributed differently across departments and across geographic regions.

Almost 65 per cent of all the men in the service in 1967 were in six departments: the Post Office (25 per cent), National Defence (14 per cent), Transport (10 per cent), National Revenue: Customs and Excise (6 per cent), Veterans Affairs, and Agriculture (5 per cent each). The six departments with the most women in them, on the other hand, contained only 55 per cent of all women in the service. Only two departments appear in both lists, and their rank order is different. The top six for women are: National Defence (18 per cent), Veterans Affairs (9 per cent), National Revenue: Taxation (8 per cent), Manpower and Immigration (7 per cent), and Comptroller of the Treasury and Unemployment Insurance Commission (6 per cent each). No other departments have more than five per cent of all males or females.[50] The men bunch up more than the women, primarily an effect of the preponderance of men in the large Post Office staff.

This 'specialization' by department on the basis of sex is partly a function of occupational segregation—different departments have different occupational mixes—but not entirely. For instance, clerical positions, which usually include a higher percentage of women, have been a male preserve in the Post Office for many years (not forever though—in the early days women filled lower level Post Office positions almost entirely, as noted earlier).

The specialization is also somewhat related to the function of departments. Around 50 per cent of all federal employees (no data are available for public service employees alone) in departments dealing with health, welfare, education, and trade and industrial development are female.[51]

Table A–3 shows the proportion of female employees in three metropolitan areas—Ottawa/Hull, Montreal, and Toronto—and in the rest of Canada. Again the distribution of males and females, differs: females are over-represented in Ottawa/Hull (where 38 per cent of all public service employees are women, compared to 27 per cent in the service as a whole) and underrepresented elsewhere. This is probably mainly a function of differences in the occupational mix required in central as compared to regional offices.

Summary

While women are represented in every broad occupational category within the public service, an overwhelming proportion—over 80 per cent—hold office or administrative support jobs. In many individual occupations there are no women, in a number of others very few, and in a small number of occupations with large populations almost all are women.

This high degree of occupational segregation by sex is the most important variable examined. It probably explains many other differences in the distribution of men and women in the public service: differences across departments, across departmental functions, and across geographic regions. It also explains a large portion of the salary differences to be examined in the next section.

SALARY AND LEVEL ATTAINED BY MEN AND WOMEN

This section will examine differences in the attainments, in level and in salary, of men and women in the public service.

Comparison by Level

Table A–4 shows the distribution by level (formerly grade) of women in 34 different occupational groups. These occupations were chosen because they contain both men and women but not, for the most part, an overwhelming majority of one or the other. In 24 of the 34 occupations, the proportion of women falls off dramatically as one moves from the lower to the higher levels. This includes Social Worker, a traditionally female occupation. (The decline here is not smooth but the 'hump' at Level 5 would disappear if one woman left or one man was promoted.)

Ten groups do not show a consistent decline in the proportion of women as level increases: Advisory Counsel, Economist, Librarian, Research Scientist, Statistician, Communication, Foreign Service Officer in External Affairs, Pharmacist, Hospital Laboratory Technician, and X-Ray Technician.

Comparison by Salary

Figures 1 and 2 show the salary distributions of full-time public service employees by sex in 1966 and 1967. The two years are shown since they span a major pay increase.

Clearly women were heavily bunched up at the lower end of the salary scale. Cumulative distributions, and comparisons between 1966 and 1967, fill in more of the picture.

In 1966, slightly over half of the women in the public service made less than $4,000 compared with 14 per cent of the men. The salary increases brought 50 per cent of the men out of this bracket (leaving 7 per cent) but only 19 per cent of the women (leaving 41 per cent). In actual numbers about 7,700 men moved up and 3,500 women.

In 1966, 67 per cent of all men made less than $6,000 compared to 94 per cent of all women. In 1967, these figures changed to 59 per cent and 90 per cent respectively, a decrease of 12 per cent for men and three per cent for women. In actual numbers, 6,428 fewer men made less than $6,000 but only 218 fewer women.

In all salary brackets above $6,000, the percentage increase of women in 1967 was considerably higher than that of men. But this percentage improvement is not as impressive as it might sound: the proportion of women making above $6,000 rose from six per cent in 1966 to 10 per cent in 1967 while the proportion of men went from 33 per cent to 41 per cent. Because there were few women there to start with, the percentage improvement was large but the proportion of women affected was only half the proportion of men (4 per cent to 8 per cent).

These differential effects of the pay increase are probably a function of both occupational segregation and of the distribution of men and women across levels within occupational groups.

The Five Figure Breakthrough

A few years ago, a five figure salary was synonymous with having 'made it' and in 1964 the Civil Service Commission requested from the Pay Research Bureau information on all women in the service making over $10,000.

Table 3 shows the proportions of men and women in the $10,000 and over bracket from 1957 to 1968, and since $10,000 is not the measure of monetary success it once was, those making $14,000 and over are compared from 1960 to 1968. To make comparison easier, ratios of male to female 'success rates' have been computed. A ratio of 100 means a man's chances of being 'successful' are 100 times the chances of a woman.

FIGURE 1 *Percentage Distribution of Full-Time Employees*, by Salary and Sex, September 1966*

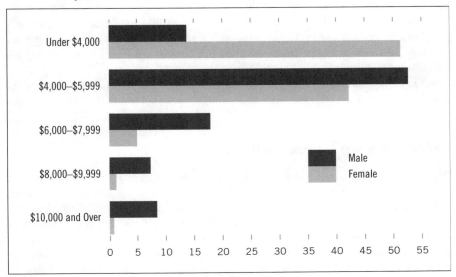

Source: Pay Research Bureau
*Under the Public Service Employment Act limited to types formerly under the Civil Service Act.

FIGURE 2 *Percentage Distribution of Full-Time Employees*, by Salary and Sex, July 1967*

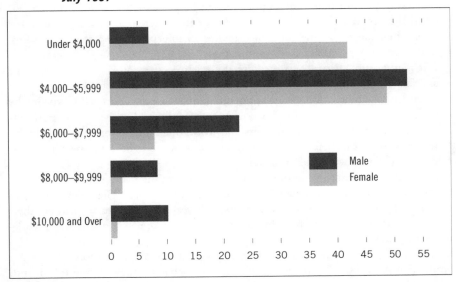

Source: Pay Research Bureau
*Under the Public Service Employment Act limited to types formerly under the Civil Service Act.

Table 3 shows a marked improvement in women's chances of reaching these top salary brackets. Between 1957 and 1965, the likelihood of a man achieving a five fig-ure salary dropped from being 115 times that of a woman to 21 times greater, an 82 per cent decrease in eight years. Between September, 1960 and March, 1968, a man's likelihood of making $14,000 or over dropped from being 133 times that of a woman down to 18 times greater, a decrease of 86 per cent in seven and a half years. This shift has been greatest in the last few years.

There is improvement in the five figure bracket, but the number of women involved is very small: in 1968 only 444 women out of a total of 43,796 made over $10,000.

Why the Differences in Occupational Success?

What factors might account for these differences in the occupational success of men and women in the public service? Salary differences are more dramatic than level differences, suggesting that occupational distribution has more influence than any differences in promotion rates or separation rates. But what accounts for the extent of occupational segregation? And what other factors might help explain the differ-ential success of men and women? Several possibilities have been mentioned, but there are others, which may affect male and female careers directly or indirectly.

All those variables which might directly influence the status and salary of an employee can be placed in four categories: capability, interests and goals (or motiva-tion), experience, and opportunity.

The first three taken together could provide an estimate of productivity or worth to the employer. The last includes both the opportunity to prove productiv-ity (access to positions) and the opportunity to be adequately rewarded (remunera-tion). If the first three cannot fully account for the differential success of men and women, then the remaining difference invites an interpretation based on the final factor: unequal opportunity or discrimination.

It is impossible actually to measure the relative effect of each factor with the data available, but a rough estimate of their relative influence is possible.

Under 'capability', for instance, do differences in education help explain the overrepresentation of women in lower status occupations? Do the split responsibil-ities of married women, between home and work, affect job performance adversely? Does the very fact of being a woman make it difficult to gain the respect and con-fidence of colleagues and subordinates?

Under 'experience', what of the separation rates of men and women—do fewer women than men stay in their jobs long enough to advance? This question relates to the work pattern of women during their adult years which, in turn, relates to their marital status and family responsibilities. Experience is one side of the coin; work-life expectancy the other.

Under 'interests and goals', what are the motivations and aspirations of working women? What do they want from their jobs and what are they willing to put into them? How many are committed to long-term careers?

Under 'opportunity', a key question remains: are there barriers to occupational

Table 3 Proportion of Men and Women in Top Salary Brackets of the Public Service, 1957–68

Date	Employee Totals		Those Earning Over $10,000					Those Earning Over $14,000				
	Men	Women	No. of men	No. of women	% women over $10,000 to total women	% men over $10,000 to total men	Ratio of male to female 'Success Rates'[a]	No. of men	No. of women	% women over $14,000 to total women	% men over $14,000 to total men	Ratio of male to female 'Success Rates'[a]
Sept., 1957	96,343[b]	37,680	96	1	.0027	.31	115					
Sept., 1958	98,883	40,001	736	5	.012	.74	62					
Sept., 1959	100,935	39,668	861	7	.018	.85	47					
Sept., 1960	94,156	36,404	1,863	21	.058	2.0	35	342	1	.0027	.36	133
Sept., 1961	97,442	38,480	2,073	26	.068	2.1	31	365	2	.0052	.37	71
Sept., 1962	1,100,062	37,236	3,088	40	.11	3.1	28	611	3	.0081	.61	75
Sept., 1963	99,970	36,007	3,309	48	.13	3.3	25	682	5	.014	.68	49
Sept., 1964	100,085	37,207	4,233	67	.18	4.2	23	1080	12	.032	1.1	34
Sept., 1965	102,071	37,560	4,966	87	.23	4.9	21	1230	16	.043	1.2	28
Sept., 1966	105,353	39,828	8,713	210	.53	8.3	16	2661	46	.12	2.5	21
July, 1967	109,246	40,999	11,004	311	.76	10.1	13	3284	54	.13	3.0	23
March, 1968	111,018	43,796	13,051	444	1.01	11.8	12	3849	86	.20	3.5	18

[a] Proportion of men in given salary bracket divided by the proportion of women.

[b] Includes 3,164 for which sex not specified.

Sources: 1957–9 figures from Service Requirements and Analysis Section, Dominion Bureau of Statistics, 1960–8 figures from Pay Research Bureau.

advancement for women with the requisite capability, motivation, and experience? Do personnel practices, co-workers' attitudes, the occupational structure create such barriers?

These four factors or sets of variables are all inter-related in a complex chain of cause and effect. For instance, the work-life expectancy of women is closely linked to their work interests. Work-life expectancy is also the forward projection of the variable 'experience'.

NOTES

1. See Tables 1 and 2 for all figures not specifically footnoted.
2. Women's Bureau, *Women at Work in Canada*, 1964 (Ottawa: Department of Labour, 1965), Table 8, p. 21.
3. 1961 *Census of Canada*, Bulletin 7.2–1 (Ottawa: Dominion Bureau of Statistics).
4. *Civil Service List of Canada*, 1885, pp. 82–122; statement by Edna Inglis in House of Commons, *Proceedings of Select Special Committee on Civil Service, 1932* (Ottawa: King's Printer, 1932), pp. 242–3.
5. *Report of the Committee on Federal Employment, President's Commission on the Status of Women* (Washington: US Government Printing Office, 1963), p. 13.
6. 'Equal Pay for Men and Women in the Civil Service', *Ministry of Labour Gazette* 63 (1955), p. 126.
7. *The Queensland Government Industrial Gazette* 68, 10 (Brisbane: S.G. Reid, 1968).
8. Royal Commission on the Civil Service, *Report of the Commissioners* (Ottawa: King's Printer, 1908), p. 14.
9. Civil Service Commission, *Tenth Annual Report*, for the year ending 31 August 1918 (Ottawa: King's Printer, 1919), pp. 13–14.
10. Civil Service Commission, *Third Annual Report*, for the period 1 September 1908 to 31 August 1911 (Ottawa: King's Printer, 1911), p. xiii.
11. 'The Commissioners have found it necessary, therefore, on the reports of the deputies as to the qualifications required in their several departments, to limit almost entirely to men, appointments in the First and Second Divisions.' From the Civil Service Commission, *First Annual Report*, for the period 1 Sept. 1908 to 31 Aug. 1909 (Ottawa: King's Printer, 1909), pp. 17–8.
12. Op. cit., 1908, p. 20.
13. See Table 2.
14. Op. cit., 1919, p. 14.
15. A writer of the time said this was also the case within the United States Civil Service. See El Bie K. Foltz, *The Federal Civil Service as a Career* (New York: G.P. Putnam's Sons, 1909), p. 293.
16. Part III, Section 38.
17. Civil Service Commission, *Annual Report, 1955* (Ottawa: Queen's Printer, 1956), p. 9.
18. *Civil Service Review* 20 (June 1947), Ottawa, pp. 148–9.
19. Stanislaw Judek, *Women in the Public Service: Their Utilization and Employment* (Ottawa: Department of Labour, 1968), Table II–2, p. 10.
20. Loc. cit.

21. According to the *Civil Service Review* of September 1946, by August of that year 'women in Ottawa were leaving the service at the rate of 550 a month, a higher turnover than the Capital had ever seen before'. This rapid exodus of women from the labour force at the end of the war was a general phenomenon. See Clarence D. Long, *The Labor Force Under Changing Income and Employment* (Princeton University Press, 1958), p. 19.

22. For instance, married women in clerical and administrative positions were not allowed to advance beyond Clerk, Grade 3. A single woman who had advanced above this was demoted to Clerk, Grade 3, upon getting married, although her duties were seldom changed. See also *Civil Service Review* 19 (Ottawa, December 1946), p. 357; and 20 (June 1947), pp. 148–9.

23. The *Civil Service Review* for 1946 provides information on regulations pertaining to veterans' preference and permanency. The rules on age limits were detailed and continually changing between 1946 and 1956. The classes most consistently affected by age limits, particularly maximum age limits, were the office support jobs: clerks, typists, stenographers, and office appliance operators. Details are contained in memoranda, circular letters, and Treasury Board minutes of the period.

24. *Civil Service Review* 19 (Ottawa, June and Dec., 1946), pp. 173 and 307. Exceptions were not made, however, to the restrictions with respect to age and marital status.

25. Ibid., 19 (September 1946), p. 237.

26. Ibid., 19 (June 1946), pp. 178–9.

27. Civil Service Commission, Competition Poster, List 1152, 13 November 1946, Competition Numbers 46–4004 and 46–3063.

28. Women's Bureau, *Women at Work in Canada* (Ottawa: Department of Labour, 1957), p. 12.

29. Women in the service upon marriage did, however, have to be re-certified. Civil Service Commission, Circular Letter 1955–30, 31 October 1955, Ref. 25–1– (Vol. 4); Civil Service Commission, *Annual Report, 1955* (Ottawa: Queen's Printer, 1956), p. 9.

30. Judek, loc. cit.

31. See Table A–1.

32. Part III, Section 33.

33. *Report of the Commission on Government Organization* (Ottawa: Queen's Printer, 1962), pp. 275, 378–9. (Henceforth referred to as the Glassco Commission.)

34. Convention III of the General Conference of the International Labour Organization, 1958.

35. Part II, Section 12.

36. Civil Service Commission, *First Annual Report,* for the period 1 September 1908, to 31 August 1909 (Ottawa: King's Printer, 1909), p. 17.

37. Glassco Commission, p. 379.

38. See, for instance, G. Winston Sinclair, 'Memorial to Alice E. Wilson', *Geological Society of America Bulletin* 77 (1966), pp. 215–18.

39. And then only because the Geological Survey made a 'tactical error [and] found itself battling the Federation of University Women', ibid., p. 216.

40. J.D. Allingham, 'The Demographic Background to Change in the Number and

Composition of Female Wage Earners in Canada, 1951–1961', *Special Labour Force Studies,* no.1, Series B (Ottawa: Dominion Bureau of Statistics, 1967); and Valerie K. Oppenheimer, 'The Interaction of Demand and Supply and its Effect on the Female Labour Force in the United States', *Population Studies* 21 (1967), pp. 239–59. With respect to the effect of reductions in household chores and shorter work weeks, see also Long, op. cit., pp. 10–11.

41. Pay Research Bureau, *Composition of the Public Service, July, 1967* (Ottawa: Public Service Staff Relations Board), p. 1.

42. Judek, op. cit., p. 13.

43. Figures are for July, 1967. Pay Research Bureau, op. cit., p. 3.

44. Since tabulations from personnel records occasionally transform males into females, the presence of the lighthouse keeper was double-checked although the others were not. The lighthouse keeper has retired since 1967.

45. *Civil Service List of Canada, 1911*, p. 306.

46. *Report of the Committee on Federal Employment,* op. cit., p. 8.

47. O.D. Duncan and B. Duncan, 'Residential Distribution and Occupational Stratification', *American Journal of Sociology* 60 (1955), pp. 493–503.

48. Edward Gross, '*Plus ça Change . . . ?* The Sex Structure of Occupations Over Time', *Social Problems, 16* (1968), pp. 198–208. When the Index was standardized to take account of differential growth of occupations, a change towards decreasing segregation (70.3 per cent to 62.2 per cent) did show up. But in terms of the number of women-and men-affected, the unstandardized Index is the relevant one.

   For comparison, the 1960 figure for *race* segregation in the American labour force was 46.8. As far as this author knows, the Index has not been computed for either sex or race segregation in the Canadian labour force.

49. For instance, the Ottawa Regional Office of the Public Service Commission restricted the job of mail clerk to men until very recently. The Public Service Commission has now drafted policy guidelines dealing with equal opportunity for women which should be helpful.

50. Pay Research Bureau, op. cit., p.4.

51. *Federal Government Employment, September, 1967,* 16 (Aug., 1968) (Ottawa: Dominion Bureau of Statistics), pp. 10–13.

Table A–1 *Proportion of Women in Civil Service Class Groups, 1960–7*

Class Group[a]	Sept 1960 Employment Total	Sept 1960 Employment Female	Sept 1960 % Female	Sept 1961 Employment Total	Sept 1961 Employment Female	Sept 1961 % Female	Sept 1962 Employment Total	Sept 1962 Employment Female	Sept 1962 % Female	Sept 1963 Employment Total	Sept 1963 Employment Female	Sept 1963 % Female
Professional	**6,050**	**421**	**7.0**	**6,178**	**456**	**7.4**	**6,695**	**471**	**7.0**	**6,672**	**479**	**7.1**
Administration	**13,791**	**1,897**	**13.8**	**14,568**	**2,078**	**14.3**	**15,021**	**2,066**	**13.8**	**15,232**	**2,081**	**13.7**
A	1,850	98	5.3	1,939	113	5.8	2,005	98	4.9	2,080	94	4.5
B	3,070	61	2.0	3,148	58	1.8	3,149	59	1.9	3,200	63	2.0
C	8,871	1,738	19.6	9,481	1,907	20.1	9,867	1,909	19.3	9,952	1,924	19.3
Technical and Inspection	**16,199**	**909**	**5.6**	**16,998**	**891**	**5.2**	**17,591**	**908**	**5.2**	**17,792**	**918**	**5.2**
Postal, Customs, and Immigration	**28,391**	**618**	**2.2**	**28,722**	**645**	**2.2**	**28,893**	**644**	**2.2**	**29,186**	**643**	**2.2**
Postal	21,371	469	2.2	21,746	487	2.2	22,167	491	2.2	22,587	483	2.1
Customs	5,953	134	2.3	5,920	143	2.4	5,685	139	2.4	5,596	145	2.6
Immigration	1,067	15	1.4	1,056	15	1.4	1,041	14	1.3	1,003	15	1.5
Office	**42,510**	**30,101**	**70.8**	**45,000**	**31,883**	**70.9**	**43,375**	**30,676**	**70.7**	**4,1341**	**29,368**	**71.0**
Clerical	25,869	14,724	56.9	27,950	16,234	58.1	26,832	15,562	58.0	25,785	15,207	59.0
Typing and Related	16,641	15,377	92.4	17,050	15,649	91.8	16,543	15,114	91.4	15,556	14,161	91.0
Service and Maintenance	**18,640**	**253**	**1.4**	**19,378**	**248**	**1.3**	**20,946**	**273**	**1.3**	**20,963**	**264**	**1.3**
Crafts and Trades	3,714	9	.2	4,085	11	.3	4,327	12	.3	4,519	7	.2
Stores and Building Service	13,320	238	1.8	13,320	231	1.7	14,793	255	1.7	14,626	252	1.7
Other Service and Maintenance	1,696	6	.4	1,973	6	.3	1,826	6	.3	1,818	5	.3
Hospital	**4,779**	**2,179**	**45.6**	**4,879**	**2,252**	**46.2**	**4,777**	**2,198**	**46.0**	**4,791**	**2,254**	**47.0**
Legislation	**200**	**27**	**13.5**	**199**	**27**	**13.6**						
Total, All Class Groups	**130,560**	**36,404**	**27.9**	**135,922**	**38,480**	**28.3**	**137,298**	**37,236**	**27.1**	**135,977**	**36,007**	**26.5**

continued

Table A–1 *(concluded)*

Class Group[a]	Sept 1964			Sept 1965			Sept 1966			Sept 19		
	Employment		%	Employment		%	Employment		%	Employment		%
	Total	Female	Female	Total	Female	Female	Total	Female	Female	Total	Female	Female
Professional	**6,871**	**498**	**7.2**	**7,154**	**547**	**7.6**	**7,712**	**627**	**8.1**	**8,034**	**624**	**7.8**
Administration	**16,537**	**2,366**	**14.3**	**17,378**	**2,438**	**14.0**	**18,383**	**1,972**	**10.7**	**22,861**[b]	**2,153**	**9.4**
A	2,338	113	4.8	2,643	135	5.1	4,444	164	3.7			
B	4,134	188	4.5	4,417	219	5.0	4,551	243	5.3			
C	10,065	2,065	20.5	10,318	2,084	20.2	9,388	1,565	16.7			
Technical and Inspection	**17,678**	**844**	**4.8**	**18,384**	**972**	**5.3**	**18,286**	**1,083**	**5.9**	**17,586**	**997**	**5.7**
Postal, Customs, and Immigration	**29,364**	**682**	**2.3**	**30,043**	**784**	**2.6**	**30,959**	**913**	**2.9**	**26,832**	**943**	**3.5**
Postal	22,855	519	2.3	23,644	619	2.6	24,993	734	2.9			
Customs	5,702	152	2.7	5,608	155	2.8	5,444	166	3.0			
Immigration	807	11	1.4	791	10	1.3	522	13	2.5			
Office	**42,179**	**30,206**	**71.6**	**42,108**	**30,197**	**71.7**	**45,669**	**32,579**	**71.3**	**51,757**[b]	**33,909**	**65.5**
Clerical	26,274	15,680	59.7	29,953	15,449	59.5	28,665	16,955	59.1			
Typing and Related	15,905	14,526	91.3	16,155	14,748	91.3	16,994	15,624	91.9			
Service and Maintenance	**19,832**	**262**	**1.3**	**19,698**	**234**	**1.2**	**19,357**	**221**	**1.1**	**18,917**	**225**	**1.2**
Crafts and Trades	4,264	8	.2	4,320	8	.2	4,192	9	.2			
Stores and Building Service	13,739	247	1.8	13,515	218	1.6	13,225	206	1.6			
Other Service and Maintenance	1,829	7	.4	1,863	8	.4	1,940	6	.3			
Hospital Legislation	**4,831**	**2,349**	**48.6**	**4,866**	**2,388**	**49.1**	**4,815**	**2,433**	**50.5**	**4,258**	**2,148**	**50.4**
Total, All Class Groups	**137,292**	**37,207**	**27.1**	**139631**	**37,560**	**26.9**	**145,181**	**39,828**	**27.4**	**150,245**	**40,999**	**27.3**

[a] For information on Class Groups, see Kathleen Archibald, *Sex and the Public Service* (Ottawa, Information Canada, 1973): 169–71

[b] Because of reclassification and resulting establishment of six new occupational categories to replace former class groups, 1967 figures had to be combined in two instances to make as close comparison as possible with previous years' figures, i.e., 15,638 employees (1,769 females) listed under the new category, Administrative and Foreign Service, have been added to Administration total, and 47,031 employees (30,946 females) in the new category, Administrative Support, to Office total. Postal Officers in the new Operational category have been added to Postal, Customs, and Immigration.

Source: Pay Research Bureau, except for July 1967 figures which were developed from data obtained from the Pay Research Bureau.

Table A–2 Proportion of Women in Public Service Occupations*, July 1967

Category and Group	Total Employees	No. of Women	% Women	Category and Group	Total Employees	No. of Women	% Women
Professional				**Professional (Cont'd.)**			
Patent Examiner 1–7	185	0	0.0	Architect 1–7	124	4	3.2
Research Management 1–3	129	0	0.0	Solicitor 1–7	125	4	3.2
Senior Scientific Officer MTS 1–3	113	2	1.8	Research Officer, Agriculture 1–5, 2A	180	6	3.3
Lecturer	50	0	0.0	Chief Statistician 1–2	57	2	3.5
Professor	39	0	0.0	Biologist 1–5	161	6	3.7
Associate Professor	37	0	0.0	Senior Advisory Counsel	52	3	5.8
Assistant Professor	35	0	0.0	Medical Officer 1–6	341	22	6.5
Examiners of Companies 1–6	31	0	0.0	Economist 1–7	273	18	6.6
Chief of Division PW 1	21	0	0.0	Actuary 1–6	14	1	7.1
Management Analyst 1–8	21	0	0.0	Scientific Officer MTS 1–3	147	12	8.2
Senior Economist 1–2	17	0	0.0	Canadian Immigration Affairs Officer 1–6	106	9	8.4
Chief of Division MTS	11	0	0.0	Combines Investigation Officer 1–6	26	4	15.3
Chief Special Programs	11	0	0.0	Statistician 1–5	309	52	16.8
Research Director, Agriculture 1–5	11	0	0.0	Citizenship Development Officer 1–5	11	2	18.1
Geologist 1–5	10	0	0.0	Pharmacist 1–4	47	9	19.2
Veterinarian 1–8	464	1	0.2	Archivist 1–5	38	8	21.0
Engineer 1–7	1,480	3	0.2	Chemist 1–5	148	39	26.4
Meteorologist 1–9	253	1	0.4	Geographer 1–5	37	10	27.0
Dental Officer 1–5	61	1	1.6	Bacteriologist 1–5	58	16	27.6
Food and Drug Officer 1–8	168	3	1.8	Junior Executive Officer	79	23	29.1
Research Officer, Forestry 1–5	155	3	1.9	Psychologist 1–2	12	4	33.3
Meteorological Officer 1–9	301	6	2.0	Language Officer 1–5, French or English	152	59	38.8
Medical Specialist 1–2	80	2	2.5	Librarian 1–5	164	106	64.6
Research Scientist 1–3	38	1	2.6	Social Worker 1–6	52	38	73.1
Research Scientist 1–4	1,291	35	2.7	Home Economist 1–4	21	20	95.2
Advisory Counsel 1–3	37	1	2.7	Dietitian 1–5	71	70	98.6

*Includes all occupational groups having a population of ten or more employees.

continued

Table A–2 *(continued)*

Category and Group	Total Employees	No. of Women	% Women	Category and Group	Total Employees	No. of Women	% Women
Administrative and Foreign Service (New)				**Technical and Inspection** (Cont'd.)			
Financial Administration 1–8	583	17	2.9	Inspector Radio Regulations 1–7	156	0	0.0
Purchasing and Supply 1–8	707	25	3.5	Grain Weighman 1–4	151	0	0.0
Organization and Methods 1–7	265	10	3.8	Grain Inspector 1–6	145	0	0.0
Welfare Programs 1–8	763	30	3.9	Inspecting Officer 1–3, Inspection Services DND	117	0	0.0
Administrative Services 1–9	1,644	121	7.4	Inspector Civil Aviation 1–5	115	0	0.0
Personnel Administration 1–9	949	100	10.5	Ship Inspector 1–5	82	0	0.0
Program Administration 1–8	8,972	1,009	11.2	Grain Trackman	81	0	0.0
Computer Systems Administration 1–6	461	68	14.8	Fruit and Vegetable Inspector 1–2	77	0	0.0
Information Services 1–6	310	72	23.2	Grain Inspection Assistant	68	0	0.0
Administrative Trainee	983	316	32.1	Inspector of Air Worthiness 1–5	55	0	0.0
				Inspector of Standards 1–7	54	0	0.0
Administrative Support (New)				Construction Supervisor 1–5	53	0	0.0
				Instructor, National Defence	40	0	0.0
Communication 1–7	679	258	38.0	Forestry Officer 1–5	39	0	0.0
Clerical and Regulatory 1–7	31,015	16,025	51.7	Fish Culture Officer 1–6	37	0	0.0
Data Processing 1–8, B–C	1,108	798	72.0	Scopewatcher	35	0	0.0
Telephone Operation 1–5	416	401	96.4	Helicopter Pilot	29	0	0.0
Office Equipment Operation	322	314	97.5	Inspector, Plant Protection 1–2	24	0	0.0
Secretarial, Stenographic, Typing 1–9 (also A–B–C)	13,269	13,044	98.3	Laboratory Animal Keeper 1–3	24	0	0.0
				Supervising Draftsman 1–3	23	0	0.0
Technical and Inspection				Retail Inspector 1–4	22	0	0.0
				District Supervisor 1–2 BTC	21	1	4.8
Fishery Officer 1–8	435	0	0.0	Land Surveyor	20	0	0.0
Inspector Standards Trade and Commerce 1–6	302	0	0.0				

continued

Table A-2 (continued)

Technical and Inspection (Cont'd.)

Category and Group	Total Employees	No. of Women	% Women
Radio Inspector 1–5	18	0	0.0
Grain Sampler Foreman 1–4	16	0	0.0
Executive Pilot 1–2	16	0	0.0
Supervising Fruit and Vegetable Inspector	15	0	0.0
Dairy Products Officer 1–4	15	0	0.0
Senior Fruit and Vegetable Inspector	11	0	0.0
Research Director, Agriculture 1–5	11	0	0.0
Proof Technician 1–2	11	0	0.0
Technician, Forest Management 1–4	11	0	0.0
Inspector, Plant Products 1–2	10	0	0.0
Air Traffic Control Trainee	10	0	0.0
Technician, Electronics 1–7	953	1	0.1
Inspector, Record of Performance 1–2	196	1	0.5
Radio Operator 1–7	599	3	0.5
Grain Sampler	143	1	0.7
Clerk of Works	120	1	0.8
Air Traffic Controller 1–9	821	7	0.8
Radio Operator 1–3	407	4	0.9
Printing and Stationery Officer 2–6	72	1	1.3
Research Officer, Forestry 1–5	155	3	1.9
Inspector of Stores 1–4	404	9	2.2
Technician, Meteorological 1–8	1,011	27	2.7
Research Officer, Agriculture 1–5, 2A	180	6	3.3

Technical and Inspection (Cont'd.)

Category and Group	Total Employees	No. of Women	% Women
Proof Assistant 1–4	69	3	4.3
Technical Officer 1–11	3,639	183	5.0
Technician 1–4	3,614	211	5.8
Air Traffic Control Assistant 1–2	54	4	7.4
Draftsman 1–6	782	59	7.5
Map Compiler and Computer 1–4	197	16	8.1
Technician, Forest Research 1–5	492	45	9.2
Photographer 1–4	53	5	9.4
Mint Officer 1–8	10	1	10.0
Computer Systems Programmer 1–7	22	4	18.1
Assistant Technician 1–3	1,192	314	26.3
Laboratory Helper	13	9	69.2
Supervising Seed Analyst	14	12	85.7
Seed Analyst	65	62	95.4

Transitional

Category and Group	Total Employees	No. of Women	% Women
Agricultural Officer 1–6	267	0	0.0
Foreign Service Officer T and C 1–8	215	0	0.0
Agricultural Commodity Officer 1–4	55	0	0.0
Auditor Excise Tax 1A	45	0	0.0
Auditor 1–5	107	1	0.9
Agricultural Products Inspector 1–4	1,249	2	0.2
Treasury Auditor 1–8	268	1	0.3
Special Investigator Taxation 1–6	181	1	0.5

continued

Table A–2 *(continued)*

Category and Group	Total Employees	No. of Women	% Women
Transitional (Cont'd.)			
Senior Officer 1–3	349	3	0.9
Auditor Excise Tax 1–7	411	4	1.0
Confidential Messenger Assesor 1–8	93	1	1.1
Assessor	998	12	1.2
Industrial Development and Production Officer 1–5	301	5	1.7
Messenger	129	4	3.1
Trade and Commerce Officer	198	9	4.5
Foreign Service Officer, External Affairs 1–10	438	27	6.2
Chief of Division, Translation Bureau 1–3	26	2	7.7
National Gallery Officer 1–5	22	6	27.3
Senior Clerk	380	137	36.1
Translator 1–6	261	98	37.5
Clerical Assistant	60	24	40.0
Supervisor, Office Services 1–3	10	4	40.0
Clerk 1–4	2,167	1,377	63.5
Interpreter	11	8	72.7
Typing and Related:			
Duplicating Equipment Supervisor 1–3	52	14	26.9
Duplicating Equipment Operator 1–4	359	160	44.6
Communicator 1–5	233	107	45.9
Electronic Data Processor 1–8	94	64	68.1
Office Composing Equipment Operator	99	85	85.9
Telephone Operator	138	120	87.0
Telephone Supervisor 1–2	10	9	90.0

Category and Group	Total Employees	No. of Women	% Women
Transitional (Cont'd.)			
Bookkeeping Equipment Operator 2–4	16	15	93.8
Calculating Equipment Operator 2–4	36	34	94.4
Typist 1–3	396	386	97.5
Steno 1–3	288	282	97.9
Steno Secretary 3	99	99	100.0
Senior Transcriber 2–3	17	17	100.0
Executive Secretary	14	14	100.0
Postal			
Supervisory Letter Carrier	2,634	0	0.0
Mail Handler	1,701	0	0.0
Railway Mail Clerk 1–5	402	0	0.0
Postal Chauffeur	67	0	0.0
Supervisory Mail Handler	13	0	0.0
Mail Despatcher	575	1	0.2
Postal Officer (Operational) 3–7	360	1	0.3
Letter Carrier	8,093	14	0.2
Postal Carrier 1–9	1,711	38	2.2
Postal Clerk 1–2	10,658	861	8.1
Postmaster	20	2	10.0
Customs			
Customs Truckman	91	0	0.0

continued

Table A-2 *(continued)*

Category and Group	Total Employees	No. of Women	% Women
Customs (Cont'd.)			
Customs Appraiser 2–5	54	0	0.0
Customs and Excise Supervisor 1–4	46	0	0.0
Special Exciseman 1–3	15	0	0.0
Customs and Excise Superintendent 1, 3–6	14	0	0.0
Computing Clerk	47	2	4.3
Customs and Excise Officer 1–3	204	18	8.8
Immigration			
Immigration Officer 1–9	87	3	
Service and Maintenance			
Crafts and Trades:			
Pump and Sanitation Services Operator 1–5	247	0	0.0
Mint Craftsman	180	0	0.0
Maintenance Supervisor 1–6	177	0	0.0
Diesel Electric Station Attendant 1–3	147	0	0.0
Airport Mechanic 1–3	59	0	0.0
Airport Maintenance Foreman 1–3	48	0	0.0
Mines Craftsman 1–5	41	0	0.0
Dockyard Superintendent	27	0	0.0
Airport Electronic Serviceman 1–3	25	0	0.0
Assitant Litho or Photo 1–3	42	0	0.0
Airway Serviceman 1–3	24	0	0.0
Dockyard Section Foreman	21	0	0.0
Service and Maintenance (Cont'd.)			
Dry Dock Plant Fireman	20	0	0.0
Dockyard General Foreman	16	0	0.0
Aircraft Mechanic 1–3	126	0	0.0
Assistant Shop and Appliance Foreman	13	0	0.0
Dockyard Shop Foreman	12	0	0.0
Lithographic Printer 3–4	12	0	0.0
Orthopaedic Appliance Foreman 1–2	10	0	0.0
Chief Operating Engineer 1–3	67	0	0.0
Stationary Engineer Heating or Power 1–4	1,907	2	0.1
Orthopaedic Appliance Maker 1–2	122	2	1.6
Maintenance Craftsman 1–4	648	3	0.5
Instrument Maker 1–5	35	1	2.9
Learner Litho or Photo	14	1	7.1
Stores and Building Services:			
Staionary Engineer Fireman	214	0	0.0
Equipment Operator 1–3	154	0	0.0
Security Guard 1–2	136	0	0.0
Storekeeper 1–2	20	0	0.0
Truckman	20	0	0.0
Dry Dock Yardman	10	0	0.0
Fire Officer 1–4	281	2	0.7
Firefighter	1,097	1	0.1
Caretaker 1–5	938	2	0.2
Storeman 1–4	1,907	9	0.5
Fireman Labourer	1,303	6	0.5
Elevator Operator	383	2	0.5

continued

Table A–2 *(continued)*

Category and Group	Total Employees	No. of Women	% Women
Customs (Cont'd.)			
Customs Appraiser 2–5	54	0	0.0
Customs and Excise Supervisor 1–4	46	0	0.0
Special Exciseman 1–3	15	0	0.0
Customs and Excise Superintendent 1, 3–6	14	0	0.0
Computing Clerk	47	2	4.3
Customs and Excise Officer 1–3	204	18	8.8
Immigration			
Immigration Officer 1–9	87	3	
Service and Maintenance			
Crafts and Trades:			
Pump and Sanitation Services Operator 1–5	247	0	0.0
Mint Craftsman	180	0	0.0
Maintenance Supervisor 1–6	177	0	0.0
Diesel Electric Station Attendant 1–3	147	0	0.0
Airport Mechanic 1–3	59	0	0.0
Airport Maintenance Foreman 1–3	48	0	0.0
Mines Craftsman 1–5	41	0	0.0
Dockyard Superintendent	27	0	0.0
Airport Electronic Serviceman 1–3	25	0	0.0
Assitant Litho or Photo 1–3	42	0	0.0
Airway Serviceman 1–3	24	0	0.0
Dockyard Section Foreman	21	0	0.0

Category and Group	Total Employees	No. of Women	% Women
Service and Maintenance (Cont'd.)			
Dry Dock Plant Fireman	20	0	0.0
Dockyard General Foreman	16	0	0.0
Aircraft Mechanic 1–3	126	0	0.0
Assistant Shop and Appliance Foreman	13	0	0.0
Dockyard Shop Foreman	12	0	0.0
Lithographic Printer 3–4	12	0	0.0
Orthopaedic Appliance Foreman 1–2	10	0	0.0
Chief Operating Engineer 1–3	67	0	0.0
Stationary Engineer Heating or Power 1–4	1,907	2	0.1
Orthopaedic Appliance Maker 1–2	122	2	1.6
Maintenance Craftsman 1–4	648	3	0.5
Instrument Maker 1–5	35	1	2.9
Learner Litho or Photo	14	1	7.1
Stores and Building Services:			
Staionary Engineer Fireman	214	0	0.0
Equipment Operator 1–3	154	0	0.0
Security Guard 1–2	136	0	0.0
Storekeeper 1–2	20	0	0.0
Truckman	20	0	0.0
Dry Dock Yardman	10	0	0.0
Fire Officer 1–4	281	2	0.7
Firefighter	1,097	1	0.1
Caretaker 1–5	938	2	0.2
Storeman 1–4	1,907	9	0.5
Fireman Labourer	1,303	6	0.5
Elevator Operator	383	2	0.5

continued

Table A–2 *(concluded)*

Category and Group	Total Employees	No. of Women	% Women
Service and Maintenance (Cont'd.)			
Watchman	102	1	1.0
Foreman, Cleaning Service 1–5	191	1	0.5
Cleaning Service Man	4,476	59	1.3
Packer and Helper	1,433	23	1.6
Airport Attendant 1–3	71	3	4.2
Maintenance Helper	101	0	0.0
Security Officer 1–2	10	2	20.0
Stores Assistant 1–2	109	93	85.3
Other Service and Maintenance:			
Plotman 1–3	191	0	0.0
Park Warden 1–2	131	0	0.0
Canal Man 1–2	118	0	0.0
Lockmaster 1–4	87	0	0.0
Greenhouseman 1–3	57	0	0.0
Farm Foreman 1–3	45	0	0.0
Poultryman 1–3	42	0	0.0
Beekeeper 1–2	42	0	0.0
Fish Culture Assistant	41	0	0.0
Bridgemaster 1–5	39	0	0.0
Fisheries Warden	33	0	0.0
Bait Depot Operator 1–3	24	0	0.0
Canal Superintendent 1–5	17	0	0.0
Chief Park Warden	16	0	0.0
Bridgeman 1–3	28	0	0.0
Gardener 1–5	157	1	0.6
Lightkeeper 1–9	637	1	0.2
Service and Maintenance (Cont'd.)			
Herdsman 1–3	76	2	2.6
Park Attendant 1–3	62	5	8.0
Hospital			
Hospital Utility Man 1–3	32	0	0.0
Remedial Physical Training Instruction	19	0	0.0
Morgue Attendant	13	0	0.0
Nursing Orderly 1–4	1,572	18	1.1
Dental Technician 1–3	26	1	3.8
Hospital Cook 1–5	244	41	16.8
Remedial Assistant Occupational Therapy 1–2	21	4	19.0
Pharmacist 1–4	47	9	19.1
Housekeeper Hospital 1–3	13	3	23.1
Technician, Clinical 1–4	51	24	47.1
Technician, X-Ray 1–4	64	34	53.1
Hospital Laboratory Helper 1–2	31	21	67.7
Technician, Hospital Laboratory 1–4	182	142	78.0
Therapist, Physical 1–5	50	47	94.0
Therapist, Occupational 1–5	31	30	96.8
Nurse Pending Registration	35	33	94.3
Nurse 1–6	1,414	1,389	98.2
Dental Nurse	72	71	98.6
Hospital Nursing Assistant	220	220	100.0
Assistant Sterile Supply Room	53	53	100.0
Total	**147,760**	**40,640**	**27.5**

Source: Pay Research Bureau.

Table A–3 Proportion of Female Employees in the Public Service in Selected Occupations in Ottawa/Hull, Montreal, and Toronto Metropolitan Areas, July 1967

Occupation	Ottawa/Hull			Montreal			Toronto			Other			All Locations		
	Employment		% Female to Total	Employment		% Female to Total	Employment		% Female to Total	Employment		% Female to Total	Employment		% Female to Total
	Total	Female		Total	Female		Total	Female		Total	Female		Total	Female	
All Occupations	42,036	15,868	37.7	15,635	3,363	21.5	13,860	3,166	22.8	78,714	18,602	23.6	150,245	40,999	27.3
In Selected Occupations															
Research Scientist	612	22	3.6	–	–	–	9	–	–	670	13	1.9	1,291	35	2.7
Medical Officer and Specialist	119	10	8.4	45	4	8.9	13	1	7.7	244	9	3.7	421	24	5.7
Economist	241	17	7.1	–	–	–	–	–	–	32	1	3.1	273	18	6.6
Statistician	296	51	17.2	–	–	–	1	–	–	12	1	8.3	309	52	16.8
Librarian	133	88	66.2	–	–	–	2	2	100.0	29	16	55.2	164	106	64.6
Administrative Services	1,045	102	9.8	80	–	–	68	1	1.5	451	18	4.0	1,644	121	7.4
Personnel Administration	692	82	11.8	43	2	4.7	50	6	12.0	164	10	6.1	949	100	10.5
Program Administration	1,332	114	8.6	940	138	14.7	1,152	174	15.1	5,548	583	10.5	8,972	1,009	11.2
Administrative Trainee	134	45	33.6	133	43	32.3	87	37	42.5	629	191	30.4	983	316	32.1
Clerical and Regulatory	11,249	6,385	56.8	2,733	1,227	44.9	2,572	1,439	55.9	14,461	6,974	48.2	31,015	16,025	51.7
Data Processing	870	604	69.4	40	34	85.0	60	54	90.0	138	106	76.8	1,108	798	72.0
Technician	1,624	148	9.1	150	2	1.4	101	6	5.9	1,739	55	3.2	3,614	211	5.8
Assistant Technician	463	147	31.7	54	8	14.8	52	18	34.6	623	141	22.6	1,192	314	26.3
Translator	238	84	35.3	22	14	63.6	–	–	–	1	–	–	261	98	37.5

Source: Prepared from data obtained from the Pay Research Bureau.

Table A–4 *Distribution by Level of Women in Selected Public Service Occupations, July 1967*

Group and Level	Total Employees	No. of Women	% Women
Professional			
Advisory Counsel			
1	11	0	–
2	18	1	5.6
3	8	0	–
Senior Advisory Counsel			
4	52	3	5.8
Total	**89**	**4**	**4.4**
Bacteriologist			
1	11	5	45.5
2	23	7	30.4
3	18	4	22.2
4	5	0	–
5	1	0	–
Total	**58**	**16**	**27.6**
Chemist			
1	33	17	51.5
2	62	20	32.3
3	38	2	5.3
4	14	0	–
5	1	0	–
Total	**148**	**39**	**26.4**
Economist			
1	37	4	10.8
2	47	4	8.5
3	33	4	12.1
4	51	1	2.0
5	57	5	8.8
6	32	0	–
7	16	0	–

Group and Level	Total Employees	No. of Women	% Women
Professional (Cont'd.)			
Senior Economist			
1	11	0	–
2	6	0	–
Total	**290**	**18**	**6.2**
Geographer			
1	13	6	46.2
2	8	3	37.5
3	8	1	12.5
4	7	0	–
5	1	0	–
Total	**37**	**10**	**27.0**
Language Officer, French or English			
1	49	30	61.2
2	62	23	37.1
3	27	5	18.5
4	11	0	–
5	3	1	33.3
Total	**152**	**59**	**38.8**
Librarian			
1	40	30	75.0
2	33	20	60.6
3	45	28	62.2
4	31	18	58.1
5	15	10	66.7
Total	**164**	**106**	**64.6**

continued

Table A–4 (continued)

Group and Level	Total Employees	No. of Women	% Women
Professional (Cont'd.)			
Medical Officer			
1	17	6	35.3
2	54	6	11.1
3	160	6	3.8
4	57	3	5.3
5	37	1	2.7
6	16	0	–
Medical Specialist			
1	38	2	5.3
2	42	0	–
Total	421	21	5.7
Social Worker			
1	1	1	100.0
2	13	11	84.6
3	19	15	78.9
4	13	7	53.8
5	4	3	75.0
6	2	1	50.0
Total	52	38	73.1
Research Scientist			
1	379	10	2.6
2	786	21	2.7
3	106	3	2.8
4	20	1	5.0
Total	1,291	35	2.7

Group and Level	Total Employees	No. of Women	% Women
Professional (Cont'd.)			
Statistician			
1	43	7	16.3
2	61	11	18.0
3	88	14	15.9
4	75	11	14.7
5	42	9	21.4
Total	309	52	16.8
Administrative and Foreign Services			
Administrative Services			
1	255	36	14.1
2	427	49	11.5
3	301	19	6.3
4	294	12	4.1
5	164	4	2.4
6	102	1	1.0
7	63	0	–
8	34	0	–
9	4	0	–
Total	1,644	121	7.4
Computer Systems Administration			
1	223	56	26.0
2	105	5	4.8
3	89	5	5.6
4	34	0	–
5	10	0	–
6	0	0	–
Total	461	66	14.8

continued

Table A–4 *(continued)*

Group and Level	Total Employees	No. of Women	% Women
Administrative and Foreign Service (Cont'd.)			
Information Services			
1	114	46	40.4
2	92	14	15.2
3	70	11	15.7
4	16	0	—
5	13	1	7.7
6	5	0	—
Total	310	72	23.2
Operation and Methods			
1	86	9	10.5
2	47	1	2.1
3	74	0	—
4	23	0	—
5	24	0	—
6	11	0	—
7	0	0	—
Total	265	10	3.8
Personnel Administration			
1	130	33	25.4
2	189	22	11.6
3	212	22	10.4
4	160	16	10.0
5	102	3	2.9
6	62	4	6.5
7	39	0	—
8	37	0	—
9	18	0	—
Total	949	100	10.5

Group and Level	Total Employees	No. of Women	% Women
Administrative and Foreign Service (Cont'd.)			
Program Administration			
1	2,589	424	16.4
2	3,966	479	12.1
3	1,253	72	5.7
4	487	18	3.7
5	306	6	2.0
6	233	7	3.0
7	108	2	1.9
8	30	1	3.3
Total	8,972	1,009	11.2
Welfare Programs			
1	175	13	7.4
2	322	10	3.1
3	110	3	2.7
4	112	3	2.7
5	22	1	4.5
6	18	0	—
7	4	0	—
8	0	0	—
Total	763	30	3.9
Administrative Support			
Clerical and Regulatory			
1	5,142	3,386	65.8
2	5,610	3,979	70.9
3	6,997	4,426	63.3
4	6,659	2,998	45.0
5	4,939	1,061	21.5
6	1,408	141	10.0
7	260	34	13.1
Total	31,015	16,025	51.7

continued

Table A—4 (continued)

Administrative Support (Cont'd.)

Group and Level	Total Employees	No. of Women	% Women
Communication			
1	164	115	70.1
2	207	63	30.4
3	232	57	24.6
4	63	19	30.2
5	13	4	30.8
6	0	0	–
7	0	0	–
Total	**679**	**258**	**38.0**
Data Processing			
1	583	503	86.3
2	98	81	82.7
3	163	95	58.3
4	93	47	50.5
5	62	28	45.2
6	34	13	38.2
7	35	5	14.3
8	13	0	–
B	2	2	100.0
C	25	24	96.0
Total	**1,108**	**798**	**72.0**
Technical and Inspection			
Technician			
1	1,357	129	9.5
2	1,119	53	4.7
3	788	19	2.4
4	350	10	2.9
Total	**3,614**	**211**	**5.8**

Technical and Inspection (Cont'd.)

Group and Level	Total Employees	No. of Women	% Women
Assistant Technician			
1	79	48	60.8
2	377	124	32.9
3	736	142	19.3
Total	**1,192**	**314**	**26.3**
Technician, Forest Research			
1	24	6	25.0
2	136	16	11.6
3	233	20	8.6
4	80	3	3.8
5	17	0	–
Total	**492**	**45**	**9.1**
Draftsman			
1	226	28	12.4
2	145	10	6.9
3	319	20	6.3
4	75	1	1.3
5	12	0	–
6	5	0	–
Total	**782**	**59**	**7.5**
Transitional			
Senior Officer			
1	190	2	1.1
2	99	1	1.0
3	60	0	–
Total	**349**	**3**	**0.9**

continued

Table A–4 *(concluded)*

Group and Level		Total Employees	No. of Women	% Women
Transitional *(Cont'd.)*				
Foreign Service Officer, External Affairs	1	63	7	11.1
	2	62	7	11.3
	3	53	1	1.9
	4	51	3	5.9
	5	65	5	7.7
	6	51	2	3.9
	7	43	1	2.3
	8	34	2	5.9
	9	10	0	–
	10	6	0	–
	Total	438	27	6.2
Translator	1	42	15	35.7
	2	60	32	53.3
	3	90	33	36.7
	4	46	13	28.3
	5	19	5	26.3
	6	4	0	–
Chief of Division, Translation Bureau	1	5	0	–
	2	9	2	22.2
	3	12	0	–
	Total	287	100	34.8
Postal				
Postal Clerk	1	657	230	35.0
	2	10,001	631	6.3
	Total	10,658	861	8.1

Group and Level		Total Employees	No. of Women	% Women
Hospital				
Hospital Cook	1	17	14	82.4
	2	150	22	14.7
	3	55	5	9.1
	4	17	0	–
	5	5	0	–
	Total	244	41	16.8
Pharmacist	1	0	0	–
	2	27	6	22.2
	3	14	3	21.4
	4	6	0	–
	Total	47	9	19.1
Technician, Clinical	1	6	6	100.0
	2	27	12	44.4
	3	15	5	33.3
	4	3	1	33.3
	Total	51	24	47.1
Technician, Hospital Laboratory	1	21	18	85.7
	2	70	58	82.9
	3	65	51	78.5
	4	26	15	57.7
	Total	182	142	78.0
Technician, X-Ray	1	6	3	50.0
	2	40	28	70.0
	3	12	3	25.0
	4	6	0	–
	Total	64	34	53.1

Source: Pay Research Bureau.

17

Service at the Pleasure of the Crown: The Law of Dismissal of Senior Public Servants

William A. W. Neilson

Abstract: The old law that public servants serve at the Crown's pleasure has a modern-day meaning for senior members of the public service facing dismissal in the wake of reorganization, cutbacks and the downsizing of governments' operations. Others discover that their services are not 'politically compatible' in the judgment of a new minister or the cabinet of a new government.

This paper reviews the law and practice of dismissal as they affect the non-union career public servants who are told by their government employer that they no longer serve at Her Majesty's pleasure. Despite adverse judicial comment and some legislative constraints, the old law persists and recent dismissals in Saskatchewan and British Columbia confirm that government employers are quite prepared to take a very strict legal approach when it serves their immediate interests in dealing with the senior public service.

The longer-run implications of these developments, and the recent interest in placing senior personnel on personal service contracts, raise important questions about the prospects for a career, non-partisan public service.

Sommaire: Le vieux principe voulant que les fonctionnaires soient soumis au bon plaisir de la Couronne présente une signification fort actuelle pour les cadres supérieurs de la fonction publique qui se voient menacés de renvoi par suite d'une réorganisation, de coupures ou d'une 'rationalisation' des programmes gouvernementaux. Certains découvrent alors que leurs fonctions ne sont pas 'politiquement compatibles', selon l'opinion du nouveau ministre ou du nouveau cabinet.

Cet article fait le point sur le droit et les pratiques touchant le congédiement des fonctionnaires de carrière non syndiqués que leur employeur gouvernemental, juge ne plus faire le bon plaisir de Sa Majesté. En dépit de critiques judiciaires et de contraintes législatives, le vieux principe subsiste. Et les congédiements effectués récemment en Saskatchewan et en Colombie-Britannique confirment que les employeurs gouvernementaux sont prêts à adopter une approche très légaliste si cela sert leurs intérêts immédiats dans leurs transactions avec les hauts fonctionnaires.

Les répercussions à long terme de ces événements et les récentes suggestions

William A.W. Neilson, 'Service at the Pleasure of the Crown: The Law of Dismissal of Senior Public Servants', *Canadian Public Administration* 27, 4 (1984): 556–75. Courtesy of The Institute of Public Administration Canada.

d'offrir aux cadres supérieurs des contrats personnels de service soulèvent d'impor-
tantes questions quant à l'avenir de la fonction publique en tant que corps profession-
nel et non-partisan.

> . . . if you live by the order in council, you die by the order in council[1]
> > *Saskatchewan cabinet minister*, 1982
>
> . . . the members want to know if they can be fired, what compensation they
> can get . . . , whether they can be forced to transfer, and whether they must
> accept lower paying jobs.[2]
> > *President, BC Government Managers Association*, 1984

This paper examines the legal position of senior members of the non-partisan public service who are dismissed 'without cause' from their career employment.
According to long-established principle, public servants are deemed to hold office at
the pleasure of the Crown. This means that government employees may be dismissed
summarily without severance pay in the absence of protective legislation.

Over the past century, federal and provincial statutes have made significant
inroads on the historic concept of service at pleasure. In the first wave of reform, public service legislation enshrined the merit principle, set up job classification systems,
and provided procedural protections to employees whose services might be terminated. Additional employment rights were introduced in the next stage of legislation,
which authorized collective bargaining in the public sector. These developments, in
very large measure, gave legal and practical effect to the principles of career service
and political neutrality in government employment. However, as we will discover,
these legal changes did not extinguish the Crown's ultimate authority to dismiss senior public servants summarily without cause. Staff cuts may be made by governments
in the name of restraint, political incompatibility or a mixture of both factors. Recent
events suggest that cabinets in several jurisdictions are quite prepared to resort to the
old law of Crown employment when it serves their immediate purposes.

In Victoria, Regina, Ottawa, and Quebec City, the subject of employment security for members of the senior public service is of more than academic interest. In
the first two capitals, dismissals of excluded personnel have reached unprecedented
levels in the wake of election victories by the Social Credit and Conservative parties
in 1983 and 1982 respectively. Similar fates have been forecast for senior members of
the federal public service with the advent of the Conservatives to power in the fall
of 1984. Reference might also he made to Manitoba, where the Pawley cabinet has
quietly replaced nearly all the deputy ministers holding office when the Lyon government was defeated in 1982.

The overall implications of these developments, particularly at the provincial
level, deserve careful analysis to gauge their wider ramifications for public service
recruitment, career expectations, and independence. In this paper, I concentrate on
the legal considerations involved in the dismissal without cause of excluded public
servants by their government employer. The visibility of recent events, combined
with limited time and resources, has forced me to limit my attention to provincial
law and practice, with particular reference to British Columbia and Saskatchewan.[3]

However, the thrust of the analysis may be extended to other jurisdictions, including the federal level. The paper does not deal with the law of dismissal for the unionized public service or for employees dismissed for cause but concentrates on the legal aspects of the arbitrary dismissal of senior public servants.

The first part of the paper reviews the common law origins of 'service during pleasure,' its restatement in provincial legislation, and the approaches taken by our courts in applying the Crown's historic right of dismissal to modern public service conditions. The second part details the recent dismissal practices of several provincial governments and relates them to the wider legal framework within which the firings have been carried out. Since severance pay guidelines and the details of most settlements are unavailable, our grasp of present reality must be based on interviews, limited documentation and cautious speculation.

There have been recent signs that some governments are turning to individual service contracts as the hiring instrument for particular senior personnel. The shift from status to contract was authorized expressly in the new Quebec Public Service Act.[4] Under its terms, the premier is authorized to contract with deputy ministers and assistant and associate deputy ministers for their services. This development and some related practices in other provinces[5] reflect a growing readiness by provincial governments and their senior personnel to negotiate in advance the details of personal service contracts, including termination provisions. We analyse these developments and their implications in the third part of this article.

THE COURTS AND PUBLIC SERVICE 'DURING PLEASURE'

The parties agree that at common law employees of the Crown retain their appointments at the pleasure of the Crown. Their employment may be terminated without notice and without any liability to pay compensation in lieu of notice. The parties also agree that this right of the Crown at common law may be abrogated in whole or in part by statute, regulation, or a term of the appointment.[6]

The origins of the present state of the law, as provided in this instance by Mr Justice MacLean of the Saskatchewan Queen's Bench in April 1984, may be traced to three British cases decided between 1866 and 1877[7] involving military officers who were dismissed from their appointments without cause or notice. In all three decisions, the courts dismissed the officers' claims and held that the Crown had an absolute right to dismiss them at pleasure, despite agreements or regulations to the contrary.

Indeed, in one case,[8] the House of Lords held that if there had been a contract, then a condition permitting dismissal at pleasure would have been included in it and if the contract had stated otherwise, then it would have been held contrary to the public interest in any event. The courts' reluctance to interfere in military matters might be explained, if not defended, by their perception of the unique nature of military service and of the necessity of an overriding support for a command structure at the expense of individual arrangements, however clearly negotiated these may be.

Were civil servants to be treated in the same manner? The watershed year was 1896 when two cases originating in distant parts of the British Empire came to

England for decision. The first case involved Mr Dunn[9] who had been hired for a three-year term as consular agent by the Queen's Commissioner for the Niger Protectorate in Africa. When he was dismissed prior to the expiry of the term, Dunn brought an action against the Crown. The English Court of Appeal simply applied the 'military model' to Mr Dunn's situation and rejected the contention that the three-year term displaced the untrammelled right of the Crown to dismiss an employee without notice or cause. A close reading of the unanimous decision suggests that the members of the court drew a direct parallel between military officers serving in the field and colonial officers serving on the frontier. In this context, it is perhaps not surprising that the Crown's absolute rights predominated over the consular agent's right to job security, at least in the absence of contrary legislative instructions.

Only a few months later, a case came before the Judicial Committee of the Privy Council involving a clerk, Mr Stuart,[10] who had been hired by the government of New South Wales. For the first time, the provisions of a modern Civil Service Act figured in the litigation. The act dealt with salaries, set up a system of appointments and promotions under the aegis of a board, provided for a classification scheme and allowed for dismissal, but only for cause. Mr Stuart was dismissed summarily without cause, sued the colonial government, won at trial and prevailed again before the Judicial Committee. In the view of the Committee, the Civil Service Act provided a security of tenure for Mr Stuart which was inconsistent with the Crown's claim that its right of dismissal could not be overridden by Stuart's contract of service.

The trial judge in the *Stuart* case identified a clear relationship between security of tenure and the establishment of an able and permanent public service. His comments were made nearly ninety years ago and bear repeating:

> It is hardly necessary for me to point out how desirable it is in the public interest that a high standard of integrity and ability should be maintained in the permanent Civil Service of the colony, and that persons of character and ability cannot be induced to enter that Service unless they have a reasonably certain tenure of their offices. Troubles have arisen in other countries out of the instability of the tenure of office of State servants, and in passing the Civil Service Act of this colony, doubtless the intention of the Legislature was, by giving to its civil servants a statutory guarantee that so long as their conduct was good they would be safe from arbitrary dismissal, to ensure to the public the stability of the Civil Service, and that high standard of efficiency which training and experience alone can give.[11]

Mr Stuart won his battle but lost the war. Promptly after the Judicial Committee's ruling, the New South Wales legislature passed a bill reinstating the unimpaired right to dismiss at pleasure.[12] According to the narrowest interpretation, the *Stuart* decision held that express legislation could take away or otherwise control the Crown's authority to dismiss public servants at pleasure. In fact, the Judicial Committee said that the right could be taken away by 'law' which would suggest that a contract of service between the Crown and the servant could override the 'at pleasure' rule.

However, it took some forty years before the Judicial Committee found an opportunity in the *Reilly* case in 1934[13] to indicate that the relationship between the Crown and its servants could well be one of contract where the attendant rights accruing to the employee would be inconsistent with the Crown's right of arbitrary dismissal. Although the remarks were not necessary to the decision, there is little doubt that they indicated acceptance of the idea that the power to dismiss at pleasure could be limited by contract. The terms of the contract might go to the length of appointment or other conditions concerning the termination of services. While it is always open to the legislature to abolish the office or otherwise set the conditions for ending the employment relationship,[14] the Reilly decision clearly leaned in favour of increased protection for public servants and a corresponding obligation on governments to honour their promises or pay compensation in lieu thereof.

Such a contract may be found in a collective agreement as well as in a personally negotiated contract. There is even an indication recently[15] that a contract may be implied in certain circumstances. As the law now recognizes that the Crown has the capacity to contract, and Crown proceedings legislation provides that it may sue and be sued on its contracts, it does not seem such a large step to say that the Crown may contract out of its right to dismiss at pleasure. The trend in Canada is certainly to recognize and enforce Crown contracts.

This line of authority was extended to a contract personally negotiated between the Attorney General for British Columbia and the province's first Rentalsman, Mr Clark. The court held that the government was bound by the actions of its minister.[16] The Crown argued that the minister lacked the authority to enter into the employment contract as the relevant statute authorized the Lieutenant-Governor-in-Council to appoint the Rentalsman. Mr Clark never had a written contract but he had been appointed as Rentalsman, at a deputy minister 1 level, for a term of five years and the terms of his appointment had been negotiated personally with the Attorney General. The continued failure of the Attorney General and his successor in office to put the contract in writing and to provide benefits promised to Clark and his deputies finally led to Clark's resignation and his successful suit for breach of contract.

Looking at the cases that have gone to court in recent years, it is clear that the trend indicated by the earlier decisions has tended to continue. There is little doubt that the right to dismiss at pleasure can he limited by statute, by collective agreement, or by contract. The court will feel free, in appropriate circumstances, to infer the terms for dismissal from the totality of the particular relationship between the government employer and the public servant. The term of appointment, written undertakings and implied commitments are among the factors considered by the courts to undercut arbitrary government actions.[17] It must be emphasized that the right of dismissal itself is in dispute.[18] The question in each case is whether the right may be exercised summarily without notice or compensation to the affected employee in question.

The case law is less clear about the situation in which the government agrees to employment terms which appear to run directly counter to the statutory language of appointment. The more cautious view is that if the statutory terms of appointment expressly refer to service at pleasure then an appointment for a fixed term of years will not bind the government if it chooses to dismiss the appointee prior to the expiry of that time.[19]

However. it is evident from the decisions that courts will generally seek to avoid this clash between 'at pleasure' and contractual terms. The trend in the law has been to restrict the Crown's right to dismiss at pleasure and to resist giving any further support to the common law's 'somewhat uncritical acceptance'[20] of the military service origins of the old rule in the context of modern government.

While this trend is well established, and more in harmony with modern reality and the public interest, it is open for a government to retain its right to dismiss at pleasure. If this is to be done, however, it seems increasingly that it should be done expressly. Otherwise the courts will be quite prepared to investigate the total circumstances of the employment relationship and to find circumstances inconsistent with the government's common law authority of arbitrary dismissal.

This trend in court decisions and judicial warnings has prompted governments to negotiate settlements with excluded employees whose appointments are being terminated. Governments may be understandably reluctant to trust their luck to the judiciary who are likely to demand a greater sense of fair play in the government's treatment of its permanent managers. By staying out of court, the Crown can continue to save the principle of 'at pleasure' tenure without running the risk of its being struck down or further eroded by the courts.

It is important to remember that court decisions involve the exercise of a considerable degree of judicial discretion. Rarely do judges simply apply clear precedent; if the case were that clear cut there would be no need for it to go to court as the result would be obvious. Where, then, do courts look for the source of their decisions? Certainly they feel a need, in general, not to be inconsistent with previous law. They are also influenced by the specific facts of each situation, particularly the way the parties have behaved. Also, although they say so less often, they are concerned with larger considerations of the public interest, such as equitable conduct, correcting for unequal bargaining power and the public interest in a professional senior public service. It is unfortunate that so much of this goes unsaid in the judgments, and we are left to speculate.

THE LEGISLATIVE CONTEXT AND DISMISSAL WITHOUT CAUSE IN PRACTICE

The Interpretation Acts of our common law provinces codify the principle of public service appointments during pleasure. In Manitoba and Saskatchewan their acts provide:

> '*Every public officer* appointed. . . by or under the authority of an enactment or otherwise, *holds office during pleasure only*, unless it is otherwise expressed in the enactment or in his commission or appointment[21] (emphasis added).

A 'public officer' for these purposes 'includes a person in the public service of the Province.'[22]

The result is that public servants are employed at the pleasure of the government subject to specific terms to the contrary found in the statute authorizing their appointment, or in the particular terms of appointment or commission (provided they are not expressly contrary to any statutory terms) or, as we have seen above, contractual terms found to be in force by a court. The fundamental principle of service at pleasure remains the bedrock of the legal basis of public sector employment.

Public service legislation customarily separates appointments into civil service commission and cabinet streams.[23] Appointments in the first category are to be made on the basis of merit, fitness, and aptitude within a framework of open competition. The statutes and their accompanying regulations normally provide for review and grievance procedures in cases of dismissal for cause. Collective agreements entered into by the government and authorized by statute frequently provide additional grievance machinery and may extend job protection on the basis of seniority or other specified factors to employees within bargaining units.

Cabinet appointees, on the other hand, involve two very separate groups: the most senior members of the public service (DMs and ADMs, for example), and partisan staff, advisers, and others who are not regarded as civil servants during their term of service. The first group and those excluded personnel appointed by the civil service commission are the subjects of this paper.

Both groups are on a tenuous footing. As public officers under the Interpretation Act and employees under the Public Service Act in British Columbia, for example, these senior public servants do not enjoy a level of employment security comparable to their organized staff. The blunt realities of the strict common law doctrine of 'serving during pleasure of Her Majesty' apply expressly to every deputy, assistant deputy and associate deputy minister in the BC public service. A 1980 amendment to the Public Service Act[24] provides that each of these appointments is to be made by the Lieutenant-Governor-in-Council and that the incumbent is to hold office during pleasure.

As we saw in the first part, a court may still force a government to honour separate contractual undertakings concerning salary and benefits if the government seeks to dispense with the services of order-in-council appointees without cause or notice. Sometimes the severance pay conditions will be standardized through regulations. This appears to be the case in British Columbia under a little known 1976 regulation[25] in which deputy ministers and other employees whose employment is terminated by cabinet order are entitled to receive a month's severance pay for each year of employment up to a maximum of six months. There was no reference to these terms (nor do they seem to have been followed in practice) when a senior official,[26] clearly speaking with cabinet authority, issued a memorandum prior to the 1983 election in which deputy ministers were promised a severance payment of up to eighteen months' salary in the event that any were dismissed after the election.

In Saskatchewan, the Blakeney government 'made a large number (some 1200) of order in council appointments during its years in office largely, though not entirely, at the senior and middle ranks of the hierarchy'.[27] Following the election in 1982, the outgoing NDP cabinet, 'wishing to assure ... reasonably generous severance provisions,' released nearly seventy order-in-council appointees, 'including executive assistants to cabinet ministers, the premier's chief political advisor, most of the premier's secretarial staff and the Cabinet press officer.'[28] Legislation in all Canadian jurisdictions expressly provides for cabinet appointment of political staff and advisers and these appointments are treated separately from public service positions including those made by cabinet order and holding office at pleasure.[29]

The legal position of this latter group was clarified soon after the new government assumed office. The Devine government, for reasons discussed elsewhere, dismissed over one hundred of these office-holders during its first year.[30] One of them was Ken Neil, appointed in July 1981 by order-in-council as director of the Northern Housing Branch of the Department of Northern Saskatchewan. He satisfactorily completed his one-year probationary period and one month later in August 1982 was dismissed by the new government. In proceedings brought by him before the Saskatchewan Queen's Bench in April 1984, the government and Mr Neil agreed that his dismissal was made without any prior notice or hearing, without just cause and unrelated to Mr Neil's employment performance. It was also accepted for the purposes of the hearing that 'the dismissal was a politically motivated act based on the perceived affiliation of the plaintiff with the previous political party forming the Government of Saskatchewan.'[31]

Counsel for Neil argued unsuccessfully that his client's completion of the probationary period had made him a permanent employee who may seek review of an arbitrary dismissal before the Public Service Commission. The court however was more persuaded by the fact that Neil had been appointed to his position by the Lieutenant-Governor-in-Council. As a result, Mr Neil could only be considered a permanent member of the 'unclassified' category of the public service whose dismissal rights and privileges were governed, in this instance, by a specific regulation that limited severance pay to one month's salary in lieu of notice.[32] In fact, the government had made an ex gratia payment of $10,419 to Mr Neil whose employment with the government had started in the classified public service in 1979. The fact of the payment was deemed irrelevant to the legal issue in dispute but, as we shall see later, reflects an approach frequently taken by governments, at least in Western Canada, when they arbitrarily dismiss career appointees and exclude management personnel whose services have been deemed contrary to the government's political leanings or surplus to its requirements.

The short result of the *Neil* case is that cabinet appointees in Saskatchewan may be summarily dismissed and cannot maintain an action for unjust dismissal. Apart from any ex gratia offer by the government, the dismissed employee is legally entitled to receive severance pay as prescribed by regulation. This entitlement in turn may be altered or extinguished by the cabinet in its law-making capacity.[33]

Nor was the court prepared to find support for Neil in the 'freedom of association' or 'liberty of the person' provisions of the Charter of Rights and Freedoms.[34] According to Mr Justice MacLean, 'order-in-council appointments to the public service frequently are politically motivated' since 'in addition to the permanent, non-political, professional staff of the civil service, elected representatives frequently must rely upon a small group of persons who share their political views and who in a broad way wish to mold our society in a particular fashion.' Given these circumstances, and the fact that Neil was presumed to have known of his 'at pleasure' status when he was appointed, the judge refused to find 'that a right guaranteed him by The Charter had been infringed.'[35]

The language of the *Neil* decision leaves open the possibility of a Charter argument in a case involving employees 'whose employment falls within the purview of the Public Service Commission.'[36] In the period since mid-1981, five public servants who had been summarily dismissed were awarded settlements in separate proceedings before the commission.[37] The Charter has not figured to date in those decisions reached after its proclamation.

The Saskatchewan Public Service Act provides a right of appeal[38] to the commission for employees dismissed by the government who were appointed into the classified service by the commission. Mr Neil was in this category from 1979 to 1981 when he was promoted to his director's position by an order-in-council. On the basis of the decisions mentioned,[39] it can be assumed that if he had been fired for the same reasons from a classified service position in 1982, Mr Neil would have been awarded an amount at least equivalent to the ex gratia payment he received as an unclassified appointee, plus substantial contributions towards his legal expenses and incidental costs. Indeed, he might have been reinstated, a remedy 'preferred in normal circumstances' by the commission whose members are 'of the view that it is not in the interest of a professional and well motivated public service for employees to be dismissed without stated cause.'[40]

However, the reinstatement of another career public servant with an exemplary performance record who had been fired without notice or cause from the same Department of Northern Saskatchewan[41] was rejected by the commission. The principal factor militating against reinstatement was the downsizing and substantial reorganization of the department planned by the government resulting in a 'destabilized environment [which] would in all likelihood make a difficult situation much worse for all concerned.'[42] One assumes the 'difficult situation' referred to the minister's firing of the employee for political reasons (although no evidence was found to indicate that he had 'involved himself in political activities which might undermine or seriously diminish or compromise his usefulness as a Research Officer').[43] The minister did not want him around and that was that. His remedy lay in 'a fair and reasonable financial settlement by way of compensation . . . for damages due to unjust dismissal'.[44]

The case confirms that a determined government, provided it is willing to pay, can get rid of any public servant.

In British Columbia, the Social Credit government has opted to handle the dismissals of excluded personnel in a different manner. These employees are the necessary casualties of an exercise in pruning or downsizing the public sector and reducing its responsibilities and operations. In January 1984 the deputy provincial secretary issued a memorandum to all deputy ministers in the BC public service entitled Policy on Staff Reduction—Excluded Employees. The policy statement applied 'to all public service employees who are not covered by the terms of a collective agreement and who become surplus to Ministry requirements.'

Notwithstanding its broad application, the policy directive was not published as an amendment to Treasury Board Order 40[45] respecting the terms and conditions of employment for excluded employees. Order 40 is silent on the policy and procedures for dealing with excluded personnel whose positions are declared redundant or surplus to a ministry's requirements. Termination of their employment ties back directly to the legal treatment of appointments during pleasure and the need to review the precise statutory authority cited in support of the government's powers of dismissal without cause.

Under the British Columbia legislation, an excluded employee may be dismissed for just cause by his minister or deputy minister.[46] Since a deputy minister is an 'employee' for the purposes of the act,[47] he could also be fired or removed by his minister for just cause without reference to the premier or the cabinet, a curious result given the vesting of the power of appointment in the Lieutenant-Governor-in-Council whose first minister, the premier, exercises firm control over senior service postings. Furthermore, this same provision in the Public Service Act would seem to permit a deputy minister to remove or dismiss for just cause an assistant or associate deputy minister (also appointed by the Lieutenant-Governor-in-Council) without further review or reference.

Dismissal for just cause, however, was not the concern of the senior managers who were the subject of the January 1984 directive. The legislation is not clear on the conditions surrounding their dismissal for other than just cause.[48] Though they are not order-in-council appointments, they lack the protection of a collective agreement and they constitute, in general terms, a group of 'employees' under the Public Service Act who serve at pleasure.

The Interpretation Act maintains this traditional framework and one is left to search for contrary signals in the Public Service Act. That statute provides[49] that the Lieutenant-Governor-in-Council retains an unimpaired authority to dismiss any employee but it does not address issues of compensation or notice for dismissals without cause. Nonetheless, cabinet clearly preserves the final authority by this provision 'to remove or dismiss any employees' and in the absence of any judicial authority on this point, the senior managers in British Columbia, strictly speaking, find themselves at the mercy of the 'at pleasure' rule as tempered by the informal arrangements proposed by the January 1984 policy directive.

The directive anticipates the offer of a severance payment but leaves open the manner of calculation and the amount of the payment itself to individual settlement. The directive is not in the form of a regulation and could be changed or withdrawn without notice.

The dismissal of senior personnel in the BC public service is now proceeding apace. In the face of cutbacks in government programs, the positions of a number of excluded personnel are being re-examined. The previous situation involving scattered individual cases of dismissal, transfers or redeployments[50] has now been supplemented by the widespread elimination of positions for excluded personnel who are declared by the deputy minister to be 'surplus to Ministry requirements' after consideration of '(a) The operational requirements of the Ministry; (b) the employee's record of performance; and (c) their abilities to perform the work remaining to be done.'[51]

The deputy minister may consider the possibility of reassigning a surplus employee to another 'suitable' excluded job within the same Ministry on the basis of his (a) qualifications and abilities; (b) level of performance; and (c) length of service.'[52]

Seniority need not be the determining factor, since the other criteria are of equal weight, and in any event, the affected manager has no claim to be considered for reassignment. That decision vests in the deputy who, in turn, is restricted to the options available within his particular ministry.

The selection process is thus idiosyncratic to each ministry through the deputy minister. There is no provision for review or appeal by persons or authorities outside the affected ministry. Each case is apparently to be handled on its own, subject to the general (and unweighted) criteria governing 'surplus' designation and the discretionary possibilities, if available, of reassignment within the ministry.

The employees who are found to be surplus to ministry requirements are not informed in advance about their status. This is because the Management Services Division, the Legal Services Branch, and a ministry representative first must 'develop a specific severance proposal to be used in discussion with the employees in question.' The severance proposal provides the basis for the ominous meeting with the deputy minister or his nominee at which the affected senior manager first learns of his fate and is 'advised that the offer of severance is good for one week.'[53]

The directive does not discuss the criteria or other factors to be considered by the government in its construction of the 'one and only' offer of severance. The sketchy evidence available to date suggests that the severance proposal may be the subject of further negotiations between the employer's Legal Services Branch and the employee's solicitor. The criteria on which the severance allowance is based bear a very close resemblance to those discussed in the BC Rentalsman decision,[54] including length of service, age, performance record, managerial level and responsibilities, employment prospects, salary level, and opportunities foregone. In this respect, the severance pay criteria appear to be similar to those used by private sector employers subject to lower limits on the maximum sums payable. This result works a hardship on longer serving personnel who, ironically, may incur greater difficulty in finding new employment. They tend to lose coming and going.

Hard figures, however, are difficult to come by, since each case is ultimately handled on a private and individual basis between the dismissed public servant or his solicitor and the government's legal adviser. In strict legal terms, any severance package proposed by the government is characterized as ex gratia on the basis that the government refuses to acknowledge the existence of a legal duty to compensate excluded personnel who are summarily dismissed without notice or cause. The 'service during pleasure' sword hangs as a threat in the background and has been sheathed only to the extent that the surplus employee is prepared unconditionally to accept the proposed severance package. Subject to the untested implications of the 1976 regulation,[55] it follows that the senior manager who cannot reach an agreement on the severance proposal must then sue the government. His claim will rest on two fronts: first, that the Crown's right of dismissal has been abrogated, in part by statute and in part by the terms of employment; and secondly, that the particular circumstances of his case merit the award of damages in excess of the severance payment and any other benefits offered by the government.

What has been the experience in British Columbia? It is difficult to be precise[56] because when severance packages are offered, it is in the government's interest to deal with terminated excluded personnel on an individual and private basis. This explains the absence of general standards or criteria. Information costs are high for each affected employee and leverage tends to favour the employer whose representatives are the only party privy to the compensation criteria and their relative weights as applied across the interdepartmental ranks of senior personnel. The surplus managers usually want to exit quietly to avoid the stigma of adverse publicity, to save legal expenses and to avoid court delays.

It would appear that settlements have been reached more easily among those managers and senior personnel who have served less than six years with the government. At the other end of the spectrum, senior managers close to retirement have accepted augmented pensions to bring them up to maximum superannuation.

There are indications, however, that some managers who have been dismissed after more than fifteen years service with the BC government have refused to accept the 'golden handshake' and will take their claims to court. Without more facts it is difficult to predict the outcome of these lawsuits. However, it is safe to assume that they will have little effect on the present firings because 'the majority of dismissed government managers will have signed releases and will be unable to sue'[57] by the time the courts have ruled.

This pattern of dismissal with compensation in lieu of notice accords closely with the practice in the private sector where corporate executives are involved. This suggests a convergence of the legal principles governing no-cause dismissals in the business and government communities—or perhaps more accurately, an appreciation on the part of government that any reliance on the 'anachronism' of the 'at pleasure' common law and general statutes [58] may not stand up before a hostile court. It remains regrettable, however, that the firings are made without the benefit of published criteria or minimum courtesies, within difficult time constraints and without any prospect of review or appeal.[59]

FROM STATUS TO CONTRACT IN THE SENIOR PUBLIC SERVICE

In British Columbia, the Public Service Act does not apply to persons appointed by the cabinet to positions designated 'as requiring special professional, technical or administrative qualifications.'[60] Under this authority, a former political assistant to the present premier was appointed government agent in Kelowna, a position normally filled by public service competition. The provision also enabled the premier to transfer his communications adviser from a pre-election deputy minister's post to a post-election contract covering the same services after questions were raised about the partisan activities of the adviser when he took a leave of absence during the campaign to work directly for the Social Credit party.

The same type of legislation also permits the appointment of political assistants, partisan advisers, and professional consultants whose viewpoints and skills are sought by ministers to help them discharge their responsibilities during their time in office. These are order-in-council appointments that are sometimes tied to detailed personal service contracts. The appointees are treated separately from public servants in respect of compensation, performance review and dismissal conditions.

In recent years, several jurisdictions have transferred the concept of contracted services into the senior non-partisan ranks of what had been hitherto the permanent public service. It is understood, for example, that the Alberta Department of Justice has hired some ten to twelve senior personnel on contract, including the Legislative Counsel. The Alberta Public Service Act[61] provides for such employment contracts and specifies that these contracts must set out the remuneration, duration and the other principal conditions of the employment relationship.

Under the new Quebec legislation,[62] deputy ministers and assistant and associate deputy ministers become 'administrators of state' in terms of their classification in the public service. Administrators of state are appointed by the premier who also has the sole authority to recommend their dismissal 'for just and sufficient cause'.[63] The legislation is silent on the issue of dismissal without cause.[64] An interesting provision of the same act allows for the engagement of a deputy minister or an assistant or associate deputy minister by contract. That person is no longer a 'public servant' for the purposes of the act.[65]

The new legislation will likely encourage the development of contracts fashioned to particular circumstances and governing salaries, fringe benefits, security of tenure, and termination arrangements. It has not been uncommon for similar personal service contracts to be bargained for by some senior management in highly visible Crown corporations.[66] Perhaps the Quebec measure represents an extension of those developments, which in turn are influenced by private sector companies in their recruitment of senior executives. In the private sector, the well-advised, sought-after senior executive seeks economic security through contractual protection against the possibility of hostile takeovers or a future squeeze-out by controlling interests.

Parallel scenarios come to mind in the senior public service in the form of newly elected governments or disenchanted ministers who seek to replace the incumbents with advisers and officials deemed to be more compatible and competent in the new circumstances. There is little doubt that the contract model could better anticipate a mutual interest in predictability and certainty. Provided there is some equality of bargaining power, appropriate termination provisions could be worked out between the parties at the outset of their relationship.

More study is required before the full ramifications of these developments can be measured and evaluated. Given the rapid turnover of deputy ministers in several provincial governments in recent years, perhaps the adoption of the contract approach simply reflects a recognition that employment in the uppermost ranks of the public service is risky and may be of limited duration. The Alberta experience in hiring senior lawyers on contract also confirms the advantages of a contract approach for attracting experienced professionals into the public service for specified duties for a fixed period of time.

The widespread application of the contract model would raise concerns for the existence of a career, non-partisan public service but for the legal planner, employment contracts reduce uncertainties in the employer-employee relationship, particularly when the question of termination or dismissal arises. Hindsight instructs us that the most appropriate time to negotiate termination provisions is at the time of hiring not firing.

In the Quebec example, the first draft of the proposed employment contract for DMs and ADMs provides for a fixed expiration date for the agreement, a right in the appointee to resign the office upon giving three months' notice and authority in the government to end the arrangement without notice 'for misappropriation of funds, faulty administration or grievous fault, or for any reason equally serious.'[67] Some ten months after the passage of the legislation in Quebec the details of its administration apparently are still being worked out. It will be important to review its implementation in the interval remaining before the Quebec election writ is issued.

I would venture the suggestion that contracted services will become more common at the middle and senior management levels of what we still call the 'public service'. We may be witnessing the thin edge of the wedge, so that the preference for contract over status becomes the norm because it is in the parties' mutual interest to establish certain and specific conditions of the employment relationship.

CONCLUSIONS

Senior public servants are normally appointed by a cabinet order-in-council or after a competition, by the public service commission or its equivalent. The first group includes deputy ministers, sometimes associate and assistant deputies, and career civil servants holding statutory posts. In the second group we find senior managers, directors and executive officers, and members of professional groups whose common attributes are management responsibilities and exclusion from union bargaining units.

Both groups are vulnerable to the full force of the historic doctrine of holding office at the pleasure of the Crown. This means that they may be summarily dismissed without severance benefits unless protection is available in legislation, regulations, the terms of their appointment or in contractual arrangements recognized by the courts. The strength of these restrictions on the Crown's right of dismissal will vary from province to province.

In addition, the constraints, where they exist, principally serve to compensate the terminated employee and do not prevent the government from firing the public servant. The remedy rests in damages and not reinstatement and it is commonplace for government employers to offer ex gratia severance payments to senior personnel who have been dismissed without cause. In other cases, the employees must resort to lawsuits to press their claims.

The common thread in both circumstances is the readiness of governments in recent years to take a very strict legal approach to their obligations as employers of the career, non-partisan public service. The resurrection of the 'at pleasure' principle and the adoption of a hardline legal stance coincides with political decisions to reduce government programs, reorganize departments, chop staff, and to favour the appointment of politically compatible executives at the higher levels.

The cumulative impact of these actions will reinforce the attractiveness of the 'at pleasure' rule to contemporary governments whose handling of senior service dismissals would be characterized as crude and inequitable in private sector circles. Without legislation to provide reasonable procural and compensation requirements, senior public servants who are fired without cause will continue to be second-class citizens compared to their organized staff and private sector counterparts.

NOTES

The research assistance of Susan Lyons is gratefully acknowledged as well as the advice and comment of conference participants.

1. Hon. Eric Bernston, Regina *Leader Post*, 27 April 1982, cited in H.J. Michelmann and J.S. Steeves, *Consolidation of Power in Saskatchewan: The Conservative Transformation of the Public Service* (Saskatoon: University of Saskatchewan, 1984, mimeo), p. 10.
2. Victoria *Times-Colonist*, 15 March 1984.
3. The Ontario practices may well be more considerate of the redundant or displaced senior public servant based upon an initial perusal of their Civil Service Commission's administrative manual.
4. Statutes of Quebec, 1983 (Bill 51), proclaimed 21 December 1983.
5. E.g., in the Alberta Public Service Act, Revised Statutes of Alberta, 1980, CP-31, s. 29.
6. *Neil v. The Government of Saskatchewan*, Sask. Queen's Bench No. 4331, 13 April 1984 at p. 12 (unreported to date).
7. *De Dohse v. R.* (1866), 66 Law Journal Queen's Bench 422 (House of Lords); *Re Tuffnell* (1876), 3 Chancery Division 164; *Grant v. Secretary of State for India in Council* (1877), 2 Law Reports, Common Pleas Division 445.
8. *De Dohse v. R.*
9. *Dunn v. R.*, [1896] 1 Queen's Bench 116 (Court of Appeal).
10. *Gould v. Stuart*, [1896] Appeal Cases 575 (Judicial Committee of the Privy Council).
11. *Stuart v. Gould* (1895), 16 New South Wales Law Reports 132 at pp. 137–8 (NSW Supreme Court).
12. Discussed in *Young v. Adams*, [1898] Appeal Cases 469 (JCPC).
13. *Reilly v. R.*, [1934] Appeal Cases 176 (JCPC).
14. *Wicks v. Attorney General of British Columbia*, [1975] 4 Western Weekly Reports 283 (BC Supreme Court).
15. *Mallett v. New Brunswick* (1982), 142 Dominion Law Reports (3d) 161 (NB Queen's Bench) aff'd (1983) 47 NB Reports (2d) 234 (Court of Appeal); see also *Jones v. City of New Westminster* (1983), 148 Dominion Law Reports (3d) 279 (BC Court of Appeal).
16. *Clark v. R. in Right of British Columbia* (1979), 15 BC Law Reports 311 (BC Supreme Court).
17. A senior Crown solicitor considers the following factors in advising his client in these cases: 1) Check terms of appointment, for example, in the relevant order-in-council—does any language directly or indirectly replace the 'at pleasure' principle? 2) Check employee's permanent file to determine if any document suggests, confirms or implies representations made to the employee in the event of dismissal. 3) Examine letters of offer and acceptance and interview senior official who hired the dismissed employee to ascertain the possibility of a personal contract between the deputy minister (for example) and the dismissed employee.

18. For example, see Public Service Act, Revised Statutes of British Columbia, 1979, c. 343. s. 48(1): 'No provision contained in this Act, or in a collective agreement between the government and a bargaining agent representing its employees, impairs the authority of the Lieutenant Governor in Council to remove or dismiss any employee.'

19. *Ison v. R. in Right of British Columbia*, BC Supreme Court, No. C 760936, 1 June 1976, Vancouver Registry; *Wuorinen v. Workers' Compensation Board*, BC Supreme Court, No. C 820524, 28 February 1983, Vancouver Registry; *Davidson v. The Queen in Right of British Columbia,* BC Supreme Court, No. C359/77, 25 January 1984, Vernon Registry.

20. Per Laskin, C. J. in *Wilson and Nova Scotia Government Employees' Association v. Civil Service Commission of Nova Scotia* (1981), 35 National Reports 103 at p. 112 (Supreme Court of Canada), a case involving legislation and a collective agreement. In an earlier decision, the late chief justice urged re-examination of 'the old common law rule . . . that a person engaged as an office holder at pleasure may be put out without reason or prior notice . . .': *Re Nicholson and Haldimand-Norfolk Regional Board of Commissioners of Police* (1979), 88 Dominion Law Reports (3d) 671 at p. 679 (Supreme Court of Canada).

21. Revised Statutes of Manitoba, 1970, c. 180, s. 18; Revised Statutes of Saskatchewan, 1978, c. 15, s. 15.

22. E.g., in the Manitoba Act, s. 19(1) (a).

23. E.g., the Saskatchewan Public Service Act, Revised Statutes of Saskatchewan, 1978, c. P–42, divides the public service into classified (Public Service Commission) and unclassified (cabinet) categories. In the BC act, see comparable results in ss. 2, 10, and 20.

24. Public Service Act, Revised Statutes of British Columbia, 1979, c. 343, s. 10.

25. *B.C. Reg.* 91/76. Gazette, Part II, 17 February 1976, pp. 109–10. The employees include executive assistants and other ministerial staff.

26. Michael Davison, chairman of the Government Employee Relations Bureau, who had deputy minister rank himself per the Public Service Act, s. 55(1).

27. Michelmann and Steeves, *Consolidation of Power in Saskatchewan*, p. 10.

28. Ibid.

29. See B.C. Public Service Act, s. 2(a).

30. Michelmann and Steeves, *Consolidation of Power in Saskatchewan*, pp. 6–15 and Appendix I for details of the positions affected by the Conservative transition.

31. *Neil v. The Government of Saskatchewan*, at p. 3.

32. *Sask. Reg.* 1754/72, Part IX, s. 9.2.

33. See also *Marshall v. Government of Saskatchewan* [1982], 3 Western Weekly Reports 244 (Sask. Queen's Bench), presently on appeal. In Ontario, a senior manager who was red-circled when his position was reclassified lost his claim of constructive dismissal without notice because the Crown has the power to dismiss at pleasure: *Malone v. The Queen in Right of Ontario* (1984), 45 Ontario Reports (2d) 206.

34. The Charter, s.2 (d): 'Everyone has the following fundamental freedoms: (d) freedom of association'; s. 7 reads: 'Everyone has the right to life, liberty and security of the person and the right not to be deprived therof except in accordance with the prin-

ciples of fundamental justice.'

35. *Neil v. The Government of Saskatchewan,* p. 12.
36. MacLean, J. referred to the separate stream of 'permanent, non-political, professional staff of the civil service' and kept them distinct from his acceptance of the government's argument that cabinet ought to be able to revoke order in council appointments in putting together 'an effective public service'.
37. Details provided in interviews. In each case, compensation was recommended for lack of notice, loss of employee benefits, and foregone vacation leave as well as an allowance for legal fees and relocation expenses.
38. Saskatchewan Public Service Act, s. 37.
39. E.g., the dismissal appeal of *Joseph Jeerakathil*, 4 March 1983 (5 pages).
40. Ibid., p. 4.
41. According to Michelmann and Steeves, *Consolidation of Power in Saskatchewan*, p. 13, the Conservatives claimed that DNS 'was exceptionally patronage-ridden' and moreover was unnecessary since they preferred to treat the province as one administrative unit.
42. *Jeerakathil* decision, p. 4.
43. Ibid., p. 1.
44. Ibid., p. 4.
45. *B.C. Reg.* 508/79, as amended by Treasury Board Orders 47, 65, 78, 97, 105, 107, 114, and 121.
46. B.C. Public Service Act, s. 48 (2).
47. Ibid., s.10 (2).
48. Ibid., ss. 46–8.
49. Ibid., s.48 (1).
50. The last two directors of the Human Rights Branch were dismissed (the first resigned). The middle appointee, Nola Landucci, sued for wrongful dismissal and settled for $24,000 while claiming that the government had 'paid out $1 million to $2 million' to settle unjust dismissals in 1982, Victoria *Times-Colonist,* 23 May 1982. The branch was abolished in 1984.
51. Deputy Provincial Secretary, Memorandum to Deputy Ministers, 24 January 1984, p. l.
52. Ibid.
53. Ibid. Apparently the deputies have now been instructed to meet with the employee personally and not send a nominee. Also the time for acceptance has been made slightly more flexible.
54. See text accompanying note 15.
55. *B.C. Reg.* 91/76.
56. Consternation, disbelief and uncertainty quickly engulf the dismissed manager. Faced with the severance ultimatum, he tends to search about for advice from close friends, and the name of a lawyer. In the author's experience, each case proceeds on a quiet, *de novo* basis. The information meeting called by the BC Government Managers' Association to help its four hundred members in Victoria on 16 March 1984 drew less than thirty-five participants. Publicity about the purpose of the meeting probably did not help attendance. The episode confirmed the managers' reluc-

tance to speak out collectively about the government's actions.

57. Provided by a solicitor retained by several dismissed public servants.

58. Recalling the description of Laskin C.J., note 19. The new Civil Service Act in New Brunswick (1984, c.5.1, s.20) provides an instructive starting point for desirable legislative reform in its simple statement that 'termination of the employment of a deputy head or an employee shall be governed by the ordinary rules of contract' in the absence of an expressly contrary statutory provision.

59. The total impact of these factors on the senior ranks of the BC public service is incalculable.

60. B.C. Public Service Act, s. 2(b).

61. Alberta Public Service Act, s. 29.

62. Quebec Public Service Act (Bill 51), Statutes of Quebec, 1983, s. 53(3).

63. Ibid., ss. 54, 60.

64. The general construction of Ch. III, Div. III on 'administrators of state' suggests that these appointees may only be dismissed with reasonable notice or compensation in lieu if 'just and sufficient cause' is not established.

65. Subject to the continued operation of the sanctions found in Ch. VII.

66. Confirmed in interviews with several directors of federal Crown corporations involved in commercial activities.

67. Draft Contract Form, government of Quebec, April 1984, paragraph 6. The proposed termination provisions are vague (to the present) about severance pay. Nor is there any requirement that the same form contract be used in every case.

PART III

Financial Management

Effective use of financial resources is no less important in the public sector than it is in private business. One of the first attempts to discuss efficiency in government in a systematic way was made by the Glassco Commission on Government Organization (1965). The commission performed a great service in challenging governments to pay more attention to efficiency. Nevertheless, the first selection in this section, by A.W. Johnson, argues that its definition of efficiency missed the mark in equating efficiency in government with efficiency in business.

A consummate public servant himself (he apprenticed with the CCF government of Tommy Douglas in Saskatchewan before going on to serve in many senior posts in the federal government), Johnson argues that there are different types of efficiency—administrative efficiency, policy efficiency, service efficiency—and that different types of organization will define those qualities in different ways. He also points out the importance of cultivating public servants' motivation to achieve efficiency. If there was any doubt about the value of revisiting the classic literature, this article should dispel it. Questions about efficiency are still widely discussed today, but it would be difficult to find a modern treatment that explores these issues more thoroughly than Johnson did, more than four decades ago.

One of the many areas where efficiency is important is the budget process. Canada was one of the first countries to experiment with the program budgeting approach pioneered in the US. Beginning with a system that it called Planning-Programming-Budgeting (PPB), the federal government then attempted to improve on that model with a new Policy and Expenditure Management System (PEMS), and then, when that became too complex and top-heavy, moved on to program reviews and business plans. Meanwhile, several other jurisdictions experimented with another American invention, called zero-based budgeting (ZBB). The late Aaron Wildavsky made his name with a book-length analysis of the budget process in the US federal government that is still regarded as the seminal work in this field, and although not Canadian he often commented on Canadian affairs. In the paper included here, written in the late 1970s, Wildavsky argues that none of the innovations noted above can meet the needs of budget-makers as well as the traditional line-item budget that lists all objects of expenditure in great detail.

Governments spend a great deal of money, and it is essential that there be adequate controls on how that money is spent. Thus another central aspect of financial management is the way the results of government activity are assessed and evaluated. The role of the auditor general has always been important, but in the 1970s legislation was passed that dramatically expanded that role. Formerly limited to the traditional attest audit—in which the main purpose was to ensure that the federal government's financial statements were accurate—now the auditor general's office took a much broader view, moving beyond basic financial auditing to comment on the ultimate value of the activities funded by government.

Sharon Sutherland has long been skeptical about this change. In the article included here she argues that it has transformed the auditor general from an external observer conducting an objective review into a political player employing techniques of dubious credibility. Her criticism is aimed partly at the incumbent of the office at the time, who in her view had his own political agenda, and partly at the techniques he wanted to employ, which she felt were poorly suited to the job.

Rodney Dobell and David Zussman pick up the latter point in their article, the last in this section. Explaining how program evaluation was conceived as a flexible but scientifically rigorous technique for assessing the economy, efficiency, and effectiveness of government programs, they then go on to suggest a number of reasons why it was not living up to expectations. They conclude by challenging us to accept the idea that evaluation is more art than science: it will never provide simple, definitive answers, but it can still play an important role in the policy-making process by stimulating debate.

It is interesting to note how many of the issues raised in these papers, all written more than twenty years ago, are still current today. There is still a tendency to define efficiency in business terms without recognizing how different the government environment is. There have been many variations on program budgeting since Wildavsky wrote his article, but it is the traditional line-item budget that has outlived all the complex variations. The role of the auditor general is still questioned from time to time, and we still have not found a completely satisfactory way of evaluating public policy.

18

Efficiency in Government and Business

A. W. Johnson

The Royal Commission on Government Organization—the Glassco Commission—has aroused an unusual interest in efficiency in government. For some, its reports—frequently unread—have confirmed a long-standing suspicion that governments always have been, and always will be, inefficient. For others the Commission's reports hold out a new hope that business-like methods can and will be introduced into government. For still others the reports reveal once again a profound misunderstanding on the part of businessmen as to the process of parliamentary government, and confirm once more the need for continuing organization and methods studies within government. For a few—the management consultants—the reports and the public interest which they have aroused create a sort of happy hunting ground where new commissions and new studies can be proposed with confidence—all of them requiring the specialized skills of the management consultant.

However heterogeneous the responses to the Glassco Commission's work, anyone who is interested in perfecting the processes of government will welcome warmly this new-found interest in government administration. Certainly we in the Institute of Public Administration of Canada do. It has been our objective, since our organization was formed sixteen years ago, to stimulate greater interest in, and more careful attention to, the problems and the potential of public administration. Oftentimes our own specialized interest, and perhaps the lack of public interest in the processes of government, have tended to propel us toward one pole of our organization—that of the purely professional society. But fortunately individual members and the governmental and corporate supporters of the Institute have cultivated and sustained the other and more important goal of our organization—that of research, of study and of teaching in the field of public policy and public administration. The work of the Glassco Commission will undoubtedly provide a further stimulus to this aspect of the Institute's work.

Having said this, I find myself wanting to sound a note of caution about the premises which seem to underlie the discussions of the Glassco reports, and indeed the reports themselves.

First, there seems to me to be abroad an assumption that 'everyone knows what

A.W. Johnson, 'Efficiency in Government and Business', *Canadian Public Administration* 6, 3 (1963): 245–60. Courtesy of The Institute of Public Administration Canada.

efficiency means'. It is simply a matter of good organization, of effective management practices, of streamlined procedures, and the like. But is this all that there is to effective government? Are there not other dimensions to 'efficiency' which are equally important to, if not more important than, the purely administrative or management aspect?

Second, the proposition seems to have been accepted, without too much critical scrutiny, that the methods by which efficiency is achieved in business are equally applicable in government—or very nearly so. There is a science of administration, in other words, which can be employed with equal effectiveness in business or in government. But is it true that the 'efficiency techniques' of business are entirely applicable in government—or at least in all phases of government? Can efficiency in the public services be achieved simply by perfecting the 'horizontal' processes—organization, financial management, personnel management, and the like? Or are there large areas of public administration where new 'efficiency techniques' must be evolved, or the conventional ones substantially adapted if the unique program problems of the public services are to be evaluated effectively?

Third, I find myself wondering, if governments are less efficient than they might and should be—and surely all of us will acknowledge that they are—why is this so? Is it enough to say that organization is defective, or that procedural practices are deficient, and they should be remedied? Or should we stop to consider whether there is in the civil service a sufficient 'efficiency motivation'—a motivation upon which we can build so as to ensure a *continuing* concern for effective operation? Or must we reconcile ourselves to the need for periodic royal commissions which will shake up the public services on these occasions, only to be followed by intervals of decline and decay? This sometimes seems to be the assumption which underlies the public discussions of the Glassco reports.

These are the questions which I want to consider tonight. Please notice that I am not pretending to analyze the Glassco Commission reports, nor to analyze the analyses that have been made of them. Instead, what I am trying to do is to question whether we really have thought through what we mean by efficiency in government, whether we really know the methods by which it can be achieved, and whether we have considered carefully enough the source of efficiency motives in government—if any.

WHAT IS EFFICIENCY?

My first question is what do we mean when we talk of efficiency? The conventional notion is clear enough: it simply means reducing administrative expenses, eliminating waste and extravagance, and speeding up service to the public. This is what I am inclined to call 'administrative efficiency'.

The notion of 'administrative efficiency' first was developed, as we all know, in private business—specifically, in manufacturing enterprises. Its pioneers—Henri Fayol and Frederick W. Taylor—were seeking to increase productivity, to maximize production, and they sought to do so by improving work arrangements. Given the production of a certain commodity, given sometimes the present technology, how could an enterprise best divide and order the processes of manufacture in order to maximize outputs and minimize inputs? The techniques they used now are well known: product simplification and standardization, production planning and control, proper division of work, the use of management improvement techniques, staff training and the development of happy staff relations, performance analysis and control, and the rest.

I do not want to elaborate on these techniques of 'administrative efficiency' right now—that will come later. My present purpose is to point out the premises upon which 'administrative efficiency' is based: this kind of efficiency takes for granted the policy decisions which created the manufacturing enterprise in the first place. 'Administrative efficiency' *assumes* that the right product is being produced; it *assumes* that the market for the product exists or can be developed; it *assumes* that the plant is properly located; and frequently it *assumes* that the technology of production being used is the appropriate technology.

But notice that if the wrong policy decisions had been made in the first place—if the plant were poorly located or the market were insufficient—not all the administrative efficiency in the world would compensate for these errors in decision-making. There is, in short, another kind of efficiency which is of a higher order than 'administrative efficiency', and that is 'policy efficiency'—the making of the right policy decisions.

In manufacturing enterprise the components of 'policy efficiency'—though it is not called that—are well known. Economic studies precede a decision to manufacture a new product—studies both of the potential market for the product, and of the manufacturing processes which will have to be developed. Feasibility studies determine the economics of the enterprise—studies which forecast the sales revenues and all of the costs of production: capital, labour, raw materials, transportation, and so on. Plant location studies compare the economics of alternative plant locations, given the differentials between the wage costs, transportation costs, and power costs of different areas. Financial analysis determines how much of the capital can be interest-bearing and how much must be equity capital in order that costs might be minimized, while at the same time retaining control in the hands of the sponsors of the enterprise. 'Policy efficiency', in short, is what the economists call proper resource allocation.

The same distinction between 'administrative efficiency' and 'policy efficiency' can be made in government. 'Administrative efficiency'—what the Glassco Commission concerned itself with primarily—consists of good organization, efficient procedures, effective financial control, proper inventory control, appropriate paperwork and systems management, and the rest. 'Policy efficiency', on the other hand, is a matter of making the right policy decisions, of selecting the appropriate programs in order to achieve the government's objectives.

Let me give a few examples. If a highway is properly located, given the trends in population distribution, travel patterns, and the rest, the taxpayers will be saved enormous sums of money in their travel costs. If welfare programs are constructed so as to return people to the active labour force, the social aid bill which the taxpayers bear will be significantly reduced. If treatment programs in mental hospitals are calculated to return patients to the community the number of mental institutions required will be controlled. If education programs produce the kind of trained labour force which the economy requires, the numbers of unemployed will be reduced. On a more sophisticated level still, if a proper balance is achieved between monetary policy, fiscal policy, and trade policy, the rate of growth of the economy will be increased, and the cost to the community of unemployment will be reduced.

Here once again, the economies of 'policy efficiency' greatly outweigh the savings which can be achieved by 'administrative efficiency'. One bad policy decision—for example, the construction of an uneconomic railway or road—will cost the taxpayer more than can possibly be saved by better control over the purchase of underwear for the armed forces.

It is important; in other words, not to be misled when we talk about efficiency. 'Administrative efficiency' unquestionably is important, but let no one think that it is the only kind of efficiency, or even that it is the most important kind.

Now let me build into this framework a third kind of efficiency— 'service efficiency'. This is an obscure phrase, I know, but it is the only one I can think of to describe 'effectiveness' as opposed to 'efficiency'.

All of us are familiar, I am sure, with the conflict which sometimes exists between administrative economies on the one hand, and the provision of better service to the public on the other. Let me give some examples. It is almost always possible to achieve economies of scale through the centralization of services, such as health and welfare. But the effect of doing so is to make the services less accessible to the public. It is always possible to enforce safety programs more efficiently by giving the safety inspectors more power, or by making the regulations more explicit; but the effect is to subject the citizen to requirements that are sometimes impractical, if not downright hostile to his freedom of action. It is frequently possible to streamline financial processes by reducing some of the controls over departmental spending, but to do so may be to reduce parliamentary control over the government and the civil service.

I acknowledge that I have collected under this heading of 'service efficiency' a heterogeneous group of public service objectives, including service to the public, responsiveness to public opinion, and the preservation of parliamentary control. But my point, I hope, is clear: efficiency in government must be measured not in economic terms alone. Equally, indeed more important, it must be measured in terms of the effectiveness with which it provides public services within the context of constitutional government. Public services must be readily and equally accessible to all citizens. They must be close enough to the citizen, in fact, that he can exert an influence upon them—adapting them to the needs of the community as the needs of the community change. The regulatory functions of the state must be discharged not for the sole purpose of protecting people and their property, but also with the purpose of preserving to the maximum extent possible the rights of the citizens being regulated. All public services must be provided and financed in such a way that the cabinet remains in control of the bureaucracy and that parliament remains in control of both. The prime measure of efficiency in government, I am arguing, is whether the government provides the public services the public wants and where it wants them, and whether the public services provided—and the public servants who provide them remain firmly in the control of the public's representatives.

Let me make one more point about 'service efficiency'. In business this kind of efficiency is less distinguishable from 'policy efficiency' and 'administrative efficiency' than it is in government. If an enterprise fails to provide what the public wants, or fails to respond to shifts in consumer tastes, an economic penalty sooner or later must be paid. Sales will decline. So 'service efficiency' in business is looked upon in economic terms. In government, however, the penalty for inefficiency in service is a political or a constitutional one: the government is defeated or constitutional processes are eroded, or both. And only a fairly perceptive observer will see the relationship—perhaps I should say the conflict—between 'administrative efficiency' and 'service efficiency'.

My first observation, then, is this: it is a mistake to judge efficiency only in administrative terms. It would be possible to have the slickest and the most streamlined government in the world, and yet to have public policies which resulted in a gross misallocation of resources, or public services which were quite incompatible with the objectives of constitutional democracy. I am not suggesting by any means that we in the Institute of Public Administration should ignore administrative efficiency: quite the contrary, it is one of our primary goals. But I do suggest that as public servants we have a responsibility to look to the broader kinds of efficiency as well— 'policy efficiency' and 'service efficiency'—if we are to serve the public well.

EFFICIENCY METHODS

If I have identified correctly the several kinds of efficiency in government, the next question is whether we know how to achieve them. It is usually assumed—I suspect that the Glassco Commission assumed—that the methods by which business achieves efficiency are equally applicable in government. This may be so. But if, on the other hand, a different approach is required in government, or a substantial adaptation of business methods is needed, we will be misled if we simply try to transplant into the public service the 'efficiency techniques' of private business. At best we will have done an incomplete job.

It is in the field of 'administrative efficiency', of course, that the approach of private business is best known. The goal as we all know, is to maximize output and to minimize expense. This means that each factor of production—labour, equipment, and so on—must be identified, and its contribution to production—its productivity—must be measured. If the productivity of a given factor, labour for example, can be increased, then the cost per unit of production will be reduced. If on the other hand, the productivity of a given factor of production has reached its limit, management may seek to substitute a cheaper production factor—equipment in place of labour, for example.

The key to this approach is measurability: you must be able to measure the inputs—man-hours, equipment hours, and so on—and you must be able to measure the outputs—units of commodity produced. Having done this it becomes possible to establish a 'standard' as to the quantity of inputs required in order to produce a given unit of output. The standard may be the average of previous levels of productivity, or it may be a target level established through controlled production experiments. In either event these standards are applied to the manufacturing process, and the various factors of production are expected to perform at the target levels.

There are, of course, techniques for raising productivity to the standards which have been set, or for raising the standards themselves. These include greater specialization in the manufacturing processes, production planning and control, improvements in organization and coordination, the simplification of work processes through work study and measurement, staff training, and so on.

These techniques were developed specifically for manufacturing operations, but they have been adapted to office operations. This has been possible wherever inputs and outputs have both been found to be measurable. Production planning and control takes the form of planning and controlling paper operations and paper flows. Work simplification takes the form of analyzing what is 'added' at each stage of the office procedure, and of eliminating steps which are found to be unnecessary. Staff training and development and space layout studies both are applied much as they are in manufacturing operations. And office equipment—notably, today, data-processing equipment—is substituted for labour where it is found to be a cheaper 'input' than are clerical man-hours.

These techniques have been found to be applicable in many office operations, but by no means in all. Wherever the output is diffuse, or does not lend itself to precise measurement, it is unlikely that these conventional efficiency techniques can be used. This is true not only in the production of office services but in the production of other services as well—legal, medical, and personal services, to name a few. The point to be noted is that business itself has found it difficult, sometimes impossible, to apply the efficiency techniques of commodity-producing industries to industries which produce services. And this is nearly always where the output does not lend itself to precise measurement.

Let me give an example to try to illustrate my point. One of the major service industries in Canada is the one which provides hospital services. Here we find a considerable differentiation in labour inputs—professional nurses, nursing aids, ward aids, orderlies, and technologists of various categories. And their inputs are measurable—they may be expressed in terms of the number of hours of direct service to patients, and the number of hours of general service. The other inputs can also be identified and measured: drugs, X-ray and other equipment, food, linen services, and so on.

But when it comes to measuring output, the matter becomes rather more difficult. The 'true output' is not easily measured. The health of a patient who leaves hospital is different—in one way or another—than it was when he entered. But it does not lend itself to precise measurement, except in the unhappiest of circumstances. So how can inputs be related to output, if the output cannot be measured?

I chose this example not only because it illustrates the difference between commodity-producing industries and service-producing industries, but also because it illustrates the adaptations than can be made to conventional 'efficiency techniques'. Hospital administrators recognized that they were unable to measure real output, so they sought some substitute, some intermediate measure. They struck on the notion of 'units of service'—the number of patient-days of care that the hospital renders.

With the patient-day as the unit of service, it became possible to differentiate between the kinds of service provided—surgical patient-days, obstetrical patient-days, medical patient-days—and to determine the inputs of labour and equipment required to provide each kind of patient-day of care.

This is the approach used in those service industries which seek to apply the conventional 'efficiency techniques'—they establish units of service and then measure the inputs required to produce a single unit of service. I want to emphasize however, that not all service industries by any means have been able to apply these techniques.

EFFICIENCY METHODS IN GOVERNMENT

Now let me return to government—the largest service industry there is. It will have become obvious that we should no more expect to be able to apply the 'efficiency techniques' of commodity-producing industries to government than we are able to apply them to other service industries. Some government services, such as large-scale paperwork operations, road building, the production and sale of electric power, and sewer and water systems, lend themselves to these 'efficiency techniques'. But a great many do not.

Consider some of the services which governments provide: public health nursing, primary and secondary schools, agricultural extension, social work services, and psychiatric research, to name a few. In each case the work inputs are measurable enough: staff time, differentiated between different classes of workers, materials used, equipment employed, travel expenses, telephone expenses, and so on.

But the output of these employees—the ultimate output—is extremely difficult to measure. This is partly because it is inherently difficult to identify and to measure, and partly because the results become apparent only several years after the services have been rendered. Here are some examples. The results of the child health clinics conducted by public health nurses become apparent only in the morbidity and mortality statistics of the future. The results of the education given in primary and secondary schools are felt only when the children involved have become active members of the labour force—and then it is difficult to compare what is with what might have been had the schooling not been given. The agricultural education given farmers by 'Ag Reps' becomes evident years later in higher and more stable crop production, but even then it is difficult to establish a clear causal relationship. The effect of social workers' efforts may never be known statistically; all we know is that certain families or young people or offenders have become active and productive members of the community. The relationship between psychiatric research and more effective treatment of the mentally ill becomes known, and even measurable statistically, but the lag between the cause and the effect is very substantial indeed.

Obviously we cannot expect to measure real output at the time the service is given and sometimes we may never be able to do so (though I think we should try much harder than we do). All we can hope to do is to measure the units of service given—and even here the exercise is sometimes futile (for example in primary and secondary education). But it *is* possible in some branches of government to measure the units of service that are provided—the number of clinics held by the public health nurse or the number of farm equipment demonstrations given by the agricultural representative—and where this is possible the conventional 'efficiency techniques' may be adapted to the needs of the public service.

My point, then, is this: the methods used by business to achieve 'administrative efficiency' may be used directly by governments only in a few areas of public service. If we are to develop 'efficiency techniques' for the rest of the service we must adapt and innovate to a very considerable extent.

'POLICY EFFICIENCY'

The same holds true of 'policy efficiency'. Business administration schools have developed a considerable body of knowledge as to how manufacturing enterprises can achieve 'policy efficiency'—they teach market analysis, plant location analysis, alternative forms of industry organization, including horizontal and vertical integration, the strategy of competition, and so on. But none of this is useful to us in the public service.

What *is* useful, however, are the underlying methods being used by businessmen. What I am talking about now—or trying to—is the use of scientific method, of rational planning. There is, of course, a lot of guesswork in the policy decisions of boards of directors, but the forward-looking firm seeks to reduce the guesswork to a minimum. The elements in decision-making are analysed and measured statistically wherever possible: market trends, changes in consumer tastes, whether involuntary or induced, trends in costs, trends in technology, the behaviour of competitors, and so on. And alternative courses for achieving a given objective are examined before a decision is made. To take a simple example, the productive capacity of an industry is expanded only after markets have been analyzed, after alternative plant locations have been examined, after alternative methods of production have been explored, and so on.

There are areas of government where the same analytical processes can easily be employed. Road location by departments of highways is a good example: public servants study traffic patterns and road-use trends, and then, using the benefit-cost analysis approach, determine the optimum location and design of a highway. This sort of approach is quite common in the engineering phases of government work though I suspect that the public is quite unaware of the use of these planning techniques.

It is more difficult to apply such planning techniques in the area of social policies though some advances have been made. It is in this area, however, where there is the greatest room for innovation and adaptation.

Let me give you some examples. Governments have assumed responsibility for the community's costs of hospitalization and, to a substantial extent, for the costs of nursing home care for the aged and the disabled. Having done so, they inevitably confront demands for enlarged facilities, as hospital utilization rises and as the population of the aged and disabled increases. Two courses are open to the government. One is to meet the demand, locating the facilities as rationally as possible, using population studies as a guide. The other is to determine whether alternative forms of care

are possible or preferable. Are there disabilities for which preventive or even earlier treatment would reduce the incidence of institutionalization? Is it possible to embark upon rehabilitation programs which would reduce the length of stay in institutions, thus increasing the 'turnover' in public institutions—to put it crudely? Is it possible to provide home-care services which would be less costly than institutionalization?

In other words, the objective is to care for the sick and the disabled, and the problem is not necessarily one of providing more capital facilities. The economic and social costs might well be lower if alternative methods of prevention, treatment and rehabilitation, were adopted.

Let me give just one more example before I go on. Everyone is concerned today with the present and potential problems of providing employment in an age of automation. And educational facilities—university, technical and vocational, and other specialized facilities—are being built at an unprecedented rate. It may well be that by sheer chance the governments involved—and all three levels of government are involved—will construct facilities which will produce a trained labour force with just the skills required for the future. But if we don't, the cost to society in unemployment and reduced levels of productivity will be enormous. To the extent that governments do, on the other hand, make rational and accurate calculations in this field, the efficiency of the economy will be greatly enhanced.

To make policy decisions such as these—and all of us could give many more examples—is to achieve efficiency in government of the highest order. But to do so requires a highly imaginative and a very skilful public service—to say nothing of the cabinets and parliaments involved. Clearly 'policy efficiency' in government is not a matter simply of adopting the techniques of business 'policy efficiency': we in government must evolve our own techniques. Moreover, we will have saved pennies and lost dollars for the taxpayer if we preoccupy ourselves solely with 'administrative efficiency'.

EFFICIENCY INCENTIVES

My first two points, then, are these: efficiency in public administration has more dimensions than just one, and it will not be achieved simply by adopting the conventional 'efficiency techniques'. Public servants must concern themselves with all three kinds of efficiency—'policy', 'administrative', and 'service'—and they must do more than merely copy the 'efficiency techniques' of business. They must adapt them and develop new ones.

My third question now comes into focus: are there in the public service sufficient incentives to efficiency? Is there the 'will' to find the 'way' to efficiency in government? The most melancholy part of public attitudes about the public service, is the assumption that there are not. We who are civil servants are, of course, inclined to dispute this, occasionally by rather pontifical pronouncements about our dedication to public service, and about our personal motivations—which we conceive to be of the highest order.

Now, I am not disputing these motivations, nor am I deriding them. They are most important. But I think the public would be relieved if they could see something more substantial, something less personal, perhaps even something less 'chancy' than individual dedication.

The question that occurs to all of us, I'm sure, is why the efficiency motivation of business is so readily accepted as being sufficient, and how it really operates. I am referring, of course, to the profit motive. Can we assume with confidence that the profit motive operates automatically in industry? If so, how is it made effective—how is it 'institutionalized'? If we had the answers to these questions we might have some clues as to where to look in the civil service for equivalent or alternative efficiency motivations.

It is probably fair to say that the profit motive in business influences primarily the owners of an enterprise, and top management staff whose effectiveness is judged largely by the profit and loss statement. And undoubtedly this motivation has a very real influence in the quest by these people for 'policy efficiency'.

But 'administrative efficiency' cannot be achieved by top management alone: in the final analysis it can be only the product of the efforts of employees who are far removed from the direct benefits of greater productivity. It is the middle management people, the foremen and supervisors, indeed the workmen themselves, who must be relied upon to introduce new procedures and methods, to improve space layout, to speed up work flows, and so on. Yet these people rarely, if ever, see a profit and loss statement, and a good many of them would be unable to interpret one if they did see it. Moreover, even if they were able to read financial statements it would be most difficult for them to discern a clear and direct relationship between 'administrative efficiency', higher productivity, and greater personal rewards. The effects of collective bargaining are more likely to be perceptible, even to foremen and supervisors.

What top management must do, then, is somehow to communicate at least to middle-management levels a 'drive for efficiency'. In some enterprises this is attempted by profit-sharing schemes. If this device were very common in private business, one might conclude that top management had in this way been able to make the profit motive operate among superintendents, supervisors, and foremen. The efficiency motivation even at these levels would then be the profit motive. But unless I am mistaken, it is a fact that profit sharing schemes are not that common in large-scale business enterprises.

What then is the 'efficiency motivation'? How does top management instill in a large corporation the desire for efficiency—a desire which may flow from the profit motive but which is capable of existing by itself? I have the impression that what happens in a well-run corporation is that a sort of 'efficiency value' is developed, and that this comes to be subscribed to by an important number of middle-management employees. The whole structure of rewards and penalties is designed to promote the efficient worker and the effective supervisor; and middle management people know that their success will be measured by the productivity of their departments. So efficiency, of and by itself, becomes the objective of the successful superintendent or foreman.

It would be idyllic to believe that this condition is produced with ease, or that it is common in all large-scale enterprises. In point of fact, businessmen themselves are not prepared to rely upon this approach alone. In addition to relating their system of rewards and penalties to employee-productivity—to the extent that their union contracts permit—business managers employ special teams whose job it is constantly to seek out improvements in organization and procedures. Work flow analysis, the examination of production processes, and all of the techniques of business engineering are used by these units to try to cut expenses and increase productivity. In smaller enterprises the services of management consultants may be used for the same end. To the extent that the 'efficiency value' has been accepted by middle management people they will welcome the work of the systems analysts; to the extent that it hasn't the 'time and motion boys' will be resented.

This oversimplification of the institutionalization of an 'efficiency motivation' in private corporations is not meant to exalt business efficiency. Anyone who has had any experience in or association with corporate enterprise knows that there is room for improvement in business administration as well as in public administration. But my point is this: it is not a perception of the relationship between 'administrative efficiency' and profits which drives middle management people or efficiency experts; it is the desire to prove their own ability to increase productivity. This is not to say that this 'drive' has no relationship to the profit motive; it is merely to say that it can motivate people who are not themselves impelled by a desire for higher profits.

This being so, it seems to me reasonable to suppose that the same kind of efficiency motivation can exist in the public service, provided there is a will on the part of governments and senior public servants to create and to develop it. Since governments are not impelled by a profit motive, the question is whether there are other impulses that will cause them to instill in the public service an 'efficiency value'.

I suggest that there are. First, it is well known that inefficiency in government, whether manifested by indolent civil servants, or obstructive red-tape, or sheer incompetence, is quick to engage public criticism. And nothing can be more damaging, politically, to governments. Even if the public were docile, or immune to inefficiency in public administration, you can be sure that parliamentary oppositions would do their best to make people aware of the deficiencies of government bureaucracy. Certainly it has been my experience that ministers of the Crown react rather quickly to the complaints of citizens or of the opposition that they have encountered slothfulness, or rudeness, or inefficiency on the part of the public service. It is the ministers and their parliamentary supporters, after all, who pay the penalty for public dissatisfaction—as it is the shareholders and the managers who are the losers when profits decline.

There is another reason, too, that ministers and senior public servants are impelled to take an interest in efficiency. All of us have learned that it isn't easy to enlarge our appropriations for the purpose of improving or expanding the programs for which we are responsible. Treasury boards and finance committees are notoriously difficult in these matters. But if we can demonstrate economies in some part of our department, the men on the treasury benches are more favourably disposed to an increase in the allotment for another part of the department. Moreover, the competition for funds is keen enough when budgets are being formulated that treasury board officials will often be told when departments feel that others are being profligate in their spending.

There is, in short, a constant competition for scarce resources in government—just as there is in the private sector of the economy—and finance officials like officials of operating departments are keenly aware of this fact. It has been my experience that this, in combination with the concern to avert public criticism, operates effectively to create in senior civil servants a real concern for efficiency.

I have said nothing about the 'service motivation' which operates in government. It is all too easy to sound pompous or righteous in doing so. But I nevertheless believe it to be true that the great majority of cabinet ministers and senior civil servants are in the public service because of a concern that government should meet the social and economic needs of the community. And because of this motivation they are just as concerned about efficiency in public administration as businessmen are about efficiency in business administration. The question is whether they succeed in communicating their concern to the middle management levels of the civil service.

The techniques that senior public servants use to instill a concern for efficiency in their division heads and supervisors are the same that private management employ. First, promotion through the higher ranks of the civil service is based, so far as I can discern, upon demonstrated ability. This, like the system of rewards used in private business tends to focus the attention of middle management people upon efficiency and effectiveness. What is often misleading, I think, is the fact that efficiency assumes different forms in the public service; the result is that it is not readily recognizable to people who are accustomed to the patterns of efficiency in business.

Second, governments, like businesses, have established special agencies for the purpose of ensuring that departments do in fact organize their work effectively. Shortly after the second World War, Organization and Methods units were established in the Government of Canada and the Government of Saskatchewan, and since then Organization and Methods units, and the use of management consultants, have proliferated in federal departments, in provincial governments, and in municipal governments. These agencies operate in much the same manner as do their counterparts in industry.

SPECIAL PROBLEMS IN PUBLIC ADMINISTRATION

I am arguing, in short, that the methods by which an 'efficiency motivation' is institutionalized in the civil service are not too dissimilar from those used in private business. Having said this, I think it is fair to observe that there are special problems which must be overcome in government.

First, some governments, notably the government of Canada, are such large organizations, and are so scattered geographically, that extra efforts are required to make the 'efficiency motivation' operative. In a sense large governments should be compared with a national railway system rather than with a compact and homogeneous industrial enterprise.

Second, departmentalization in government is fundamentally different than it is in business. Each agency of the public service tends to operate a group of programs which are differentiated clearly from those of other agencies, with the result that a single approach to efficiency becomes impossible. Moreover, because of the principle of individual ministerial responsibility, it is more difficult to impose a central or unified approach to the management of the differentiated affairs of the several departments. The result is that it is possible to find some departments that are operated more efficiently than others. And it is not always easy for the cabinet to impose 'efficiency requirements' on the weaker departments; certainly not as easy as it is for the management of a private business to do with respect to recalcitrant divisions of a relatively monolithic corporate enterprise.

Third, there is more frequently in government a conflict between 'service efficiency' and 'administrative efficiency'. I was alluding to this when I spoke of the principle of individual ministerial responsibility. Greater 'administrative efficiency' is sometimes possible, but only at the cost of diluting or modifying the arrangements of constitutional government. A cabinet is not a monolithic structure, any more than Canada is a homogeneous nation. And if individual ministers, like distinctive cultures in our nation, display a highly individual approach to the management of their affairs, it is not an easy matter, nor is it always proper, to impose a single or a unified approach. Similarly, a prime measure of success in government is whether parliamentary control is preserved and maintained. There is no doubt in my mind that financial processes in government could be streamlined if parliament's annual appropriation control were abandoned. But 'service efficiency'—the preservation of parliamentary control—must take precedence.

Special difficulties are encountered also in achieving 'policy efficiency'. It seems to me reasonable to suppose that some government programs become obsolete during the passage of time, and that superior policies could be evolved for achieving the same ends. But the plain truth is, or so it seems to me, that there are strong, built-in pressures from the electorate to retain almost any public program which you might care to mention. Equally, new policies undoubtedly are adopted which are not the most efficient way of achieving a goal—indeed the goal itself may be questionable. I'm sure, for example, that most of us could select as illustrations some of Canada's tax laws: measures which are incredibly difficult to administer, but the results of which seem not to justify the effort involved. Yet each of these was built into the tax laws to meet the pressures of some part of the electorate.

It is not for me, as a civil servant, to identify more specifically than this alleged examples of 'policy inefficiency'. I content myself with the assertion that such inefficiencies, if they do exist, are the product largely of the political process in Canada. And if in fact we are getting the kind of government which we vote for, it is simply a contradiction in terms to suggest that these policy aberrations are in fact inefficiency. They may be inefficient ways of achieving an objective, or the objective itself may be inefficient in economic terms. But as long as the policies involved are the product of democratic processes they are legitimate in themselves—they are the product of 'service efficiency'.

This brings me back to where I started, and, you will be happy to know, to where I want to stop. It is a good thing that the Glassco Commission has generated such a keen interest in government efficiency: until perfection has been achieved anyone connected with public administration will welcome this interest. But I hope that the discussions of government efficiency will not be superficial. There are, as I have said, more kinds of efficiency in government than conventional 'administrative efficiency'. Second, it is not enough simply to try to apply in the public service the efficiency techniques of private industry: adaptations and innovations are required. Third, efficiency motivations in the public service should not be dismissed as inadequate, but they must be cultivated and sharpened if we are to accomplish what seems to me an especially complicated task. I hope that the Institute of Public Administration will make an appropriate and a useful contribution to this end.

This paper was presented to meetings of the Victoria, Vancouver, Edmonton, Hamilton, and Halifax Regional Groups of the Institute of Public Administration of Canada.

19

A Budget for All Seasons?
Why the Traditional Budget Lasts

Aaron Wildavsky

INTRODUCTION

Almost from the time the caterpillar of budgetary evolution became the butterfly of budgetary reform, the line-item budget has been condemned as a reactionary throwback to its primitive larva. Budgeting, its critics claim, has been metamorphized in reverse, an example of retrogression instead of progress. Over the last century, the traditional annual cash budget has been condemned as mindless, because its lines do not match programs; irrational, because they deal with inputs instead of outputs; shortsighted, because they cover one year instead of many; fragmented, because as a rule only changes are reviewed; conservative, because these changes tend to be small; and worse. Yet despite these faults, real and alleged, the traditional budget reigns supreme virtually everywhere, in practice if not in theory. Why?

The usual answer, if it can be dignified as such, is bureaucratic inertia. The forces of conservatism within government resist change. Presumably the same explanation fits all cases past and present. How, then, can we explain why countries like Britain departed from tradition in recent years only to return to it? It is hard to credit institutional inertia in virtually all countries for a century. Has nothing happened over time to entrench the line-item budget?

The line-item budget is a product of history, not of logic. It was not so much created as evolved. Its procedures and its purposes represent accretions over time rather than propositions postulated at a moment in time. Hence, we should not expect to find them either consistent or complementary.

Control over public money and accountability to public authority were among the earliest purposes of budgeting. Predictability and planning—knowing what there will be to spend over time—were not far behind. From the beginning, relating expenditure to revenue was of prime importance. In our day we have added macroeconomic management, intended to moderate inflation and unemployment. Spending is varied to suit the economy. In time the need for money came to be used

Aaron Wildavsky, 'A Budget for All Seasons: Why the Traditional Budget Lasts' in *The Public Evaluation of Government Spending*, G. Bruce Doern and Allan M. Maslove, eds (Toronto: Butterworth/IRPP, 1979): 61–78. Reproduced with permission of the Institute for Research on Public Policy (IRPP) at www.irpp.com.

as a lever to enhance the efficiency or effectiveness of policies. He who pays the piper hopes to call the tune. Here we have it: budgeting is supposed to contribute to continuity (for planning), to change (for policy evaluation), to flexibility (for the economy), and to rigidity (for limiting spending).

These different and (to some extent) opposed purposes contain a clue to the perennial dissatisfaction with budgeting. Obviously no process can simultaneously provide continuity and change, rigidity and flexibility. And no one should be surprised that those who concentrate on one purpose or the other should find budgeting unsatisfactory; or that, as purposes change, these criticisms should become constant. The real surprise is that traditional budgeting has not been replaced by any of its outstanding competitors in this century.

TRADITIONAL BUDGETING VS ALTERNATIVES

If traditional budgeting is so bad, why are there not better alternatives? Appropriate answers are unobtainable, I believe, so long as we proceed on this high level of aggregation. So far as I know, the traditional budget has never been compared systematically, characteristic for characteristic, with the leading alternatives.[1] By doing so we can see better which characteristics of budgetary processes suit different purposes under a variety of conditions.

Why, again, if traditional budgeting does have defects, which I do not doubt, has it not been replaced? Perhaps the complaints are the clue: just what is it that is inferior for most purposes and yet superior over all?

The ability of a process to score high on one criterion may increase the likelihood of its scoring low on another. Planning requires predictability and economic management requires reversibility. Thus, there may well be no ideal mode of budgeting. If so, this is the question: do we choose a budgetary process which does splendidly on one criterion but terribly on others? Or, do we opt for a process that satisfies all these demands even though it does not score brilliantly on any single one?

A public sector budget is supposed to ensure accountability. By associating government publicly with certain expenditures, opponents can ask questions or contribute criticisms. Here the clarity of the budget presentation—linking expenditures to activities and to responsible officials—is crucial. As a purpose, accountability is closely followed by control: are the authorized and appropriated funds being spent for the designated activities? Control (or its antonym 'out of control') can be used in several senses: are the expenditures within the limits (a) stipulated or (b) desired? While a budget (or item) might be 'out of control' to a critic who desires it to be different, in our nomenclature control is lacking only when limits are stipulated and exceeded.

Budgets may be mechanisms of efficiency—doing whatever is done at least cost, or getting the most out of a given level of expenditure—and/or of effectiveness—achieving certain results in public policy such as improving health of children or reducing crime.

In modern times, budgeting has also become an instrument of economic management and of planning. With the advent of Keynesian economics, efforts have been made to vary the rate of spending so as to increase employment in slack times or to reduce inflation when prices are deemed to be rising too quickly. Here (leaving out alternative tax policies), the ability to increase and decrease spending in the short run is of paramount importance. For budgeting to serve planning, however, predictability (not variability) is critical. The ability to maintain a course of behaviour over time is essential.

As everyone knows, budgeting is not only an economic but also a political instrument. Since inability to implement decisions nullifies them, the ability to mobilize support is as important as making the right choice. So, too, is the capacity to figure out what to do, that is, to make choices. Thus, the effect of budgeting on conflict and calculation—the capacity to make and support decisions—must also be considered.

Traditional budgeting is annual (repeated yearly), incremental (departing marginally from the year before). It is conducted on a cash basis (in current dollars). Its content comes in the form of line-items (such as personnel or maintenance). Alternatives to all these characteristics have been developed and tried, though never, as far as I know, with success. Why this should be so, despite the obvious and admitted defects of tradition, will emerge as we consider the criteria each type of budgetary process has to meet.

UNIT OF MEASUREMENT: CASH OR VOLUME

Budgeting can be done not only in terms of cash but also in terms of volume. Instead of promising to pay so much in the next year or years, the commitment can be made in terms of operations to be performed or services to be provided. Why might someone want to budget in terms of volume (or constant currency)? To aid planning: if public agencies know that they can count, not on variable currency, but on what the currency can actually buy, that is, on a volume of activity, they can plan ahead as far as the budget runs. Indeed, if one wishes to make decisions now which could be made at future periods, so as to help assure consistency over time, estimates based on stability in the unit of effort—so many applications processed or such a level of services provided—are the very way to go about it.

So long as purchasing power remains constant, budgeting in cash or by volume remains a distinction without a difference. But should the value of money fluctuate (and, in our time, this means inflation), the public budget must absorb additional amounts so as to provide the designated volume of activity. Budgeters lose control of money because they have to supply whatever is needed. Evidently, given large and unexpected changes in prices, the size of the budget in cash terms would fluctuate wildly. Evidently, also, no government could permit itself to be so far out of control. Hence, the very type of stable environment which budgeting by volume is designed to achieve turns out to be its major unarticulated premise. Given an irreducible amount of uncertainty in the system, not every element can be stabilized at one and the same time. Who, then, will enjoy stability and who will bear the costs of change?

The private sector and the central controller pay the price for budgeting by volume. Budgeting by volume is, first of all, an effort by elements of the public sector to invade the private sector. What budgeting by volume says, in effect, is that the public sector will be protected against inflation by getting its agreed level of services before other needs are met. The real resources necessary to make up the gap between projected and current prices must come from the private sector in the form of taxation or interest for borrowing. In other words: for the public sector volume budgeting is a form of indexing against inflation.

Within the government, spending by agencies will be kept whole. The central budget office bears the brunt of covering larger expenditures and takes the blame when the budget goes out of control, that is, rises faster and in different directions than predicted. In Britain, where budgeting by volume went under the name of the Public Expenditure Survey, the Treasury finally responded to years of severe inflation by imposing cash limits, otherwise known as the traditional cold-cash budget. Of course, departmental cash limits include an amount for price changes, but this is not necessarily what the Treasury expects so much as the amount it desires. The point is that the spending departments have to make up deficits caused by inflation. Instead of the Treasury handing over the money automatically, as in the volume budget, departments have to request it—and their requests may be denied. The local spenders, rather than the central controllers, have to pay the price of monetary instability.

Effects of Inflation

Inflation has become not only an evil to be avoided but a (perhaps *the*) major instrument of modern public policy. Taxes are hard to increase and benefits virtually impossible to decrease. But similar results may be obtained through inflation, which artificially elevates the tax brackets in which people find themselves and decreases their purchasing power. Wage increases which cannot be contested directly may be nullified indirectly (and the real burden of the national debt reduced), without changing the ostensible amount, all by means of inflation. The sensitivity of budgetary forms to inflation is a crucial consideration.

From all this, it follows that budgeting by volume is counter-productive in fighting inflation because it accommodates price increases rather than encouraging the struggle against them. Volume budgeting may maintain public sector employment at the expense of taking resources from the private sector, thus possibly reducing employment there. There can be no doubt, however, that volume budgeting basically serves counter-cyclical purposes because the whole point is that the amount and quality of service do not vary over time, rather than going up or down in accordance with short-run economic conditions.

How does volume budgeting rate as a source of policy information? It should enable departments to understand better what they are doing since they are presumably doing the same thing over the entire period of the budget. But volume budgeting does poorly as a method of instigating change. For one thing, the money is guaranteed against price changes, so there is less need to please outsiders. For another, volume budgeting necessarily leads to interest in internal affairs (how to do what one wishes), rather than to seeking external advice (whether there are better things one might be doing). British departments unwilling to let outsiders evaluate their activities are hardly going to be motivated by guarantees against price fluctuations.[2]

TIME SPAN: MONTHS, ONE YEAR, MANY YEARS

Multi-year budgeting has long been proposed as a reform to enhance rational choice by viewing resource allocation in a long-term perspective. Considering one year, it has been argued, leads to short-sightedness—only the next year's expenditures are reviewed; overspending—because huge disbursements in future years are hidden; conservatism—incremental changes do not open up larger future vistas; and parochialism—programs tend to be viewed in isolation rather than in comparison to their future costs, in relation to expected revenue. Extending the time span of budgeting to three or five years, it is argued, would enable long-range planning to overtake short-term reaction and substitute financial control for merely muddling through. And the practice of stepped-up spending to use up resources before the end of the budgetary year would decline in frequency.

Much depends, to be sure, on how long budgetary commitments last. The seemingly arcane question of whether budgeting should be done on a cash or on a volume basis will assume importance if a nation adopts multi-year budgeting. The longer the term of the budget, the more significant inflation becomes. To the extent that price changes are automatically absorbed into budgets, a certain volume of activity is guaranteed. To the extent that agencies have to absorb inflation, their real level of activity declines. Multi-year budgeting in cash terms diminishes the relative size of the public sector, leaving the private sector larger. Behind discussions of the span of the budget, the *real* debate is over the relative shares of the public and private sectors—which one will be asked to absorb inflation and which one will be allowed to expand into the other.

A similar issue of relative shares is created within government by proposals to budget in *some* sectors for several years, and, in others, for only one year. This poses the question of which sectors of policy are to be exposed to the vicissitudes of life in the short term, and which are to be protected from them. Like any other device, multi-year budgeting is not neutral but distributes indulgences differently among the affected interests.

Of course, multi-year budgeting has its positive aspects—if control of expenditure is desired, for instance. A multi-year budget makes it necessary to estimate expenditures further into the future. The old tactic of the camel's nose—beginning with small expenditures while hiding larger ones which will arise later on—is rendered more difficult. Still, as the British learned, 'hard in' often implies an even harder out. Once an expenditure gets into a multi-year projection, it is likely to stay in because it has become part of an interrelated set of proposals which might be expensive to disrupt. Besides, part of the bargain struck when agencies are persuaded to estimate as accurately as they can is that they will gain stability, that is, not be subject to sudden reductions according to the needs of the moment. Thus, control in a single year may have to be sacrificed to maintain limits over the multi-year period. And should there come a call for cuts to meet a particular problem, British experience shows that reductions in future years (which are always 'iffy') are easily traded for maintenance of spending in the all-important present. Moreover, by making prices more prominent due to the longer time period involved, large sums may have to be supplied in order to meet commitments for a given volume of services in a volatile world.[3]

Suppose, however, that it were deemed desirable significantly to reduce some expenditures in order to increase others. Due to the built-in pressure of continuing commitments, what can be done in a single year is extremely limited. Making arrangements over a three- to five-year period (with constant prices, five per cent a year for five years, compounded, would bring about a one-third change in the budget) would permit larger changes in spending, to be effected in a more orderly way. This is true; other things, however—prices, priorities, politicians—seldom remain equal. While the British were working under a five-*year* budget projection, prices and production could hardly be predicted for five *months* at a time.

As Robert Hartman put it, 'there is no absolutely right way to devise a long-run budget strategy.'[4] No one knows how the private economy will be doing nor what the consequences will be of a fairly wide range of targets for budget totals. There is no political or economic agreement on whether budget targets should be expressed in terms of levels required for full *employment*, for *price stability*, or for *budget balancing*. Nor is it self-evidently desirable either to estimate where the economy is going and to devise a governmental spending target to complement the estimate, or to decide what the economy *should* be doing and to budget in order to encourage that direction.

In any event, given economic volatility and theoretical poverty, the ability to outguess the future is extremely limited. Responsiveness to changing economic conditions, therefore (if that were the main purpose of budgeting), would be facilitated best by a budget calculated in months or weeks rather than years. Such budgets do exist in poor and uncertain countries. Naomi Caiden and I have called the process 'repetitive budgeting' to signify that the budget may be made and remade several times during the year.[5] Because finance ministries often do not know how much is actually in the nation's treasury or what they will have to spend, they delay making decisions until the last possible moment. The repetitive budget is not a reliable guide to proposed expenditure, but an invitation to agencies to 'get it if they can'. When economic or political conditions change (which is often), the budget is renegotiated. *Adaptiveness* is indeed maximized but *predictability* is minimized. Conflict increases because the same decision is remade several times each year. Agencies must be wary of each other because they do not know when next they will have to compete. Control declines, partly because frequent changes make the audit trail difficult to follow, and partly because departments seek to escape from control so as to re-establish a modicum of predictability. Hence they obfuscate their activities (thus reducing accountability), and actively seek funds of their own in the form of earmarked revenues (thus diminishing control). Both efficiency and effectiveness suffer. The former is either unnecessary (if separate funds exist) or impossible (without continuity), while the latter is obscured by the lack of relationship between what is in the budget and what happens in the world. Drastically shortening the time frame wreaks havoc with efficiency, effectiveness, conflict, and calculation. But if immediate responsiveness is desired, as in economic management, the shorter the span the better.

CALCULATION: INCREMENTAL OR COMPREHENSIVE

Just as the annual budget on a cash basis is integral to the traditional process, so also is the budgetary base—the expectation that most expenditures will be continued. Normally, only increases or decreases to the existing base are considered in any one period. If such budgetary practices may be described as incremental, the main alternative to the traditional budget is one which emphasizes comprehensive calculation. The main modern forms of the latter are planning, programming, and budgeting (PPB) and zero-base budgeting (ZBB).

Let us think of PPB as embodying *horizontal* comprehensiveness—comparing alternative expenditure packages to decide which of them best contributes to larger programmatic objectives. ZBB, by contrast, might be thought of as manifesting *vertical* comprehensiveness: every year alternative expenditures from base zero are considered for all governmental activities or objectives treated as discrete entities. In a word, *PPB compares programs*, ZBB *compares alternative funding.*

Planning, Programming, and Budgeting

The strength of PPB lies in its emphasis on *policy analysis* to increase effectiveness: programs are evaluated, found wanting, and presumably replaced by alternatives, designed to produce superior results. Unfortunately, PPB engenders a conflict between error *recognition* and error *correction.* There is little point in designing better policies so as to minimize their prospects of implementation. But why should a process devoted to policy *evaluation* end up stultifying policy *executions?* Answer: because PPB's *policy rationality* is countered by its *organizational irrationality.*

If error is to be altered, it must be relatively easy to correct.[6] But PPB makes it hard. The 'systems' in PPB are characterized by their proponents as highly differentiated and tightly linked. The rationale for program budgeting lies in its connectedness: like programs are grouped together. Program structures are meant to replace the confused concatenations of line-items with clearly differentiated, non-overlapping boundaries—only one set of programs to a structure. This means that a change in one element or structure must result in change reverberating throughout every element in the same system. Instead of altering only neighbouring units or central control units, which would make change feasible, all are, so to speak, wired together so that the choice is, in effect: all or none.

Imagine one of us deciding whether to buy a tie or a kerchief. A simple task, one might think. Suppose, however, that organizational rules require us to keep our entire wardrobe as a unit. If everything must be rearranged when one item is altered, the probability that we will do anything in those circumstances is low. The more tightly linked and the more highly differentiated the elements concerned, the greater the probability of error (because tolerances are very small), and the less the likelihood that error will in fact be corrected (because with change, every element has to be recalibrated with every other which had been previously adjusted). Being caught between revolution (change in everything) and resignation (change in nothing) has little to recommend it.

Program budgeting increases rather than decreases the cost of correcting error.

The great complaint about bureaucracies is their rigidity. As things stand, the object of organizational affection is the bureau as serviced by the unusual line-item categories from which people, money, and facilities flow. Viewed from the standpoint of bureau interests, programs to some extent are negotiable: some can be increased, others decreased, while keeping the agency on an even keel, or, if necessary, adjusting it to less happy times without calling into question its very existence. Line-item budgeting, precisely because its categories (personnel, maintenance, supplies) do not relate directly to programs, are easier to change. Budgeting by programs, precisely because money flows to objectives, makes it difficult to abandon objectives without abandoning the organization which gets its money for them. It is better to use non-programmatic rubrics as formal budget categories, permitting a diversity of analytical perspectives, than to transform a temporary analytic insight into a permanent perspective through which to funnel money.

The good organization is interested in discovering and correcting its own mistakes. The higher the cost of error—not only in terms of money but also in personnel, programs, and prerogatives—the less the chance that anything will actually be done about them. Organizations should be designed, therefore, to make errors visible and correctible, that is to say, cheap and affordable.

Zero-base Budgeting

The ideal ahistorical information system is zero-base budgeting. The past, as reflected in the budgetary base (common expectations as to amounts and types of funding), is explicitly rejected: there is no yesterday; nothing is to be taken for granted, everything is at every period subject to searching scrutiny. As a result, calculations become unmanageable. The same is true of PPB, which requires comparisons of all or most programs which might contribute to common objectives. To say that a budgetary process is ahistorical is to conclude that it increases the sources of error while decreasing the chances of correcting mistakes: if history is abolished, nothing is settled. Old quarrels become new conflicts. Both calculation and conflict increase exponentially, the former worsening selection, and the latter obstructing correction of error. As the number of independent variables grows, ability to control the future declines (because the past is assumed not to limit the future). As mistrust grows with conflict, willingness to admit, and hence to correct, error diminishes. Doing without history is a little like abolishing memory—momentarily convenient, perhaps, but ultimately embarrassing.

Only poor countries come close to zero-base budgeting, not because they *wish* to do so, but because their uncertain financial position continually forces them to go back on old commitments. Because past disputes are part of present conflicts, their budgets lack predictive value; little that is stated in them is likely to occur. Ahistorical practices, which are a dire consequence of extreme instability and from which all who experience them devoutly desire to escape, should not be considered normative.

Policy Implications

ZBB and PPB share an emphasis on the virtue of objectives. Program budgeting is all about relating larger to smaller objectives among different programs and zero-base budgeting promises to do the same within a single program. The policy implications of these methods of budgeting, which distinguish them from existing approaches, derive from their overwhelming concern with ranking objectives. Thinking about objectives is one thing, however; making budget categories out of them is quite another. Of course, if one wants the objectives of today to be the objectives of tomorrow, if one wants no change in objectives, then building the budget around objectives is a brilliant idea. But if one desires flexibility in objectives (sometimes known as learning from experience), it must be possible to change them without simultaneously destroying the organization through the withdrawal of financial support.

Both PPB and ZBB are expressions of the prevailing paradigm of rationality in which reason is rendered tantamount to ranking objectives. Alas! An efficient mode of presenting results in research papers—find objectives, order them, choose the highest valued—has been confused with proper processes of social inquiry. For purposes of resource allocation, which is what budgeting is about, ranking objectives without consideration of resources is irrational. The question cannot be 'what do you want?'—as if there were no limits—but should be 'what do you want compared to what you can get?' Ignoring resources is as bad as neglecting objectives, as if one were not interested in the question 'why do I want to do this?' After all, an agency with a billion would not only do more than it would with a million but might well wish to do something quite different. Resources affect objectives as well as vice versa. And budgeting should not separate what reason tells us belongs together.

For purposes of economic management, comprehensive calculations stressing efficiency (ZBB) and effectiveness (PPB) leave much to be desired. For one thing, comprehensiveness takes time, and this is no asset in responding to fast-moving events. For another, devices which stress the intrinsic merits of their methods— 'this is (in)efficient and that is (in)effective'—rub raw when good cannot be done for external reasons, that is, because of the state of the economy. Co-operation will inevitably be compromised when virtue in passing one test becomes vice in failing another.

I have already stated that conflict is increased by ahistorical methods of budgeting. Here I wish to observe that efforts to reduce conflict only make matters worse by vitiating the essential character of comprehensiveness. The cutting edge of competition among programs lies in postulating a range of policy objectives small enough to be encompassed and large enough to overlap so that there are choices (trade-offs in the jargon of the trade) among them. Instead, PPB generated a tendency either to have only a few objectives, so anything and everything fit under them, or a multitude of objectives, so that each organizational unit had its own home and did not have to compete with any other.[7] ZBB produced these results in this way: since a zero base was too threatening or too absurd, zero moved up until it reached, say 80 per cent of the base. To be sure, the burden of conflict and calculation declined—but so, at the same time, did any real difference from traditional incremental budgeting.

In so far as financial control is concerned, ZBB and PPB raise the question: control over what? Is it control over the *content* of programs? Or the efficiency of a given program? Or the total cost of government? Or just the legality of expenditures? In theory, ZBB would be better for efficiency, PPB for effectiveness, and traditional budgeting for legality. Whether control extends to total costs, however, depends on the form of financing, a matter to which we now turn.

Appropriations or Treasury Budgeting

A traditional budget depends on traditional practice—authorization and appropriation followed by expenditure, post-audited by external auditors. But in many countries, traditional budgeting is not in fact the main form of public spending. Nearly half or more of public spending does not take the form of appropriations budgeting but what I shall call 'treasury budgeting'. I find this nomenclature useful in avoiding the pejorative connotations of what would otherwise be called 'back-door' spending, because it bypasses the appropriations committees in favour of automatic disbursement of funds through the treasury.

Alternatives to Traditional Appropriations

For our present purposes, the two forms of treasury budgeting which constitute alternatives to traditional appropriations are *tax expenditures* and *mandatory entitlements*. When concessions are granted in the form of tax reductions for home ownership or college tuition or medical expenses, these are equivalent to budgetary expenditures except that the money is deflected at the source. In the United States, tax expenditures now amount to over $100 billion a year. In one sense, this is a way of avoiding budgeting before there is a budget. Whether one accepts this view is a matter of philosophy. It is said, for instance, that the United States government has a progressive income tax. Is that the real tax system? Or is it a would-be progressive tax as modified by innumerable exceptions? The budgetary process is usually described as resource allocation by the president and Congress acting through its appropriations committees. Is that the real budgetary process? Or is it that process together with numerous provisions for 'back-door' spending, low interest loans, and other devices? From a behavioural or descriptive point of view, actual practices constitute the real system. Exceptions are part of the rule. Indeed, since less than half of the budget passes through the appropriations committees, the exceptions *must* be greater than the rule. And some would argue that the same could be said about taxation. If the exceptions are part of the rule, however, tax expenditures stand in a better light. Then the government is not contributing or losing income: instead it is legitimately excluding certain private activities from being considered as income. There is no question of equity—people are just disposing of their own income as they see fit in a free society. Unless whatever is, is right, however, tax and budget reformers will object to sanctifying regrettable lapses as operating principles. To them, the real systems are the ones which we ought to perfect: a progressive tax on income whose revenues are allocated at the same time through the same public mechanism. And tax expenditures interfere with both these ideals.

Mandatory, open-ended entitlements—our second category of treasury budgeting—provide that anyone eligible for certain benefits must be paid, regardless of the total. Until the legislation is changed or a 'cap' limits total expenditure, entitlements constitute obligations of the state through direct drafts on the treasury. Were I asked to give an operational definition of the end of budgeting, I would say 'indexed, open-ended entitlements'. Budgeting would no longer involve allocation within limited resources but only addition of one entitlement to another, all guarded against fluctuation in prices.

Obviously, treasury budgeting leaves a great deal to be desired in controlling costs of programs, since these depend on such variables as levels of benefits set in prior years, rate of application, and severity of administration. Legal control is possible but difficult because of the large number of individual cases and the innumerable provisions governing eligibility. If the guiding principle is that no one who is eligible should be denied, *at the cost of including some who are ineligible,* expenditures will rise. They will decline if the opposite principle—no ineligibles even if some eligibles suffer—prevails.[8]

Whether or not entitlement programs are efficient or effective, the *budgetary process* will neither add to nor subtract from that result simply because it plays no part. To the extent that efficiency or effectiveness are spurred by the need to convince others to provide funds, such incentives are either much weakened or altogether absent. The political difficulties of reducing benefits or eliminating beneficiaries speak eloquently on this subject. No doubt benefits may be eroded by inflation. Protecting against this possibility is the purpose of indexing benefits against inflation (thus doing for the individual what volume budgeting does for the bureaucracy).

Why, then, in view of its anti-budgetary character, is treasury budgeting so popular? Answer: because of its value in coping with conflict, calculation, and economic management. After a number of entitlements and tax expenditures have been decided upon at different times, usually without full awareness of the others, implicit priorities are produced *ipso facto*, untouched, as it were, by human hands. Conflict is reduced, for the time being at least, because no explicit decisions giving more to this group, and less to another, are necessary. Ultimately, to be sure, resource limits will have to be considered, but even then only a few rather than *all* expenditures will be directly involved, since the others go on, more or less, automatically. Similarly, calculation is contracted as treasury budgeting produces figures, allowing a large part of the budget to be taken for granted. Ultimately, of course, there comes a day of reckoning in the form of a loss of flexibility due to the implicit pre-programming of so large a proportion of available funds. For the moment, however, the attitude appears to be 'sufficient unto the day is the (financial) evil thereof.'

For the purposes of economic management, treasury budgeting is a mixed bag. It is useful in providing what are called automatic stabilizers. When it is deemed desirable not to make new decisions every time conditions change, for example, regarding unemployment benefits, an entitlement enables funds to flow according to the size of the problem. The difficulty is that not all entitlements are counter-cyclical (child benefits, for example, may rise independently of economic conditions), and the loss in financial flexibility generated by entitlements may hurt when the time comes to do less.

Importance of Time

Nevertheless, treasury budgeting has one significant advantage over appropriations budgeting, namely *time*. Changes in policy are manifested quickly in changes in spending. In order to bring considerations of economic management to bear on budgeting, these factors must be introduced early in the process of shaping the appropriations budget. Otherwise last-minute changes of large magnitude will cause chaos by unhinging all sorts of prior understandings. Then the money must be voted and preparations made for spending. In the United States the completion of this process—from the spring previews to the Office of Management and Budget, to the president's Budget in January, to congressional action by the following summer and fall, to spending in the winter and spring—takes from 18 to 24 months. This is not control but remote control.

'Fine-tuning expenditures', attempting to make small adjustments so as to speed up or slow down the economy, do not work well anywhere. Efforts to increase expenditure are just as likely to decrease it in the short run due to the very effort required to expand operations. Similarly, efforts to reduce spending in the short run are just as likely to increase it due to such factors as severence pay, penalties for breaking contracts, and so on. Hence, even as efforts continue to make expenditures more responsive, the attractiveness of more immediate tax and entitlement increases is apparent.

The recalcitrance of all forms of budgeting to economic management is not so surprising: after all, both spending programs and economic management can not be made more predictable if one is to vary in order to serve the other. In an age profoundly influenced by Keynesian economic doctrines, with their emphasis on the power of government spending, however, continued efforts to link macro-economics to micro-spending are only to be expected.

THE STRUCTURAL BUDGET MARGIN

One such effort is the 'structural budget margin' developed in the Netherlands. Due to dissatisfaction with the Keynesian approach to economic stabilization, as well as to disillusion with its short-term fine-tuning, the Dutch sought to develop a longer-term relationship between growth of public spending and the size of the national economy. Economic management was to rely less on sudden starts and stops of taxation and expenditure, and greater effort was to be devoted to controlling public spending. The closest the United States has come to something similar is through the doctrine of balancing the budget at the level of full employment, which almost always entails a deficit. The Dutch were particularly interested in a control device because of the difficulty of getting agreement to hold down expenditures in coalition governments. Thus, spending was to be related not to *actual* growth but to *desired* growth, with only the designated margin available for new expenditure.[9]

Needless to say, there are differences in definition of the appropriate structural growth rate, and it has been revised up and down. Since the year which is chosen as a base makes a difference, that too has been in dispute. And, as one would expect, there are disagreements over calculation of cash or volume of services, with rising inflation propelling a move toward cash. Furthermore, since people learn to play any game, *conservative* governments used the structural budget margin to hold down spending while socialists used the mechanism to increase it, for then the margin became a tool for calculating the necessary increases in taxation. Every way one turns, it appears, budgetary devices are good for some purposes and bad for others.

WHY THE TRADITIONAL BUDGET LASTS

Every criticism of traditional budgeting is undoubtedly correct. It *is* incremental rather than comprehensive; it *does* fragment decisions, usually making them piecemeal; it *is* heavily historical, looking backward more than forward; it is indifferent about objectives. Why, then, has traditional budgeting lasted so long? Answer: *because it has the virtues of its own defects.*

Traditional budgeting makes calculations easy, precisely because it is not comprehensive. History provides a strong base on which to rest a case. The present is appropriated on the basis of the past, which may be known, rather than of the future, which cannot be comprehended. Choices which might cause conflict are fragmented so that not all difficulties need to be faced at one time. Budgeters may have objectives but the budget itself is organized around activities or functions—personnel, maintenance, and so on. One can change objectives, then, without challenging organizational survival. Traditional budgeting does not demand analysis of policy; neither, however, does it inhibit it. Because it is neutral in respect of policy, traditional budgeting is compatible with a variety of policies, all of which can be converted into line-items. Budgeting for one year at a time has no special virtue (two years, for instance might be just as good or better) except in comparison with more extreme alternatives. Budgeting several times a year aids economic adjustment but also creates chaos in departments, disorders calculations, and worsens conflict. Multi-year budgeting enhances planning at the expense of adjustment, accountability, and possible price stability. Budgeting by volume and entitlement also aids planning and efficiency in government at the cost of control and effectiveness. Budgeting becomes spending. Traditional budgeting lasts, then, because it is simpler, easier, more controllable, more flexible than modern alternatives, such as ZBB, PPB, and indexed entitlements.

A final criterion has not been mentioned because it is inherent in the multiplicity of others, namely *adaptability*. To be useful, a budgetary process should perform tolerably well under all conditions. It must perform in face of the unexpected deficits and surpluses, inflation and deflation, economic growth and economic stagnation. Because budgets are contracts within governments signifying agreed understandings, and signals outside of government, informing others of what government is likely to do so that they can adapt to it, budgets must be good (though not necessarily excellent) for all seasons. It is not so much the fact that traditional budgeting succeeds brilliantly on every criterion, as that it does not fail entirely on any one, which is responsible for its longevity.

Needless to say, traditional budgeting also has the defects of its virtues: no instrument of policy is equally good for all purposes. Although budgets look back, they may not look back far enough to understand how (or why) they got to where they are. Comparing this year with last may not mean much if the past was a mistake and the future is likely to be a bigger one. Quick calculation may be worse than none if it is grossly in error. There is an incremental road to disaster as well as faster roads to perdition. Simplicity may become simple-mindedness. Policy neutrality may degenerate into lack of interest in programs. Why then has it lasted? Answer: so far, no one has come up with another budgetary procedure which has the virtues of traditional budgeting, while lacking its defects.

At once one is disposed to ask why it is necessary to settle for second or third best: why not combine the best features of the various processes, specially selected to work under prevailing conditions? Why not multi-year volume entitlement for this and annual cash zero-base budgeting for that? The question answers itself; there can only be one budgetary process at a time. It follows that the luxury of picking different ones for different purposes is unobtainable. Again, the necessity of choosing the least bad, or the most widely applicable over the largest number of cases, is made evident.

Still, almost a diametrically opposed conclusion is also obvious to students of budgeting: observation reveals that a number of different processes do in fact co-exist right now. Some programs are single-year while others are multi-year; some have cash limits while others are open-ended or even indexed; some are investigated in increments while others (where repetitive operations are involved) receive, in effect, a zero-base review. Thus beneath the facade of unity, there is in fact diversity.

How, then, are we to choose among truths that are self-evident (there can be only one form of budgeting at a time and there are many)? Both cannot be correct when applied to the same sphere; but, I think both are true when applied to different spheres. The critical difference is between the financial form in which the budget is voted in the legislature, and the different ways of thinking about budgeting. It is possible to analyse expenditures in terms of programs, over long periods of time, and in many other ways, without requiring that the form of analysis should be the same as the form of appropriation. Indeed, as we have seen, there are persuasive reasons for insisting that form and function should be different. All this can be summarized: the more neutral the form of presenting appropriations, the easier to translate other changes—in program, direction, organizational structure—into the desired amounts without turning the categories into additional forms of rigidity, acting as barriers to future changes.

Nonetheless, traditional budgeting must be lacking in some respects or it would not be replaced so often by entitlements or multi-year accounts. Put another way, treasury budgeting must reflect strong social forces. These are not mechanisms to control spending but to increase it.

'The Budget' may be annual but tax expenditures and budget entitlements go on until changed. Where there is a will to spend, there is a way to do so.

CONCLUSION

I write about auditing largely in terms of budgeting and budgeting largely in terms of public policy. The rise of big government has necessarily altered our administrative doctrines of first and last things. When government was small, so also was public spending. Affairs of state were treated as extensions of personal integrity . . . or the lack thereof. The question was whether spending was honest. If public spending posed a threat to society, it was this: that private individuals would use it to accumulate private fortunes with which to enter the economy. State audit was about private avarice. As government grew larger, its manipulation meant more. Was it doing what it said it would do with public money? *State audit became state compliance.* But when government became gigantic, the sheer size of the state became overwhelming. The issue was no longer control of the state—getting government to do what it was told—but the ability of the state to control society. Public policy, that is, public measures to control private behaviour, leapt to the fore. And that is how auditing shifted from private corruption to government compliance to public policy.

Social forces ultimately get their way, but while there is a struggle for supremacy, the form of budgeting can make a modest difference. It is difficult to say, for instance, whether the concept of a balanced budget declined due to social pressure or whether the concept of a unified budget, including almost all transactions in and out of the economy, such as trust funds, makes it even less likely. In days of old when cash was cash, and perpetual deficits were not yet invented, a deficit meant more cash out than came in. Today, with a much larger total, estimating plays a much more important part, and it is anyone's guess (within a margin of $50 billion) as to the actual state of affairs. The lesson to be drawn is that for purposes of accountability and control, the simpler the budget the better.

Taking as large a view as I know how, the suitability of a budgetary process under varied conditions depends on how well diverse concerns can be translated into its forms. For sheer transparency, traditional budgeting is hard to beat.

NOTES

This paper grew out of my collaboration with Hugh Heclo on the second edition of The Private Government of Public Money. *I wish to thank him, James Douglas, Robert Hartman, and Carolyn Webber for critical comments.*

1. But, for a beginning, see Allen Schick 'The Road to PPB: The Stages of Budget Reform', *Public Administration* 26 (Dec. 1966), pp. 243-58.
2. Hugh Heclo and Aaron Wildavsky, *The Private Government of Public Money: Community and Policy in British Public Administration*, 2nd edn (Berkeley: University of California Press, 1979).
3. Ibid.
4. Robert A. Hartman, 'Multiyear Budget Planning', in J.A. Pechman, ed., *Setting National Priorities: The 1979 Budget* (Washington, DC: The Brookings Institution, 1978), p. 312.
5. Naomi Caiden and Aaron Wildavsky, *Planning and Budgeting in Poor Countries* (New York: Wiley, 1974).
6. This and the next eight paragraphs are taken from my 'Policy Analysis is What Information Systems are Not', *New York Affairs* 4 (Spring 1977).
7. See Jeanne Nienaber and Aaron Wildavsky, *The Budgeting and Evaluation of Federal Recreation Programs; or Money Doesn't Grow on Trees* (New York: Basic Books, 1973).
8. The importance of these principles is discussed in my book, *Speaking Truth to Power: The Art and Craft of Policy Analysis* (Boston: Little, Brown, 1979).
9. J. Diamond, 'The New Orthodoxy in Budgetary Planning: A Critical Review of Dutch Experience', *Public Finance* 32, 1 (1977), pp. 56-76.

20

On the Audit Trail of the Auditor General: Parliament's Servant, 1973–1980

Sharon Sutherland

Abstract. Since 1973, important changes have been brought about in the powers of the Office of the Auditor General. The balance of our system of parliamentary government is undermined by these changes. This paper argues that the Auditor General's value-for-money campaign has taken the OAG over the line between audit and trespass on government policy. The Office's new powers have their legal basis in the new Auditor General Act of 1977, which says that the OAG can review value-for-money studies of programs. Another term for these studies is 'effectiveness evaluations'. The powers acquired in the act made the creation of the new central agency, the Office of the Comptroller General, inevitable. Among this agency's responsibilities is the duty to ensure that each of government's programs is reviewed for value-for-money, to satisfy the requirements of the Auditor General. The two agencies thus exist in a situation of mutual obligation and legitimation. The paper further argues that value-for-money audit is not an objective review technique, but involves a great deal of judgment in each of its stages of application. It is not fitting, therefore, that reports generated under its procedures should be reviewed externally, by an officer without any electoral base. This implies that government requires some form of legitimation to govern quite outside normal conceptions of parliamentary government. Next, it is argued that the techniques of classic program evaluation are themselves biased toward demonstrations of program failure. As the post of Auditor General of Canada fell vacant in September, 1980, and a new Auditor General will be appointed, the government should take the opportunity to review the responsibilities and privileges of the Office.

Once upon a time, the post of Auditor General of Canada was a position of solid respectability, but negligible political power. All year long, solemnly mindful of their position as servants of Parliament, the auditors general reviewed accounts to verify that the government's reports of its spending were a fair description of the actual expenditure history of the year. Once each year, the current incumbent of the office, having certified the Public Accounts, would table his report in the House of Commons, bringing to the notice of the members every observed instance of slack-

Sharon Sutherland, 'On the Audit Trail of the Auditor General: Parliament's Servant, 1973–1980', *Canadian Public Administration* 23 (1980): 616–44. Courtesy of The Institute of Public Administration Canada.

ness or dishonesty which fell under the auditor's ambit for report. In later years, auditors general enjoyed leavening their reports with instances of government maladroitness which were not strictly of an accountancy nature. The annual hubbub was a three-day wonder. It served to keep almost everyone honest, and was enjoyed by almost everyone. There was a certain roundness to the event, characteristic of morality plays, which might have been seen as futility by the very energetic.

All this is past. Since 1973 when the present incumbent of the Office of the Auditor General (OAG), Mr James J. Macdonell, assumed office, the federal government has been in the throes of being cured not only of waste but also of error. In some respects little seems to have changed in the course of the decade: We continually elect Liberal governments, which continually subject the bureaucracy and the 'machinery of government' to review and reform. But the role of the Auditor General has changed: where that officer began as a traditional auditor, he is now an independent figure holding the potential of considerable political power. The topic of this paper is the history of that transformation, and an analysis of its implications for the balance of the Canadian system of government. The analysis is timely because the Office of the Auditor General falls vacant in the course of the 1980–1 fiscal year. Before appointing a new incumbent,[1] it would be appropriate for the government to review the situation. Basically, the paper argues, there are two main problems to correct. One is the Auditor General's new de facto power to 'certify' *policy*, or the *substance* of expenditure decisions, in addition to the traditional comment on the probity of expenditure. The other related problem is that this power interferes with the cabinet's ability to initiate, conduct and consider appropriate analyses of the performance of its programs.

The paper will first analyse the present situation and powers of the Office of the Auditor General. Secondly, it will review how the situation came about—the rationale, strategy and events which resulted in the OAG's new 'value-for-money' powers. This is followed by a review of the evaluation methods used by the OAG in the Studies in Procedures of Cost Effectiveness (SPICE). It is argued that SPICE was a complete failure, but still achieved a strategic end. Another aspect of the Auditor General's strategy, the creation within the centre of the federal bureaucracy of the Office of the Comptroller General (OCG), is put into context with the other events. Finally, the political costs of the present situation are discussed. It should be stressed at the outset that the paper does not assess any contribution of the OAG to management of the government other than the value-for-money mandate and its effects.

NEW POWERS OF THE OFFICE OF THE AUDITOR GENERAL

The situation at present is that the Auditor General has gained through the new act defining the powers of the Office (Auditor General Act, 1977) the de facto right to assess and protest against public policy programs implemented by the government. This was accomplished by shifting to the government the burden of demonstrating legitimacy of programs. A program is legitimate in the OAG's terms when it can be demonstrated that the program has achieved the results for which it was initially set up. All programs are to be analysed for their accomplishments, as a matter of routine.

The results of a government program, the Auditor General claims, can be conclusively described in a bottom-line kind of productivity measure yielded by his Office's so-called technique of value-for-money audit. (This term has now been subsumed under the title 'comprehensive audit'.)

It must be noted that at least four important issues are intertwined from the 1977 legislation onward. One is the problem of whether it is possible via some routine and demonstrable audit technique to generate 'facts' about whether or not some public program is effectively meeting the goals which it was intended to satisfy, these goals still existing as needs. The second issue is, given that there might be such a technique, should it be initiated, controlled, and conducted by cabinet or by the bureaucracy? That is, if an objective method exists for testing the utility of programs as 'deliverers' of public policy (and therefore as tests of the accuracy or utility of partisan ideological views of society), should the reins be held by elected politicians or by non-elected bureaucrats? Who should decide whether or not to implement the 'results' of studies? Third, if no such method exists, what is the implication of having created a structure which *assumes* that conclusive knowledge can be routinely generated, then substitutes reviews of unknown or contentious truth value in the dress of the new scientific product? Finally, who or what controls the Office of the Auditor General in the quest to bring government to account? These questions are addressed below. For the moment, it is important to establish the policy outcome of the semantic, technical, and philosophic confusion surrounding these issues.

The Auditor General has claimed since 1973 that an objective technique exists and that it is definitely to be found in 'value-for-money audit', 'effectiveness audit', 'effectiveness evaluation', 'management controls', and 'program evaluation'. In essence, the technique as explored by the OAG, and reported in its Studies in Procedures in Cost Effectiveness (SPICE)[2] is a confused application of a particular kind of social science activity developed in the United States during the early 1960s. The Americans developed the genre under the general rubric of 'program evaluation' or 'program impact evaluation'. In what can be called the classic American literature,[3] the program itself is conceived of as an experimental initiative or intervention by government. A 'program' is definitionally intended to ameliorate some problem or to bring about some desirable state of affairs. The changed situation represents the 'goals' of the program. The program evaluation study is therefore the controlled, scientific observation of the program treated as an experiment.

Researchers trained in the scientific method monitor and objectively measure the *amount of change* which the program has been able to accomplish, and report outcomes in summary, quantitative terms. Such studies were to generate program reports with the status of scientific knowledge. The information could then be applied by the persons in the system holding the *authority* to act upon the knowledge. They could add, subtract, and shift resources as program feedback dictated. Clearly, the program suited to this form of analysis would be the exception rather than the rule.

The Auditor General achieved adoption of the new act in 1977. His rationale for the new value for money audit was that the government was wilfully refusing to adopt the new technique, and that this refusal contributed to the alleged utter lack of central management control over the entire federal bureaucracy. The strategy undertaken to get the new act and, later, to shore it up, seemed to work by an alternation of scare tactics with careful encroachment. In essence, the Office of the Auditor General has moved from review of accounts for probity, to review of 'systems' for adequacy, to study of the entire management milieu for soundness, to the power to insist upon review of policy substance and outcomes, challenging the utility and legitimacy of policy.

The part of the Auditor General Act of 1977 which is of interest in this critique was conferred in the two value-for-money clauses which state that the Auditor General shall call attention to cases where:

- money has been expended without due regard to economy or efficiency; or
- satisfactory procedures have not been established to measure and report the effectiveness of programs, where such procedures could appropriately and reasonably be implemented.[4]

The government was mistaken to allow these issues to be presented as management problems dealing with economy, efficiency, and effectiveness in the context of pure administration. By doing so, the political issue is clouded. The issue is that the Auditor General has in fact gained the power to judge the government's right to pursue unquantifiable aims. The assumption is that a special kind of analysis (program evaluation. according to the OAG's definition) is appropriate unless it can be demonstrated otherwise to the Office of the Auditor General. Each of the government's programs is therefore subject to legitimation.

Strategically, the OAG has only to insist that a particular program is an appropriate candidate for review. Its power is applied to the bureaucracy just under the political level, through the new Office of the Comptroller General (OCG). The formation of this Office was extracted from the Liberal government in 1978. It was carved out of the Treasury Board Secretariat and is still housed there.[5] It is headed by a government appointee at the deputy head level. The incumbent is the 'Chief Financial Officer' for government with responsibility to the Treasury Board for establishing a comprehensive system of financial management. This responsibility is to be accomplished by the Comptroller General playing an accountancy role, and also taking responsibility for the quality of *non-financial* 'management controls'. It is the second responsibility which is of interest here. It means that the Comptroller General is responsible not only for ensuring that government programs are managed with regard to economy and efficiency, but that they will be evaluated for effectiveness in attaining goals. Between the new OCG and the Audit Office there exists a situation of reciprocal legal obligation, and thus of mutual supports and legitimation. When the Auditor General calls for a review, it is up to the Comptroller General to conduct a definitive study—or to seem to be quibbling about the program's suitability for evaluation. As paper powers now stand the OAG can then authoritatively judge the quality of the evaluation. The Office of the Auditor General has the last word.

One final transformation must be noted. The value-for-money audit facet has lately been subsumed under a new title, 'comprehensive audit'. This is a multifaceted examination and review of government management. Components of this total review are accessed through the OAG's acronym FRAME:

F – Financial controls
R – Reporting to Parliament
A – Attest and authority
M – Management controls—economy, efficiency, and effectiveness
E – EDP (electronic data-processing).[6]

The fourth component, management controls, is the value-for-money audit. As was noted above, this is the only aspect of the OAG's performance being commented upon in the present critique. (In comprehensive audit language, R and A are the traditional responsibilities of Parliament's auditor.)

In summary, the Auditor General's value-for-money audit mandate operates symbiotically with the responsibility of the Office of the Comptroller General to ensure that effectiveness evaluation is conducted. The effect is an erosion of political control of public policy. This is tolerated on the assumption that program effectiveness evaluation is an established, viable audit technique which provides value-free data from the administrative level for consumption by policy-makers. Because the Auditor General has the legal power to claim that a particular program is an appropriate candidate for measurement of outcomes (with the measurement to be conducted by the bureaucracy to the Auditor General's unspecified standards), the Office's incumbent has become a powerful political actor. The Auditor General possesses a vastly reinforced ability to suggest subjects for parliamentary consideration—that is, to direct the Public Accounts Committee's inquiry to policy themes and issues of the OAG's choosing. Should the government use its control of Parliament to stifle any theme, the Auditor General has only to move to the media and the public. The recent incumbent of the Office of the Auditor General seemed to freely take his case to the public.[7] Lately, the Office has managed the impact of the annual report. The presentation of the Report is split into several stages. There is a preview with departments, so that they may negotiate their reactions to OAG recommendations. There are press conferences. There is a conspectus for parliamentarians, with the highlights of the year selected and summarized. This is tabled with the Report itself. Each Report contains a check-list for the Comptroller General, specifying government's very agenda for reply.

Parliament is in the present situation a weapon in the Auditor General's hand when he so chooses, rather than the other way about. The Office of the Auditor General controls a major agenda. Indeed, the Office of the Auditor General is a far more potent opposition than the Official Opposition. The OAG claims what it wishes to claim, and is not itself subject to exposure, accusation and examination of anything like a similar scope. As a recent commentator notes, without irony, '[f]ew if any governments anywhere in the world are subject to such accountability.' The introduction to this extraordinary statement tells us that the Auditor General

. . . sees the hypothetical danger of an auditor general abusing his power as more than outweighed by the benefits which value-for-money auditing will bestow on Canadian taxpayers. No longer will politicians or bureaucrats be able to ignore, camouflage, or suppress the true effects of their spending programs, no matter how ill-conceived or ill-fated they may be. From now on they will either provide Parliament with a factual comparison of the original objectives and actual results of such programs, or risk having their failure to do so exposed in the Auditor General's report.[8]

It is essential to answer that governments do not attain their legitimacy by being successful in all their attempts at governing. The legitimacy of government is based on the electorally expressed will of a sovereign people. The electorate puts politicians in power to pursue policy via programs. In our parliamentary system, the government is to be watched but not seriously impeded by other politicians. The Auditor General of Canada's traditional role was to assure parliamentarians through the Public Accounts Committee that the administrative arm—the bureaucracy—was complying to the letter of the government's expenditure directives. Bureaucrats were neither to pocket the public money nor to spend it without authority. Instead, our parliamentary auditor has become a conduit directly to the public *via* Parliament for so-called objective information on government policy and program *outcomes*. If knowledge is power, then so is the ability to control the process by which information is selected, certified as authentic audit knowledge, and made public.

RATIONALE FOR PURSUIT OF VALUE-FOR-MONEY AUDIT

This situation in which a non-elected officer has the power to call the government's bluff, but never himself have his bluff called, is scarcely credible in the absence of an account of why and how it was brought about. The situation seems to be the result of Mr Macdonell's desire to use the audit function in a creative way, interacting with the ambience created by the PPB system in government as a whole. Traditionally the audit function ends at disclosure of lapses. It then rests with the client for the audit to devise appropriate corrective action. But Mr Macdonell wanted to recommend systems to prevent typical kinds of lapses. He further wanted to guarantee the implementation of his recommendations by obtaining the power to check or 'audit' for whether suitable changes had been made.[9] At the same time, it seems to have occurred to Mr Macdonell that the whole program itself rather than its individual financial transactions was a suitable entity for audit. We now turn to that choice.

The choice was made possible by a second factor: the Canadian government's prior and independent adoption in 1971 of the Planning Programming and Budgeting System (PPBS) framework for presentation of its Estimates of forthcoming expenditure to Parliament. As early as 1975, the Auditor General's decision to audit programs was foreshadowed by the *Report of the Independent Review Committee on the Office of the Auditor General*.[10] (The report is generally called the Wilson Report. The committee members were in fact appointed by the Auditor General.) The report explicitly links the need for major qualitative changes in the audit function to the 'new approach to expenditure management' of the 1960s—the adoption of PPBS and the decentralization of financial control following upon the Glassco Commission's report.

PPBS was intended to make analysis (both political and bureaucratic) guide internal bureaucratic procedures by linking the products of analysis to the budgetary process. The Independent Review Committee Report provides a succinct description:

> In developing requests for future funding, departments were supposed to examine critically their current spending programs, to evaluate the effectiveness of past expenditures and to analyze the comparative cost and effectiveness of alternative methods for achieving objectives. Interest was promoted in cost benefit analysis and other quantitative techniques designed to promote superior evaluation of expenditure proposals. . . . Old techniques of detailed control were found to be inefficient and PPBS represented a major effort to respond to the problem . . . these changes reflected a recognition that in a multi-million dollar budget it was less important to ensure that every financial t was crossed and i dotted than it was to know whether funds were being spent in a manner that would ensure the achievement of the purposes for which they were made available.[11]

The problem is that PPBS was thought out for application to American government. There, as in Canada, departments develop requests for future funding for two audiences: the government which agrees to put its request in the budget, and the legislature which appropriates the public money for the department or agency. In the American context, both requests are 'real'. There, the legislature can refuse a request for funding which has already been accepted by the executive. Thus if describing the individual items of expenditure in terms of their goals can work once to justify the department to the executive, it may work again to justify the executive to the legislature.

But in a parliamentary system, the request for future funding from a department to government (the Treasury) is real, whereas the request from government to legislature is *pro forma*. Hence the intent of the government in adopting the 'purposes-and-programs' PPBS format for rolling-up expenditures for its internal use would have been to improve routine internal use of planning. It should have made programming more responsive to policy, as it were. The government's intention in using PPBS categories to describe its expenditures for Parliament must have been to improve the understanding of the House of Commons (both opposition and government backbenchers) of the government's priorities and general direction. This improved understanding would be revealed in a better quality of debate and work in the House and its committees. That is, it must surely have been intended that the PPBS program framework serve as the *only* format for planning and review of policy and its delivery through programs; as an *auxiliary* format to the line-item budget for accounting and control within the government; but *not at all* for legitimation and 'audit' for achievement of government's very purposes.

It likely did not occur to the planners in the executive that government could be taken at face value when it began in the 1971 Estimates to describe its spending by program purposes, rather than by votes detailed with the items of expenditure in functional categories. The government controls Parliament through its majority. It is therefore unthinkable that a majority of parliamentarians take an independent adversary position and authoritatively demand an accounting of spending against the scheme of purposes/programs. Parliament is supposed to hand the money over by vote, to understand and debate general purposes and departmental achievements in terms of PPBS programs, and to depend on the parliamentary auditor to review the votes' expenditure for probity and legality to certify the public accounts.

In fact it was not Parliament that picked up on the possibility of linking appropriations with results of appropriations. It was, as noted, the Auditor General. Given the breadth and technical confusion of the votes' statements, compared with the purposeful statements of the program budget, it may have seemed simpler to the OAG to audit on the latter. But the project is premised on a suppressed assumption. If the Auditor General is to assess conclusively the extent to which funds achieve the political-cum-rhetorical purposes for which they were voted, it must be through a publicly defensible, objective, scientific management technique. The subtle sands of opinion and value are the weapons of the *partisan* opposition for attacking executive spending: when all is said, the government simply outvotes the opposition and helps itself to the public purse. The opposition is paid to bark, while the rules ensure that it will not be a dog in the manger. But an auditor cannot work with rhetoric and suggestion. The corollary is that results of a proper objective audit cannot be ignored. They are authoritative within their proper sphere. The Auditor General, therefore, in auditing on programs, must have a measuring device that both government and opposition can assess and certify as conclusive.

The necessary objective technique is, of course, the effectiveness evaluation component of the OAG's value-for-money concept. It is argued to be a bottom-line technique for judging goals attainment. The Wilson Committee had recognized that there were serious problems with the identification of program purposes in such a way that they would be amenable to quantification. It also recognized that the aspects of a problem which were currently measurable were not necessarily the aspects most urgently in need of a solution. Even so, it recommended that the Auditor General be granted in his new legislation the right to report on government's effectiveness studies and 'even to make his own evaluation of program results if there is no other satisfactory way'.[12] The committee thereby specified the two most pressing tasks for the OAG's post-1975 workplan: to gain the legal power to conduct value-for-money audits of the outcomes of the government's programs; and to develop, specify, and demonstrate criteria and methodology for the conduct of a conclusive value-for-money audit.

THE PURSUIT OF THE VALUE-FOR-MONEY AUDIT MANDATE: STRATEGY AND EVENTS

The annual reports of the Office of the Auditor General provide a history of the transformation of the Office's powers. The transformation began quite tentatively: in the 1973 Report, Mr Macdonell had stated his intention to audit for remedial action taken to correct weaknesses. Neither politicians nor bureaucrats seem to have reacted to this statement. He next noted in the 1974 Report that the Financial

Administration Act (FAA) indicated how Parliament's auditor should perform both the legislative compliance audit and the matching of expenditures and revenues to certify the Public Accounts. Here one sees the foreshadowing, of the 'management controls' audit. The Auditor General's duties are to be discharged '. . . through an investigation of the adequacy of the organization, application and operation of financial controls and procedures.'[13] Section 58 of the FAA states that the Auditor General is '. . . to examine . . . and to ascertain whether . . . essential records are maintained and the rules and procedures are sufficient to safeguard and control . . .' To establish what 'sufficiency of controls' might mean, servicewide, the Auditor General then launched an investigation called the Financial Management and Control Study (FMCS), staffing it with more than thirty senior accountants from sixteen accounting firms.[14] The following year, it is noteworthy that FMCS is cited as though it were a formal discharge of Audit Office duties required under the FAA. Furthermore, the study itself has as its bottom line a clear conclusion: 'The present state of the financial management and control systems of departments and agencies of the Government of Canada is significantly below acceptable standards of quality and effectiveness.'[15]

In 1975 there is anticipation of the creation of the OCG. The 1975 Report contains some recommendations for improvement of purely financial control. Their gist is that 1) departments should take responsibility to tighten budgeting and accounting practices as suitable to their own needs and the needs for full disclosure; and 2) the responsibility for monitoring the quality of departmental efforts should be taken up in a much more determined fashion by the centre of government. The Supplement to the 1975 Report sketches how this should be done: '. . . a new senior official of the government in all matters of financial management and control' should be appointed. In the first references, Mr Macdonell recommends that this new officer, the Comptroller General, should not regard the post as a 'stepping stone to other jobs' in government.[16] That is, the mode of appointment of this new senior official should establish his independence of bureaucratic and political pressures. Also in 1975, there is a clear and open anticipation of the future importance of the value-for-money audit. The Report notes:

> . . . although budgetary control systems satisfy the legal restriction against over-spending of appropriations, they do not show managers whether the intended purposes have been attained by relating clearly stated objectives to explicit benefits measured quantitatively wherever possible.[17]

The Supplement enlarges the thought:

> Continuing programs and policies require improved evaluation to weed out the redundant, to improve the faulty and to ensure that they appropriately reflect the government's changing priorities. This involves a review of the basis for and the operation of the detailed activities, sub-activities, projects, and processes carried on within programs and an assessment of the results attained relative to costs incurred.[18]

The following paragraph notes the then-current (never implemented) plan for evaluation of policy or programs at cabinet initiative, similar to the Policy Analysis and Review of the British government. Cabinet-level evaluation is not enough, the Audit Office says: all continuing federal programs and activities should be reviewed in detail, on a cyclical basis, from a base of 'much-improved information on the various activities, their costs and their results'. The central agencies should participate as appropriate.

In 1976, the Auditor General took a different line of attack. The results of the Financial Management and Control Study led the Auditor General 'inescapably' to report that 'financial management and control in the Government of Canada is grossly inadequate.'[19] The Public Accounts Committee had earlier endorsed all the 1975 Report recommendations, but the Auditor General now re-emphasized only his requirement for a chief financial officer, the Comptroller General. The state of affairs was said to be so bad as to require urgent adjustments to the centre of the machinery of government. The task of the new central agency would be to manage government, almost as though to do so were itself solely a matter of efficiency. The new office was prescribed a number of interrelated responsibilities. It was to make the annual Estimates a sound basis for control through changes as to their form; to preside over the systems that monitor the flow of money through the government; to maintain the central accounts; to ensure that expenditure conforms to efficiency and economy, and that 'satisfactory procedures measure the effectiveness of programs where they could reasonably be expected to apply'.[20]

The 1976 Report also published the Wilson Committee's recommendations that the role of the Auditor General be substantially altered. Section 3 recommends that the Auditor General report to Parliament cases where 'money has been expended other than for purposes for which it was appropriated by Parliament or value-for-money has not been obtained for any expenditure or expenditures'.[21] Nineteen seventy-six also appears to be one of the first important years for previews of the OAG's Report. Shortly after being warned of its dramatic contents in November, the government established the Royal Commission of Inquiry on Financial Management and Accountability (the Lambert Commission).

The Auditor General's own prescription was already fully formed: a fundamental restructuring of the Treasury Board Secretariat by appointment of a chief financial officer, the Comptroller General, and a more prominent recognition of the financial function in departments and agencies. Indeed, his suggestions are virtual demands, in the context of his statement that 'unless the Government responds positively to these . . . actions [he is] convinced that the present unsatisfactory state of affairs will persist'.[23]

Nineteen seventy-seven became a banner year. Its events consolidated the Auditor General's authority over the standards and procedures of the financial function. First, there is a report of the government's promise to establish a Comptroller General to 'further strengthen administrative controls and to eliminate inefficiencies and waste'.[24] At the same time the Auditor General Act had been introduced for second reading in the House of Commons. The Wilson Committee's key recommendation for the value-for-money audit had been captured to the Auditor General's satisfaction in section 7 (2) of the new act. This section '. . . for the first time formally assigns the responsibility for this type of reporting to the Auditor General'.[25]

A third major announcement reports somewhat anti-climactically, that the new 'responsibility' has already been taken up. In anticipation of the full mandate, the Auditor General had initiated a Study of Procedures in Cost Effectiveness (SPICE) in September of 1976. It can be noted that the strategy was similar to the earlier use of the FAA to justify the first set of studies, the Financial Management and Control Study. Again the purpose was to investigate and describe management control systems in the public sector which monitor or measure economy, efficiency and effectiveness. The information which would be generated was to help the OAG develop resourcing and technical strategies for the uptake of the new duties. Again the SPICE studies were being directed by some sixty senior consultants recruited from the accounting profession under the Executive Interchange Program. Once more, the initially friendly and low-key probing would lead to 'inescapable' and roundly negative 'conclusions'.

To recapitulate, the situation at the end of 1977 was as follows: 1) the Auditor General had established that there was a need for central financial controls, and for routine, standardized monitoring (controlling) of government activities on criteria of efficiency, economy, and effectiveness in achievement of goals (the management controls); 2) the government had promised a new central agency which would have the responsibility of designing and implementing all necessary systems and controls; 3) the Auditor General had now the right to audit for these systems and controls, and the right to specify what is appropriate or reasonable, the criteria for this audit remaining undisclosed. That is, he could by 1977 comment authoritatively, without specifying standards, pending the development of audit criteria.[26] Lesser-noted changes concern timing. The new act gives the Auditor General the right to submit special reports on subjects he considers too pressing to await tabling of his annual report. In the fall of 1977, the Standing Committee on Public Accounts gained in a separate initiative a permanent order of reference: as soon as the Public Accounts and the Auditor General's reports on the Accounts are tabled, they are referred immediately to the Public Accounts Committee for study.[27]

There is still a key missing for an understanding of why and how the Auditor General ran the end run to establish the Office of the Comptroller General inside the bureaucracy. In effect, the changes which the government had made to the value-for-money clauses of the act made it inevitable. The government had not been willing to give the Auditor General carte blanche to investigate its program accomplishments and present a full report card of so-called audit observations to an entity identified only as 'Parliament'. This would have amounted, at most, to open pronouncement on policy. At the least, it would have amounted to an admission that the government's spending required some additional legitimation. Hence the defensive wording in the new Auditor General Act, cited earlier. The Auditor General was in the new act given the right to audit for the presence of satisfactory evaluation procedures, but was not himself to provide substantive comment on program outcomes. Given the government's wording, it appeared that the OAG would simply have to review the evaluations as they were generated from within, by whatever source.

Analysis would continue to be initiated by the conventional actors at a time of their choosing. Government's evasion was to have a short life. The Auditor General wanted the evaluations. The ground work had already been laid to create the OCG to monitor financial processes: that office could also be used to host and thereby entrench the program evaluation function inside government.

As it happened, events unfolded through 1976 and 1977 in a manner which had enhanced the independence and power of the Auditor General. These were the years of the scandals over the Crown corporations Polysar and Atomic Energy of Canada. These scandals were said to be 'the smoking guns which proved to the public, to the Public Accounts Committee and, ultimately, to the government that Macdonell was not posturing or indulging in alarmist tactics when he claimed that Parliament had lost, or was close to losing, effective control of the public purse.'[28] Unfortunately, smoking guns are as often a sign of discussion foreclosed as of justice triumphant.

The Auditor General made considerable strategic gain with the findings that undocumented expenditures in the millions had been made by the corporations. The government's fault took on a general aspect despite three important factors. These are: 1) that Parliament has never controlled the public purse in the sense the Auditor General suggested; 2) that the abuses took place in loosely controlled, enterpreneurial Crown corporations rather than in the ministries of government; and 3) that the abuses had to do with the ruthless pursuit of profit rather than with slack, wasteful, or dishonest financial management of departmental programs. This was the currency which bought the linch-pin for the value-for-money audit—the Office of the Comptroller General. Once more initial bargaining positions were such that the Auditor General's concessions to government did not seriously interfere with the entrenchment of the value-for-money function. Mr Macdonell had initially wanted the Comptroller General to be an independent officer, similar to the Auditor General in his autonomy. The government won the point that the new officer should be a full career member of the bureaucracy. He was not to be independent of government and bureaucracy alike by virtue of an appointment to serve Parliament.[29] The change was essentially meaningless. Regardless of what his own formal mandate might say, the OCG was bound to provision of evaluations by the terms of the 1977 Auditor General Act. In essence, with regard to the value-for-money function, the Comptroller's Office is under a franchise to the OAG.

In 1978 the Office of the Auditor General celebrated its one hundredth year. The emphasis in that year's Report is on the new Office of the Comptroller General, and on the findings of the SPICE project, by now under way for two years. Both subjects are prominently discussed in the Report's preface, which consists of letters between the then-President of the Treasury Board, Robert Andras, and Mr Macdonell. The new Comptroller General is not to be at a loss as to how to proceed: SPICE has introduced systematic value-for-money audit to government.

It should also be noticed that the Auditor General applies no caveats as to the experimental or investigatory nature of the SPICE studies (the first year of which were carried out both before and beyond the limited authorization of the new 1977 act). Instead, the 1978 Report talks strongly about SPICE findings and recommendations. These are

. . . as important as any I have reported to Parliament during my term of Office and may well be as important as any reported to Parliament since the Audit Office was established one hundred years ago. . . .

There is, in my opinion, widespread lack of due regard for economy and efficiency in the operations of the Government, and inadequate attention to determining whether programs costing millions of dollars are accomplishing what Parliament intended.[30]

As well, a new chapter opens. Another major theme of the centennial year is the need to consolidate and reshape departmental audit—all phases of review from financial audit through all types of reviews—into one 'comprehensive audit' function. The aspects of the comprehensive audit are to be applied to all activities inside government twice during the course of a three- to five-year plan: once by internal auditors working for the top departmental bureaucrat but to standards overseen by the Comptroller General, and once by the Office of the Auditor General for its reports to Parliament. It can be noted that the ground work is here being laid for departmental evaluation schemes to contain routinely a value-for-money or evaluation component for application to all programs. Further, this work will go forward on a multi-year cycle which is independent of the multi-year parliamentary or political cycle. The Auditor General as 'servant' of Parliament is no longer the servant of any particular Parliament.

EVALUATION METHODOLOGY: SPICE AS A DEMONSTRATION

It has been claimed by the OAG that the Studies in Procedures in Cost Effectiveness both generated conclusive knowledge about the state of the government, and developed evaluation methodology by serving as the test vehicle for the Audit Office's 'comprehensive methodology' in the three 'controls' aspects of management. These aspects are planning capital acquisition projects (economy), measuring and increasing efficiency, and evaluating effectiveness. In the newer comprehensive audit language, we are talking here about development of standards for conclusive audit of the fourth element of the acronym FRAME, the 'management controls' of economy, efficiency, and effectiveness. This methodology remains un-standardized despite the Auditor General's official endorsement of SPICE and the techniques supposedly developed under its aegis. The purpose of this section is to point to the major flaws of SPICE.

Were it not for the classic problem of distinguishing between politics and administration, the Auditor General's goals for SPICE and its contribution to public service management would seem unexceptionable. Managers in the public service, according to the Auditor General, are to manage public money with due regard to delivering full value for expenditure. Due regard is shown by the use of management information to achieve economy and efficiency in transactions and procedures. Further, the manager must measure *outcomes* of the initiative which the money attempted to accomplish—that is, effectiveness. A proper comprehensive audit, therefore, is a complete and independent assessment of a manager's performance. The audit

teams are to assess the management controls in the light of the special program circumstances for which they were designed.

Some few of the OAG's definitions of these terms are necessary. Economy is the
acquisition of human and material resources in appropriate quality and quantity at
the lowest cost. Efficiency is the production of the maximum output for any given
set of resources which are put into the program effort. It is important to take the third
definition, of effectiveness, in full:

> Effectiveness concerns the extent to which a program achieves its goals or
> other intended effects. For example, to increase income in a particular area, a
> program might be devised to create jobs. The jobs created would be program
> output. This contributes to the desired program effect of increased income
> which can be measured to assess program effectiveness. Of course, not all pro-
> grams are equally evaluable.[31]

Despite the seeming reasonableness, SPICE was poorly planned and poorly conducted from beginning to end. Most obviously, the manner in which the target areas
were chosen for the SPICE process, forbids the results being authoritatively reported
as representative of the multitude of organizations composing the public service.[32] It
will be recalled that SPICE was initiated in order to explore the *potential* for effectiveness evaluation. This evaluation was to be conducted under some future mandate of
the Auditor General to improve public service management. In essence, then, SPICE
was initiated as a probe to explore the technique. Exploratory studies often deliberately select extreme cases. These offer the best potential for illustration of a new technique or method. The SPICE team accordingly deliberately selected particular
programs for study. A sample which is drawn for purposes of inference is quite a different matter. If a 'scientific' study intends to make discoveries which will be representative of some larger entity, it should not pre-select 'hot' areas. A reporting-type
study should have chosen its sample from the supposed twenty-two hundred small
program elements[33] of the public service in such a way that the sample would be representative of all types of programs. The classical way of doing this is to randomly
choose the sample for review from some comprehensive master list. SPICE had it both
ways. The programs for study were hand-picked, and it was then claimed that the
SPICE results accurately described the state of management of the *whole* public service. This would be fault enough, had the government committed it, to utterly dis-
qualify the overall findings of such a report in the OAG's eyes.

Indeed, there is an ambivalence characterizing the SPICE exercise as described
and defended in the 1978 Report which is so great that, for this reader, it cumulates
into an impression of intellectual dishonesty. The impression is perhaps created by the
fact that the Report is the work of many persons rather than one, and its claims have
not been closely reconciled. Ambiguity is prominent in statements of criteria for the
individual studies, the standards to which work shall be conducted, and the rules for
avoidance of political comment by the OAG. We can now turn to the problems giving rise to this impression.

Let us begin with the criteria by which the individual audit studies of the SPICE teams were to be conducted. According to the Oxford Shorter Dictionary, criteria are characteristics attached to a thing, by which the thing can be judged or estimated. Criteria for judgment of an audit entity must be stipulated before the fact. Otherwise the auditor is under suspicion of having made up his observations on an ad hoc basis, and the attest purpose of audit is defeated. The SPICE effectiveness studies were supposed to demonstrate the usefulness and applicability of the OAG's criteria, so that the bureaucracy will know how to apply them internally. The bureaucracy's results would be later reviewed on the same criteria by the staff of the Office of the Auditor General. In his introduction to SPICE's findings, Mr Macdonell does not specify the criteria for effectiveness audit. He does however take a firm stand:

> I have observed a mystique that surrounds the question of evaluating program outcomes. Many see program evaluation as complex, esoteric and difficult, if not impossible. In plain language, we are talking about the information managers should have at their fingertips concerning the accomplishments of government programs. By and large, the Government does not have this information even though it is basic to the concept of accountability.[34]

Later statements, presumably by Office staff, are no more specific. First, program objectives and effects are to be specified as precisely 'as possible'. Secondly, those program objectives which can be measured should be identified. (In neither case is the actor who specifies or the entity identified.) The third criterion is that 'procedures to measure program effectiveness should reflect the state of the art, and be cost justified.' Fourthly, study results should be reported to departmental management, to the government, and to Parliament, in a 'manner and frequency consistent with the particular recipient's decision-making responsibilities.' Finally, the evaluation studies generated to these broad specifications should be used as an 'essential input to decisions on the future of programs.'[35] Managers and politicians are to be responsible and accountable for the use of the information and recommendations of the evaluation reports. (The Lambert Royal Commission failed to note that managers are accountable to the Auditor General, if to no one else,[36] because he has the intention to audit for their compliance with his recommendations. In a looser sense, politicians likewise can be held to account by the Auditor General, should he choose to emphasize to Public Accounts Committee that the government has not acted upon receiving alleged knowledge about a program.)

But these are not criteria. The first three are summary descriptions of some aspects of the problem. The last two insist that results must be used. It is not at all surprising that these statements show up again a few pages later as *recommendations* to the government describing what would constitute a desirable state of affairs to prepare for effectiveness evaluation.[37] That is, SPICE ends as it began: by recommending the development of criteria for the audits it has only just completed.

After criteria come the standards to which the work shall be conducted. In the places where the SPICE researchers speak of the need to develop evaluation methodology, improvement becomes a matter of degree: the effectiveness evaluation technique can be appropriately utilized in '. . . at least partial measurement of the impact of most major programs'. But when SPICE is reviewing the government's own evaluation activity, it is all or nothing: '. . . technically flawed measurements are at least useless and perhaps misleading'.[38] Two standards exist.

The remaining problem for the SPICE methodologists is to state the rules which they will follow to stay clear of commentary on the value positions taken in the political process. That is, objective criteria for routine and objective audit must not only exist, they must also be applied to the proper objects of audit. The Report itself says that the Audit Office should not comment on political themes.[39] Having stated the desirable outcome, the SPICE methodologists push on. The Report next states that the unchecked tendency for public programs to perpetuate themselves must be overcome. This political theme is laid down as a matter of simple fact. Example fares no better. SPICE might at the very least have demonstrated the OAG's tact in the choice of subjects for the individual SPICE studies. But among the thirteen abbreviated SPICE case histories published on pages 84 to 96 of the 1978 Report are studies of such politically important areas (that is, central to ongoing partisan politics) as the current government's job creation programs for depressed areas, education activity for the benefit of natives, the Parole Board's method of taking decisions to parole federal convicts, tax enforcement activity, the bilingualism program, the Regional Development Incentives Act, and job retraining programs for the unemployed. As SPICE saw it *none* of the government's prior attempts to assess the usefulness of these initiatives had been completely satisfactory. Only two departments were found to have measured 'significant' program outcomes, and their studies were technically deficient. The few studies that went forward to senior management were so flawed as to be substantively misleading, and, for some reason, '. . . the communication of such reports to Parliament is rare'.[40]

Enough has been said to establish that SPICE did not create an objective methodology for the review of public programs to establish the extent to which programs have met their objectives. Nor did SPICE succeed in choosing programs for review at a level of analysis which would stay clear of partisan-political values. But not only does the Auditor General continue to insist that an objective technique exists; he has created the Office of the Comptroller General, one of whose tasks is to ensure that the mechanism shall become embedded in government. It is perhaps tempting to ask whether the Comptroller's team will succeed where SPICE failed. But the question is strategically naive. SPICE was an intellectual failure but still a political success. The intellectual failure did not matter because SPICE 'results' were not necessary. The OAG had already accomplished its goal: to establish the mechanism for automatic, 'bottom-line' policy review inside the bureaucracy. The existence of the objective technique does not matter if it is generally accepted that objective review is possible, that departments will provide analytic products under the new name, that the OCG orchestrates their provision, and finally, that the OAG defines and guarantees the activity.

ROLE OF THE OFFICE OF THE COMPTROLLER GENERAL

Has the Auditor General succeeded in entrenching a program evaluation function in the heart of bureaucracy—the new central agency of the Comptroller General—so that bureaucracy and government shall become self-inhibiting? The question can be broken into two. First, is it possible in principle that the Office of the Comptroller General might develop an objective methodology through which it will be possible to assess conclusively the outcomes of all public programs? What would it mean if it could? Secondly, if such a method for developing conclusive knowledge cannot be developed, what are the implications of a continuation of the present situation? This can be described as a situation in which there is ostensibly an expectation that an objective methodology can and will be developed, plus a continuing authority for the Office of the Comptroller General to enforce the conduct of current state-of-the-art program evaluations to satisfy the requirements of the Auditor General.

Let us take possibilities first. The kind of activity which the Auditor General demands is social scientific research applied to the problem of describing whether, or to what extent, public programs have met their goals. This is not the place to rehearse the debate on the potential of social scientific research to generate demonstrable knowledge or to solve practical problems. It is enough to indicate a few of the major difficulties which beset classic program evaluation as just one type of applied research. There are problems of the following types:

- difficulties about specifying goals; it may be counter-productive or inappropriate (for example, for political reasons) to specify them, they may not be representable with even rough accuracy by simple indicators which in the case of multiple goals will be incommensurable, and the goals may properly change or be changed in the course of carrying out the program;
- difficulties stemming from lack of knowledge about social causation and hence a lack of theory to focus the evaluation research (leaving only the symbolic value-laden political rhetoric as a broad guide to suggest mechanisms for test);
- difficulties about replicating programs, and thereby carrying over to one program lessons learned from an earlier program (and related difficulties due to ever-changing contexts of program application);
- difficulties about organizing and maintaining in a bureaucracy or a political system a 'memory' for any lessons at all; and
- difficulties about using the results of one-shot studies when these results are not overwhelmingly confirmed by ordinary knowledge or common sense, or by other research.

There is some evidence that the first and current incumbent of the Office of the Comptroller General, Mr Harry Rogers, has some respect for the thorns in these problems. Mr. Rogers does not himself seem to hold the view that a technique exists by which absolute facts will be generated:

... you could get into a situation where the department had relied on its management consultants but the auditor, also involved with management consultants, would come up with a different answer. Who would resolve the two answers, both of which were arrived at, using very acceptable methods, by two sets of consultants?[41]

During 1980, the Office of the Comptroller General professed its 'reasonableness' as to the standards and costs of the evaluation studies. It is clear that the OCG does not expect the bureaucracy to routinely generate classic, conclusive studies of high scientific value. There had been to this date no ascertainable move to set up a central recording system for preservation, retrieval and cross-referencing of individual findings of departmental studies. Indeed, this lack is tantamount to admission that perhaps most of the studies generated under the evaluation policy will be context-bound management-type reviews. While this catholicity is entirely appropriate to the variety in the field for study, it is not appropriate to the second order of general policy requirement.[42]

COSTS OF THE STATUS QUO

The OCG's reasonable-man approach to the problem generates a serious dilemma. If program evaluation is not conducted to one standard methodology, so that two analysts working on the same program or program element, following the same sets of steps, will come up with the same result, why should we still call it an audit technique? And if studies which pass as program evaluations contain elements of professional judgment for which ministers must take responsibility, why should the Auditor General get to review them? The Auditor General has the legal authority to demand and to review evaluation studies, and to comment authoritatively upon them. As paper powers now stand, therefore, on the argument of this paper, the external auditor of the government for Parliament is to be routinely supplied with judgmental management information. For example, the OAG would have to be privy to a minister's order that his departmental officers disregard efficiency to pursue some higher-order policy-cum-political value. Otherwise the bureaucracy would bear the brunt of criticism of seeming inefficiency.

Will such a thing come to pass? It is unfortunate either way. If the OAG is made privy to management information, a non-elected officer and his staff have become influential at the heart of decision-making. What is more likely to take place is that less and less crucial analysis at the intersection of policy and program will be committed to paper. (It is not at all clear how the value-for-money initiative will fit with the freedom of information act proposed in 1980.) Analysis may well become less formal, and therefore less subject to critical review internally as well as externally. The government in effect will be much less free to initiate, conduct, and implement its own analyses for the achievement of its own purposes. It will be less free to experiment with programs for their policy utility. Instead, government is driven into a continual defensive posture, as is the bureaucracy. When the analytic product demanded must always be 'program evaluation', both will protect themselves with analyses which they have no intention of using. The result will be a proliferation of inappropriate and/or superficial analysis, and a retreat of effective power from the paper-bound corridors. Another related result will be an increase in the size of government, to feed the dance of the papers.

In effect, the Auditor General has become a compulsory management consult-ant to government with something that consultants are not supposed to have—the last word and the use of the client's overhead. Democratic political control is eroded. There is no need to argue whether this is important to some degree, it is important *per se*. The Auditor General has breached the principle of political accountability for the actions of the government. The cost of pretending that judgmental reports are generating a conclusive kind of scientific knowledge is clear. It is that the Office of the Auditor General has acquired a routine power to meddle in the process whereby policy is delivered to the public. What will the outcome be, one may ask?

Even little Red Riding Hood recognized the wolf once the bonnet was off. Public servants as a rule are very cautious about giving the appearance of pursuing politically relevant values independently of their political masters. Probity dictates that the public servant behave so that he or she cannot be accused of either partisan preference or partisan jealousy, because of the public causes they espouse. The Office of the Auditor General is perhaps qualitatively different from most government appointments, in that a link to the public is suggested by making the reporting relationship to Parliament. But this is intended for defence only, to protect the Office's incumbent from the influence of the party of government. It is not intended to establish the Office as an active political force in its own right. It is therefore important that the incumbent of the Office not give the impression of being moved by political values or interests which would fit with a partisan preference. His audit observations must be beyond suspicion of partisan taint.

To answer the question posed, then, Mr Macdonell's purpose in wanting to entrench the program evaluation function at all levels of government is surely to push big government into cutting itself back to small government, indeed small-c conservative-type government. This is made utterly clear, for one example, in a speech he presented to the annual conference of the Institute of Public Administration held in August 1979, in Winnipeg.[43] The speech is a polemic for small government, in which the authorities are the conservative thinkers Milton Friedman and F.A. Hayek. In mid-1980, Milton Friedman was acting as a consultant to both Mr Ronald Reagan in the United States and Mrs Margaret Thatcher in Great Britain. The Auditor General's speech caricatures bureaucrats as fanatic spenders of money which they regard as 'wampum'. This argument is supported by reference to the *New York Times* on the American bureaucracy; similarly the Auditor General sees the cure in the American 'tax revolt' of Proposition Thirteen. He calls personal income tax deduction at source '. . . this insidious and monstrous bureaucratic strategem.' He recommends that citizens should pay personal income tax in phased lump sums, presumably to maximize resentment. In one breath he maintains that he is not political. In the next he speaks approvingly of 'right-wing' governments in Britain and elsewhere, including the Canadian provinces, perhaps misapprehending that 'right' merely stands for 'correct' in the phrase. In this speech he also maintains that his new comprehensive audit does for non-profit organizations what the bottom line does for business—it establishes one simple measure of viability derived from some form of cost-benefit analysis. It is a contingent social fact that these sentiments are also held by that tendency of modern political thought dubbed neo-Conservatism. It is this writer's considered opinion that the sentiments of this speech are nothing short of astounding when voiced by a public servant. They are campaigning-type conservative values.

Further, so long as the OAG and OCG retain their confusing shared guidance of the evaluation function, these values will be entrenched in government. Even where evaluation studies are conducted as applied social research on the best possible model, they will operate in a biased manner to yield results claiming that programs are ineffective.

The defence of this view is simple. In traditional research the null hypothesis is tested: in program evaluation the null hypothesis is that the causal intervention of the program has made *no difference* to the problem which the program was designed to solve. But the internal logic of scientific research is such that its own errors and inadequacies work to dilute results. This dilution is intended in the scientific method to ensure caution: it will stop the researcher from overturning the null hypothesis and making a false claim about the effectiveness of some cause. Therefore, the foregone conclusion of sloppy or badly defined applied research is that 'nothing works' whether or not this is true. And it is historically true that program evaluation conducted in government overwhelmingly results in sloppy research. American experience since 1960 has generated a great deal of evidence[44] for this contention. When the burden is on government to demonstrate effectiveness, but when nothing can be shown to work, the slide from technical statements to prescription is easy. If one cannot *cure* some problem, then why spend money on the people who suffer the problem? To spend money on lost causes suggests that one thinks money is 'wampum'. The problem set is such that redistributive aims tend to be lost to consideration.

In assessing the importance of this outcome, pragmatists tend to concede the principle, but argue that a systematic bias toward small government will in fact have no real impact on the direction of our society. There are two parts to the pragmatists' argument. First, they say that it must be realized that the expenditure budget of the federal government consists of a blend of statutory and discretionary expenditures, in proportions of roughly 60 to 40.[45] Therefore, the government is already locked into the greater part of its expenses. Further, expenditure may well be the least significant of the instruments that elected politicians can wield in pursuit of either small or big government. Tax expenditure and regulation may be more important, more hidden, ways of creating winners and losers in terms of society's wealth and privileges.[46] Therefore, any impact will be at the margins. The second leg to the argument is that the significant areas of social expenditure are in the provincial jurisdiction under the division of powers specified in the British North America Act. The provinces are in charge of welfare, health care, education and the administration of the courts and the civil law. The pragmatic conclusion is that the entire issue is a storm in a teapot. The Auditor General may have achieved a kind of personal fame, inconvenienced the bureaucracy and dumbfounded a few politicians, but he has had and can have no real impact on the nation or on policy for any part of the nation's citizens.

A simple review of the federal jurisdictions is rebuttal enough. Among federal areas are the entire criminal justice area, including the RCMP and the penitentiaries, unemployment insurance, immigration policy, and all the spending in the Department of Secretary of State through which a sense of the shared cultural identity of the nation is fostered. The federal jurisdictions are socially important in themselves.

Nor are the provincial jurisdictions safe from the value-for-money logic. Most of the provinces, encouraged by the Auditor General of Canada, have themselves adopted some form of value-for-money legislation for their provincial legislative auditors.[47] Nor is the expenditure budget the only permanent focus for control. Mr Macdonell has provided for the establishment of the Canadian Comprehensive Auditing Foundation to further studies in the area of value for money. From this base, he may yet move on to evaluate tax expenditure and regulation, and to require the OCG to do so for government. It appears that the funds for the Foundation are to come out of funds allocated for ordinary official audit.[48]

The political cost of the value-for-money audit is therefore clear. As a nation, we stand to have entrenched philosophical conservatism inside government, regardless of the partisan stamp of the elected government. We stand to have much routine analysis, and many public servants to provide the analysis, but fewer public services. We stand to have a public service raised in an ethos, not of providing services to the public, but of watchfulness and suspicion toward other members of the service. Neither are the costs of the value-for-money initiative negligible in terms of opportunities for improvement foregone, absolute financial costs, and costs levied against the sense of credulity of the members of the bureaucracy itself.

The recommendation for control of the value-for-money initiative is clear: any such function should be initiated and provided its terms of reference by a minister of the government. The political masters cannot cast off the task of managing the very arm of government to the limb itself, nor can they delegate the management task to a third actor. The evaluation function is value-laden in each of its aspects. It is therefore properly a political function. The government should choose its own targets for analysis, and consume results at its own rate. It should be responsible, as it is accountable to the electorate.

One can only hope that the government will rescue the Comptroller from his Siamese twinship with the Auditor General. This must be done soon, for the new function is being established quite rapidly. The more unreasonable the Auditor General looks, the more reasonable the Comptroller looks with the approach to 'realistic' evaluation. By the fall of 1980, more than half the major departments had acted to establish the evaluation function, despite the lack to that date of coherent standards about what evaluation might be. Further, the important second-order issues, those general policy concerns which this paper has tried to address, had yet to be aired in a public debate.

NOTES

The author wishes to thank David Braybrooke, Bruce Doern, Michael Jordan, Alan Maslove, and James O'Connor for their comments and criticisms on earlier drafts of this paper.

1. The Auditor General is appointed by the government, but is an officer of Parliament. He holds office 'during good behaviour', which means in effect that he cannot be removed by the government of the day.
2. Auditor General of Canada, *100th Annual Report to the House of Commons* (Ottawa: Supply and Services, 1978). The thirteen summarized SPICE assessments of programs for effectiveness evaluation are published on pp. 84–96.

3. See, for example, Donald T. Campbell, 'Reforms as Experiments'; in F.G. Caro, ed., *Readings in Evaluation Research* (New York: Russell Sage Foundation, 1977); James Coleman, *Policy Research in Social Science* (Morristown, NJ: General Learning Corp., 1972); Edward A. Suchman, *Evaluative Research: Principles and Practice in Public Service and Social Action Programs* (New York: Russell Sage Foundation, 1967), and David Nachmias, *Public Policy Evaluation: Approaches and Methods* (New York: St. Martin's Press, 1979). For a less selective approach to program evaluation see Joseph S. Wholey, et al., 'Evaluation: when is it really needed?' (The Urban Institute: Washington, DC, March 1977), and Joe E. Nay et al., 'If you don't care where you get to, then it doesn't matter which way you go'; in Clark C. Abt, ed., *The Evaluation of Social Programs* (Beverly Hills: Sage, 1977) pp. 97–120. For a Canadian work on program evaluation, see Leonard Rutman, ed., *Evaluation Research Methods: A Basic Guide* (Beverly Hills: Sage, 1977).

4. The Auditor General Act, 7(2)(d) and (e). For the full text of the act, see the 1978 *Report*, Appendix A, pp. 585–9.

5. See J.M. Jordan and S.L. Sutherland, 'Assessing the Results of Public Expenditure: Program Evaluation in the Canadian Federal Government', *Canadian Public Administration* 22, 4 (Winter 1979), pp. 581–609.

6. For an introduction to comprehensive audit, see Auditor General of Canada, *Conspectus of the 100th Annual Report to the House of Commons* (Ottawa: Supply and Services, 1978), Appendix A, 'Comprehensive Auditing for Parliament: A New Cyclical Approach', pp. 77–96. The FRAME acronym is also displayed and discussed in Chapter 11 of the 1978 report.

7. See, for example, 'Zero-base budgets switch is healthy, Macdonell says', *The Globe and Mail*, 30 August 1979, p. 8; Rita Scagnatti, 'The Auditor-General's story follows a low-profile road', *The Citizen*, 14 July 1979, p. 13; Carol Goar, 'Last blast: Macdonell's final report reflects anger with government', *Ottawa Journal*, 9 November 1979, p. 9.

8. Sonja Sinclair, *Cordial but not Cosy: A History of the Office of the Auditor General* (Toronto: McClelland and Stewart, 1979), p. 125 (emphasis added). In the fall of 1979, the Office bought up 1,500 copies of this book from the publisher for about $22,500 and gave them to all staff, provincial auditors and some accounting firms. See Frank Howard's Bureaucrats, *The Citizen*, 6 September 1979, p. 2.

9. See, for example, *Report of the Auditor General at Canada to the House at Commons for the Fiscal Year 1973* (Ottawa: Supply and Services, 1973), p. 5:

   . . . While I shall report to the House of Commons on such matters as required by Section 61 of the Financial Administration Act I intend to report also on the action taken to remedy detected weaknesses. I further intend to have the revised procedure monitored for an appropriate period to ensure that the remedial action is, in fact, achieving the desired results.

   See also Sinclair, *Cordial but not Cosy*, p. 111:

   His objective, as he saw it, was to improve financial management in government; and his best hope of succeeding was not by chasing down individual instances where money had gone down the drain, but by recommending systems to prevent future leaks, asking departments to comment on his suggestions, finding out what if anything was being done to correct the situation and placing the combined evidence before the Public Accounts Committee.

10. *Report of the Independent Review Committee on the Office of the Auditor General of Canada* (Ottawa: Information Canada, 1975). The committee members were accommodated in OAG premises. An 'independence wall' was installed. See Sinclair, *Cordial but not Cosy*, p. 115.

11. *Report of the Independent Review Committee*, p. 23.

12. Ibid., p. 35.

13. 1974 AG *Report*, p. 3.

14. Ibid., p. 69.

15. 1975 AG *Report*, p. 4.

16. *Supplement* to the 1975 AG *Report*, pp. 124, 125.

17. 1975 AG *Report*, p. 4.

18. *Supplement* to the 1975 AG *Report*, p. 53.

19. 1976 AG *Report*, p. 9.

20. Ibid., pp. 14–15.

21. Ibid., pp. 209–19.

22. See Sinclair, *Cordial but not Cosy*, pp. 143–4.

23. 1976 AG *Report*, p. 9.

24. 1977 AG *Report*, p. 8.

25. Ibid., pp. 18–19.

26. See also the 1978 AG *Report*, p. 34, and Sinclair, op. cit., p. 124.

27. See the Auditor General Act. On the changing role of the Public Accounts Committee, Eric Adams, 'The Public Accounts Committee in the Accountability Process: Background Paper for Parliamentarians', Research Branch, Library of Parliament, June 1978 (updated 1979) is very useful.

28. Sinclair, *Cordial but not Cosy*, p. 175.

29. For a discussion of these issues, and testimony by Mr Macdonell and Mr Andras on the status of the Comptroller General of Canada, see the *Minutes of the Proceedings and Evidence of the Standing Committee on Miscellaneous Estimates* for 16 March 1978. Mr Rogers was a witness before the same committee on 27 April 1978, when he outlined his game plan for the OCG.

30. 1978 AG *Report*, p. 3.

31. Ibid., p. 34.

32. Definitions of the public service abound. The Auditor General covers the bodies named in the Financial Administration Act (section 55) whose financial statements must be included in the Public Accounts. Ronald Robinson, in his 'Developing Value-for-Money Methodology: The Study of Procedures in Cost Effectiveness', in Office of the Auditor General, *Comprehensive Auditing—Planning for Century II: Centennial Conference Proceedings* (Ottawa: Minister of Supply and Services, December 1978) clearly describes the SPICE process.

33. What constitutes a program is arbitrary. At one level, there are the 170 large programs of the Main Estimates. The Comptroller General has adopted another scheme. He sees Estimates programs as sub-divided into 'chewable chunks' or 'program components': unidimensional (one purpose) clusters of activities which can be related to unique organizational entities. He estimates that there are 2,200 of these making up the federal government. See Harry Rogers, 'Program Evaluation in the Federal

Government' in G. Bruce Doern and Allan M. Maslove, eds, *The Public Evaluation of Government Spending* (Toronto: Institute for Research in Public Policy, 1979), pp. 79–81, and Harry Rogers, 'Management Control in the Public Service', *Optimum* 9, 3 (1978), pp. 17–25.

34. 1978 AG *Report*, p. 9.
35. Ibid., pp. 81–2.
36. One of this journal's readers has objected to my thesis, saying that the Lambert Commission endorsed the OAG's interpretation of its mandate and its pursuit of the value-for-money power. In fact, the Commission's report is rather vague on the topic of evaluation. It can be read, however, as advocating political control of the evaluation function. See *The Royal Commission on Financial Management and Accountability: Final Report* (Ottawa: Minister of Supply and Services, 1979), p. 97, recommendation 6.1 and pp. 130–2, recommendations 7.21 and 7.22. One of the Committee members, Professor J.E. Hodgetts has gone on record as frankly opposing the value-for-money audit. See 'Onus for Government Accountability "falls on deputy ministers and MP's"', *The Citizen*, 9 June 1979, p. 18. Professor Hodgetts said the AG was then 'approaching the thin line between auditing and encroaching on government policy'. He further said that: the Lambert Commission 'consciously recommended against setting up a new growth industry in federal auditing . . .'
37. 1978 AG *Report*, p. 84.
38. Ibid., p. 81.
39. Ibid., p. 79.
40. Ibid., pp. 83–4.
41. Office of the Auditor General of Canada, *Comprehensive Auditing*, p. 165.
42. On the systemic level, the commitment to control is open-ended and non-evaluable. Departments at present are expected to 'find' the funds for program evaluation from their administrative budgets, ironically making themselves look less efficient in the process. Those parts of the OAG's and OCG's organizations which perform effectiveness or value-for-money related tasks are not reported distinctively in the Estimates.
43. See James J. Macdonell, 'Value-for-Money: The Accountability Equation', a paper presented to the annual conference of the Institute of Public Administration of Canada, Winnipeg, 29 August 1979. This speech was later tabled with the Miscellaneous Estimates Committee and is available in the Minutes (Issue No. 16, 8 November 1979).
44. Of great value is the census of evaluation activity of the US Federal Government in 1974, reported in Ilene N. Bernstein and Howard E. Freeman, *Academic and Entrepreneurial Research: The Consequences of Diversity in Federal Evaluation Studies* (New York: Russell Sage, 1975). See also Gerald Gordon and Edward V. Morse, 'Evaluation Research', *Annual Review of Sociology,* 1 (1975), pp. 339–59. Also useful is Anne L. Schneider and Peter R. Schneider, 'Evaluations and Decision-Makers: Perceptions of the Evaluation Process', Contract report from the Law and Justice Planning Office, Washington, and the Law Enforcement Assistance Administration. January, 1977. (The LEAA was disbanded in 1980.)
    For a more sympathetic approach, but essentially the same conclusion, see Richard E. Brown, ed., *The Effectiveness of Legislative Program Review* (New Brunswick, NJ:

Transaction Books, 1979), pp. 142–3. The book contains a number of case studies of major evaluations conducted by state auditors for their legislatures, and a review of outcomes. The few higher-quality experimental and quasi-experimental studies whose findings have been surprising and/or of political relevance—the Coleman report, the studies of Headstart and the Guaranteed Annual Income experiments for examples—have started whole research traditions and spurred bitter partisan controversy rather than decisive, successful, technical intervention. These studies are discussed at length in several recent American critiques of applied social science. See, for example, Martin Rein, *Social Science and Social Policy* (Penguin, 1976); I.L. Horowitz and J.E. Katz, eds, *Social Science and Public Policy in the United States* (New York: Praeger, 1975); Charles Frankel, ed., *Controversies and Decisions: The Social Sciences and Public Policy* (New York: Russell Sage, 1976); and C.E. Lindblom and D.K. Cohen, *Usable Knowledge: Social Science and Social Problem Solving* (New Haven and London: Yale University Press, 1979).

45. See Treasury Board of Canada, Federal Expenditure Plan 1979–80 (Ottawa: Minister of Supply and Services, 1979).

46. See G. Bruce Doern, ed., *The Regulatory Process in Canada* (Toronto: Macmillan. 1978); Alan Maslove, 'The Other Side of Public Spending: Tax Expenditures in Canada'; in Doern and Maslove, *Public Evaluation of Government Spending*, pp. 149–69; and G. Bruce Doern, ed., *Spending Tax Dollars: Federal Expenditures 1980–81* (Ottawa: School of Public Administration, Carleton University, 1980).

47. See R.A. Denham, 'New Public Sector Audit Legislation in Canada', *Canadian Public Policy* 4, 4 (Autumn 1978), pp. 474–88, and, also Simon McInnes, 'Improving Legislative Surveillance of Provincial Public Expenditures: The Performance of the Public Accounts Committees and Auditors General', *Canadian Public Administration* 20, 1 (Spring 1977), pp. 36–86.

48. The Canadian Comprehensive Auditing Foundation, based in Ottawa, is to be a research organization to further audit methodology and the pedagogy for imparting audit skills. Its official date of inception was May 1980. The provincial and federal legislative auditors are the main participants, with some private sector representation. British Columbia, Alberta, Ontario and the federal government have explicit value-for-money legislation, with most of the other provinces' legislative auditors pursuing similar activities under an 'any other matters' type of clause.

The Foundation itself might be said to be a good example of seemingly uncontrolled government growth through unexamined spending. Frank Howard says in his Bureaucrats column (*The Citizen*, 19 September 1980, p. 2) that the Foundation's budget is to come from a 1 per cent tithe from the operating budgets of the federal and provincial auditors, some $280,000 annually, he speculates. As well, CIDA is said to have tentatively committed $500,000 for an international program aimed at third world countries. (See also Minutes of the Miscellaneous Estimates Committee, 12, 26 June 1980, p. 1217.)

21

An Evaluation System for Government: If Politics Is Theatre, Then Evaluation Is (Mostly) Art

Rodney Dobell and David Zussman

In addressing the topic 'Evaluating Evaluation in Today's Government', it has seemed appropriate to take a somewhat philosophical and abstract view of the subject. Intending simply to stimulate discussion, we have stated the argument baldly, without attempt to embrace all the nuances and qualifications (which anyway is an evident impossibility in anything short of a very fat book).[1] As in the C.M. Drury paper[2] we develop in particular the fact that the process of policy analysis (including policy and program appraisal, or evaluation) is subject to both procedural impediments, arising out of the fact that the work takes place in an organizational and political context, and to analytical limits arising out of the lack of analytical criteria or relevant information to guide the key choices to be faced.

'Evaluation' has become part of the rhetoric of government, and a glamorous addition to the repertoire of the pop-art experts on the three day workshop circuit ($1,000 per participant, coffee included). There have been many declarations about the need for, and the firm determination to ensure rational analysis and searching evaluation to support government decisions. Those of us with relatively short memories in the system go back to the old *Financial Management Guide* accompanying the Treasury Board's Directive MI–3–66, which had the declared objective 'to promote more effective and economical operations by the greater use of financial management techniques', including program budgeting, 'required to give Parliament, the executive and management a clear insight into the primary purposes of departmental operations so that alternatives may be evaluated and policy decided'. Or to the speech by C.M. Drury on 8 June 1970 in the House describing 'the various measures the government has taken in recent years to improve or increase the efficiency and effectiveness of the public service' and indicating that 'what is required, and what has been lacking, is a continuing program of evaluation. This we have started . . .'[3]

As part of this process, Treasury Board decisions in the mid-1970s provided a mandate for departmental evaluations to be reported to the board, and cabinet itself introduced the so-called Cabinet Evaluation Studies program.

More recently, one recalls TB 1977–47 and the ringing declaration from the

Rodney Dobell and David Zussman, 'An Evaluation System for Government: If Politics Is Theatre, Then Evaluation Is (Mostly) Art', *Canadian Public Administration* 24, 3 (1981): 404–27. Courtesy of The Institute of Public Administration Canada.

1978 Speech from the Throne (under the heading 'Openness and Social Responsibility') that '[i]n the further promotion of open and efficient government, a proposal will be placed before you to provide for the review by Parliament of evaluations by the government of major programs'.[4]

The federal government was not alone in all this, of course; many provincial governments have been pursuing similar initiatives. In 1979, for example, the then chairman of the Treasury Board in British Columbia wrote to his colleagues to inform them of a plan endorsed by Treasury Board 'for implementing a more rigorous approach to the evaluation of the effectiveness and efficiency of Government programs'.[5]

Clearly there has been no lack of good intention. But realization seems always to dangle tantalizingly in the future. Now in 1981, the federal government is still at the beginning of a new round, with assurances that twelve departments out of fifty-eight agencies and departments covered by TB 77–47 have adequate evaluation functions, and six are working toward that goal with plans acceptable to the Office of the Comptroller General.

On this point, Mr. James Brophy, an official in the OCG explained to the Miscellaneous Estimates Committee that the OCG are not the experts on all the programs of the government, but 'are, purportedly, the experts on how to do program evaluations'. Departments, having carried out evaluations according to the precepts of the OCG (and having in mind 'definitions of good or bad impacts and effects determined to some extent by the government') would then make decisions as to whether programs should be discontinued or expanded.[6]

Unfortunately, Mr Rogers had to inform the committee that it would not be possible for the committee or other MPs to see the evaluations, or to know departmental evaluation plans, or even to know what programs are now evaluated. Mr Rogers did, however, invite Mr McGimpsey 'to status the committee by giving a brief read-out of where the "Information for Parliament Project" now stands.'[7] This project, it appears, is designed to revise the form of the Estimates so as to relate money expenditures to output or achievement in the Estimates document. But it too is still at the stage of work on model statements in five pilot departments.

Thus, it seems that nothing much has yet happened as a result of all the successive initiatives since MI–3–66. We will spare the reader the catalogue of expressions of user dissatisfaction, and also the long series of expositions outlining why it should have been evident to every thoughtful observer that the environment for the implementation of evaluation activities would prove overwhelmingly hostile. The flavour is captured by the observation of D.G. Hartle, 'where program evaluation has been carried out, it has had minimal effect on budgetary decisions;'[8] or in the United States by James Anderson, 'I am unable to think of a government program that has been terminated as a consequence of an unfavourable systematic evaluation effort;'[9] or by Hartle again, 'Foolishly, I didn't take into account the fundamental systems which make many planning (evaluation) groups virtually useless.'[10] More generally, Robert H. Haveman, formerly a member of the staff of the Joint Economic Committee of the US Congress, has suggested that 'policy analysis answers questions that few legislative policy-makers are interested in either asking or having asked.'[11] Similar observations abound.

A solid decade—almost two—has gone into changing the words and the forms. Yet even the most dedicated do not argue that evaluation efforts have led to decisive results or significant government action.

FACTORS

There are at least three reasons commonly cited to explain why the aura of disillusion and despond is so widespread amongst the people who looked for results from the massive efforts poured into successive assaults on evaluation problems. The first is a lack of agreed theory and purpose.

In fact, different groups were looking for very different sorts of results, and attached different meanings to the word 'evaluation'. When a diverse clientele holds widely differing expectations, it is not surprising that most will be disappointed.

The second is that people and groups and large organizations offer all sorts of resistance to any efforts to entrench ongoing processes of evaluation. A vast, sometimes entertaining, literature has grown up on the politics of bureaucracy, on incentive systems and pay-off rules in organization, on communication flows and social networks in offices, and on the manifold possible failures of implementation. Even simple fault-tree analysis would suggest that when there are so many things that can go wrong in the course of evaluation studies and so many things that must all go right all at once if such studies not only are to be done but also to be read, it is unlikely that success can come frequently.

The third reason, the one on which we will focus the last half of this paper, is that the attempt to establish comprehensive evaluation systems, or even comprehensive evaluation studies, to serve cabinet and Parliament, failed to consider the true nature and information needs of the user. It is not possible to provide the relevant information in the garb of a conventional evaluation study.

Let us look briefly at each of these three concerns, which bear on the questions to be asked at each level of an evaluation system designed to meet the needs of various clienteles.

Fragmented Theory

Politicians have often seen program evaluation as a means for solving the problem of measuring (and increasing) efficiency and effectiveness in government programs. C.M. Drury, as mentioned earlier, stated his support for evaluation efforts in announcing a new policy 'to provide Ministers and their Departments with the authority and the machinery with which to better discharge their responsibility to the Cabinet and to the House for the effectiveness of their programs and the efficiency of their administration.'[12] Mr Bechard in 1979 expressed interest in program evaluation when he stated that 'the regular monitoring of the on-going performance of programs is an essential element in the governmental management process.'[13] The most recent Speech from the Throne returned to the theme in suggesting that 'improving the efficiency of the federal government is as important an objective of these reforms as reducing the deficit'.[14]

A different emphasis is suggested by the remarks of other politicians; for example, Perrin Beatty, as a member of the former Conservative cabinet, advocated 'legislation to determine whether or not the programs that have been put into place by Parliament were serving the purposes for which they were designed'.[15] In 1979, James Fleming suggested that Parliament had been promised 'the opportunity to review evaluations of major programs which would ensure that honourable members had an on-going opportunity to be part of a review process'.[16]

Many benefits were seen by the politicians to flow from all this activity, both that related to the management process and that related to parliamentary oversight. Delegation and devolution of authority would be enhanced; inflation rates would be lowered by reducing unnecessary government spending; identification of services which could better be offered by the private sector would be possible; the budget deficit would be reduced.

To any public expectations created by such announcements should be added those created by the exhortations of the professional community, illustrated, for example, most recently by the recommendations of the Wilson Committee, the Auditor General, and the Lambert Commission. To argue so vehemently the need for an integrated financial management information system is, by implication, to promise great benefits from linking the Program Forecasts to the Estimates and thence to the Public Accounts, and monitoring progress against multi-year operational plans.[17]

Yet again, different expectations were held by those who interpreted evaluation to be an instrument for performance appraisal. To link discussion of program evaluation with accountability of senior executives seemed to imply the existence of an objective procedure for identification (and subsequent reward) of good management. This impression finds support in the Lambert Commission Report, which would strengthen the accountability of public servants, and in the D'Avignon Report, which proposed a revamped appraisal system.[18]

Thus, not only improved government management and greater public or parliamentary scrutiny, but also strengthened appraisal and accountability of officials as managers were expected. Indeed, under the general heading of 'evaluation' appeared to fall *ex ante* evaluation in support of decisions as to future policy action, retrospective *ex post* evaluation to appraise past decisions or to examine the continuing benefits of current programs, managerial evaluation for operational control of on-going programs, appraisal of feasible alternative program designs, appraisal of managerial performance as part of an incentive system based on executive accountability, provision of information to Parliament to guide decisions whether to vote supply and thus continue particular programs, and overall general accountability to Parliament and the public. But what machinery was to serve these purposes? Here again, it is important to distinguish at least three quite different approaches, which reflect the way program evaluation developed as a research activity within the social sciences and which offer one possible reason for the confused expectations mentioned above. Unlike many management tools which have become popular over the years, program evaluation developed independently from at least three different academic disciplines instead of from one theoretical base.

Among the first program evaluators to gain public prominence were social psychologists and sociologists in their capacity as assessors of the US 'Great Society' programs of the middle and late 1960s.[19] Most of these evaluation studies attempted to incorporate the conventional research methodologies of the discipline, particularly experiments using control and experimental groups as a means for measuring program impacts. Typically, these studies would attempt to measure selected dependent variables before and after the policy initiatives to be appraised were introduced, as a means for establishing a link between the intervention and the policy outcome.

Some practitioners attempted to solve methodological problems by devising a series of 'quasi-experimental' conditions to eliminate the need for control groups or for pre-test measures, but each time such improvements were made the soundness of the underlying method was called further into question. More important, social experiments raise possible ethical problems, since individuals are randomly assigned to control and experimental groups, thus denying some of the subjects the potential benefits of the policy being evaluated. Significant also is the possible invasion of subjects' privacy in an attempt to gather suitable information about a program's effects.

Experimental studies present additional problems. It is almost impossible to control all of the possible factors which might have some influence on the outcomes of a government program. As a consequence, most experiments depend on heroic assumptions concerning the randomness of errors in order to retain the integrity of the methodology. Moreover, in the most common ways of conducting the work, the relative impacts of the program under consideration on the experimental and the control groups are not easy to identify since, as conventionally employed, statistical theory is essentially conservative and places the burden of proof on the intervention.[20]

The second major approach to program evaluation has been developed by accountants and economists. In general, economic analysis emphasizes the relative costs, both direct and indirect, of attaining policy objectives by alternative methods of program delivery. One of the most powerful of these techniques is benefit–cost analysis, which is simply a comparison of the discounted value of a flow of social benefits with a flow of social costs associated with each policy option.[21] Benefit–cost analysis is most usefully and easily applied to the study of capital projects. But it has been applied with varying degrees of plausibility to many other types of public sector problems, including manpower training, foreign aid, agricultural subsidy programs, and the like.

On the surface, the method is extremely attractive. It has a strong theoretical base, and is conceptually tight in the sense that all assumptions and factors are clearly identified. Consideration of true opportunity costs and the importance of timing are emphasized. But the goals and objectives of the policy being evaluated must be clearly identified if benefit–costs analysis is to be useful, while unfortunately, the objectives of government programs are often poorly stated, contradictory, weighted in an unknown manner, and difficult to measure. Programs are not necessarily designed to attain their stated objectives, for a number of reasons, including a possible desire to mask the program's true intentions and to appear to serve a wider constituency. In addition, economic studies place a heavy burden on the evaluator to identify legitimate policy alternatives from among many possibilities; the act of choice represents, for the evaluator, normative judgment about what is a reasonable and fair alternative. Indeed, benefit–cost and cost-effectiveness analyses involve a substantial number of such normative statements (e.g., discount rate, benefits, costs, shadow prices, time frame) which cannot be justified on objective grounds or by appeal to generally accepted accounting principles.

Thus even when these studies are complete, the results are never definitive; decision-makers are still forced eventually to formulate decision rules on their own.

The third type of program evaluation could be considered essentially a marketing approach, conducted in an eclectic fashion without any reference to a theoretical framework. It is essentially concerned with process, or the way in which a particular program or policy has been implemented. The methodology used to support this approach varies from surveys of staff and client to participant-observation studies. Each evaluation is approached on an ad hoc basis and, as a consequence, the results are difficult to replicate.

It seems likely that monitoring efforts of this sort provide the bulk of the information on which management personnel base decisions to modify program delivery systems or on-going operations. But there is little common ground in the analytical methods used, and there is no need to develop the discussion of this class of evaluation studies further.

The essential point is that there are many techniques of use in program evaluation and these stem from diverse origins. For our purposes most can be considered as falling within the hypothesis-testing approach, the economic evaluation approach, or the process-control approach. These, while essentially complementary rather than in conflict, grew up separately and this accounts for much of the confusion in expectations as to the results of evaluation efforts.

Behind this confusion also lies a further problem, however, one which we must address later in this paper. This is the appeal to different underlying models or ideal patterns of organization. The overwhelming influence in discussion of management in government is, not surprisingly, the tradition of private sector management practices and principles. In the attempt to graft evaluation activities onto government operations, this private sector management model has run squarely into the principles and practices of parliamentary government with its traditions of ministerial responsibility.

It seems clear that the public perceives the private sector as having management methods far superior to the public sector.[22] The Glassco Report was outspoken in this view. More recently, both the Lambert Commission and the D'Avignon task force indicated their preferences for private sector models, and advocated further transfer of business management systems to the public sector.

We deal later with the question whether these systems apply as fully in a public sector environment as is often thought. But the existence of these different models is important, along with the differing expectations and different theoretical traditions discussed above, in understanding why little progress can be claimed for evaluation in government to date.

More concrete concerns arise in the process of implementing evaluation activities, and it is to these that we now turn.

Problems of Implementation

On the reasons why previous initiatives in evaluation seem never to have been successfully implemented, hindsight abounds. A compelling account of experience in the United States is contained in the Brookings publication written by Charles Schultze on his retirement as Director of the Bureau of the Budget following the election of President Nixon in 1968.[23] Experience from the same era was the source of the well-known work by Graham Allison which points to the significance of structural or organizational considerations as well as the important roles played simply by personality and individual values in government action on policies and programs.[24] Accounts of Canadian experience are given by Hartle and Good, among a growing number of others.[25]

There is no need to do more than offer a reminder of this extensive literature on the importance of bureaucratic games, formal and informal pay-off rules or incentive systems, procedural constraints leading to distortions in collective decision processes, and so on. The point is simply that evaluation takes place within a political and organizational context which drives analysis and analysts to an essentially adversarial role. We take for granted the accuracy, in essential respects, of the processes of 'partisan mutual adjustment' which Lindblom describes.[26]

Within such a framework of advocacy, the bureaucratic incentives do not press in the direction of continuing searching evaluation. Considerable emphasis can properly be placed on Doug Hartle's much-repeated observation that asking the public service manager to subject his operations to recurrent comprehensive evaluation is like asking a dog to carry the stick with which she or he will subsequently be beaten. There were few rewards perceived to be associated with the process of evaluation in the climate of the sixties and early seventies. The reluctance of managers interested in expanding programs and policy development to embrace evaluation activities is understandable.

Moreover, as Harry Rogers has pointed out to us, some practical problems should not be overlooked. There was little systematic effort devoted to appropriate training of managers concerned with evaluation, and no follow-through. Though activities like the Treasury Board-sponsored Quantitative Analysis Course provided thorough grounding for a small number of senior analysts, and managers of analysts, it provided no help to the vast bulk of managers who would have to use the work. At the same time, major central agencies created no models and provided few examples on which managers elsewhere could base their ideas. The Planning Branch of the Treasury Board Secretariat was a voice in a hostile wilderness.

Beyond bureaucratic incentives and mechanical obstacles, however, was the absence of political incentives to encourage any implementation of evaluation activities. The significance of this barrier can be appreciated by contrast to the present situation where public concerns about inflation and public pressures for restraint have led to structural changes emphasizing new roles for the offices of the Auditor General and the Comptroller General, and to new decision processes centred on the Policy and Expenditure Management System (PEMS). This latter, coupled with public commitments by the government to broaden provisions for disclosure of information, has created a demand for evaluation activities which was absent until now.

(What is particularly intriguing—although it cannot be developed at any length here—is the observation that the PEMS approach to a cabinet decision may lend itself particularly to an emphasis on cost-effectiveness evaluation.[27] Compared to the 'bottom-up' optimization of the PPBS methods, the envelope system emphasizes a 'top-down' rationing process. This substitution of rationing for full-scale rational allocation places the burden of decision on the ministers in each envelope committee, but simultaneously restricts the allocation of resources by the arbitrary division of expenditures into envelopes in the absence of the program evaluation information a full-scale PPBS approach promised to provide. Nevertheless, a conscious emphasis on rationing of a fixed expenditure envelope does shift responsibility for evaluation from a simple 'guardian' agency to the committee of ministers as a collectivity, and hence creates a more general demand for evaluation efforts.)

Thus, problems of implementation arose essentially because of the absence of strong public pressures for restraint in spending and hence the absence of any institutional or procedural framework for evaluation. In a new era of altered public perceptions, with apparently greater concern for private disposable income than for an expanded 'social wage', the political incentive for greater evaluation efforts exists.

Inherent Limits

Implementation problems cannot, however, be blamed for all the difficulties. Analytical work, especially program evaluation, encounters some inherent limits. We are not referring here to methodological difficulties of the kind referred to by Hatry or Majone[28] in their reviews of pitfalls of analysis. Nor are we referring simply to recognized limits on available data, on limits to communications channels or information-processing capacity, or even to obvious limits on the ability of ministers and senior officials to absorb relevant information and take considered decisions in the time available.

Rather, we are alluding here to the profound uncertainty which surrounds any significant policy or program decision, the unavoidable absence of definitive criteria for resolving problems of public choice, and hence, to the impossibility of arriving, by analysis, at definitive recommendations relevant to the problems actually faced in the formation of public policy.

It would be interesting to pursue this philosophical question at greater length, but that is obviously impossible here. Some attempt to deal with the implications in the context of economic policy and social policy formation is developed in two recent papers by Dobell;[29] the problem is set out at greater length in the recent book by Cohen and Lindblom.[30]

In the language they use, the point of this section can be summed up in the simple observation that professional social inquiry for social problem-solving is not the same thing as evaluation and monitoring for management of public programs. Public and professional expectations may have confused the two activities and different methodological origins may have contributed to this confusion. Different models of management may underline problems of implementation, and in any case implementation must inevitably be difficult in any organization where entrenched interests or established pay-off rules are threatened by evaluation activities. But neither confusion over purpose nor problems of implementation can fully explain the failure of evalu-

ation efforts to date; there are inherent limits to the capacity of any system to generate what Harry Rogers refers to as 'simply the information managers should have at
their fingertips concerning the accomplishments of government programs'.

RESOLUTION

Recognizing the costs of introducing still further terminology, we think it is important to distinguish *formative evaluation*—monitoring and feedback activities which
enable managers to improve performance by adjusting operations and redesigning
programs—from *summative evaluation*—comprehensive assessments of the degree of
success achieved by programs.

In the former, the deputy minister and departmental management will be the
clients. The information provided by these evaluation efforts will permit informed
decisions on ways in which departmental programs may be adapted to achieve specified program goals within all the ground rules laid down by Parliament and cabinet.
In such decisions, in which the concern is to choose amongst alternative techniques
to achieve specified goals, an accepted body of analytical principles and methods can
be brought to bear. For the most part, the criterion of productive efficiency is paramount; cost-effectiveness measures might often be developed according to generally
accepted methods. The degree of coverage or take-up or penetration of target groups
can be estimated; client response or satisfaction can be appraised by familiar survey
techniques. In all this, the evaluation procedures urged by the Auditor General have
a role to play, and the plans and procedures disseminated by the OCG are applicable.

This feedback loop designed to yield information for management purposes is
illustrated in the lower portion of Figure 1.[31]

In the case of summative evaluation, the client is not the program manager or
the deputy minister, and the purpose is not to adapt a program to a changing external environment or to amend expenditure levels. Rather, the client is initially cabinet and ultimately the whole community, and the purpose is to appraise the
continued validity of program goals against alternative goals and social objectives.
Productive efficiency and resource costs must be weighed against social justice.
Equity and distribution, personal roles in the processes of decision, perceptions of
involvement or alienation are at stake, and the procedures of comprehensive audit
have little application. Principles and methods of analysis will differ as widely as the
values individuals will bring to the assessment.

It is, of course, not implied that analysis is irrelevant in all this; quite the contrary. Rhetoric and persuasion must be based on substantive knowledge, and political scientists are the last group to whom political choices should be entrusted. The
real opportunity costs of 'political judgments' must be known and seen. But useable
knowledge in this context will not, in general, come from the evaluation processes
we have been discussing; or indeed, from any established body of conventional technique based on generally accepted professional principles.

If this argument is plausible, it follows that a fundamental duality of management
problems in the public service must be recognized. Decision support systems for
good management of an agency are different from mechanisms for political account-

Figure 1—*Framework for Program Evaluation and Policy Analysis: A Schematic Representation*

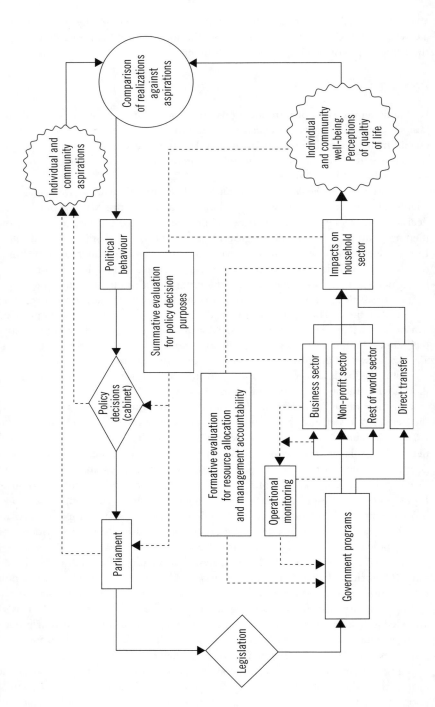

ability to Parliament and the public. Evaluation procedures modelled on integrated financial management systems and based upon efficiency in resource use are essential for the first, and (almost) useless for the second.

Obviously, it becomes necessary for us to explain why evaluation systems which are so central to corporate management are unable to carry the burden proposed for them in government. All one can do is summarize in slightly different fashion arguments which have been made before.

There seem to be two major reasons why we all have the impression the appraisal of performance in business is more direct and reliable than in government. The first is the possibility of 'single-issue' voting—purchasers may be concerned about a complex cluster of qualities and services, but they purchase, voluntarily, one item at a time. Thus, the degree to which goods or services are successful in meeting expectations (or at least commanding the acceptance) of consumers is clearer than any of the messages to be read from voting behaviour. The second is a signaling mechanism more reliably tied to successful performances. Whereas the bottom line may not be a good measure of short-term performance of business managers, the longer-term financial viability of a business is presumably in large part a reflection of successful management decisions in anticipating and responding to changing customer needs in an evolving environment.

More generally, referring to Figure 2, one might speculate that the basis of market mechanisms (depicted on the top of the diagram) is responsiveness to individual needs or preferences; the basis of government operations (depicted on the bottom) is financing through the tax system; this latter coercive mechanism is responsive to individual preferences only to the extent that long-term political legitimacy can be thought to be bound up with a general acceptance of the government which in turn reflects individual appraisals of separate government programs; it is a crude and global test at best.

Thus, it may be argued that government operations are subject to no discipline corresponding to the long-term discipline of the market which ties corporate survival to successful response to individual preferences as measured by a voluntary allocation of income.

This argument is a little like the ecological argument that systems require a long-term, self-correcting mechanism more than momentary optimization (fine tuning). Business has a self-correcting mechanism which says that firms which cannot realize revenues sufficient to cover costs go bankrupt; governments do not have a comparable test of acceptance. For example, consider a case like that of the Chrysler Corporation, where social concerns move away from covering production costs to preserving employment rather than closing down, the firm seeks public financing. But the ability to cover production costs (with adequate return) used to be the test of whether the operation was 'in the public interest'. What is the comparable test for the evaluation of government programs? Referring to Figure 2, it appears clear that none of the methods based on individual votes—either through markets or terminals—is likely to be usable; nor does appraisal based on shadow prices and imputed willingness to pay seem feasible; only political acceptability appears usable as a test of the public interest.

Figure 2—*Spectrum of Potential 'Signaling' Mechanisms (The feedback loop)*

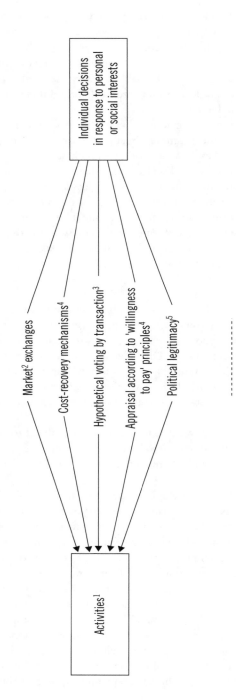

1   Mechanisms for allocation of resources to meet individual or community needs by providing goods and services.

2   'Voluntary' allegiance to products through willing payments of disposable income sufficient to cover costs of production.

3   In principle, a referendum on each program decision could signal the public will as directly as a market transaction (except for 'free-rider' problems)

4   Benefit-cost analysis and similar procedures substitute an 'imputed' transaction in place of observed market exchanges or cost-recovery procedures.

5   'Voluntary' allegiance to a system which determines disposition of private income through taxes and the coercive powers of a tax system.

6   Beyond simple user charges there exist many ingenious mechanisms developed in the literature on public choice.

Figure 3—*Elements of the Public Sector Management System*

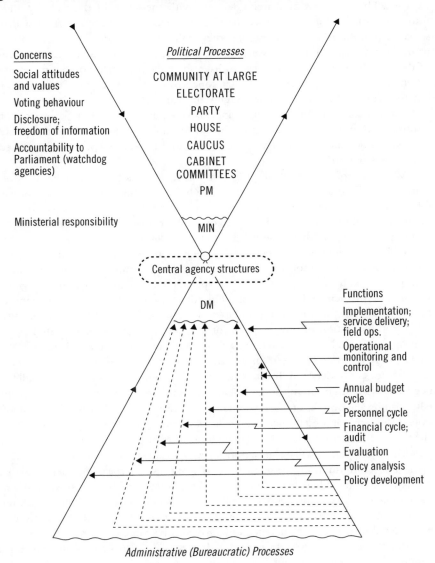

Concerns

Political Processes

Social attitudes
and values

Voting behaviour

Disclosure;
freedom of information

Accountability to
Parliament (watchdog
agencies)

COMMUNITY AT LARGE
ELECTORATE
PARTY
HOUSE
CAUCUS
CABINET
COMMITTEES
PM

Ministerial responsibility

MIN

Central agency structures

DM

Functions

Implementation;
service delivery;
field ops.

Operational
monitoring and
control

Annual budget
cycle

Personnel cycle

Financial cycle;
audit

Evaluation

Policy analysis

Policy development

Administrative (Bureaucratic) Processes

This leaves the issue as ultimately one of organizational structure: Does information flow differently, or are executives responding to different incentives, if one
organizes activity in a market or a government setting? We leave that question as an
exercise for the reader.

Looking at the problem in a more traditional manner, as illustrated in Figure 3,
one might argue that private sector problems stop at the neck of the hourglass. The

private sector manager is accountable to his or her board in a clear-cut and definitive way. The concerns of shareholders are with the value of their equity and its future growth. To the extent that shareholders become more concerned with the social responsibilities of corporations, they will, of course, demand an accounting from their managers on these issues. But the key feature remains, in that the owners of the corporation can be expected to have shared, rather than conflicting, interests when it comes to appraisal of the vital concerns of the enterprise. Thus, while the chief executive officers may be in roughly the same situation as the deputy minister so far as management of the agency and management decisions are concerned, the evaluation of policy and major programs according to the criteria of the political process can be ignored in a private sector setting. More clear-cut financial and economic tests will suffice.

We have argued, then, that evaluation efforts have not been notably fruitful to date, and we have set forth some reasons. We have also argued that a major source of difficulty has been the failure to distinguish evaluation for monitoring and adjustment of operations (where a private sector model helps) and evaluation for political accountability (where that same private sector model hurts).

If this argument is accepted, the approach to an evaluation system for government follows almost automatically. It entails simply confining the management systems prescribed by the OAC/OCG to their appropriate domain (program management within a department) while instituting full public accountability of departments and ministers through fuller reporting and provisions for increased parliamentary scrutiny.

On the question of how a system of evaluation might be orchestrated, we can sum up the critical points by referring to the well-known 'Deputy's Lament': When I talk to my minister, he doesn't hear; when he hears, he doesn't listen; when he listens, he doesn't understand. In the OAC 'model' system, this sequence of roadblocks need not arise in communicating evaluation efforts to deputy heads. When analysts talk about evaluation results they will be heard, because the hearer will have commissioned the work and estabished the terms of reference and be recognized to be the client. When the work is heard, it will be listened to, because the system of executive performance appraisal will assign significant weights to success in matters of management and administration; the incentives to make use of evaluation results will be strong because the efficient conduct of agency business will be rewarded. And when the evaluation story is listened to, it will be understood because effective communication will be accepted as the key feature of good analytical work. Promotion of a professional mystique and tolerance of jargon will be rooted out from the system.

But this evaluation system is designed to provide management information to deputy heads and departmental managers. It does not discharge the government's responsibility for accountability to Parliament and the public. An evaluation system cannot do so. An evaluation process cannot do so. Good analytical work can help; but the only guarantee of any progress in establishing accountability of government to the public is open access to all relevant information. Public debate of government objectives and programs on the basis of unfettered critical scrutiny of program data as well as departmental program evaluation results is what's necessary to accountability. The key is to get the internal analyses into the public domain for review, and get the outside independent analysts into a position to conduct their own analysis of the facts relating to government programs.[32]

In such a system, the obligation to answer in public for the conduct of departmental activities would be imposed on ministers through more substantial annual departmental reports, greater staff support to permit more searching scrutiny by parliamentary committees, and an expectation that deputy heads, as a fundamental part of their executive responsibilities, would produce for parliamentary scrutiny a full accounting for the nature and impacts of departmental programs. The promise in the 1978 Speech from the Throne remains to be kept—but in its own right, not as part of a budget process or a revision to the form of the Estimates. Of course, a persuasive demonstration of the sincerity of the government of the day in the matter of this promise would be simply to make the departmental 'strategic overview' document submitted each 31 March to the relevant policy committees public as discussion papers.

In order to deal with the obvious practical difficulty, however, it has to be recognized that no analytical effort, directed at program evaluation or otherwise, can work at the scale of the most general national choices. It needs little effort to see that the decision channels of the federal government are clogged at present, that neither the information-handling capacity nor the decision-taking capacity is there to deal with the full range of resource allocation, stabilization, distributional, social, and procedural problems assumed by the federal government. The solution, in one way or the other, must be to decompose these problems to a scale against which analytical tools and human reason can be brought to bear.

The obvious form of decomposition is delegation of resource allocation decisions to individual economic agents acting through market mechanisms. As Vickers points out, this has the apparent merit of 'guaranteeing personal economic freedom—or so much personal freedom as is deserved by the market's impersonal assessment of one's economic value to one's fellows'.[33]

But there are also other ways by which the scale of government decisions might be reduced. The new expenditure management system, for example, accomplishes this goal by a largely arbitrary decomposition of total expenditures into a number of sub-totals (envelopes) to be managed separately by individual cabinet committees. One approach (due to John Fryer of BCGEU and the CLC) to burgeoning problems of labour relations might be to force resolution of conflicts over historical relativities within an enterprise onto a single bargaining unit forced to bargain for all employees, within an overall consultative framework. Decentralization of authority and regionalization of federal government operations have long been advanced as one way to make the scope of decisions—and decision support systems—manageable. A constitutional framework which would see matters of economic development handled locally and matters of distribution handled federally has been proposed to avoid the need for the exercise of federal power to decide the location of every service station and every port in the nation. With appropriate decomposition of the problem, and delegation of powers, a government evaluation system having some robustness, if not full optimality, becomes feasible.

Of course, as Vickers also points out, social mechanisms based on the assumption of independent atomistic individuals depend on very special circumstances. 'The ballot box, like the market, is a device for optimizing solutions of conflict, where accord is assumed to be possible. Radical conflicts cannot be so resolved. . . . Such individual autonomy in matters of value can be combined with social coherence only in societies in which consensus on values remains consistently high.'[34] We do not pursue the question whether contemporary society displays sufficiently high consensus on values to accommodate autonomous individuals in something less than a dictatorial centralized state.

CONCLUSION

We do not wish, in this note, to suggest any case against formal evaluation activities in government. We do not mean to imply that economic considerations and efficient use of resources are irrelevant to major government decisions. Indeed, we see a crying need for more analysis—more substantive statistical evidence, more appeal to facts and logic arrayed analytically, even symbolically, for greater effectiveness—both in the practice of public administration, and in the study of public administration. What we propose is intended to lead to greater appeal to evaluation and analysis by concentrating these efforts where they have a chance of being useful and used.

When we speak of evaluation as art, we do not deny the importance of extensive and careful work on program evaluation. Indeed, the view we espouse assigns paramount importance, in the end, to the analyst. As Lord Keynes, himself an accomplished public servant, observed long ago:

> The ideas of economists and political philosophers, both when they are right and when they are wrong, are more powerful than is commonly understood. Indeed the world is ruled by little else. Practical men, who believe themselves to be quite exempt from any intellectual influences, are usually the slaves of some defunct economist. Madmen in authority, who hear voices in the air, are distilling their frenzy from some academic scribbler of a few years back. I am sure that the power of vested interests is vastly exaggerated compared with the gradual encroachment of ideas. Not, indeed, immediately, but after a certain interval; for in the field of economic and political philosophy there are not many who are influenced by new theories after they are twenty-five or thirty years of age, so that the ideas which civil servants and politicians and even agitators apply to current events are not likely to be the newest. But, soon or late, it is ideas, not vested interests, which are dangerous for good or evil.[35]

What's wrong with the view that we should leave major government decisions to political judgments untroubled by concerns for 'rational decision' is the failure to recognize that productive efficiency is a fundamental element of individual human welfare. To waste resources, to employ them in less than their best use, is irresponsible. It is a failure of stewardship which leaves us and future generations poorer than we need be. We need the information which lets us weigh the welfare loss due to economic inefficiency against the welfare gains due to pursuit of other goals.

Unfortunately, we cannot have everything we need. There are some laws of nature we must live with, no matter how much our hopes might lead us to rebel against them. We have learned to accommodate to the limits imposed by the laws of thermodynamics, and the laws of motion, and even the basic law of economics ('There is no such thing as a free lunch', sometimes expressed mathematically as $T(O) = (O)$).

The same sort of limits apply when it comes to what we can know about government programs. The motive which led to the social indicators movement was simple: economic indicators could not account for growing unrest in a time of rising material well-being, and the search for measures which better captured perceptions of the quality of life spread. But this search encountered inevitable confrontation with the limits on human knowledge: as the indicators demanded became ever more comprehensive and general, the ability to link them with any specific program or action or decision by government faded entirely.

So too with evaluation in government. The motive which led to this work was simple and laudable: those who make decisions on behalf of the community need relevant information on which to base those decisions. But inevitably, the unavoidable natural limits are encountered: as the size of the community grows, and the scale of the decisions expands, the scope of the relevant information broadens to embrace all human experience.

If it were possible to bring equity and redistribution, satisfaction with the perceived quality of life, and concern for the relation of the individual to the apparatus of the state, all within the ambit of pure productive efficiency, then tests of effectiveness in public policy might be brought within an agreed methodology. Generally accepted principles of analysis could be established; departments and agencies could observe them, the OCG could monitor them, and the Auditor General could report to Parliament on areas where the government's monitoring seemed inadequate. If it were . . . But this brings us around to the position of the economist advising the group of hungry castaways on a desert island, looking helplessly at the store of tinned food shipwrecked with them. 'Assume this coconut is a can-opener, and proceed as follows . . .'

Just as a coconut is not a can-opener, so evaluation is not a methodological key to resolution of basic social dilemmas. What we should expect from evaluation is more competent detailed work and less philosophy; more method and less methodology; more disclosure, more openness, more parliamentary and public scrutiny, more access to facts and debate over substance.

The conference organizers posed to us a number of questions, of which two seemed to us critical: What information is relevant? and, What can legitimately be expected of evaluation efforts? In this note we have tried to suggest first that for the program manager the relevant information is contained in formative evaluation results bearing on the operations of the program within all the constraints of imposed goals, designs, and procedures, while for ministers and MPs and members of the community, the relevant information includes all that changes our perception of a program's nature and impact in our society. We have also suggested, we hope, that great expectations for evaluation work can legitimately be held where the tools are appropriate to the task.

Thus, in this setting, one recognizes that politics is theatre—the use of rhetoric and leadership and persuasion to mobilize support for the great projects of the nation. Public policy formation is participation in a poker game—anticipation and bluff, with strategic action in pursuit of an undisclosed agenda in the face of competing actors. And in this setting, analysis must in part be advocacy—an advisor behind every player—while evaluation is art—an attempt to mobilize ideas to help the audience see problems and solutions in a new perspective. Not art for art's sake, but to change our view of the world, and our actions in it.

There really is little new to say on the subject of evaluation. It is time we stopped talking about it and got on with doing some, based on data in the public domain and analysis open to public scrutiny.

Though there is little new to say, of substance, we have tried in these remarks to suggest a slightly different perspective. We start from Harry Rogers' remark that the OCG seeks merely to institute procedures and practices which ensure that managers in government have the information they need to manage responsibly. We add Stafford Beer's definition that 'information is what changes us'. We recognize politics as theatre, and we try to reconcile ourselves to evaluation as art.

Measured by his impact on social policy, Charles Dickens must be rated a good analyst. He wrote well, and in an extended evaluation of contemporary social programs, marshalled the evidence in such a way as to change the way his generation viewed the nature of society and its obligations. By the same criterion, Siegfried Sassoon and Wilfrid Owen and Stephen Spender changed the way people appraised estimates of the costs of military activity, as John Steinbeck altered views of social programs in the 1930s, and Woody Guthrie shaped impressions of labour relations policy. Television coverage of marches in Mississippi or skirmishes in Vietnam, and Washington Post coverage of Watergate, changed the way the current generation appraises the integrity and trustworthiness of administrators and politicians.

We conclude, in light of all the things which Lindblom and Hartle and all report to us, that analysis and evaluation must take place in a courtroom setting, not a classroom setting. That—with all its implications about advocacy, bargaining and partisan mutual adjustment—seems clearly to be a fact of life. There is little point in continuing to debate methodology in this setting. The next time IPAC sponsors a conference on evaluation, it should not be on evaluation of procedures to appraise the processes by which somebody attempts an evaluation. No criticism of this present seminar is implied by that remark—no doubt the topic is interesting and timely. But it is also time to move forward. Let us hope that the next time we meet it will be to debate the validity of two or three concrete appraisals of particular major programs.

In other words, the plea from our end of the academic community wouldbe to quit talking about plans and intentions and procedures, and get on with the work. And let the rest of the world in to see that work, so as to draw its own conclusions about how valid that work is, and how effective are the programs appraised. Truth has never been effectively pursued or persuasively spoken in any other manner.

NOTES

1. Had we written a book, it might, with luck, have looked somewhat like Aaron Wildavsky's *Speaking Truth to Power* (Boston: Little, Brown; 1979), with a substantial lacing of Kenneth Cohen and Charles E. Lindblom (*Usable Knowledge*, [New Haven: Yale University Press, 1979]), and Geoffrey Vickers (*Freedom in a Rocking Boat*, [Harmondsworth: Penguin, 1970]). Our starting point in the Canadian literature is the classic C.M. Drury piece contributed to the first issue of *Canadian Public Policy*, and, in addition for ARD, the impact of a dozen years working and talking with Prof. D.G. Hartle on these and related topics will be evident.
2. C.M. Drury, 'Quantitative Analysis and Public Policy Making', *Canadian Public Policy* 1, 1 (1975), pp. 89–96.
3. House of Commons, *Debates*, 8 June 1970, p. 7858.
4. Ibid., 11 October 1978.
5. Letter to his cabinet colleagues from the Honourable Evan Wolfe, then Chairman of the Treasury Board.
6. Miscellaneous Estimates Committee, Minutes, 27 October 1980, 23, pp. 32–4.
7. Ibid., p. 23: 11.
8. *Financial Post*, 9 September 1975.
9. J.E. Anderson, *Public Policy Making*, 2nd ed. (New York: Holt, Rinehart and Winston, 1979).
10. *Saturday Night*, March 1976.
11. P.H. Haveman, 'Policy Analysis and the Congress: An Economist's View', *Policy Analysis* 2, 2 (1976), p. 247.
12. House of Commons, *Debates*, 8 June 1970, p. 7858.
13. Ibid., 11 February 1979, p. 3336.
14. Ibid., 14 April 1980, p. 6.
15. Ibid., 11 December 1979, p. 2247.
16. Ibid., 16 February 1979, p. 3339.
17. For further information see: Canada, *Report* of the Independent Review Committee on the Office of the Auditor General of Canada, 1975; Canada, Office of the Auditor General, *Report*, 1979; Canada, Royal Commission on Financial Management and Accountability, *Final Report*, 1979.
18. Performance appraisal does, in principle, have a link with program evaluation, although the relationship is tenuous. Public evidence of the federal government's interest in bringing program and performance evaluations together is their recent decision to grant bonus pay to 'exceptional' managers. Presumably, the government by this action expected to improve program effectiveness by rewarding program efficiency through an incentive system. Unfortunately, as Zussman has argued elsewhere (see 'Bonuses, Performance and Program Evaluation in the Public Sector', *Canadian Psychologist*), there has never been any demonstrable link between performance, measured by efficiency or productivity indicators, and levels of compensation—specifically bonuses—at the executive level either in the private or public sector. Thus, it seems unlikely that these recent actions will significantly increase government efficiency.

19. Although evaluation research can be traced back to the writings of early social scientists, in the United States, the rediscovery of social problems in the early 1960s led to a renewed interest in program evaluation research. For example, early studies covered delinquency prevention projects (R. Marris, and M. Rein, *Dilemmas of Social Reform* [New York: Athonton Press, 1967], pp. 191–207), education evaluations resulting from the Elementary and Secondary Education Act of 1965 (J. Coleman, 'Evaluating Educational Programs', *The Urban Review*, 3, no. 4, 1969), and demonstration programs such as Head Start (U. Cicarelli, *The Impact of Head Start*, vol. 1 [Executive Summary], [Bladensburg, Maryland: Westinghouse Learning Corp., June 1969], p. 1–11).

20. It is sometimes argued (see, for example, the recent article by S.L. Sutherland, 'On the Audit Trail of the Auditor General: Parliament's Servant, 1973–1980', *Canadian Public Administration*, 23, 4 [1980], pp. 616–44 [also reprinted as Chapter 20 in this book]) that the techniques of classic program evaluation are themselves biased toward demonstrations of program failure. This argument, however, reflects a lack of understanding of the logic in the classic Neyman–Pearson approach to statistical tests of hypothesis or the more recent Bayesian approach to decision analysis. In either case the risks of failing to reject the null hypothesis when it is false are weighed against the risks of incorrectly rejecting the null hypothesis when it is true. Neither risk can be avoided and decisions must be taken in light of the costs and consequences of committing one or other. Bias toward a failure to reject the null hypothesis creeps in only because of a tradition of work by people who don't understand the tools they use, and hence, tend toward 'conventional' significance levels. Indeed, it could be argued that traditions of 'data-mining' and repeated tests on the same data base bias current methods toward reporting of some 'significant' results when no such conclusion is warranted. (It is, after all, of little interest to journals to print papers which do not report significant results.) So the alleged bias against identification of causal linkages may be an illusion.

21. Financial management, project appraisal, and like techniques reflect the community's essential concern with efficient use of resources. Material well-being is important and efficiency is a critical first step toward greater welfare.

    Social benefit-cost techniques, it should be recognized, stem from the same basic concern with efficiency in the use of scarce resources. The transition from the financial management techniques of the private corporation to a benefit-cost appraisal appropriate to a public body may seem substantial, and many an accountant may feel uncomfortable with some of the results. But essentially, this step involves only the substitution of social costs and values for observed market prices where there is reason to believe the two differ, and recalculation of all flows to reflect the viewpoint of the new clientele—the citizens of Canada—in place of the shareholders, when it comes to deciding what truly are costs or benefits as opposed to transfers. Valuing goods and services at true opportunity costs, and appraising the outcome from the perspective of the whole community, may yield very different estimates of the worth of a program from those generated by conventional analysis of financial data. But it still says little about the acceptability of the program to the community, or the legitimacy of the political decision which brought it about.

22. The public's perceptions of the public sector's ability to provide services has been the subject of a number of government-sponsored task forces. The results of one study commissioned by a recent task force are reported in D.R. Zussman, 'The Image of the Public Service in Canada' *Canadian Public Administration* 25, 1 (1980).

23. C. Schultze, *The Politics and Economics of Public Spending* (Washington, DC: The Brookings Institution, 1968).

24. G.T. Allison, *Essence of Decision: Explaining the Cuban Missile Crisis* (Boston: Little, Brown and Company, 1971).

25. D.G. Hartle, *Public Policy Decision Making and Regulation* (Montreal: Institute for Research on Public Policy, 1979), and *Expenditure Budgetary Process in the Government of Canada* (Toronto: Canadian Tax Foundation, 1976); D. Good, *The Politics of Anticipation: Making Canadian Federal Tax Policy* (Ottawa: Carleton University, 1980).

26. Charles E. Lindblom, *The Policy-Making Process* (Englewood Cliffs, NJ: Prentice-Hall, 1968).

27. As Aaron Wildavsky has observed in a comment on this paper, however, the interaction of budgetary ceilings of this kind with evaluation activities represents an interesting topic for further exploration.

28. H. Hatry, 'Pitfalls of Evaluation' in G. Majone, and E.S. Quade, *Pitfalls of Analysis*, International Institute for Applied Systems Analysis (Toronto: John Wiley and Sons, 1980) pp. 159–78; G. Majone, 'An Anatomy of Pitfalls', in ibid., pp. 7–21.

29. A.R. Dobell, 'Formation of Economic Policy and the Division of Economic Powers', *Policy Options* 1, 3 (1980), and 'Social Policy Making in the 1980s: Elements and Issues', OECD Conference on Social Policies in the 1980s, October 1980.

30. Cohen and Lindhlom, *Usable Knowledge*.

31. Versions of this diagram appear in a number of places, including the OPMS Manual published by the Treasury Board Secretariat, and an interesting survey paper prepared by T.R. Robinson 'A General Framework for the Evaluation of Social Security Policies: A Canadian Overview', Staff Working Paper 7505, Department of Health and Welfare, 1975. So far as we know, the first version (without any reference to information flows) was prepared by Dobell in D.G. Hartle's boardroom in the Confederation Building, for purposes of a paper on financing of post-secondary education. The point then was to emphasize that a variety of government programs authorized by Parliament work through a variety of channels to affect the well-being of the household sector, and that appraisal of their success is a complex issue reflecting a variety of political forces. The message has not changed much in the subsequent ten years.

32. Thus, our answer to the question 'Who should do these evaluations?' is that in the case of summative evaluation (designed to answer the question 'How well are we responding to the problem?') we should all do it—academics, journalists, parliamentary staff, the community at large—much more than we do. We should do it case-by-case, randomly, as events arise, but on the basis of full and open access to the relevant information. In the case of formative evaluation (designed to answer the question 'How can this program be made better?'), we have no substantial quarrel with the approach advocated by the OAG and proposed by the OCG. This work should be available to the program manager reallocating resources within the pro-

gram, to the deputy reallocating resources within the department (and thus internalizing inter-program spillovers), and to the policy committees reallocating resources within an envelope (and thus internalizing interdepartmental spillovers). Notice that in this sort of formative evaluation, one may find an ineffective program receiving greater resources—because they are needed—or reduced resources—because they are not deserved; at this level, no paradox exists.

33. Vickers, *Freedom in a Rocking Boat*, p. 23.

34. Ibid., p. 24.

35. J.M. Keynes, *General Theory of Employment, Interest and Money* (New York: Harcourt Brace, 1935).

PART IV

Policy and Administration

This last section focuses primarily on problems of program administration and policy implementation. Most of the selections were written in the 1980s, when these issues began to attract more attention, but two are considerably older: these are of particular interest given the current popularity of 'public choice' or 'rational choice' theory. All the articles in this section are the work of academics, or former academics, among them some of the best-known names in Canadian public administration.

The first selection, by Peter Aucoin and Herman Bakvis, focuses on the perennial organizational problem of centralization and decentralization, cast here in terms of differentiation and integration and applied both to public organizations and to the very Canadian issue of regional economic development. The theoretical issues are addressed mainly in the early and concluding parts of the article. Students unfamiliar with the 'golden age' of federal–provincial relations and the period of rational planning in Canadian public policy will find this an excellent summary (for more detail we recommend Donald Savoie, *Federal–Provincial Collaboration: The Canada–New Brunswick General Development Agreement*, and Richard French, *How Ottawa Decides*).

The theme of intergovernmental relations is further developed in Stefan Dupré's 'Reflections on the Workability of Executive Federalism'. This paper, prepared for the Royal Commission on the Economic Union and Development Prospects for Canada (MacDonald Commission, 1985), offers a valuable overview of the history behind the tensions that continue to trouble relations between different levels of government in Canada today. It also includes an extensive case study on education and occupational training that will be of interest to anyone concerned with preparing the labour force for an uncertain economic future.

Perhaps the most insightful comment ever made about bureaucracy is 'Parkinson's Law': that work expands to fill the time available. In their article Albert Breton and Ronald Wintrobe suggest some variations on Parkinson's theme, drawn from economic theory. Readers may find parts of their article challenging, but it is not necessary to understand the economic theory behind it to grasp their argument. This paper remains one of the best theoretical explanations ever offered of a set of principles that continues to resonate for students and practitioners alike.

The next article, by Ted Morton and Les Pal, looks at one of the most signifi-cant changes brought about by the Charter of Rights and Freedoms: today many pol-icy decisions are in effect made by judges and produce outcomes that are not necessarily consistent with the intentions of the traditional policy-makers—politi-cians and bureaucrats. According to Morton and Pal, the reason for this inconsistency is that judges make their decisions on individual cases, whereas policy-makers must think about classes of cases. This paper reminds us that what is right in one single case may not make for optimal public policy. Although it was written before the 'equal-ity rights' in section 15 of the Charter came into effect, the logic of its argument is still powerful. An update would be a valuable addition to the academic literature.

The following article is also relevant today. Michael Prince and John Chenier trace the initial phases of the decline in policy planning that over time led to the de-staffing of policy planning units and eventually the virtual elimination of the policy planning function itself. In the absence of long- and often even medium-term plan-ning, governments lurch from one policy crisis to another, making 'just in time' deci-sions, and citizens pay the price. If planning ever does receive a new mandate, this article could serve as a blueprint of what to aim for.

What Mark Sproule-Jones calls 'coordination' may be better known today as 'horizontal management'. Focusing on water-quality planning in BC's Lower Fraser River region, he explores the complex interactions of three levels of government between themselves and with the private sector—interactions that go well beyond simple contracting. Today, when governments are increasingly interested in public–private partnerships (often known as PPP), the experience he documents offers many useful lessons.

We conclude with Ken Woodside's article on policy instruments—an area in which Canada has made an international contribution. Another possibility might have been Bruce Doern and Richard Phidd's classic work defining policy instru-ments, but we decided on this one because the choice between tax expenditures and tax subsidies has been so central to the ideological debate about economic policy in Canada. That choice—made by the Minister of Finance every time a budget is pre-pared—may seem fairly simple, but it has profound implications for public policy, public administration, and income distribution.

22

Organizational Differentiation and Integration: The Case of Regional Economic Development Policy in Canada

Peter Aucoin and Herman Bakvis

Abstract: Over the past two and a half decades regional development policy and administration has gone through at least five distinct stages: in 1961 the government started with a number of uncoordinated boards and agencies; in 1969 it created the high profile and centralized Department of Regional Economic Expansion (DREE); a few years later (1973), DREE was decentralized and became more low key in its approach; in 1978 the government struck the centralized Board of Development Ministers, supported by the Ministry of State for Economic Development (MSED), to revamp the national economy while maintaining DREE in its decentralized format; and in 1982 DREE was abolished and the Cabinet Committee for Economic and Regional Development (CCRED), headed by a Minister of State for Economic and Regional Development and supported by a Ministry of State for Economic and Regional Development (MSERD), was given the responsibility of integrating economic and regional development activities of all line departments. The logic of and reasons for the 1982 reorganization are assessed. Although innovative, particularly with regard to the placement of a Federal Economic Development Coordinator (FEDC) in each province, the reorganization does not necessarily mean improved regional policy. Major obstacles are identified which may serve to prevent the objectives of the reorganization from being realized.

On 12 January 1982 the Government of Canada announced a major re-organization of its various economic development policy portfolios and their supporting agencies.[1] The reorganization signalled the termination of a portfolio and department that, since 1969, had been the government's flagship in the field of regional economic development policy, namely the Department of Regional Economic Expansion (DREE). Given the economic exigencies of early 1982, this major reorganization was viewed in some quarters as tantamount to reshuffling the deck chairs on the Titanic. A fair amount of skepticism and criticism thus greeted the government's announcement, especially with regard to the ostensible aim of making all the economic development portfolios (e.g., Transport, Agriculture) responsible for regional economic development. The purpose of this article is to examine the reasons for and logic of this

Peter Aucoin and Herman Bakvis, 'Organizational Differentiation and Integration: The Case of Regional Economic Development Policy in Canada', *Canadian Public Administration* 27, 3 (1984): 348–71. Courtesy of The Institute of Public Administration Canada.

reorganization in the field of regional economic development policy. To this end, we describe the organizational and policy developments which led to this most recent reorganization: most recent, that is, because in this field of public policy and administration there has been an evolution of successive organizational regimes. Our thesis is that the reorganization constitutes a logical response to the perceived need for increased differentiation and integration in this policy field in light of the increasing priority given to the development of strong central agencies to support the collegial structure of the cabinet that has emerged over the past two decades.[2] We do not argue, however, that the regional economic development policies of the federal government will necessarily be improved as a consequence of this reorganization because there are clearly major obstacles which can easily undermine the intended consequences.

Our paper is divided into five sections. The first section describes briefly the initial efforts of the federal government to establish organizations and policy to deal with regional economic development in Canada up to and including the establishment of the portfolio and Department of Regional Economic Expansion in the late 1960s and its development in the 1970s. The second section describes, again briefly, organizational changes in the 1970s as they relate to the larger field of economic development policy, of which regional economic development policy was but one element. The third section focuses on the organizational integration of economic and regional development policies, culminating in the establishment of the Ministry of State for Economic and Regional Development (MSERD). The fourth section examines the structures and processes of MSERD as a decentralized central agency with a focus on Federal Economic Development Coordinators (FEDCs) and their regional offices in the ten provinces. The final section provides an analysis and assessment of the reorganization in light of prior experience, especially with respect to the role played by DREE, and current political circumstances.

REGIONALISM, REGIONAL POLICY, AND DREE

While the concept of regionalism encompasses several dimensions, three are particularly relevant in the Canadian context. First, there is the political dimension of regionalism. We have a federal system of government which in large part reflects differing regional identities, cultures, and partisan preferences. In turn, federal institutions tend to reinforce and enhance these identities by virtue of the considerable autonomy enjoyed by provincial governments which, it is argued, make ample use of the levers of power available to them to engage in province-building.[3] The general consequence is what we can refer to as 'intergovernmental governing': in virtually any jurisdiction both levels of government have some role, whether it be in education, fisheries, or economic management.

The second is the spatial dimension of the national economy. It encompasses two aspects: regional effects of national policy and regional disparities in resources and economic opportunities. The effects of inflation, interest rates, and unemployment differ widely in different parts of the country while basic structural differences between regions and provinces in terms of resources, markets, and per capita income have existed from before confederation down to the present.[4]

The third dimension relevant to our study concerns the organization of the federal government. By the very nature of their activities many of the line departments have a large number of their employees based outside of Ottawa. Although there are obvious implications for span of control when administrative units are widely scattered, geographic dispersal is not the same as organizational decentralization.[5] It is possible and perhaps even desirable to decentralize the operations of a government department, using geography as a basis, with a view to making the organization more effective or at least regionally sensitive. This sort of decentralization, however, has not been extensively practised by the federal government, and the decentralization of DREE, to be discussed below, stands as an exception rather than the rule.

The three dimensions of regionalism outlined above have affected Canadian political and administrative life since confederation. However, with the possible exception of the Prairie Farm Rehabilitation Act of 1935, there was no such thing as a formal regional development policy by the federal government until 1957, the various ad hoc payments made to provinces over the years notwithstanding. The Diefenbaker government passed the Agricultural and Rural Development Act (ARDA) in 1961 and in 1962 created the Atlantic Development Board (ADB), thereby ushering in a decade of regional policy that was characterized by unclear political direction and philosophy and dependent upon a number of uncoordinated boards and agencies for the delivery of programs. Although ARDA was aimed at rural rather than regional development and was initially administered through the Department of Agriculture, the designated depressed rural areas were specifically located in the prairies and the Atlantic provinces. Furthermore, Alvin Hamilton, Minister of Agriculture at the time, conceived of rural development in distinctly regional terms, favouring growth in the regions themselves.

When they came to power in 1963, the Liberals expanded these programs rather than abolishing them. To ARDA they added the Fund for Rural Economic Development (FRED).[7] The Liberals were somewhat less committed to Alvin Hamilton's shibboleth that 'no one should have to move because of rural poverty' and more prone to see rural development in terms of adjustment and mobility. Nevertheless, the Pearson government did create the Area Development Agency (ADA) to help bring jobs to people in depressed regions rather than vice versa; and in 1965 the ambit of the ADA was extended when it was superseded by the Area Development Incentives Act which deliberately favoured the poor regions. Generally it is important to note that during the 1961–9 period there were ambiguities in philosophy and tensions within and between the different programs and agencies concerned with regional development; above all there was a general lack of coordination.

Most programs were delivered by means of boards, agencies or, in certain instances, Crown corporations, and lines of accountability often were not clear. Most of the boards and agencies did report to or operate within the confines of line departments: ADA became part of the newly created Department of Industry in 1963; ARDA was first administered through Agriculture and then in 1964 was moved to the new Department of Forestry and Rural Development. The placement of a program, moreover, was often determined on political grounds. The ADB was put by the Liberal government first in Secretary of State and then in Transport, the initial placement and subsequent shift coinciding with the move of Jack Pickersgill, the senior minister from Newfoundland, from one to the other. It was only when Pickersgill left the cabinet in 1967 that the ADB found a logical home in Forestry and Rural Development.[8] In early 1965, the Special Planning Secretariat was established within the PCO with responsibilities for coordinating and directing all departmental policies for Canada's 'war on poverty', and this included regional poverty. The Secretariat, by virtue of being located within the PCO, had no funds or operational responsibilities. Its efforts at coordination of the different programs were described as 'absolutely abortive' and it was dissolved in 1967.[9]

In summary, during this period, in spite of the proliferation of regional programs there was no single department whose sole or primary function was to promote and implement regional policy and there was a lack of coordination between the different programs and agencies. The argument that certain line departments were at least regionally sensitive by virtue of having responsibilities for some of these agencies has to be discounted by the fact that the agencies in question were frequently regarded as poor cousins and their location in any given department was often anomalous. The commitment on the part of the federal government to doing something about regional disparities continued unabated. This commitment culminated in the 1969 establishment of DREE and ushered in a new, albeit brief, phase of centralized control and program delivery. The new department took over existing programs such as ARDA–FRED and ADA, and had as its responsibility the design and implementation of regional development programs. It was a line department with its own funds to spend; but it was also expected to cooperate with and, when authorized by cabinet, to coordinate activities of other departments in order to achieve stated goals.[10]

In the first few years of its existence ADA took a highly centralized approach to the problem of regional development. Regional officers of ARDA–FRED lost their signing authority and were no longer permitted to deal with provincial planning agencies, agencies whose existence and growth in many instances had been encouraged by earlier ARDA–FRED policies and money. Federal–provincial consultative mechanisms at the regional level were abolished; consultation was now strictly between Ottawa and the provinces; and in many instances the provinces themselves were bypassed or ignored when federal policy initiatives were introduced into the regions.[11] Within a few years DREE was forced to backtrack when a number of the provinces were successful in applying political pressure on Ottawa. A number of the more rigid policies had to be adapted and readjusted after the fact in order to fit local conditions, illustrating the difficulties inherent in the centralized design and implementation structure.

In 1973, after an elaborate review, DREE's operations were revised considerably with the introduction of a new policy orientation and a decentralized organizational structure.[12] Regional policy became more multi-dimensional and projects were more widely distributed throughout the provinces, a change from the earlier stress on the 'growth pole' concept which restricted development opportunities to large urban centres and projects to the provision of infrastructure and industrial incentives. Projects were now on a smaller scale but would encompass a wider range of sectors and be distributed throughout any given province.[13] The multi-dimensional aspect recognized the fact that regional development encompassed a wide range of highly differentiated activities.

The reorganization itself comprised two aspects: decentralization of the department, and adoption of the so-called General Development Agreement (GDA) approach. Decentralization was achieved by establishing four regional offices, complete with administrative, financial, and policy analysis support and headed by assistant deputy ministers. The ten provincial offices were also strengthened; and all development ideas, whether from Ottawa or the province, were henceforth channelled through the provincial offices. Both provincial directors-general and regional ADMs were given discretionary authority to approve projects up to fairly generous limits.[14] The GDA approach, in turn, reinforced the effect of the decentralization. The GDA was basically an enabling document which stated the general goals to be pursued over a ten-year period; subsidiary agreements then gave effect to these broadly defined goals by outlining the specific objectives and the means to attain them. Unlike earlier DREE initiatives, the GDAs were designed to be joint endeavours by Ottawa and the provinces. Once a GDA had been approved by both the federal and provincial governments it was then administered by the Canada–Province Development Committee. Subsidiary agreements also required cabinet approval at both levels. These agreements were then implemented by joint management committees with equal representation from both governments, including the provincial director-general of DREE and a senior provincial bureaucrat. There were *no* politicians on either the development or management committees.[15]

The GDA era was unique in many respects, especially in light of the heightened level of competition and conflict between Ottawa and the provinces during the 1970s. The popularity of the GDAs with the provinces can be explained by the fact that in some provinces the federal government was willing to pay up to 90 per cent of project costs; and furthermore a number of low and medium priority items of the provinces could be brought under the GDA umbrella and hence receive funding. Once the GDA and various subsidiary agreements were in place, DREE and provincial officials worked together with relatively little political interference. This blissful state of affairs, however, was misleading; inherent in these arrangements were lodged major problems which in the long run helped to bring about the downfall of DREE.

First, there developed dissatisfaction on the part of political leadership at both levels of government with DREE programs. At the provincial level, politicians in some provinces felt that they had very little influence over programs once they were in place. At the federal level some ministers did not like their inability to influence DREE expenditures. These concerns were in good part animated by envy on the part of line departments, which saw DREE initiating projects in their own areas of jurisdiction while they themselves had to operate with restricted budgets. Equally important perhaps were the more general concerns by the federal government over the perceived lack of political credit and visibility for all the roads, canneries and strawberry farms funded by DREE. This concern became particularly acute during the early 1980s with respect not only to DREE but also other programs such as medicare and post-secondary school financing.[16]

From an organizational perspective, a major federal concern was that DREE was not proving to be terribly effective in coordinating and integrating the activities of other line departments. Particularly in taking a multi-dimensional approach, it was expected that the activities of line departments deemed to be relevant to development in a particular province would be coordinated or 'bent' by DREE. The department had a certain amount of financial clout but no overall coordinating authority to override line department decisions. It could only offer to purchase the necessary program components from the appropriate line department and in a number of crucial situations this technique proved to be inadequate. The line departments in turn felt relatively little need to pay much attention to regional concerns, and indeed one common sentiment was that DREE existed to take care of regional issues and, therefore, line departments did not need to concern themselves with these responsibilities.[17]

In many respects DREE fell between a number of stools. It had neither the financial wherewithal to finance large-scale multi-dimensional projects, nor the political or administrative authority to coordinate and integrate the multifarious activities of other departments so as to be able to achieve the same objectives. Furthermore, by having insulated itself from direct political authority, and in having attracted a certain amount of envy on the part of other departments, it left itself highly vulnerable. When most of the ten-year GDAs were about to expire, and in the atmosphere of federal–provincial conflict over the constitution and fiscal transfers, matters became ripe for change. These conditions, however, were perhaps necessary but not sufficient to explain the demise of DREE. We need to take account of other developments in Ottawa and to place the problems confronting DREE, particularly in its relations with other line departments, in the broader context of policy and expenditure management and overall strategies for economic development.

THE STRUCTURES AND PROCESSES OF NATIONAL ECONOMIC DEVELOPMENT POLICY

The establishment of DREE, its subsequent decentralization, as well as its efforts to have other line departments participate more effectively in regional development were but elements in a larger system of economic development policy-making and administration. Within this larger system, there emerged through the 1970s an increased concern for greater coordination of the wide range of departments and agencies whose programs, expenditures, and regulations related to economic development.[18] By the late 1970s the federal government did have several mechanisms in place to provide for coordination as well as co-operation and consultation. The cabinet committee system, a number of 'horizontal' or coordinating portfolios, an enlarged complex of central agencies, and a program budgeting system had been put in place in order to promote greater collegial decision-making and thereby increased coordination in policy development and program management.[19] Notwithstanding these organizational innovations, however, there remained a number of deficiencies in the organization of the federal government, particularly with respect to economic development policy.[20]

First, no single portfolio, not even Finance, was considered able to exercise sufficient leverage to define, let alone to integrate, the field of economic development policy. Economic development was a function of several portfolios including

Industry, Trade and Commerce, Regional Economic Expansion, Science and Technology as well as the several resource-based departments and agencies. Secondly, the cabinet committee system was not structured in such a way as to focus or integrate decision-making at this level on the broad subject of economic development policy. Thirdly, an effective 'interface' between the government and the private sector was not considered to be helped by this highly differentiated departmental structure. Fourthly, the increased dispersal of federal line departments to the regions had occurred over the years with what some thought was insufficient attention to the need for policy coordination in the field. Lastly, the decision-making system throughout the federal government did not appear to provide for a sufficient integration of policy and expenditure decision-making. These last three perceptions of shortcomings of structure and process had implications for fields other than economic development policy but for a number of reasons they were perhaps most obvious and acute in this field.

In August of 1978, the Prime Minister decided to effect major budget cuts in federal spending while at the same time giving highest priority to new initiatives in the area of economic development. This new fund for economic development programs during a time of restraint meant, of course, that intense interdepartmental competition could be expected for these discretionary funds and there was concern that the existing machinery of government was incapable of providing the desired degree of coordination and integration. These concerns had been addressed in the Privy Council Office and at least three major options for change were considered:

1. a new 'super' department, providing for the integration of Industry, Trade and Commerce, Regional Economic Expansion, and Science and Technology;
2. a strengthened interdepartmental committee based on the above noted interdepartmental review process; and
3. a 'board' of ministers.[21]

This third option was presented to the Prime Minister shortly after his August decision and, in November, along with a cabinet shuffle, a new Board of Economic Development Ministers was created. This board of ministers was composed of the Deputy Prime Minister, the Minister of Finance, and the President of the Treasury Board, the latter two as ex officio; the ministers of Energy, Mines and Resources, Science and Technology, Labour, Regional Economic Expansion, Employment and Immigration, National Revenue and Small Business, Industry, Trade and Commerce; and the newly created portfolio of the Minister of State for Economic Development as president of this new board. The president and board were provided a Ministry of State for Economic Development, a support staff to serve both this new portfolio and new cabinet committee.[22]

The roles of this new portfolio, cabinet committee and central agency secretariat constituted an organizational innovation in a number of respects. Most important, in general terms, was the fact that this new structure integrated at the ministerial level functions which under the existing cabinet committee system had been separated, namely policy and expenditure decision-making. The board was not only a new cabinet committee for economic development policy, it was also a sectoral cabinet committee with powers to allocate expenditure resources for the programs of the departments within its sector. In this latter respect, the board has assumed powers which heretofore were located with a horizontal cabinet committee separate from the other cabinet committees, namely the Treasury Board. Concomitantly, at the official level, the secretariat to serve the Board, the Ministry of State for Economic Development, performed central agency—or staff—functions previously performed by the Privy Council Office and the Treasury Board Secretariat for the sectoral cabinet committees and the Treasury Board respectively. To this end, all ministers on the board, and not just the president, were briefed by the ministry on the policy and expenditure implications of proposals to be considered by them. In that particular field of economic development policy there now was not only a cabinet committee but, equally important, a minister and Ministry of State with general powers of policy coordination and integration for this newly defined field of federal government policy. In practical political terms, moreover, the Prime Minister made it clear, by virtue of the selection of the individuals to head both the portfolio and its secretariat, that this new organization would be endowed with the necessary political and bureaucratic power.[23]

Although there were obvious political reasons in 1978 to question the federal government's commitment to these innovations, doubts about the organizational rationality of this change were to a certain extent laid to rest when the Progressive Conservative government of Prime Minister Joe Clark reorganized the structures and processes of the federal decision-making system using this innovation as its model. Although the board lost its title and became the Cabinet Committee on Economic Development, its mandate and powers remained essentially the same, especially in respect to the integration of policy and expenditure decision-making.[24] By the time the Liberal party returned to power, the concepts of sectoral cabinet committees headed by ministers of state with their own central agency secretariats and of an integrated policy and expenditure management system were clearly established as the organizational principles upon which the executive decision-making system was predicated.[25]

THE INTEGRATION OF ECONOMIC AND REGIONAL DEVELOPMENT POLICY-MAKING AND ADMINISTRATION

The establishment of the Cabinet Committee on Economic Development, the Ministry of State for Economic Development, and the policy and expenditure management system did not substantially transform the roles of the portfolios or departments involved in the field of economic development policy. Rather, these innovations were imposed upon the existing structure. Within this new system, however, the minister and the Department of Regional Economic Expansion operated in a political and bureaucratic milieu which highlighted the strengths and weaknesses of the federal government's organization for regional economic development policy. The mandate of DREE had been a sweeping one even if its powers had been limited. Its regional economic development responsibilities included industrial development, which brought it often into conflict with Industry, Trade and Commerce, but they also extended beyond: indeed, its responsibilities (if not authority) extended widely to encompass the specific concerns of a number of federal government departments, especially those in the major resource fields, which also brought it into conflict with them. DREE's objective was to alter the spatial distribution of economic development activities and, accordingly, to adjust or bend national programs to fit regional needs.

Although, as noted earlier, DREE's capacity to coordinate, in an authoritative manner, the activities of other federal departments and agencies was extremely limited, politically and bureaucratically it did possess two assets which gave it some leverage. First, its decentralized structure in tandem with the GDA approach enabled it to develop effective relationships with provincial governments at the bureaucratic level. These relationships in the regions often afforded it the opportunity to initiate proposals and to see them well advanced before many of the affected political and bureaucratic officials in Ottawa, other than in its own department, were brought into the decision-making process. Secondly, the expenditure process as it related to the subsidiary agreements, given their federal-provincial character, was structured in such a way that DREE could draw on a separate fund. This fund, in some respects, constituted an expenditure envelope assigned exclusively to regional economic development programs.

Each of these assets, however, was also a liability for both Regional Economic Expansion and the federal governments efforts in regional economic development. Opposition from other ministers and departments to the regional economic development fund was inevitable once expenditure restraint set in, simply because restraint severely limited the amount of new or discretionary monies that could be allocated to programs proposed by other ministers and departments. The ability of DREE to support its new programs or projects provoked the obvious envy and even resentment of others. At the same time, these other ministers and departments did not welcome the efforts of DREE to bend their programs and expenditures to promote regional economic development. DREE could not dictate such programs or expenditure-bending, but it did have some leverage through the expenditure incentives of its development fund. While some success was achieved by virtue of this approach, its value was considered to be marginal at best and counterproductive at worst in at least two respects. First, Regional Economic Expansion's mandate and activities were regarded by other ministers and departments as those of a distinct portfolio and department. Therefore, as noted earlier, little or no effort was made by others to consider the regional economic development dimensions of their programs or expenditures. Given that these programs and expenditures have major effects on regional economic development, their importance clearly outweighs the marginal effects which DREE could have on regional economic development, even with its GDAs and other programs. Moreover, with many of the infrastructure requirements for regional economic development accomplished through these agreements by the end of the last decade, the perceived need to address the regional dimensions of these other programs and expenditures had become more critical. DREE had considerable responsibility in this regard, but precious little in the way of authority or power to fulfill them.

The second disadvantage of this structure and process was that DREE's mandate was limited to regional economic development which did not extend to economic development generally. In this sense, again, it was no more than one line department among many. At the same time, the establishment of the board and then the Cabinet Committee on Economic Development with its minister and Ministry of State for Economic Development was a recognition of the need for coordination in this field, a field that clearly embraced regional economic development. This new system provided the required focus but was simply imposed on top of the previous regime. This approach, as would be expected, quickly raised questions about the logic of maintaining those elements of the previous regime whose defects led to the establishment of the new arrangements.

The organizational response to the perceived need to integrate more fully regional economic development policy and economic development policy involved extensive changes in three areas. First, the regional programs of DREE and the industry, small business and tourism programs of IT&C were amalgamated through the establishment of a new Department of Regional Industrial Expansion. (The trade branch of IT&C was transferred to a reorganized Department of External Affairs.) Both DREE and IT&C were thus dismantled as portfolios and departments. Secondly, the Cabinet Committee on Economic Development and the Ministry of State for Economic Development were renamed to signify the intention of the government that 'the regional perspective be brought to bear on the work of all economic development departments and in all economic decision-making by the Cabinet':[26] hence the Cabinet Committee on Economic and Regional Development and the Ministry of State for Economic and Regional Development. The regional focus of the government was to be enlarged to include all regions of the country, and now to be designated as corresponding to the boundaries of the provinces. To this end, all sectoral departments in this field were directed 'to improve their regional capabilities and to build the regional dimension into their internal policy development and decision-making processes', now that 'responsibility for economic development in the regions . . . [would] not be the distinct mandate of a single department'.[27] These departments were expected to take advantage of 'the availability of specialized personnel (individuals already in regions and now part of DREE)' to assist them in carrying out this directive of the Prime Minister.[28] What this meant, of course, was that departments were to decentralize not only in respect to their operations, as many had done or begun to do, but, more important, in respect to their policy analysis and development functions.

The third major element in the reorganization, and an innovation of critical importance, was the establishment of a system of regional offices in each province as part of the Ministry of State for Economic and Regional Development organization. These offices, headed by a Federal Economic Development Coordinator of 'senior rank', have four main functions:

> to provide an improved regional information base for decision-making by the Cabinet Committee on Economic and Regional Development (CCERD), for use particularly in the development of regionally sensitive economic development strategies;

to give regional officials of sector departments a better understanding of the decisions and objectives of the Cabinet;

to better coordinate the implementation of government decisions affecting economic development in the regions;

and to develop regional economic development policies for consideration by Cabinet.[29]

This innovation is of critical importance because it is the decentralized organization of the ministry that, in large part, is meant to ensure that the advantages which obtained with the decentralized DREE are maintained, while the disadvantages which obtained with the limited capacity of DREE to coordinate other line departments are overcome. This decentralization of a central agency is novel in the Canadian experience and its success, or lack thereof, will depend upon a number of factors, a subject to which we now turn.

THE ROLES OF FEDERAL ECONOMIC DEVELOPMENT COORDINATORS AND REGIONAL OFFICES

Crucial to the roles of Federal Economic Development Coordinators (FEDCs) and their regional offices, and their capacity to perform their functions effectively, are the roles of MSERD in the policy and expenditure management system (PEMS).[30] MSERD's roles in this system should enable it to have a major influence on both the determination of the strategies and priorities of the economic and regional development policy sector, as established by its cabinet committee, and the specific policy and expenditures decisions of this committee. It should have this influence in the former set of decisions by virtue of its coordinating role in the preparation of departmental 'strategic overview' and 'operational plans' and its own preparation of the entire sector's 'policy outlook'; its influence in the latter set of decisions would emanate from its provision to all members of the committee of 'assessment notes'—that is, brief and concise analyses of departmental proposals which assess each proposal within the context of the government's policies, priorities, and resources. In short, MSERD functions as a support staff for this cabinet committee as a collective decision-making body and exercises a policy coordinating role *vis-à-vis* the departments in this sector on behalf of its minister with respect to his role as Minister of State for the entire sector and as chairman of the cabinet committee.[31]

Within this context, the roles of the FEDCs and their regional offices are clearly those of a central agency. Although these roles represent the decentralization of a central agency, the four functions to be performed by it, as noted in the previous section, do not differ in kind from the central agency functions performed by the central office. However, the decentralization of MSERD does enable MSERD to undertake central agency functions in the field, functions which could not be carried out in the absence of decentralization. Given the cabinet committee's and MSERD's responsibilities for regional economic development, decentralization constitutes an essential element in this structure and process. Regional perspectives must be obtained by MSERD through other than decentralized line departments, and regional economic development policies must be developed, in part at least, by staff in the regions.

The functions performed by the FEDCs and their regional offices involve three principal tasks. First, these officials must be able to develop a solid grasp of the particular characteristics, needs, and opportunities extant in their provinces as they relate to government policies, priorities, and resources. This understanding is essential if they are to contribute a regional perspective to MSERD's policy outlooks and assessment notes. Although easier said than done, such an understanding is crucial to the effective performance of their central agency roles. Secondly, these officials, and especially the FEDCs, must be able to coordinate the implementation of federal decisions within the region without intervening in the actual management of programs. Again, the role of central agency officials is to effect coordination but not to engage in second-guessing the decisions of program managers. Thirdly, MSERD officials in the field must be able to facilitate effective federal–provincial co-operation and public sector–private sector consultations without infringing on either the regular bureaucratic processes of such relations or usurping the regular processes of department-client relations.

The success of the FEDCs and their regional offices will depend on at least three sets of relationships: within MSERD, that is between headquarters and the field; between the FEDCs and their officials and the regional officials of the line departments; and between the FEDCs and their offices and provincial governments and the private sector. We shall deal briefly with each of these in turn.

The relationships within MSERD require that the FEDCs be fully involved in the work of MSERD. As central agency officials with responsibilities that encompass the full spectrum of MSERD's responsibilities, albeit for a particular region, the FEDCs need to be informed of the thinking that is taking place within their headquarters. This requirement constitutes a significant challenge, notwithstanding the sophisticated technologies of communication at the disposal of MSERD. The FEDC must not be allowed to become either 'our man in Havana' or a federal 'spokesman' for his or her province. Neither role will serve the purposes for which a decentralized MSERD was established.

Two features of the established structures and processes of MSERD are meant to avoid these undesired outcomes. First, the position of the FEDCs within the structure of MSERD is a senior one. The FEDCs are clearly more than regional directors. They do not report to assistant deputy ministers but are included within the central management structure of the ministry along with the deputy secretaries for policy, operations, and projects. Secondly, the FEDCs have the right and responsibility to provide an input to the preparation of the principal policy memoranda which are given to all ministers on CCERD. Since such memoranda constitute the lifeblood of MSERD as a central agency, the FEDCs are, at least in theory, strategically involved in the policy and expenditure management system.

The relationships of the FEDCs and their officials to the regional officials of line departments require that the former work closely with the latter both to draw upon their expertise in their various departmental areas and to promote a sensitivity to regional economic development concerns in the development and implementation of departmental programs. It could be argued that the regional offices of MSERD must remain small, in terms of professional staff, if each of these objectives is to be achieved; otherwise, the temptation 'to do in the office' what should be done in departments will be great and, in any event, efforts to promote the required sensitivity to regional concerns will become diffused with too many MSERD officials involved.

Again, the same two features noted in the case of the first set of relations may serve to counter any development toward too many central agency officials in the field, that is in the regional offices. First, the capacity of the regional office to provide the required coordination demands that the FEDC play a major role in all efforts at coordination because it is the FEDC who wields bureaucratic clout. The FEDC thus has an incentive, if he or she wishes to be effective, to be involved in such efforts and thus not to spend the time on internal regional office management which would be required by a large staff. Secondly, the role of the FEDC in MSERD's operation of the policy and expenditure management system is supposed to give him or her the leverage necessary to promote the desired sensitivity to regional economic development concerns on the part of regional officials in line departments. Since the FEDC provides input to MSERD's assessment notes, regional officials of line departments should have an incentive to ensure that they provide a regional perspective to departmental proposals with regional implications, given that the FEDC will be in a position to comment on them. It is in their department's interests, in short, that they develop the capacity to provide the required regional perspective and that such perspectives not be upstaged by advice that is rendered by the FEDC.

The third set of relationships that must be established is between the FEDC and the regional office and provincial governments on the one hand and the private sector on the other. In respect to both of these relations the role of the FEDC must be clearly established as one in which he or she is acting, and is seen to be acting, by the other parties in such relationships as a 'field representative of a central agency'. This role is one of coordination and not of operational management. As such, it must be recognized that the FEDC cannot speak either for the Cabinet Committee on Economic and Regional Development or for individual ministers and their line departments. He or she is not, in short, a 'prefect' for the federal government. On the other hand, the FEDC must be able to assure both a provincial government and the private sector in the province that he or she is able to effect the required coordination of federal activities as they relate to their particular concerns.

In our view in order for a FEDC to accomplish the latter task, it will be necessary that both MSERD and the individual FEDCs achieve the first two required sets of relationships—that is, those internal to MSERD and those internal to the federal government in the sector encompassed by the Cabinet Committee on Economic and Regional Development. This sector of the federal government, in other words, must get its own act together if external relationships are to be effectively established. To the extent that there is inter-organizational competition or uncertainty within this sector, external relationships will suffer.

ANALYSIS AND ASSESSMENT

The government's reorganization in the field of regional economic development policy was received in many quarters with considerable skepticism and criticism. The Senate Committee on National Finance virtually accused the government of abandoning its responsibilities for assisting the least developed regions.[32] The Atlantic Provinces Economic Council (APEC) echoed these concerns and argued that DRIE constituted an inadequate replacement for DREE.[33] Robert Stanfield claimed that because the federal government was so preoccupied with national economic considerations lesser concerns like the well-being of the poorer regions had been set aside.[34]

In every instance those who are critical of the reorganization which took place in January 1982 point to the decrease in federal government allocation to DREE over the past several years, particularly as a percentage of total federal government expenditures, and to the shift of expenditures away from Atlantic Canada toward the west. The point that we would make in this regard is that these expenditure patterns were well advanced prior to 1982.[35] These were the result of policy decisions and it is obvious that the presence of DREE did little to prevent these decisions from being made. More significant in our view, however, is the perception on the part of the skeptics that the reorganization involved essentially the substitution of DRIE for DREE. In one sense perhaps this perception is not unexpected; even the well-informed observer tends to identify with line departments which implement programs, deliver services, and distribute government funds. To many, therefore, what DREE once did is now to be done by DRIE, albeit with a more diffused mandate because it is responsible for both regional *and* industrial expansion.[36] Those in the less-developed regions who have long regarded regional economic development as being either in unfair competition with, or a lower priority to, national industrial development can perhaps be excused if they view the reorganization as one which has sacrificed regional economic development on the altar of national industrial development, whatever the title of the transformed department of industry.

This perception, however, may be misplaced in some respects. DRIE does assume some of the former responsibilities of DREE but, without repeating what we have described in previous sections, the reorganization involves much more than this. Most important, it designates regional economic development as a central concern of the cabinet committee for this policy sector (CCERD) and the ministry of state (MSERD) that serves it. Secondly, it demands that all line departments in this sector, including DRIE, assume responsibility for the regional dimensions of national economic development policies and programs. In short, regional economic development is supposed to become an integral part of economic development policy with a structure and process to provide for this integration. Regional economic development is no longer the principal mandate of one line department; nor has DRIE replaced DREE in this respect, even if it is one of the more important of the line departments in this sector.

Every reorganization, even those that are not subject to criticism and skepticism, brings with it its own set of obstacles which must be overcome if its organizational advantages are to be realized. In the case of major reorganizations, these obstacles will be encountered at a number of levels both intra-organizationally and inter-organizationally. The organizational system created in January 1982 must deal with at least four potential obstacles.

First, this new system must overcome the resistance of line ministers and their departmental officials to the intrusion of the regional dimension into their specific departmental mandates and operations. The integration of regional and national economic development policies through CCERD and MSERD will have been for naught if the differentiation of regional economic development policy among line departments does not take place.[37] Resistance to this intrusion of the regional dimension on the part of ministers and their officials is of course inevitable. It will be overcome only if there is present both the commitment of the leaders of the government, especially the Prime Minister, and incentives and sanctions for those who design and deliver programs. MSERD, to be sure, has a certain clout not only in Ottawa but also in the regions; but while this clout is necessary for the new system to work, it is not sufficient. At neither the ministerial level within CCERD, nor at the bureaucratic level within this sector, can the minister or Ministry of State for Economic and Regional Development demand that the ministers and their departmental officials fall into line without the explicit and continued support of the Prime Minister, the Cabinet Committee on Priorities and Planning, and officials in the Prime Minister's Office and the Privy Council Office. If political priority is not given to the regional dimensions of the national economic development policies of these departments, then regional concerns will lose out, as the DREE experience demonstrated.

If political priority is given to regional development within economic development policy, a second potential obstacle may well be an overload on the decision-making system that results in process constipation and paralysis by analysis. In order to avoid these organizational pathologies, and assuming that priority is given to regional development, MSERD must succeed in formulating a reasonably coherent regional economic development strategy. Such a strategy will be required if CCERD and MSERD are to cope not only with the volume of program proposals from the several line departments which potentially could be involved, but also with the implications of these proposals for the government's priorities in this integrated field, including their interregional and federal-provincial dimensions. This strategy, in other words, should consist of a basic framework of priorities and criteria with which MSERD can assess policy and expenditures proposals, and CCERD can make decisions, with some measure of policy coherence. If MSERD does not succeed in this respect, its coordinating role will be to no avail: the system will break down under the weight of its own design.

The third potential obstacle involves the relationship between this new formal system for regional economic development policy and the long-standing informal system of regional ministers.[38] How this new system relates to the informal powers which have traditionally been granted to regional ministers is not clear. What, for example, will be the outcome when a proposal for a particular province emanating from this new system runs counter to the political priorities of a regional minister for that province? Or, to take the opposite example, what happens when a regional minister attempts an end-run around the CCERD/MSERD apparatus because his or her pet project does not fit with the provincial economic development perspective adopted by CCERD for the region? These are not merely theoretical questions; indeed, there is some evidence to suggest that tensions between the new formal system and the longstanding informal system have already emerged, as of course might have been expected. With respect to the Atlantic region, these tensions are clearly significant given the number of so-called regional ministers with very specific local ties. If a significant number of regional program or expenditure decisions are made outside of the CCERD/MSERD process, the credibility of the FEDCs in the regions will be undermined and the integrity of the regional policy and expenditure management system will be jeopardized. We are not saying that the political dimension should be overridden, far from it; the alternative of the FEDC turning into a kind of French prefect would be equally destructive for other reasons. But it is necessary for the political and organizational dimensions of regional policy to be integrated into a common coordinating framework. Perhaps in the long run we may see the development of regional ministers of state who would then play an important role in the CCERD. At the moment, of course, not all regional ministers are members of the CCERD.

The final major obstacle lies in the area of intergovernmental relations. Allan Tupper argues that the reorganization, in conjunction with Ottawa's wish for enhanced control over economic development, will result in a heightening of federal–provincial conflict.[39] Again it is important to note here the distinction between the policies pursued by government and the structures used to deliver them. The two are related, but it is misleading to say that one determines the other. With reference to federal–provincial consultation in general, the introduction of MSERD's regional offices will probably have a differential effect depending upon the province. Some provinces may feel that the FEDC acts as a buffer and thereby hinders direct communication between the province and Ottawa, particularly if the province has been accustomed to communicating with Ottawa on a minister-to-minister basis. On the other hand the Maritime provinces may have reasonably fond memories of both the ARDA–FRED and DREE–GDA periods when there was close liaison between local federal and provincial officials. MSERD's regional offices clearly draw on this tradition and the FEDC has a clear mandate to establish relationships with provincial officials as well as with non-governmental groups in the region. At the same time there is nothing to prevent the provincial government from dealing directly with ministers or officials in Ottawa. In a sense communication might be enhanced by the province approaching both Ottawa and the FEDC.

With respect to future economic development agreements with the provinces, the federal government has taken a more aggressive stance, which suggests shades of the 1969–71 DREE period when policy initiatives were tendered to provinces on a take it or leave it basis. However, the present policy orientation (which is still far from being firmly set) and the organizational structures differ in three crucial respects. First, the early DREE approach was highly centralized; the provincial offices played little or no role in the negotiations between DREE and the provincial governments. In the present case, the FEDCs appear to be playing an important role, both directly and indirectly, in the negotiating of new Economic and Regional Development Agreements (ERDAs) to replace the expiring GDAs. There is opportunity for the federal government both to be better aware of provincial needs and demands and to design agreements that fit the needs of particular provinces.

The second point relates to the aim of the federal government to achieve greater control over regional policy. In part the aim is improved integration of all economic development programs, both national and regional, something which was difficult to achieve under the GDA approach. As well, the desire for greater control reflects a further federal unhappiness with the GDA experience, namely the inadequate return on investment in terms of political credit and visibility. This may well have been the most important factor underpinning the abandonment of the GDA approach. But it is worth noting again that the additional problem was the perceived lack of political control on the part of some ministers and a decline in accountability. This problem was also of concern to some provincial politicians, though it was most likely construed as a problem of personal influence rather than accountability to their provincial legislatures. Perhaps the greater potential for federal–provincial conflict is one of the trade-offs that has to be made in having greater visibility and accountability.

The third point is that the federal goal of greater control over, and credit for, regional development policies neither precludes nor excludes negotiations with provinces as to which government will be responsible for what program component in any given economic development agreement. It does appear to be the wish of the federal government to coordinate its policies with those of provincial governments, and to do so under the rubric of ERDAs presently being negotiated with the provinces by the sectoral departments, under the coordination of MSERD. There probably will be more continuity from the GDA period and greater room for negotiation than many people allow for. To argue that this means the ushering in of a new and harmonious era of federal–provincial relations is clearly unrealistic. Yet other than massive concessions on the part of the federal government towards Newfoundland and Quebec, among other provinces, there is probably very little that any kind of reorganization or policy reorientation could achieve to reduce federal–provincial conflict in the present circumstances.

In summary, will the reorganization result in a better regional policy? In one sense this question is virtually impossible to answer, given the widely diverging views on what constitutes appropriate and effective regional policy. Economists such as Anthony Scott have pointed to the example of the United States where the reduction in regional disparities over the past four decades has been much greater than in Canada, in spite of the absence of either a regional policy or a redistributive federal equalization program.[40] Factor mobility of both labour and capital is viewed as responsible for this state of affairs. Other economists, such as John Graham, have argued that in Canada these factors do not operate in the same way or to the same extent, particularly with respect to labour mobility.[41] Whatever the merits of these economic arguments, what can be said is that in Canada it is politically imperative to have a visible regional policy. Over the years, and well before the introduction of regional policy programs, the federal government has acceded to a variety of monetary demands from not only Quebec but many of the other provinces as well. This practice has long been embedded in Canadian political tradition, and most recently a general commitment to reducing regional disparities has been entrenched into the constitution.[42] No political party competing for national office in Canada would seriously entertain the abolition of regional policy (or equalization and other transfer programs) as party policy.

In monetary terms, the test of an effective regional policy might be the extent to which government resources can be channelled into regional projects and programs through the ERDAs. The potential funds lie not just in the newly established regional fund but also in the 'A' base of line department budgets and in any policy reserve fund. It has been estimated, for example, that doubling the amount of money that Supply and Services spends in the Atlantic region would represent far more than DREE was ever capable of mobilizing in this region. In theory, at any rate, MSERD's mandate is that these resources in the 'A' base and the policy reserve fund can be mobilized or bent for economic development purposes should suitable opportunities arise in a given region. It has also been stated that MSERD will concentrate on a limited number of opportunities in each province but on a fairly large scale.[43] Although we will not judge the appropriateness of these policies, we can say that there is potential for much more in the way of actual resources being devoted to regional programs. Whether this potential will be realized only time will tell. As noted earlier, much will depend upon its political priority assigned to regional development policy, especially by the Prime Minister, and the formulation of a coherent regional development strategy.

From the management side, and to comfort those who argue that the best regional policy is no regional policy, it can be said that under the policy and expenditure management system employed by MSERD there is greater opportunity to identify contradictory policies. That is to say, regional policies which are clearly detrimental to national economic policies now stand a better chance of being identified and corrected; and the converse—that is, the identification of possible perverse regional effects of national policies—would also he true. Whether decision-makers will act on this sort of information is another question, but it does appear that at present there is greater likelihood they will have this information before them, which was not always the case previously.

POSTSCRIPT

On 30 June 1984, Prime Minister John Turner announced 'measures to strengthen the role of Ministers and to streamline the Cabinet decision-making system'. These measures included the elimination of the portfolio and central agency that was MSERD and, as well, the use of assessment notes. In effect, the new Prime Minister reversed the policy of Prime Minister Trudeau which had given increased emphasis to the development of strong central agencies to support cabinet decision-making.

With the elimination of MSERD, responsibility for regional development policy was given to a new minister of state for regional development, a portfolio under the aegis of the Minister of Regional Industrial Expansion. An 'office' for regional development policy, operating out of DRIE, will serve this new minister of state and the FEDCs, now called federal coordinators, will report to this minister. This apparatus will be responsible for the coordination of the ERDA process, with CCERD continuing to be responsible for approving ERDAs and subagreements as they are negotiated by relevant departmental ministers.

At this time the precise roles of the new, and clearly junior, minister of state for regional development are not certain nor, in particular, is his relationship with the minister for DRIE. There are suggestions that the latter wishes to take over responsibility for regional development policy and the 1984 changes indicate that he may be successful in this. On the other hand, there is every indication that regional ministers will be given greater power within the new Prime Minister's cabinet. How these two developments will mesh remains to be seen. The same can be said for the roles and positions of the federal coordinators in each province. In any event, it is now clear that the 1982 reorganization did not overcome all of the obstacles which we have outlined in this article. Prime Minister Turner, in effect, decided that the logic of this reorganization needed to be turned on its head.

NOTES

An earlier version of this paper was presented at the Canadian Political Science Association Annual Meeting, Vancouver, BC, June 1983. Financial support from Dalhousie University's Research Development Committee, using funds supplied by the Social Sciences and Humanities Research Council of Canada is gratefully acknowledged. The authors are currently continuing their research on the subject for the Royal Commission on the Economic Union and Development Prospects for Canada. This present paper is based on research conducted prior to their work for the commission.

1. Office of the Prime Minister, Release, 'Reorganization for Economic Development', 12 January 1982. It should be noted that the formal legislation for the reorganization (Bill C–152) was not passed by Parliament and enacted until the fall of 1983.
2. For a theoretical account of this general subject, see Paul R. Lawrence and Jay W. Lorsch, 'Differentiation and Integration in Complex Organizations', *Administrative Science Quarterly* 12, 1 (June 1967), pp. 1–47.
3. Alan C. Cairns, 'The Governments and Societies of Canadian Federalism', *Canadian Journal of Political Science* 10, 4 (December 1977), pp. 695–725.
4. There is an extensive literature on this topic. See especially the chapters by Paul Fox, 'Regionalism and Confederation', and Thomas Brewis, 'Regional Development in Canada in Historical Perspective', in N.H. Lithwick, ed., *Regional Economic Policy: The Canadian Experience* (Toronto: McGraw-Hill Ryerson, 1978). Recent evidence on regional disparities is provided in the Economic Council of Canada, *Living Together, A Study of Regional Disparities* (Ottawa: Supply and Services, 1977).
5. This distinction is not always clearly made. The best single work in this area remains James Fesler, *Area and Administration* (Birmingham: University of Alabama Press, 1949). See also Sidney Tarrow, 'Introduction' in Tarrow et al., *Territorial Politics in Industrial Nations* (New York: Praeger, 1978) pp. 1–27. On the geographic dispersal of Canadian federal departments, see J.E. Hodgetts, *The Canadian Public Service* (Toronto: University of Toronto Press, 1973), pp. 219–38.
6. Anthony Careless, *Initiative and Response: The Adaptation of Canadian Federalism to Regional Economic Development* (Montreal: McGill-Queen's University Press, 1977), pp. 71–8, 109.
7. Ibid., p. 72.
8. Ibid., p. 114.
9. Cited in Careless, *Initiative and Response*, p. 162.
10. For a discussion of the legislation creating DREE, see Richard W. Phidd and G. Bruce

Doern, *The Politics and Management of Canadian Economic Policy* (Toronto: Macmillan, 1978), p. 326–8.

11. Careless, *Initiative and Response*, pp. 85–9.

12. Phidd and.Doern, *Canadian Economic Policy*, pp. 328–9.

13. Donald J. Savoie, 'The General Development Agreement Approach and the Bureaucratization of Provincial Governments in the Atlantic Provinces', *Canadian Public Administration* 24 (Spring 1981), p. 119.

14. In the case of directors general it was up to $500,000 for individual projects; for regional ADMs it was $1,500,000; Phidd and Doern, *Canadian Economic Policy*, p. 327.

15. Donald J. Savoie, *Federal–Provincial Collaboration: The Canada–New Brunswick General Development Agreement* (Montreal: McGill-Queen's University Press, 1981), p. 29.

16. Sheilagh M. Dunn, *The Year in Review 1981: Intergovernmental Relations in Canada* (Kingston: Institute of Intergovernmental Relations, 1982), ch. 3.

17. See former DREE minister Donald Jamieson's comments, as cited in Halifax *Mail-Star*, 1 November 1982, p. 7. Also Report of the Standing Senate Committee on National Finance, *Government Policy and Regional Development* (Ottawa: Supply and Services, 1982), p. 75.

18. See Richard French, *How Ottawa Decides* (Toronto: Canadian Institute for Economic Policy, 1980), and Phidd and Doern, *Canadian Economic Policy*.

19. See G. Bruce Doern and Peter Aucoin, eds., *Public Policy in Canada* (Toronto, Macmillan, 1979).

20. See G. Bruce Doern and Richard Phidd, 'Economic Management in the Government of Canada: Some Implications of the Board of Economic Development Ministers and the Lambert Report', a paper prepared for the Canadian Political Science Association, 30 May 1979, Saskatoon, Saskatchewan.

21. Ibid.

22. See French, *How Ottawa Decides*, pp. 123–9.

23. Ibid., p. 126.

24. Ibid., pp. 134–42.

25. See R. Van Loon, 'Stop the Music: The Current Policy and Expenditure Management System in Ottawa', *Canadian Public Administration*, 24 (Summer 1981), pp. 175–99, and his excellent analysis of how the PEMS system works in practice, 'The Policy and Expenditure Management System in the Federal Government: the First Three Years', ibid., 26 (Summer 1983), pp. 255–85.

26. Office of the Prime Minister, Release, 12 January 1982, 'Reorganization for Economic Development', p. 1.

27. Ibid., 'Background Paper', p. 3.

28. Ibid., p. 4.

29. Ibid.

30. The analysis in this section is based primarily on confidential interviews carried out in January through April 1983.

31. See R.W. Crowley, 'A New Power Focus in Ottawa: the Ministry of State for Economic and Regional Development', *Optimum* 13, 2 (1982), pp. 5–14; also Crowley, 'The Design of Government Policy Agencies: Do We Learn from Experience?' *Canadian Journal of Regional Science* 5, 1 (1982), pp. 103–22.

32. Report of the Standing Senate Committee on National Finance, pp. 74–6.

33. Atlantic Provinces Economic Council, 'Analysis of the Reorganization for Economic Development: Background and Policy Directions', Halifax, October 1982.

34. As quoted in Halifax *Mail Star*, 1 November 1982, p. 7.

35. Initially back in 1969, DREE's expenditures represented 2 per cent of the federal budget; by 1980–1 this percentage had been reduced to half. Furthermore, in 1970–1 the proportion of DREE's budget allocated to the Atlantic region was 53 per cent; by 1980–1 this proportion had dropped to 36 per cent. Atlantic Provinces Economic Council, 'Analysis of the Reorganization for Economic Development', pp. 13–14.

36. See, for example, 'Ottawa's merger sets the (alarm) bells ringing', *The Globe and Mail*, 21 February 1983, p. B1.

37. For a discussion of some of the difficulties DRIE has encountered in this respect, see 'DRIE still awaits its place in cabinet sun', *Financial Post*, 18 September 1982, p. 1.

38. This, of course, is a tension inherent in the political-administrative relationship generally. The divergence between political needs and the exigencies of economic policy is discussed in E. Tufte, *The Political Control of the Economy* (Princeton: Princeton University Press, 1978). On the dangers of designing a planning and coordinating system which excludes the political dimension, see H.R. van Gunsteren, *The Quest for Control: A Critique of the rational-control-rule approach in public affairs* (London: Wiley, 1976).

39. Allan Tupper, *Public Money in the Private Sector: Industrial Assistance Policy and Canadian Federalism* (Kingston: Institute of Intergovernmental Relations, 1982), pp. 105–6.

40. A.D. Scott, 'Policy for Declining Regions: A Theoretical Approach', in Lithwick ed., *Regional Economic Policy*, pp. 46–67. Thomas Courchene most clearly favours migration as a means to alleviate provincial economic inequalities. See his 'Interprovincial Migration and Economic Adjustment,' ibid., pp. 74–101.

41. John Graham, *Fiscal Adjustment and Economic Development* (Toronto: University of Toronto Press, 1963).

42. The Constitution Act, 1982, Part III, 36(1).

43. See 'DRIE still awaits its place in cabinet sun'.

23

Reflections on the Workability of Executive Federalism

J. Stefan Dupré

In recent years, interaction among federal and provincial first ministers has fallen into a state of disarray. At the level of ministers and officials, federal–provincial relations have become so varied and complex that they defy generalization. As a long-time national sport, executive federalism, like the post-expansion NHL, has become the subject of anxious hand-wringing by many of its practitioners and much of its audience. This essay, written by one of the latter, but enriched by the insights of a small number of experienced practitioners,[1] probes the workability of executive federalism. By workability, I do not mean the capacity of executive federalism, on any given issue or at any given time, to produce federal–provincial accord as opposed to discord. Because executive federalism is rooted in what Richard Simeon has labelled succinctly the 'political independence' and the 'policy interdependence'[2] of our federal and provincial governments, it is these governments that make the fundamental choices to agree or disagree. Whether executive federalism works involves not whether governments agree or disagree, but whether it provides a forum (or more accurately a set of forums) that is conducive, and perceived to be conducive, as the case may be, to negotiation, consultation, or simply an exchange of information.

A major theme of this essay is that the workability of executive federalism is to an important degree a function of the manner in which the executives of our federal and provincial governments operate. This is explored in an introductory way under the heading Executive Federalism and Intragovernmental Relations, and probed further in the next two sections, one entitled Federal–Provincial Functional Relations, the other Federal–Provincial Summit Relations. These sections probe selective circumstances under which executive federalism has been a more-or-less workable mechanism of federal–provincial adjustment. The final section of this essay, titled Prescriptions for Workable Executive Federalism, proposes procedural and substantive directions that executive federalism might seek to follow for the balance of this century.

EXECUTIVE FEDERALISM AND INTRAGOVERNMENTAL RELATIONS

The fundamental facts of Canadian constitutionalism are federalism and the cabinet-parliamentary form of government. The first means that the Canadian territorial divi-

J. Stefan Dupré, 'Reflections on the Workability of Executive Federalism', *Intergovernmental Relations*, vol. 63: 1–32. © University of Toronto Press. Reprinted by permission of the publisher.

sion of power takes the form of two constitutionally ordained levels of government, each endowed with distinct yet often overlapping jurisdiction. The second means that executive and legislative institutions, through the constitutional conventions of responsible government, are fused in such a manner that what Thomas Hockin calls 'the collective central energizing executive' (cabinet) is the 'key engine of the state'[3] within each of the federal and provincial levels of government.

The Canadian version of the rise of the modern administrative state yields progressively larger and more potent federal and provincial bureaucracies, formally subordinated to their respective cabinets, and growing federal–provincial interdependence as each of these levels of government, driven by its energizing executive, actualizes the jurisdictional potential conferred upon it by the Constitution. With almost Sophoclean inevitability, the resulting need for a non-judicial mechanism of adjustment is met by what Donald Smiley so aptly calls executive federalism, 'which may be defined as the relations between elected and appointed officials of the two orders of government in federal–provincial interaction . . .'[4] Smiley includes relations among the elected and appointed officials of provincial governments under the umbrella of executive federalism, but this essay will refer to such purely interprovincial relations as 'executive interprovincialism'. This is in part to stress the fact that relations between governments that share identical jurisdiction are different from relations between governments that share divided jurisdiction, in part to acknowledge that executive interprovincialism has not infrequently been a provincial response to executive federalism.

'The relations between elected and appointed officials of the two levels of government' are taken as the constant that defines executive federalism. Executive federalism has been categorized in the literature from the standpoint of outcomes, as cooperative or conflictual federalism. From the standpoint of actors, it has been called summit federalism (relations among first ministers and/or their designated ministerial or bureaucratic entourage) and functional federalism (relations among ministers and/or their officials). From the standpoint of participating governments, it has been labelled multilateral (the federal and all ten provincial governments), multilateral–regional (the federal government and the governments of some, normally contiguous, provinces), and bilateral (the federal government and a single province). These labels—and others—will be used where appropriate in the text of this essay; all, however, are deemed conceptually secondary to the notion of executive federalism as embodying the relations between the elected and appointed officials of the energizing executives of our federal and provincial levels of government.

It is this simple notion that permits me to observe that executive federalism, as a mechanism of federal–provincial adjustment, cannot be divorced from intragovernmental considerations, i.e., from the structure and functioning of the 'collective central energizing executives' with which the conventions of the Constitution endow Ottawa and each of the provinces. Without altering one iota of the constitutional conventions that give them their central energizing force, cabinets can operate in vastly different ways. Thus, for example, at any given point in time, there will be differences in the manner in which cabinets operate in Ottawa, as distinct from large provinces, and as distinct from small provinces. Such differences, which may be accentuated by the role of political, especially prime ministerial, personalities and by the complexion of different governing parties, will be acknowledged as this essay proceeds. More important to a general consideration of executive federalism are historically distinguishable modes of cabinet operation. I shall distinguish three such modes of cabinet operation. The first, which I choose to label the 'traditional' mode, is one in which cabinets can be said to operate primarily as what Jean Hamelin calls 'chamber(s) of political compensation'.[5] This mode of cabinet operation antedates the rise of the modern administrative state and, for that matter, of executive federalism. Here, cabinet ministers, given the limited scope of their respective governments, preeminently articulate and aggregate matters of regional or local political concern, and are primarily in the business of dispensing patronage. The extent to which the federal cabinet, in this mode of operation, can itself provide a mechanism of federal–provincial adjustment has been sketched aptly by Donald Smiley.[6] The second and third modes of cabinet operation, which respectively accompany the rise and then the maturation of the modern administrative state, are the ones that are material to executive federalism. I shall call the second the 'departmentalized cabinet' and the third the 'institutionalized cabinet'.

The 'departmentalized' cabinet at once reflects and abets the rise of the modern administrative state. Government departments, allocated among ministers as their respective portfolio responsibilities, are the prime depositories of public sector expansion and of the special expertise which fuels and responds to expansion. The functions assigned to a department make it the natural focus of discrete client interests, and the inputs of these departmentally oriented clientele groups interact synergistically with the 'withinputs' of the department's expert bureaucrats. For ministers, this interaction breeds 'portfolio loyalty' both because they perceive that their effectiveness is judged by their departmental clienteles and because they depend on departmental expertise for policy formulation and implementation. Subject to greater or lesser degrees of prime ministerial direction, ministers are endowed with a substantial measure of decision-making automony which redounds to the benefit of their departmental clienteles and bureaucracies. In the departmentalized cabinet, a minister is of course always a member of what by constitutional design is a collectively responsible executive but, as James Gillies puts it so well, 'the principle of Cabinet collective responsibility [is] based on the commonsense notion of confidence in one's colleagues, rather than on the concept of sharing of knowledge or decision-making.'[7]

In the 'institutionalized' cabinet, by contrast, various combinations of formal committee structures, established central agencies, and budgeting and management techniques combine to emphasize shared knowledge, collegial decision making, and the formulation of government-wide priorities and objectives. 'The major thrust,' Smiley writes, 'is to decrease the relative autonomy of ministers and the departments working under their direction.'[8] More than this, the institutionalized cabinet generates distinguishable categories of ministers; what Douglas Hartle calls the 'central agency' ministers and the 'special interest' ministers.[9] The portfolios of the former, in Hartle's words, 'cut across special interest lines for they reflect the several dimensions of the collective concerns of the Cabinet.'[10] Meantime, the ministers in the second category continue to pursue, 'as they are expected to pursue, the special interest of special interest portfolios.'[11] In this setting, intragovernmental decision making becomes not only collegial, but acquires a competitive, adversarial flavour.

The original Canadian home of the institutionalized cabinet is the Saskatchewan of Premier T.C. Douglas, and its best documented manifestations are those of the Pearson–Trudeau–Clark–Trudeau era in Ottawa. With substantial variations, both spatially and temporally, the institutionalized cabinet has as its theme the quest to make contemporary government decision making manageable. It arises initially as the response to the perceived defects of the departmentalized cabinet in the face of the range, complexity, and interdependence of the decisions that contemporary governments are called upon to make. Once in place, it can be adjusted into a variety of configurations as the quest to make contemporary decision making manageable continues to be pursued with all the intensity of the quest for the Holy Grail. From one perspective, effectively articulated by Peter Aucoin, the institutionalized cabinet subjects special interests to the welcome challenge of greater scrutiny and increased competition.[12] From a contrary perspective, articulated with similar effectiveness by James Gillies, the institutionalized cabinet can so dissipate the input of special interests into the policies which affect them that it threatens to undermine the doctrine of government by consent.[13]

Which perspective is more nearly correct (and both may have enormous elements of validity) is less important for an essay on the workability of executive federalism than the stark fact that the intergovernmental relations between elected and appointed officials of our two levels of government are bound to be affected by the very different intragovernmental relations that characterize the departmentalized and institutionalized modes of cabinet operation. To expound, let us consider federal–provincial functional relations and federal–provincial summit relations. In each instance, the transition from the departmentalized to the institutionalized cabinet has fundamental implications, as do the various configurations which institutionalized cabinets can acquire.

FEDERAL–PROVINCIAL FUNCTIONAL RELATIONS

From the 1920s into the 1960s, the Canadian story of income security, social services, health care, vocational education, transportation infrastructure, and resource development is a tale in which federal–provincial functional relations play a starring role. True to the operation at each level of government of the departmentalized cabinet, executive federalism rests upon relations between program officials, deputy ministers, and ministers from federal and provincial departments with overlapping or complementary missions. The relations are financially lubricated by numerous conditional grants which apply the federal spending power to individual programs that frequently, but not invariably, aspire to national standards. When categorized in terms of outcomes, federal–provincial relations are justifiably labelled as cooperative federalism.[14] The ingredients of these relations can be readily enumerated to yield what I choose to call the 'functional relations model' of executive federalism. Each element in the model is remarkably conducive to the formation and maintenance of what Albert Breton and Ronald Wintrobe call 'networks,' that is to say, 'trust relationships or trust ties',[15] along intergovernmental lines.

- The appointed federal and provincial program officials involved in functional relations share common values and speak a similar vocabulary as a result of common training in a particular profession or discipline, e.g., Public Health, Social Work, or Education.
- Departmentalized cabinets make it likely that the commonalities that characterize functional relations at the level of program officials will percolate to the deputy ministerial and ministerial levels. In the departmentalized setting, deputy ministers often will have risen through the ranks of their departments, thus sharing the outlooks of their program subordinates. As for ministers, the relatively uninhibited portfolio loyalties bred by the departmentalized cabinet induce a coincidence of views, notwithstanding their diverse political and professional backgrounds. Furthermore, the measure of decision-making autonomy which ministers enjoy as members of their departmentalized cabinets means that there is minimal likelihood that federal–provincial accord at the ministerial level will be questioned or reversed by first ministers or cabinets.
- The trust relationships generated by the above two elements draw ongoing sustenance from the longevity of the federal–provincial structures within which functional relations are conducted. Enhancing as they do the likelihood of repeated transactions over long periods of time, these stable structures, to borrow the words of Breton and Wintrobe, 'increase the future return to investments in trust.'[16] They ensure that federal and provincial ministers, deputy ministers, and program officials, at any given point in time, have a stake in their future relationships.
- The financial lubricant supplied by conditional grants serves to aid and abet trust relationships in that the resulting program activity at the donating and recipient levels of government enhances bureaucratic careers and ministerial reputations. Such grants also insulate program activity from budgetary competition to the extent that they generate the familiar lock-in effect ('we are locked in by promises made to the provinces') at the federal level, and the equally familiar carrot effect ('50-cent dollars') at the provincial level.
- Special interests (e.g., those focused upon public health, welfare, or education) achieve virtual representation in the processes of executive federalism through the associational ties of department officials and the loyalty of ministers to their clientele-oriented portfolios.

If the four decades of federal–provincial functional relations, from which the above model is derived, can indeed be labelled an era of co-operative federalism, the evident exception is Quebec. But this exception supports rather than undermines the importance of the model's components. To the extent that Quebec officials shared professional backgrounds similar to those of their counterparts from Ottawa and the anglophone provinces, their distinctive academic formation was anything but tantamount to the common school ties (corresponding to the restricted number of professional faculties then found in English-speaking universities) worn by anglophone program officials. Moreover, in the Quebec version of the departmentalized cabinet, ministerial autonomy was severely circumscribed by the prime ministerial style of Maurice Duplessis and by the government-wide objective, founded on widely shared respect for classical as opposed to cooperative federalism, of protecting provincial jurisdiction and indigenous institutions. Again, in that Quebec did not uniformly exclude itself from functional arrangements, it is to be noted that the temporal longitude of federal–provincial structures, coupled with the open-ended availability of conditional grants, permitted selective shopping by the Quebec government and accommodated its acquiescence to programs of its choosing, normally in the domain of income maintenance. Finally, with respect to special interests, the extent to which Quebec's self-imposed exclusion from federal–provincial functional relations enjoyed societal support is testimony to the segmentalist orientation,[17] driven by linguistic barriers, of this province's elites.

As the decade of the 1960s unfolded, federal–provincial functional relations underwent a significant metamorphosis. This metamorphosis paralleled and reflected the transition within governments from the departmentalized to the institutionalized cabinet. The budgetary distortions which conditional grants generated through their 'lock-in' and 'carrot' effects, once discovered by rationalized budgetary processes, spelled the demise of these grants on a grand scale. Equally consequential was the extent to which functional relations had to adapt to broader governmental considerations, acquired bilateral dimensions, and were forced to accommodate sudden shifts in personnel and structures. A few sketches, culled from the realms of social assistance, manpower training, and regional development are illustrative.

Social Assistance

The successful negotiation of the Canada Assistance Plan (CAP), in the period 1963–6, wrought the termination of several categorical conditional grant programs in favour of a broad shared-cost approach to income security and social services for persons in need. Rand Dyck's instructive account of the negotiations makes it abundantly clear that the long-standing relations among federal and provincial deputy ministers of welfare enveloped the emergence of CAP in a co-operative atmosphere.[18] However, Dyck notes that federal welfare officials, along with a number of their provincial counterparts, were oriented on professional grounds to favour a shared-cost design that would stimulate the achievement of high national standards. These views were overridden in favour of flexibility by federal central agencies sensitive to broader federal-provincial issues. (Dyck names the Department of Finance, Treasury Board, the Privy Council Office, and the Prime Minister's Office.[19]) The outcome was a CAP which relegated the matter of interprovincial discrepancies to the unconditional, fiscal capacity-related equalization payments of the *Fiscal Arrangements Act*, left welfare standards to the budgetary processes of provincial governments, and accommodated Quebec demands to the point where its opted-out position in the realm of social assistance became largely symbolic. What the CAP episode illustrates are:

- the continuing importance of long-standing trust ties among functional officials;
- a new central agency presence in federal–provincial functional relations; and

- the capacity of central agency influence to contribute to a harmonious federal–provincial outcome linked to considerations that lie beyond specialized
  professional norms.

The Social Security Review, launched in 1973, yields a different sketch of functional
relations coloured by a different manifestation of the institutionalized cabinet. The
origins of the Social Security Review lay partly in the Ottawa–Quebec jurisdictional
discord (which eventually aborted the Victoria Charter in 1971), and partly in the
capacity of policy analysis (epitomized by Quebec's landmark Castonguay-Nepveu
report) to articulate the attractiveness of sweeping welfare reform, which, through a
guaranteed annual income, would reconcile income maintenance with equitable
work incentives for low-wage earners. The Review is distinctive because a significant
number of its participants were by design individuals without social welfare backgrounds. This was visibly symbolized in the person of the then newly appointed federal deputy minister of welfare, A. W. Johnson, previously secretary of the Treasury
Board (Johnson's minister, Marc Lalonde, had been principal secretary in the Prime
Minister's Office prior to his entry into electoral politics); and it was tangibly mani-
fest in the involvement, in both federal and provincial delegations, of economists and
manpower officials, as well as of social welfare specialists. According to Johnson's
account of the first two years of the Review, the diverse backgrounds of the participants eventually yielded a degree of mutual education. This was preceded, however,
by time-consuming discord, bred by the extent to which 'those concerned with
employment and employment services were inclined to be suspicious of (social work)
phrases like "fullest functional potential" and the social workers tended to regard the
manpower people as being excessively preoccupied with employment rather than the
"whole person"'.[20]

Once federal–provincial functional relations are called upon not only to accommodate central agency influence, but to open their channels to individuals who articulate their positions from the standpoint of diverse professional backgrounds, there is
reason to temper one's expectations of what they are capable of producing. And in
the result, the failure of the Social Security Review to produce a guaranteed annual
income invites the further consideration that, as it proceeded, this exercise unravelled
an agenda item whose ramifications were simply too broad to be accommodated at
any level of federal–provincial relations short of the summit. The government-wide
concerns that can be injected into functional relations by central agency personnel
do not obviate the competitive features of collegial decision-making within the institutionalized cabinets of individual governments. Programs with an intimate bearing
on the guaranteed annual income, like federal and provincial minimum wage laws,
federal unemployment insurance, and provincial workers' compensation, are the preserve of agencies other than welfare departments. This being so, Keith Banting's verdict that the Social Security Review 'was doomed from the outset by
interdepartmental barriers at both levels'[21] has great weight. The institutionalized cabinet reduces departmental autonomy in a quest to make contemporary decision making manageable. However, pursuing this quest in the framework of competitive
collegiality and finding the Holy Grail remain two quite different things. The sources

of the failure of the Social Security Review include interdepartmental tensions within each of the respective levels of government. And incidentally, to those who criticize executive federalism as an essentially closed process, Banting offers a telling rejoinder when he writes: 'The politics of executive federalism focus the full glare of government and public attention on *intergovernmental* coordination failure. In comparison, *intragovernmental* failures languish in the twilight of cabinet discretion.'[22]

This triggers a final observation with respect to the Social Security Review. Its one strong note of federal–provincial accord was sounded early in its existence, and produced a new source of asymmetric federalism: provincial configuration, i.e., provincial capacity to alter, within limits, the rates of benefits paid by the federal family allowance program. The point is that this achievement involved a program entirely within the portfolio of Health and Welfare Canada. A few years after the termination of the Review, the provincial gratification with which configuration had been received, particularly by Quebec, was undone by a unilateral federal measure—in the realm of taxation. Quebec had chosen a provincial configuration of family allowances that increased the rate of allowances with the rank of a child in the family. However, the Child Tax Credit, initiated in 1979, took no account of child ranking and was accordingly incongruent with Quebec social assistance benefits that had been integrated with the provincially configurated family allowances.[23] The resulting discord over federal unilateralism was quite as real as the fact that the source of federal unilateralism lay outside the welfare portfolio. In the circumstances, tax policy takes on the guise of an external event that impinged negatively on trust ties between federal and provincial welfare ministers.

Manpower Training

The design of the federal Adult Occupational Training Act of 1967 was in part the product of the major retreat from conditional grants sounded by summit federal-provincial fiscal concerns. It was also in part the outcome, at the highest level of federal economic policy making, of a unilateral decision to transform the vocational training of adults into an adjunct of employment policy.[24] Unveiled by Prime Minister Pearson at the federal-provincial summit conference of 1966, adult occupational training terminated almost 50 years of conditional grants in the realm of vocational education and assigned the use of training as an employment policy tool to the newly created Department of Manpower and Immigration. This initiative ended the functional relations long articulated by the vocational education divisions of provincial departments of Education and the Training Branch of the federal Department of Labour. The Branch's practice of recruiting its personnel from the ranks of provincial vocational education specialists had ensured the prevalence, across divided jurisdiction, of shared professional norms. The Technical and Vocational Training Advisory Council, the structure within which federal-provincial trust ties had flourished during its 25 years of existence, was dissolved. Henceforth, through what was couched simultaneously as a constitutional claim and an effort to disentangle federal–provincial relations, the federal government would purchase, at full cost, training courses for adults, selected by its employment placement counsellors on the basis of these counsellors' assessments of their clients' aptitudes and future employment prospects. The desired training could be purchased either from public institutions under provincial control or from private sources.

That the federal manpower design of the mid-1960s never became reality is poignantly apparent from the fact, almost 20 years later, that this Commission listed as an unmet challenge the provision of 'timely opportunities for retraining in order to enable working Canadians to adapt to changes resulting from technological innovation and competition.'[25] The fate of the federal design was sealed within months of its unveiling by a provincial victory which stands as an early exhibit in the annals of competitive, as distinct from co-operative, federalism.[26] In brief, what happened was that provincial departments of education successfully interposed themselves between federal adult training and public postsecondary institutions, forced federal officials to deal with them as 'exclusive brokers' of training courses, and used their exclusive brokerage to eliminate private-sector training programs as potential competitors. The ingredients of the provincial educationists' success included:

- support from the highest levels of their governments in a setting where the establishment of new postsecondary institutions (CAATs, CEGEPs, community colleges) enjoyed province-wide priority, and the task of orderly institutional development brooked no outside interference;
- their own close relations with college administrators who, in turn, possessed strong local and community ties; and
- federal inexperience with training programs and institutions, coupled with an incapacity to assess, let alone forecast, manpower needs.

Early on, the federal manpower initiative stimulated vigorous recourse to executive interprovincialism. It gave impetus to the formation of the Council of Ministers of Education in the summer of 1967, and to the initial prominence of the CME's Manpower Programs Committee as an interprovincial *cum* educationist counterstructure in the realm of adult training. As for federal-provincial relations, the federal design had been based on little by way of formal structure: the federal aim was to substitute buyer-seller relations for those of executive federalism. A multilateral body, known first as the Federal–Provincial Meeting of Officials on Occupational Training for Adults, and subsequently as the Canada Manpower Training Program (CMTP) committee, was intended originally simply to ease exchange of information; but it immediately became a forum where federal and provincial officials divided themselves along professional lines, between federal economists bent on training as an adjunct of employment and provincial educationists wedded to the development of the 'whole person'. In short order, provincial insistence upon exclusive brokerage forced the formation, along increasingly structured lines, of bilateral federal–provincial committees. It was in these committees that the 'purchase' and 'sale' of training became a negotiated, shared-cost planning process subservient, most especially in the case of Ontario, to provincial institutional and enrolment strategies.

In that bilateralism is a fount of asymmetry in federal–provincial relations, it permits more or less cooperative or conflictual atmospheres to prevail in different provincial contexts. Significantly, it appears that the Ottawa–Quebec relationship in adult training proved at least a partial exception to otherwise conflictual relations at the functional level. In this instance, the provincial side of the bilateral relationship was articulated not by educationists, but by officials of the Quebec Department of Manpower and Immigration, whose professional backgrounds parallelled those of their federal counterparts. Recalling the times, a senior Quebec Manpower official noted that the conflict between economists and educationists, which elsewhere plagued federal–provincial functional relations, had instead emerged in Quebec as an intragovernmental conflict around the provincial cabinet table.[27] This invites the observation that cabinets are endowed with means of conflict resolution which federal–provincial bodies can never possess.

Regional Development

Thanks to the scholarship of Anthony Careless and Donald Savoie, there exists a relative wealth of information on the nexus between federal-provincial functional relations in the realm of regional development and the emergence of institutionalized cabinets at each of these levels of government. Careless concentrates on the years 1960–73 and traces regional development from its genesis in the ARDA of Diefenbaker and Hamilton, through the first era of the Department of Regional Economic Expansion (DREE).[28] Savoie, focusing exclusively on New Brunswick, takes up where Careless leaves off and sketches the course of regional development under what, in 1973, became a radically reorganized and deconcentrated DREE.[29] While a few paragraphs cannot do justice to the richness of the Careless and Savoie accounts, it is illuminating to highlight the essential thrust of what their works uncover.

ARDA (which stood initially for the *Agricultural Rehabilitation and Development Act* passed in 1961) was basically farm-oriented and spawned projects which 'concentrated upon dealing with land and resources in order to improve the farmer's well-being'.[30] Operated with the provinces on a shared-cost basis, ARDA involved intergovernmental transactions conducted on a bilateral basis by the federal Department of Agriculture and its provincial counterparts along the lines of the traditional federal–provincial functional relations model.

The initial ARDA lasted only until 1964 when, with only the acronym retained, the Agricultural and Rural Development Act was legislated into being along with a special Fund for Rural Economic Development (FRED). As their names suggest, ARDA–FRED moved beyond farming to the much more encompassing realms of rural poverty and thus embraced a planned approach to regional development. ARDA–FRED was made the responsibility of a new federal department, Forestry and Rural Development, and launched a very different set of federal–provincial functional relations. These relations were to be articulated not by agriculture officials, but by planning specialists. And because the scope of ARDA–FRED was such that it embraced numerous provincial departments, it called for a government-wide planning capacity at the provincial level. Accordingly, the federal government under ARDA–FRED assisted especially the smaller and poorer Maritime Provinces in developing their own initial versions of the institutionalized cabinet. The resulting program agencies, planning secretariats, or improvement corporations were linked to premiers' offices, cabinet committees, or both. The consequent provincial planning capacity was viewed by federal personnel as a positive step which they had helped to induce and signalled the emergence of new bilateral networks of like-minded federal and provincial officials.

As these networks formed, however, the institutionalization of the federal cabinet was unfolding apace. The advent of PPBS (Program Planning Budgeting System), with its emphasis on program objectives, and the 1966 reorganization that yielded a separate Treasury Board Secretariat and Department of Finance, each with its own minister, gradually impinged upon the Department of Forestry and Rural Development. The mission of Treasury Board officials focused upon efficiency and effectiveness in the pursuit of defined objectives, while Finance acquired direct influence over the priority to be accorded to such objectives, notably in the striking 'of a balance between economic proposals for maximizing "welfare" (regional aid) and those for "efficiency" (national productivity)'.[31] Then came the new decision-making cabinet committees launched by Prime Minister Trudeau in 1968, and the enhanced role of the Privy Council Office as the manager of the committee system and the PCO's intolerance for 'lack of effective interdepartmental relations in the federal government'.[32] In the face of this configuration of events, structures and concerns, the Department of Forestry and Rural Development gave way, in 1969, to the new Department of Regional Economic Expansion.

Geared to the insistence that federal spending must effectively and visibly pursue federally designed objectives and federally determined priorities, the Department of Regional Economic Expansion (DREE) shifted the focus of regional development away from rural poverty and toward industrial and urban growth, with emphasis on public works and jobs. At this juncture, the officials of the provincial planning agencies found at one and the same time that their Forestry and Rural Development network had disappeared and that their planning premises no longer coincided with those of Ottawa. As bilateral relations degenerated into an atmosphere of proposal and counter-proposal, it became increasingly clear that DREE's preferred style would be to by-pass provincial central agents altogether in favour of direct dealings with individual provincial departments. As a result, DREE succeeded in imposing this style to varying degrees in different provinces (indeed to the point where, in Nova Scotia, the provincial planning secretariat was dissolved). Lying behind DREE's success was not only the fiscal leverage of federal spending, but the impatience of provincial cabinet ministers with the planning agents of their own institutionalized cabinets.

Within a decade, regional development had moved from bilateral networks of federal and provincial agriculture officials to bilateral networks of planning officials to a setting in which a new centrally oriented federal department was penetrating provincial departments and writing off province-wide concerns. Then in 1973, the grounds shifted once again. In the wake of ministerial and deputy ministerial shuffles, and of the Liberal minority government produced by the 1972 election, DREE suddenly perceived itself as excessively insensitive to the provinces. It also discerned, through internal review, that regional development, whose focus had already shifted from farming to rural poverty, and thence to industrial and urban growth, should again acquire a new orientation. This time the orientation would be 'the identification and pursuit of development opportunities'.[33] The quest that this implied was to be shared with provincial governments and, to ensure on-site federal involvement, DREE was deconcentrated into provincial offices, each headed by a Director-General with substantial decision-making authority. Operating under the umbrella of a ministerial General Development Agreement with a ten-year lifespan, each provincially based DREE Director-General was designated the prime negotiator of subsidiary agreements with the provinces, these agreements being the 'action pacts'[34] pursuant to which spatial or sectoral development projects would be undertaken.

Savoie's detailed study of federal–provincial relations under the Canada–New Brunswick General Development Agreement sketches an original portrait precisely because DREE's deconcentration was without parallel in Canadian administrative history. Launched on their shared quest to identify and pursue economic opportunities (whatever they might be), DREE's field personnel, headed by its Director General in Fredericton, and their provincial counterparts, headed by the Secretary of the New Brunswick Cabinet Committee on Economic Development, formed trust ties based upon 'being purpose- or result-oriented.'[35] However, an alliance between federal field personnel, who are remote from Ottawa headquarters, and provincial officials, who are proximate to provincial politicians and senior bureaucrats, exposed a gap between slow decision making at the federal level and quick decision making at the provincial level. In addition to their proximity to the cabinet of a small province, provincial officials possessed 'carrot effect' leverage from the shared-cost nature of development projects (in the New Brunswick case, a leverage which could be as high as 20-cent dollars). Faced with the consequent ease with which provincial decisions could be extracted, the federal government could only compromise its own decision-making apparatus. At DREE headquarters, officials often found their involvement 'limited to reviewing subsidiary agreements and this only after the agreements [had] been fully developed and agreed upon by provincial DREE and provincial government officials'.[36] As for the federal Treasury Board, it was left in a position where rejection or revision 'would in fact not only be rejecting or revising a proposal from a federal department, but also one that [had] been approved by a province, in the case of New Brunswick, by the Cabinet'.[37] Meantime, federal operating departments, on whose economic missions DREE–New Brunswick agreements impinged, found that they were not infrequently by-passed or compromised.

Early in 1982, the DREE of the General Development Agreements fell before one more federal attempt to make the decision making this department had circumvented manageable. DREE's reincarnation, merged with elements of the former Department of Industry, Trade and Commerce into the Department of Regional Industrial Expansion (DRIE), was accompanied by the deconcentration of a central agency called the Ministry of State for Economic and Regional Development (MSERD). This central agency, itself created a scant four years earlier to serve the conflict-ridden cabinet committee on economic development, was in turn slated for dissolution upon John Turner's accession to the office of prime minister in the summer of 1984. As for the General Development Agreements, they were allowed to die a natural death upon the expiration of their ten-year terms. Their replacement, named Economic and Regional Development Agreements, called upon the field officials of MSERD to play a key role (this role was made moot by the intended abolition of MSERD). About the only thing that could be said with certainty, as of mid-1984, was that the federal-provincial networks formed under the deconcentrated DREE had been destroyed.

Executive federalism, during the era of that deconcentrated DREE, displayed elements strongly reminiscent of the tradition-derived model of federal–provincial functional relations. Federal and provincial officials found common ground in the imperative to produce results out of their vague mandate to identify and pursue economic opportunities. The nine-year life of the bilateral structure, in which they articulated their relationship, reinforced trust relations. The financial lubricant of cost sharing was copiously available. However, at least in the New Brunswick case, the provincial officials were central agents, not departmental personnel, and the federal DREE officials, given the wide scope of regional development, did not represent a department upon which clienteles with clear-cut functional interests focused. The result was, particularly in the negotiation of sectoral subagreements (e.g., agriculture, forestry),[38] that the societal interests most directly affected had neither direct nor virtual representation. The capacity of DREE officials to circumvent the federal decision-making process, coupled with the carrot-effect leverage, which the provincial central agents could deploy *vis-à-vis* provincial departments, only reinforced this outcome. It appears that it was only when regional development projects were more spatial than sectoral that active consideration of affected societal interests entered into federal-provincial negotiation. In New Brunswick, these were the spatially defined interests of the Acadian northeast, with their partisan links to the Liberal cabinet in Ottawa, and of the anglophone southwest, with their partisan links to the Conservative cabinet in Fredericton.[39]

FEDERAL–PROVINCIAL SUMMIT RELATIONS

Federal–provincial summit relations are epitomized in the media-haunted conferences of the 11 first ministers, but they have come to encompass also a variety of central agency ministers and officials. This being the case, they are strongly conditioned by the extent to which, within governments, the quest to make decision making manageable is eminently prime ministerial. In this regard, it is to be noted both that first ministers are the chief architects of their own institutionalized cabinets, and that they alone can elect to change or by-pass the decision-making structures and processes of these cabinets at any given time, and on any particular matter.

Federal–provincial summitry has fallen into a state of disarray. The starring role in how this came about must be assigned to the all-too-familiar conflicting forces that first ministers have so audibly articulated: Quebec nationalism/independentism, post-OPEC Western Canada assertiveness, Ontario's defence of its economic pre-eminence, Atlantic Province resentments, and federal counteroffensives to perceived excesses of provincialism. All these forces roosted at the federal–provincial summit table during the constitutional review exercise of 1980–1. Their continuing saliency, exacerbated by the fact that the outcome of the constitutional review was declared illegitimate by the Government and Legislature of Quebec, finds expression in the extent to which first ministers have become prone to talk past each other from their respective capitals, rather than with each other on the basis of their policy interdependence. It is tempting to conclude that federal–provincial summit relations, having fallen into such disarray, can be rescued, if at all, only by new political personalities and governing parties with new orientations. After due reflection, I have personally succumbed to this temptation. My confession openly made, I shall probe summit relations, for the purpose of this section, principally in the context of their longest-standing agenda item, fiscal arrangements. The lengthy history of these particular relations enables us to discern how summitry can be workable; the present condition of these once workable relations aptly demonstrates the recent magnitude of summit disarray.

The taxing, spending, and borrowing activities of government have always given a special status to Departments of Finance (or Treasury). Long before the rise of the institutionalized cabinet and the coining of the term 'central agency', Finance Departments stood out as horizontal portfolios whose government-wide scope made them readily available adjuncts of first ministers. The war-conditioned initiation of tax rental agreements in 1940 gave to fiscal matters what turned out to be a regular quinquennial place on the agenda of federal–provincial summitry. By 1955, once the financial exigencies of recent and anticipated public-sector growth were apparent, the first ministers naturally turned to their finance officials in order to equip their fiscal conferences with an expert infrastructure. Thus was born the Continuing Committee on Fiscal and Economic Matters, to which was added a Tax Structure Committee of finance ministers in 1964 and then, beginning in the late 1960s, the still ongoing practice of pre-budget formulation meetings of ministers of finance.[40]

With these underpinnings, federal–provincial summit relations, through the devising of the 1977–82 Fiscal Arrangements, achieved results that are well known: divorce of tax collection agreements from intergovernmental transfers and tax sharing; orderly reallocations of income tax room between the federal government and the provinces; unconditional equalization payments geared to provincial fiscal capacity, as measured by a representative tax system; curtailment of conditional grants, and the development, initially, of a shared-cost and then, of a block-funding approach to health and postsecondary education; and accommodation of income tax reform through federal revenue guarantees to the provinces.[41] The path to these achievements was often acrimonious. Thus, for example, the 1967–72 Fiscal Arrangements, while they did not provoke united provincial opposition, were never endorsed by a summit meeting.[42] The 1977–82 Arrangements, which did receive summit endorsement in December 1976, previously had provoked a provincial common front.[43] What remains constant is that first ministers, whether or not they endorsed a particular set of Arrangements and however heated their periodic disagreements, had come to perceive their relations, underpinned as they were by finance ministers and officials, to be workable. The elements of this workability can be readily enumerated so as to comprise a 'fiscal relations model' of federal–provincial summitry.

- Financial issues are inherently tangible and quantifiable. Accordingly, the parameters within which they are discussed can often be delimited within the bounds of common-sense bookkeeping (e.g., the question of tax room for the provinces is constrained by the fiscal capacity required to make federal equalization payments; and the extent to which provincial natural resource revenues can enter into an equalization formulation is confined by reference to what constitutes a tolerable growth rate in the size of the federal equalization bill). Also, the bounds of any particular issue can be narrowed and even resolved through easily measured saw-offs (e.g., the provincial common front, which formed in 1976 around a revenue guarantee termination payment of four personal income tax points, was bargained down to one point in tax room and one point in cash).[44]

- Finance officials share not only the common vocabulary of macroeconomic analysis, but also the common outlook (the 'treasury mentality') bred by their roles as governmental fiscal managers. These characteristics, once situated under the umbrella of the long-lived Continuing Committee on Fiscal and Economic Matters, are conducive to the formulation of trust ties.

- Network formation among finance ministers is facilitated by the trust ties among their officials and abetted by their common preoccupations with revenue, and with managing the spending ambitions of their cabinet colleagues.

- From first ministers down to finance officials, the fixed maximum five-year term of fiscal arrangements means that any particular configuration of issues, however disputed, must once again be opened to review. This simultaneously eases the climate of consultation ('nothing is forever') and invites reinvestment in trust ties.

What happens to this 'fiscal relations model'? Its effective operation remains abundantly apparent in the design of the 1977–82 Fiscal Arrangements and, most particularly, the Established Programs Financing (EPF) feature of these arrangements. The block funding of health and postsecondary education disentangled federal rates of spending from provincial rates of spending, and vice versa. As such, EPF contributed to the quest to make the spending of each order of government manageable. It is precisely what might be expected to emerge from an intergovernmental network of finance ministers and officials. The summit consensus of December 1976 testifies to the continuing influence of this network on first ministers, not least when two circumstances are recalled. First, the Parti Quebecois had come to power in the autumn of 1976. Second, in the preceding summer, outright provincial rejection of Prime Minister Trudeau's minimalist constitutional patriation package had signalled the full awakening of western provincial governments to constitutional issues and their consequent rejection of the Victoria amendment formula.

But December 1976 marked the last hurrah of the fiscal relations model. Its outline is barely discernible in the fashioning of the 1982–7 Fiscal Arrangements. From David Perry's account, it is apparent that negotiation among finance ministers and officials had little impact on any component of these arrangements other than equalization.[45] Here, the main result was a five-province representative average standard in lieu of the initial federal proposal for an Ontario average. For the rest, the fiscal relations model was inoperative. This is due in part to the weakening of the position of the Department of Finance within the federal government. It is more especially due to the fact (perhaps because of this weakness?) that the government of Canada chose to pursue its counter-offensive against provincialism beyond the constitutional review and into the fiscal domain.

By the mid-1970s in Ottawa, the institutionalization of the federal cabinet had attenuated the hegemony of Finance as the key horizontal portfolio in fiscal and economic management. Indeed, competition among central agencies, notably Finance, the Treasury Board Secretariat, and the Privy Council Office, was a documented reality.[46] The emergence, as the 1970s blended into the 1980s, of yet two more central agencies, the Ministry of State for Economic (later, Economic and Regional) Development and the Ministry of State for Social Development, engendered further competition for the Department of Finance in the decision-making processes of the Government of Canada. As Douglas Hartle asked pointedly in noting these developments, 'Is it credible that Finance has as much impact on federal–provincial fiscal relations and on economic and social development policies as it had when it was the over-all "economic manager" of the federal government?'[47]

The relative waning of the Department of Finance (and with it the fiscal relations model), in the devising of the 1982–7 Fiscal Arrangements, was signalled with the appointment of the Parliamentary Task Force on Federal–Provincial Fiscal Arrangements (the Breau Task Force) in 1981. This innovation could be viewed— and justified—as a positive step because it involved members of Parliament in the pre-legislative process and opened the fiscal arrangements to interest group involvement. But it also unleashed an Ottawa-centred view of the fiscal arrangements, in particular of its EPF (Established Programs Financing) component. The EPF block cash payment was perceived as lacking an acceptable basis in accountability to Parliament. Moreover, the Breau Task Force proved to be a federal magnet for interest groups dissatisfied with provincial spending and policies in health care and postsecondary education. It met, as Rod Dobell has noted, 'the desire of provincially based interest groups operating in areas falling within provincial jurisdiction to appeal to the federal government for action [standards, criteria, rules, whatever] to offset the impacts of provincial government spending [and legislative] priorities.'[48]

At this juncture, it became apparent, at the highest political levels of the federal government, that the abandonment of block funding could be pursued in the name of parliamentary accountability and responsiveness to interest group demands— demands whose allure was enhanced in turn by polls demonstrating public antipathy toward user charges and extra billing by physicians for insured services. The upshot, after a stopgap extension of EPF for the first two years of the 1982–7 Fiscal Arrangements, was the Canada Health Act of 1984. And the potent appeal, especially in an election year, of the values of accountability and responsiveness, was dramatically underlined by the all-party support given to the passage of this act in the House of Commons.

A starkly unilateral federal initiative endorsed by the prime minister, the Canada Health Act emerged not from the Department of Finance, but from the collegial processes of cabinet decision making, served now not only by the Privy Council Office and its offshoot, the Federal–Provincial Relations Office, but by the Ministry of State for Social Development as well. In essence, the act lays down a code of provincial government conduct toward insured hospital and medical services. User charges and extra billing by physicians are deemed a violation of the code, and are henceforth subject to measured reductions in the EPF cash transfer to the offending provinces. Furthermore, compliance with the code requires a province to enter into a formal agreement with medical practitioners and dentists with respect to their compensation, and to the resolution of compensation disputes through conciliation or arbitration. Failure to comply entails reductions in the cash transfer, that are left for the federal cabinet to determine.[49]

These details starkly spell the demise of block funding, and with it the disentanglement of provincial from federal spending. Beyond spending, the very manner in which provinces choose to deal with health care practitioners becomes subject to federal fiscal intervention. What emerges is a fundamental reorientation of federal–provincial fiscal arrangements that has completely circumvented summit consultation and its underlying networks of finance officials and ministers. Thus does the disarray in federal–provincial summitry, exacerbated by the conflicting forces so apparent in the constitutional review, now embrace the fiscal arrangements that stood for decades as the staple agenda item of first ministers' conferences. One more point needs to be made.

The Canada Health Act fits the mould of federal counter-offensives to perceived excesses of provincialism. In this instance, however, the perceived excess at which the counter-offensive takes aim lies outside the mainstream of those which the Government of Canada sought to counter in the constitutional review. There, the perceived excesses converged around matters of economic policy. The slogan 'Securing the Canadian Economic Union' was the subtitle of the federal position paper on economic powers.[50] The economic union is to be secured from what are deemed to have been, for about a decade, balkanizing and unilateral provincial incursions into the economic realm, in the form of a wide variety of protectionist measures and province-centred industrial and resource development policies. The Canada Health Act, for its part, has nothing to do with countering such provincial economic incursions. It constitutes a federal counter-offensive to provincial policies in the social realm of health care, policies which are a mixture of fiscal, cost-control, and professional compensation considerations. As such, the act is defensible in the name of accountability and responsiveness to interest group demands for equity. Meantime, however, the provincial incursions that have been perceived to affect the economic union are themselves defensible on the same grounds. Are not protectionism and province-centred development policies a reflection of provincial responsiveness to interest group demands, and of the ultimate accountability of provincial governments to their electorates? Viewed in this light, the condition that leaves the 11 ministers with their summit interaction in disarray is, if nothing else, deliciously ironic. And the irony will be compounded if postsecondary education comes to join health care as the subject of a code of provincial conduct, a matter under active internal consideration in Ottawa both before and after the 1984 election campaign.

The present condition of summit disarray casts a shadow over all manifestations of executive federalism. Nonetheless, I persist in holding the view, especially under favourable assumptions regarding personalities and governing parties, that this condition is not intractable. I insist, however, on stressing that the path to renewed workability, especially where interaction among the first ministers is concerned, does not lie in one more comprehensive attempt to 'get the Constitution right'. This is because I consider that any summit process called upon to devise the 'right' Constitution is too likely to fail in the attempt, even allowing for sweeping changes in the dramatis personae of first ministers. When we include the 1968–71 route to the aborted Victoria Charter along with the 1980–1 exercise that yielded (only after Supreme Court assistance) the Constitution Act of 1982, it is apparent that multilateral summitry has failed twice to: achieve central institution reform; disentangle the division of jurisdiction; and recognize the historical mission of Quebec in the cultural domain. Setting aside whether or not these reforms were desirable in principle, I find a straightforward explanation for this double failure in what I call a 'constitutional review model' of federal–provincial summitry. It is, in all respects, the diametrical opposite of my fiscal relations model.

- Constitutional issues, being symbolic and abstract rather than tangible and quantifiable, are not amenable to readily measurable trade-offs.
- The officials who underpin constitutional review deliberations include law officers who, to the extent that they view their respective governments as legal clients, may tend to magnify jurisdictional jealousies rather than reduce them on the basis of shared professional values.
- The horizontal portfolio ministers most closely involved are federal and provincial Ministers of Justice and Attorneys-General whose portfolios include recourse to adversarial processes before the courts, and who are therefore prone to examine constitutional proposals in this light.
- The whole process of a comprehensive constitutional review exercise focuses the attention of all participants, from first ministers down, on the 'one last play' that will be the constitutional engineering feat of comprehensive change. The anticipated proximity of this last play depreciates investment in long-term trust.
- Because it is known that the 'one last play' yields a quasi-permanent end result, given the rigidity of the amendment process, negotiations are inherently more tension ridden than when 'nothing is forever'.

My 'constitutional review model' demonstrates all the reasons why the last thing I would prescribe for the current disarray in federal–provincial summitry is another comprehensive attempt at constitutional review. In the vocabulary of economics, the transaction costs are enormous, and the opportunity costs are likely to engulf all other matters that should occupy the summit agenda. I am mindful that these already include a constitutional item: the native rights that are mandatorily on the summit agenda by virtue of section 37 of the Constitution Act of 1982. Then there is the challenge of legitimating that very act in the eyes of the Government and National Assembly of Quebec.

The issue of native rights is confined rather than all-encompassing; it therefore offers the summit the opportunity to record an initial success in the use of our governmentally dominated amendment formula which might subsequently be emulated in other, similarly confined areas. As for the legitimation of the Constitution Act of 1982 in Quebec, I suggest that that likelihood is directly related to the extent to which it can be decoupled from any kind of comprehensive constitutional review. I suggest that the most salient points involve, in the first place, rewriting section 40 so that reasonable federal compensation would accompany provincial opting out of future amendments, beyond those restricted to educational and other cultural matters; and, secondly, acknowledging the existence of a Quebec veto. Both amendments are subject to the section 41(e) requirement of unanimity. In neither case do I see a multilateral summit of first ministers capable of playing a useful initiating role. I regard these as matters for bilateral summitry between Ottawa and Quebec, accompanied by informal soundings of other first ministers in their capitals, but sustained on a bilateral basis to the point where agreed-upon texts would be ready for submission as government resolutions to Parliament and the Quebec National Assembly. Summit accord could then be sought for identical submissions to the other legislatures. Without such accord, the resolutions could be passed by Parliament and the National Assembly, leaving the nine English-speaking provinces the choice to ratify, within the three-year limit of section 39(2), what would finally legitimize the Constitution Act of 1982 *a mari usque ad mare*. If this scenario leaves me sounding like someone who recoils from burdening the agenda of summitry with constitutional matters, I stand guilty as charged. I look elsewhere than in the constitutional domain as I seek workable federal–provincial relations.

Prescriptions for Workable Executive Federalism

Having turned my back on the constitutional domain, where shall I look for workability in executive federalism? First, I will extract what I consider to be the moral of my stories of functional and summit relations, and on this basis formulate a number of propositions for first ministers in their roles as the heads of our 'central energizing executives'. I will then outline a prescription addressed to summit relations as such, one which has found favour with the experienced practitioners of executive federalism, who have given me the benefit of their insights. Finally, I will make a few observations concerning the potential of executive federalism in coming to grips with substantive economic and fiscal issues.

Two Tales of Executive Federalism

I have told a story of federal–provincial functional relations according to which there was a time, lasting until the mid-1960s, when these relations had sufficient commonality to be explained by a simple conceptual model. Thereafter, functional relations galloped off in several directions, as witnessed by examples which, though restricted in number, suffice to convey that wide variability in such relations has become a matter of fact. My tale of summit interaction, for its part, was about relations which, when fiscal arrangements were on the agenda, could be explained by another model, valid as late as the mid-1970s. These relations then bogged down in a state of disarray.

So much for my tales; what is their moral? When all is said and done, the moral of my stories is that the formation and maintenance of networks (i.e., trust ties) between the appointed officials of the two orders of government play a fundamental role in the workability of federal–provincial interaction. Trust ties can be a function of shared professional training and norms, as in the functional relations model; they can be a function of geographical proximity and of shared desire to extract results from a vague mandate, as in the case of the deconcentrated DREE of 1973–82, and they can be a function of the shared vocabulary of macroeconomic analysis and a common interest in managing the spending ambitions of operating departments, as in the fiscal relations model.

Trust ties are communicable to ministers; even more so when ministers possess a measure of independent decision-making autonomy in their portfolios, instead of being oriented to collegial decision-making processes within their cabinets. Finance ministers are a special case. Presiding as they do over the original and historically most potent central agency, they are in a position to capitalize on the trust ties among their officials, to the extent that they have primacy of access to first ministers. Once this primacy is hedged by competing central agencies (especially by central agencies under other central agency ministers, who vie for their own access to their first ministers) finance ministers are in danger of becoming 'central agency ministers like the others'. The utility of finance officer networks thus will be dissipated.

The moral of my stories is simple enough. If it evokes a sense of nostalgia for the 'good old days' of departmentalized cabinets, when operating department ministers enjoyed decision-making latitude and finance ministers presided over a horizontal portfolio unchallenged by insurgent central agencies, so be it. I happen to believe that future cabinet reorganizations, especially in Ottawa, can well afford a touch of nostalgia. I also believe, however, that in one form or another institutionalized cabinets are here to stay. The multiplicity, complexity, and interdependence of the decisions which contemporary governments are called upon to make demand both cabinet committees and central agencies. They ensure that the quest to make decision making manageable will remain ongoing and will lead to continuing experimentation with forms and processes, and this will extend beyond the executive and into legislative assemblies, if only because institutionalized cabinets, in attenuating the autonomy of 'special interest' departments and ministers, generate a need for new channels of interest group consultation, new adjustments designed to accommodate the desideratum of government by consent. All of this has implications for the workability of executive federalism to which first ministers especially should be sensitive and which I choose to address by means of a handful of practical propositions.

- Central agencies per se are not inimical to the conduct of federal–provincial functional relations among ministers and officials. The case of the Canada Assistance Plan demonstrates that central agents can constructively inject government-wide concerns into functional relations. The key distinction to be observed is between occasional appearances to communicate or clarify general policy and ongoing participation in the process of consultation or negotiation. The latter is to be reserved for departmental ministers and officials.
- Once central agents (and for that matter officials from different departments

with different professional backgrounds) enter a domain that has hitherto been the preserve of functional interaction among particular operating ministers and departments, as in the Social Security Review, then first ministers have reason to be concerned that the agenda item involved is too broad to be handled short of summit processes. Such an item is better placed before the first ministers themselves or before central agency ministers, who have been given a specific prime ministerial mandate to coordinate the departments involved with the item concerned (e.g., a guaranteed annual income).

- First ministers can virtually guarantee unworkable federal–provincial relations if, by design or inadvertence, the officials charged with articulating the positions of the two orders of government do so on the basis of the clashing norms of different professions. Manpower training is an excellent case in point. If professional norms clash and the matter cannot be confined to one professional group, intergovernmental consultation or negotiation by administrative generalists is to be preferred. Outstanding interprofessional differences are best left to fester or be resolved around each government's cabinet table. In line with this thought, I cannot resist the parenthetical insertion that I have long found incomprehensible the federal government's occasional plaintive request for an entree into the Council of Ministers of Education. More than an interprovincial club, the CME is a club of professional educationists and fated to remain so for as long as primary and secondary education continue to dominate provincial education portfolios, which they will. Professional faculties of education stand in splendid isolation from the universities in which they are located. This fact speaks eloquently about containing one's expectations of what an educationist club could usefully contribute to manpower economics or scientific research and development.

- When the possibility of internal governmental reorganization appears on a first minister's agenda, he should actively consider its potential implications for workable federal–provincial relations. An internal reorganization that destroys an established federal–provincial network (e.g., the dismantling of the deconcentrated DREE in 1982), or that nips an incipient intergovernmental network in the bud (e.g., the replacement of the Department of Forestry and Rural Development by the centralized DREE of 1969), involves costs in foregone trust ties. These costs might have been avoided if the desiderata prompting the proposed change (visibility, closer adherence to Treasury Board guidelines, whatever) had first been communicated clearly to the federal–provincial networks as criteria to which their interactions should adapt. On the other hand, a reorganization might yield a new agency in order to enhance the internal priority that a government wishes to accord to a particular function. If that government's position in a particular federal–provincial interaction is currently less than constructively articulated, consideration should be given to assigning that role to the new agency (e.g., the new Ontario Manpower Commission in the Ministry of Labour might logically assume the key role in federal–Ontario training relations).

- The institutionalization of cabinets means that departmental ministers and officials are less effective conduits for the claims of client interest groups than was once the case. By the same token, the capacity of special interests to achieve a degree of virtual representation in many forums of federal–provincial interaction has gone the way of the functional relations model. An enhanced use of parliamentary committees to ventilate group interests beckons on both counts. If recourse to such committees poses a particular problem in matters of federal–provincial interaction, this is because interest groups are not necessarily prone to follow the jurisdictional flag when the opportunity of open hearings presents itself. The more impressive problem that lurks behind parliamentary committees is asymmetry in group presentations. The Breau Task Force, implicated as it is in the current federal–provincial fiscal disarray, was a magnet for public spending coalitions; on the other hand its companion Task Force on Pension Reform, another inherently federal–provincial matter, attracted groups closely identified with the case for fiscal restraint.[51] First ministers should consider, and indeed might well consult on, the manner in which legislative committees examining matters of federal–provincial import could be equipped with terms of reference that attract the widest appropriate spectrum of contending views. So that parliamentarians might themselves have the opportunity to view federal–provincial relations writ large, rather than through the terms of any particular committee assignment, there might be merit as well in making an annual federal–provincial relations debate a set feature of each legislature's agenda, as with the Throne Speech and the Budget.

The above propositions can be considered as easily by first ministers in their respective capitals, as they can be at a summit conference. There is much to executive federalism below the formal interaction of first ministers themselves. My propositions are meant to sensitize the heads of our governments to what can be done with respect to federal–provincial interaction generally. What of their own interaction?

Toward Routinized Federal–Provincial Summitry

The good news about the recent disarray in federal–provincial summit relations is that the contending party leaders in the 1984 federal election campaign all promised to do something about it. While anyone who is familiar with the value of Canadian electoral promises has reason to call for the proverbial grain of salt, the prospect that this low-cost promise will be fulfilled by the landslide victor of the 1984 election is enhanced by the honeymoon he has been accorded by his provincial counterparts. The accompanying fact that Prime Minister Mulroney is engaged in producing, at an apparently measured pace, his own version of the institutionalized cabinet, yields a situation that is brimming with potential. Given the recent disarray in federal–provincial summitry, I have been inspired by those experienced in the practice of executive federalism, to advance the view that the most portentous outcome of an early post-election summit would be agreement to hold annual first ministers' conferences as routine events each year. Such routinized conferences are as laden with potential as they are devoid of glamour. Their attractiveness lies precisely in being both.

Where being devoid of glamour is concerned, routine annual summits would not supplant any first ministers' meetings that must take place (e.g., on the constitutional matter of native rights), or that might take place on any momentous agenda item (e.g., fiscal arrangements). Their explicit purpose would be to make summit interaction a commonplace event. Their potential agenda would extend to any matters that already involve, or should involve, federal–provincial interaction at any level, from that of officials to that of first ministers. Their informal atmosphere would stress consultation and exchange, not negotiation. Emphasis on the fundamentally routine nature of the events would contain public and media expectations. It should involve an undertaking among first ministers that routine meetings do not include televised proceedings, or invite pre- or post-conference posturing by the participants.

As for the potential of routine annual summits, several considerations are worth highlighting.

- Because the matters that could appear on the agenda of routinized meetings potentially embrace anything of federal and provincial concern, preparation for each such meeting will necessitate close and ongoing interaction on the part of senior central agency officials situated in first ministers' offices or cabinet offices. The pressure on these officials to 'show results' by extracting manageable annual agendas from their vague mandate should abet the formation of trust ties and promote workable proceedings.
- The nexus between federal–provincial interaction and intragovernmental organization, illustrated by the propositions I addressed to first ministers earlier in this essay, provides a practical if not invariably palatable menu for interchanges among the very individuals who, at the apex of their respective cabinets, share incentives to make manageable their own decision making, and the formal powers of organizing and reorganizing their governments.
- Regularly recurring events have the capacity to gather their own momentum and to evoke constructive patterns of behaviour. The latter range from mutual sensitivity, in areas where governmental actions unavoidably overlap, to identifying opportunities for disentanglement, which might, in time, become the subject of individual constitutional amendments. Supremely, I dare to hope that routinized summitry would breed and nurture among first ministers what J.A. Corry calls 'constitutional morality',[52] a behaviour pattern that focuses on the norms, as distinct from the mere legalities, of federalism; a pattern that seeks simultaneously to capitalize on the socioeconomic forces that bind a federation, and on those that demand decentralization.

Economic and Fiscal Issues

A prescription which calls for routinized summitry is one which focuses on a process that is incremental and that takes a long-run view of federalism. If it finds favour in the eyes of some experienced practitioners of federal–provincial diplomacy and selected political scientists, is this not because it is so congruent with the shared background and norms of what—let's face it—is just another professional group (if indeed the adjective 'professional' is even applicable)? What about the urgency of economic issues in a Canada which, with its double-digit unemployment rate at the head of a long list of alarming symptoms, has its abundant share of the end-of-the-century problems besetting all advanced capitalist and social democratic systems?

Executive federalism must indeed come to grips with economic issues. It is hardly within my purview, and even less within my competence, to analyze the substance of these issues. Nonetheless, I do not hesitate to venture two sets of observations concerning the potential of executive federalism in coming to grips with substance. The first involves the importance of containing one's expectations of what might be called 'multilateral economic summitry', and of searching out agenda items that hold at least some promise of early success. The second, whose relative urgency is easily measured by the fact that the next set of fiscal arrangements spans the years 1987–92, seeks to galvanize fiscal summitry into renewed and reoriented coherence.

I have several reasons to contain my own expectations of what multilateral summit relations can achieve with respect to economic issues writ large. For one thing, there is the track record of summitry with respect to the regionally most divisive economic issue in recent years: energy. Here, the intractable manner in which Premier William Davis of Ontario chose to present the position of energy consumers (not least during the Clark government interlude) guaranteed that summit negotiations must be confined to bilateral interaction between Ottawa and the producing provinces, rather than pursued on the agenda of the 11 first ministers.[53] For another, there is the elaborate exercise in multilateral economic summitry of 1978, complete with ministerial and other working groups. In Michael Jenkin's words, 'The results of the conferences tended to be either agreements on general principles that later turned out to hide very real differences, or agreements on isolated issues which did not, in themselves, add up to a coherent program of political action.'[54] More generally, it is a fact that provincial premiers have been prone to use economic conferences as vehicles for charging the federal government with economic mismanagement, while the Government of Canada has perceived many provincial economic positions as an affront to its primacy in the economic realm. Once again, personality changes might rectify this situation, but it should be borne in mind that any summit conferences called in the near term to deal with 'the economy' are bound to be major media events, replete with opportunities for political posturing. Such conferences, if they are to have any chance of meeting public expectations, will be in need of restricted agenda items, selected with an eye to their potential for eliciting consensus and demonstrating movement.

One possibility lies in regional development, now perhaps even more disoriented than after DREE's demise in 1982, because the Ministry of State for Economic and Regional Development has been dissolved. Federal–provincial interaction in regional development necessarily hinges in the main on bilateral relations, but a multilateral economic summit might well address in principle the future orientation of bilateral agreements. Michael Trebilcock, in a recent address to the Ontario

Economic Council, suggestively raised the possibility that the thrust of future agreements might concentrate preferably on economic adjustment rather than development.[55] What he calls 'General Adjustment Agreements' would focus upon adjustment costs arising from freer international trade and reduced barriers to internal trade.

Then there is the possibility of seeking summit approbation of Michael Jenkin's proposal for a continuing structure at the level of ministers and officials, which he calls the Canadian Council of Industry and Technology Ministers.[56] Bearing in mind that within governments (notably within the federal government) tensions among economic portfolios have been painfully apparent, I do not foresee that a CCIT has the same potential for trust ties as the long-standing Continuing Committee on Fiscal and Economic Matters. It beckons nonetheless, especially to screen what might or might not provide workable agenda items for future economic summits, and to assist in staffing the more informal, routinized summit meetings.

My own favourite, subject to a heavy discount for this very reason, is the possibility of economic summit deliberations on manpower training. What could be sought here is what is within the capacity of first ministers as heads of government to grant: federal–provincial interaction by ministers and officials concerned not with education, but with training as an employment placement and economic adjustment tool. The functional conflict, which reverberated some 20 years ago when the federal government attempted a serious initiative in this regard, arose in what I established earlier in this essay was a context peculiar to the times. In the mid-1960s, employment and training for employment had not acquired the overtones of the moral and ethical imperative that they possess today. And now that non-university postsecondary institutions are firmly established and mature, they no longer justify provincial insulation from outside influence—be these called 'federal', 'economic', or 'labour market' influences. If I discern a problem with placing manpower training on the agenda of an early economic summit, it is because this restricted agenda item may be swept up in the controversy of a Canada Health Act approach to post-secondary education. Having prescribed, in a suggestive vein, possibilities for workable economic summitry in the near term, I conclude by addressing what I consider to be the most pressing matter of substance for the processes of executive federalism: the fiscal arrangements for 1987–92.

The Canada Health Act, as I have already pointed out, leaves executive federalism in a position that is nothing if not deliciously ironic. Here is a federally devised code of provincial conduct, to be implemented through the application of the federal spending power, in the realm of social policy. This initiative came on the heels of a quite different federal thrust, one which, in the context of the constitutional review, sought to establish greater federal primacy in the realm of economic policy. Having largely failed in the latter, the Government of Canada successfully undermined provincial primacy in the realm of social policy. Here, surely, is Corry's principle of constitutional morality turned on its head. And it has its own economic downside. As Thomas Courchene observes:

> With health costs already representing over 30 percent of some provincial budgets and escalating rapidly, with the likelihood of even more cost increases

arising from the combination of increasingly expensive diagnostic treatment and an aging population, and with a concerted effort by numerous health-related associations to be covered under the universal health plan, it would appear that increased innovation and experimentation is essential in order that more efficient ways of delivering health care can be found. Already much in the way of provincial experimentation is ongoing. . . . To the extent that the Canada Health Act serves to promote uniformity rather than flexibility and to favour conformity rather than innovation, it is clearly a move in the wrong direction.[57]

Putting Corry and Courchene together, the Canada Health Act is a *massive thrust* in the wrong direction. To be sure, it can be justified on grounds of accountability and responsiveness to interest group pressures. But so can any of a number of provincial interventions in the economic realm, including protectionist interventions, which generate costs that are not simply imposed on provincial electorates, but are externalized (i.e., borne elsewhere in the country). As Robert Prichard puts it so well, the externalities that flow from such interventions 'are affected by a fundamental illegitimacy that does not apply, at least in theory, to federal intervention'.[58] The parallel illegitimacy of the Canada Health Act is that health costs are largely internalized within provinces and yet will be driven by a federal code. Thus a code applies where it has no basis in constitutional morality or economic rationality and is non-existent with respect to matters where it is warranted.

It is this precarious and anomalous situation which, in my view, cries out for rectification in the fiscal arrangements of 1987–92. The outcome that is earnestly to be desired is one in which a code of provincial conduct is withdrawn from the realm of social policy and applied instead in the realm of protectionist economic policies. The long-standing network of finance officials and ministers must be galvanized to probe once again the relative roles of tax sharing and fiscal transfers in matters of social expenditure. If the federal spending power is to be used to secure adherence to codes of provincial conduct, let this be examined in the realm of conduct that has perverse economic consequences, not where decentralized experiments in cost control are to be desired.

I fully appreciate that to transpose codes of conduct from social to economic policy will be a matter of the utmost political delicacy. The toothpaste, so to speak, is well out of the tube on two counts: any federal prime minister knows that the Canada Health Act enjoys significant support, and any provincial first minister knows equally well the forceful stake of special interests in provincial economic protectionism. What will be central is nothing more nor less than the extent to which first ministers, jointly and severally, can discern that grand abstraction, the public interest, as distinct from particular interests. The test I pose to executive federalism, from the level of finance officials to the summit, involves 1987–92 fiscal arrangements that will at least move in the direction of constitutional morality and economic rationality. The movement, as distinct from the outright resolution, is what is of supreme importance. Because in fiscal arrangements, as distinct from constitutional reform, 'nothing is forever,' the 1992–7 arrangements will present a further opportunity. What should be accomplished between now and 1987 is the move-ment, not without difficulty or even acrimony, as testimony to the reactivated work-ability of executive federalism.

Notes

This study was completed in December 1984. I gratefully acknowledge the comments on an earlier draft of Alan Cairns of the University of British Columbia, Richard Simeon of Queen's University, and the following University of Toronto colleagues: Anthony Careless, Douglas Hartle, Albert Johnson, and Peter Russell.

1. Richard Simeon, on behalf of the Royal Commission on the Economic Union and Development Prospects for Canada, assembled a Working Group on the Mechanisms, Process and Politics of Intergovernmental Relations whose members were David R. Cameron, J. Peter Meekison, Claude Morin, and Donald Stevenson. The author served as the group's *animateur,* and Karen Jackson as its *rapporteur.*

2. Richard Simeon, 'Intergovernmental Relations and the Challenges to Canadian Federalism', *Canadian Public Administration* 23 (1980): 21.

3. Thomas A. Hockin, *Government in Canada* (Toronto: McGraw-Hill Ryerson, 1976), p. 7.

4. Donald V. Smiley, *Canada in Question: Federalism in the Eighties,* 3rd edn (Toronto: McGraw-Hill Ryerson, 1980), p. 91.

5. Jean Hamelin, *The First Years of Confederation* (Ottawa: Centennial Commission, 1967) cited in Donald V. Smiley, 'Central Institutions', in *Canada and the New Constitution: The Unfinished Agenda,* vol. 1, edited by Stanley M. Beck and Ivan Bernier (Montreal: Institute for Research on Public Policy, 1983), p. 36.

6. Smiley, 'Central Institutions,' pp. 28–9 and pp. 34–5.

7. James Gillies, *Where Business Fails* (Montreal: Institute for Research on Public Policy, 1981), p. 84.

8. Smiley, *Canada in Question,* p. 277.

9. Douglas Hartle, *Public Policy Decision Making and Regulation* (Montreal: Institute for Research on Public Policy, 1979), p. 72.

10. Ibid.

11. Ibid.

12. Peter Aucoin, 'Pressure Groups and Recent Changes in the Policy-Making Process', in *Pressure Group Behaviour in Canadian Politics,* edited by A. Paul Pross (Toronto: McGraw-Hill Ryerson, 1975), pp. 174–92.

13. Gillies, *Where Business Fails,* p. 137.

14. Donald V. Smiley, *Constitutional Adaptation and Canadian Federalism Since 1945,* Document 4, Royal Commission on Bilingualism and Biculturalism (Ottawa: Queen's Printer, 1974), ch. 8.

15. Albert Breton and Ronald Wintrobe, *The Logic of Bureaucratic Conduct* (Cambridge: Cambridge University Press, 1982), p. 78.

16. Ibid., p. 75.

17. Albert Breton and Raymond Breton, *Why Disunity? An Analysis of Linguistic and Regional Cleavages in Canada* (Montreal: Institute for Research on Public Policy,

1980), pp. 58–60 and *passim.*

18. Rand Dyck, 'The Canada Assistance Plan: The Ultimate in Cooperative Federalism,' *Canadian Public Administration* 19 (1976): 587–602.
19. Ibid., p. 592.
20. A.W. Johnson, 'Canada's Social Security Review 1973–75: The Central Issues', *Canadian Public Policy* 1 (1975): 471.
21. Keith Banting, *The Welfare State and Canadian Federalism* (Kingston and Montreal: McGill-Queen's University Press, 1982), p. 80.
22. Ibid., p. 82.
23. Louis Bernard, 'La conjoncture actuelle des relations intergouvernementales,' in *Confrontation and Collaboration: Intergovernmental Relations in Canada Today,* edited by Richard Simeon (Toronto: Institute of Public Administration of Canada, 1979), p. 103.
24. J. Stefan Dupré et al., *Federalism and Policy Development: The Case of Adult Occupational Training in Ontario* (Toronto: University of Toronto Press, 1973), *passim.* Save where otherwise noted, the account of manpower training is drawn from this book.
25. Royal Commission on the Economic Union and Development Prospects for Canada, *Challenges and Choices* (Ottawa: Minister of Supply and Services Canada, 1984), p. 47.
26. Alan C. Cairns, 'The Other Crisis of Canadian Federalism,' *Canadian Public Administration* 22 (1980): 175–95.
27. Claude Mérineau, assistant deputy minister of Manpower, Government of Quebec, oral commentary at a seminar on adult occupational training given by J. Stefan Dupré at the Centre for Industrial Relations, McGill University, 29 January 1974.
28. Anthony G.S. Careless, *Initiative and Response: The Adaptation of Canadian Federalism to Regional Economic Development* (Montreal: McGill-Queen's University Press, 1977).
29. Donald J. Savoie, *Federal–Provincial Collaboration: The Canada–New Brunswick General Development Agreement* (Montreal: McGill-Queen's University Press, 1981).
30. Careless, *Initiative and Response,* p. 72.
31. Ibid., p. 131.
32. Ibid., p. 164.
33. Savoie, *Federal–Provincial Collaboration,* p. 28.
34. Ibid., p. 30.
35. Ibid., p. 155.
36. Ibid., p. 134.
37. Ibid.
38. Ibid., pp. 48–57.
39. Ibid.. pp. 55–7 and 70–85.
40. Smiley, *Canada in Question,* pp. 95–6.
41. Perrin Lewis, 'The Tangled Tale of Taxes and Transfers', in *Canadian Confederation at the Crossroads,* edited by Michael Walker (Vancouver: Fraser Institute, 1978), pp. 39–102.
42. Richard Simeon, *Federal–Provincial Diplomacy: The Making of Recent Policy in Canada* (Toronto: University of Toronto Press, 1972), pp. 259–62.
43. A.S. Rubinoff, 'Federal–Provincial Relations: Is Our Conduct Changing?' paper

presented to the annual conference of the Institute of Public Administration of Canada, Victoria, BC, 17–18 September 1977.

44. Ibid., p. 22.

45. David B. Perry, 'The Federal–Provincial Fiscal Arrangements for 1982–87', *Canadian Tax Journal* 31 (1983) pp. 30–4.

46. Richard D. French, *How Ottawa Decides: Planning and Industrial Policy-Making 1968–1980* (Ottawa: Canadian Institute for Economic Policy, 1980).

47. Douglas G. Hartle, *The Revenue Budget Process of the Government of Canada: Description, Appraisal and Proposals* (Toronto: Canadian Tax Foundation, 1982), pp. 66–7.

48. Rod Dobell, 'Alternative Consultation Processes: Prospect for 1987 and Beyond', notes prepared for discussion at the Ontario Economic Council conference, 'Ottawa and the Provinces: The Distribution of Money and Power', Toronto, 14–15 May 1984, p. 13.

49. Ibid., pp. 7–11.

50. Hon. Jean Chretien, Minister of Justice, *Securing the Canadian Economic Union in the Constitution* (Ottawa: Minister of Supply and Services Canada, 1980).

51. Dobell, 'Alternative Consultation Processes', p. 2.

52. J.A. Corry, 'The Uses of a Constitution', in Law Society of Upper Canada, Special Lectures, *The Constitution and the Future of Canada* (Toronto: Richard De Boo, 1978), pp. 1–15.

53. Jeffrey Simpson, *Discipline of Power* (Toronto: Personal Library, 1980), pp. 179–203.

54. Michael Jenkin, *The Challenge of Diversity: Industrial Policy in the Canadian Federation*, Science Council of Canada Background Study 50 (Ottawa: Minister of Supply and Services Canada, 1983), p. 128.

55. Michael J. Trebilcock, 'The Politics of Positive Sum', notes prepared for discussion at the Ontario Economic Council conference, 'Ottawa and the Provinces: The Distribution of Money and Power', Toronto, 14–15 May 1984.

56. Jenkin, *The Challenge of Diversity*, p. 175.

57. Thomas J. Courchene, 'The Fiscal Arrangements: Focus on 1987', notes for an address to the Ontario Economic Council conference, 'Ottawa and the Provinces: The Distribution of Money and Power', Toronto, 14–15 May 1984.

58. J. Robert S. Prichard, with Jamie Benedickson, 'Securing the Canadian Economic Union: Federalism and Internal Barriers to Trade', in *Federalism and the Canadian Economic Union*, edited by Michael J. Trebilcock et al., Ontario Economic Council Research Studies (Toronto: University of Toronto Press, 1983), p. 49.

24

Bureaucracy and State Intervention: Parkinson's Law?

Albert Breton and Ronald Wintrobe

Abstract. Parkinson's Law is the popular idea that bureaucrats or administrators are bound to multiply. The basis for the Law was Parkinson's observation that, in some organizations, the number of administrators continued to increase even when the organization, as measured either by its output or the size of its direct labour force, was declining. This paper first considers two popular explanations of this phenomenon: the political monopoly model and the model of bureaucrats as budget maximizers. The authors show that neither of these theories is capable of providing a satisfactory explanation of Parkinson's observations. They then outline a new and more general theory of bureaucracy, in which bureaucrats maximize power, not by maximizing budgets, but by accumulating the loyalty of their subordinates and that of interest groups and the media. The paper then shows that this model does provide a consistent and indeed commonsense explanation of Parkinson's observations. All declining organizations might be expected to become top-heavy with administrators, as Parkinson predicted, but the process need have nothing to do with bureaucratic expansionism. The paper concludes by stressing the important policy implications of Parkinson's Law for the rational administration of government in an era of declining budgets.

Work expands to fill the time available for its completion.

—C.N. Parkinson

Whether it is because of, or perhaps despite, their witty presentation, the ideas of C. Northcote Parkinson have had considerable influence on contemporary thinking about public administration. Indeed, we venture to suggest that the Parkinsonian notion that bureaucrats can expand their empires and simultaneously reduce their workloads, so that the typical public servant heads a large staff which does very little, is probably the most popular view among ordinary citizens of what goes on in the public sector.

Perhaps more surprisingly, the dominant approach in the new political economy, which applies economic theory to problems of the public sector, is also the Parkinsonian idea that bureaucrats are essentially empire-builders, or in more precise

Albert Breton and Ronald Wintrobe, 'Bureaucracy and State Intervention: Parkinson's Law?', *Canadian Public Administration* 22, 2 (1979): 208–26. Courtesy of The Institute of Public Administration Canada.

language that bureaucrats maximize the size of the bureau under their control.[1] This idea was put forth in a very elegant and systematic way by William Niskanen, an economist who was himself a former senior bureaucrat in the US Office of Management and Budget.[2] Milton Friedman has recently promoted the notion which we label the 'strong' version of Parkinson's Law below—the idea that when bureaucrats expand their empires, they actually manage to *reduce* the level of services they provide to the public.[3]

Parkinson's Law also carries with it a delightful policy implication, namely that one can cut government spending and at the worst suffer no reduction in government services, and in the strong version, actually get more of them. In an age when both scholars and ordinary citizens are concerned that governments may have grown too large, as symbolized most dramatically by the recent vote for Proposition 13 in California, *Parkinson's Law* certainly makes good reading.

For all these reasons, we thought it worthwhile to take Parkinson's Law seriously, and to see if it was true that, as is sometimes asserted, it makes good economics as well as good reading.

The paper is organized as follows. Since there are a number of different versions of the Law, both in Parkinson and in interpretations of him, section 1 presents several alternatives, and then isolates one version, which we believe captures more than the others the essence of Parkinsonian thinking. Previous explanations of the Law are then discussed in sections 1 and 2. Neither of these explanations—Friedman's monopoly model of the public sector, nor Niskanen's model of a budget-maximizing bureau can account for the Law in a satisfactory way. A new approach is needed, and section 3 therefore outlines, in rough fashion, a new model of bureaucratic power which we have been developing over the past several years, and then applies this model to Parkinson's Law. Section 4 concludes the paper.

1. THE 'STRONG' VERSION OF PARKINSON'S LAW

There are a number of alternative hypotheses all of which have been referred to at one time or another as Parkinson's Law. To consider them, one must first divide the work force of any organization into two components, a bureaucratic or administrative component, A, and a direct labour component, L. These two are commonly distinguished in the statistics on private firms. In government, the distinction is often less clear, but sometimes it is easy to make; for example, in military organizations, the L are the ones who do the fighting, and the A are the ones who do not.

Three alternative Parkinsonian hypotheses with respect to the behaviour of A are:

- A expands by a constant factor over time;
- the ratio A/L is increasing over time; and
- A sometimes expands at the same time as both L and the output of the organization decline.

The first version is roughly true at least for recent history, but unremarkable, since L has also expanded and the growth in the number of administrators may be explained simply by the growth of the economy. The second version is somewhat more striking, and also true. However, the evidence is that the growth in the A/L ratio has been most pronounced in chemical and engineering firms, by all accounts among the most dynamic and technically progressive sectors of the economy.[4] Seen in this light, the standard explanation of the increase in A/L in terms of changes in the productivity of administrative tasks such as coordination appears more promising than one along the line of bureaucratic expansionism.

The third hypothesis is the most striking, arguably the one which most captures the spirit of Parkinson's thought, and is henceforth our subject. Parkinson illustrated this hypothesis with the case of the British Navy. He observed that, from 1914 to 1928, the number of ships in the Navy declined by 67 per cent, and the number of officers and men by 31.5 per cent, but the Admiralty officials (the A) *increased* over this period by 78 per cent, providing, as Parkinson notes, 'a magnificent navy on land.'[5]

Later, in a series of lectures entitled 'The Essential Parkinson', Parkinson described another (so far as we know fictitious) case of a German industrial group with a headquarters staff of two thousand which had all its factories destroyed by enemy action. However, he reports, 'It was then discovered that the administrative staff were working just as hard as ever, even when there was nothing left to administer. Here was gratifying proof, in practice, of what I had described in theory.'[6]

To Parkinson, a top-heavy administration was associated with the decline of an organization or a state. Looked at this way, the third hypothesis is simply an implication of the first combined with the occurrence of some other event which causes a decline in the fortunes of the organization. Thus, if administrators are bound to multiply, and continue to do so even when there is an exogenous decline in the size of the direct labour force, we will observe an increase in A at the same time as both L and output decline.

This interpretation, in which the bureaucracy plays essentially a passive role in the process of the decline of an organization (since all they do is to keep on multiplying, like rabbits) is not the only one possible. Recently, Milton Friedman has popularized an alternative explanation (first proposed by the physician Max Gammon) in which the increase in the number of administrators is the cause of the organization's decline. Gammon summarizes his 'Theory of Bureaucratic Displacement' as follows:

> In a bureaucratic system . . . increase in expenditure will be matched by fall in production. . . . Such systems will act rather like black holes in the economic universe, simultaneously sucking in resources, and shrinking in terms of 'emitted' production.[7]

In Friedman's own words, in a bureaucratic system, 'useless work drives out useful work'.[8]

As examples of this process, Friedman cites, in addition to the British National Health Service over the period 1965–73 which was the subject of Gammon's analysis, the US school system from 1971–2 to 1976–7, and as a case of Parkinson's Law operating in reverse, the New York City government from 1976–7 where cuts in the number of government employees allegedly resulted in higher levels of service.

We do not cite these cases because they in any sense represent serious 'evidence' which points to the operation of Parkinson's Law. The reason for citing them may be made clearer if we look at the story of 'black holes' themselves in physics. Physicists sometimes conjecture the existence of a phenomenon not on the basis of observation, but because its existence is required by their theory. As we understand it, in the case of black holes, their existence was initially predicted by theoretical physicists but doubted by the majority of the physics profession. Subsequently, their existence was confirmed by observation, and this fact added to confidence in the entire theory.

The peculiar nature of Parkinson's Law, an economic 'black hole', is that far from being in some sense required by neoclassical economic theory, it stands in absolute contradiction to it. The contradiction is easily established. The basic postulate of economic theory is that of rational behaviour. Applied to the standard model of the production of goods and services, with two factors, labour and (say) capital, this leads to the definition of a region of production which is uneconomic, namely where the quantity of one factor (e.g., labour), is so large relative to that of the other that it is counter-productive: its marginal productivity is negative. In this region, a reduction in the quantity of labour employed will both reduce costs (since labour has a positive price) and increase output. As long as the organization has some goal or purpose other than the growth of its own administrative component, no rational manager will ever continue to operate with these factor proportions. Hence the standard prediction that production in this 'region' will never be observed.

Now, what we have called the strong version of Parkinson's Law is precisely the assertion that the number of administrators may become so large relative to the quantity of direct labour that the organization in question is operating in the uneconomic region. This is why officials who expand the size of their staff find themselves working harder than ever after this growth to accomplish precisely the same task as before. On the theoretical grounds outlined, economists therefore consistently deny the relevance of the law to private organizations.

With respect to public organizations a most curious phenomenon occurs. Many economists will accept Parkinson-type observations on the flimsiest evidence as a standard example of the workings of the public sector. Friedman's article is a case in point.

The difference, it is said, is that the public sector is organized monopolistically, while the private sector is competitive. However, although each bureau has, to a greater or lesser degree, a monopoly on the services it provides to citizens, bureaucrats are accountable to their political masters, and there is certainly competition among political parties for office. Moreover, bureaus compete against each other for funds from the ruling government. Consequently, one would expect that inefficient bureaucrats would find themselves displaced by more efficient ones, either by transfers of personnel or by territorial encroachment. And a political party which tolerated inefficiency would find itself displaced from office. In short, if one is disposed to, one can, in the competition among bureaucrats for funds or amenities, and in the competition among political parties for office, glimpse the operation of that same ghostly invisible hand which is said to ensure efficiency in the private sector.

Of course, it could still be argued that the public sector is, for a number of possible reasons, less competitive than the private sector.[9] Assume this to be the case. Indeed, for purposes of argument, ignore the previous discussion and assume that it is a monopoly—in other words, that representative democracies, despite appearances, are really dictatorships. *We would still not expect to observe the operation of Parkinson's Law.* For the theorem that organizations do not operate in the unproductive region is a consequence not of competition, but of rational behaviour. Why would a dictator have so many administrators that they are counter-productive? If he were a 'perfect' dictator, that is, if the public sector were operated entirely for his benefit (it does nothing but build monuments to him), why should he both pay more for his administration and have fewer monuments built for him than he could have otherwise?

We conclude that Friedman's government monopoly model can't account for Parkinson's Law. Only if the monopoly power in the government is held entirely by the bureaucracy, and the bureaucracy cares only about the size of its own bureaus, does this explanation of Parkinson's Law appear plausible. Let us turn to that model.

2. THE BUDGET-MAXIMIZATION MODEL

William Niskanen's book *Bureaucracy and Representative Government* represents the major step forward in the development of Parkinsonian ideas of bureaucratic behaviour. Niskanen retained the Parkinsonian idea that a bureaucrat wants to maximize the size of his budget. But by embedding this hypothesis into a formal economic model of a bureau, analogous to the standard economic model of the firm, Niskanen was able to develop the implications of this model in a systematic way.

Niskanen's model is simply the logical development of two assumptions: bureau heads desire as large a budget for their bureau as possible; and bureau heads are monopolists, so they get the budget they desire, subject only to the constraint that this budget cannot exceed the total value to citizens of the bureau's services.

To understand the second assumption, note that even a monopolist cannot raise his price without losing some of his customers, and at some point, the price charged can be so high that everyone would rather go without his product than pay for it. Similarly, politicians are responsive to the wishes of citizens, and both politicians and citizens have some notion of what they are willing to pay for government services, and if a monopoly bureau requests a budget which is larger than the total value of the service to them, they will prefer not to have the service at all rather than accede to the bureau's demand.

But neither citizens nor politicians can be expected to know the true costs of the bureau's services. As long as the total costs of the service are less than its total value to citizens, the bureau head can fool the citizens and the politicians by pretending that public services cost more than they really do, or by deliberately seeking out expensive production processes and pretending that these are the only ones available. The most obvious example of this process is the often-alleged behaviour of the Pentagon with respect to new weapons, the argument being that only the most expensive weaponry available could truly make the United States 'secure'.

To show the implications of Niskanen's model, we need to develop these ideas more rigorously. One version of Niskanen's model is shown in Figure 1. The demand for the bureau's services is depicted as DD′. For simplicity assume that DD′ represents the true demand by citizens, and that politicians have learned their wishes and translated this demand into the funds they are willing to allocate to the bureau at different possible prices for the service. The true marginal costs of the service are MC, and therefore the optimum level of the service from both citizens' and governing politicians' points of view is where DD′ = MC, namely output level OV, with a budget of OVNL.

OVNL, however, is not the optimum output from the point of view of the bureau head, who desires as large a budget as possible. One way for the bureau head to exploit his position as a monopoly supplier of the service is to use expensive production processes with declining cost curves. Thus, imagine the same service can be provided by a process with marginal costs like AB. The bureau head can present this cost curve to the politicians as the true minimum costs of the service, in which case politicians will choose output OQ rather than OV and provide the bureau with a total budget of AMQO.

Assuming the bureau head can successfully fool his political master in this way, where will the process end? Only where the bureau's cost curve has been artificially shifted up and twisted so as to lie identically on DD′. In equilibrium, the output of the bureau is equal to OX and its budget equal to the entire area under the demand curve (OXD). At that point, the bureau extracts all of politicians' and consumers' surplus from its provision of the service. The value of additional output to politicians and to citizens is zero, and it is only this which prevents the bureau from expanding any further.

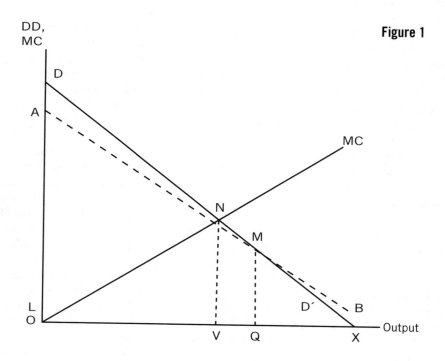

Figure 1

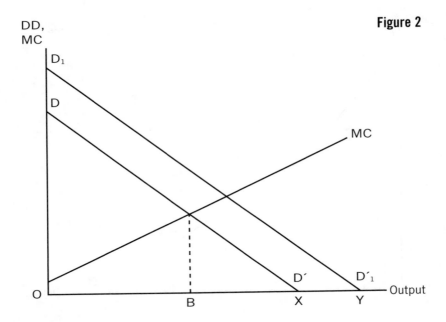

Figure 2

We have criticized this model elsewhere,[10] especially with respect to its statement of the constraint on bureaucratic maximization, and do not wish to repeat those criticisms here, except to note that politicians are not as helpless in the face of bureaucratic distortions as the simple Niskanen model suggests and as Niskanen now recognizes,[11] We want instead to consider whether the model can explain Parkinson's Law.

Niskanen's model does appear to provide a convenient explanation of the first version of Parkinson's Law: that bureaus expand by a constant factor over time. (We do not know whether Niskanen himself would subscribe to this application of his model.) Since the constraint on budget-maximization is the citizens' demand curve, once the bureau's budget has expanded to OXD, no further expansion is possible. However, if citizens' and politicians' demands were to increase, for example, because of growth in population or in real income, so that the demand curve shifts to the right, this permits a further expansion by the bureau. Thus, in Figure 2, if the demand curve shifts from DD′ to D_1D_1′, the bureau can increase its budget from OXD to OYD$_1$. Consequently, if citizens' demands were to grow over time at a fairly constant rate we would observe the first version of Parkinson's Law. Note that technological improvements in the bureau's ability to deliver its output would not alter this growth, since the bureau's costs are entirely determined by the demand curve.[12]

Can Niskanen's model also account for the strong version of Parkinson's Law? There is no distinction between administrators and direct labour in Niskanen's model, but one can still ask if it is possible in that model for the size or budget of the

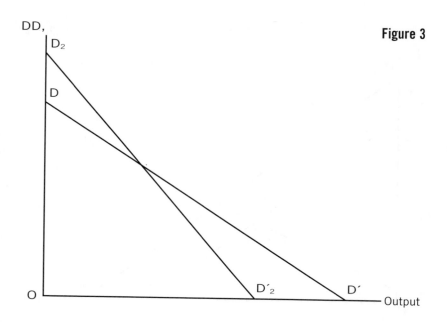

Figure 3

bureau to increase at the same time as its output declines. This will indeed happen, Niskanen shows,[13] if there is a fall in the elasticity of demand for the bureau's services. In Figure 3, the demand curve for the bureau's output changes from DD′ to D_2 D_2', implying that the bureau provides a smaller output in exchange for a larger budget.

A little reflection will surely convince anyone that, while this is plausible as a theoretical prediction, it does not account for Parkinson's observations. Recall that the period over which the number of ships and officers of the Royal Navy declined, while Admiralty and other officials increased, is the period from 1914 to 1928. It can scarcely be argued that the 'need' for defence and therefore for the Navy was larger after the war had ended than it was at its inception. Yet this would be Niskanen's proposition. Moreover, Parkinson was surely right in assuming that, the war being over, there was a fall in the demand for the services of the Navy.

What happens to a budget-maximizing bureau when there is a fall in the demand for its services? Look at Figure 2 again, but assume that the initial demand for the bureau's services is the curve D_1D_1'. In equilibrium, the bureau will have adopted production processes with large fixed costs so that its cost curve is exactly the same as D_1D_1', and its budget is OD_1Y. Now assume a decline in the demand for the bureau's services, so that the new demand curve is DD′. With costs equal to D_1D_1', and demand equal to DD′, the demand curve lies entirely below the bureau's cost curve, and the bureau cannot deliver any output for a price that citizens or politicians are willing to pay. Indeed, at these 'prices' *politicians desire none of the bureau's output, and the bureau will disappear!*

On the other hand, if the bureau's costs had not been distorted initially, but remained at MC, the bureau would still exist after the drop in demand (its output would be OB).[14]

The point we wish to make is not that bureaus tend to disappear every time there is a drop in the demand for their services, but that this is a logical implication of the pure budget-maximization model. What it shows is that however appropriate budget-maximization might be as a strategy in times of increasing demand, it is a very risky one to use if there is ever going to be a possibility of budget cuts. The reason is that distortions in costs are not easily reversible. So a bureau which adopts expensive production processes with large fixed costs to take advantage of an increase in demand will be stuck with those same processes when demand drops. Now, whatever else bureaucrats have been accused of, no one has ever suggested that they are indifferent to their own survival. Our analysis shows that the budget-maximizing strategy proposed by Niskanen is inconsistent with that aim. It follows that budget-maximization cannot be a general representation of the preferences of bureaucrats.

3. A New Model of Bureaucratic Power

If it is conceded that Parkinson did point to bureaucratic phenomena which it would be interesting to explain, then we require an alternative to either the Friedman-type monopoly model or Niskanen's hypothesis of budget-maximization. In the course of the past year or so we have been developing a new, and, we believe, more general model of bureaucracy. In this section, we intend to first outline some of the basic ideas of that model in a non-technical way, and then to apply our reasoning to Parkinson's Law.

In common with previous writers, we assume that bureaucrats maximize power. This assumption corresponds to the assumption in the standard theory of the firm that businessmen maximize profits, or politicians maximize their chances of election, and is neither any more nor any less realistic than those assumptions.

Power for a bureaucrat is defined as his ability to obtain policies with the characteristics he desires. To understand this, note first that in line with previous work by Breton,[15] we define the entire output of the public sector as consisting of a set of policies, such as national defence policies, censorship, bilingualism, snow removal, and so on. The definition of policies is very broad and is simply one way of describing the output of the public sector.

Second, policies may be thought of as consisting of characteristics which appeal either to bureaucrats, to citizens, or to politicians. To illustrate, consider a tariff structure policy. Some of the characteristics associated with that policy are: 1) a stimulation of the production of goods which are substitutes for goods in the protected sector; 2) an increase in the earnings of labour in the protected sector; 3) a greater opportunity for the inefficient and the mediocre to survive; 4) an increase in public revenues; 5) more jobs will be created and maintained in the public sector; 6) some additional discretionary power is given to senior bureaucrats who have to administer the tariff structure; 7) the ability to discreetly reward friends and punish foes either by a change in the tariff rate, in the tariff list, or in the mode of administration of the tariff law; 8) with the need to coordinate the tariff structure with the tariff structure of other countries, international contacts, travel abroad and all the amenities which such travel entails becomes necessary.

Similar lists could be constructed for other policies. The important points we wish to make are that public policies possess a myriad of characteristics, some of which appeal more to bureaucrats, others to citizens and still others to politicians; and that the more power a bureaucrat has, the more those characteristics he likes will tend to be incorporated into public policies.

So bureaucrats maximize power, not merely because they like power per se, though that is of course possible, but because they can use or 'spend' power to obtain policies with more of the characteristics they desire, in the same way that people accumulate wealth, not for its own sake, but for the goods and services that wealth will buy.

How do bureaucrats spend their power? There are a number of well-known instruments which bureaucrats use to obtain policies with characteristics they desire. To list the main ones: 1) distorting information, or distorting commands as they flow through or across hierarchical levels; 2) leaking information to other bureaus, to the media or interest groups, or to the political opposition; 3) distorting the 'speed' of implementation of programs, and more generally distorting the costs of policies as they are implemented.

Thus, the inevitability of some random distortion of information as it flows through the chain of command makes it possible for bureaucrats to selectively distort information in a self-serving way—that is, to withhold information which is damaging to policies they prefer and to exaggerate information favourable to those policies and *vice versa* for policies they dislike. Alternatively, information may be leaked to the media, to pressure groups, or to the political opposition for purposes of pumping up or deflating the demand by citizens for policies. Finally, the costs of policies may be distorted: the simplest way to sabotage a policy one dislikes is to allocate personnel to do the job whose qualifications are formally adequate, but who are known to be incompetent to carry it out. And such practices as formal slowdowns and 'work to rule' are merely extreme cases of the more common and more subtle practice whereby policies which are disliked are endlessly held up through red tape, the need for formal clearances and perhaps formal coordination with other departments, et cetera. If, on the other hand, the bureau particularly favours a policy, there are numerous ways in which the bureau can bypass formal routines to produce it with what will appear to be amazing rapidity.

There is a common principle behind all of these strategies, and we have called it the principle of *selective efficiency*. A bureau head has power when information distortion, leaks and distortions in costs occur only when he wants them to (i.e., when he can control the efficiency level at which the bureau operates). The wider the range of efficiency over which the bureau can be made to operate at his discretion, and the greater control which the bureau manager has over that range, the greater his power.

A crude way to conceptualize the process of selective efficiency is to imagine that a bureau can be operated at three speeds: fast, normal, and slow, and that to have power in the organization is to have one's finger on the switch. To the extent that a bureau head has this control, governing politicians will find it in their interest to incorporate characteristics he desires into public policies in exchange for more efficient production by the bureaucracy. Bureaus therefore may be thought of as 'internal' pressure groups, who implicitly press for the policies they want by altering the efficiency with which different policies are produced.

How can a bureau head accumulate the control over the bureau's efficiency level which we have identified with power? To understand this process, note first that none of the instruments of selective efficiency can be used effectively by the bureau head without the systematic co-operation of others—either that of his subordinates, interest groups, the media, or other bureaus. But, with respect to his subordinates, a bureau head's formal powers of command do not extend to practices of selective efficiency. If he wants their cooperation to leak a document, to sabotage a policy, or to bypass formal procedures in the interests of doing something quickly, there must be something in it for them as well as for him. The same is more obviously true for potential allies such as interest groups, the media and members of other bureaus.

But few policies will have characteristics which appeal in equal measure to all of these groups. As long as they continue to act in isolation from one another, they will seldom have any influence on the policies of the public sector. What is needed to obtain power is for them to agree to exchange cooperation with one another, thus at one time acting in common to pursue an objective which the bureau head desires, in exchange for an explicit or implicit commitment on his part to return the favour later. Thus, for example, within the bureau itself, subordinates may be expected to readily co-operate with a superior beyond their formal responsibilities, since he has much to offer them in return (e.g., a promotion), if only they believe that he will in fact reciprocate in the future.

The obstacle to this cooperation is the fact that there is no guarantee that promises made now will be kept later. The problem is that on the one hand everyone benefits (has more power) from exchanging co-operation, but on the other hand there is no mechanism by which payment may be made except the promise of future cooperation, and what is to prevent an unscrupulous bureaucrat from cheating on the transaction by reneging on his commitments? Consequently, in bureaucratic systems, as in other relationships where there are significant possibilities of cheating, people trade only with those whom they trust. Accordingly, a bureau head who seeks the co-operation of his subordinates or that of other groups in the pursuit of his policy aims must first earn their loyalty by demonstrating to them that he can be trusted.

This process is undoubtedly very complex, and we do not pretend to have understood it fully. But it is clear that loyalty must be built, trust must be earned. And one way for a bureau head to build trust with subordinates, or with other potential allies such as the media or interest groups, is to fight for a policy which is in their interest, rather than his own. Thus a bureau head invests in loyalty on each occasion in which he demonstrates the value to him of a longer-term relationship by foregoing an opportunity for himself in order to benefit another party, or by giving to that party without demanding something in return. The amount 'invested' is simply the value of the foregone opportunity or of the gift and the yield is the enhanced belief on the beneficiary's part that the first party is reliable.

There are two margins along which trust can be accumulated: the first is the amount invested in a single relationship (the extent of intensity of trust) and the second is the number of relationships invested in. Changes in the environment faced by an individual will alter his optimal investment pattern, by changing the returns to investment along these two margins. For example, in an open, mobile and relatively impersonal society, large investments in the extent of trust in a small number of relationships are seldom warranted at the same time as the profitability of a wider span of 'contacts' is increased. To give examples in bureaucratic organizations, the British civil service is relatively small and closed relative to that in the American federal government and it has been alleged that bureaucrats in the British system trust each other a great deal more than do those in the American; at the same time, they do not have contacts with as many of their peers as does the typical American bureaucrat.[16]

To the extent that trust has been established, a bureau head can ask his subordinates to cooperate with him in either implementing a policy especially rapidly, or with agonizing slowness. He can ask an interest group to promote an objective of his, and they will do so. He can leak information to the media, and they will print it. Cooperation is forthcoming, to the extent that they trust him, because to that extent they are confident that he will reciprocate in the future.

A bureaucrat therefore accumulates power by accumulating capital in the form of *networks*—lines of trust and mutual confidence. These networks amount to the isolation of a set of contacts, along which repeated interaction takes place. By restricting interactions to those with whom one has had previous dealings or with whom one expects to deal in the future, the costs of 'policing' transactions (preventing cheating) are reduced. Since there are gains from trade, there are benefits from being part of the network, and therefore the threat of being dropped from the network constitutes an effective sanction.

The existence of networks within hierarchical organizations (often called the 'informal organization' by sociologists and organization theorists) has been documented for many different types of organizations. They exist in private business firms (Dalton, 1959), Soviet enterprises (Berliner, 1952), as well as in government bureaus (Heclo, 1977; Heclo and Wildarsky, 1974). In all cases we suggest that their purpose is to facilitate trade by facilitating credit. This ability to trade gives their members power over the policies of the organization.

Our model of bureaucratic power may be summarized in two key propositions. First, the amount of power possessed by a bureaucrat is directly related to the extent to which he can obtain the co-operation of others (his subordinates, other bureau head, the media, pressure groups, et cetera) in the system to achieve his own policy aims. The reason is that it is this co-operation which facilitates the practice of selective efficiency, and it is only by this practice that bureaucrats can get policies adopted by the government which they desire, but neither politicians nor citizens want. Secondly, bureaucrats obtain this cooperation by investing in the loyalty of groups whose cooperation they want. In economic terms, power is simply a form of capital, and the process by which it is accumulated is formally the same as that for any capital good.

We turn now to the application of this model of bureaucratic power accumulation to Parkinsonian problems. Two questions are considered. First, is maximizing power equivalent to multiplying one's subordinates, so that bureau heads are indeed motivated to expand their organizations as much as possible? And secondly, and more importantly, is the model consistent with the strong version of Parkinson's Law?

In our framework, a bureau head would want to increase the size of his bureau only if this implies an increase in his power. This will be true only if he can by so doing increase the size of the group with which he can establish some trust or loyalty, and who will be willing to co-operate with him. If the bureau were initially very small, he would indeed wish to hire more men (build an empire) if only because initially it is undoubtedly easier (less costly) to build loyalty with subordinates than with others. If this remained true as the bureau continued to expand, our model would be identical with Parkinson's First Axiom: 'An official wants to multiply subordinates, and not rivals.'

But as the bureau expands in size, so does the division of labour within the organization and Parkinson's Second Axiom comes into play: 'Officials make work for each other'. So in Parkinson's analysis, although one reason for increasing the size of the bureau is to reduce the head's workload, an official finds himself working harder than ever to accomplish the same task even after the growth in his empire.

In our framework, the effect of the increase in the division of labour as size expands is to increase the costs of accumulating power over the bureau. As the division of labour increases, so does the number of groups whose loyalty must be invested in and maintained to have the same amount of control over the organization as before.

To be sure, in both large and small organizations the co-operation of only one sub-group is necessary to create a bottleneck which slows down the entire organization. But to speed up the bureau's operation requires the co-operation of every major group, and this is clearly more difficult to obtain in the larger organization. A bureau head who can only slow down his organization is vulnerable to territorial encroachment from other, smaller and more flexible bureaus, and leaves himself open to possible replacement.

The other instruments of selective efficiency are similarly affected by size. Cliques are formed within the bureau against the head and he increasingly becomes the victim, rather than the generator, of leaks to the media and to other outside groups and of distorted information within the bureau.

We conclude that, after a point, expanding the size of the bureau reduces power rather than increasing it. We should not be surprised at this conclusion. Few would contend that, in Canada, senior officials in the Department of Health and Welfare are more powerful than those in Finance, yet this is what is implied by a model in which size is equated with power. In our model, bureaus differ in power because they differ in the resources and opportunities available for building networks. Thus, some positions offer access to information which is of considerable interest to the media, others do not; some bureaus produce policies which are of considerable interest to other bureaus and to powerful pressure groups, others do not. Hence, there is no reason, in our way of thinking, to associate power merely with size of personnel.

Let us now turn to a more detailed consideration of Parkinson's Law. To consider the strong version of Parkinson's Law within the framework of this model, assume a decline in demand for the organization's output. Divide the organization à la

Parkinson into administrative and direct labour components (A and L). Administrators typically have one characteristic not remarked by Parkinson: they possess skills which are organization-specific, and therefore are less likely to be dismissed in times of slack demand for the organization's services.[17] Assume further that at least some members of the L have co-operated beyond the call of duty with those at senior levels of the bureau in the past, who are therefore indebted to them.

Now consider the rational behaviour of the head of an organization which is (temporarily or permanently, he has no way of knowing) in decline. Since the demand for the organization's output has fallen, the work force has to be cut. The cuts have to come from among the L and not the A, and they have to be made according to some general rule such as seniority. The loyal L will be aware that, if they are dismissed, they will never be repaid for the loyalty in which they have invested in the past. The only way they can be reasonably sure of staying with the organization is to be promoted to the A. So they 'call in their loans' and demand promotion so as to avoid being cut.

The bureau head, or others at senior levels in the bureau who are in debt to the L, are also aware that dismissal of the L according to any objective criterion will not discriminate between those who have been loyal in the past and those who have not. If they do not promote the loyal L, they will suffer a loss of power in two ways: they lose their loyal L; and those who remain in the organization will observe that loyalty did not, in the end, turn out to be worth much. Hence the senior bureaucrats' future promises will be immediately discounted, and their ability to rebuild their power permanently impaired, in literally the same way that anyone who fails to repay his obligations will have difficulty getting a loan in the future. Hence they, too, will want to promote their loyal L.

The rational thing to do is therefore to promote the loyal L to A and fire the required number of the remaining L. We will observe a decline in L, decline in output, and an increase in A—the strong version of Parkinson's law.

Lest one thinks the explanation contrived, we hasten to point out to the academic reader that he can probably observe the process right now in his own organization. We first observed it when we were curious as to why, the demand for economics courses being so strong despite the general decline in enrolments, there seemed to be no funds available to hire new staff in many universities. One reason suggested was that those departments where the demand was weakest had seen the writing on the wall and prematurely promoted their assistant professors to tenured positions to make them immune from dismissal.

A number of other aspects of the process call for more detailed comment. As the example of universities illustrates, the process has a definite end point, namely when all debts have been cleared. Unlike Parkinson's version, the model here therefore does not predict a continuous expansion in the A, but a once-and-for-all expansion. The process need not be exactly as described above, and can take many alternative institutional forms. The basic problem is to discriminate between the loyal and the non-loyal L, and one obvious way to do this is to reorganize the bureau. Whatever other functions reorganization permits during a period of a decline in demand (and we do not deny that there may be some), it does permit this discrimination to take place, by creating new slots among the A for the loyal L, and eliminating the positions of some of the other L. Reorganization is thus a means of clearing debts and settling accounts within an organization.

Governor Jerry Brown of California is currently planning to reorganize the local governments there, on the avowed purpose of creating a 'leaner' government for the future Small-is-Beautiful era, but our prediction is for a government which is indeed leaner at the bottom, but fatter around the middle.

Parkinson's own example of the British Navy is a particularly simple case. The L who were still alive after the war were presumably not promoted to the A to avoid dismissal, but simply as a reward for loyal service. And the L were not expanded to their former strength again because so large a force was no longer required after the end of the war. We would expect all military organizations to go through the same process— in other words, become top-heavy in the period after the end of a major war.

Most organizations reduce their output by dismissing their employees, and not because they are killed in a war. For them, the fuller analysis given here is necessary. Were Parkinson's Law considered relevant only for military organizations, of course, that analysis would not be needed. This brings us to our final point. There is no reason why the strong version of the Law should not apply to *all* organizations, private as well as public. Bureaucrats in private firms are no less concerned with accumulating power than their public counterparts. And loyalty is no less important for accumulating power and obtaining influence over the policies of private organizations than in public ones.

Parkinson himself was surprised at the reaction of businessmen to his theory:

> I originally supposed that this administrative burden was peculiar to governments. It had existed, I knew, in the later phases of Roman and Moghul Empires. But the publication of *Parkinson's Law* brought me a stream of correspondence, much of it from people engaged in commerce and industry. Writing from a variety of offices in the most distant and various countries, they all wrote, in effect, 'How did you come to know about *our* organization?'[18]

4. CONCLUSION

The basic question we want to close with is this: If we have in a sense succeeded in rehabilitating Parkinson's Law, need we accept the policy implications drawn from it by Friedman and others? Can a cut in government spending possibly result in an increase in output?

If the argument of this paper is correct, the answer is clearly no. A top-heavy administration, in our framework, is a symptom of decline, and not its cause. We have shown that neither the top-heavy administration nor the decline need result from or in any way be associated with bureaucratic expansionism. To put it differently, it is the cut in expenditures or the decline in demand itself which results in a top-heavy administration and not the other way around. And the reason is simply that bureaucrats will seek to implement cuts in ways that are least damaging to their power in the long run.

Notes

Financial support from the Killam Foundation is gratefully acknowledged. This is a revised version of a lecture delivered by Ronald Wintrobe at the Conference of the Institute of Public Administration of Canada, Quebec City, 29 August to 1 September, 1978.

1. See for example, Anthony Downs, *Inside Bureaucracy* (Boston: Little, Brown, 1967) and William Niskanen, *Bureaucracy and Representative Government* (Chicago: Aldine, 1971).

2. W. Niskanen, op. cit.

3. Milton Friedman, 'Gammon's Black Holes', *Newsweek*, 7 November 1977.

4. See the evidence in R.E. Chester, *A Study of Post-War Growth in Management Organizations* (OEEC, 1961).

5. C.N. Parkinson, *Parkinson's Law and Other Studies in Administration* (New York: Ballantine Books, 1957).

6. C.N. Parkinson, *The Essential Parkinson* (New Delhi: Federation House, 1970).

7. Max Gammon, *Health and Security* (London: St Michaels, 1976).

8. Friedman, op. cit.

9. A plausible argument along these lines is presented in Gordon Tullock, 'Barriers to Entry in Politics', *American Economic Review* (May 1964).

10. See Albert Breton and Ronald Wintrobe, 'The Equilibrium Size of a Budget-Maximizing Bureau', *Journal of Political Economy* (January–February 1975).

11. W. Niskanen, 'Bureaucrats and Politicians', *Journal of Law and Economics* (December 1975).

12. In 'Bureaucrats and Politicians', Niskanen does suggest an alternative explanation—that the monopoly power of bureaus has increased over time as governments have become increasingly centralized. But this explanation obviously does not apply to cases such as Canada, where much of the growth of government has been at the provincial level.

13. Niskanen, *Bureaucracy and Representative Government*, pp. 71–2.

14. It is true that as a long-run comparative static proposition, the new equilibrium output for a budget-maximizing bureau after the drop in demand is OX rather than zero. But there is no way that the bureau, having distorted its cost curve to look like $D_1D'_1$ can deliver any output once demand has fallen without violating its constraint—that the budget be no greater than the total costs of the services promised. Thus, there is no way the bureau can 'get to' the new equilibrium from this point. Of course, one may say that bureaucrats would realize this danger and not distort their cost curves fully to look like $D'_1D'_1$. But that is just the point we are making.

15. See Albert Breton, *The Economic Theory of Representative Government* (Chicago: Aldine, 1974).

16. See Hugh Heclo and A. Wildavsky, *The Private Government of Public Money* (London: Macmillan, 1973) and H. Heclo, *A Government of Strangers* (Washington: The Brookings Institution, 1977).

17. See G.S. Becker, *Human Capital* (New York: National Bureau of Economic Research, 1964) for the theory of specific human capital.

18. Parkinson, *The Essential Parkinson*, p. 26.

25

The Impact of the Charter of Rights on Public Administration

F.L. Morton and Leslie A. Pal

Abstract: It is generally accepted that the Charter of Rights and Freedoms, and in particular its section 15 'equality rights', will significantly affect Canadian public policy and administration. We argue that the principal change wrought by the Charter will be that judges, applying judicial methods of reasoning, will have the final say on many policy problems formerly managed exclusively by administrative institutions, applying administrative methods of reasoning.

The article compares these 'institutional logics' through close examination of two documents, both addressing the issue of sex discrimination in maternity benefits under the Unemployment Insurance Act (UI). The first document, obtained through the Access to Information Act, is a 1978 briefing memorandum to the Canadian Employment and Immigration Commission advising on the likely outcomes of the impending Supreme Court decision on the *Bliss* case. The female plaintiff in *Bliss* alleged that UI maternity benefits violated the Canadian Bill of Rights equality provisions. The second document is an influential law review article on the *Bliss* case by Professor Marc Gold. Addressing the same policy problem, the documents come to very different conclusions. By using these documents as examples of administrative and judicial reasoning, we demonstrate how different assumptions about the nature of 'discrimination', sources of authority, the weight of financial considerations, the relevant facts, and institutional mandates will tend to lead to conflicts between the courts and administrators.

The adoption of the Charter of Rights and Freedoms in April 1982 added a new dimension to Canadian politics. Henceforth all legislation, administrative rules and regulations, and administrative behaviour must be consistent with the rights enumerated in the Charter. Contrary to first impressions, the principal impact of the charter of Rights and Freedoms is not the creation of new rights, bur rather a new way of making decisions about rights in which judges will play a central and authoritative role.[1] Almost all of the rights enumerated in the Charter existed prior to 1982.[2] It is from a practical or operational point of view that the novelty of the Charter is great-

F.L. Morton and Leslie A. Pal, 'The Impact of the Charter of Rights on Public Administration: A Case Study of Sex Discrimination in the Unemployment Insurance Act', *Canadian Public Administration* 28, 2 (1985): 221–44. Courtesy of The Institute of Public Administration Canada.

est. Its practical effect is to create a second tier of policy review, in which all legislative and administrative decisions are subject to review by judges, to ensure conformity with the Charter.

While it is widely acknowledge that this broadened scope of judicial review will
increase judicial participation in the policy-making process, no one has tried to describe
precisely how or why judicial enforcement of rights differs from traditional legislative
or administrative treatment.[3] It has simply been assumed that judges will view and
define rights differently than legislators or administrators. The purpose of this article is
to provide a better understanding of the characteristics of judicial decision-making that
are likely to lead to conflict with administrative decision-makers. Our method is to
closely compare two documents that address the same policy problem from two different perspectives, one judicial and the other administrative. The policy problem is the
conflict between the maternity benefits provisions of the Unemployment Insurance Act
(UI), 1971, and the equality rights section of the 1960 Bill of Rights. This conflict was
the central issue in a 1978 Supreme Court of Canada decision, *Bliss v. A.-G. Canada*,
which held that the UI exclusion of pregnant women from regular unemployment benefits did not violate the right to 'equality before the law'.[4]

The *Bliss* case served as a catalyst for the two documents compared in this article. The first is a confidential, internal policy memorandum of the Canada
Employment and Immigration Commission (CEIC) recently obtained through the
Access to Information Act. This memorandum was written prior to the Supreme
Court's decision and advised the commission on the probable outcome of the *Bliss*
case and available policy options. We treat this policy memorandum as an example
of administrative reasoning. The second document is a widely cited law review article that criticizes the Court's decision in *Bliss*, argues for a much broader conception of equality rights, and accordingly recommends that the offending sections of
UI should be declared inoperative by the courts.[5] While the model of judicial analysis advocated in this article was addressed to the 1960 Bill of Rights, it is now a leading contender for adoption under the reworded 'Equality Rights' section of the
1982 Charter of Rights.

These documents create the opportunity to compare two examples of administrative and judicial response to the same policy problem—the allegation of illegal sex-
based discrimination in an income security program.[6] Through a comparative analysis
of these documents, we substantiate the existence of two different kinds of 'institutional logic'. We suggest that these differences are not unique to this particular case
study, but can be generalized to form a useful theory of inherent conflict between
Charter-based judicial behaviour and traditional administrative behaviour.[7]

MATERNITY BENEFITS AND EQUALITY RIGHTS

Maternity benefits first became available in Canada under the 1971 UI Act, though
there had been earlier pressures to include them in the program. These pressures had
been resisted largely on the grounds that maternity benefits were incompatible with
the actuarial principles governing UI as an insurance program. UI was intended to
provide benefits to bona fide members of the labour force who were involuntarily

unemployed, who had made the required contributions, and who were capable of and available for suitable work. UI officials and politicians presumed that pregnancy was physically debilitating to the degree that a woman was incapable of working in the weeks surrounding the birth of her child. As well, it was assumed that childcare responsibilities consequent to birth made most mothers unavailable for work, even if they might be physically capable. Finally, pregnancy had a voluntary aspect which seemed to make it inappropriate for inclusion under UI.[8]

The 1962 Gill Committee report on UI recommended against maternity benefits on these grounds, and suggested that the administrative 'rule of thumb' that disqualified pregnant claimants for six weeks before and after the date of birth be expanded to eight weeks. Continued review of this problem through the 1960s however led to the inclusion of maternity benefits in the 1971 UI Act as a 'special benefit'.[9] The new maternity benefits were governed by sections 30 and 46 of the act. Section 30 provided for fifteen weeks of UI benefits upon proof of pregnancy, but only on the following conditions: claimants had to have had (i) twenty weeks of insurable employment in the last fifty-two and, (ii) ten weeks of employment in the twenty weeks immediately preceding the thirtieth week before the due date. This second condition came to be known as the 'magic ten' rule, and effectively limited maternity benefits to women who were working prior to their conception. This was deemed to be a valid test of bona fide attachment to the labour force, a logical prerequisite of UI. The magic ten rule also prevented women from entering the labour force after conception simply to qualify for UI maternity benefits several months later at the time of delivery. Section 46 disentitled pregnant claimants from regular UI benefits around the time of delivery if they could not qualify under section 30. Section 46 thus ensured a distinction between maternity and regular benefits. The intended effects of sections 30 and 46 on a working woman with a normal (i.e., forty weeks) pregnancy is illustrated in Figure 1.

Figure 1 *Maternity Benefits under the 1971 Unemployment Insurance Act*

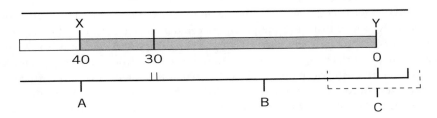

Under the 1971 act, a pregnant woman was required to have ten insurable weeks of employment in the twenty-week period (A) immediately preceding the thirtieth week before her expected date of confinement (B). Since a normal pregnancy lasts forty weeks from the date of conception (X) to the expected due date (Y), the magic ten rule meant that a claimant must have been working at or around the time of conception. Section 46 of the act prohibited benefits to pregnant claimants who did not meet the magic ten rule for a period commencing eight weeks before the expected date of confinement and ending six weeks after the actual date (C). This coincided with the maximum period for which maternity benefits could be paid.

The magic ten rule made the eligibility requirements for maternity benefits the strictest of any in the UI program. Regular UI benefits, for example, required only eight weeks of insurable employment. Feminist groups criticized this, and the issue finally came before the courts in the Stella Bliss case. Bliss had been dismissed by her Vancouver employer allegedly because she was pregnant, but Bliss successfully appealed to the British Columbia Human Rights Commission and was reinstated. In February 1977 she applied for UI maternity benefits, but failed to meet the magic ten rule, even though she had had twenty weeks of insurable employment in the last fifty-two. Bliss continued to work until 12 March, gave birth on 16 March, and then reapplied for UI benefits on 22 March, claiming that she was capable and available for work. The CEIC considered the application as one for maternity benefits, rejected it on the same grounds as before, and denied regular UI benefits because of section 46.

Bliss appealed on the grounds that section 46 violated the Canadian Bill of Rights' guarantee of 'equality before the law'. The case came before the Supreme Court of Canada, which in October 1978 decided against Bliss. The Court ruled that section 46 did not violate the equality provisions of the Bill of Rights because Bliss had not been denied 'equality in the application and administration of the law.'[10] This procedural interpretation of the equality provision was buttressed by the Court's assertion that any discrimination arising from sections 30 and 46 was due to 'nature' and not the legislation itself.

In the early months of 1978, in anticipation of the Supreme Court's decision in the *Bliss* case, the Benefit Policy Branch of the CEIC prepared a memorandum on the impact of an adverse decision and available options.[11] The CEIC memorandum correctly predicted that the Supreme Court would uphold sections 30 and 46, but also noted that this would be a 'Pyrrhic victory' because it would lead to political pressures to amend maternity provisions under the act. It proceeded to consider five 'operational alternatives' to the prevailing benefit provisions, and ultimately recommended revising section 46 to allow the payment of regular benefits if availability and capability could be demonstrated.[12]

A very different conclusion was reached in 1980 by Professor Marc Gold, in an influential *Osgoode Hall Law Journal* article on the Bliss case and equality rights. Gold persuasively argued that since the purely procedural meaning attributed to 'equality before the law' in Bliss still allowed for discriminatory laws, the Supreme Court should adopt a stricter, more substantive meaning. Gold advocated adopting a recent innovation from American jurisprudence known as the 'middle tier' or intermediate scrutiny test. According to this test, 'Laws that do differentiate on an enumerated basis should be evaluated closely to determine whether or not they are supported by good reasons.' Whether or not 'good reasons' existed would be determined by judges using a 'sophisticated balancing test'.[13] The factors to be balanced included 'the nature of the legislative classification, the importance of the benefit denied, and the importance of the government's reason for tailoring the law as it did'.[14] Armed with this new test for equality before the law, Gold concluded that the Supreme Court should have struck down both sections 30 and 46 as lacking sufficient reason and thus illegal.[15]

The Gold article's importance lies in the possibility that under the equality provisions of the new Charter of Rights, the Supreme Court will adopt a similar middle tier approach. Largely in response to intense lobbying by feminist organizations, the Charter's section 15 equality provisions were intentionally rewritten to force judges to apply a more demanding test than procedural fairness and equality. All legal commentaries on the Charter agree that if Bliss had arisen under the new Charter that sections 30 and 46 would have been held unconstitutional. These same commentators agree in recommending that the Supreme Court adopt some sort of middle tier scrutiny—or reasonableness test—similar to that used by Gold in order to make section 15 workable.[16]

How did the CEIC memorandum and the Gold article come to such different conclusions on the same issues? We suggest that the two documents exemplify two different logics or modes of reasoning, one administrative and the other judicial. In short, what was reasonable from the administrative perspective was seen as unreasonable from the legal perspective. Through a comparison of the Gold article with the CEIC memorandum, we can test for the presence of inherent differences between the judicial and the administrative approaches to policy problems. The comparison also discloses the kinds of conflicts that may arise between judges and administrators over section 15.[17] Our purpose is to elaborate these differences, and to warn against some of the problems associated with judicial policy-making. It is not our intention to defend one mode as inherently superior to the other.

COMPARISON OF DOCUMENTS

Discrimination

The most obvious and direct point of conflict between social benefit programs and the Charter of Rights is the issue of discrimination. The Charter, in the form of the section 15 equality rights, forbids it, while discrimination, in the dictionary sense, is required by almost all social benefit programs. The *Bliss* case is a representative example of the collision of these two conflicting mandates.

Discrimination, in its dictionary sense, simply means the process whereby different states or conditions are discerned or selected. In the administration of social policy, this ability to discriminate is essentially the process of deciding, in terms of the act, what are like cases and what are not. Most social programs deliver certain benefits to a target population. As well, the same programs may deliver a variety of benefits or a graduated scale of benefits. This means that program administrators must discriminate in two senses. They must discriminate their target population—e.g., youth, the elderly, citizens, women, babies, the poor, the rich—from everyone else. Then they often must be able to discriminate sub-populations within the overall target population who will receive different kinds or levels of benefits.

In UI the first distinction corresponds to the necessity of discriminating between labour force participants and non-participants. Traditionally labour force participation has been determined by whether a person is searching for and available for work, and capable of work if a job is offered. Within this broad target population, however, the program goes on to discriminate among various degrees of labour force attachment ('major' or 'minor'), as well as the different types of unemployment. For example, those who are unemployed because they quit their jobs without just cause are treated differently from those who are laid off.

Beginning on 17 April 1985, the day on which section 15 of the Charter took effect, all such distinctions must not 'discriminate' in a manner that violates the following right:

> Every individual is equal before and under the law and has the right to the equal protection and equal benefit of the law without discrimination and, in particular, without discrimination based on race, national or ethnic origin, colour, religion, sex, age or mental or physical disability.

As noted above, section 15 was worded in a manner expressly designed to force judges to review more than procedural fairness in the 'application and administration' of the laws. Judges will now be required to determine whether the law itself discriminates. Any statutory or administrative use of one of the enumerated grounds of discrimination will certainly constitute a prima facie case of illegal discrimination, although one that can perhaps be rebutted if judges can be persuaded that it is a 'reasonable' discrimination. Illegality is not limited, however, to the statutory use of race, religion, sex, etc. The 'equal benefit of the law' clause, designed specifically to overturn the logic of the Bliss decision, seeks to extend illegality to the discriminatory impact or effect of an otherwise permissible classification. Section 15 thus has the potential to subject almost all legislative and administrative classifications to judicial review. For even if a statute or regulation does not explicitly use one of the enumerated grounds of discrimination, it could still be scrutinized for unequal and thus discriminatory impact.

This was essentially the case in *Bliss,* where the impugned sections of UI did not discriminate between men and women, but between pregnant and non-pregnant persons. Bliss's argument, further elaborated by Gold, was not that the classification itself discriminated, but that its negative effect fell disproportionately, indeed exclusively, on women. It is at this point that what seems a reasonable and fair distinction from an internal, administrative perspective, can he seen as unfair and invidious discrimination from the judicial–civil liberties perspective.

In the context of the internal logic of the UI Act, the stricter requirements for maternity benefits appeared reasonable and predictable. The requirement of 'major attachment' (twenty weeks of insurable employment rather than eight), for example, was not limited to maternity benefits, but also applied to sickness benefits. Both maternity and sickness benefits differed from regular UI benefits by not requiring the recipient to be available for and capable of working. This is why they were designated 'special' benefits. Because they were more generous or 'forgiving' in this respect than regular UI benefits, they were intentionally limited to those with a longer period of attachment to the labour force. It was reasoned that such persons both deserved and needed the benefits more than persons with a shorter attachment to the labour force. In both the maternity and sickness benefits programs, the stricter criteria were also defended as lowering costs and reducing the likelihood of abuse. The magic ten rule was unique to the maternity benefits program, but it was the result of similar considerations of prior contributions, need and economy. Finally, the section 46 disqualification simply codified the pre-1971 administrative 'rule of thumb' presumption about availability and capability. In the process, it changed what had been a rebuttable presumption into an irrebuttable presumption. This was justified on the grounds of administrative efficiency, since there had been so few successful rebuttals under the old rule of thumb. In sum, the additions of sections 30 and 46 to UI in 1971 were presented as a generous extension of an entirely new package of benefits to working women, while its various restrictions seemed to be dictated by actuarial soundness and program logic.

From the judicial–civil liberties perspective, however, the new maternity benefits sections did not appear so generous nor the attendant restrictions so benign. As Gold is quick to point out, pregnancy benefits had the most stringent qualifying restrictions of any UI benefits: twenty weeks plus the magic ten. Since only women could be affected by these requirements, Gold is able to make a prima facie case of sex discrimination. Secondly, section 46 made it impossible for a pregnant applicant who failed to meet the strict criteria for section 30 benefits to collect regular UI benefits, even if she were otherwise qualified. This was Stella Bliss's predicament. The assumption that at and around the delivery date a pregnant woman is both incapable of and unavailable for work could not be rebutted by factual demonstration. A woman such as Bliss, who lost her job because of pregnancy, but was in fact still available for and capable of working, would be denied the regular UI benefits to which she would otherwise be entitled. Since this disadvantage could apply only to women, Bliss, Gold, and others have argued that section 46 also constituted an illegal instance of sex discrimination.

Sources of Institutional Authority

These two different responses to the problems raised in the Bliss case are explicable in large part by the different sources of authority and different purposes that govern and guide the behaviour of judges and administrators. For an administrator, the enabling statute defines both the source of his authority and purpose of his activity. By contrast, a judge's authority stems from the written constitution, and his mandate is to protect the enumerated rights of individuals. Starting from different points and directed by different purposes, it is not surprising that judges and administrators often recommend different solutions to the same problem.

All bureaucratic activity begins and ends with reference to 'the act'. Every department, commission, or agency of government has as its basis a statute that defines the structure, responsibilities and goals of the organization. The act serves several important functions from the bureaucrat's point of view. First, it sets out the scope of bureaucratic authority, and thus creates the possibility of action. It makes the bureaucrat's actions legal and legitimate. Within the bureaucratic psychology, the act takes on a central importance as the first mover in the official universe, the source of existence and energy. For this reason, officials are extremely reluctant to ignore or violate the act, even if it is badly drafted or otherwise flawed. A second function of the legislation is to express or codify the goals of a given public policy. Such goals are necessary to give direction to the exercise of administrative discretion on a day-to-day basis. In sum, officials need both a basis of authority and a purpose. Both of these are supplied by the legislation that governs their activity.

The UI Act fulfills both of these functions. It sets out fairly detailed program parameters, and outlines the structure and responsibilities of the commission that administers the act. The combination of sections and subsections defines the purpose of UI as ensuring against loss of earnings due to involuntary unemployment incurred by regular members of the labour force. This simple description distinguishes UI from other types of service delivery for the same problems. It is, first and foremost, an insurance program. However much the Canadian system has moved away from strict actuarial principles, this aspect of the program imposes many constraints. There must be contributions and these contributions must roughly balance benefits paid out. Potential for abuse and fraud must be minimized. The risk insured must be relatively specific and well defined. There is room for administrative discretion in determining what counts as 'earnings', 'involuntary unemployment', or 'regular member of the labour force', but the purpose of UI entails clear conceptual limits to the exercise of this discretion. The program could never pay out benefits not related to some form of contribution, or pay these benefits to people who had no intention of seeking employment. In expressing goals, the act outlines the program's rationale and logical foundation. The act and its meaning therefore play a central role in administrative logic.

Judges draw their authority and sense of purpose from very different sources. Under the Charter, judges are directly empowered to consider the constitutionality of all federal and provincial statutes and regulations, and to strike down as being 'of no force or effect' any that are inconsistent with the rights enumerated in the Charter.[18] This mandate places judges, or at least the judges of the Supreme Court of Canada, on an equal footing with Parliament and the provincial legislatures. Administrators, by contrast, draw their authority from the statutes, and are clearly the creatures of the legislative body.

The perspective and attitudes of judges and administrators are coloured by these differences in the sources of their authority. One entails a subordination of administrative discretion to legislative purpose, while the other encourages judicial assertiveness and creativity. The supremacy of the written constitution over ordinary statutes encourages a boldness that is uncommon in administrative decision-making. These differences are reflected in the very different solutions recommended to the *Bliss* case by the CEIC memorandum and by Gold.

The CEIC memorandum shows a consistent concern for maintaining continuity with and fidelity to the legislative purpose embodied in sections 30 and 46. The memorandum begins by situating the Bliss dispute in the context of the evolution of the UI Act, from the pre-1971 rule of thumb that excluded most pregnancy claims, to the 1971 changes effected by sections 30 and 46. After canvassing a number of possible responses to a Supreme Court decision striking down section 46, the CEIC memorandum recommends a preferred response: amend section 46 to allow women whose unemployment is caused by pregnancy/childbirth to apply for regular benefits pursuant to section 25 if they failed to qualify for the special maternity benefits of section 30. Since section 25 requires proof of both availability and capability, this recommendation really only amounts to a revival of the old pre-1971 rule of thumb.

The memorandum goes on to argue the advantages of this response, and they strongly reflect the traditional administrative imperatives: achieving consistency with legislative intent, minimizing additional expenditures, eliminating the grounds for any future legal challenge, and ensuring political acceptability.[19] The CEIC memorandum concludes with an interesting caveat. Acknowledging that 'there might be considerable pressure to abolish section 46 quickly', the memorandum recommends that 'the unknown magnitude of abuse might make it more prudent to only consider this question in the comprehensive review and study of all maternity provisions under the Act'.[20]

Both the content and the spirit of the CEIC recommendations contrast sharply with the judicial solution recommended by Gold. Gold argues that the courts should unilaterally strike down not just section 46 but also section 30's stricter qualifications for maternity benefits. Gold shows little concern for the additional costs that such changes would incur. Nor does he share the administrator's respect for consistency with the original legislative intent. Indeed, he flatly declares that Parliament's original intention was wrong:

> The Unemployment Insurance Act took a step in the right direction by recognizing the concept of maternity benefits, but it erred in treating pregnancy as a special case distinct from other temporary medical conditions. The Court should have insisted that the same regime apply to maternity benefits as applies to illness benefits. [21]

Such public defiance of parliamentary judgment is rare amongst civil servants, at least those who value their careers. And while it is also rare in pre-Charter judicial behaviour in Canada, American experience indicates that when judges are armed with a constitutionally entrenched Bill of Rights, they can become much less deferential to legislative judgment.

COSTS VERSUS RIGHTS

Maximizing the efficient use of limited resources is a major factor in administrative decision-making. New program proposals are always accompanied by cost analyses, and are almost never assessed simply in terms of equity or principle. If decisions involve significant new costs, they must be considered at higher levels, often even by the minister. This is especially true of insurance-based programs such as UI, where a balance between premiums paid in and benefits paid out is a practical necessity, at least over the medium term. In the case of UI, cost consciousness is further heightened by the administrators' awareness that there is considerable public criticism of UI for not being cost-efficient. The increasing concern over the problem of government expenditure growth, to which UI is a major contributor, has further strengthened this bureaucratic reflex.

By contrast, costs are at best a secondary consideration for the courts. Under the Charter of Rights, judicial inquiry is narrowly focused on the question of whether or not a right exists or has been violated. As Donald Horowitz has pointed out,

The initial focus on rights is also a serious impediment to the analysis of costs, for, in principle at least, if rights exist they are not bounded by considerations of cost. If a person possesses a right, he possesses it whatever the cost.[22]

This difference in perspective is very much in evidence in the Gold and CEIC treatment of the *Bliss* case.

In anticipation of a possible adverse Supreme Court decision striking down section 46, the CEIC memorandum projected the additional costs to be in the vicinity of $20–$25 million in regular benefit payments.[23] The memorandum characterized this amount as a 'considerable amount of money in potential benefit payouts'. The memorandum went on to note a variety of secondary costs that would be incurred by making the necessary changes to UI brochures, claims packages, and audio-visual materials.[24] From the commission's perspective, the seriousness of the issue was in direct proportion to the additional costs that it might incur.

The commission's response to this problem was to work up a list of possible 'operational alternatives' to an adverse judicial decision—a task that occupies the largest single section of the memorandum. Horowitz has noted that listing policy options is the archetypical legislative/administrative response to a policy problem, and one that reflects the primacy of costs in the legislative/administrative calculus.[25] This cost consciousness is also reflected in the final recommendation to the CEIC—to amend section 46 to allow women to claim regular benefits if they can satisfy the section 25 criteria of being both available for and capable of work. In listing the advantages of this approach over the others considered, the memorandum declares that, 'The proposal should not result in significant expenditures for the Commission in terms of benefits or operational cost.'[26]

These concerns for conserving limited resources contrast sharply with Gold's approach. There is no canvassing of alternatives for the most cost-effective solution to the problem. Indeed, Gold's single-minded focus on the question of rights leads to a rather different perception of what the problem is. While Gold is aware that his proposed judicial resolution of the Bliss case may entail additional costs, he is not deterred by it. With reference to the problems of guarding against abuse without the section 46 exclusion, he simply declares, 'When important rights are at stake, arguments of efficiency cannot be allowed to prevail.' And when he goes on to recommend that the Supreme Court strike down the stricter requirements for section 30 benefits, he declares that, 'If it is the case that women are being treated unfairly by the Act as it now stands, the increased cost is the price that must be paid.'[27]

Scope and Consistency

One reason that judges are prone to ignore administrative costs is the much narrower focus of judicial inquiry. The traditional 'adjudication of disputes' function of courts concentrates judicial focus on the particular case before the court. The mandate of the court is to settle this dispute justly. Administrators, by contrast, must think in terms of *all* potential cases arising under a given regulation, not one case in particular. The scope of their concern must of necessity be broader, and they must try to maintain consistency across all cases in terms of legislative intent. While fairness is one factor in the administrative calculus, it must be balanced against considerations of legislative intent, administrative efficiency, and accompanying costs.

The narrower focus of judicial inquiry is reinforced by the judges' distance from and unfamiliarity with the social and policy milieu within which the case arises. The traditional methods of judicial fact-finding further compound 'this abstraction of the case from its more general social context'. The adversary process is designed to elicit only 'historical facts', a factual account of what actually transpired between the two parties to a specific dispute. By contrast, administrators and other policy-makers are less interested in what happened in this or that particular case, than in the general run of cases. Sound public policy is based on a knowledge of 'social facts', or 'recurrent patterns of behaviour'.[28] Because of traditional rules of evidence, judges are rarely able to collect and acquaint themselves with social facts.[29] The result is that in many cases, judges try to infer more general patterns of behaviour from the one set of facts that they do know. That is, they simply assume that the case before them is representative. This is a wholly gratuitous assumption and is often false.[30]

In recent years the Supreme Court has taken important steps to try to insure that it is better informed of the social facts that surround its constitutional decisions. The Court had been sharply criticized for deciding important constitutional cases in a virtual factual vacuum and without any knowledge of potential policy impact.[31] Perhaps in response to these criticisms, in the 1970s the Supreme Court began to make more extensive use of 'legislative history' such as Hansard, government white papers, and other forms of 'extrinsic evidence'.[32] In its first Charter decision, Justice Estey, writing for a unanimous court, made use of scholarly commentary from law journals, and cited with approval the trend of 'broadening the scope of the record in constitutional cases before this court'.[33] These developments notwithstanding, the judicial use of social facts remains problematic. Even in the case most celebrated for its novel use of extrinsic evidence—the 1976 *Anti-Inflation* Reference—the judges made scant use of the economic data they received. Finally, even in the unlikely event that judges possess the identical social facts as administrators, it is still possible that they would draw different conclusions, because of the different institutional biases already described.

These differences of perspective are very much in evidence in the CEIC memorandum and the Gold article. While Gold concedes that section 46 might have as its purpose 'the protection of the fund against . . . fraud and abuse', he counters that there is 'no question of fraud in circumstances like those of Mrs Bliss', since she was only claiming ordinary (not maternity) benefits and was willing and able to work.[34] What Gold passes over here is the question of determining whether Mrs Bliss's claim to meet the requirements of being available for and capable of working were true, and the administrative costs of making such determinations, not just for Mrs Bliss but for all similar applications.

Referring to the same situation, the CEIC memorandum found it to be much more problematic. The main problem here would be in the application of section 25 to pregnant claimants filing for regular benefits. It is to be expected that there could be an increase in abuse in that some women, not eligible for maternity benefits, could dishonestly assert that they were available and capable in order to receive regular benefits. There would be little the commission could do about this as the control feature specifically designed to prevent it (section 46) would have been struck down by the Supreme Court.

The CEIC memorandum goes on to argue that the problem of abuse 'could well be significant', and that it would be further compounded by the Commission's legal inability to determine if the claimant were in fact pregnant. The memorandum concludes by characterizing such a situation as 'very difficult' to control. In addition to the potential for fraud, the commission identified another problem in demonstrating capability for work through medical certificates as 'the reluctance [of doctors] to issue large numbers of medical certificates for this purpose'. A final problem was that 'the certificate would only state that the claimant was capable as of that day and would be useless for any subsequent period'.[35]

In sum, considerations of administrative efficiency and preventing abuse play a major role in the CEIC's analysis of the issues raised by Bliss, but are completely absent from Gold's treatment of the same issues. Because he deals 'at retail' with the individual case before him, Gold argues that Stella Bliss should be treated the same as other applicants for 'ordinary' benefits. From the 'wholesale' perspective of the administrator, such a procedure seems prone to abuse, complicated to administer, and expensive. This disagreement is not unique to the *Bliss* case, but can be understood as the predictable consequence of the different mandates, different focuses, and different factual knowledge of judges and administrators.

Probabilistic Versus Last Case Reasoning

Yet another aspect of the single-case focus of judicial inquiry is what Horowitz has described as the 'last case' character of legal reasoning. Last case reasoning refers to the tendency of lawyers and judges to concentrate on the unusual or exceptional case, rather than the general run of cases. By contrast, Horowitz ascribes a 'probabilistic' style of reasoning to policy-makers, a tendency to concentrate on the typical case, and to design policies that work most of the time for most people. In designing the qualifying criteria for benefit programs, for example, Horowitz points out that it is often counterproductive to concentrate on or even to accommodate the exceptional case.

The section 46 exclusion is a good example of this phenomenon. From the UI–CEIC perspective, section 46 covered the general run of cases. Working women who were regular members of the labour force could meet the section 30 requirements, and thus were not usually affected by section 46.[36] For those who failed to meet the section 30 requirements, experience under the pre-1971 rule of thumb demonstrated that very few women who were unemployed by reason of pregnancy or recent childbirth could prove that they were capable of and available for work. Thus, they could not qualify for regular UI benefits even in the absence of section 46. Section 46 would thus have a minimal impact on working women, was simple to understand and to administer, and was cost-efficient. Any casualties of section 46's irrebuttable presumption (such as Stella Bliss) were simply the marginal cost of its other advantages.

What is a marginal cost from the program administrators' perspective becomes the central focus in the judicial forum. The judge is concerned not with what happens most of the time to most of the people, but with what happened to the individual before him. Gold's approach to the *Bliss* case illustrates this tendency. First, Gold is principally concerned with the plight of Mrs. Bliss. To the extent that he addresses the issues of discrimination against women in general, he mistakenly assumes that Bliss is representative of most working women. Secondly, Gold treats sections 30 and 46 as separate issues. In separating what in practice are two parts of a whole, he obscures the policy logic that links the two. Gold then formulates the central legal issue raised by section 46 as follows: 'Is there a good reason for denying Mrs Bliss ordinary benefits contemplated by the Act?'[37] Having abstracted Bliss's case from the treatment of women generally, and having further isolated section 46 from section 30, it is hardly surprising that Gold concludes that section 46 does indeed discriminate against Bliss in particular and women in general.

The policy-maker is likely to perceive great irony and even perversity in the suggestion that section 46 discriminates against women. From this perspective section 46 cannot he separated from section 30. Together, they constituted a dramatic expansion of UI benefits for working women, with no corresponding increase in contributions. Section 46 by itself adversely affected a small proportion of female workers. Indeed, with respect to disproportionate or discriminatory impact on the sexes, an equally plausible case could be made that it is men who are discriminated against. Men are excluded, a priori, from the benefit program with the least strict requirements in all of UI—one that waives the traditional requirements of availability and capability. Moreover, male workers help to pay for a benefit program—the most expensive of all the special benefit programs—from which they cannot individually collect benefits. Indeed, male workers as a group have always contributed much more in UI premiums than they have drawn in benefits, while the opposite is true of female workers. In short, UI *as a whole* constitutes a net transfer to women.[38] No doubt there are a number of good and defensible reasons for this pattern, but it undermines the force of the claim that section 46 discriminates against women.

It would be reassuring to assume, as Gold seems to, that favourable judicial judgments on single cases will 'tidy up' legislative programs such as UI, that 'correcting' the exceptions will improve the general rule. On this view, judicial review could complement administrative decision-making, not conflict with it. While this happy coincidence may sometimes occur, there are good reasons to doubt that it will be the norm. First, any single case may be more or less extreme, more or less rare. When a judge undertakes to redesign social benefit or regulatory programs based on a single case, he risks basing his decision on a highly unusual set of circumstances. Bliss's case was not unique, but neither was it typical. Secondly, such decisions are likely to have secondary and unanticipated consequences for other aspects of the program. Most programs or policies consist of a web of rules, each intertwined with the other, and all drawing their rationale from the overall purpose(s) of the program. To outsiders, including judges, this web may be only dimly intelligible. While a judicial decision involving an unusual case may improve one rule, it may simultaneously upset the balance among the rest.

In UI, for example, we have noted that there was already a net transfer from male contributors to female beneficiaries. If Gold had actually been a judge, his attempt to rectify the discrimination against women that he found in sections 30 and 46, would have actually increased the discriminatory effect of UI as a whole on male contributors. Most social benefit and regulatory programs share the characteristic of constituting a complex matrix of interrelated rules. As a result, judicial tinkering in one area may create unanticipated and sometimes equally troublesome consequences in other areas of the program. While this may occur with administrative tinkering as well, the generalist character of judges makes judicial law reform more prone to unanticipated consequences.

Institutional Mandate

A final difference in the approaches of administrators and judges to the same policy problems is found in their institutional mandates. The effect of institutional mandate is admittedly intangible and difficult to isolate, but this does not preclude helpful generalizations about inherent differences between the behaviour of judges and administrators, differences rooted in the structural differences of courts and administrative agencies.

The mandate of judges and administrators is quite different. Under the Charter, the judges are in effect placed as watchdogs over legislative and administrative conduct. The judicial mandate is to enforce the broadly worded liberties and rights of the Charter. In the minds of some jurists, this amounts to an invitation to translate natural law into positive law, or morality into public policy.[39] Stated this baldly, such a proposition is fraught with serious problems of the authority and the competency of judges to undertake such law-making. But even after all the necessary qualifications have been added, there remains a broad incentive for judges to conceive their purpose under the Charter as promoting a 'more just' society.

This is a heady mandate indeed, and in the United States there is evidence that it has affected federal judges' perception of their role and function. According to one defender of judicial activism, 'an elite tradition animates the federal judiciary, instilling elan and a sense of mission in federal judges . . .'[40] A recent opinion survey study also found that American 'legal elites' consistently supported more libertarian positions than the mass public or community leaders.[41] This sentiment is sometimes expressed as a consequence of the superior institutional competence of courts 'to move us in the direction of a right answer' in human rights issues.[42] However this phenomenon is described, it contributes to the aggressive posture assumed by federal judges toward Congress and especially state legislatures.

The political considerations that govern the exercise of administrative discretion are quite different. In theory, bureaucrats are explicitly subordinated to their political superiors, usually in the form of the responsible cabinet minister. While in practice bureaucrats often enjoy considerable autonomy from ministerial control, they know that there are limits to this independence. While administrators, like judges, have their personal opinions about larger issues of social justice, they are explicitly discouraged in most instances from translating these opinions into public policy. Rather, they are constrained by their legal subordination to the cabinet, and their statutory mandate to implement parliamentary purpose. Administrators provide opinions on technical matters and the probable political repercussions of policy options, but their personal political convictions are unimportant.

These differences are reflected in the CEIC memorandum and the Gold article. The CEIC memorandum repeatedly raises the threat posed to political support by the impending Supreme Court decision in *Bliss*. The concept of political support is used in multiple senses to denote public support for UI generally, support for Liberal government policy, and cabinet support for the CEIC and its staff. These of course are all related from the staff's point of view. In assessing the probable impact of an adverse Supreme Court decision, the memorandum accords the second highest priority to the political impact. The memorandum warns that even if the legality of section 46 is upheld, it would probably be 'politically expedient to amend section 46', because such a court decision would likely serve as a catalyst to increase public criticism of the act. On the same theme, it is noted that one of the advantages of an adverse decision would be to remove 'one cause of increasing criticism of the Commission'. A bit further in the memorandum, one of the operational alternatives considered is to abolish sections 30 and 46, and 'to allow maternity benefits to be paid as sickness benefits'. While the memorandum sees some merit in this approach, it ends by cautioning that this course of action could be seen by women's groups 'as an attempt to deprive women of an acquired right and therefore meet with considerable opposition.' Finally, in assessing the advantages of its recommended course of action—to amend section 46 to accommodate cases such as Bliss—the memorandum stresses that it would be 'politically and socially acceptable' and that 'women's groups and civil liberties groups would probably also approve it'.[43]

Such considerations of political expediency and political support are not to be found in Gold's analysis of the problem. In concluding that both section 30 and 46 should be declared illegal instances of sex discrimination, Gold reveals the much broader premise of his position:

> Underlying this argument is the belief that, if women are to enjoy equal opportunity to participate in social life, the social value of child-bearing ought to be given full currency in the law. . . . Indeed, a revolution must take place in the way in which the role of women in our society is perceived.[44]

While Gold is quick to concede that such a change will require 'a systematic approach', and not just piecemeal changes to UI, this does not mean that the court should not intervene. 'The better way is not the only way,' he quips. In short, Gold thinks that judges, armed with the Bill of Rights, and now the Charter, have their own special role to play in hastening the 'revolution'.

It is true that to date most Canadian judges have not shown much enthusiasm for using the Charter to become architects of social reform. The reasonable limitations clause of section 1 signifies that no right is absolute, and invites the judges to be sensitive to a government's policy reasons for limiting an enumerated right.[45] However, the significance of this early judicial deference to legislative judgment is not clear. No doubt it reflects the continued influence of the tradition of judicial self-restraint engendered by over a century of Canada's unique form of parliamentary supremacy. The question is whether this tradition will sustain itself under the new regime of constitutional supremacy and enhanced judicial authority.

A tradition is really no more than the collective habits of a generation. The generation of judges, lawyers, and scholars who gave such cautious and narrow interpretation to the 1960 Bill of Rights is giving way to a new and younger generation of Canadian lawyers. This new generation, men and women like Marc Gold, has been inspired by the social reform decisions of the Warren Court in the United States, and aspire to create a Canadian version. The adoption of the Charter of Rights in 1982 was a crucial first step in this direction. Aided and abetted by interest groups who share a similar political vision, it is doubtful that future Canadian judges can completely resist the opportunity to play the role of architects of social reform offered by the Charter of Rights. By contrast, there is continued pressure to reduce the discretion and autonomy of public administrators.

CONCLUSION

The *Bliss* case and the related documents discussed in this article reveal sharp differences in the way courts and administrators process policy problems. This case study has examined one program, unemployment insurance, and an aspect of that program, maternity benefits. But the problems raised by the old sections 30 and 46 of the UI Act are routinely addressed by administrators of most social programs in Canada. For example, various youth programs explicitly discriminate on the basis of age in the distribution of special benefits. Is this the kind of age discrimination prohibited by section 15 of the Charter? UI also discriminates on the basis of residence and the level of local unemployment. Two unemployed workers with identical work histories can receive quite different levels of benefits depending upon where they live. Will judges agree that there are sufficient 'good reasons' to justify this type of different treatment of similarly situated individuals? Social assistance programs also provide different types and levels of benefits depending on characteristics such as age, disability, family status and need. Is it 'reasonable' that in certain cases an elderly, disabled person should receive less in social assistance benefits than a single mother with school-aged children? Problems of this sort can be endlessly multiplied.

Further problems arise from the fact that in many cases uniform application of an economic or social program will have different effects on different sub-populations of the general public. In other words, equal treatment can produce unequal results because of differences between the groups affected. In UI prior to the 1971 reforms, the requirements of ability and availability clearly had a disproportionately negative impact on married working women of child-bearing age. Conversely, the maternity benefits provisions introduced in 1971 had a similarly unequal impact on male workers. Would either of these policies violate the right to the 'equal benefit of the law' guaranteed by section 15?

The point is not that programs of this sort are indefensible, but that the intended and even unintended discriminatory aspects of most public policies reflect the logic of the statute and the exigencies of administration. The need to discriminate among target populations, the need to consider the most efficient distribution of limited resources, the need to remain consistent with program logic, the enabling statute, and the wishes of the legislature, all confront the public official as he administers programs. These amount to nothing less than an 'institutional logic' of public administration, irrespective of the specific policy or program in question.

A very different logic may now guide judicial inquiry under the section 15 equality rights of the Charter, especially if Gold's middle tier mode of analysis is adopted. The courts, and the Supreme Court in particular, will be encouraged by the Charter to apply a new logic, a logic of rights rather than of costs, of justice rather than efficiency, ultimately the logic of the Charter rather than the enabling statute. Charter-based legal reasoning leads, as the Gold article suggests, to conclusions very different from those reached by administrators. This clash of logics is likely to occur no matter who the judges or administrators happen to be.

It would be misleading to conclude that this conflict is simply the clash of justice against administrative efficiency. Judges do not have a monopoly on justice, but only on a particular method—a very individualistic method—of posing and answering questions of justice. While this distinctive judicial method may well serve the ends of justice in resolving traditional kinds of criminal and civil disputes, it does not follow that it is well suited for designing the eligibility rules and benefit structures of social programs. As our analysis of Gold's solution to the Bliss case indicates, judicial intervention to remove an injustice in one area of a program may actually exacerbate anomalies or discrimination in other areas. Moreover, administrative efforts to efficiently utilize the taxpayers' money and to follow legislative intent are not devoid of justice. The morality of individual rights must be juxtaposed with the morality of government by consent of the governed.

NOTES

1. This is the thesis of Peter H. Russell, 'The Effect of a Charter of Rights on the Policy-Making role of Canadian Courts', *Canadian Public Administration* 25 (Spring 1982), pp. 1–33.
2. There are several important exceptions. Section 6, dealing with 'mobility rights', can be said to create rights that did not exist before. The same is true of section 23, minority language education rights; section 25, aboriginal rights; and section 23(2), the conditional exclusionary rule. The new wording of 'equality rights' in section 15 seems to necessitate a new meaning to the traditional concept of 'equality before the law'. Section 10(b) takes a traditional right, the right to counsel, and extends it: the right to be informed of the right to counsel. For a more detailed account, see Peter W. Hogg. 'A Comparison of the Canadian Charter of Rights and Freedoms with the Canadian Bill of Rights', in Walter S. Tarnopolsky and Gerald A. Beaudoin, eds, *The Canadian Charter of Rights and Freedoms: Commentary* (Toronto: Carswell, 1982), pp. 2–24.
3. This issue has been partially addressed by Tom Flanagan 'Policy-Making by Exegesis: The Abolition of "Mandatory Retirement" in Manitoba', *Canadian Public Policy*, 11 (March 1985), pp. 40–53.
4. *Bliss v. A.-G. Canada* [1979] 1 S.C.R. 183, 92 D.L.R. (3d) 417.
5. Marc Emmett Gold, 'Equality Before the Law in the Supreme Court of Canada: A Case Study', *Osgoode Hall Law Journal* 18, 3 (1980), pp. 336–427.

6. Strictly speaking, of course, the Gold article is not a judicial approach but rather a law review article. However, it is still reasonable to characterize it as a judicial approach for purposes of comparison. Its 'reasonable basis' method of analysis is the approach of the US Supreme Court, and Gold clearly advocates that it should become the approach of the Canadian Supreme Court. Indeed, Gold 'retries' the case using this approach and 'rules' in favour of Bliss. Finally, most of the best-known commentators on the Charter have recommended that the Supreme Court adopt this mode of analysis for interpreting the equality rights section of the Charter. (See below and footnote 16.) Since the Charter did not take effect until 17 April 1985, it remains to be seen whether the Supreme Court will follow this advice. To the extent that it does, then the problems elaborated in this article are likely to be realized.

7. We restrict our analysis to program administration, leaving aside regulatory activity and state enterprise. The Charter will undoubtedly affect these aspects of administration as well, but they are beyond the scope of this inquiry.

8. Report of the Committee of Inquiry into the Unemployment Insurance Act (Ottawa: Queen's Printer, 1962), pp. 30–1.

9. These changes had been recommended by a study published in 1968, *Report of the Study for Updating the Unemployment Insurance Programme* (Ottawa: Unemployment Insurance Commission, 1969), 2, Chapter 9; and a white paper released in 1970, *Unemployment Insurance in the 70s* (Ottawa: Department of Labour, 1970).

10. This interpretation had been established by the earlier Supreme Court decision in *A.-G. Canada v. Lavell and Bedard*, 33 D.L.R. (3d) 481 (1973).

11. Canada Employment and Immigration Commission, Benefit Policy Branch, 'A Discussion Paper Concerning the Aftermath of the Supreme Court Decision', 1978. Acquired through the Access to Information Act. Hereinafter referred to as CEIC Memorandum.

12. CEIC Memorandum, pp. 30–1. The alternatives were: revert to the pre-1971 policy; repeal section 46 and pay the applicable benefit; amend section 30 and eliminate the 'magic ten' rule; amend section 25(b) to allow maternity benefits to be paid as sickness benefits; and to rewrite section 46 to allow the collection of regular benefits if availability and capability could be demonstrated.

13. Gold, 'Equality Before the Law', pp. 382–3.

14. Ibid., p. 411.

15. Ibid., pp. 415 and 422. 'The question that must he addressed is whether there are good reasons for distinguishing in this way between maternity benefits and all other benefits available under the UI Act.'

16. In an article written after the Charter was adopted, Gold himself advocates essentially the same flexible approach to section 15 that he urged in his earlier article on *Bliss*. See Marc Gold, 'A Principled Approach to Equality Rights: A Preliminary Inquiry', in E.P. Belobaba and E. Gertner, eds, *The New Constitution and the Charter of Rights: Fundamental Issues and Strategies, Supreme Court Law Review* (1982), pp. 131–94, especially 151–54. A similar approach is advocated by W.S. Tarnopolsky, 'The Equality Rights', in Tarnopolsky and Beaudoin, *The Charter*, pp. 395–442, at 422; and Peter W. Hogg, *Canada Act Annotated* (Toronto: Carswell, 1982), pp. 50–1.

17. Section 15 of the Charter did not take effect until 17 April 1985. This three year

moratorium was intended to allow all governments to conduct an audit of existing statutes to discover and to correct any probable infractions of the new equality rights. The Government of Saskatchewan recently released a discussion paper concerning its audit. The audit revealed that the three most common types of discrimination were sex, age, and mental or physical disability. See 'Compliance of Saskatchewan Laws with the Canadian Charter of Rights and Freedoms', Department of Justice, Government of Saskatchewan, September 1984.

18. Charter of Rights and Freedoms, sections 33, 52.
19. CEIC Memorandum, p. 31. The memorandum listed the following advantages: '(1) The periods provided for by sections 30 and 46 would once again be the same as was the intent of the legislator in 1971, (2) The inequity caused by the present section 46 would be eliminated, (3) Persons would not be able to receive maternity and regular benefits at the same time, (4) The maximum number of benefits weeks for maternity would continue to be 15 as set out in Section 22(3a), (5) All fifteen weeks of maternity benefits would have to be drawn in the prescribed period, (6) Claimants not having the "magic ten" weeks would be able to draw regular benefits providing they could also prove availability and capability or prescribed illness, injury or quarantine, (7) Minor attachment claimants would be able to draw regular benefits providing they could prove availability and capability, (8) All the elements which gave rise to the Bliss case would be rectified, (9) The proposals should be politically and socially acceptable assuming it were properly explained and publicized. Women's groups and civil liberties groups would probably also approve it, (10) The proposal should not result in significant expenditures for the Commission in terms of benefits or operational costs.'
20. CEIC Memorandum, p. 34.
21. Gold, 'Equality Before the Law', p. 426.
22. Donald L. Horowitz, *The Courts and Social Policy* (Washington, DC: The Brookings Institute, 1977), p. 34.
23. CEIC Memorandum, pp. 14–5. The immediate costs using 1977 figures would be $9.8 million. The higher figure accounts for the anticipated increase in the number of claim applications if the section 46 restrictions were removed.
24. Ibid., pp. 15–6.
25. Horowitz, *The Courts and Social Policy*, p. 34.
26. CEIC Memorandum, pp. 30–1.
27. Gold, 'Equality Before the Law', pp. 416, 425.
28. Horowitz, *The Courts and Social Policy*, p. 45.
29. The rule against hearsay evidence, for example, normally prohibits the introduction of books and reports that might provide a better picture of the social facts. Nor does allowing exceptions to the hearsay rule solve this problem. See ibid., pp. 48–9.
30. Ibid., pp. 46–7.
31. See Paul Weiler, *In the Last Resort: A Critical Study of the Supreme Court of Canada* (Toronto: Carswell, 1974), pp. 156–63.
32. See Peter Hogg, 'Proof of Facts in Constitutional Cases', *University of Toronto Law Journal* 26 (1977), p. 386.
33. *Law Society of Upper Canada v. Skapinker* [1984] D.L.R. (4th), p. 180.

34. Gold, 'Equality Before the Law', p. 416.
35. CEIC Memorandum, pp. 23–4.
36. Recent analysis indicated that 77 per cent of maternity benefit claimants had over forty weeks of insurable employment before their claim. In other words, the magic ten rule does not exclude many women from collecting maternity benefits. See Employment and Immigration Canada, *Unemployment Insurance in the 1980s* (Ottawa: Minister of Supply and Services, 1981), p. 68.
37. Gold, 'Equality Before the Law', p. 415.
38. See Employment and Immigration Canada, Strategic Planning and Policy Group, 'Distributive and Redistributive Effects of the UI Program', Technical Study 10 of *Unemployment Insurance in the 1980s* (Ottawa: Employment and Immigration Canada, August 1981), p. 15.
39. See Walter Berns, 'Has the Burger Court Gone Too Far?' *Commentary*, 78 (October 1984), p. 27. Berns quotes a Federal Appeals Court judge to the effect that 'the Warren Court taught the country that there need be no "gulf between the law and morality."' The most radical of the Warren Court activists, the late Justice William Douglas, is said to be 'esteemed in liberal circles precisely because . . . he "dared" to raise the question of what was good for the country and then to translate (or at least try to translate) his answers into constitutional law.'
40. Burt Neuborne, 'The Myth of Parity', *Harvard Law Review* 90 (1977), p. 1105.
41. See Herbert McCloskey and Alida Brill, *Dimensions of Tolerance: What Americans Believe About Civil Liberties* (New York: Russell Sage Foundation, 1983).
42. Michael J. Perry, *The Constitution, the Courts, and Human Rights* (New Haven: Yale University Press, 1983), p. 102.
43. CEIC Memorandum, pp. 12–32.
44. Gold, 'Equality Before the Law', p. 426.
45. In its only two Charter decisions to date—*Law Society of Upper Canada v. Skapinker*, [1984] D.L.R. (4th), p. 161, and *Southam Inc. v. Hunter*, 17 September 1984, unreported—the Supreme Court has expressly avoided interpreting the section 1 reasonable limits clause.

26

The Rise and Fall of Policy Planning and Research Units: An Organizational Perspective

Michael J. Prince and John A. Chenier

Abstract. Some observers have suggested the success of policy planning and research units depends upon the receptivity of the political system to rationality. Others have put forward personality traits such as 'flair' and 'diplomatic style' as the major determinants of policy unit effectiveness. Neither of these would seem to provide an adequate explanation for the Canadian experience. This paper concentrates on the profile which a policy unit might assume in any given organization. A two-dimensional model is presented based on the degree of initiative and the degree of visibility of policy units. Against the background of the model, the experience of these units in the Canadian federal bureaucracy suggests that while most start as highly visible and proactive, they later tend toward being invisible and reactive.

With a view to the future, a distinction is made between the policy development function and the policy unit. If policy development and analysis is to survive, greater use must be made of a task force approach. If permanent policy units are to survive and be effective, they should adopt a modest role and profile.

INTRODUCTION

Government bureaucracies in Canada have undergone many significant institutional and policy process changes over the past decade. One of the most striking developments has been the introduction of a large number of personnel and procedures, often within new units, to initiate, develop, and analyse policies and programs. For present purposes, we refer to these new structures as policy planning and research units.

Policy planning and research units are government 'staff' organizations, generally responsible for analysing and proposing new policy and program initiatives in order to improve the process and content of government performance. More specifically, these units are intended to assemble and analyse information for the planning and formulation of policy; identify future policy problems and objectives; and consider the likely future implications of ongoing programs in the medium and long term.[1]

The intellectual, technical, and political constraints facing organizational

Michael J. Prince and John A. Chenier, 'The Rise and Fall of Policy Planning and Research Units: An Organizational Perspective', *Canadian Public Administration* 23, 4 (1980): 519–41. Courtesy of The Institute of Public Administration Canada.

reforms in government are well recognized in the literature.[2] Unfortunately, the impact of organizational factors on new policy planning and research structures, and related issues of organizational politics and behaviour, have received less attention. Little theoretical or empirical analysis has been done on how organizational variables effect the success or failure of these policy structures. As one group of writers recently noted:

> The 'problem' of the apparent irreconcilability of rational approaches to the policy decision within the political context of the policy making process has been a matter of concern to several writers, and there have been attempts to re-orientate analysis and model building to take more account of the political process of policy evaluation. Nevertheless the main result has been to emphasize the legitimated political arena rather than internal organizational politics.[3]

The politics of the organizational setting in which policy advisers work 'are rarely explicitly included in policy models'.[4] Organizational politics in the policy planning process can include actors' perceptions as related to their roles and their environments, considerations of feasibility in both a rational and subjective sense, negotiations between advisers and clients, agency philosophies, institutional interests, administrative processes and routines, and patterns of organizational power.[5]

In this article we will identify and examine some key organizational dimensions which influence the successful adoption of policy units and propose a framework for the analysis of such reforms. Against a background of the framework, evidence will be presented related to the introduction of policy units in the Canadian federal bureaucracy. The experience of these units highlights the significance of organizational factors on attempts of reform. The article concludes with some recommendations to enhance both the policy planning function and the performance of policy planning units.

Policy Unit Profiles

Policy planning units can assume a wide array of profiles and roles. There are, of course, a number of factors which are important to consider in studying these structures, and which could account for variations in the assumed role. Factors that can have important consequences for the success of any given policy unit include: the role conceptions and skills of officials; the nature of the organization in which the unit is located; and the presence of other advisory structures internal and external to the organization.[6]

For our purposes, however, we are concerned with two aspects of organizational structure and behaviour, which seem to us to be particularly important for an understanding of policy planning and research structures in government. All organizations carry out some functions or activities and all conduct interactions with their environment. Hence activity and interaction constitute two major dimensions which can be used for examining policy units. The first aspect we shall examine therefore is the type of activity, operationalized in terms of the degree of *initiative* a unit has in generating proposals. The second is the *visibility* of the unit to other actors in the organization. Both of these organizational factors can be viewed as dimensions or continua along which are various degrees. The concepts of initiative and visibility call attention to the functional nature of administrative reforms and their interorganizational implications.

Degree of Initiative

The diverse activities of policy planning units can be compared and considered in terms of the degree of initiative a unit has in generating new proposals. Policy units can be placed along a continuum where at one end are units whose sole task is to analyse proposals generated by persons outside of the unit, while at the other end are units which, in themselves, are the source of all new innovative proposals in the organization. The former type will be referred to as reactive units and the latter will be called proactive units. As one moves along the continuum between the two, the responsibility for developing innovative proposals becomes more or less centralized in the unit.

A reactive unit does not serve as a source of innovative policy or program ideas; it merely appraises and maybe responds to suggestions emanating from other parts of the organization. For a number of reasons which will be discovered below, this type of policy unit encounters the least amount of resistance from other actors in the organization. The major factor which limits the usefulness of a reactive unit is the quality and quantity of the proposals flowing in from the rest of the organization. If other units of the organization lack the resources—both time and intelligence—to develop proposals, the effectiveness of, and the need for, this type of unit will be minimal. In such cases, there is a greater likelihood that the organization will establish a unit responsible for generating new ideas of its own, namely a proactive unit.

A proactive unit has, in its extreme form, a monopoly in the elaboration of innovative proposals in the organization. Such a unit may be considered necessary in cases where the organization does not have or has not demonstrated a capacity to produce the strategies required to keep pace with changes in the environment. In a less extreme form, it may be established in order to generate competing alternatives to those which are emanating from other units within the organization. Whatever the reasons for the creation of such a unit, we will argue that the acceptance of the unit and its proposals is difficult to procure.

Visibility

The second organizational aspect we are concerned with is the visibility of a policy unit to other actors in the organization. In part, visibility is a function of size of the unit. The more personnel engaged in a function, the harder it is to disguise the work or, conversely, justify the lack of tangible output. In addition to size is the frequency and location of boundary exchanges, that is, the various interactions between a unit and its immediate task environment. Finally, and most important, is the nature of the role and impact in the policy process (in either a reactive or proactive sense).[7]

Different combinations of these factors will result in substantial variations in the visibility of a policy unit from nearly invisible to highly visible.

A unit that is relatively invisible does not interact with other units. It receives no input and delivers no output to other parts of the organization. Its sole contact for these items is the line manager whom it serves. On the other hand, a highly visible unit has an explicit role in the decision-making process of an organization. This role involves direct contact with other units in the organization, usually conducted at an 'equal functionaries' level. All outputs, whether reactive or proactive, are clearly seen to issue from the unit.

There are many points along the continuum of visibility. For purposes of illustrating some of these, consider the following three mandates for a reactive type unit:

- to receive all proposals, assist the manager in the preparation of the agenda, and relay messages from senior management to the other units and vice versa;
- to review all proposals to see that they conform to well-known and accepted criteria, such as clearly stated objectives, costs, and so forth;
- to send a proposal back to the originating unit until the policy unit deems it to be ready for discussion by senior management.

A progression through the above illustrations demonstrates a much more visible and explicit role in the decision-making process.

A Model

The degree of initiation (reactive-proactive) and the degree of visibility (invisible–visible) focus on two key organizational facts of life for a policy planning and research unit. These two factors can be combined to produce a framework for studying the form and nature of policy planning and research structures. Figure 1 shows a two-dimensional model with the degree of visibility along the vertical axis and the degree of initiation along the horizontal axis.

There exists, of course, a large number of possible combinations of visibility and initiative that any individual unit can and may assume. Policy units at points A, B, C, and D as depicted in Figure 1 would be polar types or extremes of the two factors under consideration. Actual units in organizations may or may not resemble any of these four types. However, these formulations are useful as standards for locating specific units along the continua and for determining how a particular unit compares with other units.

Type A, in the upper left-hand corner of the model represents policy units which are highly visible with a reactive function. Such units would have a clearly articulated mandate to review and, if necessary, temporarily reject all proposals arriving from other groups in the organization and would have frequent direct boundary exchanges with line personnel. Type A units would not, however, have a mandate or resources to produce their own proposals for innovation.

Units lying between type A and B would be highly active in the policy process and, aside from having the mandate to review the proposals of others, would also have

Figure 1

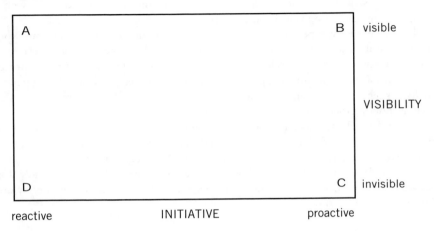

some resources to undertake the study and development of their own proposals.

Type B units are highly visible units which have a monopoly on proactive behaviour and thus are considered to be the source of all innovative proposals in the organization. This arises primarily because all of the 'slack resources' such as person years, analytical facilities, and so forth which might be used for these purposes are channelled into the policy unit. Type B units may also perform a 'door opener' role by encouraging and supporting the articulation by, and access of, external groups to the policy process.

Between types B and C would lie units of varying visibility in the policy process. As mentioned earlier, their degree of visibility would depend on the extent to which the outputs were identified with the unit, and the frequency and depth of interaction with other parts of the organization in the formulating of work plans, soliciting of information or feedback for the development of proposals. Concern (and thus visibility) would be expected to increase with the importance of the work being done by the unit. Once again, this type of unit would maintain a monopoly on the resources directed toward policy development and innovation.

In the lower right-hand corner of the model, one would find invisible, proactive units—type C. Like type B, these units are the source of all innovative proposals in the organization. At the same time, however, a type C unit keeps a very low profile by operating through management, with the advice and information not being identified as coming from the unit. This type of unit would tend to have few personnel.

Units lying between types C and D would tend to be small and have a very low profile in the policy process. They would advise the manager on proposals flowing from other parts of the organization, while at the same time, devote resources toward the solution of a modest number of key issues.

In the lower left-hand corner are invisible and reactive units—type D. These units would not prepare any proposals of their own but simply react to those prepared by other groups in the organization. Moreover, the type D unit would submit all its advice to a senior line manager, and any comments on proposals would be seen by other groups to come from this individual.

Units between types D and A would vary in the degree of visibility but would perform only a reactive function. Such a unit might be responsible for the circulation of documents and the collection of papers for committees, the gathering of facts, or might have a mandate to apply agreed, neutral criteria (for example, proper format) to such documents. In other words, an increase in both boundary exchanges and role in policy process takes place.

This model suggests a number of relationships between degree of initiative and visibility which we feel aids in defining and understanding the development of policy units. It also suggests a number of questions. With regard to the Canadian experience, is there evidence which suggests the prevalence of certain types? What consequences ensued from the choices made? What effect has this had on policy units in the federal government?

CANADIAN EXPERIENCE

Before the 1960s, policy and program planning functions in the federal public service were not housed in special structures but were performed by administrators and management through informal or ad hoc means.[8] During the 1960s and early 1970s most federal government agencies and departments set up structures specifically to perform policy planning and other staff support functions. In the main, these structures or units were first established in and around the central agencies of the federal public service.

In 1971 Simon Reisman, then Deputy Minister of Finance, described to a Senate Committee the planning efforts in the federal government as follows:

> Each of the departments of Government has some personnel who are charged with the task of looking further ahead, trying to anticipate some of the longer term problems. My predecessor said he found that his efforts in this regard were always frustrated by the emergence of a whole series of problems from day to day. I also find that is happening, but I am making a real effort to have people who do look at the long term.
>
> More important than what happens in individual departments is, I think, the apparatus of the Government decision-making process. The introduction into the Cabinet system of the Planning Committee of Cabinet over which the Prime Minister presides, and it is the body at the decision-making level which tries to pull in a good deal of the longer-term thinking and analysis, and tries to mesh that into some kind of coherent total policy.[9]

Indeed, the creation of departmental policy planning units was, to a large extent, a direct response to a series of developments in the executive-bureaucratic arena.[10]

The introduction of a system of Planning, Programming, and Budgeting (PPB) throughout the federal government is an example. In October 1966 Treasury Board issued a guide for Financial Management that set out a policy of moving towards program budgeting.[11] The intention of PPB was to have departments submit program forecasts which set specific objectives, assessed alternative ways of achieving objectives, framed budget proposals in terms of programs aimed at achieving objectives, stated yearly plans for program achievement and multi-year cost projections of programs, and supplied data for monitoring program performance. In 1968 the cabinet committee system was reorganized with the creation of a Priority and Planning Committee chaired by the Prime Minister. There was also the advocacy of a more 'rational' approach to policy-making by Prime Minister Trudeau and some of his key advisers, exemplified by the development of a planning capacity in the Prime Minister's Office. In part, the large growth in policy planning and research units in federal agencies reflected the optimism of the 1960s about improving government's performance with analytical systems oriented techniques and structures.

The Privy Council Office was reorganized and a Plans Branch was established in 1968–9. A Planning Branch was established in the Treasury Board Secretariat in 1969 to develop and apply techniques and methodologies in effectiveness and efficiency evaluation of government programs, and strategic planning. The Planning Branch in conjunction with certain departments conducted program evaluation studies, and provided briefings and guidelines in order to encourage departments to develop their own skills and organizations for planning and analysing programs. The Board also encouraged departments to establish units staffed with specialists in the use of analytical techniques by making available senior executive (SXE) and economist statistician (ES) positions especially for policy development, planning, and evaluation.[12]

At the central agency–department level policy units were viewed as a means to ensure that better analysis came to cabinet committees from departments. In order that the central planning and decision-making process in and around cabinet operated effectively, the quality of departmental submissions needed to be improved. Thus, central agency officials saw a need to improve policy development skills in departments, and to have people in departments who could interact with the PCO.

In addition, the creation of departmental policy units is an illustration of the 'Poyser Principle'—which postulates that when central agencies increase their capacity for control the departments will respond with capacity to cope with and perhaps neutralize the new demand from the central agencies. Indeed, planning units in departments were often created to protect and advance ministerial and departmental interests in the executive and central bureaucratic arena.[13]

Initially, most departments established units at the upper levels of departmental hierarchies at the rank of 'staff' assistant deputy minister (ADM) or equivalent. For example, the Post Office in 1969 established a Strategic Planning Branch reporting directly to the deputy minister. The same year, External Affairs created a Policy Analysis Group reporting to the under secretary. In 1971 Industry, Trade and Commerce created the position of ADM Industrial Policy; in the same year, the Department of the Environment established an ADM Policy, Planning and Research Branch; and in 1972 the Department of National Defence established both a Policy

Branch and an Evaluation Branch at the ADM level. These units were generally intended to be highly visible and proactive. In other terms, units were located at or near the apex of organizational hierarchies, their size was not insignificant, and they were expected to have direct exchanges with other groups both inside and outside the organization. Moreover, units usually had an explicit mandate in the policy and management processes to promote corporate planning and resource coordination.

After the rapid proliferation of staff ADM level policy planning units in the late 1960s and early 1970s, there followed a period when departments began locating units within operating divisions at the program ADM, director general, or director level. Examples include Customs and Excise, which established a planning group in the Customs Operations Branch in 1973; the Department of the Environment which set up a Policy and Program Development Branch in Environmental Management Services in 1974; and the Secretary of State which established a Policy Branch in the Citizenship Section in 1975. More recent years have witnessed a decline in the creation of policy units, and an increase in the reorganization and transfer of existing staff resources into the middle levels of departmental management.

This spread of units within individual departments and agencies partly demonstrates the Poyser Principle on an intra-organizational basis. Furthermore, management thinking in the federal public service tended to support such a dispersal. The general administrative opinion on the location of support services is perhaps best captured in a paper by R.H. Dowdell.[14] In examining the issue of whether all managers should have their own support resources Dowdell says:

> In theory, every officer with major management responsibilities should have his own staff to provide him with specialist advice and service. This is the best way to ensure that he has access to them and that they are fully knowledgeable about the activities he is responsible for, and the problems inherent in them. [15]

Hence, policy units in government departments were seen as providing dedicated support services to managers of various ranks, including those at branch level. By the mid 1970s there were at least 3,500 planners in the major departments of the federal government.[16]

Even where substantial resources had been allocated to policy units, certain intended activities, particularly proactive functions, were not performed. Personnel from many policy units believed that a proactive role conflicted with their other functions and their needs, especially in the early years of operation, to develop good relations with line officials. In the words of a director of planning and evaluation in the Department of National Health and Welfare:

> Not much of the analyst's time will be spent in developing high policy for others to implement or even in generating 'a new idea'. An effective analyst will play the roles of facilitator, expediter, and change agent, not only arranging initial key events but following through, gathering information and setting the stage to avoid delays.[17]

These more modest roles were seen by planners as necessary to avoid 'causing concern', to ensure that 'the right persons have input', and because planning analysts frequently lack detailed knowledge of the policy subject matter.[18] And, as Arnold J. Meltsner points out, policy analysts 'will be disenchanted when they find that all power does not reside at the top. Most significantly, they will not know much about the operating programs of the agencies. As outsiders they will have a hard time learning from people at the bottom.'[19] Thus, organizationally less threatening reactive functions have been emphasized by many units at the expense of more proactive activities. This trend was reinforced as new policy units were established throughout departments and the advisory marketplace became more 'competitive'.[20]

The performance of a 'firefighting' role in a number of units, whether intended or not, has dominated and in some cases prevented the development of more active staff services.[21] This problem could not be solved simply by keeping units separate from the heat of day-to-day concerns. The survival of policy units usually depended upon a judicious mix of short- and long-term work and not being left out in the cold.

In summary, it can be said that most government agencies and departments established policy units to perform long-term policy thinking, analysis and formulation. The size of these reflected a general attitude that policy units should be modestly endowed with the number of person-years required to achieve a substantial core of skills necessary for the performance of their duties. However, as the 1980s begin, policy units are increasingly viewed by some as a waste of resources and many have been significantly reduced in size while some have been eliminated altogether. What, then, can we learn from this experiment in administrative reform and rationality? How have organizational forces influenced the development of policy units in the Canadian federal bureaucracy?

THE RISE AND FALL OF POLICY UNITS

An atmosphere of good intentions is not enough to ensure the success of a policy unit. Even if everyone agrees on the need for policy development and analysis, there may not be a consensus on where it should be done within the organization or how it should be done. The issues of the location and role of these personnel and resources are central to the debate surrounding policy units.

The experience to date in Canadian government, combined with certain elements from organization theory, suggest to us a hypothesis concerning evolution of policy units. Policy units are likely to start with relatively high visibility and intentions of a high proactive role (plus high hopes) but will have a tendency to move toward a more reactive role with a lower degree of visibility. At any one time there are probably policy units with various combinations of initiative and visibility. However, we believe there are a number of forces acting upon policy units which have influenced their origins and their direction of development.

Upward Forces

Why were so many of the new policy units given such high visibility and proactive roles? What factors led the decision-makers to almost consistently opt for what appears to be the most difficult type of unit to successfully adopt? A number of items suggest themselves.

First, the organizational and political worlds were steeped in an era of rationality. In Ottawa, this approach to government and management included a felt need for greater efficiency and effectiveness, clearer objectives and thus stronger political direction.[22] Kirby and Kroeker have noted that a prevailing attitude in the federal government during the late 1960s, 'was that virtually all major crises were events of the past. Solutions existed for all problems if only adequate structures and processes were in place to anticipate, to plan and to co-ordinate government activity.'[23]

'Corporate planning' and 'cybernetic systems' were thought to be necessary and achievable for all. A growing emphasis on 'turbulent environment' and 'feedback loops' called for units to process information and ascertain new directions for the organization to follow, and design better ways to get there. Cybernetics assumes a steering capacity and the collecting and processing of information necessary to guide this steering activity. Thus, units performing these functions were placed near the top of the organization to provide advice to those doing the driving.[24]

Secondly, while the *task* which these units were to perform might have been a sharp break from the past, the establishing of policy *units* can be viewed as an incremental step from the tradition (or previous practice) of the senior adviser or staff officer so prevalent in the military. In part, highly visible policy units were justified on the basis of providing advisory support to senior departmental management. Madar and Stairs, in discussing the reasoning behind the corporate location of the Policy Analysis Group in External Affairs, report that:

> PAG was established as a unit responsible to the under-secretary, partly in recognition of the under-secretary's central importance in the department's administrative and policy processes, partly because PAG's activities, like those of the Press Office, are potentially significant enough to warrant a direct formal link, partly because a group with such an over-arching purview has no natural niche further down in an organization structured around regional and functional specialties, and partly . . . because it was desirable at the time to have not just a planning staff, but a highly visible one. As the department's permanent head, the under secretary is the leadership to be served.[25]

Thirdly, if changes in the direction of the organization and/or the means of delivery were expected it may be in the interest of the senior manager to remain neutral in any staff-line frays which develop. As Anthony Downs has pointed out, the manager uses conflict generated in the line-staff confrontation to achieve marginal change while, at the same time, maintaining good relations with his or her line managers.

A large staff can function as a control mechanism 'external' to the line hierarchy, promote change in opposition to the line's inertia, and act as a scapegoat deflecting hostility from its boss.[26] After a discussion of the differences between line and staff Downs continues:

> These differences . . . generate an inherent conflict between them that allows

their mutual boss to use one as a scapegoat in dealing with the other. Thus, by getting his staff members to press the line to make changes he really wants himself, he can deflect most of the resulting resentment to them and retain the loyalty of his chief line subordinates.[27]

This calls for an ability for the policy unit to fight its own battles at the senior levels of the bureau, thus requiring a high degree of visibility.

Fourthly, is the matter of obtaining an effective unit. The main requirement was the acquisition of skilled personnel which when combined yielded the necessary breadth of knowledge. Thus, it was argued that the levels had to be sufficiently senior in both rank and pay to attract the persons with the requisite skills. As well, the unit had to be of sufficient size and mix of skills so as to provide a 'critical mass' for the purposes of multi-disciplinary, synergistic output. Hence, number and rank of personnel often forced the unit up the hierarchy to the top levels of the organization.[28]

Fifthly, the demands from outside the organization and at the cybernetic centre of government, as mentioned earlier, namely the PCO, PMO, and TBS, required a functional equivalent in the other organizations. The early policy units were given a high visibility because they were to provide departmental responses to central agency initiatives. On the other hand, the departments themselves were looking for ways to counteract the developments in the central agencies. Once again, this called for a highly visible unit located near the top of the organization.[29]

As well as the factors examined above, those officials inside policy units themselves were highly motivated to adopt a visible and proactive role.

In administrative thinking during the late 1960s one of the major arguments for policy units was that administrators tended to neglect longer-term planning and research. Policy units were seen as necessary to ensure that these staff functions were done in government. Hence, units were granted and assumed considerable initiative in setting their work programs and providing advice.[30] Policy units were also seen as an institutional device to inform public servants of new ideas and techniques. The rationale for units providing advice on their own initiative has been succinctly stated by R.H. Dowdell:

> The responsibilities of support units are not effectively exercised if they merely respond to manager's requests for advice and service. They are frequently aware of needs and impending problems before the manager is, and should go to him with information, advice and proffered assistance whenever they feel there is a reason to do so.[31]

Managers and administrators have their own work and daily affairs to do and suggesting work for policy units often comes low in their priorities. In addition, some officials take the view that suggesting work topics and new areas of policy action is not part of their job. They believe their job is to execute policy and to explain existing programs, not to suggest policy.

Thus, as staff or advisory organizations, part of the role of policy units is to propose ideas and projects. Such organizations, often with an 'organic' internal structure, emphasize the ability to detect new issues, especially those transorganizational in nature, and information needs. As policy units are new organizations with a comparatively novel role, other officials—potential clients—frequently have only a vague idea of the role of a unit and its possible use to them. For purposes of organizational survival and effectiveness, therefore, unit staff must suggest work and ideas to show other officials the uses of their unit.

Given the existence of these factors and conditions, it is not surprising that policy units were generally created as highly visible and proactive bodies. Obtaining such a profile was easy; maintaining it was not.

Downward Forces

A number of forces combined to change the role of policy units substantially and perhaps permanently. What was the nature of these forces and were these forces inevitable in the Canadian federal bureaucracy? The key issues which appear to be the major contributors to the role displacement exhibited by policy planning and research units are: the absence of agreed criteria for determining the essential elements of good policy; the difficulties of recruiting suitable personnel; the lack of attention to different departmental needs; the problems seemingly inherent in line-staff differentiation; and the absence of sustained commitment and support from senior management. What follows is a discussion of these.

First, due to a shortage of skilled and experienced persons in policy analysis, the recruitment of the necessary staff posed a major problem for policy units. In the words of a past chairman of one departmental policy unit:

> The Policy Analysis Group has been less successful than originally expected in bringing together persons with disparate backgrounds, partly because people with special skills as well as good judgment and general competence are much in demand. Moreover government regulations and recruitment practices do not make it easy to attract outsiders for temporary periods . . . or to swap officials with other departments.[32]

The shortage of skilled research and policy planning specialists meant that in the early 1970s many units were not fully staffed and/or had to settle for less than the best. Those units not adequately staffed lacked the required critical mass 'to permit intense depth study of significant problems, application of different disciplines of knowledge, and diversity in approaches'.[33] Many units began and remain today at a size too small to permit much work being initiated. Furthermore, many persons appointed to senior and middle level planning positions were recruited directly from the academic and private sectors. As a result, many planners had little in-depth knowledge of the structures and processes of government or the realities of bureaucratic bargaining. All of these personnel factors presented difficulties for the credibility and the work capacity of policy units.

A second factor operating was the different perspective normally held by persons in policy units from those in other parts of the organization. This differing perspective often resulted in problems of communicating and promoting understanding. Such a situation was evident with respect to the functioning of many policy units in the Canadian government. Policy units were organizationally distinct from the structures responsible for line management. While this arrangement mini-mized the danger of policy units becoming bogged down in day-to-day operations, it also raised problems of coordination and communication between administrators and policy advisers. The creation of these units often introduced another organiza-tional structure into the system, and institutionalized previously implicit or diverse functions.

This institutionalization introduced crucial differences in the role responsibilities between policy advisers and line managers.[34] These differences presented difficulties for policy units in obtaining their intended profile. The role of policy advisers was to consider the future and to view programs in 'systems' terms. Policy advisers were expected to develop new policies and innovative program designs by using analytical and conceptual techniques like 'thinking the unthinkable'. Their role called for behaviour that critically evaluated current activities and advocated changes. In con-trast, line managers and officials administer programs in the here-and-now, and view their program responsibilities primarily in functional terms. The role of line managers is to ensure the ongoing delivery of programs, by using pragmatic and operational tools. They are likely to point out the practical problems in any proposals for change made by policy advisers.

In another important sense, policy advisers were not everyday bureaucrats. Personal differences between advisers and other public servants probably reinforced line management resistance toward policy units. Compared with other public ser-vants, persons recruited to planning units in the early seventies were generally younger, higher paid and more highly educated, with many coming directly from academia. In short, they were 'whizz kids'.[35]

Both these organizational role and interpersonal differences created potential barriers to understanding and co-operation between policy unit staff and line offi-cials. As Lawrence and Lorsch have pointed out, this increased differentiation calls for enhanced integrative mechanisms which serve to minimize or control the conflict stemming from these differing perspectives.[36] In the case of policy units in the federal bureaucracy, it would appear the main responsibilities for this necessary integration rested with the traditional managerial hierarchy. In the absence of additional integra-tive efforts, many line managers perceived these new policy units as eroding their own advisory role and as intruding on their operational activities. Policy advisers thus faced problems in obtaining the necessary information, advice and support in order to perform their expected role.[37]

Thirdly, maintaining a highly visible and/or a proactive profile in a unit requires a large and sustained expenditure of influence and commitment by senior officials. Yet the evidence seems to suggest that top departmental officials and cabinet minis-ters, even those most committed to policy and program analysis in principle, were not prepared in practice to expend the necessary resources and influence to maintain or even implement proactive and or highly visible policy processes.[38] For example, lack of support from some deputy ministers has kept policy units isolated from manage-ment and decision-making processes. There are at least three reasons for this situation. First, as noted earlier, some deputy ministers created policy units primarily because of pressures from the central agencies or promises of new senior executive positions from Treasury Board. Secondly, certain deputy ministers are known more for their administrative skills than for an interest or competence in planning and policy advice, and 'may have little faith in "professional analysts" as distinct from experienced program officials'.[39] Thirdly, other deputies, while sympathetic to the policy unit concept, may not have confidence in the incumbent planning director and staff, and may feel unable to replace them. A 1974 Treasury Board study found that this did happen, especially in departments where deputy ministers inherited a policy unit from their immediate predecessor.[40]

Due to the imbalance of power between policy units as staff and other line officials in the absence of senior management support, units were required to assume a less visible and more reactive role. Richard Hall has clearly expressed the implications of this power relationship:

> In order to accomplish anything the staff must secure some cooperation from the line. This requires giving into the line by moderating proposals, overlooking practices that do not correspond to rigid technical standards, and in general playing a rather subservient role in dealing with line. If this is not done, the staff's suggestions would probably go unheeded. This in turn would make their output zero for the time period, and their general relevance for the organization would be questioned.[41]

Thus, considerations of gaining organizational support and legitimacy have influenced the development of policy planning units, and the application and sophistication of policy planning techniques has been less than originally intended.

Fourthly, there was the very basic question of the need for these units. Policy units were apparently created to help public organizations cope with a rapidly changing or turbulent environment. Not many would argue against the position that the internal environment of the federal public service was undergoing significant change—new management systems, new language requirements, new organizations not to mention policy planning units, indeed, for some it seemed a 'topsy-turvy' place.[42] True, some major policy changes did take place over the period in question but how many of these were simply one-shot affairs?

For many departments, the environment was reasonably placid given the lack of the competitive market place. Yet the departments were all treated the same. The policy unit model was a general one promoted and adopted throughout the federal bureaucracy. Differences in departmental needs, environments and functions were not seen to be crucial factors in the decision to establish policy units.

At the Department of External Affairs, for example, a period of relative stability shortly ensued after the creation of its policy analysis group in 1970:

> After the completion of the foreign policy review of 1970, and the work on Canada–United States Relations in 1971–72, there was an inevitable period of drift. The department, after all, had endured several years of review and

appraisal. New directions were apparently set. There was little appetite for further reflection. The need was to get on with the job.[43]

In such circumstances, policy units were hard pressed to find line managers within their departments willing to initiate or suggest ambitious planning studies. Units therefore turned to far more modest and reactive functions such as speech-writing, firefighting, and commenting on aspects of current policies.[44]

Finally, another downward force was the inability of policy analysts to determine generally accepted criteria as to what constitutes good or sound policy. The absence of such criteria, in conjunction with the related points above, denied policy units full access to their major source of influence within the organization, namely, 'expert power'.[45] The reasons why policy units fell short of their intended power base of expertise are well illustrated in the following conundrums. Were policy units the guardians of rationality or experts in understanding political forces? Could they be both? Could they be either? Were they to promote the science of policy analysis or the art of reasoned judgment? Was the former possible? Was the latter absent before their arrival? How does the policy adviser know when to provide a timely response as opposed to indepth analysis? How does one add clarity to the muddy waters of conflicting, vague, and multiple objectives? Should the adviser try to balance considerations of administrative feasibility, political acceptability, and public need? If so, how?

These questions demonstrate the morass of policy analysis. There would appear to be no one best way to proceed through the swamp of competing views and methodologies. Thus, policy advisers confront the subjectivity of their craft when they realize there is no codebook, no universally agreed principles to perform their role. This ambiguity diminishes policy units' expertise as a source to influence other officials and organizations in government.[46]

The downward forces we have noted—the shortage of qualified staff, staff-line differences, the comparatively weak power base of planning units, the dispersal of power and resources within complex organizations, the withdrawal of management support, environmental stability, the subjectivity of planning, and an abdication of proactive roles by policy analysts in order to gain support from line officials—all these presented serious problems for those units attempting to maintain a highly visible and proactive profile.

Outcomes: Equilibrium or Extinction?

Given these downward forces, what happens to highly visible proactive units? Firstly, it has been observed that the policy units' functions have been dispersed downward in the organization. Where once the 'corporate unit' had a monopoly on the resources to be directed toward the development of new policy and initiatives, now a number of policy units, smaller in size, have been established throughout the organization and attached to line branches.

As well, corporate units have often been forced into a more reactive, sometimes a pure secretariat role. Most have assumed a lower profile and undertaken a predominantly firefighting role. In general their mode of operation is skewed toward attitudes and behaviours of a conflict-avoidance nature. This requires low visibility and a prudent minimum of proactive behaviour. In the present era of fiscal restraint, and, in part because of a lack of tangible and significant contributions, the size of these units has often decreased; vacancies are left unfilled.

Some units which cannot or choose not to flow with these downward forces risk loosing the oracle status they seek. They become divorced from the decision-making process within the organization and assume the role of organizational ornament. One can observe two forms of these ornaments. The first, the 'sadly amusing unit' persists in turning out elaborate policy analysis and initiatives which go unheeded by any persons in the organization. Such planning units 'build up their own enclaves and justify their existence by being busy doing their own thing.'[47] The second type of ornament is the 'sinking ship', where the personnel who haven't yet abandoned the unit have long since stopped trying to keep it afloat. The major advantage of both types is that they can still be used to impress visitors as a symbol of the foresight and capabilities of the organization.[48]

In summary, the expectations for policy units were very high in the early stages of their development. But as a consequence of a number of factors explored above, both the role and the utility of most units have settled at a more realizable level. This level is considerably lower than first envisioned. It seems reasonable, therefore, to speak of the rise and fall of policy units in the Canadian federal bureaucracy.

Conclusions

What then does this suggest for the future of policy development and analysis in general, and policy units in particular? First of all, it is quite possible, indeed, sometimes necessary, to separate the two. The policy development function does not necessarily require a policy unit, nor, it would seem, does a policy unit often develop policy, at least not that which is implemented. If these circumstances exist, then it becomes desirable to reassess the role of policy planning and research units, and design new structures to perform the major policy functions.

The framework presented here calls attention to organizational factors that have previously often been ignored in the policy studies literature. Its application to the experience of policy units in the Canadian federal bureaucracy demonstrates that attempts to rationalize the policy process are inextricably linked to the organizational context in which policy analysis operates. A consideration of such factors as visibility and initiative contributes to an understanding of policy planning and research units. Much of the politics of policy reform is the politics of organizational behaviour.

Our analysis and that of others suggests that, over time, policy units become the victims of organizational infighting, slowly losing any effectiveness in the policy process, while at the same time often acquiring a more passive, less visible role. Eventually, like the boy who cries wolf, their words lose their effect on the listeners. Surely one would be better off without such a sentry, for when the wolf is truly there, it is time for action, not ignorance.

The need for organizational innovation and adaptation is much dependent on the relative stability of an organization's environment. For many, if not most, public sector organizations, the environment is fairly placid. Major new ventures are the exception rather than the rule, and many of these bubble through the system for years before bursting on the scene. In many cases, innovation is a cyclical affair, a major shake up, some new policy initiatives, then business as usual until the next readjustment several years hence.

Such situations would seem ideally suited to temporary and periodic policy development and analysis, or, in other words, a task force approach to innovation. Such an approach, though not a panacea, has several advantages. While perhaps it might suffer from the 'watering-down' syndrome found in some client–consultant relationships,[49] these seldom compare to the debilitating effects to which permanent units are exposed. Secondly, such an arrangement facilitates the involvement of line personnel to a greater degree, thus enhancing the prospects for eventual implementation. Thirdly, the infrequency of the activity is likely to draw more attention to the outcomes. Fourthly, resource utilization is improved. Additional features which could result are better analyses of ongoing programs and stronger commitment of top management, but these would depend largely on the contract between senior management and the task force.

But is a temporary capacity sufficient? Some might well inquire about the capability to react to an emergency situation of environmental turbulence. At the same time, attention should be paid to the time when the emergency has passed and the unit still remains. Perhaps more importantly, attention should also be focused on the ability to meet emergencies in the future. Is the organization better or worse off for having kept the unit in place? While inconclusive, our research suggests that the intra-organizational warfare which often accompanies the intervening periods of environmental peace leaves the organization and the policy unit disarrayed and ill-prepared to cope effectively with new external uncertainty. Thus, in many instances, there are few rewards for maintaining a high-powered, high-profile policy unit within the organization on a permanent basis.

However, this does not mean that management should forfeit the benefits of staff advice. Rather, it suggests a more realistic appraisal on the limits to the activities of such actors. In doing so, management may well reduce impediments to the adoption of innovation in the future.

Such an approach calls for small units with a low profile, serving, perhaps, as a secretariat, but most likely as a firefighter and intelligence network for senior management. It should lean much more toward the senior staff officer concept rather than the corporate think-tank image. The duties assigned might better tend toward the ad hoc rather than the programmed function. In large measure, this would seem to be where policy units end up, at any rate. The suggestion, therefore, is that it may be better to start in the short run where one is likely to arrive in the long run and, in the process, spare the generation of a good deal of ill-will.

We suspect that many government agencies have already determined the problem. However, a strong commitment to the current advisory structure, particularly the vested interests of policy staff themselves, has launched another effort to increase the leverage of these units within their own departments. Primarily, the mechanism to be adopted is the development of a common data base: a mutually accepted view of what has to be done. It is hoped that the development of such a framework would enable policy units to have an impact on policy initiatives within their departments and ensure that these initiatives concur with this shared view. Whether this most recent venture will lead to a new equilibrium or push these units closer to extinction is uncertain. While we wish them well, we believe this attempt to revive the pro activity of policy units will be met by an equal increase in countervailing organizational forces.

Notes

1. For a detailed discussion of policy planning and research units, see Michael J. Prince, *Policy Advice and Organizational Survival* (Farnborough: Gower Publishing Co., 1983).
2. See, for example, the conventional explanation of obstacles to rational policy and decision making represented in the works of Herbert Simon, *Administrative Behavior*, 3rd edn (New York: Free Press, 1976), and Charles E. Lindblom, *The Policy-Making Process* (Englewood Cliffs, NJ: Prentice-Hall, 1968).
3. Sue Jones, Colin Eden and David Sims, 'Subjectivity and Organizational Politics in Policy Analysis', *Policy and Politics* 7, 2 (April 1979), p. 147.
4. Ibid., p. 147. A notable exception is the study by Arnold J. Melstner, *Policy Analysts in the Bureaucracy* (London: University of California Press, 1976).
5. On the bureaucratic or organizational politics approach to the study of public policy and administration, see Graham T. Allison, *Essence of Decision* (Boston: Little, Brown, 1971); W.I. Jenkins, *Policy Analysis* (London: Martin Robertson, 1978); Richard W. Phidd and G. Bruce Doern, *The Politics and Management of Canadian Economic Policy* (Toronto: Macmillan, 1978); Kim Richard Nossal, 'Allison Through the (Ottawa) Looking Glass: Bureaucratic Politics and Foreign Policy in a Parliamentary System', *Canadian Public Administration* 22, 4 (Winter 1979), pp. 610–26; and David A. Good, *The Politics of Anticipation: Making Canadian Federal Tax Policy* (Ottawa: School of Public Administration, Carleton University, 1980).
6. Prince, *Policy Advice and Organizational Survival*, chapters 4 and 5.
7. A similar approach to assessing the influence of policy planning staff is given by Linda P. Brady, 'Planning for foreign policy: a framework for analysis', *International Journal* 32, 4 (Autumn 1977), pp. 829–48.
8. For a brief discussion of how planning and research activities traditionally took place in federal government departments, see James Eayrs, *The Art of the Possible* (Toronto: University of Toronto Press, 1961), pp. 151–9; and J.E. Hodgetts, *The Canadian Public Service* (Toronto: University of Toronto Press, 1973), p. 213–15. On the personalized style of the federal public service generally, see M.J.L. Kirby and H.V. Kroeker, 'The Politics of Crisis Management in Government: Does Planning Make Any Difference?' in C.F. Smart and W.T. Stanbury, eds, *Studies On Crisis Management* (Toronto: Butterworth, Institute for Research on Public Policy, 1978), pp. 182–6.
9. S.S. Reisman, Deputy Minister of Finance, Senate of Canada, Standing Committee on National Finance, *Growth, Employment and Price Stability* 22, 29 June 1971, p. 42.
10. See G. Bruce Doern and Peter Aucoin, eds, *The Structures of Policy-Making in Canada* (Toronto: Macmillan, 1971); and M.J.L. Kirby, H.V. Kroeker and W.R. Tescke, 'The Impact of Public Policy-Making Structures and Processes in Canada', *Canadian*

Public Administration 21, 3 (Fall 1978), pp. 407–17. As well, many of the following observations are based on interviews conducted by one of the authors and reported, in part, in Michael J. Prince, 'Policy Advisory Groups in Government Departments', in G. Bruce Doern and Peter Aucoin, eds, *Public Policy in Canada* (Toronto: Macmillan, 1979), pp. 275–300.

11. Canada, Treasury Board, *Planning Programming, Budgeting Guide* (Ottawa: Queen's Printer, 1966).

12. See Prince, 'Policy Advisory Groups in Government Departments', and Richard D. French, *How Ottawa Decides* (Toronto: James Lorimer, 1980).

13. On the 'Poyser Principle', see Donald V. Fowke, 'Toward a General Theory of Public Administration for Canada', *Canadian Public Administration* 19, 1 (Spring 1976), p. 36. On its relevance to the development of policy planning units see, for example, Daniel Madar and Denis Stairs, 'Alone on Killers' Row: The Policy Analysis Group and the Department of External Affairs', *International Journal* 32, 4 (Autumn 1977), pp. 727–55. Madar and Stairs argue that the Policy Analysis Group at External was 'established largely for cosmetic reasons related to the organizational defence of the department' (p. 738).

14. R.H. Dowdell, 'The Relationship of Support Units to Operating Units', *Optimum* 2, 4 (1971). pp. 4–14.

15. Ibid., p. 9.

16. Report on *Departmental Planning and Evaluation Groups in the Federal Government* (Ottawa: Treasury Board Secretariat, Organization Division, July 1976).

17. David F. Bray, 'The Analyst, the Manager and the Fit of Operations to Policy Intent', *Optimum* 8, 1 (1977), p. 59.

18. Ibid., pp. 59–60.

19. Meltsner, *Policy Analysts in the Bureaucracy*, p. 288.

20. Interviews; on the concept of 'competitive advice', see Edward S. Flash, Jr, *Economic Advice and Presidential Leadership* (New York: Columbia University Press, 1965). See also Prince, *Policy Advice and Organizational Survival*, Chapter 7.

21. See *Report on Departmental Planning and Evaluation Groups in the Federal Government*.

22. Michael Pitfield, 'The Shape of Government in the 1980s: Techniques and Instruments for Policy Formulation at the Federal Level', *Canadian Public Administration* 19, 1 (Spring 1976), pp. 8–20.

23. Kirby and Kroeker, 'The Politics of Crisis Management in Government', p. 183.

24. This brave new cybernetic and systems world was represented by, among others, K. Deutsch, *The Nerves of Government* (London: Collier-Macmillan, 1966), and Y. Dror, *Public Policy Making Reexamined* (San Francisco: Chandler, 1968). For its impact on the federal government, see G. Bruce Doern, 'Recent Changes in the Philosophy of Policy-Making in Canada', *Canadian Journal of Political Science*, 4, no. 2 (1971), pp. 243–64, and George R. Lindsey, 'Operational Research and Systems Analysis in the Department of National Defence', *Optimum* 3, 2 (1973), pp. 44–54.

25. Madar and Stairs, 'Alone on Killers' Row', pp. 744–5.

26. Anthony Downs, *Inside Bureaucracy* (Boston: Little, Brown, 1967), p. 154.

27. Ibid., p. 155.

28. Indeed, the widespread creation of planning units contributed to marked growth in

senior executive and equivalent positions in the early 1970s. See the *Report on Departmental Planning and Evaluation Groups in the Federal Government*.

29. Interviews. See Madar and Stairs, 'Alone on Killers' Row', p. 738.

30. Prince, 'Policy Advisory Groups in Government Departments' pp. 281–2. On the nature of developing a research program see, for instance, Irving K. Fox, 'Planning and Management of Environmental Research Programs', *Optimum* 4, 4 (1973), pp. 38–49.

31. Dowdell, 'The Relationship of Support Units to Operating Units', p. 8. See also David F. Bray, 'The Analyst, the Manager and the Fit of Operations to Policy Intent', pp. 60–1, who argues that planning analysts should initiate topic selections and proposal developments.

32. G.A.H. Pearson, 'Order Out of Chaos? Some Reflections on Foreign-policy Planning in Canada', *International Journal* 32, 4 (Autumn 1977), p. 763.

33. Yehezkel Dror, *Design for Policy Sciences* (New York: Elsevier, 1971), p. 91.

34. See P.R. Lawrence and J.W. Lorsch, 'Differentiation and Integration in Complex Organizations', *Administrative Science Quarterly* 12, 1 (June 1967); Patricia A. Rea, 'A Study of Re-organization and the Implementation of the Planning and Development Group in Transport Canada—1974–1977', MA thesis, School of Public Administration, Carleton University, 1978; Bray, 'The Analyst, the Manager and the Fit of Operations to Policy Intent'; and Meltsner, *Policy Analysts in the Bureaucracy.*

35. Prince, 'Policy Advisory Groups in Government Departments', pp. 288–90.

36. Lawrence and Lorsch, 'Differentiation and Integration in Complex Organizations'.

37. Rea, 'A Study of Re-organization and the Implementation of the Planning and Development Group in Transport Canada—1974–1977', pp. 85–90, *Report on Departmental Planning and Evaluation Groups in the Federal Government,* pp. 35–9, and interviews.

38. See Madar and Stairs, 'Alone on Killers' Row', pp. 745–6, Richard D. French, *How Ottawa Decides,* pp. 151–2, and Walter Baker. *The Elusive IPB System,* Case Program in Canadian Public Administration (Toronto: IPAC, 1977). This study examines the aborted attempt to institute Integrated Planning and Budgeting (IPB) in the federal Department of Public Works. Baker was ADM Planning and System in the Department of Public Works in the early 1970s.

39. *Report on Departmental Planning and Evaluation Groups in the Federal Government*, p. 33. On the different role skills of deputy ministers see also, Michael Pitfield, 'The Shape of Government in the 1980s', p. 17, and Royal Commission on Financial Management and Accountability, *Final Report* (Ottawa: Supply and Services Canada, 1979), Chapters 10 and 12.

40. Ibid., p. 33. For a different and useful assessment of interpersonal factors, particularly with regard to the importance of the relationship between the organization head and the leader of the policy unit, see Brady 'Planning for foreign policy'. From her analysis one can conclude that the mobility of ministers and deputies would have a serious impact on the activities of policy units.

41. Richard H. Hall, *Organizations, Structure and Process*, 2nd edn (Englewood Cliffs, NJ: Prentice-Hall, 1977), p. 216.

42. H.L. Laframboise, 'Administrative Reform in the Federal Public Service: Signs of a

Saturation Psychosis', *Canadian Public Administration* 14, 3 (Fall 1971), pp. 303–25.

43. Pearson, 'Order out of chaos?', p. 764.

44. Ibid., p. 765. See also, Madar and Stairs, 'Alone on Killers' Row', pp. 742–3.

45. The seminal piece on types of power is John R.P. French, Jr, and Bertram Raven, 'The Bases of Social Power', in Dorwin Cartwright and A.F. Zander, eds, *Group Dynamics: Research and Theory* (New York: Harper and Row, 1960), pp. 607–23.

46. See Douglas G. Hartle, 'The Public Servant as Advisor: The Choice of Policy Evaluation Criteria', *Canadian Public Policy* 2, 3 (1976), pp. 424–38, and Richard D. French, *How Ottawa Decides,* chapter 2.

47. J.Q. McCrindell, 'Some reflections on administrative reforms in the federal government', *Optimum* 6, 2 (1975), p. 57.

48. See Aaron Wildavsky, 'If Planning is Everything, Maybe it's Nothing', *Policy Sciences* 4 (1973), p. 146.

49. See Charles H. Ford, 'Developing a successful client-consultant relationship', *Optimum* 5, 4 (1974), pp. 38–53.

27

Coordination and the Management of Estuarine Water Quality

Mark Sproule-Jones

INTRODUCTION

It is still often assumed, by economists and students of public administration, that coordination of non-market interdependencies can be facilitated only by means of an hierarchical chain of command. Yet evidence about the provision of policing services (McDavid, 1974; E. Ostrom et al., 1974) and of solid waste collection in metropolitan areas (Savas, 1976) indicates that substantial coordination takes place between agencies and organizations in a non-hierarchical fashion, such as through contracting and bargaining. This paper will, among other things, present evidence to show that substantial coordination can also take place, in a non-hierarchical fashion, in the management of estuarine water quality.

The paper will also make a contribution to the economic analysis of bureaucratic behaviour. It will suggest a series of hypotheses about the efficiency advantages of a number of interagency and interorganizational arrangements, on the basis of evidence about estuarine water quality management for the Lower Fraser River. Currently, public choice theorizing about inter-organizational arrangements is limited largely to that of contracting.

It must be noted that the water quality of an estuary has the characteristics of a public good. It is both jointly produced and jointly consumed by persons engaged in social and economic activities in a basin, some of these activities being 'in-the-channel' uses and some 'on-the-land' uses.

Because of the large number of marketable goods and services made possible by activities carried on in most river basins, one expects to find, in the first place, a large number of individual persons and a large number of locally owned, provincially owned, nationally owned and perhaps internationally owned corporate persons and groups jointly involved in the production and/or consumption of water quality. One also expects to find, secondly, a large number of local, regional, provincial, national, and international agencies of government jointly involved in the production and/or consumption of water quality, either because (1) they are involved in the production and/or consumption of marketable goods and services provided by the basin; or

Mark Sproule-Jones, 'Coordination and the Management of Estuarine Water Quality', *Public Choice* 33, 1 (1979): 41–53. With kind permission from Springer Science and Business Media.

because (2) they are involved in the regulation (for allocative, stabilization or redistributive reasons) of the production and/or consumption of marketable goods and services; or because (3) they are involved in the production and/or consumption of public goods and services. In other words, a multiplicity of individuals and organizations (government and private) will contribute in different ways, toward the production and consumption of water quality, and no one individual or organization will possess a monopoly in its production or a monopsony in its consumption. Such a social, organizational and institutional network may be called a 'provision system' (Gregg, 1974). Similar complex provision systems appear to exist for the delivery of goods and services other than water quality (e.g., E. Ostrom, 1973).

Because water quality is jointly produced and jointly consumed by a multiplicity of individuals, groups, and organizations, one would expect to find in any water quality provision system a set of coordinative institutional arrangements to link and regulate the interdependencies in production and consumption. Yet many analyses of water quality and environmental management assert there is a lack of coordination of these interdependencies. Thus Cram (1971, p. 163) asserts that 'administration of Canadian water resources . . . [is] hampered by confusion and lack of coordination.' Ouellet (1969, p. 83) claims there is 'general agreement' that one of three major sources of water management problems in Canada is 'the huge multiplicity of agencies dealing with water matters, and the general lack of coordination among these agencies'. And, as a third example, Franson et al. (1976, p. 84) conclude with an assertion that 'communication between the agencies responsible for different aspects of water management seems to be lacking.' Such conclusions as these have led to a variety of proposals for establishing a single basin-wide authority to coordinate the interdependencies (e.g., Beecroft 1966, Kneese and Bower 1968; MacNeill 1971; Haefele 1973).

The apparent difference between what one should expect to find in any water quality provision system and what many studies assert does not occur calls for systematic empirical verification of the extent and kinds of coordinative arrangements, if any, between and among producers and consumers of water quality. It is one of the objectives of this paper to provide such a verification by examining the experience of the management of water quality in the Lower Fraser River of British Columbia.[1] This objective is also warranted because a substantial body of theoretical literature reasons that coordination may take place, not simply through a single hierarchical chain of command, but through a variety of interorganizational and interpersonal agreements, contracts, and bargains (see, especially, V. Ostrom, 1974).

The paper has a second objective. Previous studies indicate that contractual arrangements can yield efficiency advantages in the public sector.[2] But previous studies do not assess the relative advantages of other kinds of interorganizational and interpersonal arrangements within the public sector or between public and private sectors. This paper will make a number of preliminary and suggestive inferences about the relative advantages of a number of implementation mechanisms, including contracting, that are exhibited in the water quality provision system of the Lower Fraser River. In other words, a number of suggestive hypotheses will be generated on the basis of a typology of interorganizational arrangements, constructed in turn by a careful scrutiny of the variety of implementation mechanisms exhibited in the provision system. The study of public sector efficiency may well benefit, at this stage in its development, by such an inductive methodological strategy.

The paper will proceed as follows. In the next section, a number of methodological procedures for data collection and analysis are summarized. Section three presents the findings on the number and extent of interorganizational arrangements. Section four presents and illustrates the typology of implementation mechanisms and hypotheses about procedures for coordination of the interdependencies in production and consumption of water quality. The final section makes a number of concluding statements about the findings of the study in the light of its twin objectives.

METHODOLOGY

As part of a larger study of water quality management for the Lower Fraser River of British Columbia, 100 elite interviews were conducted in the Spring of 1975 of individuals working within some 54 public and private organizations with activities and uses of the Basin in question. The interviews were selected by a snowball sampling procedure from an initial list of 14 persons nominated by judges on the basis of their significance in the provision system. The individuals were asked to name and indicate the nature of their contacts and interactions with individuals in other organizations, public and private. In order to counteract the limitations of recall of an interviewee during the time of interview, respondents were given a list of organizations with whom they were expected to have frequent interactions and asked to nominate individuals in these organizations with whom they interrelated. Also written agreements were used to supplement this basic source of data, and occasionally arrangements were recalled by the counterpart to a particular elite member in another organization in the system. It is possible that some unwritten and non-recalled interactive arrangements were not recorded by these procedures, and if so the number and type of coordinative arrangements would be biased downwards.

The existence of coordinative arrangements for a water quality matter between two organizations in the provision system were categorised as a single arrangement, even though two organizations may have a number of dyadic relationships (such as for information sharing and the contractual use of a laboratory facility). Also, coordinative arrangements that did not pertain to water quality matters for the Lower Fraser itself were excluded from the analysis. These procedures were again employed as a validity check against overestimating the extent and types of coordinative arrangements exhibited in the provision system. In other words, the findings on the number and extent of interorganizational arrangements summarized in the next section of the paper are probably underestimated as a result of a number of deliberate methodological procedures.[3]

THE NUMBER AND TYPES OF COORDINATIVE ARRANGEMENTS

Our data reveal that 781 coordinative arrangements existed between the 54 organizational members of the water quality provision system as of the Spring of 1975. The organization with the most coordinative arrangements, the Pollution Control

Branch,[4] has linkages with 46 of the 53 other members. At the other extreme, two organizations, the Towboat Owners Association[5] and Rivtow Straights Ltd,[6] have only one routinized linkage with other organizations. Table 1 presents some summary statistics on the frequency of coordinative arrangements in the system. These data provide one indicator to belie the argument that a lack of coordination is associated with a multiplicity of organizations for the management of river basin water quality.

Table 1 *Summary of coordinative arrangements*

No. of organizations:	54
No. of organization linkages:	781
Mean no. of linkages:	14.46
Standard deviation:	9.96

It might be argued that the absolute number of linkages between organizations is an insufficient indicator of the presence of coordinative arrangements that can make some difference in the activities of the provision system as a whole. Consequently, our data on linkages are classified into three types of coordinative arrangements, irregular, regular, and integrated coordination. These types of coordinative arrangements are defined as follows. Irregular coordination exists when one or more organizations will make available a service to one or more other organizations on an occasional and non-planned basis. For example, as a response to allegations from one medical health officer in 1974, the Marine and Civil Engineering Section 7 sampled the bottom material, the stockpile of dredge spoils and the water in the outside channel of Ladner Harbour (one of the smaller harbours on the River) for the existence of coliforms. Or to take another example, the Canadian Wildlife Service[8] will provide occasional consultative services to SPEC 'Central',[9] such as on the estimated effects of small scale oil spills on birds.

Regular coordination exists when one or more organizations will make its services available to one or more other organizations on a frequent but again non-planned basis. For example, the Land and Water Quality Group[10] will frequently contact the Vancouver Department of Permits and Licenses[11] to inform them of new industrial processes and other new potential sources of wastes for the city's sewers. Again, as another example, Water Rights Engineers[12] will frequently meet with BC Wildlife Federation[13] officials and officials from the Fish and Wildlife Branch[14] to discuss and dispute rival claims about required minimum flow levels in streams and tributaries in the Lower Fraser.

Integrated coordination exists when one or more organizations will provide the same service to one or more other organizations in the system on a regular and planned basis. For example, one leading multinational forest product company has a regular and planned agreement with SPEC 'Central', whereby the latter will complain to the Pollution Control Branch if it is made aware of contraventions (or presumed contraventions) of the Pollution Control Act by the company's competitors in the industry. In return, company officials will articulate the concerns of the environmental group at the company Board level. A second example would be the routine monitoring of dredge spoils by the Marine and Civil Engineering Section to count the number of salmon fry killed, and to schedule its annual channel maintenance dredging program in off-migratory seasons for salmonoids, in response to the concerns of the Habitat Protection Directorate of the Fisheries and Marine Services.[15]

Table 2 *Number and proportion of coordinative types*				
	Coordinative types			
Summary statistics	Irregular	Regular	Integrated	Total
Total number	245	140	396	781
Means	4.54	2.59	7.33	14.46
Standard deviations	3.33	2.42	6.43	9.96
Percentages	31.37%	17.93%	50.70%	100.00%

Table 2 summarizes the number and proportion of irregular, regular, and integrated coordinative arrangements for the 54 organizations in the water quality provision system.

Table 2 reveals that almost 400 of the coordinative arrangements between organizations in the provision system, a number amounting to 50 per cent of the total arrangements, involve not just frequent interaction but frequent and planned provision of services by more than one organization. Again it cannot be said that there is no coordination in the provision system in question. Moreover, it may also be said that, because only 31 per cent of the arrangements are infrequent, that coordination does not take place sporadically and in an unplanned fashion.

It might finally, be argued that coordinative arrangements across governmental levels and between governmental levels and the private sector are merely of the sporadic kind, and consequently not of major importance in institutionalizing the interdependencies between organizations. In other words, regular and integrated coordination across levels of government and between government and the private sector are significantly constrained by constitutional and/or political considerations. Table 3 does indeed indicate that there is a weak association (Cramer's V = 0.23) between government level (and private sector) and type of coordinative arrangement, with the provincially owned organizations in particular much more likely to enter integrated coordinative arrangements. However, Table 4 indicates that some of this association can be accounted for by differences between governmental organizations and private ones. Governmental agencies are more likely than private ones to rely on integrated rather than other types of arrangements. Again, the weight of the evidence would indicate that any weaknesses in the performance of the provision system do not appear to be associated with a lack of coordination, and that constitutional and/or political constraints make only a small difference in the proclivity of govern-

Table 3 *Type of arrangements by government level and private sector*

	Level								
Type	Provincial[1]		Federal[2]		Local/Regional		Private		Private	
	N	(%)	N	(%)	N	(%)	N	(%)	N	(%)
Irregular	71	(26.30)	63	(31.66)	40	(30.77)	71	(39.01)	245	(31.37)
Regular	26	(9.63)	23	(11.56)	34	(26.15)	57	(31.32)	140	(17.93)
Integrated	173	(64.07)	113	(56.78)	56	(43.08)	54	(29.67)	396	(50.70)
Totals	270	(100)	119	(100)	130	(100)	182	(100)	781	(100)

Chi Square = 83.43 $p \leq 0.01$ V = 0.23

Notes: 1. Includes medical health officers, who are joint provincial-local officials.
2. Includes the International Pacific Salmon Fisheries Commission, which has federal appointees (+ US appointees) as commissioners.

Table 4 *Types of arrangements by government or private sector*

Type	Government		Private		Total	
	N	(%)	N	(%)	N	(%)
Irregular	174	(29.05)	71	(39.01)	245	(31.37)
Regular	83	(13.86)	57	(31.32)	140	(17.93)
Integrated	342	(57.10)	54	(29.67)	396	(50.70)
Totals	599	(100.01)	182	(100)	781	(100)

Chi Square = 48.88 $p < 0.01$ V = 0.25

mental organizations to enter into integrated coordination arrangements across levels of government.

In sum, our data indicate that there is substantial coordination within the provision system, that the coordination is not sporadic and unplanned, and that it can take place both across and within government and privately owned sectors. In other words, there is little empirical evidence to substantiate the assertions of much literature on water quality management that a lack of coordination exists within the institutional arrangements for, at least, this particular river basin.

Procedures for Coordination

The methods or procedures for coordination are instructive for two reasons. First, they illustrate the range of techniques available for taking into account the mutual interdependencies between provision system members. More important, previous studies have focused their attention either on hierarchical decision-making or on contracting between organizations, yet it appears that many of the procedures for coordination are less formalized than either of these two alternatives, and that a substantial element of 'government' (in a generic sense) consists of arrangements and interactions between public and private organizations that are not captured by either alternative.[16] Consequently, a five-fold categorization or typology of non-hierarchical arrangements within the water quality system is now discussed and illustrated, and a number of suggestive hypotheses advanced as to the relative benefits and costs for the policy in question. The arrangements are categorised by their degree of formalization, from the most formal arrangement, contracting, through referrals, committees, working agreements, to the least formal arrangement, tacit agreements.

Contracts between organizations in the provision system are formal mechanisms by which one organization will provide a packageable service to one or more other organizations on a *quid pro quo* basis. Often, the contracts are constructed on a fee-for-service basis, and an extensive market operates for the sale and purchase of consultative engineering and biological services in the Lower Fraser. Contractual relationships exist in the private sector, such as between industrial effluent permit holders (or applicants) and private consultants for engineering design and effluent monitoring. They exist between governmentally owned organizations and privately owned organizations, such as between the Harbour Commissions and private dredging firms for dredging other than regular channel maintenance. And they exist between purely governmental organizations for 'support' services. An example of the last phenomenon is the use of laboratory support services by the Land and Water Quality Group which purchases laboratory services of different kinds from the Provincial Ministry of Agriculture, the Federal Inland Waters Directorate, the Federal Department of Agriculture, the BC Water Resources Chemistry Laboratory, as well as from the laboratory it jointly operates with Federal Fisheries and Marine Services. Contracts are, in other words, a frequently used and often an effective set of indicators of the value of a range of services provided by members of a water quality provision system.

However, it may be hypothesized that there are incentives on organizations in the public sector to provide support services to other agencies free or below going market rates. First, such services tend to be over-used and an incentive is generated to overexpand the agency, subject to the constraints of the budgetary process.[17] This hypothesis is consistent with the conclusion of the works of Niskanen (1971) and others, but does not require assumptions about the preferences of politicians and hence fits better with the empirical realities of parliamentary systems. Secondly, when such support services are overused, it increases the discretion of bureaucrats to 'set priorities' amongst a variety of users. A number of theorists have generated conclusions about the behaviour of agencies consistent with empirical realities on the basis of postulated (but not theoretically derived) assumptions about bureaucratic discretion (Migue and Belanger, 1974). In other words, despite the global efficiencies of contracting for support services at market rates in the public sector, such a procedure for coordination may be underused because of advantages accruing to agencies and bureaucrats from providing such services free of charge or below going rates.

A second, but less formal procedure, for implementing coordinative arrangements between organizations in the water quality provision system for the Lower Fraser River is that of referrals. These are mechanisms whereby one or more organizations provide information and consultative services to other organizations in response to a formal request, but without a negotiated *quid pro quo.* They can be multilateral information and consultancy systems or bilateral ones between only two organizations in the provision system. An example of the former, and the most extensive system in operation in the provision system in question, is the Pollution Control Branch referral system, when the application for an effluent disposal permit (or permit change) is referred by the Pollution Control Branch (a) to six Provincial agencies; (b) to the particular field offices of these Provincial agencies if the head offices wish, and they usually do; (c) to the Federal Environment Protection Service and hence to two Federal agencies and their field offices, and to the International Pacific Salmon Fisheries Commission; (d) to the particular municipality and regional district in which an outfall is located; and (e) by virtue of the publication of the application in the *BC Gazette,* to the BC Wildlife Federation, SPEC, and the BC Environmental Council (three interest groups that monitor the Gazette), all of which may refer further to their member organizations. Comments on the application, as well as technical information on likely impacts of the application if available, are then transmitted back to the PCB either directly or through tortuous channels, and the PCB mayor may not include the comments of an agency in its negotiations with the applicant.

Many other multilateral and bilateral referral systems exist in the provision system, and an example of a bilateral referral system is the schedule of channel maintenance dredging operations transmitted by the Marine and Civil Engineering Section to the Habitat Protection Directorate for comment.

Such referral systems have the advantage of reducing the transaction costs for an organization in finding out and commenting on the routine operations of another organization in the provision system. But this advantage must be weighed against the disadvantage to an organization of having some of its economic resources and activities tied up in processing such referrals; the Habitat Protection Section, for example, has three full time personnel engaged in processing merely the PCB referrals alone. It may be hypothesized that many agencies in the system prefer not to weigh the benefits and costs of responding to referrals, in the light of the expected value of the referring organization adopting the position of the organization in question. Instead, it appears that many agencies prefer to use the disadvantages as an argument or budget strategy, while complaining about a lack of coordination in the absence of a *quid pro quo* attached to such referral systems.

Standing and *ad hoc* committees are a third mechanism by which the interdependencies of organizations in the provision system are coordinated. An example of a standing committee is the Technical Planning Committee of the Greater Vancouver Regional District which consists of 21 administrative representatives from member municipalities, the District itself, and Provincial and Federal agencies, and which, on occasion, can serve as a forum for information exchange and integrated activities that bear upon water quality matters for the Lower Fraser. An example of an *ad hoc* committee would the Task Force established in the Winter of 1974–5 to investigate the causes of a duck kill in the Ladner area of the basin, a committee which consisted of administrative representatives of the Canadian Wildlife Service, the Land and Water Quality Group, the Habitat Protection Section, and the BC Ministry of Agriculture.

Committees are flexible and explicit forums for negotiation and bargaining between interdependent interests. They operate under rules of willing or unanimous consent, with the consequences that each represented interest is taken into account in decision making but at the cost of (on occasions) extended transaction and bargaining costs (Buchanan and Tullock, 1962). However, because not all interdependencies are symmetric and equivalent between provision system members, there is an incentive on some organizations to avoid such mechanisms except where established by statute. In other words, as in the case of contracts, committees appear to be an underexploited mechanism for coordination.

A fourth kind of procedure used to implement the interdependencies between organizations in the provision system is that of working agreements. Working agreements are arrangements between individual personnel in one or more organizations to provide mutually beneficial services. Personnel in the Provincial Habitat Protection Section and the Habitat Protection Directorate will usually, for example, consult over PCB permit applications (or permit change applications) and submit similar comments to the PCB referral system; sometimes these informal interactions will involve the clientele groups of these agencies, such as the BC Wildlife Federation, or involve other personnel in the 'fishing industry', such as staff members of the International Pacific Salmon Fisheries Commission. So important are these working agreements, often arranged on the telephone, that a large portion of administrative expertise appears to consist of establishing 'trap lines' and maintaining such contacts in other organizations in the provision system. Working agreements are flexible mechanisms for dealing with interdependencies when they arise, but they can constitute an entry cost for new personnel in the system as they learn about who does what, alone or jointly, in the various organizations in the system. Environmental interest groups, without relative permanency in executive positions, appear least able to bear these entry costs.

Finally, it must be noted that arrangements between organizations are occasionally implemented by tacit agreement. That is, one organization may undertake or not undertake a particular activity, because its personnel know that *another* organization is undertaking or not undertaking such activities.[18] For example, it appears that until 1971, there was a tacit agreement that the primary responsibility for the management of the salmonoid fishery in the Lower Fraser would fall on the International Pacific Salmon Fisheries Commission, and that the Federal responsibilities would be primarily for the management of salmonoids in other estuaries. Personnel changes in organizations (international, federal, and provincial) in the provision system has been one factor that has now changed this tacit agreement. It is difficult to place any estimate on the number of tacit agreements in the system because such a mechanism of coordination 'may occur below the threshold of conscious design' for many members in the provision system (Fiesema, 1967, pp. 123–4). However, their usefulness and importance for coordinating interdependencies depends on stability among and between user interests in the basin, a condition which is violated in most estuaries, including the Fraser.

In short, the irregular, regular and integrated coordinative arrangements between organizations in the provision system are implemented by a number of mechanisms that vary in their degree of formalization. It appears that contracting and committees offer some efficiency advantages in that they can signal, register, and provide procedures for the coordination of a range of market and non-market interests found in any River Basin. However, it also appears that there are incentives on agencies often to avoid such mechanisms, and resort instead to referrals, working agreements and tacit agreements that do not possess the same kinds of advantages. It seems doubtful that parliamentary systems possess the kinds of self-correcting political mechanisms to eliminate these latter incentives (Sproule-Jones, 1975).

CONCLUSION

Evidence has been presented to show that there is extensive coordination between public and private organizations interested in and affected by water quality conditions in the Lower Fraser River. This conclusion is contrary to many assumptions and statements in literature on water quality management. It is also contrary to many of the assumptions and statements to be found in the literature on public administration and provides yet more evidence, from another policy field, to indicate that hierarchy is neither a necessary nor a sufficient condition for coordination of interdependencies in production and/or consumption.

A number of suggestive hypotheses have also been raised about the relative advantages and disadvantages of five kinds of coordinative mechanisms found in the provision system in question. These hypotheses have been generated in an inductive fashion from a careful scrutiny of interorganizational and interpersonal interactions, and while they are consistent with the assumptions and/or conclusions of a number of previous public choice analyses of bureaucratic behaviour, they require further empirical verification to confirm their warrantability. It is also to be hoped that subsequent public choice theorizing about bureaucratic behaviour will move beyond studies of hierarchical decision-making and contracting between organizations, and include other forms of interorganizational arrangements that appear to constitute such a large element in 'government'.

NOTES

The author wishes to acknowledge the help of Irving K. Fox and Kenneth G. Peterson of the Westwater Research Centre at the University of British Columbia in facilitating research on water quality management for the Lower Fraser River, some findings from which are reported in this paper. A Canada Council Research Grant (No. 66–0208) financed part of the research.
1. A descriptive overview of the uses of the estuary will be found in Fox (1976).
2. A recent overview of these studies will be found in Niskanen (1975).
3. Further details on the methodology and details about the activities and objectives of the organizations in the provision system may be obtained from the author.

4. This organization is a Provincial agency that is primarily concerned with implementing Province-wide effluent standards. Consequently, its major activities in the Basin consist of reviewing changes in permits, and monitoring compliance with permit regulations, from some 88 individual and 4 collective point sources of effluent discharge.

5. This is a trade association of 75 per cent of all towboat operators engaged in the transportation of forest products on the River. Its major activity is in lobbying for the control of sawlog debris, largely because of the increasing insurance costs of damaged vessels.

6. This is a private company engaged in log transportation and storage, ship building and repair, freighting and barge transportation. It also administers some foreshore and upland leases from federal and provincial agencies.

7. This is a Federal agency with a primary concern for maintaining navigation channels (through its annual dredging program) or improving navigation and moorage facilities (by contracting out dredging programs).

8. This is a Federal agency that is primarily concerned with administering the Canada–US Migratory Birds Convention Act (1966) which protects certain insect-eating migratory birds.

9. The Scientific Pollution and Environment Control Society—'Central'—is the provincial office of the largest conservationist interest group in the Basin.

10. A Federal agency that conducts receiving water studies in connection with specific effluent discharges and other *ad hoc* projects.

11. This is a City agency that, *inter alia*, implements the City by-law setting effluent standards for industrial discharges to municipal sewers.

12. These are field officers of a Provincial agency that issues water licenses, and compliance with their terms, for a variety of beneficial uses.

13. The central office for over 140 rod and gun clubs in the Province.

14. A Provincial agency that provides mainly consultative services on the biological effects of site specific developments in the Province.

15. This is a Federal agency that provides mainly consultative services on the biological and water quality effects of site specific developments out of its primary mission for the protection of salmon spawning, feeding, and stop-over areas.

16. Notable exceptions in the literature are the works of Friesema (1971), McDavid (1974), and the ongoing studies of Elinor Ostrom and associates.

17. Work-load statistics and the queueing of cases being a frequently used justification during this process.

18. See, especially, Friesema (1967), pp. 123–4.

References

Beecroft, Eric. *The Municipality's Role in Water Management* (Montreal: Canadian Federation of Mayors and Municipalities, 1966).

Buchanan, James M. and Gordon Tullock. *The Calculus of Consent* (Ann Arbor: University of Michigan Press, 1962).

Cram, John S. *Water: Canadian Needs and Resources* (Harvest House Press, 1971).

Fox, Irving K. in Anthony H. J. Dorcey, (ed.), *The Uncertain Future of the Lower Fraser* (University of British Columbia Press, 1976), pp. 5–19.

Franson, Robert T., et al. 'The Legal Framework for Water Quality Management in the Lower Fraser River of British Columbia,' in N.A. Swainson ed. *Managing the Water Environment* (University of British Columbia Press, 1976), pp. 54–95.

Friesema, H. Paul. *Metropolitan Political Structure* (University of Iowa Press, 1971).

Gregg, Phillip M. 'Units and Levels of Analysis: A Problem of Policy Analysis in Federal Systems', *Publius* 4 (1974), pp. 87–108.

Haefele, Edwin T. *Representative Government and Environmental Management* (Johns Hopkins Press, 1973).

Kneese, Alan V. and Blair T. Bower. *Managing Water Quality: Economics, Technology, Institutions* (Johns Hopkins Press, 1968).

MacNeill, James W. *Environmental Management* (Information Canada, 1971).

McDavid, James C. 'Interjurisdictional Cooperation Among Police Departments in the St. Louis Metropolitan Area', *Publius* 4 (1974), pp. 35–58.

Migue, Jean-Luc and Gerard Belanger. 'Toward a General Theory of Managerial Discretion', *Public Choice* 17 (1974), pp. 27–42.

Niskanen, William A. *Bureaucracy and Representative Government* (Aldine, 1971).

—— 'Bureaucrats and Politicans', *Journal of Law and Economics* 18 (1975), pp. 617–44.

Ostrom, Elinor. 'On the Meaning and Measurement of Output and Efficiency in the Provision of Urban Police Services', *Journal of Criminal Justice* 1 (1973), pp. 93–112.

—— et al. 'Defining and Measuring Structural Variations in Interorganizational Arrangements', *Publius* 4 (1974), pp. 87–108.

Ostrom, Vincent. *The Intellectual Crisis in American Public Administration,* rev. edn (University of Alabama Press, 1974).

Savas, E.S. 'Solid Waste Collection in Metropolitan Areas.' in Elinor Ostrom ed., *The Delivery of Urban Services: Outcomes of Change* 10 (Urban Affairs Annual Reviews, Sage Publications, 1976).

Sproule-Jones, Mark. *Public Choice and Federalism in Australia and Canada* (Australian National University Press, 1975).

28

The Political Economy of Policy Instruments: Tax Expenditures and Subsidies in Canada

Kenneth Woodside

The rapid growth in the size of government since the Second World War has been accompanied by an explicit and widespread use of policy instruments to intervene in the operation and change the character of the economy. While intervention was already practised by Canadian governments prior to the war, the espousal of Keynesian economic doctrine by the political élites during and after the war resulted in an expanded use of interventionist techniques by politicians and officials. The growing intervention by governments has made analysts of all political persuasions aware of and interested in the actions of politicians and the institutions of government in attempting to influence the working of the economy. This relationship between political and economic factors is the focus of study in political economy. One approach involves an examination of the ways that different policy instruments used by government involve different political processes and are used to solve the problems of different social and economic groups. It can be argued that politicians and officials face a market in policy instruments, and that a range of factors will contribute to their choice.[1]

Governments may attempt to regulate certain activities in order to eliminate or minimize undesirable behaviour. Alternatively, governments may prefer to provide a service through a public or crown corporation either de novo or as a result of some method of nationalization. Governments may also attempt to change or influence behaviour through some form of fiscal activity such as monetary or taxation policy-making or through the spending of public funds. Each of these policy instruments may be used separately or in some combination as a means of satisfying a mix of policy goals. In this essay I will undertake a comparative analysis of the different political processes that encompass two of these policy instruments, the tax incentive, and the expenditure subsidy.

A tax incentive, or tax expenditure as it has come to be described in recent years, is a provision within the tax statutes that affords special treatment for certain designated types of income or wealth. This special treatment takes the form of a reduction in tax liability; it is called a tax expenditure because the recipient benefits by the

Kenneth Woodside, 'The Political Economy of Policy Instruments: Tax Expenditures and Subsidies in Canada' in *The Politics of Canadian Public Policy*, Michael M. Atkinson and Marsha A. Chandler, eds. © 1983 University of Toronto Press: 173–97. Reprinted by permission of the publisher.

amount of the reduction in taxes. A subsidy is a direct payment made by government to individuals or organizations that satisfy certain conditions.

Each of these two policy instruments can be used to achieve a diverse range of goals. Expenditure subsidies may be used to assist Canadian shipyards in building, repairing, or converting ships, or to encourage multinational automobile companies to set up parts production facilities in Canada rather than in the United States, Europe, or in Southeast Asia. Expenditure subsidies may also be used to supplement the incomes of low-income pensioners or to provide family allowances. The diversity of such expenditures is matched by tax incentive provisions. While taxes have traditionally been thought of as instruments to raise revenue, over the past few decades they have also been used to pursue a wide range of other goals. For instance, the traditional personal income tax system with its standard deductions related to family size and dependency has been further complicated by deductions aimed at promoting home ownership and establishment of retirement savings plans. Similarly, tax incentives have been introduced to encourage the installation of pollution abatement equipment by industry and to promote the location of industry in the less developed areas of Canada.

In the next section I will discuss the general character of these two policy instruments and attempt to relate their characteristics to the management of conflict and other general goals of politicians. In the third section I will assess the extent to which the instruments are used. The fourth section will compare the different political processes within the government and Parliament that produce the two different types of policy output. In the fifth section this comparison will be extended to the political process outside the government and Parliament in order to assess differences in the responses of constituent groups to each policy instrument as well as the broader income distribution implications of each type of policy instrument. In the sixth section some of the administrative and efficiency considerations of any choice will be discussed. Finally, some proposed reforms of the tax policy process and the 1981 effort to eliminate some tax expenditures will be considered. The focus is largely on the federal government. This reflects the character of Canada's taxation system, where most tax expenditures have been introduced by the national government and provincial taxes are expressed as a function of the federal tax.

POLICY CHARACTERISTICS: TAXES AND SUBSIDIES

In recent years the wide use of tax incentives has become a topic of growing controversy. Public-finance specialists, in increasing numbers, have begun to distinguish between the normal tax structure—those sections necessary to the revenue-raising function of the tax structure—and what they call tax expenditures.[2] The purpose of the distinction has been to highlight the use of tax measures as a form of expenditure and to distinguish it from the usual revenue-raising function. While there are difficulties associated with this distinction, tax expenditures may be defined as special provisions in the tax statutes, applicable to particular types of business or sources of income, which result in those designated types of income being taxed at a lower rate than would otherwise be levied.[3] We will use the terms 'tax expenditure' and 'tax incentive' interchangeably. Tax incentives are viewed by most public-finance practitioners as being conceptually equivalent to expenditure subsidies, except that the former are administered through the tax system. Although some tax expenditures are difficult to reformulate in the terms of an expenditure subsidy, they do represent deviations from a normal rate of tax and thus involve a tax saving, which is passed on to those who are eligible to receive it. The net result of a tax expenditure is that tax revenue that ordinarily would have been collected by the government is not collected.

This is a crucial difference between tax expenditures and expenditure subsidies. Whereas the subsidy involves money that comes to a recipient from the government in the form, for instance, of a grant—a transaction that involves government ownership and control over the money prior to receipt of the grant—the tax expenditure involves money that the government has not taken from the recipient, which suggests that the recipient has been and remains the owner of those funds. The tax expenditure is thus a less direct form of government action, involving the failure to do something (i.e., to tax income at the regular rate) that the government supposedly would otherwise have done. In a mixed economy with a strong private sector and supported by widely held beliefs in free enterprise, the directness or indirectness of governmental action may be an important factor in policy instrument choice.

A second and related difference between tax expenditures and expenditure subsidies concerns their visibility. While expenditures will be funded through the Consolidated Revenue Fund, to which all taxpayers have contributed, and leave an audit trail that clearly ties them to government action, the tax expenditure involves forgone revenue, the cost of which appears less obviously to be a burden on other taxpayers.[4] The visibility or relative invisibility of government behaviour is important because, when government acts, its behaviour is discriminatory. Government interventions are bound to benefit one group more than another.[5] They are both a response to and a source of conflict within society and, as a result, the extent to which the government is seen to be favouring or abusing any group or individual may well rebound to its disadvantage.

The importance of the visibility or relative invisibility of the exercise of government power, therefore, is that this exercise of power entails winners and losers, and thus conflict. The extent to which the action is easily associated with the government can become an important variable in government decision-making. Incumbent politicians normally will seek to minimize the level of conflict focused on them in order to enhance their chances of staying in office. The desire to be re-elected, to promote one's career, and to reward one's allies usually leads to efforts by politicians to control and minimize the level of conflict created by the interventions of their governments.[6]

The two characteristic differences between tax expenditures and expenditure subsidies—their directness or indirectness and their visibility or relative invisibility—are obviously closely related. The more indirectly a government policy instrument operates, the less visible the government's actions will probably be. A policy instrument that is more direct in its application will make the source of the policy more visible. These underlying differences are reflected in and enhanced by the political processes that produce the different forms of intervention.

THE CANADIAN EXPERIENCE

Before proceeding with a comparison of the political processes and characteristics that differentiate the use of tax expenditures and subsidies, a brief assessment of the extent of their respective use is necessary. First, evidence will be provided on the amounts of money being spent by Canadian governments, especially the federal government, through expenditure subsidies and tax expenditures. Second, we will examine the extent to which tax expenditures and subsidies have been growing in relative importance. It will be seen, first, that huge sums of public funds are being dispersed by both expenditure subsidies and tax expenditures and, second, that in recent years the growth in tax expenditures has substantially exceeded the growth in expenditure subsidies.

The federal government spent just over $53 billion in fiscal year 1979–80. This money was spent on a wide range of objects from government salaries, police protection, and welfare payments to medical services and subsidies to corporations. While it is difficult to determine what proportion of this spending subsidized non-governmental activities, about $10 billion went for income maintenance activities and over $5 billion for economic development and support.[7] When people talk about government spending, they are usually referring to this accounting for expenditures. Indeed, until very recently it was the only accounting available. However, as we have already argued, there is another type of expenditure accomplished through the tax system. In 1979 the federal government published its first description of these tax expenditures. According to the estimates provided, the federal corporate and personal income tax structures alone incorporated special provisions which reduced tax revenues by almost $26 billion, a sum equal to almost one-half of federal expenditures for that fiscal year.[8] Furthermore, this Tax Expenditure Account did not include all tax incentives—many were omitted or not accounted for 'because of resource constraints and data limitations'.[9]

While previous estimates of the size and scope of tax expenditures were often controversial with respect to both their methodology and conclusions and while the federal government estimate is inconclusive in character, it is useful to review the findings of this literature. The first attempt to measure tax expenditures was made by the Royal Commission on Taxation, which estimated the revenue cost of a selected number of corporate income tax measures and several other personal income tax exemptions at 16 per cent of the total governmental revenue for 1964 derived from personal and corporate income taxes.[10] A decade later, David Perry estimated that all corporate income tax expenditures for 1973 cost Canadian governments 67 per cent of the total federal and provincial corporate income tax revenues collected.[11] In a subsequent study, Roger Smith estimated slightly higher ratios of 74.9 per cent and 68.7 per cent of corporate tax revenues for 1974 and 1975 respectively, using the same tax measures studied by Perry.[12] A study done by the National Council of Welfare estimated that a sum equivalent to 62 per cent of federal and provincial personal income tax revenue in 1974 had been disbursed in the form of tax expenditures.[13] In a subsequent study, the council estimated that twenty personal income tax expenditures alone cost the federal government $7.1 billion in 1976, a sum $800 mil-

lion greater than the federal deficit for that year (whose size was, at the time, the subject of great controversy).[14] The National Council of Welfare studies, however,
included a number of exemptions that usually are considered to be part of the normal income tax structure, not tax expenditures. Allan Maslove estimated that 31 per
cent of personal income tax revenue had been lost as tax expenditures in 1976, a sum
over 50 per cent higher proportionately than that estimated by Jonathan Kesselman
for 1973.[15] Given the introduction of a large number of exemptions and deductions
in the intervening years, these two estimates are roughly compatible.[16] In assessing all
the studies, the obvious conclusion is that while the federal government has spent
substantial sums as expenditure subsidies, it has disbursed at the same time large
amounts as tax expenditures. Indeed, in areas such as economic development, tax
spending has exceeded expenditure subsidies, at least in recent years.[17]

Not only do tax expenditures amount to substantial sums when compared to
government expenditure subsidies, they have also been growing at a faster rate.[18]
Edward Tamargo estimated that tax expenditures had grown by 42 per cent from
1976 through 1979 as compared to a 30.4 per cent growth rate for expenditures.[19]
Roger Smith, in a projection of Kesselman's analysis for 1973 through 1976, found
that personal income tax expenditures increased by 50 per cent in 1974, 18 per cent
in 1975, and 34 per cent in 1976.[20] Richard Bird, as reported by Smith, estimated federal and provincial corporate tax expenditures at 37 per cent of total corporate tax
expenditures collected in 1964 by both the federal and provincial governments.[21] In
1973 David Perry estimated federal and provincial corporate tax expenditures at
about 67 per cent of total federal and provincial corporate taxes for that year; while
Roger Smith's extension of Perry's analysis to 1975 set the value of corporate tax
expenditures at almost 69 per cent of total federal and provincial corporate tax revenues.[22] All of these studies indicate that, compared to expenditure subsidies, tax
expenditures have been growing at a relatively rapid rate in recent years. This surge
in tax spending has occurred at the same time that a heightened sensitivity to and
gradual reduction of government expenditures has been developing.

THE POLITICAL PROCESSES IN GOVERNMENT AND PARLIAMENT

In comparing the processes through which tax incentives and subsidies are devised
within the government and passed by Parliament, the most important element may
well be the range of interests and actors that play an influential role in each area of
the policy-making process and must be accommodated. Taxation policy decision-
making is guided by and carried on within the parliamentary tradition of budget
secrecy. This doctrine constrains open discussion of proposed tax changes even within
the cabinet, and therefore provides fewer opportunities for opponents of a measure
to intervene before the government is committed to a position by the finance minister in his budget speech. As well, it reduces the ability of the government's tax officers to obtain outside advice on possible alternatives.[24] The result is that tax policy
decisions are made by a small number of officials within the Department of Finance
and are less directly subject to the scrutiny of interested parties.[25]

In the case of subsidies, such wide-ranging scrutiny is the norm. All proposals are subject to review and analysis by the appropriate department, the policy-sector committee, the Treasury Board and its secretariat, and cabinet.[26] Departmental proponents of a measure will have to confront and justify its costs to the Treasury Board Secretariat. Subsidies normally involve complicated inter-departmental negotiations, and consequently their approval is more awkward. The net result is that decision-making power over tax policy is highly concentrated, and that more actors and a wider range of interests are involved in the review of subsidy decisions. The new system of 'policy envelopes' introduced by the Conservative government in 1979 encompasses both tax expenditures and subsidies, so that tax incentives sought by departments other than Finance must undergo more rigorous review procedures involving the policy sector committee, the Treasury Board, Finance, and cabinet.[27] However, Finance's ability to introduce independently new tax incentives and expand or reduce others has not been affected by this new system. While the authority of the Department of Finance in tax policy may have been somewhat eroded over the last decade, the department continues to operate within a policy process comparatively well insulated from many political pressures.[28]

A second factor differentiating the political processes of tax incentives and subsidies within the government is the implications of each for policy administration. All tax measures are administered by officials in National Revenue although in some cases the use of a tax incentive may have to be approved by the relevant department. Thus, while an accelerated capital cost allowance for pollution abatement equipment was introduced in 1965, it was not until 1970 that claimants needed certification by Environment Canada to establish eligibility.[29] Subsidies are usually administered by the department normally responsible for the relevant area of activity. The result may be badly administered policy when tax incentives are used in place of subsidies because the government administrators may be more concerned with the integrity of a provision as a tax measure than they are with its cost-effectiveness or its implications for the policy area generally.

Third, recent developments in the character and complexity of federal-provincial relations make tax expenditures more attractive as a policy instrument for the federal government. In most areas of government policy apart from taxation the federal and provincial levels of government pursue highly interdependent policy strategies, and unilateral action by one level of government can be a source of concern and ill will for the other level.[30] Co-operation has been increasingly difficult to obtain because of the conflict between pressures of province-building and nation-building.[31] However, while subsidies may be introduced only after lengthy negotiation between the federal and provincial governments, the federal government can still act unilaterally in the area of taxation. While the sales tax dispute of 1978 and the 1980 proposals for resource taxation may be harbingers of a more complicated and interdependent taxation policy process in years to come, this area remains one in which federal autonomy, both de jure and de facto, is high.[32] Since tax expenditures appear less intrusive as a result of their more indirect character, federal action through the tax structure is usually construed to involve less interference with provincial government responsibilities. The irony of this is that federal tax expenditures may not only involve intrusions into provincial areas of legislative competence but may also entail a loss of revenue to the province because of shared tax bases and the provincial tax levies being calculated as a percentage of the basic federal tax.[33]

A fourth area of comparison relates to the character of information available to the public concerning the use of tax expenditures and subsidies. Until 1979 the government published no data on the cost of tax measures beyond the occasional estimate of the cost of a new provision for the first year, which would be presented in the budget statement. Since 1979 the government has published an annual Tax Expenditure Account, but these documents leave much to be desired. The tax expenditure estimates are far from complete; they show no totals for even sub-categories of tax expenditures, and they are full of disclaimers as to the ultimate value of the exercise despite the large sums involved.[34] The costs of subsidies, on the other hand, are detailed annually in the main or supplementary estimates and, unlike tax expenditures, are audited by the auditor-general. Further, descriptions of the purposes and goals of subsidies, while not above criticism themselves, tend to be better documented than tax expenditures.[35] The relatively greater visibility of subsidies contributes to the apparently greater interest of MPs and even prime ministers in the examination of subsidies, and thus makes the introduction of new subsidies somewhat more subject to comment and evaluation, if not control, within Parliament.[36]

A fifth and final area of comparison with respect to the political processes involved in tax expenditures and subsidies relates to the political process within Parliament. At first glance the differences in process are substantial, although, as we shall see, there are grounds to question the extent to which one process is more effective as a means of control than the other. Changes in tax incentives are normally introduced into the House through the budget speech. Until that time the proposals will have been kept secret from all but a few officials within the Department of Finance and, as budget day approaches, the prime minister and finally cabinet.[37] The proposed tax changes will not have been debated within the government party caucus. Still, once the changes are introduced through the budget, the government normally regards itself as committed to the stated position, and for this reason is quite inflexible toward admendments.[38] The budget proposals will receive detailed committee examination from the Committee of the Whole, in which the opposition is unable to call expert witnesses or conduct hearings. The result of this procedure is that proposed tax expenditures are subject to relatively little scrutiny once they are introduced. Even where a tax measure includes a time limit providing for its expiration, the tax expenditure is regularly extended with little comment.[39] Moreover, some tax changes can be introduced by regulations issued through order-in-council as a result of provisions in the Income Tax Act.[40] In this way parliamentary review can be avoided almost entirely. Subsidy proposals will have been subject to much more open discussion and analysis within the government and within the caucus and, on introduction to the House, are referred to a standing committee for detailed examination after second reading. The standing committees can receive testimony and evidence from outside experts and can even meet if the House is not sitting.[41] Once passed, the estimated cost of a subsidy will always be reflected in the estimates as long as it is in place and even though the measure itself does not receive specific examination frequently.

These differences suggest that tax expenditures are subject to significantly less careful examination and control by Parliament than are subsidies. While in general it is true that the scrutiny of tax proposals is less far-reaching, many questions have been raised about the effectiveness of parliamentary control over the expenditure process. Various critics have noted a long list of problems with the House of Commons standing committees, including poor attendance by MPs, a lack of expertise and background knowledge which might make MPs' committee questioning effective, an excessively high turnover in committee membership that makes expertise difficult to acquire and does not allow good working relationships to develop, excessive control over committee work by the government, inadequacies in the format of the estimates as they are received by the House and the committees, and a lack of interest on the part of MPs in really controlling spending costs.[42] By the time that the estimates reach the House, they have already gone through a long negotiation process and reflect a balance of interests reached within the government, thus making the government more resistant to adjustments in its plans.[43] The Royal Commission on Financial Management and Accountability reported in 1979 that 'ministers and officials consider review of Estimates, for example, a waste of time'.[44] Finally, many government expenditures, both statutory and non-statutory, are far from easily changed because they reflect a consensus of the federal and provincial governments at a particular point in time or are necessary to provide for the orderly operation of the country.[45]

Looking back over the argument so far, it is clear that tax expenditures are the product of a political process subject to a more concentrated and narrowly based range of interests, that they offer more freedom to the federal government within the context of inter-governmental relations, that their costs are somewhat less visible, and that their passage through the House of Commons is easier and involves less careful scrutiny. These features make tax expenditures attractive to some elements of the government in that, depending on what the government is attempting to achieve, it can act more decisively and less conspicuously through the tax system.

Among these factors the relatively lesser visibility of tax expenditures as compared to expenditure subsidies is of great importance. It perpetuates the existing pattern wherein a narrow range of interests are influential in tax policy making and it generates less pressure to increase the scrutiny of tax expenditures by Parliament and to produce more information about tax preferences for public evaluation. The lack of visibility also generates less concern over conflicts and inconsistencies in departmental responsibilities and makes the provincial governments either less willing or less able to oppose tax reductions that interfere with their jurisdiction while benefiting their constituents. To the extent that visibility and an openness of the policy process to the broadest range of interests possible are positive features of a healthy and balanced policy, the characteristics of the process of legislating tax expenditures do not contribute to the healthy functioning of a democratic state.

THE POLITICAL PROCESSES BEYOND GOVERNMENT AND PARLIAMENT

Looking at the political process more broadly, a first area of comparison is the distributive and equity implications of each policy instrument. Can choice of policy instrument affect who gets what when? Distributive implications can be seen in three areas: with respect to individuals, with respect to corporations, and as between Canadians and non-residents.

In the case of the distributive implications of each instrument for individuals, it must be cautioned that tax expenditures or incentives are not necessarily regressive, nor are expenditure subsidies necessarily progressive. Indeed, there are some measures of each kind in each category. However, as tax expenditures are usually structured, few can be described as progressive. This is because of the way that most of them are designed, and especially because of what is called the 'upside-down effect' of tax expenditures where those with the largest incomes receive the greatest absolute benefit.[46] Tax expenditures are normally available through an exemption of income from taxation, a deduction from taxable income, a credit against taxes payable, or a reduction in the rates applicable to certain income. A common feature is that one must have taxable income in order to receive any benefit. Moreover, the more income one has, the better off one is likely to be.[47] As a consequence, a tax expenditure with social-policy implications (such as a deduction for child care or health care expenses against taxable income) will provide the greatest benefit to those with the largest income because their high income makes them subject to higher rates of tax under the progressive income tax structure. Tax expenditures by their very nature, therefore, tend to be regressive in character.[48] While many expenditure subsidies such as subsidies to shipbuilders or pulp and paper firms are likely to be equally advantageous to the well-to-do, a subsidy can be more directly targeted to benefit individuals equally despite variations in their incomes, or indeed especially to benefit those with the lowest incomes. It is largely through the use of subsidy instruments that most social security and welfare payments are implemented, although the 1978 introduction of a refundable child tax credit is a small step toward making tax expenditures more useful to those with lower incomes.[49]

With respect to corporations, tax expenditures tend to be of more financial benefit to large firms than to small firms. Taxes are not paid on tax expenditures (they are usually paid on subsidies or grants). A corporation must make a profit in order to be able to make use of the tax expenditure. The larger and more regular the profit, the greater will be the benefits of these tax expenditures. Thus, since small, private, Canadian-controlled corporations pay taxes at the rate of 25 per cent of taxable income they will benefit less from tax expenditures that reduce their taxable income than larger and more profitable corporations paying tax at the normal rate of 46 per cent. Further, tax expenditures that reduce the cost of capital or reduce the cost of borrowing money to take over another firm will benefit the larger firms that are better able consistently and effectively to use the tax saving potential that such actions generate.[50] Subsidies can be made available to firms regardless of income and profitability, and the benefits available to the recipient company may even be geared to provide more benefits for the less well-off firm.

Finally, there are the differential benefits available to residents and non-residents as a result of tax expenditures and subsidies. Distinctions between the two groups, while mentioned on occasion in the tax code, have not been the rule, and indeed the most general and valuable tax expenditures (especially those provided for the resource industries) have tended to provide greater benefit to non-resident corporations and individuals. The Royal Commission on Taxation estimated that 78 per cent of the revenue derived from its recommended eliminations of tax expenditures would have been extracted from non-residents.[51] The high degree of foreign owner-ship in the manufacturing sector also ensures that the generous tax expenditures available to that sector will be particularly useful and valuable to non-residents.[52] Subsidies, such as those proposed in 1980 for the oil and gas sector by the federal government, can be more effectively and carefully targeted and designed so that for-eign firms are not eligible or only eligible under special circumstances.[53] However, in practice it is not clear that subsidies to the corporate sector have been used much more frequently to aid resident over non-resident firms. The favouring of Canadian residents over non-residents may put Canada in conflict with its obligations under GATT not to discriminate against foreign investors.

In reviewing the distributive implications of tax expenditures and subsidies it is evident that the tax system as a means of program delivery works to the advantage of wealthier rather than poorer individuals and corporations. Although tax measures could be designed to reverse this impact, in practice this has not been the case. While subsidies have been used for the whole range of distributive programs, it is through them that governments have sought to assist the less fortunate individual and corpo-ration.[54] The character of tax expenditures is reflected in the political process that generates them. David Good has described the making of Canadian federal tax pol-icy as the product of an informal process dominated by the interests of business groups and (to some degree) their interpretations of likely outcomes, all of which is balanced against the financial requirements of the government.[55] The mutual trust and informality in the process would appear to work to the advantage of those who are well organized, able to maintain a continuing presence, and establish relations of 'mutual trust', those who share a common perspective with Finance officials, and those who command resources that the government needs or wishes to influence.

A second area of comparison closely related to the first is the regional impact of programs implemented through the two policy instruments. In Canada, the regional distribution of government spending has become an important factor in assessing the desirability of that spending. The government has established and developed programs such as those administered by the former Department of Regional Economic Expansion that are particularly intended to encourage economic development in areas of low growth. The expansion of regionally sensitive subsidy programs proceeds despite the considerable doubt that exists as to their effectiveness or desirability in strictly economic terms.[56] While tax expenditures such as the investment tax credit work to the advantage of emerging firms or firms expanding in less economically developed regions, subsidies have the advantage of helping firms whether or not they are profitable. Subsidies may also be useful to small and new firms in a poor cash-flow situation. Tax expenditures can allow government to act with less concern for the regional impact of a policy. Since a subsidy is a more visible policy instrument than a tax incentive, by using the subsidy the government will not only be attempting to promote business in the less economically developed regions but will be seen to be doing so. The greater visibility of subsidies makes them more symbolically satisfying for the federal government in a time of heightened regional sensitivity. Tax expenditures do not usually require that a firm be located in a particular part of the country; as a result, they allow the government to act with less concern for the regional impact of its policy.

A third area of comparison flows directly out of the greater visibility of subsidies as government programs. The growth of anti-government sentiment in the 1970s and the concomitant emphasis on government expenditures as a measure of the weight of government activity has encouraged proponents of new or expanded programs to pursue their goals through other policy instruments. Since the costs of tax expenditures have not been as well documented, increased reliance on tax expenditures to implement government programs has been a less visible, less conflictual way of expanding government action. As a result, the appearance of government restraints reflected in expenditure cuts could coexist with actual program expansion through the use of new or broadened tax incentives.[57] The pressures for government restraint also made subsidies a less dependable form of aid, as they were more readily subjected to pressures for delay as a measure of spending restraint and, unlike tax expenditures which are administered by National Revenue, they might require the creation of a new bureaucratic apparatus to administer the program.[58] Because tax expenditures do not appear in the estimates, they are less subject to restraint and, indeed, governments have received little credit for restraint in this area. In fact, tax expenditures may appear costless to their proponents. Until the publication of the 1979 Tax Expenditure Account there was no official tabulation of the costs of tax expenditures, and there is evidence that the costs of tax incentives were not monitored with any care.[59] Most tax expenditures are not subject to any limits, and even where there are limits (as with the investment tax credit) they apply only to the individual applicant and are not a global budgetary restraint for the program as a whole.[60] Whether the new envelope system will alter the perception that tax spending is free and is somehow not tied up with the issue of 'big government' is difficult to say, but it seems unlikely that the proponents of budgetary austerity will override the defenders of political opportunism.

Fourth, businessmen usually are more hostile to government subsidy programs. Subsidies are seen to involve excessive intervention and interference with management prerogatives and are 'tainted' by association with other government expenditure programs such as unemployment insurance, welfare, or financial aid to troubled companies. Subsidy programs generally involve procedures to establish eligibility and some degree of control over the actual spending of the subsidy. Substantial discretion is left in the hands of government administrators, and there exists a concomitant threat of interference in the management of the firm's subsidized activities. If governmental assistance is to be received, the preferred policy instrument is a tax expenditure. Tax incentives leave the initiative more clearly in the hands of the private sector beneficiary, especially where the tax expenditure is itself a rather broad and open-ended incentive, and there is the appearance of less governmental interference with management decisions.[61] The word 'appearance' is important in this context because the tax expenditure, if it is effective, obviously involves interference and intervention by government in that satisfying the conditions necessary to use it may have altered the course of action a corporation would otherwise have followed. The underlying desire, therefore, is to diminish the visibility and directness of government support.

Thus, the federal government Ministry of State for Science and Technology in its January 1981 statement on research and development policies, planning, and programming explicitly recognizes the preference of businessmen for government assistance through the tax system rather than as a form of subsidy.[62]

In order to highlight the significance of the greater discretion afforded government officials in expenditure programs, it is useful to compare briefly the differential treatment of individuals charged with income tax and social security fraud.[63] The income tax structure and its administration has been subject to the rule of law since 1948; the statute and subsequent regulations are published, and interpretations and court rulings are public.[64] Social security administration and adjudication is much more subject to discretion, is less open to outside assessment, and affords less protection of the rights of individuals. Rulings by social assistance review boards or by administrators are either unpublished or, if published, are so attenuated that it may be difficult to determine just what principles of law are being followed.[65] The right of search is more extensive in areas of suspected social security abuse than in cases of income tax evasion, and the likelihood of being convicted and incarcerated is much higher. The fact that the income tax system is the main vehicle of assistance for the well-to-do while expenditure subsidies are used to implement social security policies affecting less fortunate individuals is no doubt a critical factor in the different rights that exist in each area of law.

A fifth area of comparison relates to the government's wish to be more or less closely associated with some course of action. The greater visibility of government involvement entailed by subsidies as opposed to tax incentives may influence the choice of policy instrument. If a government has a public commitment to certain policies, it may not want excessive attention focused on deviations from that course. Similarly, the character of a government party's voting constituency may affect the degree of openness with which it will want to be seen courting the support of certain groups: depending on who is in receipt of the benefits, there may be ideological or practical reasons to choose one instrument over another. As we have argued, for instance, businessmen see tax incentives as more of a free-market solution than subsidies, while a new tax exemption will not be of much help to poor people who lack the requisite income to take full advantage of it.

ADMINISTRATIVE AND EFFICIENCY CONSIDERATIONS

Tax incentives take effective immediately upon their introduction into Parliament and thus, in theory, permit a government to respond quickly to a problem. Subsidies only come into effect after they have been passed into law. The speed of delivery of the measures, however, may not reflect these procedures. In the 1970s, for instance, a pattern developed whereby budgetary provisions might take up to a year to be finally passed into law, with the result that while the measure was itself effective immediately, the exact wording of the statute remained unclear. In consequence, the value of the tax expenditure was undercut because of uncertainty about the final wording. While subsidies are subject to a slower process of introduction, the discretion they normally give to administrators allows for a more flexible, less legally bound approach. Further, while tax incentives can in theory be introduced quickly, evidence suggests that much of their impact is subject to considerable time lags and that as a result the cure may have its greatest impact after the problem has become less serious. Moreover, the tax system is structured to provide benefits on an annual basis, whereas subsidy payments can be scheduled with closer attention to the real needs of the recipient. The net result is that subsidies can be a more flexible and responsive policy instrument than tax incentives.

A second difference between the two measures involves their relative efficiency. There is a growing literature that suggests that tax incentives are inefficient and overly costly to government.[66] Subsidies are easier to target than tax expenditures, especially when the object is a narrow sector or group, and they are subject to much closer supervision.[67] (While this closer supervision can make subsidies more cost-effective than tax expenditures, it is also a major source of irritation for many businessmen.) The relative inefficiency of tax expenditures is not just a result of lack of supervision and the excessively wide definition of many tax incentives. It is also a consequence of the increased complexity of the Income Tax Act, where incentives are piled on incentives and many tax expenditures may operate (or fail to operate) in unexpected ways because of unanticipated interaction with existing provisions. In addition, the dense language of the act makes it difficult to be aware of available opportunities. This is less of a problem for larger firms than it is for small private corporations, who may be unable to afford the legal or accounting expertise necessary to interpret the act. Clearly there are grounds to question the efficiency of tax expenditures and to advocate the use of subsidies as a more cost-effective alternative. This thinking is reflected in the new emphasis on investment grants in the federal Petroleum Incentives Program.[68]

In one important area, however, tax expenditures may be preferable to subsidies. Recently, countervailing duties have been levied against the exports of several Canadian firms such as Michelin and Honeywell by the United States government as a result of subsidies paid to the companies. It may well be that the high visibility of subsidies has disadvantages in international trade in that the subsidies threaten to trigger countervailing duties from Canada's trading partners and especially from the United States.

In conclusion, it is argued that tax expenditures do not have the administrative advantages over subsidies that are sometimes ascribed to them. Moreover, tax expenditures tend to be relatively costly and inefficient as instruments of policy. To some extent this higher cost results from government's attempt to create indirectly an environment favourable to certain undertakings. By choosing this oblique course of action, the government may unintentionally fund other unrelated activities through the tax system.

CONCLUSIONS AND RECONSIDERATIONS

This analysis has suggested that substantial differences exist between tax incentives and subsidies. On the one hand, tax expenditures are less visible and less subject to constraint, offer more freedom for a government to act decisively and inconspicuously, are a means of assistance for the well-to-do and for successful large corporations, appear to be without cost to the federal government, and are seen (by the corporate sector especially) not to involve intervention in the economy. On the other hand, subsidies are much more cost-efficient, can be subject to much closer controls on cost and conditions of use, go through a more broadly based and open process of policy formulation, and are commonly the means of redistributive social policies.

These differences raise several points worthy of further discussion. First, a focus on policy instruments alone ignores the substance of a policy. What we want to consider, therefore, is the way in which these two components of the policy process—the substance and the instrument—interact. Second, how did these policy instrument differences evolve? Tax expenditures and subsidies do not necessarily have to take their present form. A tax incentive need not be subject to the 'upside-down' effect. The existing differences reflect to some degree the residue of policy development over the decades. The Income Tax Act, for instance, has evolved in response to a narrower range of interests than can be said of many subsidy policies. Third, what will be the impact of possible reforms of the tax policy process that have been gaining in popularity over the last decade? Finally, what can be learned from the 1981 budget and the tax reforms proposed in that document?

The first question might be posed as follows: does the use to which each type of policy instrument is put produce the differences between them? Are tax incentives less visible because they are the preferred instrument for providing social benefits to the well-to-do and to successful corporations? Are subsidies more visible and open to scrutiny because they are used to aid the poor and to subsidize less successful businesses? These questions mirror one of the perennial disputes in political analysis: how important are political institutions as determinants of public policy outputs?[69] While it is not my purpose to come to grips with this broader question, it is worth noting that many subsidy programs, like tax incentives, are also consistently able to avoid serious political attention. On the one hand, grants to the pulp and paper and to the shipbuilding and repair industries are routinely subject to relatively little public intervention and outsider review. On the other hand, the greater scrutiny usually given to subsidies makes policies that benefit the poor more easily attacked and the benefits of these programs less secure. Tax policies beneficial to the poor, to the very limited extent to which they exist in the Income Tax Act, appear to be better shielded from opposition. In general, assistance to the well-to-do and to successful large corporations is relatively free from criticism and secure in the availability of benefits whether it takes the form of a subsidy or a tax expenditure. The subsidy policies that usually draw the most fire from critics are those such as welfare, unemployment insurance, and DREE grants that assist businesses in the poorer regions of the country. The choice of policy instrument may have an independent impact where policies that benefit the lower income categories are implemented through tax expenditures. Therefore, while the choice of instrument is an important factor in determining the character of the political process that evolves, the substance of the policy is also important. Many of the differences between tax expenditures and expenditure subsidies may have less to do with the instrument used to implement the policy than with the substance of the policy being implemented. On these grounds the scope for substantial change in policy content as a result of procedural changes may be smaller than some analysts have suggested.

The second question relates to the origins of differences between policy instruments. Policies pursued by social democratic parties in North America and Western Europe normally have been paternalistic in their solutions to social issues, focusing on correcting specific problems. The progressive income tax was initially seen by radical groups on the left as a means of destroying the capitalist state. The moderate social reformers, whose subsequent influence has been widespread, were less interested in destroying capitalism and preferred a more direct and paternalistic instrument than was available in the tax system. Moreover, at the time that these new social policies were gathering support, the income tax still was narrowly focused on those earning high incomes. Pressure for increased redistribution through taxation would have antagonized the upper classes and threatened the successful implementation of new expenditure programs. As a result, new redistributive policies introduced by left-wing parties were subsidy policies. Since 1940, however, the redistributive character of the tax system has declined significantly. This occurred because the rapid spread of the income tax net during the Second World War to encompass most of the working population (who are now taxed at relatively high rates) was continued into the postwar period, and because of the sharply increased use of corporate and personal income tax expenditures over the same years. A lack of attention to tax policy developments by social democrats made it easier for the tax system to develop subject to a much narrower range of political interests, largely those of the affluent. This conjunction of historical and social factors served to sharpen and even increase the intrinsic differences between tax incentives and subsidies. Only over the last decade or so has there been any appreciable growth in awareness of what has happened in the area of tax policy. In recent years both social reformers and government officials have begun to take a fresh look at the wealth of tax expenditures that have taken root within the Income Tax Act.

In the face of continuing and growing pressures to open up the tax policy-making process, it is interesting to speculate on the implications of the many recent proposals for reform. It appears that for many observers the closed and secretive character of federal tax policy-making undermines the legitimacy of the resulting decisions. Calls for reform have usually been heard in periods of dissatisfaction with federal economic leadership and in the face of controversial tax measures being proposed by the Department of Finance. The overall thrust of these reform proposals is to open the tax policy process to greater and more intense scrutiny at a stage when the government can back away safely from unpopular initiatives. Some possible reforms include relaxing the restraint of budget secrecy to allow more consultation with tax professionals outside government prior to delivery of the budget, special or permanent advisory committees to review possible budget alternatives, and changing procedures in the House of Commons to allow a committee either to consider budget proposals in the context of their broad policy implications or to examine them on a clause-by-clause basis.[71]

The various proposals suggest different implications for the tax policy process. In general, if the impact of the reforms is to increase consultations with tax professionals, the result would reinforce the influence of the existing tax community. This would make subsequent tax increases on capital and high incomes more difficult to implement; it would increase the obstacles to eliminating or reducing the value of existing tax expenditures, and might increase pressure to expand them. However, reforms that bring into the tax policy-making process viewpoints that are usually excluded might produce policy outputs more representative of the full range of interests within Canada. Several other implications deserve notice. A more open policy-making process would create additional delays for the implementation of tax measures, but it seems likely that improvements in policy would offset any costs of delay. Further, the federal government might find it more difficult to resist pressures from the provincial governments to be more responsive to provincial concerns.

A brief look at the Liberal budget of November 1981 and its aftermath is useful as a means of putting taxation politics into some perspective. In the 1981 budget, Finance Minister Allan MacEachen proposed the closing off and reduction of a number of tax expenditures in conjunction with a reduction in personal income tax rates. Among the proposed changes were a reduction in the first-year capital cost allowance for depreciable assets, taxation of a number of employee benefits that had been exempt, limitations on the deduction of interest costs, elimination of tax deferrals through income-averaging and capital gains reserves, and an end to the capital gains exemption for more than one principal residence per family. These changes were accompanied by reductions in the personal income tax rates that largely benefited those with high incomes. Almost immediately there were cries of outrage as the budget came under attack. It was criticized for its failure to include new tax expenditures (for example, a provision for the deductibility of mortgage interest). The removal of existing tax expenditures was described as an attack on investment incentives. The competence of officials in the Finance Department was impugned. Within months Finance had made significant concessions in withdrawing from many of its initial positions through the provision of transitional relief and 'grandfather' clauses. Further retractions or adjustments were expected in subsequent budgets.

The struggle was particularly revealing of the character of tax politics. The distribution of benefits from tax expenditures favours those with high incomes, especially non-salaried incomes. The dominant actors in tax politics are the groups and individuals who receive these benefits. Finance recognized this factor in concentrating its rate reductions in the high-income categories. The implication of this struggle, as well as the earlier attempt at tax reform in the period from 1969 to 1971, is that if the government is serious about reducing tax expenditures it must either carry on with its reforms despite the attacks of opponents or it must mobilize new support to offset the opposition of aggrieved interests. Equally important, the government must show more care in authorizing future tax expenditures; once in place, they will be difficult to reduce or eliminate.

NOTES

1. R.W. Phidd and G. Bruce Doern, *The Politics and Management of Canadian Economic Policy* (Toronto: Macmillan 1978), ch. 14. Roger Smith has argued that governments

are increasingly aware of the opportunity to choose one or the other as policy instruments. See Roger S. Smith, *Tax Expenditures: An Examination of Tax Incentives and Tax Preferences in the Canadian Federal Income Tax System,* Canadian Tax Papers no. 61 (Toronto: Canadian Tax Foundation 1979), p. 8.

2. Stanley S. Surrey, 'Tax Expenditure Analysis: The Concept and its Uses', *Canadian Taxation* 1, 2 (Summer 1979), pp. 3–14, and Stanley S. Surrey, *Pathways to Tax Reform* (Cambridge: Harvard University Press 1973). Also see Smith, *Tax Expenditures.*

3. The basic difficulty with tax expenditure analysis lies in trying to distinguish between those tax provisions that are subsidies or incentives intended to encourage some particular result and those that are integral to the revenue-raising function. The problem of revenue loss estimation for tax expenditures is one shared with all government programs. On this question, see the symposium on tax expenditures in *Canadian Taxation* 1, 2 (Summer 1979). Also see Smith, *Tax Expenditures*, pp. 1–6, and Stanley S. Surrey and Paul R. McDaniel, 'The Tax Expenditure Concept and the Legislative Process', in *The Economics of Taxation* ed. Henry J. Aaron and Michael J. Boskin (Washington: The Brookings Institution 1980), pp. 123–44. Critics of the tax expenditure concept and its application argue that the tax expenditure was initially intended as an instrument of budget reform and that it has been perverted into a way of increasing tax progressiveness by emphasizing the costs of tax preferences of all kinds. On this argument see Seymour Fiekowsky, 'The Relationship of Tax Expenditures to the Distribution of the "Fiscal Burden"', *Canadian Taxation* 2, 4 (Winter 1980), pp. 211–19.

4. Ibid., 215.

5. The different political relationships of government to the various groups and sectors of a society are at base, the critical feature distinguishing the liberal-democratic, corporatist, and socialist state systems.

6. Smith, *Tax Expenditures*, 1.

7. Edward Tamargo, 'Comparing Direct Spending and Tax Spending', *Canadian Taxation* 1, 4 (Winter 1979), pp. 42–5.

8. *Government of Canada Tax Expenditure Account* (Ottawa: Department of Finance 1979), pp. 33–46.

9. Ibid., p. 27.

10. Smith, *Tax Expenditures*, p. 16.

11. David B. Perry, 'Corporate Tax Expenditures', *Canadian Tax Journal* 24, 5 (Sept.–Oct. 1976), pp. 528–33.

12. Smith, *Tax Expenditures*, pp. 18–19 (see Tables 2a and 2b).

13. *The Hidden Welfare System* (Ottawa: National Council of Welfare 1976).

14. *The Hidden Welfare System Revisited* (Ottawa: National Council of Welfare 1979), pp. 1–2.

15. Allan M. Maslove, 'The Other Side of Public Spending: Tax Expenditures in Canada', in *The Public Evaluation of Government Spending,* ed. G. Bruce Doern and Allan M. Maslove (Toronto: Institute for Research on Public Policy 1979), pp. 149–68, and Jonathan R. Kesselman, 'Non-Business Deductions and Tax Expenditures in Canada: Aggregates and Distributions', *Canadian Tax Journal* 25, 2 (March–April 1977), pp. 160–79.

16. Smith, *Tax Expenditures*, 15, 22.

17. Edward Tamargo, 'Comparing Direct Spending', 44.

18. *Tax Expenditure Account*, 1979, p. 30, and Allan Maslove, 'The Other Side of Public Spending', p. 157.

19. Edward Tamargo, 'Comparing Direct Spending', pp. 42–5.

20. Smith, *Tax Expenditures*, p. 22.

21. Ibid., p. 16.

22. Ibid., pp. 18–9; and David B. Perry, 'Corporate Tax Expenditures', pp. 530–2.

23. W. Irwin Gillespie and Allan M. Maslove, 'The 1980–81 Estimates: Trends, Issues and Choices', in *Spending Tax Dollars: Federal Expenditures, 1980–81,* ed. G. Bruce Doern (Ottawa: Carleton University, School of Public Administration 1980), pp. 23–48.

24. Donald R. Huggett, 'The Budget Process and Income Tax Changes', in *Report of Proceedings of the Twenty-Ninth Tax Conference,* 21-3 Nov. 1977, pp. 20–40; and David A. Good, *The Politics of Anticipation: Making Canadian Federal Tax Policy* (Ottawa: Carleton University, School of Public Administration 1980). Huggett notes (pp. 22–3) that a new method of getting around the budget secrecy problem has evolved inadvertently. Increasingly in the 1970s the minister ended up submitting budgetary legislation and then resubmitting it later, thus allowing the government to respond to criticisms of the first effort.

25. Ibid., ch. 3 and pp. 152–6.

26. Ibid.: also see Douglas G. Hartle, *The Expenditure Budget Process in the Government of Canada,* Canadian Tax Papers no. 60 (Toronto: Canadian Tax Foundation 1978), ch. 2.

27. *The New Expenditure Management System* (Ottawa: Department of Finance 1979), p. 10.

28. *Government of Canada Tax Expenditure Account* (Ottawa: Department of Finance 1980), pp. 2–4. On the question of the decline in the authority of the Department of Finance, see Douglas G. Hartle, *The Revenue Budget Process of the Government of Canada: Description, Appraisal and Proposals,* Canadian Tax Paper no. 67 (Toronto: Canadian Tax Foundation 1982), p. 33.

29. Joan Allin, 'The Tax Subsidy for Pollution Abatement Equipment', *Canadian Taxation* 1, 2 (Summer 1979), pp. 47–50.

30. Richard Simeon has presented a strong case for the need to 'disentangle' the two levels of government. See 'The Federal-Provincial Decision-Making Process', in *Intergovernmental Relations* (Toronto: Ontario Economic Council 1977), pp. 25–38.

31. For an example see R. Brian Woodrow, Kenneth Woodside, Henry Wiseman, and John B. Black, *Conflict over Communications Policy,* Policy Commentary no. 1 (Montreal: C.D. Howe Institute 1980), pp. 29–74.

32. See Thomas E. McDonnell, 'The Tax Reform Process: Comments on the Report of the Tax Legislative Process Committee', *Canadian Taxation* 1, 4 (Winter 1979), pp. 27–9.

33. According to the Fiscal Arrangements and Established Programs Financing Act, 1977, all provinces except Quebec levy their personal income tax as a percentage of the basic federal tax. In the case of the corporate income tax, all provinces except Ontario and Quebec (and soon Alberta) share the same corporate income tax base as that of the federal government. The federal government collects the revenue for both levels of government, and provincial corporate taxes are expressed as a percent-

age of the federal taxable income. See Robin W. Boadway and Harry M. Kitchen, *Canadian Taxation Policy*, Canadian Tax paper no. 63 (Toronto: Canadian Tax Foundation 1980), p. 116. A major exception to this lack of concern is in the area of resource taxation where the western provincial governments have been especially concerned that federal resource taxations interfere with and reduce their control over revenue from their resources. However, in areas of non-resource income and personal income taxation there is little evidence of continuing concern apart from the rare case such as the battle over tax reform from late 1969 through the end of 1971.

34. Government of Canada, *Tax Expenditure Account*, December 1979, pp. 27–8. It is noteworthy that the government has not committed itself to the publication of an annual tax expenditure account as is the case in the United States.

35. For a discussion of some of the criticisms see *Report of the Royal Commission on Financial Management and Accountability* (Ottawa: Ministry of Supply and Services 1979), chs 6, 21, and 22.

36. See Huggett, 'The Budget Process', p. 28; Good, *The Politics of Anticipation*, p. 134; *Report of the Royal Commission on Financial Management and Accountability*, pp. 386–7, 399.

37. Good, 'The Politics of Anticipation', pp. 152–6; Hartle, *The Expenditure Budget Process,* pp. 24–33. The finance ministers will, of course, receive many suggestions and requests from MPs and representatives of non-governmental groups but the Finance officials must play the role of good listeners and avoid giving hints about what the government might or might not do.

38. Good, *The Politics of Anticipation*, pp. 121–61. As mentioned in n. 24 the trend in the 1970s was for many budget proposals to be resubmitted; in the process some controversial measures (such as the 1978 proposals to remove special tax provisions for self-employed professionals and athletes) were substantially revised.

39. For instance, the two-year write-off for manufacturing and processing machinery and equipment introduced in 1972 was extended indefinitely in 1974 with relatively little comment.

40. A general example of tax changes introduced by regulations is found in the capital cost allowance rates and the designation of qualified investments eligible for consideration under an existing tax provision.

41. *Report of the Royal Commission on Financial Management and Accountability*, p. 406.

42. Ibid., chs 6, 21, and 22; Robert J. Jackson and Michael M. Atkinson, *The Canadian Legislative System,* 2nd rev. ed. (Toronto: Macmillan of Canada 1980), pp. 99–102, 107–9; Paul G. Thomas, 'Parliament and the Purse Strings', in *Parliament. Policy and Representation,* ed. H.D. Clarke, Colin Campbell, F.G. Quo, and Arthur Goddard (Toronto: Methuen 1980), pp. 160–81.

43. *Report of the Royal Commission on Financial Management and Accountability*, p. 384.

44. Ibid., p. 399.

45. Ibid., pp. 100–3 and Hartle, *The Expenditure Budget Process,* 36–8.

46. Neil Brooks, 'The Tax Expenditure Concept', *Canadian Taxation* 1, 1 (Jan. 1979), pp. 31–5, and Gerard M. Brannon, 'Tax Expenditures and Income Distribution: A Theoretical Analysis of the Upside-Down Subsidy Argument', in *The Economics of*

Taxation, ed. Henry J. Aaron and Michael J. Boskin (Washington: The Brookings Institution 1980), p. 87. It is true, however, that the smaller absolute gains for those in the lower income categories may in fact produce larger gains proportionately.

47. Surrey, *Pathways to Tax Reform*, pp. 134–8.

48. A regressive measure is one that benefits high-income earners more or costs them less than it does low-income earners.

49. The refundable child tax credit is unique because those below the tax threshold (i.e., those without taxable income) receive a credit for each child which comes in the form of a payment from the government. The value diminishes as income increases beyond a certain maximum. Thus the benefits tend to be concentrated on those with lower incomes, although Brigitte Kitchen has noted that families near the median income level benefit the most. See Brigitte Kitchen, 'The Refundable Child Tax Credit', *Canadian Taxation* 1, 3 (Fall 1979), pp. 44–51. An attempt to introduce a second refundable credit ended in December 1979 with the defeat of the Crosbie budget. This was the refundable energy tax credit. For discussion of its redistributive character see Andrew Doman, 'The Effect of Federal Budgetary Policies 1978–80 on the Distribution of Income in Canada', *Canadian Taxation* 2, 2 (Summer 1980), pp. 112–22.

50. Richard M. Bird, *Tax Incentives for Investment: The State of the Art* (Toronto: Canadian Tax Foundation 1980), pp. 52–3. Also see R.P. Simon, 'The Efficacy of Recent Corporate Income Tax Reductions for Manufacturing—An Unsimulated View', *Canadian Tax Journal* (March–April 1974), pp. 160–5.

51. *Report of the Royal Commission on Taxation*, vol. 6 (Ottawa: Queen's Printer 1966), p. 69.

52. Bird, *Tax Incentives for Investment*. In this regard Bird places particular weight on the heavy use of capital cost allowances, investment tax credits, and reduced rates of taxation.

53. *The National Energy Program*, 1980 (Ottawa: Department of Energy, Mines and Resources 1980), pp. 38–41.

54. Many expenditure subsidies are not particularly redistributive because they are not sufficiently focused on the poor. Thus the unemployment insurance revisions of 1971 'provided virtually no fiscal benefits for the poorest families'; W. Irwin Gillespie, *In Search of Robin Hood* (Montreal: C.D. Howe Research Institute 1978), pp. 18, 25, 40–2.

55. David A. Good, *The Politics of Anticipation*, pp. 11–78, 92, 108, 188.

56. For instance, see R.S. Woodward, 'The Effectiveness of DREE's New Location Subsidies', *Canadian Public Policy* (Spring 1975), pp. 217–30; D. Usher, 'Some Questions about the Regional Development Incentives Act', *Canadian Public Policy* (Autumn 1975), pp. 557–75; and *Industrial Incentives Programs in the Atlantic Region* (Halifax: Atlantic Provinces Economic Council 1976). A more recent example of dissatisfaction with DREE programs can be found in David Crane, 'Ottawa wastes investment funds, economists say', *Toronto Star*, 25 November 1980.

57. Gillespie and Maslove, 'The 1980–81 Estimates', 44; Ken Woodside, 'Tax Incentives vs. Subsidies: Political Considerations in Governmental Choice', *Canadian Public Policy* (Spring 1979), pp. 248–56.

58. Wolfe Goodman in 'The Small Business Credit: A Panel Discussion', *Canadian*

Taxation 1. 2, pp. 44–5. Attacks on 'big government' virtually never involve a reference to the number of tax expenditures or the amount of revenue forgone through the tax system. See, for example, the following instances: *Toronto Star,* 17 June 1976; 11 November 1975, and *The Globe and Mail,* 20 November 1975, 18 March 1976, 18 May 1976, and 14 December 1976.

59. Good, *The Politics of Anticipation*, p. 82. Also see the *Toronto Star*, 15 September 1979. On the reasons for the introduction of the tax expenditure account, see Hartle, *The Expenditure Budget Process,* pp. 14–5.

60. *Tax Expenditure Account*, 1979, p. 31. Not all expenditure subsidies have limits, however. The 1980–1 plan to provide grants for exploration and development by the oil industry is essentially open-ended and therefore limited only by the degree to which the industry responds to the incentives.

61. David Vogel, 'Why Businessmen Distrust Their State', *British Journal of Political Science* (Jan. 1978), pp. 45–78; and Leonard Silk and David Vogel, *Ethics and Profits: The Crisis of Confidence in American Business* (New York: Simon and Schuster 1976), ch. 2.

62. *R & D Policies, Planning and Programming* (Ottawa: Ministry of State, Science and Technology 1981), p. 24.

63. Reuben Hasson, 'Tax Evasion and Social Security Abuse—Some Tentative Observations', *Canadian Taxation* 2, no. 2 (Summer 1980), pp. 96–108. This excellent article is part of a useful symposium on the subject.

64. Ibid., pp. 106–8; also W. Goodman, 'Panel Discussion: Tax and Social Security Abuse', *Canadian Taxation* 2, 2 (Summer 1980), pp. 109–11, and Robert W. Davis, *Capital Cost Allowances,* Studies of the Royal Commission on Taxation, 21 (Ottawa: Queen's Printer 1967).

65. Hasson, 'Tax Evasion and Social Security Abuse'.

66. Bird, *Tax Incentives for Investment,* pp. 32–45.

67. *Tax Expenditure Account*, 1979, p. 31.

68. *Petroleum Incentives Program: The Basic Rules—A Framework* (Ottawa: Department of Energy, Mines, and Resources 1980).

69. Two examples of a large literature on this question are Arthur Maass, *Area and Power* (Glencoe: The Free Press 1959) and J. Roland Pennock, 'Agricultural Subsidies in England and the United States', *American Political Science Review* 61, 3 (September 1962), pp. 621–33.

70. For instance, see Paul Addison, *The Road to 1945* (Quartet Books, London 1977), pp. 117–8 and the interview with Stuart Holland in Bertram Silverman, 'The Crisis of the British Welfare State', *Challenge* (September–October 1980), pp. 33–9.

71. A review of many of these proposals can be found in Hartle, *The Expenditure Budget Process,* pp. 47–60. Also see the Tax Legislative Process Committee, 'The Tax Legislative Process', *Canadian Tax Journal* 26, 2 (March–April 1978), pp. 157–82, and John B. Stewart, *The Canadian House of Commons: Procedure and Reform* (Montreal: McGill-Queen's University Press 1977), pp. 101–8, 277–81. Also see *The Budget Process* (Ottawa: Department of Finance 1982).